second edition

Modern Christian Thought

Volume I
The Enlightenment
and the Nineteenth Century

JAMES C. LIVINGSTON

The College of William and Mary

Prentice Hall   Upper Saddle River, New Jersey 07458

Livingston, James C.
    Modern Christian thought / James C. Livingston.—2nd ed.
        p.   cm.
    Includes bibliographical references and index.
    Contents: v. 1. The Enlightenment and the nineteenth century.
    ISBN 0-02-371423-9
    1. Theology, Doctrinal—History—Modern period, 1500–   I. Title.
BT27.L58 1997
230′.09′03—dc20   96-3409
                                                                   CIP

Acquisitions editor: Angela Stone
Editorial/production supervision, interior design: Jenny Moss
Copy editor: Susan Korb
Buyer: Lynn Pearlman
Photo researcher: Sherry Cohen

This book was set in 10/12 Palatino by Carlisle Communications, Ltd., and was printed and bound by RR Donnelley & Sons Company. The cover was printed by Phoenix Color Corp.

Text and photo credits appear on pages 417–418, which constitute a continuation of the copyright page.

© 1997, 1992, 1988 by Prentice-Hall, Inc.
Simon & Schuster/A Viacom Company
Upper Saddle River, New Jersey 07458

Printed in the United States of America
10   9   8   7   6   5   4   3   2   1

ISBN 0-02-371423-9

Prentice-Hall International (UK) Limited, *London*
Prentice-Hall of Australia Pty. Limited, *Sydney*
Prentice-Hall Canada Inc., *Toronto*
Prentice-Hall Hispanoamericana, S.A., *Mexico*
Prentice-Hall of India Private Limited, *New Delhi*
Prentice-Hall of Japan, Inc., *Tokyo*
Simon & Schuster Asia Pte. Ltd., *Singapore*
Editora Prentice-Hall do Brasil, Ltda., *Rio de Janeiro*

Brief Contents

Contents

Chapter 11
The Ritschlian Theology and Protestant Liberalism   270

Chapter 12
Movements of Recovery and Conservation:
The Princeton Theology   299

Chapter 15
Kierkegaard and Nietzsche:
Toward the Twentieth Century 384

Preface

This is the first volume of a two-volume revised edition of the text *Modern Christian Thought,* first published over a quarter of a century ago. Both the sustained interest in the first edition and its need for a substantial revision and expansion led to the decision to publish this new version in a two-volume paperback edition. This first volume covers the Modern period from the Enlightenment through the nineteenth century. The second volume includes chapters on the important movements, theologians, and religious writers of the twentieth century, including recent developments at the end of the century.

Teaching modern Christian thought for many years convinced me of the need for a text that covers in some depth the important intellectual developments in the history of modern Western Christianity, including movements and thinkers in both the Catholic and Protestant traditions. There are texts that survey the history of Christianity, including the Modern period, and there are others that deal with Protestant or Catholic thinkers, but no text that attempts a study of the major figures and movements in both traditions in Europe and America since the beginning of the Modern era.

Each chapter concerns itself with a distinctive movement or school of thought and is relatively independent. The chapters follow essentially the same format. First, the context or historical setting of the movement or group of thinkers is briefly traced—for example, the background of Romanticism and Darwinism—followed by a longer exposition of the distinctive ideas of the movement *as exemplified in the thought of a few representative thinkers.* The goal has been the selection of exemplary figures—Kant, Schleiermacher, Möhler, Newman, Ritschl—rather than a comprehensive, and necessarily cursory, survey of numerous thinkers.

Second, the text makes extensive use of important and illustrative quotations from primary sources so that the reader can be engaged by a seminal thinker's own ideas. The reader is then assisted in understanding the particular writer's meaning and import through further elucidation and critical analysis. An effort has been made to include figures—e.g., Reimarus, Lessing, Drey, Herrmann, Blondel—who have played critically important roles in modern Christian thought but who often are given little or no attention.

The book concentrates on developments in historical, philosophical, and apologetical theology, that is, with the encounter between Christian ideas and modern philosophy, history, and the natural sciences. It is not concerned with the development of particular doctrines per se, or with liturgical and moral theology. This is why the book gives special attention, for example, to such movements as the Tübingen School, the Neo-Thomistic Revival, and Modernism in its treatment of modern Roman Catholicism. It also explains the inclusion of such figures as Voltaire, Feuerbach, and Nietzsche. I agree with Nikolai Berdyaev's assertion that many of the great modern philosophers are "Christian" philosophers in the sense that without Christianity much of their philosophical work would have been very different and that without such thinkers, e.g., Hume, Kant, and Hegel, Christian thought would not be exactly where it finds itself today.

The book begins with the Enlightenment for two reasons, one substantive, the other more practical. I have followed the lead of Ernst Troeltsch and others in the conviction that the real beginning of *modern* Christian thought is traceable to the scientific and philosophical revolutions of the seventeenth and eighteenth centuries and not to the Reformation, which was still largely medieval in outlook. The practical reasons for beginning with the Enlightenment are that several excellent, up-to-date studies of the Reformation period are available and that the attempt to deal adequately with developments in Christian thought from the fifteenth century invites superficiality.

There now is widespread conviction that in the latter decades of the twentieth century we have moved into a new post-Modern era and that Christianity in the future will reveal thought forms and ways of doing theology that are radically different from the forms that we have come to identify with either the Medieval or Modern periods. Doubtless others see the history of the Modern period from a different perspective, but I view it as a watershed in Christian history that continues to have a profound influence in the twentieth century. It represents a series of severe crises marked by creative responses and advances. The last three hundred years have witnessed some of the most serious intellectual assaults against Christianity in its history—challenges that, nevertheless, have been met with extraordinary resilience.

Because the book is concerned with distinct movement of religious thought, it does not attempt

a systematic study of the historical development of certain key themes—e.g., God, Christology, the doctrine of human nature, and so on. Nevertheless, the reader will note that the volume concentrates on a few problems that have emerged again and again in the modern history of Christian theology. These include the problem of religious authority, whether it is to be concentrated in the individual reason, in the Church, or in the Bible; the issues that have emerged from the critical study of the Bible and Church history, especially the problem of the historical Jesus and the development of doctrine; the question of our knowledge of God and God's relation to the world; and the relation of Christianity to other faiths. These problems continue at the center of theological discussion today.

In undertaking a project that covers such a range and variety of movements, theologians, philosophers, and writers in the modern history of Christianity, I am acutely conscious of both the difficulties involved in the selection process and my considerable indebtedness to the many scholars whose valuable studies of particular movements and thinkers are the foundation of this book. In thinking about how this new edition might best be recast I was helped in part by the excellent recent overviews of nineteenth-century Protestant and Catholic thought by Claude Welch, B. M. G. Reardon, and others. My indebtedness to the many authorities on specific thinkers is, needless to say, very great. Unfortunately, they are too many to mention here. Specialists in the field will easily recognize their presence in the notes and bibliographies.

I am immensely obligated to several colleagues in this field who read portions of the text or the penultimate draft of the entire first volume. The meticulous care for detail that was undertaken by these readers proved indispensable, and most of the suggestions for revision, deletions, and additions made eminent sense and were incorporated into the text. Some proposals for the inclusion of additional thinkers or themes had to be resisted due to the constraints of space. I, of course, take full responsibility for the book's final substance and form. One or more chapters were read by Richard Crouter, Joseph Fitzer, Terry Foreman, Mark Fowler, Darrell Jodock, Earl McLane, and Mark Noll. A late draft of the entire book was read by Garrett Green, Darrell Jodock, and Paul Misner.

I also wish to take this opportunity to thank others who assisted me with this project. Staff personnel at the Swem Library of the College of William and Mary, the Cambridge University Library, the Catholic University of America Library, and the Western Theological Seminary Library were always prepared to help. My wife Jackie typed drafts of several chapters and assisted with other editorial details. Tammy Cooper, secretary in the Department of Religion, prepared most of the final drafts on the word processor while carrying out all of her other responsibilities and working under deadlines. My daughter Susannah, a seasoned editor, gave most chapters careful scrutiny and suggested many improvements. Aylin An assisted with the processing of permissions.

Finally, I wish to express my appreciation to several editors: Maggie Barbieri for her initial support for my undertaking this new two-volume edition; Ted Bolen and Angela Stone for their support and encouragement; and Susan Alkana and Jenny Moss, who have been of invaluable assistance while this volume was in the latter stages of preparation and production.

James C. Livingston

Introduction
Modernity and Christianity

This book is an exploration of modern Christian thought since the Enlightenment of the eighteenth century. We begin with the Enlightenment because our understanding of Christianity, in its relationship with Western culture since the eighteenth century, has undergone a revolutionary—though often unperceived—development. Christianity has been powerfully influenced by our culture's secular explorations of the world, society, and the self. This may be neither an obvious nor an undisputed judgment, and so more must be said briefly about it here. It is a conspicuous, though implicit, theme in the chapters that follow.

When one uses terms such as "Modernity," "Modernism," or "the Modern Age," two or three fundamental questions immediately present themselves. One, of course, is the definitional question. In the last years of the twentieth century, a rather heated debate has occurred in intellectual circles concerning the nature of Modernity and what constitutes Modernity or Modernism. This has been prompted in large part by what appears to be the ever-increasing opinion that we now are living in a *post-Modern* age, one that has, in crucial respects, repudiated the leading convictions and values of Modernity. And, for those who maintain this position, it often implies a rejection of the guiding assumptions and the legacy of the Enlightenment.

This debate is complicated, however, by the fact that scholars in the fields of art and literature identify the emergence of Modernism with the cultural revolution that erupted at approximately the beginning of the twentieth century and which we associate in art with the revolt of Cubism, Picasso, the Dadaists, and Surrealists, and in literature with James Joyce's *Ulysses* and T. S. Eliot's *The Waste Land*. In this temporal framework Modernity or Modernism turns out to be a relatively short-lived movement, having given way to a new post-Modern cultural sensibility in art, architecture, and literature—as well as in philosophy and religion.

Many historians, however, essentially reverse the temporal perspective and trace the concept of "Modern" back as far as the fifth century C.E., when the Latin word "modernus" was used to distinguish the new Christian era from the Roman and pagan past. The idea of "Modernity" is also associated in the minds of many historians with the Renaissance, primarily with its "discovery" of the "modern" individual consciousness, reflected for example in its portraiture and in Petrarch's *Ascent of Mont Ventoux*.

Moreover, historians long have traced the beginning of "the Modern Age" to the Protestant Reformation and the political and cultural hallmarks of the period: the emergence of the printing press, the birth of the middle class, incipient capitalism, the rise of the nation-state, and, of course, Luther's bold assertion of individual conscience against the claims of traditional authority. Now, all of these historical developments represent important elements of cultural change that have helped to shape "Modernity." History, after all, is a continuous process.

The fact remains that the word "modern" has been used again and again throughout Western history in periods when there was an acute consciousness of a contrast with the previous age, the sense of the emergence of a new epoch provoking a war between the "ancients" and the "moderns." The founders of German Romanticism, Friedrich Schlegel and others, spoke of the spirit of the new literature and sensibility as *das eigentümliche Moderne,* the peculiarly or properly Modern, in contrast to the Neo-Classical. That is, the use of the word "modern" simply has meant that which is new in contrast with what is ancient or traditional. This suggests, of course, that what is modern for one age may well be regarded as passé by the next. Used in this sense, the "modern" is a highly relative and fluid idea. And it is the case that the term "Modernism" generally has been used to identify a cultural movement or program that sees itself, or is viewed by others, as upholding what is perceived as "modern" in contrast to what is habitual, traditional, orthodox, or taken for granted. In Lionel Trilling's phrase, the Modernists represent an "adversary culture," such as the Cubists in art and the Catholic Modernists in theology in their opposition to, respectively, conventional representation in painting or traditional Scholasticism in theology.

While not denying in the least that what we understand today as constituting "Modernity" can trace some of its features to the cultural innovations of the Renaissance and, especially, the changes in religious belief and sensibility occasioned by the Protestant Reformation, the premise of this text is that *modern* Christian *thought* can best be understood as beginning with the formidable changes in our world-view that were occasioned by the intellectual ferment unleashed in the scientific, philosophical, and historical challenges of the Enlightenment. I follow the historian Ernst Troeltsch and others in the contention that, while the Reformation included modern elements, it was essentially a modification of Medievalism. Troeltsch called the Reformation a "second blooming" of the Middle Ages, but what was genuinely modern about the Reformation only emerged *after* classical, orthodox Protestantism was profoundly challenged by the intellectual and social revolutions of the seventeenth and eighteenth centuries.

Christianity's responses to these profound revolutions were varied. One response was a complete, or at least substantial, capitulation to these secular currents in the form of an *accommodation* of Christian thought and institutions to "modern" ideas. In this book we will encounter instances of this kind of response. A second response was vigorous *resistance* to Modernity or Liberalism, which frequently involved either a retreat into a cultural and intellectual ghetto, a "fortress mentality," as we see in certain "fundamentalist" movements today, or highly sophisticated strategies of repristination or restoration of an older tradition of orthodoxy. In different ways and degrees, we see this latter response in such nineteenth-century efforts as the Oxford Movement, the Neo-Scholastic revival in Catholicism, and the Princeton Theology and its sequel in later evangelical movements within Protestantism. We have included these movements in this text because they specifically address what they see as the threats of Enlightenment Modernity to Christian thought and its institutions. A third and rather more pervasive response was the effort to preserve most of the classical tradition of Christian thought but to *reinterpret* it in constructive new ways so as to ensure its congruence and coherence with the received knowledge of modern science, history, and social experience. Many of the programs and movements discussed in this text will exemplify this type of response.

What is it that Troeltsch and other historians of Christian thought see as constituting "the Modern World"? There was, first, the emergence of the *secular state.* In its struggles with the Church, the modern state became acutely aware of its own power and the necessity of establishing its own constitutions, laws, and judicial and administrative functions on a secular basis—that is, to free itself from ecclesiastical domination. This was initiated in the American and French revolutions and carried forward in the subsequent political struggles of the nineteenth century. During this period the Church was divested—slowly but steadily—of its political power and influence. Allied with the growth of the secular state was a fast-accelerating secular economic capitalism, enhanced by a secular natural science that, with technological advance, transformed every dimension of our being. These lent confidence to the belief that our world is intelligible and open to progressive advancement.

Most significant, however, is the fact that modern politics, economy, art, and science all assume an autonomous individualism, the freedom of individual persons and groups to choose, analyze, test, and question. Both institutionally and morally, medieval culture was largely under the dominion of ecclesiastical authority. Modern culture opposes the dominance of Church authority or, more importantly, any purely externally imposed, divinely given standards of belief and behavior. As Troeltsch writes:

> Even where new authorities are in principle established, or in practice followed, the respect accorded to them arises from purely independent and rational conviction; and even where the older religious convictions hold their ground, their truth and their binding force are . . . primarily based on inner personal conviction, not on submission to authority as such.[1]

This growth of individual autonomy and its corollary, the spirit of critical inquiry, has brought about a further characteristic of Modernity: the growing and increasingly pervasive constriction of human interests to matters that bear on life in this present world. "In consequence," as Troeltsch observes, "all the factors of the present life acquire an enhanced value and a higher impressiveness, and the ends of life fall more and more within the realm of the present world and its ideal transformation."[2] This is not to claim that "Modernity" implies the triumph of a thoroughly secular consciousness and cultural ethos. We are far from it in many contexts. It does, however, advance the claim that the Christianity that has emerged within and in response to the Modern Age is, in significant ways,

very different from Christianity in its origins and through the seventeenth century. It is the burden of this text to show how this has become so by highlighting those intellectual movements and challenges that have played such a critical role in the shaping of a distinctive *modern* Christian thought.

One last matter requires comment. All too often, "Modernity" has been identified with the Enlightenment—or, more candidly, with a caricature of the Enlightenment—resulting from selective attention to those thinkers and writings that represent the most egregious excesses of eighteenth-century rationalism, abstraction, materialism, or belief in an inevitable historical progress. The Enlightenment was, of course, a far more complex and variegated phenomenon. Just as there were various Romanticisms, so there were Enlightenments sharing certain crucial ideals but also reflecting distinctive thought processes. But, more to my point, "Modernity" has not been shaped exclusively by the Enlightenment. The Modern Age also is deeply infused with the spirit, feelings, and values of various Romanticisms, with the ideas and sensibility we find in Wordsworth and Coleridge, in Hamann and Hegel, in Lamennais and Newman, in Kierkegaard and Nietzsche, or in the divided psyche of Chateaubriand.

The case can still be made that we are living today in the "Modern" world that came into being in the eighteenth and nineteenth centuries. Jacques Barzun has shown that early Romanticism helped to bring into being later adumbrations of Romanticism in literary Naturalism and Realism and beyond. So, I believe, can we see in manifestations of contemporary post-Modernism—its critique of metaphysics and the claim to possess incorrigible foundations of knowledge and belief, its attention to how rationality and knowledge are embedded in distinctive languages and cultures, and its critique of liberal individualism—that all these have their roots in the fertile soil of both the Enlightenment and Romanticism, which, respectively, have shaped our complex and pluralistic modern world. Only the passage of time and historical distance will, of course, enable us to judge decisively whether post-Modernism is a late representation of Modernity, or whether it will be seen as a genuine turning point in Western consciousness.

NOTES

1. Ernst Troeltsch, *Protestantism and Progress: The Significance of Protestantism for the Rise of the Modern World* [1912] (Minneapolis, 1986), p. 24. On the theme of "Modernity," also see Troeltsch's essay "The Essence of the Modern Spirit" [1907], in *Religion in History* (Minneapolis, 1991), Chap. 15.

2. Troeltsch, *Protestantism and Progress,* p. 26.

Chapter 1
The Enlightenment
and Modern Christianity

Immanuel Kant

"Enlightenment," wrote Immanuel Kant, "is man's release from his self-incurred tutelage. Tutelage is man's inability to make use of his understanding without direction from another.... *Sapere aude!* ('Dare to know.') 'Have courage to use your own reason!'—that is the motto of the enlightenment."[1]

The term "Enlightenment" signifies that period of European history from the close of the Thirty Years War (1648) to the French Revolution. In the realm of ideas, it is often designated as that era of modern thought from Francis Bacon's *Novum Organum* (1620) to Kant's *Critique of Pure Reason* (1781). It is the age which brought together the humanistic spirit of the Renaissance and the scientific revolution of the seventeenth century and thereby ushered in what we call "the modern world." It was this period of roughly a century and a half that witnessed a general change in world-view of the most wide-ranging and deepest significance.

This study begins with the contention that the *modern* history of Christian thought begins not with the Reformation of the sixteenth century but rather with that movement of the eighteenth century known as the Enlightenment. All history is continuous, and the periodization of history into discrete epochs or world-views is never completely successful. Nevertheless, it is correct to say that there is more in common between the world-views of the thirteenth and sixteenth centuries than between those of the sixteenth and nineteenth. Between the sixteenth and nineteenth centuries a revolution occurred in our understanding of ourselves and our world that caused a sharp break with medieval civilization and ushered in the modern epoch.

A. C. McGiffert has expressed this change in the following way:

> The whole world of thought and culture was transformed. . . . the dependence upon supernatural powers, the submission to external authority, the subordination of time to eternity, and of fact to symbol . . . the somber sense of the sin of man and the evil of the world, the static interpretation of reality, . . . the belief that amelioration can come only in another world beyond the grave—all of which characterize the Middle Ages—were widely overcome and men faced life with a new confidence in themselves, with a new recognition of human power and achievement, with a new appreciation of present values.[2]

What happened between the Reformation and the French Revolution were two revolutions of far-reaching importance. The first was the scientific transformation that came as a result of the work of Copernicus, Galileo, and Newton. What it did was to deprive humanity of its traditional place and value in the world, making individuals aware of both their "grandeur and misery" in a vast, mechanical universe. The second revolution was that of Descartes. What Descartes did was to make doubting the first principle of philosophy and the model for all the sciences. Together these movements brought about a significant shift in humanity's understanding of itself and its situation in the world.

What occurred in the seventeenth and eighteenth centuries was the development, imperceptible and yet pervasive, of a world-view strikingly different from either classical or medieval culture. From the point of view of Christianity, this new modern epoch can be characterized as a culture emancipating itself from ecclesiastical and theological authority. The Enlightenment represents the loosening of the state and society from ecclesiastical control and the emergence of a culture increasingly secular in character. The theories and sanctions of modern social and political life no longer are derived from biblical revelation or Church authority but independently arrived at by natural reason and social experience. An essential feature of the Enlightenment and of our modern culture since the eighteenth century is the growing separation of Western civilization from the authority of the Church and theological dogma.

Underlying this whole movement is a renewed awareness and trust in humanity's own capacities or initiative and appreciation of, interest in, and hope for human life on this earth. Reason largely supersedes revelation as the supreme court of appeal. As a result, theology faced a choice of either adjusting itself to the advances in modern science and philosophy and, in so doing, risking accommodation to secularization, or resisting all influences from culture and becoming largely reactionary and ineffectual in meeting the challenges of life in the modern world. The history of modern Christianity is thus frequently viewed as the history of the secularization of the West.[3]

The historian Carl Becker advises us that if we are to understand the inner spirit of any age, we should look "for certain unobtrusive words." A brief look at some of the "unobtrusive" words common to the Enlightenment can give us a clearer picture of that age as well as a keener awareness of the heritage of the Enlightenment which, despite the recent attack and scorn of some critics, remains a vital part of our own contemporary experience.

AUTONOMY

More than anything else the Enlightenment marks a revolt against authoritarianism and the emergence of individual reason and conscience as the primary arbiters of truth and action. While every age has produced remarkable individuals who have challenged the accepted authorities of their day by appeal to individual conscience, the Enlightenment is characterized by the spread of the spirit of autonomous reason far beyond the confines of the intellectual salons, especially among the burgeoning middle class.

The term "autonomy" (*autos* self + *nomos* law) means self-governed. It involves "man's release from his self-incurred tutelage"—from the inability to reason and to will without sanctions imposed from outside the self. John Locke describes the ideal of autonomy in his portrayal of the genuine lover of truth. Of such persons there is, remarks Locke, "one unerring mark, viz., the not entertaining of any proposition with greater assurance than the proofs it is built upon will warrant. Whoever goes beyond this measure of assent, it is plain . . . loves not truth for truth's sake, but for some other end."[4]

The ideal of the Enlightenment is, then, the duty of not entertaining any belief that is not warranted by rational evidence, which means by the assent of autonomous reason rather than biblical or ecclesiastical authority. Autonomy, therefore, is that faculty which the reason and the will possess of being their own lawgiver. Opposed to autonomy is heteronomy (*heteros* = other) or the imposition of sanctions or authority on oneself from outside, which one would not impose on oneself if one were free, i.e., truly rational. Thus autonomy is the foundation of all true liberty. But autonomy does not mean freedom "to do as one pleases," for that could mean subjection of the will to what is merely particular and immediate. Rather, autonomy—and thus true liberty—is achieved only when the individual reason and will are in accord with universal laws of reason. One prominent form of heteronomy, or slavery, is evident in obedience to divine commands simply because some external authority, i.e., the Bible or the Church, demands obedience to such laws—laws which appear to the autonomous reason to be arbitrarily imposed. For the Enlightenment, the will or law of God can only be followed autonomously—only when the divine commands can be transformed into general laws which can become universal, rational axioms of behavior. No longer, then, is authority simply imposed arbitrarily from without; authority now depends on its inherent ability to produce rational conviction.

REASON

The eighteenth century is rightly known as the Age of Reason. But the age was dominated by a peculiar kind of reason. It was not the abstract reason of classical rationalism. The *philosophes,* it is true, looked to the rationalist Descartes as the one who had liberated the mind from blind authority. But

Descartes's reason was too speculative and abstract. The model of reason in the Enlightenment was the empirical, experimental reason of Francis Bacon and John Locke. What was required was *an examination of the facts of experience.* Reason was now called upon to serve a critical function according to the model of contemporary natural science. As Cassirer points out, in the eighteenth century philosophic method came to be patterned after Newton's "Rules of Philosophizing" rather than Descartes's *Discourse on Method*—on analysis rather than on pure deduction.[5] Thus Voltaire exhorted his contemporaries: "We must never make hypotheses; we must never say: Let us begin by inventing principles according to which we attempt to explain everything. We should say rather: Let us make an exact analysis of things. . . ."[6] Equipped with this new instrument of analysis, humanity could examine, weigh, sift, and compare the facts again and again until it could discern the true from the false, the contingent and particular from the necessary and universal.

Reason was no longer a given heritage, an intellectual treasury. It now was conceived of as a vital, progressive force. Reason was no longer defined by its effects, a distinct body of truth, but by its function, by its ability to bind and loose, to separate fact from opinion. Ideas, beliefs, even our understanding of what constitutes facts change, but reason as a function is what remains immutable and universal. This was the great discovery and the source of the excitement and optimism of the age. Because misfortune and suffering arise very largely from ignorance, it was believed reason could cast its light into the darkness of superstition and deceit and bring humanity its long-anticipated enlightenment and happiness.

NATURE

For the philosophers of the Enlightenment, what was "reasonable" was also "natural," grounded somehow in the very nature of things. The equation of the reasonable and the natural can be traced very largely to the new science of Newton. For Newton the laws of nature were orderly and uniform, always and everywhere the same. Likewise, what is reasonable in human affairs is what is natural, i.e., what is universal beneath the divergences of culture and outward appearance. What was called for, then, was the excision of all the beliefs and practices that had taken hold as a result of humanity's deviation from nature. Society had become artificial, the victim of all kinds of heteronomous influences—the monarch, the church, the conventions of society—which had destroyed freedom and corrupted natural integrity. The *philosophes* felt like Alceste in Molière's *The Misanthrope.* They itched to "unmask" the hypocrisy and artificiality of the times and yearned to flee to what they believed to be the simplicities of nature—that state in which humans existed before they were corrupted. This "state of nature" was very largely a cherished figment of the eighteenth-century imagination. Some thought they discerned it in earlier times, in a more rustic age when humans had simple needs that could easily be satisfied. Locke, Diderot, and others thought they perceived this natural state in far-off places such as China, America, and Tahiti. The belief spread that in these distant lands there lived a society of "noble savages" who were superior to the Europeans because they lived in accordance with Nature. Even the skeptical Voltaire thought of Confucius as exemplifying the simplicities of the natural individual guided by reason. Little did he know what a bourgeois *gentilhomme* Confucius really was!

The extent to which Nature and her rational laws were reverenced, even divinized, is evidenced in d'Holbach's paean, *Système de la Nature:* "O thou," cries Nature to humanity,

> Dare to enfranchise yourself from the trammels of superstition. . . . denounce those empty theories which are usurpers of my privileges; return under the dominion of my laws. . . . It is in my empire alone that true liberty reigns. . . . Return, then, my child, to thy fostering mother's arms! Deserter, trace back thy wandering steps to Nature. She will console thee for thine evils; she will drive from thy heart those appalling fears which overwhelm thee. Return to nature, to humanity, to thyself.[7]

This could very well have served as a naturalistic surrogate for the Parable of the Prodigal Son.

MELIORISTIC OPTIMISM

Nature reflects not only great rational simplicity but also order and regularity. It was Newton who discerned the beautiful symmetry of nature—an order and harmony which is not always immediately apparent. Frequently what we regard as evil or out of joint from our immediate point of view is not so in the general order of things. What looks at a distance as indeed very gray may be a rosy pink on closer examination. Our vision is too limited to take in the complex whole. Alexander Pope thus reminded his age that

> All are but parts of one stupendous Whole
> Whose body Nature is, and God the soul . . .
> All Nature is but Art unknown to thee;
> All chance, direction, which thou canst not
>   see;
> All discord, harmony not understood;
> All partial evil, universal good;
> And spite of Pride, in erring Reason's spite,
> One truth is clear, Whatever is, is right.[8]

For Pope the world is like a vast canvas of Rembrandt, filled with shadows and eerie blackness. Yet, if we concentrate not only on these large patches of darkness but on the whole, we see that the shadows are indispensable to Rembrandt's art. The seeming evil or darkness is a kind of good in that it is a necessary constituent of the whole. Perhaps this is not the most perfect world conceivable, but it is in Leibnitz's words "the best of all possible worlds."

Leibnitz's imposing argument for "all is well" was widely held, but not everyone in the eighteenth century was enamored of Leibnitz's optimism. Voltaire had been drawn to Leibnitz's theodicy, but news of the Lisbon earthquake in which thousands died on All Saints' Day, 1755, turned him against the cold abstractions of the German. In 1756 Voltaire composed a poem entitled, *The Lisbon Earthquake: An Inquiry into the Maxim "Whatever Is, Is Right."* In the preface to the poem, Voltaire points out that, impressive as they are, views such as those of Leibnitz and Pope are a perverse justification of the status quo. Why, after all, should one seek to remove evil if this is actually the least evil of all possible worlds?

If this world, such as it is, be the best of systems possible, we have no room to hope for a happy future state. If the various evils by which man is overwhelmed end in general good, all civilized nations have been wrong in endeavoring to trace out the origin of moral and physical evil.[9]

In Voltaire's opinion, Leibnitz and Pope are apostles of hopelessness because they feel no need to change the human situation. Voltaire's hope lay not in the present but in the future:

All *may* be well; that hope can man sustain,
All *now* is well; 'tis an illusion vain.[10]

Voltaire's optimism is a melioristic optimism—a hope oriented, like that of most of the *philosophes,* to the future betterment of the human race.

Jean Jacques Rousseau was impressed by Voltaire's poem on the Lisbon disaster and had himself begun to approach the problem from a new perspective that has had far-reaching significance for Christian theology. Rousseau saw no need to explain away the present evil state of humanity; nor did he find it necessary to trace such an evil condition back to an original Fall of Adam. Rousseau introduced the distinction between "natural man" and "civilized man." The natural individual is in a state of innocency in that he or she has not yet been tempted to subject others to his or her will. Rousseau believed it is the compulsions of human society that cause us to become egotistical and acquisitive and that lie at the root of our misery and inhumanity to others. But for Rousseau, as later for Marx, such an acquisitive, heteronomous society was not humanity's inevitable fate. In the *Social Contract* he envisioned a community in which the individual will and the "general will" are one: i.e., an autonomous society in which individual liberty is in perfect accord with the common good.

Cassirer points out the significance of Rousseau's hope:

When the compulsory form of society, which has hitherto prevailed, falls and is replaced by a new form of political and ethical community—a community in which every member, instead of being subjected to the arbitrary will of others, obeys only the general will which he recognizes and acknowledges as his own—then the hour of deliverance has arrived. But it is futile to expect this deliverance from without. No God can bring it about for us; man must rather become his own deliverer and in the ethical sense his own creator. Society heretofore has inflicted the deepest wounds on mankind; yet it is society too which through a transformation and reformation can and should heal these wounds.[11]

The kind of melioristic hope in the future of the human race, which we find in Voltaire and Rousseau, lies at the heart of the modern doctrines of development and progress.

PROGRESS

Chastened optimists like Voltaire and Rousseau held out a fervent hope for the advance of posterity to a condition in accord with nature and reason. Progress would not be easy, but for most of the *philosophes* it was inevitable.

Self-interest, ambition, vainglory, . . . inundate the earth with blood. Yet in the midst of their voyages manners are gradually softened, the human mind takes enlightenment, separate nations draw nearer to each other, commerce and policy connect at last all parts of the globe, and the total mass of the human race . . . marches always, although slowly, towards still higher perfection. . . .[12]

The feeling was widespread that the "new age" was in the imminent future, for signs indicated that the decisive battle in the age-old struggle between superstition and reason had been won. Signs of the victory were the advancements of science and the application of scientific method to politics and to social problems. There was, however, a tendency to join with a belief in inevitable progress the paradoxical idea that until the time of Bacon, Newton, and Locke people had lived for almost two thousand years in utter darkness. Many agreed with Condorcet who, in *The Progress of the Human Mind,* traced the persistence of superstition and error to the triumph of Christianity.

Contempt of human sciences was one of the first features of Christianity. It had to avenge itself for the outrages of philosophy; it feared that spirit of investigation and doubt, that confidence of man in his own reason, the pest alike of all religious creeds. . . . The triumph of Christianity was thus the signal for the entire decline of both the sciences and of philosophy.[13]

According to Condorcet, the seventeenth century had turned the tide, and the stage was now set for the new age, which he called the "tenth *époque,*" in which the progress of the human mind was assured. With deep, religious feeling, Condorcet expressed his hopes in the inauguration of the "tenth *époque.*"

How consoling for the philosopher . . . is this view of the human race, emancipated from its shackles, released from the empire of fate and from that of the enemies of its progress, advancing with a firm and sure step along the path of truth, virtue, and happiness! It is the contemplation of this prospect that rewards him for all his efforts. . . ."[14]

For writers like Condorcet, hope for posterity became a kind of eschatological substitute for the traditional Christian hope in the Kingdom of God. "Posterity," said Diderot, "is for the philosopher what the other world is for the religious." Just as Rousseau had offered a secular answer to the Christian doctrine of the Fall and Redemption, so did Diderot and Condorcet provide a this-worldly hope in the future in place of an other-worldly expectation—in an earthly city in which there will be no more "mourning nor crying nor pain anymore, for the former things will have passed away." The end of human life now falls exclusively within the present world and its ideal transformation.[15]

TOLERATION

The concern for religious toleration in the eighteenth century was as much due to the exhaustion which set in after the religious wars of the two previous centuries and to the growing resentment and indifference to the dogmatic claims of revealed religion as to a sincere and broad-based interest in the establishment of civil liberties. Nevertheless, the late

seventeenth century produced a number of treatises, including Roger Williams's *Bloudy Tenent of Persecution* (1644), Milton's *Areopagitica* (1644), Locke's *Letters on Toleration* (1689), and the writings of Pierre Bayle, all of which had considerable influence in shaping eighteenth-century sentiment.

For the writers of the Enlightenment, the great enemy was not religion but dogmatism and intolerance. Bayle had emphasized that "the obstacles to a good examination do not come so much from the fact that the mind is void of knowledge as it is full of prejudice." Following the model of science, in which "truth" is gradually discovered and ever-changing, Bayle argued that there is no "truth" which is at any time so absolutely certain as to justify the suppression of contrary views by force. Even a belief that seems to be wrong must be tolerated because it might possibly prove to be right. Bayle's influence on the French Encyclopedists was considerable, and his views on toleration were frequently repeated by them. Following Bayle, Diderot writes:

The mind can only acquiesce in what it accepts as true. The heart can only love what seems good to it. Violence will turn man into a hypocrite if he is weak, into a martyr if he is strong. . . . Teaching, persuasion, and prayer, these are the only legitimate means of spreading the faith.[16]

Locke argued similarly. Once you allow that civil governments can enforce religious uniformity among their citizens, you have conceded the same right to London, Geneva, and Rome. But it is clear that these places hold different religions to be the true one, in which case it follows that you have conceded the right of forced uniformity to false religions as well as the true one. What makes such a position doubly ridiculous is that people's eternal fate is solely dependent upon the place of their birth or residence rather than on the intrinsic or proven truth of their religious allegiance. It follows, in Locke's argument, that religious toleration will, in the long run, give the true religion the best chance of capturing the minds and hearts of a people. It is only false religion that has anything to fear from the tests of reason and experience. Because the truth of religion cannot be absolutely determined by purely theoretical criteria, such as the appeal to proofs of historical fact or logical argument, but is dependent upon internal conviction and moral suasion, religious toleration is all the more imperative.

The view that toleration is required by the very fact that the truth claims of the historical religions cannot at present be indubitably proved is the moral of Lessing's famous fable of the three rings in his drama, *Nathan the Wise.* According to the fable, it was the custom in an ancient Eastern family for the father to bequeath to his son a ring which "possessed the secret power to make the owner loved of God and man." At last the ring came to the father of three sons, all of whom he loved alike. And so to each of the three he gave the ring, two being perfect imitations. The father died, and each of the sons considered the other two deceivers.

> But all in vain, the veritable ring
> Was not distinguishable—
> Almost as indistinguishable as to us
> Is now—the true religion.

The sons brought their case before a judge who, about to throw out the difficult case, recollects:

> But stop; I've just been told that the right ring
> Contains the wondrous gift to make its wearer
>   loved,
> Agreeable alike to God and man,
> That must decide, for the false
> Rings will not have this power.

The judge then gives the sons this sage advice:

> But my advice is this:
> You take the matter as it stands.
> If each one had his ring straight from his
>   father,
> *So let each believe his ring the true one.*
> *'Tis possible your father would not longer tolerate*
> *The tyranny of this one ring in his family,*
> *And surely loved you all—and all alike,*
> *And that he would not two oppress*
> *By favoring the third.*
> Now then, let each one emulate in affection
> Untouched by prejudice. *Let each one strive*
> *To gain the prize of proving by results*
> *The virtue of his ring,* and aid its power

> With gentleness and heartiest friendliness,
> With benevolence and true devotedness to
>   God;
> And if the virtue of the ring will then
> Have proved itself among your children's
>   children,
> I summon them to appear again
> Before this judgment seat,
> After a thousand thousand years.
> Here then will sit a judge more wise than I,
> Who will pronounce.[17] (Italics added.)

Lessing was reminding his readers that they must be tolerant in religious matters for two quite different reasons. God, in his compassion, could not suffer the tyranny of one dispensation which would give special favor to one son, for God loves all his sons—and all alike. Lessing is, nevertheless, advocating religious toleration for another reason. One of the rings (religions) is in fact the genuine one, but the decision as to which one it is must wait until some future time when its truth can be made clear by its fruits, by "the proof of the spirit and the power." Meanwhile the practitioners of each religion should assume their faith to be the true one and seek to commend its truth through virtuous conduct.

Such were some of the "unobtrusive" convictions that permeated the thinking of eighteenth-century Europe—convictions very largely secular in origin and character. The appeal to autonomous reason and conscience, the melioristic optimism with its attendant discontent with existing conditions of political and economic injustice, the undogmatic temper with its appeal to what is natural and universal and to tolerance in matters of belief, all of this reflects a break with both medieval Catholic civilization and Protestant orthodoxy.

The Enlightenment was also to run its course; and its understanding of nature, humanity, and God required correction and supplementation. Today we are living in a quite different world, and yet the problems that Christianity continues to face in the realms of historical and philosophical theology can, by and large, trace their beginnings to the intellectual effervescence of the eighteenth-century Enlightenment.

NOTES

1. I. Kant, "What Is Enlightenment?" trans. and ed. L. W. Beck (Chicago, 1955), p. 286.
2. *The Rise of Modern Religious Ideas* (New York, 1921).
3. See, for example, J. H. Nichols, *History of Christianity, 1650–1950* (New York, 1950).
4. *Essay Concerning Human Understanding,* ed. A. S. Pringle-Pattison (Oxford, 1934), Bk. IV, Chap. 19.
5. E. Cassirer, *The Philosophy of the Enlightenment* (Boston, 1960), p. 7.
6. Voltaire, *Traité de Metaphysique,* Chaps. 3, 5. Quoted in Cassirer, op. cit., p. 12.
7. Baron d'Holbach, *Système de la Nature,* Part II, Chap. 14.
8. "An Essay on Man," Epistle I, from *Poetical Works,* ed. H. F. Carey (London, 1872).
9. *The Works of Voltaire,* Vol. X, Part 2, St. Hubert Guild ed. (1901), 5–7.
10. Ibid., p. 18.
11. Cassirer, op. cit., pp. 157–158.
12. A. R. J. Turgot, *Discourse at the Sorbonne, The Life and Writings of Turgot,* ed. W. Walker Stephens (London, 1895).
13. Quoted in C. Frankel, *The Faith of Reason* (New York, 1948), p. 134. Frankel should be read as a corrective to the views of C. Becker in his *The Heavenly City of the Eighteenth Century Philosophers.* Without denying that many of the *philosophes* were naively optimistic about the future, Frankel points up, correctly, that their concern to apply scientific method to social problems was a valuable and enduring contribution. See especially his defense of the much-maligned Condorcet, Chap. 7.
14. *Sketch for a Historical Picture of the Human Mind,* trans. June Barroclough (London, 1955).
15. For an excellent statement of this changed perspective, see Becker, op. cit., Chap. 4, "The Uses of Posterity"; and R. R. Palmer, "Posterity and the Hereafter in Eighteenth Century French Thought," *Journal of Modern History* (June 1937).
16. Diderot, in the article "Intolerance," *Encyclopedia: Selections,* ed. T. Cassirer and N. Hoyt (New York, 1965), p. 148.
17. Trans. by Williams Jacks (Glasgow, 1894).

SUGGESTIONS FOR FURTHER READING

I

For general accounts of ecclesiastical history *and* theological movements in the Modern period, the following can be consulted:

Ahlstrom, Sydney E. *A Religious History of the American People* (New Haven: Yale University Press, 1972). The best one-volume work on the subject.

Cragg, Gerald R. *The Church in the Age of Reason, 1648–1789* (New York: Penguin Viking, 1974). A brief but scholarly account of this critical period.

Jedin, Hubert, and John Dolan. *History of the Church* (New York: Crossroad, 1965–1981).

Vol. 7. *The Church in the Age of Absolutism and Enlightenment*

Vol. 8. *The Church between Revolution and Restoration*

Vol. 9. *The Church in the Industrial Age*

Vol. 10. *The Church in the Modern Age*

The fullest account in English of Roman Catholicism in the Modern period, but not strong on thought.

Vidler, Alec. *The Church in an Age of Revolution* (New York: Penguin Viking, 1974). A brief, well-written account of major movements of the nineteenth century.

II

For general works on the history of ideas and Christian thought in particular:

Baumer, Franklin L. *Modern European Thought: Continuity and Change in Ideas, 1600–1950* (New York: Macmillan, 1977).

Smart, Ninian, et al. *Nineteenth Century Religious Thought in the West,* 3 vols. (Cambridge: Cambridge University Press, 1985). Individual studies of thinkers and movements from Kant to Max Weber by experts on each subject.

On Protestant Thought:

Dillenberger, John, and Claude Welch. *Protestant Christianity: Interpreted through Its Development,* 2d ed. (New York: Macmillan, 1988). A brief, lucid account of major developments by two experts, with a concentration on thought.

Thielicke, Helmut. *Modern Faith and Thought* (Grand Rapids: Eerdmans, 1990). An interesting study of Christian thought from Descartes to Ernst Troeltsch by a leading German Protestant theologian.

Welch, Claude. *Protestant Thought in the Nineteenth Century.* 2 vols. (New Haven: Yale University Press, 1972, 1985). The standard work in English that covers more than a single country from 1799 to 1914.

On British Thought:

Reardon, B. M. G. *From Coleridge to Gore: A Century of Religious Thought in Britain* (London: Longmans, 1971). The best up-to-date survey of British religious thought of the nineteenth century with major, but not exclusive, attention to Anglican developments.

On Roman Catholic Thought:

For Catholicism there is no work in English comparable to Welch's study of Protestant thought. For accounts of Catholic movements and thinkers, consult the following:

McCool, Gerald A. *Catholic Theology in the Nineteenth Century: The Quest for a Unitary Method* (New York: Seabury, 1977).

O'Meara, Thomas F. *Church and Culture: German Catholic Theology 1860–1914* (Notre Dame: University of Notre Dame Press, 1991).

Reardon, B. M. G. *Liberalism and Tradition: Aspects of Catholic Thought in Nineteenth Century France* (Cambridge: Cambridge University Press, 1975).

These works are advanced, but they cover major figures.

III

Among the many books on the general history of ideas during the period of the Enlightenment, the following are highly recommended:

Becker, C. L. *The Heavenly City of the Eighteenth Century Philosophers* (New Haven: Yale University Press, 1962). A delightful, controversial interpretation of eighteenth-century thought. For an appraisal of Becker's view, see *Carl Becker's Heavenly City Revisited,* ed. R. O. Rockwood (Ithaca: Cornell University Press, 1958).

Cassirer, E. *The Philosophy of the Enlightenment* (Boston: Beacon Press, 1960). Perhaps the profoundest philosophical interpretation of the Enlightenment. Very readable but requires some background knowledge.

Gay, Peter. *The Enlightenment: An Interpretation* (New York: Alfred Knopf, 1966). Written by one of the leading authorities on the thought of the eighteenth century.

Hazard, Paul. *The European Mind, 1680–1715* (New Haven: Yale University Press, 1953).

———. *European Thought in the Eighteenth Century* (New Haven: Yale University Press, 1954). Hazard's studies are a literary achievement in addition to being authoritative and stimulating. Not for the beginner.

Manuel, Frank. *The Eighteenth Century Confronts the Gods* (Cambridge: Harvard University Press, 1959). A learned study that also covers figures of the Counter-Enlightenment.

Schmidt, James, ed. *What Is Enlightenment? Eighteenth Century Answers and Twentieth Century Questions* (Berkeley: University of California Press, 1996). Contains valuable documents on the eighteenth-century debate followed by seventeen studies by twentieth-century historians and philosophers.

Chapter 2
The Religion of Reason

John Locke

The eighteenth century inaugurated what we call the "modern age." We are, in essential ways, children of the Enlightenment, largely imbued with its spirit, dedicated to many of its ideals. We are modern, and not medieval, persons whose religious faith has passed through the analytical fires of the age of reason. We have passed through it and have become something else, but we cannot deny our inheritance. The Reformation was still largely medieval, not modern. The movements which followed in the late sixteenth and early seventeenth centuries—the Catholic Counter Reformation, Calvinism, and Lutheranism—tended to emphasize, even more than the medieval period, insistence on doctrinal orthodoxy and ecclesiastical authority. The seventeenth century was a period of Protestant "scholasticism"—a time not of evangelical enthusiasm, but of

defining and systematizing sound doctrine. The Reformation had sought to return to what it thought to be the original purity of the Christian faith, and so the great reformers were in many respects negative and iconoclastic in their attacks upon the Catholic tradition. It was left to the next generations of theologians, individuals like Melanchthon, to define, systematize, and conserve the purity of doctrine rediscovered by Luther and Calvin. To allow error to continue was to fail to carry out the very intention of the Reformation. The difficulty was, of course, to agree upon what the Reformers meant by their teaching and what constituted purity of doctrine.

The late sixteenth and most of the seventeenth century is a history of long and bitter theological controversies on the Continent and in England.

Today we can better appreciate some of the issues that were the cause of such contention and divisiveness. Nevertheless, A. C. McGiffert is basically correct when he says that seventeenth-century theology

in spite of many differences in detail, was very largely that of the Middle Ages. . . . The reigning philosophy was that of Aristotle, as understood by the medieval schoolmen, and the supernatural realm was conceived in the same objective and realistic fashion. Compared with that of the Middle Ages, Protestant scholasticism was much more barren and at the same time narrower and more oppressive. . . . Of the new science and philosophy that were making headway in the world outside they took no account.[1]

Although it appears to be basically true that Protestant scholasticism was taking little account of the revolutionary movements in science and philosophy, imperceptibly these movements were having their effect on the consciousness of the age. Post-Copernican science, influenced by the dualism of the philosophy of Descartes, sharply severed the medieval unity of the Book of Nature and the Book of Scripture. This was to have a profound effect on Christian thought.

There were, however, two aspects of Protestant scholasticism in particular that helped usher in the religion of reason in the eighteenth century. First, seventeenth-century scholasticism was itself highly rationalistic in spirit and practice. Theological truth was arrived at not through religious experience but, rather, by logical deduction from certain first principles. The test of truth was that of rational consistency. The question became not whether Christianity was to be judged by rational standards, but, rather, what were to constitute the rational standards by which religion should be tested. Karl Barth correctly has remarked that in many respects the seventeenth-century orthodox rationalists and the eighteenth-century heterodox modernists were really bedfellows at heart. As we shall see, the move from orthodox supernaturalism to Deism was not as difficult as it might appear.

The second feature of seventeenth-century orthodoxy, instrumental in setting the stage for eighteenth-century Deism, was its divisiveness.

Europe was worn out from a century of religious wars and persecutions, frequently based on theological issues of concern to only a very few. The theological conflicts in England ended with the Act of Toleration of 1689. There now was a desire to find some common religious foundation upon which all rational persons could agree, despite their differences. Reasonable persons of all Christian sects could agree that the Scriptures were to be honored. But here the agreement ended, for these reasonable individuals could not agree on the interpretation and application of the Bible. Was it possible to bring the revealed principles of the Bible wholly within the sphere of reason itself? Thus began the long and involved modern history of the problem of reason and revelation, philosophy and the Bible.

Lord Herbert of Cherbury

An important attempt to answer this question was made by Edward Lord Herbert of Cherbury (1583–1648). Herbert was a soldier and diplomat during the Thirty Years War, a bloody conflict fought over religious differences. Herbert recognized that the great issue of his time was how to resolve religious conflict and bring about peace. The problem was to find some agreed-upon criteria of religious belief. "What," he asked, "shall the layman, encompassed by the terrors of diverse churches militant throughout the world, decide as to the best religion? For there is no church that does not breathe threats, none almost that does not deny the possibility of salvation outside its own pale. . . . Who will be the witnesses, who will be appointed judge of these controversies?"[2]

Herbert saw that some universal criterion of religious truth was required, since "the wretched terror-stricken mass have no refuge, unless some immovable foundations of truth resting on *universal consent* are established, to which they can turn amid the doubts of theology and philosophy." Herbert explored the teachings of all the ancient religions, making an inventory of those teachings that were common to all of them and that were grounded on common reason. His inductive researches supported the contention that God "has bestowed common notions [*notitiae communes*] upon men in all ages as media of his divine universal providence."3 These universally shared religious ideas, imprinted by God on the human mind for all time, are five in number:

1. That one God exists.

2. That God ought to be worshipped.

3. That the practice of virtue is the chief part of the worship of God.

4. That humans have always had an abhorrence of evil and are under an obligation to repent of their sins.

5. That there will be rewards and punishments after death.

In his great work, *De Veritate* (1624), Herbert set forth these axioms of universal natural religion which, he believed, could be agreed upon by all regardless of the positive (historical and dogmatic) differences among their many faiths. He further believed that a religion based on such principles would lead to religious harmony, or at least to toleration, rather than dissension and bloodshed. As J. S. Preus notes, Herbert's significance lies in the fact that while his agenda was theological, "his universalism entails a complete freedom from the necessity of 'saving' the biblical framework and its primal history or of incorporating it into the construction of an authentic religion."4

Herbert does not deny a role for, say, biblical revelation, only that of revelation's exclusive claim. Any purported revelation must be tested by the universal consent and those "common notions" implanted by a universal Providence. Herbert makes a distinction that challenges the Christian orthodoxy of his time, namely, that there could be a difference between what is contained in the Bible and the "Word of God." He writes: "Not every religion which proclaims a revelation is good, nor is every doctrine taught under its authority always essential or even valuable. Some doctrines due to revelation may be, some ought to be, abandoned. In this connection, the teaching of Common Notions is important; indeed, without them it is impossible to establish *any standard of discrimination in revelation* or even in religion."5

Lord Herbert is proposing that one must approach the Bible with certain rational presuppositions or an interpretive key that will separate the wheat from the chaff in the Bible. These ideas were attractive to many writers in the eighteenth century, and Lord Herbert came to be known as the "Father of Deism."

In England in the seventeenth century, there were a number of influential writers who, like Herbert, sought to find a common platform on which all persons of faith (or at least all Protestants) could agree. William Chillingworth's *Religion of Protestants, A Sure Way of Salvation* (1637), although written as a defense of Protestantism, nevertheless sought to make the Bible the sole guide of faith and to minimize all beliefs and practices not defined by the Scriptures.

> Take away this persecuting, burning, cursing, damning of men for not subscribing to the words of men as the words of God. . . . I say take away tyranny and restore Christians to the first and full liberty of captivating their understandings to Scripture only; and as rivers when they have a free passage run only to the ocean, so it may well be hoped, by God's blessing, that universal liberty, thus moderated may quickly reduce Christendom to truth and liberty.6

Chillingworth assumed the authority of the Bible as a matter upon which all Christians were agreed. As long as no one questioned that tenet, all was well. But the fact was that the several sects could not agree upon the interpretation of Scripture. Was it not necessary to go back even further for a principle other than Scripture that was common to all Christians? The issue was joined. By the end of the seventeenth century most of the ablest religious thinkers were divided into two camps. The orthodox or rational supernaturalists insisted on the unique role of revelation and on the distinction between what could and what could not be known by the exercise of reason alone. The more radical thinkers, who came to be known as Deists, rejected the necessity of revelation and insisted on the sufficiency of the unaided natural reason in religion. The development of this controversy is an interesting one, and the outcome of the battle was truly "epoch-making," for it led directly to the skepticism of David Hume and eventually, in France, to a more militant atheism. Many of the issues raised by the Deist controversy are still with us, in slightly different guise, in the latter years of the twentieth century.

RATIONAL SUPERNATURALISM

John Tillotson

Chillingworth found a very able successor in John Tillotson, Archbishop of Canterbury. Tillotson (1630–1694) was the most famous preacher of his day, and his sermons and other writings were widely read and admired in the eighteenth century. The Archbishop was a leader in the controversy over the claims of the Roman church, and his attack upon Roman beliefs was avowedly rationalist. In fact, Hume was later to found his essay "Of Miracles" on Tillotson's favorite argument against Catholic Transubstantiation—namely, that the doctrine is contrary to the testimony of all our senses. "Nothing," says Tillotson, "ought to be received as a revelation from God which plainly contradicts the principles of natural religion."[7] No argument will prove a doctrine to be divine "which is not clearer and stronger than the difficulties and objections against it."[8] Religious beliefs are to be tested like any other propositions—by rational evidence.

According to Tillotson, the function and end of religion is found in the fact that it provides divine sanctions for morality. These sanctions are found in natural religion which teaches us (1) that there is a God, (2) that He requires that humankind live virtuously, and (3) that God will reward the righteous and punish the wicked. If Tillotson could reduce religion to so few principles of natural religion, why is he included among the rational supernaturalists? Part of the answer is that Tillotson did not believe that natural religion alone proved effective. It required the supplementation of revelation. Revelation clarifies the truths discerned by natural reason and makes for their more effective reception. "Natural religion is the foundation of all revealed religion and revelation is designed simply to establish its duties."[9] According to Tillotson, first, we can know an alleged revelation is genuine if it does not contradict the principles of natural religion and, second, if the reasons for supposing it a revelation are stronger than those reasons that can be brought against it.

Tillotson's rational supernaturalism is also evident in his defense of Christianity on the basis of the argument from miracle. In his sermon on "The Miracles Wrought in Confirmation of Christianity," the Archbishop asks: "In what circumstances and with what limitations are miracles a sufficient testimony to the truth and divinity of any doctrine?" His answer is that

> there are two things [that] must concur to give the mind of man full satisfaction that any religion is from God. First, if the person that declares this religion give testimony of his divine authority, that is, that he is sent and commissioned by God for that purpose. And secondly if the religion which he declares contain nothing in it that is plainly repugnant to the nature of God. . . . *For though a doctrine be never so reasonable in itself, this is no certain argument that it is from God if no testimony from heaven be given to it; because it may be the result and issue of human reason and discourse; and though a doctrine be attested by miracles, yet the matter of it may be so unreasonable and absurd . . . that no miracles can be sufficient to give confirmation to it. . . .*[10] (Italics added.)

If, then, there is a concurrence of the "testimony of divine authority" and "nothing in it [the miracle] that is repugnant to the nature of God," then the miracle is "the principal external proof and confirmation of a doctrine."[11]

Today Tillotson's proof of Christianity from miracle would be regarded with astonishment by many because he is arguing that the proof of the faith lies in the miracles which attended its beginnings and were accomplished *specifically* to confirm its unique claims. To many modern believers there is something wooden about such an external, miraculous proof and something very wrong in Tillotson's conception of the function and purpose of the miracle stories in the Gospels. Yet Tillotson combined in his rational supernaturalism those characteristics which exemplified much of the orthodox rationalist thinking of his day: the conviction that nothing is to be accepted that does not commend itself to our natural reason, and the belief that miracles are entirely reasonable and often can be adduced as certain proof of divine revelation. These characteristics are best seen in the writings of the foremost rational supernaturalist, the philosopher John Locke.

John Locke

John Locke (1632–1704), regarded by many as the most important of the English philosophers, thought of himself as a devout and orthodox Christian. He accepted the authority of both reason and the Bible and never saw any serious difficulty in serving both masters. In the introduction to his great work, *An Essay Concerning Human Understanding* (1690), Locke says that his purpose was "to enquire into the original certainty and extent of human knowledge, together with the grounds and degrees of belief, opinion and assent. . . ."[12] Toward the very end of this long but lucid work, Locke turns to the question of the nature and extent of our genuine knowledge of religion. In Book IV, Chapter 17, Locke makes an important distinction among what is "above, contrary and according to reason."

> 1. *According to reason* are such propositions whose truth we can discover by examining and tracing those ideas we have from sensation and reflection, and by natural deduction find to be true or probable.
> 2. *Above reason* are such propositions whose truth or probability we cannot by reason derive from those principles.
> 3. *Contrary to reason* are such propositions as are inconsistent with or irreconcilable to our clear and distinct ideas. Thus the existence of God is according to reason; the existence of more than one God is contrary to reason; the resurrection of the dead above reason.[13]

Genuine religious knowledge can be discovered by natural reason and in those propositions that are above but not contrary to reason. Assent to propositions that are "above" reason is the assent of faith to truths of revelation. Locke makes the following distinction between reason and faith:

> *Reason,* as contradistinguished from faith, I take to be the discovery of the certainty or probability of such propositions or truths, which the mind arrives at by deductions made from such ideas which it has got by the use of its natural faculties, viz. by sensation or reflection.
> *Faith,* on the other side, is the assent to any proposition, not thus made out by the deductions of reason, but upon the credit of the proposer, as coming from God in some extraordinary way of communication. This way of discovering truths to men we call *revelation.*[14]

Locke says that revelation may give a man genuine knowledge which is also discoverable by man's natural reason.

> I say, that *the same truths may be discovered and conveyed down from revelation which are discoverable to us by reason.* . . . So God might, by revelation, discover the truth of any proposition in Euclid. In all things of this kind there is little need or use of revelation, God having furnished us with natural and surer means to arrive at the knowledge of them. For the knowledge we have that this revelation came at first from God, can never be so sure as the knowledge we have from the clear and distinct perception of the agreement or disagreement of our own ideas.[15]

Revelation may, however, give us knowledge that is above reason,

> there being many things wherein we have very imperfect notions, or none at all; and other things, of whose past, present or future existence, by the natural use of our faculties, we can have no knowledge at all: these being beyond the discovery of our natural faculties and above reason, are, when revealed, *the proper matter of faith.* Thus that part of the angels rebelled against God, and thereby lost their first happy state: and that the dead shall rise and live again: these, and the like, being beyond the discovery of reason, are purely matters of faith, with which reason has, directly, nothing to do.[16]

Although such revelatory knowledge may be "above reason," revelation can never be assented to which is "contrary to reason."

> Whatever God hath revealed is certainly true; no doubt can be made of it. This is the proper object of faith: but whether it be a divine revelation or no, reason must judge; which can never permit the mind to reject a great evidence to embrace what is less evident, nor allow it to entertain probability in opposition to knowledge and certainty. There can be no evidence

that any traditional revelation is of divine original, in the words we receive it, so clear and so certain as that of the principles of reason. And therefore *nothing that is contrary to, and inconsistent with, the clear and self-evident dictates of reason, has a right to be urged or assented to, as a matter of faith wherein reason hath nothing to do.*[17]

The question which remains to be answered is, How do we know that propositions given in revelation ("above reason") are to be given our assent? That is, what reason have we for accepting "the credit of the proposer" who claims that certain truths were offered by revelation? Locke deals with this problem in Chapter 19 of Book IV, entitled "Of Enthusiasm." Locke sees "enthusiasm" as a third, though fallacious, "ground of assent," along with reason and revelation. It is that ground of assent which in effect "takes away both reason and revelation, and substitutes . . . the ungrounded fancies of a man's own brain. . . ."[18] The enthusiasts are those who "cannot be mistaken in what they feel . . . . they are sure because they are sure, and their persuasions are right, only because they are strong in them."[19] "But," says Locke,

> to examine a little soberly this internal light and this feeling on which they build so much: the question here is, How do I know that God is the revealer of this to me; that this impression is made upon my mind by his Holy Spirit and that therefore I ought to obey it?[20]

The enthusiasts are caught in a vicious circle, for they claim the veracity of a revelation because they firmly believe it and they believe it because it is a revelation!

Locke's answer to the "enthusiast" is the following:

> Light, true light in the mind is or can be nothing else but the evidence of the truth of any proposition; and if it is not a self-evident proposition, all the light it has, or can have, is from the clearness and validity of those proofs upon which it is received. . . . God, when he makes the prophet does not unmake the man. He leaves all his faculties in their natural state, to enable him to judge of his inspirations, whether they be of divine original or no. . . . If he [God] would have us as-

sent to the truth of any proposition, he either evidences that truth by the usual methods of natural reason, or else makes it known to be a truth which he would have us assent to by his authority, and convinces us that it is from him, by some marks which reason cannot be mistaken in. . . . Every conceit that thoroughly warms our fancies must pass for an inspiration, if there be nothing but the strength of our persuasions, whereby to judge of our persuasions. If reason must not examine their truth by something extrinsical to the persuasions themselves, inspirations and delusions, truth and falsehood, will have the same measure, and will not be possible to be distinguished. Thus we see, the holy men of old, who had revelations from God, had something else besides that internal light of assurance in their own minds to testify to them that it was from God. They were not left to their own persuasions alone, that those persuasions were from God, but had outward signs to convince them of the Author of those revelations.[21]

What the holy people of old had that convinced them of the veracity of their revelations were "outward signs." For Locke the reasonableness of revelation depends, then, upon "outward signs," i.e., upon the external evidence of prophecy fulfillment and miracle. The sole purpose of such miracles is to give assurance that a person is a messenger of God and thereby to confirm the divine origin of the revelation.

> It is to be considered, that divine revelation receives testimony from no other miracles, but such as are wrought to witness his mission from God who delivers the revelation. All other miracles that are done in the world, how many or great soever, revelation is not concerned in.[22]

In 1695 Locke published *The Reasonableness of Christianity* in which the general principles of the *Essay* are applied directly to the Christian faith. In this little book Locke examines the Bible both to discover the essence of Christianity as revealed by Christ and to prove the reasonableness of Christ's credentials as a messenger of God. Locke's study of Scripture leads him to reject much of traditional Christian belief which he finds contrary to reason, but also to the discovery that Christ and his apostles taught only two things necessary for salvation: (1) belief that Jesus is the Messiah sent from God for our redemption and (2) the necessity of repentance and the bringing forth of the fruits of repentance by following a righteous life. What, asks Locke, could be more reasonable than this? The reasonableness of these truths revealed by Christ are clearly proved by two "external signs": (1) the fulfillment of the Messianic prophecies and (2) the performance of miracles.

For Locke the proof of prophecy is apparently the successful fulfillment of the prediction. Jesus simply fits the description of the one whose coming was foretold. I. T. Ramsey contends that Locke actually presents a form of intuitive proof from prophecy fulfillment.

> May not Locke . . . have implied that in bringing alongside the person of Jesus the Messiah label, there strikes us an aptness and appropriateness of the kind which strikes us when, for example, we see at long last the island corresponding to the map we have pondered for years, or the lost piece in the jigsaw which is just what we had been told to expect. In other words, though Locke never says so, is it not possible that even in thinking of the Messiah as a descriptive label which fitted Jesus, Locke was appealing to some kind of disclosure situation . . . to something he called "intuition". . . ? May not intuition play the same part for propositions which are "above reason" as demonstration does in the case of propositions which are "according to reason"? In this case the broad reasonableness of Christian assent would lie in its intuitive character.[23]

In the light of modern biblical research, the idea of Jesus's "fitting" the Messianic label is an especially difficult ground for proof for the simple reason that Jesus did not fit most of the Messianic labels in circulation. Locke's model of the "disclosure situation" is too simple to fit the facts. However, Locke's evidence from prophecy fulfillment might still be reasonable if the concept of "disclosure situation" is broadened.

> It must now be an intuition which arises when a number of different labels are seen to fit an object to which none of these alone are adequate, such as is the

case when we become intuitively aware of a cone by seeing various projections of it, or of a mountain by seeing various single aspects of it. Our previous map and jigsaw examples are too simple.[24]

That Locke was not involved in a crude empirical proof from prophecy and miracle is even clearer in his remarks concerning miracle. Miracles are credentials which, being plainly observable events, make reasonable the propositions of their performer. Locke appears at times to argue that if two people utter propositions which call for our assent, the more reasonable assent simply depends upon the size or power of the miraculous act. This, however, is not Locke's view. In the *Third Letter on Toleration,* Locke compares the power of a miracle with that of civil power and argues that the power of miracle is of quite a distinct kind. Again commenting on Locke's view, I. T. Ramsey says that for Locke

> the power of a miracle is not measurable power, it is not power according to law. This means, I suggest, that a miracle must be given the same compelling power as belongs to an intuition. . . . Then Locke can justly say (as he does) that to distinguish between a pretended revelation and that which is truly divine "we need but open our eyes to see and be sure which came from [God]."[25]

Ramsey rightly indicates that for Locke the compelling power of divine miracle is intuitively disclosed. Unlike his successors, the Deists, Locke appears to have desired to preserve not only reasonableness but also mystery as an irreducible component of the Christian faith.

The Reasonableness of Christianity was concerned with separating the essential articles of faith from the plethora of dogmas and rites with which "writers and wranglers in religion have filled it" and to indicate the reasonableness of Christ's credentials as the instrument of God's revelation. Having accomplished this, Locke turns, at the conclusion of the work, to certain objections that were yet to be met. The first difficulty had to do with those who lived before the time of Jesus Christ. If men are justified by God for believing Jesus to be the Messiah "what shall become of all mankind, who lived before Our

Saviour's time; who never heard of his name and consequently could not believe in him?"[26] The answer, says Locke, is "obvious and natural."

> Nobody was or can be required to believe what was never proposed to him to believe. . . . All then that was required before his [Messiah's] appearing in the world was to believe what God had revealed, and to rely with a full assurance on God for the performance of his promise. . . .[27]

The greater difficulty has to do with those "who, having never heard of the promise or news of a Saviour, have had no thought or belief concerning him." Locke's answer is that those who were never in a position either to accept or to reject Christ's revelation would be illuminated by that natural reason which is God's gift to all his children.

> God had, by the light of reason, revealed to all mankind, who would make use of that light, that he was good and merciful. The same spark of the divine nature and knowledge of man, which making him a man, showed him the law he was under as a man; showed him also the way of atoning the merciful, kind, compassionate Author and Father of him and his being, when he had transgressed that law. He that made use of this candle of the Lord, so far as to find what was his duty, could not miss to find also the way to reconciliation and forgiveness, when he had failed his duty.[28]

Having admitted this much concerning the sufficiency of the religion of natural reason, Locke is required to answer why revelation is needed at all. Locke concludes *The Reasonableness of Christianity* with five arguments for revelation. All five are variations on the single theme that in human history revelation has proved practically useful and even necessary.

The rational supernaturalists Tillotson and Locke both agreed that natural religion is good as far as it goes, but that, practically, it has always needed to be supplemented by revelation. Christian revelation makes our natural piety and duties plain, and the glory of Christian revelation lies in the fact that, while it serves to clarify and empower, it does so without contradicting or altering the findings of natural reason. The rational supernaturalists also agreed

that the essentials of Christian revelation could be reduced to a very few doctrines and that these doctrines provided the divine sanctions for morality.

The second stage in the development of eighteenth-century theology was entered when those contemporaries of Locke, who came later to be called Deists, challenged the claim that the divine sanction for morality required a special revelation—i.e., that a true natural religion demanded the particular teachings of Christianity.

DEISM IN ENGLAND

John Locke had maintained a place for those things that, while not contrary to reason, were, nevertheless, "above reason." Locke appears to have desired to preserve mystery as a genuine element in Christian faith. Most of Locke's successors were eager, however, to exclude all mystery from revelation. This is evident in the work of John Toland, a man who considered himself a disciple of Locke.

John Toland

John Toland (1670–1722) was a graduate of Edinburgh and studied at Leyden and at Oxford where he was supported financially by a group of Protestant dissenters. While at Oxford he wrote his first and most important book, *Christianity Not Mysterious* (1696). In this book Toland follows a position that might appear similar to that of Locke's *Essay.* However, unlike Locke, he does not allow for truths which are "above reason." Toland narrows Locke's three classes of natural religion, superstition, and revelation to two; for "according to reason" (natural religion) and "above reason" (revelation) are, for Toland, essentially of the same class. Thus, Toland rejects the possibility of the revelation of truths which, in themselves, are beyond the compass of reason. Toland admits that no one in his day would hold that reason and revelation are contradictory, but, perhaps with Locke specifically in mind, he continues,

> very many affirm that though the doctrines of the latter cannot in themselves be contradictory to the principles of the former, as proceeding both from God; yet,

John Toland

that according to our conceptions of them, *they may seem directly to clash:* And that though we cannot reconcile them by reason of our corrupt and limited understandings; yet from the authority of Divine Revelation, we are bound to believe and acquiesce in them; or as the Fathers taught them to speak, *to adore what we cannot comprehend.*[29]

Toland's sharp reply to this view is that such a "famous and admirable doctrine is the undoubted source of all the *Absurdities* that ever were seriously vented among Christians. Without the pretence of it, we should never hear of Transubstantiation and other ridiculous Fables. . . ."[30]

But if we are never to assent by faith to what is "above reason," are we not saying that faith is no longer faith but knowledge? Toland answers that if knowledge means understanding what is believed, then faith is, indeed, a form of knowledge. Does not then such a notion of faith as knowledge render revelation useless? Toland answers:

But pray, how so? for the question is not whether we could discover all the objects of our *Faith* by

Ratiocination: I have proved on the contrary that no matter of fact can be known without *Revelation*. But I assert, that *what is once revealed we must as well understand as any other matter in the world, Revelation being only of use to enform us while the evidence of its subject persuades us.* Then reply they, *Reason* is of more dignity than Revelation. I answer, just as much as a *Greek Grammar* is superior to the *New Testament;* for we make use of Grammar to understand the language and of Reason to understand the sense of that book. But, in a word, I see no need of Comparisons in this case, for *Reason* is not less from God than *Revelation;* 'tis the Candle, the Guide, the Judge he has lodged within every man that cometh into this world.[31]

Toland argues that reasonable facts or truths may be discovered by us for ourselves or may be made known to us by the testimony of others which may be given by revelation. But in either case *revelation is never mysterious or incomprehensible once it is known.* Revelation is perfectly rational but concerns events that otherwise have not fallen under our observation or within our experience.

Most of the Deists of the late seventeenth and early eighteenth centuries sought to show that God's perfection demands a way of salvation open to all persons and that positive (historical) revelation, being limited to special times and peoples, lacks universality. The true religion must be equally accessible to the natural reason of humanity at all times and places. The most complete exposition of this Deistic view was made in Matthew Tindal's *Christianity as Old as the Creation,* a book regarded as the culmination of the constructive phase of English Deism and referred to as "the Deist's Bible."

Matthew Tindal

Matthew Tindal's life (1655–1733), as a Fellow of All Souls College, Oxford, was peaceful and respectable in comparison with the tumultuous and bohemian life of Toland. In 1730, at the advanced age of seventy-three, Tindal published the first volume of *Christianity as Old as the Creation.* At his death three years later he left the manuscript of a second volume which was quietly destroyed by a bishop, fearful of its probable influence. The bishop's action, revealing an all-too-common intellectual timidity on the part of ecclesiastics, was not justified, however. The first volume elicited 150 replies, including William Law's *The Case of Reason* (1731), Bishop Berkeley's *Alciphron* (1732), and, most important, Bishop Butler's *Analogy of Religion* (1736).

Tindal's book begins with two a priori principles on which his whole case is built. First, God is eternally the same, infinitely wise and good. What originates with a perfect, all-wise God must itself be perfect. Thus an absolutely perfect religion cannot be altered or increased or decreased. Second, human nature is always the same and unalterable in itself. Hence, God's perfect religion must dispense its truth equally to every person at all times. Historical revelation can add nothing to a religion that is absolutely perfect, universal, and unchanging.

> If all own that God, at no time, could have any motive to give laws to mankind but for their good; and that he is at all times equally good, and at all times acts upon the same motives, must they not own with me, except they are inconsistent with themselves, that his Laws at all times must be the same?[32]

God in his infinite goodness desired that everyone should come to a knowledge of true religion. If we assume that Christianity is the only true and perfect religion, then it must have been created for all of humankind from the beginning. The name "Christianity" may be of more recent origin, but the essentials of the Christian religion must have existed from the creation. From the beginning God has given humanity the means to know and practice Christianity, the "means" being reason, that faculty that separates us from the beasts. God has created us rational creatures, that through this capacity we might know what constitutes the very law and will of divine reason. According to Tindal, what is offered to us as God's will must be reasonable and what is reasonable must itself be judged by reason. Nothing then can be admitted into Christianity except what our reason tells us is worthy of God.

> The Holy Ghost can't deal with men as rational creatures, but by proposing arguments to convince their understandings, and influence their wills, in the same manner as if proposed by other agents; for to go beyond this would be making impressions on men, as a seal does on wax; to the confounding of their reason,

and their liberty in choosing; and the man would then be merely passive, and the action would be the action of another Being acting upon him; for which he could be in no way accountable: but if the Holy Ghost does not act thus, and Revelation itself be not arbitrary; must it not be founded on the Reason of Things? And consequently, be a *Republication,* or Restoration of the Religion of Nature?[33]

Since Tindal holds that God has provided us at all times with the means of knowing what he requires, then natural religion and true, revealed religion cannot differ in substance but only in the manner in which each becomes known.

> I think too great a stress can't be laid on Natural Religion, which, as I take it, differs not from Revealed but in the manner of its being communicated. The one being the internal, as the other the external Revelation of the same unchangeable will of a Being, who is alike at all times infinitely wise and good.[34]

According to Tindal, since God must have dealt equally with all humanity, it follows that doctrines not revealed to all cannot be doctrines imposed by God. With this principle in hand, Tindal makes a clean sweep of all those doctrines and practices of the church that cannot stand up to the scrutiny of natural reason. With shrewd and bitter sarcasm, Tindal jests at the "superstitions" of the Bible and the Roman Church. What right, he asks, has a Papist who rubs a dying man with oil to laugh at the Indian who thinks it will conduce to his future happiness to die with a cow's tail in his hands?[35] Like his French counterpart, Voltaire, Tindal discloses a completely uncritical admiration for the Chinese while jeering unmercifully at the beliefs and practices of the Jews and Christians.

For Tindal all beliefs and practices must be judged not only by natural reason but by their ability to promote human happiness. God's purpose in creation was not for His own glory or advantage, but the happiness of His creatures. God thus demands of us only what will contribute to our perfection and happiness.

> Whoever so regulates his natural appetites as will conduce most to the exercise of his reason, the health of his body and the pleasures of his senses taken and

considered together (since herein his happiness consists) may be certain he can never offend his Maker; who, as he governs all things according to their natures, can't but expect his rational creatures should act according to their natures.[36]

The end of religion, then, is morality, for true religion consists "in a constant disposition of mind to do all the good we can, and thereby render ourselves acceptable to God in answering the end of our creation."[37] The only difference between morality and religion is that morality is "acting according to the reason of things considered in themselves," while religion is "acting according to the same reason of things considered as the rule of God."[38] Anything in religion that is not required of our moral life should be removed, for the more one "is taken up with the observation of things which are not of a moral nature, the less he will be able to attend those that are."[39]

Tindal is willing to call everything in religion superstitious and dangerous which is not directly conducive to morality.

> As long as men believe the good of society is the supreme law, they will think it their duty to be governed by that law; and believing God requires nothing of them but what is the good of mankind *will place the whole of their religion in benevolent actions* . . . but if they are made to believe there are things which have no relation to this good, necessary to salvation, they must suppose it their duty to use such means as will most effectually serve this purpose, and that God, in requiring the end requires all those means as will best secure and propagate it. And 'tis to this principle we owe the most cruel persecutions, inquisitions, crusades and massacres.[40]

With Tindal, Christianity is reduced to the practice of virtue. Religion becomes the recognition of our moral duties as divine commands. Here Tindal arrives at a conception of religion and of Christianity that Immanuel Kant will adopt in his book on *Religion Within the Limits of Reason Alone.* With Tindal the center of focus has shifted from the religion of the older rationalism to the religion of practical reason, that is, a reason that does not seek to prove God and immortality, but to show that

these beliefs are implicit in our human moral consciousness. The rational supernaturalists had conceded too much, and it was left for Tindal to discredit their appeal to a special revelation. Tindal's shift to a theism based on practical reason was perhaps unconsciously due to the inherent weakness of the rational basis of the Deists' position itself. In any case, Tindal's own book reflects both the shaky foundation of rationalistic theism and, at the same time, the beginnings of a move in a quite new direction. In remarking on the change that occurred between Locke and David Hume, Leslie Stephen points to the pivotal role of Matthew Tindal in the decline of rational supernaturalism.

> It was in vain that, after exhausting their eloquence to prove the competence of human reason and the absolute clearness and simplicity of religious truth, writers of that school laboured to establish some narrow standing-ground for revelation. They had, in their own opinion, raised such immovable pillars for the support of morality, that the old-fashioned props became first superfluous and then offensive. When their necessity was no longer felt in practice, men had leisure to remark upon their antiquated and grotesque design, and to observe how inadequate they were for the task imposed upon them. So far Tindal's victory was undeniable; though his own flank was equally liable to be turned, and his antagonists were not slow to perceive their advantage. So long as the controversy was confined within the prescribed limits, nothing could run more easily than Tindal's logic.[41]

As long as the issues were kept within the prescribed limits, Deism won the day. However, in their slashing offensive against the orthodox, the Deists failed to examine their own fortifications. It was not long after the appearance of *Christianity as Old as the Creation* that Deism itself faced devastating attacks on two fronts. On the one hand, there were the defenders of orthodoxy, such as Bishop Butler, who sought to demonstrate the difficulties in belief in natural religion, thereby enhancing belief in revelation; on the other flank, there emerged the great skeptic David Hume. But before examining at length the critique of the religion of reason, we must take a brief look at Deism in France and Germany.

DEISM IN FRANCE: VOLTAIRE

There is a certain truth in the statement that the religion of reason had its origins in England but was made popular in France. The French *philosophes* were not formal philosophers but were, by and large, literary individuals, zealous popularizers and disseminators of the new knowledge which they believed would emancipate society from ignorance and fanaticism.

French Deism was much less theoretical and constructive than English Deism, although the former drew heavily from the latter for its weapons. The situations of the two countries explain in part the differences in the development of rational religion. In England, religious toleration allowed for freedom of expression which even encouraged dialogue between the Deists and the representatives of orthodoxy and the established Church. In France, these conditions did not exist. The Catholic Church opposed free thinkers uncompromisingly and could call upon the State for assistance in repressing religious heterodoxy. The *philosophes* felt they were an embattled minority, standing against the forces of darkness: intolerance, fear, and superstition. The constant threat of persecution and repression gave to French Deism a militant, scurrilous, and yet devious quality that is predominantly negative in character. In speaking of Voltaire, G. R. Cragg describes well the tone and tactics of French Deism in general as follows:

> This lurking threat of persecution explains a certain oblique disingenuousness in Voltaire, a readiness to hide behind the authority of others and to imply that he accepted more than he really did. He was sometimes abusive, sometimes cringing. He used abuse when he felt brave; he resorted to lies when he felt timid. But it also accounts for the violence, even the extravagance, into which the champions of reason and common sense allowed themselves to fall. When it was safe to do so, they attacked the strongholds of superstition with volcanic energy. Nothing was so sacred as to escape their ribald criticism, nothing so mysterious as to defy their constant analysis.[42]

The French *philosophes* popularized the views of the English Deists by reducing the often-tedious verbiage of the English dissertations to clear, crisp, and often witty pronouncements that were immediately grasped with a self-evident authority. The man who best exemplifies the phenomenon of French Deism is François Marie Arouet, who is known to us by his adopted name, Voltaire.

Voltaire (1694–1778) was for over half a century one of the most important influences on European thought and life. He was not a philosopher but a poet and dramatist turned critic and sage, whose pen changed the life and institutions of his native France.

Voltaire's religious beliefs have long occupied scholars.[43] Alfred Noyes, among others, has argued that Voltaire was a good Roman Catholic.[44] Others have claimed Voltaire for Protestantism and for atheism. By picking and choosing from his writings, which span half a century, Voltaire can be made to champion everything from militant atheism to orthodox Catholicism. This is due not only to his long and active life but to his holding, with Emerson, that "a foolish consistency is the hobgoblin of little minds." He had a tough, pragmatic mind and, like most great individuals, the courage to change. Voltaire's writings have been aptly described as a "chaos of clarities." Nevertheless, most Voltaire scholars hold that the French sage was, through his mature life, a vague, mystical, and even emotional Deist.

Voltaire's early Deism is a simple natural religion, skeptical of speculation, but firmly convinced that the rationality of the Newtonian universe justifies belief in the existence of a divine intelligence behind it. This is evident in his first attempt at a summation of his philosophic beliefs, the *Traité de Métaphysique,* written about 1734. In this essay Voltaire offers two arguments for the existence of God—the argument from design and the argument from the necessity of a first cause. In offering his argument from design, Voltaire uses the analogy between God and the watchmaker, an analogy which William Paley would later make famous in his *Natural Theology* (1802). The marvelous adaptation of means to particular ends, says Voltaire, argues for a designer.

> When I see a watch whose hands mark the hours, I conclude that an intelligent being has arranged the

springs of this machine so that its hands will mark the hours. Thus, when I see the springs of the human body, I conclude that an intelligent being has arranged these organs to be received and nourished for nine months in the womb; that the eyes are given for seeing, the hands to seizing, etc., but from this sole argument I cannot conclude anything further than that it is probable that an intelligent and superior being has skillfully prepared and fashioned the matter.[45]

In typical rationalist fashion Voltaire offers his second argument for the existence of God, the argument from the necessity of a first cause.

> I exist, hence something exists. If something exists, then something must have existed from all eternity; for whatever is, either exists through itself or has received its being from something else. If through itself, it exists of necessity, it has always existed of necessity, it is God; if it has received its being from something else, and that something from a third, that from which the last has received its being must of necessity be God. . . . Intelligence is not essential to matter, for a rock or grain do not think. Whence then have the particles of matter which think and feel received sensation and thought? It cannot be from themselves since they think in spite of themselves; it cannot be from matter in general, since thought and sensation do not belong to the essence of matter: hence they must have received these gifts from the hands of a Supreme Being, intelligent, infinite, and the original cause of all beings.[46]

Voltaire's conclusion in *Traité de Métaphysique* is that "In the opinion that there is a God there are difficulties; but in the contrary opinion there are absurdities."[47] In an article entitled *Théiste* in the *Dictionaire Philosophique,* Voltaire sums up his religious faith in a single page that could well serve as the Confession of Faith of Deism:

> The theist is a man firmly persuaded of the existence of a Supreme Being equally good and powerful, who has formed all . . . existences; who perpetuates their species, who punishes crimes without cruelty, and rewards virtuous actions with kindness.

> The theist does not know how God punishes, how He rewards, how He pardons; for he is not presump-

tuous enough to flatter himself that he understands how God acts; but he knows that God does act and that He is just. The difficulties opposed to a providence do not stagger him in his faith, because they are only great difficulties, not proofs; he submits himself to that providence, although he only perceives some of its effects and some appearances; and judging of the things he does not see from those he does see, he thinks that this providence pervades all places and all ages.

> United in this principle with the rest of the universe, he does not join any of the sects, who all contradict themselves. His religion is the most ancient and the most extended, for the simple adoration of a God preceded all the systems in the world. . . . He believes that religion consists neither in the opinions of incomprehensible metaphysics, nor in vain decorations, but in adoration and justice. To do good—that is his worship; to submit oneself to God—that is his doctrine. The Mohammedan cries out to him: "Take care of yourself, if you do not make the pilgrimage to Mecca." "Woe be to thee," says a Franciscan, "if thou dost not make a journey to our Lady of Loretta." He laughs at Loretta and Mecca; but he succours the poor and defends the oppressed.[48]

Until 1751 Voltaire refrained from any public attack upon Christianity. Here and there he would jab and mock at the foibles and fanaticism of the Church, but most of his religious writings consisted of praises of natural religion and pleas for mutual tolerance and understanding. However, for over twenty years after 1751 Voltaire published a torrent of pamphlets and essays, scathing in their denunciation of Christianity. The causes of this declaration of war are not all known; three events in the decade following 1751 are certainly important. These events were the suppression of the *Encyclopédie,* for which Voltaire had written several articles; the facile theological explanations of the Lisbon earthquake of 1755, and the execution of Jean Calas, the Huguenot (Calvinist Protestant), in 1762, unjustly condemned on the charge of having killed his son to prevent his conversion to Catholicism.

Ecrasez l'infâme—"Crush the infamous thing"— was the battle cry heard throughout Europe. Voltaire became so intoxicated with the slogan he even used it, in abbreviated form, as a signature: "Ecr. linf." What did Voltaire mean by *l'infâme* that required to be crushed? Four possibilities have been argued with some plausibility: fanaticism, Catholicism, Christianity, and religion. It is clear, however, that to the end of his life Voltaire expressed genuine, deep religious convictions. It is also evident that the object of his attack went beyond fanaticism in general and was primarily an assault on the doctrines and practices shared by Catholics and Protestants alike. *L'infâme* was quite certainly Christianity in any of its orthodox, institutional forms, whether found in Geneva or Rome.

Voltaire's declaration of war was the *Sermon of the Fifty,* written at the court at Potsdam. The *Sermon* and other writings of this period are vehement and cynical tracts whose critical insights now appear quaint but nevertheless reveal that Voltaire was *au courant* of the most advanced biblical criticism of his age. He pokes fun at the outmoded science and primitive morals of the ancient Hebrews, relating story after story of the lies, murders, and fornications of the noble Jewish patriarchs.

> What will you say of the holy King David, the king who found favour in the eyes of the God of the Jews, and merited to be an ancestor of the Messiah? This good king is at first a brigand, capturing and pillaging all he finds. Among others, he despoils a rich man named Nabal, marries his wife and flies to King Achish. During the night he descends upon the villages of King Achish, his benefactor, with fire and sword. He slaughters men, women, and children. . . . When he is made King he ravishes the wife of Uriah and has the husband put to death; and it is from this adulterous homicide that the Messiah—God himself—descends![49]

Voltaire delights in pointing out the incongruities and contradictions in the Bible. Here are just a few examples:

Adam and Eve:

> On the sixth day God makes man and woman; but the author, forgetting that woman has been made already, afterwards derives her from one of Adam's ribs. Adam and Eve are put in the garden from which four rivers issue; and of these rivers there are two, the Euphrates and the Nile, which have their sources a thousand miles from each other.

Noah and the Flood:

> [God] wished to save Noah and ordered him to make a vessel of poplar wood, three hundred cubits in length. Into this vessel were brought seven pairs of all clean and two pairs of the unclean. . . . You can imagine what would be needed to feed fourteen elephants, fourteen camels, fourteen buffaloes, and as many horses, asses, deer, serpents, ostriches . . .!

Jesus:

> In the first place, Jesus is described as a descendant of Abraham and David, and the writer of Matthew counts forty-two generations. . . . Luke also gives a genealogy, but he assigns forty-nine generations after Abraham and they are entirely different generations. To complete the absurdity, these generations belong to Joseph and the evangelists assure us that Jesus was not the son of Joseph. Would one be received in a German chapter on such proofs of nobility?[50]

Voltaire ends the *Sermon* by imploring:

> May the great God who hears me—a God who certainly could not be born of a girl, nor die on a gibbet, nor be eaten in a morsel of paste, nor have inspired this book with its contradictions, follies, and horrors—may this God have pity on the sect of Christians who blaspheme him![51]

Voltaire's attack on *l'infâme* never varied. The illustrations changed, but the sermon remained the same. Often the long explications of biblical passages are tedious and tendentious, but here and there they are lightened by brilliant and outrageous humor. What drove Voltaire to such feverish polemics was his conviction that organized Christianity supported irrational superstitions whose vulnerability to rational refutation led only to fanaticism. With psychological insight Voltaire recognized that fanaticism was usually the reaction of weakness covering up its seething uncertainty by forcefully suppressing the opposition. "If you were fully persuaded you would not be intolerant. You are intolerant only because deep in your heart you feel that you are being deceived."[52] The only way to reduce the evils of fanaticism was to unmask superstition, thus freeing humanity from the source of its spiritual malaise: "In a word, less superstition, less fanaticism; and the less fanaticism, less misery."[53] Voltaire regarded most of the doctrines of the Christian tradition—the Incarnation, the Atonement, the Trinity, the Eucharist—as superstitious folly and the principal source of persecution and suffering of nonconformists and skeptics. His comments on the Trinity will suffice.

Here is an incomprehensible question which for over sixteen hundred years has exercized curiosity, sophistical subtlety, bitterness, the spirit of cabal, the rage to dominate, the rage to persecute, blind and bloodthirsty fanaticism, barbaric credulity, and which has produced more horrors than the ambition of princes, which indeed has produced enough. Is Jesus Word? If he is Word, did he emanate from God, is he coeternal and consubstantial with him, or is he of similar substance? Is he distinct from him, or not? Is he created or engendered? Can he engender in turn? Has he paternity or productive virtue without paternity? Is the Holy Ghost created or engendered, or produced? Does he proceed from the Father, or from the Son, or from both? Can he engender, can he produce? Is his hypostasis consubstantial with the hypostasis of the Father and the Son? and why, having precisely the same nature, the same essence as the Father and the Son, can he not do the same things as these two persons who are himself? I certainly do not understand any of this; nobody has ever understood any of this, and this is the reason for which people have slaughtered one another![54]

Voltaire wanted to purify religion of *l'infâme,* of dogmatic Christianity. He felt that health could be restored to society only when the infection of fanaticism was eliminated. Yet Voltaire was aware of the dangers of depriving the masses of their inherited religion, for it was the foundation of their moral sanctions and restraints. Though aware of the social utility of an unquestioned religious tradition,[55] Voltaire was willing to take the chance that the untutored masses could be enlightened: "We know that our enemies have been crying for centuries that one must deceive the people; but we believe that the lowest people are capable of knowing the truth."[56] Christianity could not be exterminated immediately, however.

Such is the miserable condition of man that the true is not always the advantageous. . . . It would doubtless be desirable to overthrow the idol, and to offer God purer homage, but the people is not yet worthy of it. For the present it is enough to contain the Church in its limits. The more laymen are enlightened, the less harm priests will be able to do. Let us try to enlighten even them, to make them blush for their errors, to lead them gradually to becoming citizens.[57]

In the place of Christianity, Voltaire envisioned a new religion: a rather vague, popular form of Deism. Doctrine would be reduced to belief in one just God, whose service was the practice of virtue. Worship would be simple and would consist primarily in praise and adoration and lessons in morality. To the end of his life, Voltaire held to his rational faith in God, despite the fact that his atheist supporters in Paris were now to turn on him in scorn and dismiss the old man with: "*Il est un bigot, c'est un déiste!*" In these last years Voltaire attacked the materialism of d'Holbach and in *We Must Take Sides* (1772) offered rational arguments for God reminiscent of the *Traité de la Métaphysique.*

The character of Voltaire's rational faith, which remained with him throughout his mature years, is nicely indicated in an incident that took place in his eightieth year. One morning in May 1774, Voltaire awakened before dawn and with a visitor climbed a hill near Ferney to see the sunrise. Reaching the top exhausted and overcome by the beauty of the glorious morning scene, Voltaire took off his hat, knelt down, and exclaimed, "I believe, I believe in you, Powerful God, I believe!" And then, getting to his feet, he told the visitor dryly: "As for monsieur the Son and madame His Mother, that is a different story!"[58]

THE RELIGION OF REASON IN GERMANY

The early German *Aufklärung* was in several ways quite different from the comparable movements in England and France. For one thing, the philosophical roots of the German Enlightenment were in the tradition of the rationalism of Gottfried Leibnitz (1646–1716) and Christian Wolff (1679–1754), rather than the Anglo-French empiricism of John Locke. By the middle of the eighteenth century, the Leibnitz-Wolff philosophy had taken on the proportions of a universal program for bringing all human thought and activity before the bar of reason—a deductive model of reason, ruled by the formal principle of noncontradiction and the metaphysical principle of sufficient reason.

Christian Wolff and J. S. Semler

Christian Wolff was a professor of philosophy at Halle and a thorough rationalist, although not antireligious. He was a popularizer of Leibnitz's religious philosophy and had great influence on German universities at the time. Wolff represents the early stages of the religion of reason in eighteenth-century Germany. His position on reason and revelation is similar to that of the rational supernaturalists in England: Wolff makes the distinction between truths that can be known by natural reason alone and those truths that are above reason and are given in revelation. The latter include such doctrines as the Trinity and the Incarnation, but since no revealed religious doctrine can be contrary to reason, it is reason that must determine the criteria by which a true revelation can be recognized.

The criteria would include the principles that the doctrines of revelation cannot conflict with the necessary truths of reason, that they be worthy of what we understand to be a rational understanding of God, and that the necessity of their being known for the well-being and salvation of humanity be shown. Wolff accepted the evidential role of miracles because he believed them to be consistent with divine reason and design, but he sharply delimited their number in a world governed by natural law. That is, God would disrupt the known order of nature only for the most compelling reasons. For Wolff, the fundamental teachings of natural religion, with a few necessary supplements, are found in the Bible. All of this he sets forth in his *Theologia Naturalis* (1736–1737).

German philosophical theology after Wolff moved in a more radical direction toward *neology*. Similar to the English Deists, the *neologians* wholly rationalized the content of revelation, although they retained a belief in its practical necessity. Particular

revealed doctrines, however, were fair game for dismissal if they were found to be unreasonable, by which the neologians meant not in conformity with one's experience, especially one's moral certainties. On these grounds, many of the orthodox Christian doctrines—original sin, predestination, vicarious atonement, the eternity of punishments—were rejected.

Among the most important of the neologians was J. S. Semler (1725–1791), professor of theology at Halle. He was influenced by the English Deists and, though raised in a Pietist environment, as a young man became strongly averse to Pietism. Semler is considered the "father" of the historical critical study of the Bible. His specialty was critical work on the biblical canon, which he saw as made up of various strata and genres of literature and the product of numerous historical factors—many parts of which are devoid of spiritual import and inspiration. He distinguished sharply between dogmatic theology and the religion of the Bible, broke with the orthodox doctrine of verbal biblical inspiration, and held that Jesus and the apostles "accommodated" their teaching to the cruder thought-world of their own day. Therefore, it was crucial to distinguish between the husk and the spiritual kernel of the Old and New Testaments. Semler followed Matthew Tindal in asserting that the essence of the religion of the Bible is to be found in the moral teachings of Christ. While he remained a pious Christian, he essentially reduced the content of biblical revelation to what he found to be both reasonable and in accord with moral experience.

English and French influences on the German *Aufklärung* were not, however, insignificant in the religious sphere. Frederick the Great of Prussia (1712–1786) was particularly drawn to French and English thought. This free-thinking and skeptical monarch was for several years friend and patron of several philosophers, including Voltaire who lived at the court of Potsdam where, as we have seen, he wrote his anti-Christian *Sermon of the Fifty*. Locke was a favorite philosopher of the Prussian monarch, and he encouraged the study of the Englishman's works. The effect of English and French thought in Germany was especially important in the development of a third and later stage of the German Enlightenment. John Toland had traveled through

Germany, visiting the courts of Hanover and Berlin. In 1741 Tindal's *Christianity as Old as the Creation* appeared in German. It is perhaps not surprising that a Deism more hostile to Christianity would also emerge in Germany, one that would find revealed Christianity not only unnecessary but a fraud. Such a position we find in H. S. Reimarus.

H. S. Reimarus

The most prominent of the German Deists was Hermann Samuel Reimarus (1694–1768), a professor of oriental languages in Hamburg. Only three of his works appeared during his lifetime, the most important being an essay entitled "The Leading Truths of Natural Religion," his deistical replacement for what he considered a discredited form of Christianity. At his death he left a four-thousand-page manuscript on which he had labored for twenty years. The work was so controversial that it remained unpublished until the philosopher G. E. Lessing obtained permission from Reimarus's daughter to issue it on the condition that the author's name not be divulged. The manuscript was originally entitled *An Apology for the Rational Worshippers of God,* but Lessing published only seven portions of it as the *Wolffenbüttel Fragments,* claiming that he had found the anonymous fragments at Wolffenbüttel where he was serving as librarian.

Armed with rationalist assumptions, Reimarus's *Apology* subjects the whole biblical history, and thus Christianity, to critical analysis. The third fragment, entitled "The Passage of the Israelites through the Red Sea," is a witty, Voltairean exposé of the account of the Exodus from Egypt. If the biblical narrative is correct, Reimarus calculates that three million Israelites passed through the Red Sea (one warrior to every four others). This would mean that if the Israelites moved in a column ten deep, the length of the column would have been 180 miles and would have taken nine days to cross at a minimum! In the fifth fragment, "On the Resurrection Narrative," the inconsistencies in the Gospel narratives are analyzed with the conclusion that the conflicting accounts indicate that the miracle itself is an imposture.

With his seventh and last fragment, "On the Intentions of Jesus and His Disciples," Reimarus left

for his successors what Albert Schweitzer has called a "magnificent overture in which are announced all the motifs of the future historical treatment of the life of Jesus."[59] Schweitzer may exaggerate, but Reimarus bequeathed to modern theology far more than a destructive, rationalistic critique of the New Testament, although it was so interpreted by Christian theologians of all persuasions at the time. The significance of Reimarus's seventh fragment rests on the fact that it presents an impressive naturalistic, historical account and explanation of the origins of Christianity. For all of its limitations, it remains important, even today, for the issues that it raises. Reimarus focuses on what twentieth-century Christian scholars recognize as, perhaps, the fundamental issue for any doctrine of Christology, namely, the tension between the historical reality and message of Jesus and the Church's memory and portrayal of him in the New Testament.

Reimarus sets Jesus squarely in his first-century Jewish context, especially in the setting of Jewish Messianic eschatology. Jesus's ideas about God and redemption were those of a first-century Jewish apocalyptic visionary who believed that, as God's chosen Messiah, he was to deliver his people from their captivity under foreign domination. Jesus's cry from the Cross, "My God, my God, why hast Thou forsaken me?" was an expression of his defeat and utter disillusionment. In later years, Christians, unknowingly, read the New Testament through the early Christian community's theological doctrines about Christ. This became the basis of present-day Christian catechetic instruction that the Christian learns as a child. It assumes that Jesus taught it as a body of doctrine and that he demanded that one believe it if one is to be saved. "However," Reimarus writes, "by 'faith in the gospel' Jesus simply meant a trusting in him and in the news that he had proclaimed, that now under him the kingdom of the Messiah was to begin."[60]

According to Reimarus, the Jewish Jesus appropriated all of the titles that were associated with his vocation as prophet and Messianic king beloved of God, including that of the Son of God. But, Reimarus insists, Jesus meant no more by the latter title than that of the humble Son of man, an entirely human figure. "When Jesus calls himself God's Son, he means to imply only that he is the Christ or

Messiah particularly loved by God, and thus he does not introduce to the Jews any new doctrine or mystery." Moreover, Jesus's disciples believed only that he was a great worldly king who would establish a powerful kingdom in Jerusalem. The failure of that Messianic mission and Jesus's inglorious death on the Cross shattered the disciples' expectations. Faced with a crisis, the apostles concocted the account of Jesus as the expected Jewish suffering savior who came to redeem humanity from sin and who would be raised on the third day. The resurrection story was thus a fraud, perpetrated by the disciples after they had stolen Jesus's body from the tomb. And so it happened that Jesus's mission and message—that of a discredited apocalyptic fanatic—was reshaped by the disciples' invention of an entirely new religion, wholly foreign to Jesus's own intention.

A related, more plausible and influential, consequence of Reimarus's apocalyptic portrayal of Jesus is his conclusion about the failure of Jesus's preaching of an imminent coming of the *eschaton,* the end of this world, and the inauguration of the kingdom of God. The delay in the speedy return of the Messiah to establish his kingdom necessitated, Reimarus claims, the entire reformulation of Jewish theology and its transformation into Christian doctrine by the early community. This claim is recognized today by many New Testament scholars.

Reimarus's hypothesis, that Christianity's origin can be traced to a disreputable fraud, is naturally rejected by Christian scholars, and it has been countered by more compelling historical accounts and explanations. Nevertheless, Reimarus, despite his long obscurity, initiated several lines of historical inquiry that influenced not only G. E. Lessing and D. F. Strauss, as we will see, but a great deal of New Testament scholarship since the beginning of the twentieth century. Reimarus's importance lies, first, in his effort to place Jesus squarely in his Jewish thought-world. That has been an enduring theme in modern scholarship, with crucial implications for Christology. Second, he anticipates later scholarship in seeing the problem of the tension, if not the disparity, between the actual historical Jesus of Nazareth and the Christ of developing Christian dogma. This has remained a persistent and perplexing issue for historical theology for the past two hundred years. It often is referred to as the problem

of the "Jesus of history" and the "Christ of faith." Finally, Reimarus is the first modern biblical scholar to champion what has come to be called "consistent eschatology." That is, he asserts that Jesus's person and message are severely distorted when cut loose from the religious world-view of radical first-century Jewish apocalypticism. This thoroughgoing eschatological understanding of Jesus and Christian origins was to dominate New Testament studies in the first half of the twentieth century under the leadership of scholars such as Johannes Weiss and Albert Schweitzer. Despite the need for modifications and corrections, it is a position that cannot be ignored in any account of the historical Jesus, the beginnings of Christianity, or in matters having to do with several Christian doctrines, for example, Christology and eschatology.

Reimarus was a man held in high honor among his contemporaries. Few, if any, outside the inner circle of friends and family, were aware of the radicalness of his ideas or the passionate feeling and even hatred that flamed in his breast. He died a seemingly serene and certainly peace-loving professor, preferring that his thoughts remain concealed rather than cause controversy and unrest. The editor and publisher of the fragments of his *Apology,* G. E. Lessing, was a man of different temperament who soon found himself in a heated controversy.

G. E. Lessing

Gotthold Ephraim Lessing (1729–1781), whom we have met as the author of *Nathan the Wise* and defender of religious toleration, is perhaps the most representative and influential figure in the German Enlightenment. He has been best known as a dramatist and literary and art critic but, as recent studies have shown, his influence on modern theology has been very great. As we shall see, this is now apparent in the writings of Kierkegaard and of theologians concerned with the issues of revelation and history.

Lessing was the son of an orthodox Lutheran pastor. At seventeen he was sent to the University of Leipzig to study theology but soon gave up theology for his real passion—the theater. In 1769 Lessing was offered the post of librarian at the Duke of Brunswick's library at Wolffenbüttel, and in 1773 he began publishing a series of *Contributions to Literature and History* from the Ducal Library. Among these *Contributions* were the fragments from the *Apology* of Reimarus. Lessing recognized that Reimarus's criticism must result in either the destruction or the entire rethinking of the idea of revelation. The publication of the fragments stirred a controversy that consumed the last five years of Lessing's life. Lessing's own attitude toward the *Fragments* was ambivalent. He rejected the strict rationalist proofs of religion offered by Reimarus and did not hold Reimarus's scornful view of the positive, historical religions. However, he believed Reimarus had rendered a very important service to religion in freeing Christianity from its false supports. At the end of the *Fragments,* Lessing appended his own "Editor's Counterpropositions" in which he expressed his own attitude to such destructive criticisms.

> And now enough of these fragments. Any of my readers who would prefer me to have spared them altogether is surely more timid than well instructed. . . .
>
> For how much could be said in reply to all these objections and difficulties! And even if absolutely no answer were forthcoming, what then? The learned theologian might in the last resort be embarrassed, but certainly not the Christian. To the former it might at most cause confusion to see the supports with which he would uphold religion shattered in this way, to find the buttresses cast down by which, God willing, he would have made it safe and sound. But how do this man's hypotheses, explanations, and proofs affect the Christian? For him it is simply a fact—the Christianity which he feels to be true and in which he feels blessed. . . .
>
> In short, the letter is not the spirit and the Bible not religion. Consequently, objections to the letter and to the Bible are not also objections to the spirit and to religion. . . . Moreover, religion was there before a Bible existed. Christianity was there before the evangelists and apostles wrote. A long period elapsed before the first of them wrote, and a very considerable time before the entire canon was complete. . . . The religion is not true because the evangelists and apostles taught it; but they taught it because it is true. The written traditions must be interpreted by their inward truth and no written traditions can give the religion any inward truth if it has none.[61]

The publication of the *Fragments* brought about a series of replies from the orthodox, especially from the Hamburg pastor, Johann Goeze, who was committed to defending Christianity by the use of the kind of evidential arguments, e.g., miracles, used by the rational supernaturalists. Goeze justly felt that the Reimarus *Fragments* would upset the simple believers, but he recognized the "Counterpropositions" of Lessing as an even greater danger to the faith. Goeze's attack provoked a series of eleven violent articles from Lessing, entitled *Anti-Goeze.* These articles reveal Lessing's brilliant invective but little of his own religious thought. Lessing's most important reply to his orthodox critics was "On the Proof of the Spirit and of Power," addressed to J. D. Schumann of Hanover, who had sought to counter the Reimarus *Fragments* with traditional arguments from miracle and prophecy.

"On the Proof of the Spirit and of Power" is a critique of the proof of Christianity from the historical testimony of miracles and fulfilled prophecy. The assumptions underlying Lessing's argument reflect his own "critical" use of reason to attack the orthodox and the older rationalism alike. He accepts, at least tactically, Leibnitz's distinction between the necessary truths of reason and the contingent truths of sensory experience. The truths of reason, which are assumed to be of a higher order, express relations that obtain among ideas that are always and everywhere the same. "Truths of reason," said Leibnitz, "are necessary and their opposite is impossible; those of fact are contingent and their opposite is possible."[62] Truths of reason are a priori and absolutely certain. Truths of fact are dubitable and therefore cannot serve as proof. To Lessing this is exactly the point. The orthodox theologians have been arguing for the indubitability of Christianity on the basis of miracle and prophecy, both of which are dependent upon historical testimony. But unqualified certainty, if not possible even for one who has personally experienced the alleged events, clearly is not indubitable when dependent on the testimony of others' experience. In preparing the way for Søren Kierkegaard's discussion of the relative advantage of the disciples at first and second hand, Lessing's argument proceeds as follows:

Fulfilled prophecies, which I myself experience, are one thing; fulfilled prophecies, of which I know only from history that others say they have experienced them, are another.

Miracles, which I see with my own eyes, and which I have the opportunity to verify for myself, are one thing; miracles of which I know only from history that others say they have seen them and verified them, are another.

If I had lived at the time of Christ, then of course the prophecies fulfilled in his person would have made me pay great attention to him. If I had actually seen him do miracles . . . I would willingly have submitted my intellect to his, and I would have believed him in all things in which equally indisputable experiences did not tell against him.

Or: if I even now experienced that prophecies referring to Christ or the Christian religion . . . were fulfilled in a manner admitting no dispute; if even now miracles were done by believing Christians which I had to recognize as true miracles: what could prevent me from accepting this proof of the spirit and of power?

But . . . I live in the eighteenth century, in which miracles no longer happen. . . . The problem is that this proof of the spirit and of power no longer has any spirit or power, but has sunk to the level of human testimonies of spirit and power.

If then this proof of the proof (the contemporary reality of miracle) has now entirely lapsed . . . how is it expected of me that the same inconceivable truths which sixteen to eighteen hundred years ago people believed on the strongest inducement, should be believed by men to be equally valid on an infinitely lesser inducement?[63]

Lessing anticipates the answer, namely, that we believe on the basis of the testimony of reputable historians. But

what is asserted is only that the reports which we have of these prophecies and miracles are as reliable as historical truths ever can be. And then it is added that historical truths cannot be demonstrated: nevertheless we must believe them as firmly as truths that have been demonstrated.

To this I answer: who will deny (not I) that the reports of these miracles and prophecies are as reliable as

historical truths ever can be? But if they are only as reliable as this, why are they treated as if they were infinitely more reliable?

And in what way? In this way, that something quite different and much greater is founded upon them than it is legitimate to found upon truths historically proved.

If no historical truth can be demonstrated, then nothing can be demonstrated by means of historical truths.

That is: *accidental truths of history can never become the proof of necessary truths of reason.*[64]

The orthodox theologians had not only proved, for example, the resurrection of Christ on the basis of historical testimony, but, worse, had "jumped" from this dubitable historical fact to a completely different class of truths.

If on historical grounds I have no objection to the statement that Christ raised to life a dead man; must I therefore accept it as true that God has a Son who is of the same essence as himself? . . . To jump with that historical truth to a quite different class of truths, and to demand of me that I should form all my metaphysical and moral ideas accordingly . . . if that is not a "transformation to another kind," then I do not know what Aristotle meant by this phrase. . . . *That, then, is the ugly broad ditch which I cannot get across, however often and however earnestly I have tried to make the leap.* If anyone can help me over it, let him do it, I beg him, I adjure him. He will deserve a divine reward from me.[65] (Italics added.)

Lessing's argument in "On the Proof of the Spirit and of Power" is meant to provoke. Scholars vary in their claims regarding it; some assert that the argument is confused and questionable; others interpret it as the work of a master ironist, depriving his opponents of any "result." Demonstrating Lessing's intention or possible faulty reasoning is not, however, our concern here; it is rather to see Lessing's own positive solution to the problem he posed.

What, then, binds Lessing to the teachings of Christ, if not the proof of his authority through miracle and prophecy? Simply the teachings themselves. The teachings are not authoritative because they are found in a sacred book; the book is sacred because it speaks an inward truth that existed long before the

Bible. "Is the situation such that 'I should hold a geometrical theorem to be true not because it can be demonstrated, but because it can be found in Euclid'?"[66] No, of course not. "When the paralytic feels the beneficial shocks of the electric spark, does it worry him whether Nollet or Franklin or neither of them is right?"[67] Again, no.

> These fruits I may see before me ripe and ripened, and may I not be satisfied with that? The old pious legend that the hand which scatters the seed must wash in snail's blood seven times for each throw, I do not doubt, but merely ignore it. What does it matter to me whether the legend is false or true? The fruits are excellent.[68]

If there be any "proof" of religion, it must be "the proof of the spirit and of power," i.e., of personal experience. And history serves a vital role in experience, for it is the rough husk in which the kernel of truth is given to us to be appropriated. History is the necessary vehicle of the truth which, because it is always and everywhere the same, must also be then and there, here and now, i.e., locatable in the particular, contingent events of history. Lessing, then, does not hold that the "necessary truths of reason" are evident without regard to time and space. Rather he makes an implicit distinction between "accidental truths of history" and "truths of history." Accidental truths of history, which cannot become proofs of necessary truths of reason, are, as Karl Barth has rightly suggested, "to be understood as such particular, concretely unique historical truths, about which I am merely informed by others. I have not myself encountered them, I have not myself experienced them as true."[69] On the other hand, "truths of history can become proof for me of necessary truths of reason, but only when they are not merely 'accidental' historical truths, but have become necessary to me."[70] When experienced as "necessary to me," such historical truths have "the proof of the spirit and of power." The proof of religion rests not in the historical events as such but through the personal experience of the "inner truth" mediated through these concrete historical events.

Is this "inner truth" of religion confined to the events of the biblical record? No, for "religion was there before a Bible existed. . . . It must be possible that everything the evangelists and apostles wrote could have been lost, and yet that the religion which they taught would have continued."[71] Because there is this primordial foundation of religious truth which is before and after the Bible, the kinds of radical doubts raised by Reimarus concerning the veracity of the biblical narratives are really irrelevant. Thus Lessing can conclude the essay by saying: "My wish is: May all who are divided by the Gospel of John be reunited by the Testament of John. Admittedly, it is apocryphal, this testament. But it is not on that account any the less divine."[72]

In *The Education of the Human Race,* published in 1777, Lessing outlines his view of history and progressive revelation. This work, so unlike the Deism of his time, shows his appreciation of historical revelation and the transcendent vocation of the historical religions, especially Hebraism and Christianity. Yet it is also evident that Lessing envisions a future in which the positive religions, including Christianity, are superseded by a more sublime, eternal gospel. Lessing's rationalism, it appears, is ambiguous, perhaps even contradictory. Passages in the *Education of the Human Race* imply that positive revelation inevitably passes over into and is replaced by reason. "Revelation," he writes, "gives man nothing which he could not also get within himself . . . gives nothing to the human race which human reason could not arrive at on its own."[73] What education is to the autonomous individual, revelation is to the whole of the human race; revelation only brings it to light more swiftly and easily. Similarly, as in education, not all knowledge can be imparted at once, so God has maintained a certain order in his revelation.

As Lessing proceeds to detail God's educative process, it becomes evident, however, that he believes historical revelation can tell us things that autonomous human reason never can learn for itself, that escape the grasp of reason. According to Lessing's conception of the revelatory process, the first humans were endowed with the belief in one God. This idea did not retain its original purity, however, and humanity fell into idolatry and polytheism. And these retrograde beliefs might have persisted for millennia if God had not selected a people for his special education. These were the ancient Hebrews. Yet such a race in its infancy is capable of receiving only an infant's instruction. "Every primer is only for a certain age. . . . A better instructor must come and tear the exhausted primer from the child's hands—Christ came! . . . That portion of the human race, which God had wished to embrace in one plan of education, was ripe for the second great step."[74]

For seventeen hundred years the New Testament has served as the second, better primer for the human race. Yet, in the course of time, the New Testament, too, will serve its turn. Newer and better conceptions of the Divine Being and of our own nature will come. "It will assuredly come! The time of a new eternal gospel, which is promised us in the primers of the New Covenant itself."[75] New teachers (the neologists, such as the Deists) claim to have advanced beyond this second primer. But Lessing is cautious; the advent of the "new eternal gospel" still lies in the distant future. It is better that the neologists return once more to the second primer; that they examine whether that which they "take only . . . for superfluous verbiage in the teaching, is not perhaps something more."[76] Rather than dismissing aspects of the New Testament too assertively, Lessing advises that these new thinkers seek out the rational idea concealed in the mysteries of, for example, the Trinity, original sin, and the atonement. "Why should we not, too, by means of a religion whose historical truth, if you will, looks dubious, be led in a similar way to closer and better conceptions of the divine Being, of our own nature, of our relation to God, *which human reason would never have reached on its own?*"[77] Here Lessing perceives reason as developing necessarily under the divine tutelage of a positive revelation. Deists, such as Tindal and Reimarus, are therefore judged as too hasty in their dismissal of the educative role of positive revelation—and, in their own cramped and pedantic rationalism, closing off the spirit and the power and hence the paths of religious development in the future.

Lessing's deep respect for the positive religions, and the crucial educative role of the special divine revelations in history, set him apart from many of the religious thinkers of the Enlightenment. He is able to distinguish between abiding religious and contingent historical truth, but at the same time he can find rational truth conveyed within the historical and mythic content of Christian faith—while refusing simply to *equate* this content with the doctrine of the natural religion of the Deists.

Finally, however, Lessing looks beyond Christianity for the coming of what he calls the "Eternal Gospel"—a gospel that will transcend the inadequate, historically conditioned and obscure truths of the second primer. For Lessing, the goal of the "Eternal Gospel" is the achievement of moral autonomy—"when man . . . will not need to borrow motives for his actions from this future [the time of the new Eternal Gospel]; for he will do right because it *is* right, not because arbitrary rewards are set upon it, which formerly were intended simply to fix and strengthen his unsteady gaze in recognizing the inner, better rewards of well-doing."[78]

Lessing is and is not a true *Aufklärer*. His attitude toward the Enlightenment faith in reason appears ambiguous. Perhaps it is more accurate to say that his understanding of reason *and* revelation has been *historized*. That is, he has created a new synthesis of the necessary truths of reason and the historical whereby the rational *is realized in and through history*. Not surprisingly, it is often noted that Lessing's principal contribution to modern theology is his conception of religion's deep-rootedness in history. And so he is a critical figure in challenging the Enlightenment's unhistorical approach to religious truth and the equally static, abstract view of the Bible shared by both the orthodox and the rationalists since the seventeenth century. Lessing anticipated the later Idealist theme of progressive revelation and the distinction between positive historical fact and its philosophical truth, between the husk or letter of Scripture and its spiritual kernel embedded in it. Lessing, therefore, represents a different and new world from that of Voltaire and Toland. As Ernst Cassirer suggests,

> Religion, according to Lessing, belongs neither to the sphere of the necessary and eternal nor to that of the merely accidental and temporal. It is both in one; it is the manifestation of the infinite in the finite, of the eternal and rational in the temporal process of becoming. With his thought Lessing has reached the turning point of the real philosophy of the Enlightenment.[79]

CONCLUSION

Despite the differences that did exist among the apostles of the religion of reason, there were many things they held in common which set them apart from those who came before and after. First, they believed religion was essentially a simple matter. There was a general desire, even among the supernaturalists, to reduce religion and Christianity to a very few doctrines and even fewer practices. Sacraments and rituals often were regarded as useless, even dangerous distractions. Locke argued for Christian revelation on the grounds that it did away with the "pompous, cumbersome ceremonies" of the Jews and the priests. The eighteenth century was anticlerical and antiecclesiastical. Institutional Christianity was considered the instrument of wily priests. As Voltaire expressed it, "the first divine was the first rogue who met the first fool."

It was generally agreed that Christianity was simple and that its essence lay in providing divine sanctions for morality. Religion was very largely confined to the performing of one's moral duties conceived of as divine commands. Endowed with a free will, one could, it was presumed, choose the good and avoid evil. Nature and humanity were thus taken from the Fall. It was assumed that humans could come to the truths of religion by the exercise of reason, and, discerning these truths, would naturally pursue the good. Future rewards and punishments would be determined solely by one's conduct on earth. Implied in such a view was the attitude that religion was solely a matter between the individual and God and therefore a highly individualistic affair. Consequently, the Church was thought of as a voluntary association.

There emerged in the eighteenth century several distinct views of the historical role of the Christian religion which have had a continuing significance in the modern quest to understand the nature and essence of Christianity.[80] Out of the debates of the eighteenth century there emerged the central question: What is Christianity? What constitutes its essence? Does it include the whole heritage of the centuries, or the teachings of Jesus, or the apostolic teachings? A number of views were expressed. The first view held that Christianity was a corruption of true religion and, therefore, an evil to be opposed

and eradicated. This was the view taken by most of the French *philosophes* and by the historian Gibbon. Christianity's influence was seen as largely pernicious and the positive doctrines as fraudulent superstitions. Culture and society would be far better off without this nefarious influence. *Ecrasez l'infâme!*

A second view identified Christianity with the religion of nature. Christianity, when purified of many of its historical accretions, was seen as a *republication* of the original religion of nature, which is open to all by the light of natural reason. This was the view of constructive Deism, of men like Toland and Tindal, and later the view taken by Kant. The essence of Christianity is none other than that of the religion of reason, but couched in the more or less imperfect form of an historical tradition. Beneath the historical illustration lies the essential and universal truth which is evident to all persons of reason. According to this view, historic revelation is a mere convenience or concession to human weakness.

A third view distinguished historic Christianity from natural religion by conceiving of the former as a necessary supplement or higher type. This was the view of the theologians of the Middle Ages but is restated in the Enlightenment by the rational supernaturalists such as John Locke. Natural religion is excellent and legitimate as far as it goes but, for one reason or another, is not sufficient. It needs the supplementation of certain supernatural doctrines which are found only in special revelation in Scripture. For Locke such special revelation is evidenced in the outward signs or divine warrants for the claim that Jesus is the Messiah. Only in Scripture are these supernatural warrants given— hence the need for special revelation "above" but not "contrary" to natural reason.

Finally, there was the attempt to conceive of Christianity as one historic stage in the progress toward a perfect, universal religion which lies in the future. This view is represented in Lessing's *Education of the Human Race* and was to become a popular view in the nineteenth century. Here Christ or Christianity is not seen as the historic republication of the original religion of nature or as the full and complete revelation of divine truth. Christianity has led humans one step further in their pilgrimage toward that "new eternal Gospel which is promised . . . in the New Testament itself."

Christianity is neither the original nor the final religion, for it, too, will give place to the universal religion of the future.

All four of these views of Christianity will continue to find exponents in the nineteenth century. Underlying all of them—even though imperceptibly—is a new concern for history, for establishing the originality, the warrants, or the relative and transitory character of Christianity by an appeal to history. The Enlightenment was, it is true, an age of reason, but its empirical spirit did not allow it to remain in a world of rational abstractions. It initiated a new historical consciousness which does not come into the full light of day until the nineteenth century. But before we consider the beginnings of the new spirit of the nineteenth century, we must give some attention to the final breakdown of the religion of reason.

NOTES

1. A. C. McGiffert, *Protestant Thought before Kant* (New York, 1962).
2. Lord Herbert of Cherbury, *De Religione Laici* (1645), ed. and trans. Harold L. Hutchison (New Haven, 1944), pp. 86, 101–102.
3. Lord Herbert, *De Veritate*, 3d ed.(1645), trans. M. H. Carré (Bristol, 1937), pp. 117, 118.
4. J. Samuel Preus, *Explaining Religion* (New Haven, 1987), p. 34.
5. Herbert, *De Veritate*, p. 289.
6. W. Chillingworth, *Religion of Protestants* (1638), p. 198.
7. J. Tillotson, *Sermons*, I, 225. Quoted in L. Stephen, *English Thought in the Eighteenth Century* (New York, 1927), p. 78.
8. Ibid.
9. J. Tillotson, *Works* (London, 1857), II, 333.
10. Tillotson, *Works*, III, 493ff. Quoted in McGiffert, op. cit., p. 197ff.
11. Ibid.
12. J. Locke, *An Essay Concerning Human Understanding*, ed. A. S. Pringle-Pattison (Oxford, 1956), p. 9.
13. Ibid., p. 354.
14. Ibid., p. 355.
15. Ibid., p. 356.
16. Ibid., p. 357.
17. Ibid., pp. 357–358.
18. Ibid., p. 360.
19. Ibid., p. 361.
20. Ibid.
21. Ibid., pp. 362–363.
22. J. Locke, *A Discourse of Miracles*, in *The Reasonableness of Christianity*, ed. I. T. Ramsey (Stanford, 1958), p. 80.
23. Introduction, *Reasonableness of Christianity*, p. 13.
24. Ibid., p. 14.
25. Ibid., p. 15.
26. Ibid., p. 52.
27. Ibid., pp. 52–53.
28. Ibid., p. 55.
29. J. Toland, *Christianity Not Mysterious*. Quoted in Creed and Boys Smith, *Religious Thought in the 18th Century* (Cambridge, 1934), p. 17.
30. Ibid.
31. Ibid., p. 20.
32. M. Tindal, *Christianity as Old as the Creation*. Quoted in Creed and Boys Smith, op. cit., p. 34.
33. Ibid., pp. 33–34.
34. Ibid., p. 32.
35. M. Tindal, *Christianity as Old as the Creation*, p. 111. Cited in Stephen, *English Thought in the Eighteenth Century*, I, 140.
36. Tindal, op. cit., p. 14.
37. Ibid., p. 18.
38. Ibid., p. 270.
39. Ibid., p. 125.
40. Ibid., p. 134.
41. Stephen, op. cit., pp. 144–145.
42. G. R. Cragg, *The Church in the Age of Reason: 1648–1789* (New York, 1961), p. 240.
43. A survey of the various positions that have been argued is found in René Pomeau, *La religion de Voltaire*. See also Peter Gay, *Voltaire's Politics* (Princeton, 1959), pp. 389–391.
44. Alfred Noyes, *Voltaire* (1936). On March 31, 1769, before witnesses, Voltaire did sign an affirmation that he wished to die in the Roman Catholic religion.
45. Voltaire, *Works*, XXI, 239.
46. Ibid., pp. 240–241.
47. Cited in J. H. Randall, Jr., *The Making of the Modern Mind* (New York, 1926), p. 296.
48. Voltaire, *Works*, VII, 82–83.
49. *Sermon*, in J. McCabe, ed., *Toleration and Other Essays by Voltaire* (New York, 1912), p. 168.
50. McCabe, *Toleration*, pp. 170, 177. Voltaire proceeds similarly in *The Questions of Zapata* (1767). The es-

say purports to be a series of questions put to a committee of theologians by a professor of theology at the University of Salamanca.

51. Ibid., p. 182.
52. Voltaire, *Notebooks,* pp. 452. Quoted in Gay, *Politics,* p. 251.
53. *Philosophical Dictionary,* article "Superstition," ed. H. I. Wolff (New York, 1924), p. 298.
54. *Philosophical Dictionary,* article "Arius". Quoted in Gay, *Politics,* p. 253.
55. On numerous occasions Voltaire wrote of the social utility of religion. A story about Voltaire reveals both his humor and practicality. D'Alembert and Condorcet were dining at Ferney and during the course of the dinner were making antireligious remarks. Voltaire stopped them, sent the servants out of the room, and said, "Now, messieurs, you may continue. I was only afraid of having my throat cut tonight. . . ." Cited in Gay, *Politics,* pp. 262–263.
56. Cited in ibid., p. 263.
57. Ibid., p. 271.
58. Ibid., p. 241.
59. Albert Schweitzer, *The Quest of the Historical Jesus* [1906] (New York, 1964), p. 26.
60. H. S. Reimarus, "Concerning the Intention of Jesus and His Disciples," in *Reimarus: Fragments,* ed.

Charles H. Talbert (Philadelphia, 1970), pp. 75–76.
61. *Lessing's Theological Writings,* ed. Henry Chadwick (Stanford, 1957), pp. 17–18.
62. *Monadology,* Everyman ed., p. 9.
63. *Lessing's Theological Writings,* pp. 51–53.
64. Ibid., p. 53.
65. Ibid., pp. 54–55.
66. *Theological Writings,* III, 127. Quoted in K. Barth, *From Rousseau to Ritschl,* p. 136.
67. *Lessing's Theological Writings,* pp. 17–18.
68. Ibid., p. 55.
69. Barth, op. cit., p. 137.
70. Ibid., pp. 137–138.
71. *Lessing's Theological Writings,* p. 18.
72. Ibid., p. 56.
73. Ibid., p. 83.
74. Ibid., p. 93.
75. Ibid., p. 96.
76. Ibid., pp. 93–94.
77. Ibid., p. 95.
78. *Lessing's Theological Writings,* p. 96.
79. E. Cassirer, *The Philosophy of the Enlightenment,* p. 194.
80. Here the author is dependent on the analysis of William A. Brown in *The Essence of Christianity* (New York, 1908).

SUGGESTIONS FOR FURTHER READING

I

For general accounts of the Religion of Reason and its context in the eighteenth century, the following are especially recommended:

Cragg, G. R. *Reason and Authority in the Eighteenth Century* (Cambridge: Cambridge University Press, 1964). An excellent survey of English theology in the Age of Reason—from Locke through the Deists, Butler, Hume, Wesley, and others.

Creed, J. M., and Boys Smith, J. S. *Religious Thought in the 18th Century* (Cambridge: Cambridge University Press, 1934). A good collection of brief texts illustrating the religious thought of the period. Helpful since many of the texts are difficult to come by.

Gay, Peter. *Deism: An Anthology* (Princeton: Van Nostrand Company, 1968). Readings from the works of the leading Deists with helpful introductions.

Graf Reventlow, H. *The Authority of the Bible and the Rise of the Modern World* (Philadelphia: Fortress Press, 1985). Valuable but advanced study of English developments from Herbert of Cherbury through the late phases of Deism.

McGiffert, A. C. *Protestant Thought before Kant* (New York: Harper, 1962). Chapter 10 contains an excellent survey of eighteenth-century theological rationalism.

Mossner, E. C. *Bishop Butler and the Age of Reason* (New York: Macmillan Company, 1936). Mossner places Butler in the context of the religious thought from Locke to Hume, especially in relation to the Deist controversy.

Randall, J. H., Jr. *Making of the Modern Mind* (New York: Houghton Mifflin Co., 1926). Chapter 12 contains an interesting, brief account of the Religion of Reason.

Stephen, Leslie. *English Thought in the Eighteenth Century,* Vol. I (New York: G. P. Putnam's Sons, 1927). The fullest and ablest account of eighteenth-century English theology available.

Waring, E. Graham. *Deism and Natural Religion* (New York: Ungar, 1967). A good collection of Deist writings.

II

The works of Cassirer, Gay, and Hazard listed in the Readings for Chapter 1 and those listed above contain useful accounts of the thinkers discussed in this chapter. For specialized studies of these same thinkers, the following are recommended:

Lord Herbert of Cherbury

Bedford, R. D. *The Defense of Truth: Herbert of Cherbury and the Seventeenth Century* (Manchester: Manchester University Press, 1979).

Carré, Meyrick H., trans. with intro., *De veritate* (Bristol, 1937).

Preus, J. Samuel. *Explaining Religion* (New Haven: Yale University Press, 1987). Chapter 2 contains an interesting treatment of Herbert of Cherbury.

John Locke

Ramsey, I. T. "Editor's Introduction" to John Locke, *The Reasonableness of Christianity* (Stanford: Stanford University Press, 1958).

Yolton, John W. *John Locke and the Way of Ideas* (Oxford: Oxford University Press, 1956). Good account of the influence on religion of Locke's philosophy.

Voltaire

Baumer, Franklin. *Religion and the Rise of Skepticism* (New York: Harcourt, Brace, 1960, 1969). Chapter 1 contains a lively account of French skepticism in the Age of Reason.

Gay, Peter. *Voltaire's Politics* (Princeton: Princeton University Press, 1959). Chapter 5 contains a superb account of Voltaire and religion.

Torrey, Norman. *Voltaire and the English Deists* (New Haven: Yale University Press, 1930; Archon Books, 1967). Fine study of the major English Deists as well as Voltaire.

John Toland

Daniel, Stephen. *John Toland: His Mind, Manners and Thought* (Toronto: University of Toronto Press, 1984).

Sullivan, Robert E. *John Toland and the Deist Controversy: A Study in Adaptations* (Cambridge: Harvard University Press, 1982).

H. S. Reimarus and G. E. Lessing

Allison, Henry E. *Lessing and the Enlightenment* (Ann Arbor: University of Michigan Press, 1966). Places Reimarus in relation to Lessing and the wider eighteenth-century context. The fullest study of Lessing on religion in English.

Beck, Lewis White. *Early German Philosophy: Kant and His Predecessors* (Cambridge: Harvard University Press, 1969). Chapter 14 contains a brief, able account.

Chadwick, Henry. "Introduction" to *Lessing's Theological Writings* (Stanford: Stanford University Press, 1957).

Schweitzer, Albert. *The Quest of the Historical Jesus* (London: A. & C. Black, 1910; New York, 1964). Schweitzer's assessment of Reimarus's significance for later New Testament scholarship and the question of the historical Jesus.

Talbert, Charles H., ed. "Introduction" to *Reimarus: Fragments* (Philadelphia: Fortress Press, 1970). Translation of "Concerning the Intention of Jesus and His Teaching" with the most up-to-date account of Reimarus in English.

Chapter 3
The Breakdown
of the Religion of Reason

David Hume

Like the Temple of Reason in Notre Dame de Paris, the popularity of the cult of reason was relatively short-lived. This was because reason has a way of turning upon itself. The Enlightenment proved, finally, to be as much the critic as disciple of rationalism, a point too often missed by recent critics. Thinkers such as Rousseau, Joseph Butler, Hume, and Kant, all of whom remained true children of the eighteenth century, were led in quite different ways to question the very foundations of the rationalist credo. The religion of reason was in a sense consumed in the fires of its own analysis.

The failure of the religion of reason was occasioned by a number of factors. First, it was unable to attract the masses. It was too abstract, too intellectual in spite of its claim to simplicity. It was devoid of feeling and the aesthetic sense which, even though unarticulated, is required of any religious

faith that expects a wide appeal. Deism also lacked unity. The radical demands of autonomy were liberating but did not contribute to *fraternité,* to a sense of a common bond of faith and worship. The chief reason, however, for the decline of Deism is that it was dismantled by its own analytical tools. In this chapter we will examine some of the major developments in the breakdown of the eighteenth-century religion of reason and of efforts to establish new grounds of religious faith and belief.

JEAN JACQUES ROUSSEAU

The historic significance of Jean Jacques Rousseau (1712–1778) lies, in part, in the fact that he was largely responsible for shifting the discussion of nature, humanity, and God to a new plane by freeing reason from its isolation from feeling and willing. In this Rousseau was a precursor of Romanticism. The discovery of feeling, will, and the affections as being indispensable ingredients in human life forced Rousseau to disassociate himself from many of his rationalist contemporaries, particularly from those *philosophes* who identified themselves with a mechanistic philosophy or the materialism of d'Holbach. The passion and melancholy of Rousseau's own life are symptomatic of his break with the rationalist spirit of his age. Lytton Strachey testified accurately to the historic uniqueness of Rousseau when he said that Rousseau

> possessed one quality which cut him off from his contemporaries, which set an immense gulf betwixt him and them . . . . He belonged to another world—the new world of self-consciousness, and doubt, and hesitation, of mysterious melancholy, and quiet intimate delights, of long reflexion amid the solitudes of Nature, of infinite introspections amid the solitudes of the heart.[1]

In short, Rousseau imbued the rationalist temper with the powerful force of feeling. In this he contributed to the demise of the older rationalist credo and to the construction of a religious faith grounded in our moral sentiments.

Rousseau's own religious pilgrimage was a stormy one. Born in Geneva into a family of Calvinists, Rousseau had early aspirations toward being a preacher. His Protestant, Genevan childhood was unusually significant in the development of his mind and character in his maturity. Yet at sixteen he ran away to Savoy where, seemingly without difficulty, he converted to Catholicism. He was then sent to Madame de Warens of Annecy, an attractive young woman who combined zeal for the Catholic religion with a notable lack of restraint in affairs romantic. Through Madame de Warens's insistence, Rousseau found himself at the monastery at Turin where he was baptized and received into the Roman Church. During his stay at Turin, Rousseau gained the friendship of several priests, including the Abbé Gaime, whose piety so impressed him that he later served as one of the models for Rousseau's Savoyard Vicar in his novel *Emile*. Rousseau lived with Madame de Warens for the better part of a decade,

during which time she served him as both mother and mistress. In 1845 at the age of thirty-three, Rousseau moved to Paris, a fervent though heterodox Catholic. There his faith was tested in the long struggles with the atheists and materialists. He came out of the ordeal a Deist, but with the flame of religious sentiment still burning. He now felt that reason was incapable of substantiating most of the traditional dogmas of Christianity, but he was equally certain, against the d'Holbach circle, that reason gave evidence of a providential deity.

In 1754 Rousseau once again visited Geneva and returned to the Protestantism of his childhood. In these years Rousseau was troubled continuously with religious questions and sought out a Genevan cleric, Pastor Vernes, as a confidant to whom he could unburden his mind. This, too, failed when Vernes proved to be unbending in his biblical orthodoxy. During this period of lonely, spiritual searching, Rousseau vowed he would find a faith that would be satisfying. The product of that resolve was "The Profession of Faith of the Savoyard Vicar" (1762), regarded by some as the masterpiece of his pen.

The "Profession of Faith" is inserted into the fourth book of Rousseau's longer work *Emile,* his novel on the principles of a natural education. The inclusion of the religious profession in *Emile* was no accident, either of form or substance. The novel form allowed Rousseau a more concrete, personal way of expressing his own religious creed while calling upon the reader to test the author's own deeply felt sentiments with his or her own religious experience. The substance of Rousseau's religious profession is also entirely consistent with the educational doctrine he sets forth in the earlier books of *Emile*. Rousseau insists that all genuine knowledge or insight must be acquired by the pupil for him or herself. It cannot be achieved through a detached, mechanical process of rote book learning. In every field of knowledge, true understanding comes only through personal experience. We learn, Rousseau insisted, by doing. And so it is in our religious understanding. Religious faith is sterile and perfunctory unless it is grounded in personal experience. Religious conviction is nothing but a certainty arrived at by the individual self in its encounter with the world.

The "Profession" opens with the kindly, unorthodox Vicar of Savoy speaking to a young boy who has fled from Geneva to Rome and, having changed religions, is filled with uncertainty and distress. The Vicar assures the boy that he does not want to argue with him or even convince him. "It is enough for me to show you, in all simplicity of heart, what I really think. Consult your own heart as I speak; that is all I ask."[2]

In many respects the Savoyard Vicar's profession is similar to that of other eighteenth-century Deists. For example, Rousseau includes a discussion on revelation and Scripture in which the difficulties encountered in the evidential claims of all special revelations are made abundantly clear. The boy, perplexed by the conflicting claims of rival positive religions, asks the vicar for guidance in this matter. The Vicar replies that since we are offered so many revelations, each claiming for itself the truth, one of two things must obtain.

> Either all religions are good and pleasing to God or if there is one which he prescribes for men, if they will be punished for despising it, he will have distinguished it by plain and certain signs . . . alike in every time and place, equally plain to all men, great or small. . . .[3]

But, in fact, neither condition obtains. None of the positive religions admit the truth of their rival's claims. One religion must then be true. But how do I find out? God has spoken? To whom has he spoken? To humans. Why, then, have I heard nothing? God has instructed others to make himself known to you. But I would rather have heard from God; then I should be secure from fraud. For what other persons tell me is so contradictory. But God protects you from fraud by showing that his messengers come from him. How so? By miracles. Where are these miracles? In books. And who wrote the books? Humans. And who saw the miracles? Those who bear witness to them. What! Nothing but human testimony. Nothing but other persons to tell me what others have told them![4] This, says the Vicar, is the answer that the positive religions are always giving. Since this is the situation, one has no choice but to test all the religions!

Consider, my friend [says the Vicar] the terrible controversy in which I am now engaged; what vast learning is required to go back to the remotest antiquity, to examine, weigh, confront prophecies, revelations, facts. . . . What exactness of critical judgement is needed to distinguish genuine documents from forgeries, translations with their originals; to decide as to the impartiality of witnesses . . . that nothing has been added, altered or falsified.[5]

And when a person has managed to surmount all these obstacles and has come to regard certain miracles as genuine, he or she faces a greater question: How does one know such genuine miracles are of God, since the Bible convinces us that the devil is a miracle worker, too? The answer given is that those miracles are genuinely of God which the message certifies. "So when we have proved our doctrine by means of miracles, we must prove our miracles by means of doctrine. . . . What think you of this dilemma?"[6]

The Vicar's conclusion concerning the claims and counterclaims of the historical religions is that he finds in them objections and contradictions which he cannot overcome and therefore must maintain "an attitude of reverent doubt."

> I call to witness the God of Peace whom I adore, and whom I proclaim to you, that my inquiries were honestly made; but when I discovered that they were and always would be unsuccessful, and that I embarked upon a boundless ocean, I turned back, and restricted my faith within the limits of my primitive ideas. . . . I closed all my books. *There is one book which is open to every one—the book of nature. In this good and great volume I learn to serve and adore its Author.* If I use my reason, if I cultivate it, if I employ rightly the innate faculties which God bestows upon me, *I shall learn by myself to know and love him,* to love his works, to will what he wills and to fulfil all my duties upon earth. . . . What more can all human learning teach me?[7] (Italics added.)

Rousseau, like his beloved Vicar, was forced back to what he came to regard as the only reliable book, the book of nature, by which he means his own natural self. Reduced, like Descartes, to doubting all, he learned to restrict all inquiries to what concerned himself,

> to admit as self-evident all that I could not honestly refuse to believe, and to admit as true all that seemed to follow directly from this; all the rest I determined to leave undecided, neither accepting nor rejecting it, not yet troubling myself to clear up difficulties which did not lead to any practical ends.[8]

Beginning then with only those truths which compel consent, Rousseau's Vicar goes on to establish certain principles of belief that, like his critique of the positive religions, are reminiscent of the then-reigning Deism. First, beginning with reflections on his own existence, he arrives at the conviction that just as in all humanity there is the principle of free judgment which is the origin of our spontaneous actions, so in the world at large one must go back to some first, spontaneous, willful cause. "I think that a will moves the universe and animates nature. That is my first article of faith." The second article of belief arises out of the order and harmony of nature which points to an *intelligent* first cause: "If the movement of matter reveals to me a will, the movement of matter according to certain laws reveals to me an intelligence; that is my second article of faith." The third article has to do not with God but with the uniqueness of humanity in the order of nature. Reflecting on the conflict in the individual between reason and the passions, the Vicar concludes that our intelligent faculty is free and independent of the body. "Man is free in his actions and as such is animated by an immaterial substance; this is my third article of faith."

From these three convictions the Vicar goes on to deduce other religious convictions, such as the explanation of evil in God's world and the immortality of the soul. All this sounds very much like the natural theology of the age, which it is. And yet Rousseau infuses his religious apology with a new *sensibilité* that is foreign to most of the rationalism of his time. It is this new religious sentiment that is important and needs closer examination.

In the "Profession of Faith" Rousseau seeks to found religion on what he sometimes calls the "inner light" or "feeling" or "conscience." The apparent vagueness of these terms has led some scholars to dismiss Rousseau's philosophy of religion with such epithets as "romantic enthusiasm" and "emotional Deism." In the twentieth century, Rousseau's theory of religion has been interpreted much more favorably, and the importance of his philosophy of religion in the general history of ideas has been accurately assessed.[9] What Rousseau means by sentiment and feeling has nothing to do with sentimentality or effusive emotion. It is closer to an intuitive disclosure or innate moral sense. Rousseau was convinced that the questions of theism, such as the existence and nature of God and the immortality of the soul, could not be answered if the intellect was called upon without the guidance of our inner sentiments and moral experience. Like St. Augustine and Pascal before him and John Henry Newman after him, Rousseau recognized that religious certitude comes not from abstract reasoning alone but from what Newman was to call the "illative sense"—from a convergence of rational evidences, religious intuition, and moral conviction. Reason cannot produce assent to religious beliefs until it is in harmony with our affections and conscience. This is made clear in what appears to be Rousseau's appeal to the rational arguments for God from the necessity of a first, voluntary cause and from the order of nature. Rousseau calls upon his reader to "compare the special ends, the means, the ordered relations of every kind," but then he adds,

> *then let us listen to the inner voice of feeling; what healthy mind can reject its evidence?* Unless the eyes are blinded by prejudice can they fail to see that the visible order of the universe proclaims a supreme intelligence?[10]

Not, says Rousseau, if the eyes of the rational mind are in harmony with the inner voice of feeling.

For Rousseau there are two requisites for any affirmation of religion. The first is that religious ideas, doctrines, or convictions be related to and a reflection upon our personal experience.

> I see God everywhere in his works; I feel him within myself; I behold him all around me; but if I try to find out where he is, what he is, what is his substance, he escapes me and my troubled spirit finds

nothing. Convinced of my unfitness, I shall never argue about the nature of God unless I am driven to it by the feeling of his relations with myself.[11]

God is known only as he is known *pro me,* only as he is known through my religious feeling. The second requirement of religious doctrine is that it be related to my moral sentiments. Other concerns are idle speculation.

> I believe that the world is governed by a wise and powerful will; I see it or rather I feel it, and it is a great thing to know this. But has this same world always existed, or has it been created? Is there one source of all things? . . . I know not; and what concern is it of mine? When these things become of importance to me I will try to learn them; till then I abjure these idle speculations, which may trouble my peace but cannot affect my conduct. . . .[12]

Theology, as Rousseau sees it, is moral theology. What does not affect our action we can respect in silence or regard with humble skepticism, "but," says Rousseau, "this skepticism is in no way painful to me, for it does not extend to matters of practice. . . . I only seek to know what affects my conduct."[13]

The Savoyard Vicar's final advice to the youth epitomizes Rousseau's own faith.

> My son, keep your soul in such a state that you always desire that there should be a God and you will never doubt it. Moreover, whatever decision you come to, remember that the real duties of religion are independent of human institutions; that a righteous heart is the true temple of the Godhead; . . . remember there is no religion which absolves us from our moral duties; that these alone are really essential. . . .[14]

For Rousseau, man's moral conscience is a natural sentiment, a feeling of the heart, not an acquired idea.

> The decrees of conscience are not judgements but feelings: Although all our ideas come to us from without, the feelings by which they are weighed are within us. . . . To know the good is not to love it; this knowledge is not innate in man; but as soon as his reason leads him to perceive it, his conscience impels him to love it; it is this feeling that is innate.[15]

Conscience is, then, our true guide, for to obey conscience is to obey that which is innately part of our very nature. These moral sentiments of the heart cannot lead to emotional anarchy because the conscience isn't the mere product of our bodily passions. And this moral sense in us, according to Rousseau, has been essentially the same irrespective of time and place. Like the love of our own good, which is prior to all knowledge in us, there are in the depth of the soul innate sentiments of justice and virtue, native to us long before we have any knowledge of good and evil.

This innate sentiment of conscience is, for Rousseau, the true image of God in humanity. It is the sole link between this ambiguous human creature and the holy God.

> Conscience! Conscience! Divine instinct, immortal voice from heaven; sure guide for a creature ignorant and finite indeed, yet intelligent and free; infallible judge of good and evil, making man like God! In thee consists the excellence of man's nature and the morality of his actions; apart from thee, I find nothing in myself to raise me above the beast. . . .[16]

To interpret Rousseau's doctrine of religion as a sentimental nature mysticism is to misunderstand his concept of nature. Rousseau did not deify the natural world. It is true that he speaks passionately about nature, and nature serves him, as it did the poet Wordsworth, as the occasion for eliciting religious feeling. But the foundation of Rousseau's religious faith is the natural conscience, and the fruition of that faith is moral action. The traditional proofs of natural theology are cold abstractions, lacking in conviction when divorced from our moral sentiments. As Kant was to show with much greater clarity a few decades later, humans cannot bridge the chasm between nature and God by pure reason alone. Moral conscience, not nature, is the only mediator between God and humanity.

Rousseau brings to complete realization the religious autonomy of the Enlightenment. But, as is evident, in so doing he also points ahead to those movements of the nineteenth century in which religious doctrine is grounded not in abstract, rational demonstration but in personal experience. A twentieth-century philosopher evaluates Rousseau's contribution to the philosophy of religion as follows:

The significance of Rousseau's philosophy of religion for cultural history can be described in a single phrase: he eliminated from the foundation of religion the doctrine of *fides implicita.** No one can believe for another and with the help of another; in religion everyone must stand on his own. . . . Neither Calvinism nor Lutheranism had ever radically overcome the doctrine of the *fides implicita;* they had only shifted its center by replacing faith in tradition with faith in the Word of the Bible. But for Rousseau there existed no kind of inspiration outside the sphere of personal experience.[17]

That Cassirer has focused on the crux of Rousseau's view of religion is evidenced in a letter Rousseau sent to Jacob Vernes, the young minister in Geneva who had questioned Rousseau's unorthodox attitude toward Scripture. Rousseau replied:

I have told you many times: no man in the world respects the Gospel more than I. It is to my taste the most sublime of all books. . . . But in the end, it is just a book. . . . No, my good friend, it is not on a few scattered pages one ought to go seek the law of God, but in the heart of man, where His hand has deigned to write: "O man, whatsoever man thou art, enter into thyself, learn to consult thy conscience and thy natural faculties, thou wilt then be just, good, virtuous, thou wilt incline thyself before thy master, and thou wilt participate in his heaven in an eternal blessedness."[18]

Rousseau is significant in the modern history of religion because he strove for a conception of reason more consonant with human experience than the narrow rationalism of the critical Deists. His contribution to the development of a more adequate basis of religious conviction is great, as we shall see when we come to Kant and to the Romantic Movement.

The rationalist pretensions of critical Deism were not only opposed by Rousseau but also came under severe attack in England in the middle decades of the eighteenth century. William Law, in *The Case of*

Reason (1731), and Bishop Berkeley, in *Alciphron* (1732), raised serious questions about the model of abstract reason by which Deists like Tindal dictated what could and could not serve as warrants of belief. Law pointed out that Tindal's conception of a perfect natural reason, by which individuals can test all truth claims, is an a priori assumption which has no grounds in actual experience.

An enquiry about the light, and strength, and sufficiency of reason to guide and preserve men in the knowledge and practice of true religion is a question as *solely* to be resolved by *fact and experience,* as is the enquiry about the shape of a man's body or the number of his senses. And to talk of a light and strength of reason, natural to man, which fact and experience have not yet proved, is egregious nonsense . . . so their cause ought to be looked upon to be vain and romantic, as if they had asserted that men have senses naturally fitted to hear sounds and see objects at all distances though fact and experience has proved quite the contrary.[19]

The most effective of these critiques of natural religion came from the pen of Bishop Joseph Butler, who in 1736 published his *Analogy of Religion, Natural and Revealed.* Butler's book proved so devastating in its exposure of the weaknesses of the Deist doctrine that no one of the opposition attempted a reply. Butler's *Analogy,* more than any other writing, brought to a close the debate between Deism and traditional Christianity. But the good Bishop's *Analogy of Religion* had an unexpected and ironic influence. Meant to restore confidence in the truths of Christian revelation, its somber, unblinking reminders of the defects of nature proved to be only more fuel for the fires of skepticism. For the likes of David Hume, the difficulties of belief in natural religion were easily convertible into an attack upon the claims of Christian theology as well. As we will see, Butler's negative method of arguing, by seeking to establish the probabilities of revelation by stressing the difficulties in natural religion, appeared to less pious minds to lead to general skepticism concerning all rational arguments for theism. It would be left to Immanuel Kant to construct out of the skepticism of Hume and the moral philosophy of Rousseau a new basis of religious faith.

**Fides implicita* refers to assent to the truths taught by the Church even though one has no knowledge of what these teachings are about or the evidence of their truth.

JOSEPH BUTLER

Joseph Butler (1692–1752) was raised a Presbyterian but, before entering Oxford, joined the Church of England. He was a precocious youth and corresponded with the elder Samuel Clarke on metaphysical problems while he was still a schoolboy. At Oxford Butler found the "frivolous lectures and unintelligible disputations" unsuitable and was persuaded to take holy orders. In 1719 he was appointed preacher at Rolls Chapel in London. The product of this assignment was *Fifteen Sermons Preached at Rolls Chapel,* published in 1726 and generally acknowledged as establishing Butler as one of the preeminent English moralists. The *Sermons* also ensured the success of Butler's ecclesiastical career. In 1736, he became Clerk of the Closet to Queen Caroline and that same year published *The Analogy of Religion.* Although he published nothing more, his ecclesiastical position steadily improved. He was successively Bishop of Bristol, Dean of St. Paul's, London, Clerk of the Royal Closet to George II, and Bishop of Durham. He died in 1752, at the age of sixty, having lived a life of exemplary moral and intellectual integrity. He was, in Leslie Stephen's words, a man "honest enough to admit the existence of doubts, and brave enough not to be paralysed by their existence."

In the Advertisement to *The Analogy of Religion,* Butler acknowledges that it had come to be taken for granted that Christianity is "discovered to be fictitious" and "a principal subject of mirth and ridicule." His purpose is to show that such was not the case and that there were good grounds for not doubting the truths of Christianity.

The *Analogy* is addressed to those Deists who would readily concede the existence of God as a moral governor of the world but were skeptical of the particular claims of Christianity. Butler's procedure is to show that the Deist belief in God, the author of nature, when coupled with consideration of the facts of our experience of the natural world, would lead one to acknowledge that perhaps belief in revelation is no more difficult than belief in the claims of natural religion. That is, if the Deists are going to appeal to the evidences of nature, they must in honesty appeal to the whole of nature—and that means warts and all!

The Deists' chronic complaint was that if God had revealed himself in the Scriptures, he would not have allowed for such ambiguities and contradictions. He would have spoken plainly and not left us in such perplexity. But, says Butler, look at nature without your rose-tinted glasses. There you will observe just as many ambiguities and defects in proving God as you will find in the Bible, for both are full of difficulties and, when examined, these difficulties prove to be of the same kind. Neither nature nor the Bible gives us indubitable proof of the claims of theism. Both are baffling to our limited minds. And so for us finite beings, "probability is the very guide of life." Like the American philosopher William James, Butler holds that religious claims cannot rise above the level of probability, so

> if the result of examination be, that there appears **on the whole,** any the lowest presumption on one side, and none on the other, or a greater presumption on one side, though in the lowest degree greater; this determines the question; . . . and in matters of practice, will lay us under an absolute and formal obligation, in point of prudence and of interest, to act upon that presumption or low probability, though it be so low as to leave the mind in a very great doubt which is the truth.[20]

Having shown that the evidences of nature, too, are only probable, Butler sums up his analogical method by quoting from the Church Father Origen that "*he, who believes the Scripture to have proceeded from him who is the Author of nature, may well expect to find the same sort of difficulties in it, as are found in the constitution of nature.*"[21] The whole design of Butler's argument is therefore

> to show that the several parts principally objected against in this moral and Christian dispensation . . . are analogous to what is experienced in the constitution and course of nature . . . that the chief objections which are alleged against the former are no other than what may be alleged with like justice against the latter, where in fact they are found to be inconclusive; and that the argument from analogy is in general unanswerable, and undoubtedly of weight on the side of religion.[22]

What, then, are these analogies that Butler finds unanswerable and which will weigh the probabilities in favor of the traditional religious claims? We cannot survey all of the analogies drawn by Butler in this long and carefully argued book; indication of a few will suffice for our purposes.

Butler begins with the question of a future life, a subject of which we know very little. But consider for a moment nature and the several changes which it undergoes without being destroyed, and see what analogy here might be drawn with our own death and whether it is probable that we survive such a change in our condition. We would all concede that it is a general law of nature that the same creatures exist in degrees of life and experience, in one period of their being greatly different from other periods: "The states of life in which we ourselves existed formerly in the womb and in our infancy, are almost as different from our present in mature age as it is possible to conceive any two states or degrees of life can be."[23] Butler goes on then to suggest that because we have powers of enjoying pleasure and suffering pain before birth, it is *sufficiently probable* that we shall retain these powers after death, especially since no one actually knows what death is. But is there not a difference in these two states, for does not death bring to an end the physical organism? A living agent is not, contends Butler, to be confused with its physical effects. The organs of our body, such as the eye or the limbs, are only instruments which the living agent makes use of to perceive and move. But there is no evidence that the dissolution of these organs is the destruction of the perceiving or moving agent. From this Butler infers (illicitly surely)

> that the destruction of several of the organs and instruments of perception and of motion . . . is not their (the agents') destruction shows demonstratively that there is no ground to think that the dissolution of any other matter will be the dissolution or destruction of living agents.[24]

If we follow the analogy of nature, we may look upon our death as in some respects like our birth "which is not a suspension of the faculties which we had before it, or a total change of the state of life in which we existed when in the womb, but a continuation of both, with such and such great alter-

ations." So, similarly, "death may immediately . . . put us into a higher and more enlarged state of life as our birth does; a state in which our capacities and sphere of perception and of action may be much greater than at present."[25]

Butler argues that we can also know something of the nature of the government of the future life from our observation of the government of our natural lives. We observe that our present life is governed by moral justice. Pleasure and pain are the natural effects of our actions. Intemperance will bring disease, temperance health. Our civil life is analogous. Civic happiness and misery are dependent on our moral conduct. By analogy this life can also be seen as a period of probation for the next. Just as infancy, childhood, and youth are a necessary discipline for maturity, so the present life is a state of moral discipline for the next:

> The fact of our case, which we find by experience, is that [God] exercises dominion or government over us at present, by rewarding and punishing us for our actions. . . . And thus the whole analogy of nature . . . most fully shows that there is nothing incredible in the general doctrine of religion, that God will reward and punish men for their actions hereafter.[26]

To the objection that the moral government of this life seems to be fairly obscure, Butler humbly acknowledges that both nature and revelation are shrouded in mystery. But assuming, with the Deists, that God does exercise a moral government over this world, we can be assured, on the basis of strong probability, of a similar government in the future life, but equally "beyond our comprehension."

But what about the biblical miracles? Had not the Deists mounted a concerted attack on the evidential value of miracles as contrary to natural law? Yes, but implied in the Deist argument is the inference that while revelation is contingent and mysterious, nature is uniform and transparent in its intelligibility. This, according to Butler, is where the Deists deceive themselves, i.e., in assuming that we know nature. What we experience in nature is but a mere point when compared with the whole plan reaching throughout eternity past and future. Yet the fact that things are beyond our experience "is no sort of presumption against the truth and reality of them" for there are innumerable things in the constitution of the universe "which are beyond the natural reach of our faculties."[27] We should not, then, presume against miracles of Scripture on account of their being unlike the known course of nature, "for there is no presumption at all from analogy that the *whole* course of things, naturally unknown to us, and *everything* in it, is like to anything in that which is known."[28] Nature teems with puzzles. We know some of her laws, "but we know in a manner nothing by what laws, storms and tempests, earthquakes, famine, pestilence, become the instruments of destruction to mankind."[29] These laws are so unknown to us that "we call the events which come to pass by them, accidental." It is only from our experience of a portion of nature as exhibiting general laws that we conclude the same for the mysterious remainder. If this be our inference concerning our knowledge of nature, then, Butler argues, it

> is sufficient for answering objections that God's miraculous interpositions may have been, all along in like manner, by *general* laws of wisdom. . . . These laws are unknown indeed to us; but no more unknown than the laws from whence it is that some die as soon as they are born, and others live to extreme old age. . . .[30]

Butler thus concludes:

> Upon the whole then: The appearance of deficiencies and irregularities in nature is owing to its being a scheme but in part made known. . . . Now we see no more reason why the frame and course of nature should be such a scheme, than why Christianity should. . . . And from all this it is credible that there might be the like appearance of deficiencies and irregularities in Christianity, as in nature. . . . And these objections are answered by these observations concerning Christianity; as the like objections against the frame of nature are answered by the like observations concerning the frame of nature.[31]

Butler uses the same method of analogy to defend the particularity of Christian revelation. To attack Christianity because revelation is not given equally to all persons everywhere at all times is sophistical. God's providential wisdom recognizes that his self-revelation needs be different for different peoples and changing circumstances. Nature demonstrates that a system such as this world implies great variety and change. Even if revelation were universal, it would not result in uniformity for

> from men's different capacities of understanding . . . their different educations and other external circumstances . . . their religious situations would be widely different and the disadvantage of some in comparison of others, perhaps, altogether as much as at present.[32]

It is just because the condition of humanity is so varied and its knowledge so imperfect that humans are in need of special revelation. Christianity does not contradict the religion of nature; rather it is a "republication" of natural religion "adapted to the present circumstances of mankind" and "containing an account of a dispensation of things not discoverable by reason."[33] It is true, then, that much found in revelation is not readily apparent to our reason—which explains just why revelation is needed. But to complain of the mysteries of revelation is not to distinguish it from natural religion, for nature, as we have seen, is full of dark irrationalities and melancholy uncertainties. Such is the good Bishop's conclusion.

Butler's *Analogy* is valuable because it demonstrated with powerful consistency that natural religion had no privileged position over Christian revelation because of the former's perfect rationality. The perfection of nature was no more obvious than the perfection of biblical revelation. Belief in God, the author of nature, required the same convergence of probabilities as belief in the God of Christian revelation. As Butler would say, taken *on the whole* there is no more reason to doubt the testimony of Scripture than the testimony of natural reason.

The weakness of Butler's *Analogy* lay in the fact that he assumed that his contemporaries' faith in natural religion was so strong as to be unshakable in the face of his negative method of argument. Butler failed to see that his method was a two-edged sword—that it is not the most promising argument for revelation to say that because nature is a mess of riddles, we cannot expect revelation to be any clearer! This may equalize the difficulties in the rational warrants that are offered in defense of Deism and of Christianity; but on the other hand, it might lead those with slightly different sentiments to the conclusion that both Christianity and natural religion are irrational. The convictions of many Deists were so attenuated as to need very little to turn them into skeptics. "It seems not to have occurred to the good Bishop," remarks Leslie Stephen, "that if natural religion were, rationally considered, on no firmer a foundation than revelation, there might be some men willing to reject them both."[34]

Butler's *Analogy*, though printed in several editions in his own lifetime, had a mixed reception due to the dangerous ambiguity of its argument. The year after its publication the Deist Thomas Chubb used Butler's theory of probability and analogy to show that it could be used to justify all forms of belief. He pointed out that Butler's use of analogy might

> possibly prove a very dangerous experiment because perhaps the same kind of reasoning may answer the same purpose to every scheme of religion.... For what difficulty is there that attends either the popish or Mahometan, or the pagan religion, but artful and inquisitive men may find out something or other in nature which they can call a difficulty and represent as analogous to it? And perhaps the application may be as just as in the former case.[35]

A few years later a remarkable pamphlet was issued by Henry Dodwell the Younger, entitled *Christianity Not Founded on Argument* (1742). Dodwell's book maintained in effect that religious faith has nothing to do with reason but is an appeal to authority and internal illumination by the Holy Spirit. He claimed that rational theology actually produced infidelity rather than conviction and, like Anthony Collins before him, suggested that no one ever thought of doubting the existence of God before reading Samuel Clarke's rationalistic defense of theism in the Boyle lectures. If religion were a matter of rational proof, says Dodwell,

> the excellent *Analogy of Reason and Revelation** lately communicated might induce me yet more powerfully to acknowledge at least a very great and specious ap-

*An obvious reference to Butler's *Analogy.*

pearance of truth in its traced connections and inferences. ... But when I consider all these enlightening lucubrations as proofs actually insisted upon ... as that which any part of the evidence of Christianity is to stand upon or depend for its support ... I cannot but draw to myself very different consequences. ... They suggest strongly to me that a position can never be a *necessary truth* which stands in need of any such farfetched apologies and labored accounts to reconcile and explain it.[36]

So it was that, contrary to his intentions, Butler's labored apology for Christianity served the cause of skepticism, religious irrationalism, and fideism. It was but a short way to David Hume, who knew Butler's work as early as 1736, and whose writings in the next few decades were to prove to be the final death blow to the religion of reason. But it was Law, Dodwell, and especially Bishop Butler who served as significant links between the Deism of Tindal and its downfall at the hands of Hume.

DAVID HUME

The writings of David Hume (1711–1776) stand with the works of Kant as a watershed in the history of philosophical theology. Although some of his writings did not have as wide an influence on theology during his own lifetime as he himself expected, all subsequent philosophical theology, that dares to call itself by that name, has had to take Hume's inquiries into account. Hume was raised in the strict Calvinist environment of eighteenth-century Scotland, but at an early age shed the Calvinist influences of his home. His later reputation as a charitable and virtuous man of unusual excellence appears to owe nothing to a personal religious faith. He never experienced the soul-searching *angst* and spiritual uncertainties that mark what William James called the "twice born" man.

In his maturity Hume found religion not only personally unnecessary but historically, in the main, a malignant influence. At the end of his essay on *The Natural History of Religion,* he concluded that if you examine the religious principles which have prevailed in the world "you will scarcely be persuaded that they are anything but sick men's dreams."[37]

Hume was not, however, an atheist. In fact, the agnostic Scotsman was shocked and amused at the dogmatic atheism of the Parisian *philosophes*.[38] Yet Hume had no belief in a personal providence or special revelation or in any specifically religious duties. What he called religion was "little more than a repudiation of all superstition," and knowledge of God was for him reducible to "one simple, though somewhat ambiguous, at least undefined proposition: that the cause or causes of order in the universe probably bear some remote analogy to human intelligence."[39]

A vivid depiction of Hume's "natural irreligion" is given in James Boswell's account of his last interview with the dying philosopher. The subject of immortality was broached. Hume indicated that he had no belief in an after-life, for it was "a most unreasonable fancy." The prospect of annihilation gave him no uneasiness, for he did not wish to be immortal. The reason, Hume drolly replied, was "that he was very well in this state of being and that the chances were very much against his being so well in another state." Boswell concludes his reminiscence by saying:

> Mr. Hume's pleasantry was such that there was no solemnity in the scene; and death for the time did not seem dismal. It surprised me to find him talking of different matters with a tranquility of mind which few men possess at any time. . . . I left him with impressions which disturbed me for some time.[40]

Hume's writings proved to be as unsettling as his personal presence.

The fact is, however, that Hume did not relish controversy and had no desire to be a Scottish Voltaire dedicated to crushing *l'infâme*. As early as 1737, Hume "castrated" his *Treatise of Human Nature* by excising all theological controversy from the book in order that "it shall give as little offence as possible."* However, a decade later Hume resolved to include theological considerations in his *An Inquiry Concerning Human Understanding* (1748), for these matters lay at the very heart of his philosophical doctrine.[41]

---

* Hume was especially concerned not to give offense to the esteemed Dr. Butler.

Of Miracles

Eighteenth-century apologetics concentrated on two basic theistic proofs: the argument from miracle and prophecy and the argument from design.[42] It is not coincidental that Hume includes an extensive discussion of both of these "proofs" in Sections X and XI of the *Inquiry*. The essay "Of Miracles" (X) had its precursor in the original "Reasonings Concerning Miracles" which had been left out of the *Treatise* in deference to Dr. Butler. Hume apparently still felt that he must proceed prudently, for he begins the essay with the *imprimatur* of the Archbishop of Canterbury by referring to John Tillotson's "concise and elegant" argument against the *real presence* in the Eucharist as the model for his own reflections.

Hume begins the essay by reasserting the premise of his whole "experimental method," namely, that experience be our only guide in reasoning concerning matters of fact. Experience admittedly is not infallible; there are all imaginable degrees of assurance from the highest certainty to the lowest possible probability. "The wise man, therefore, proportions his belief to the evidence." The wise person must weigh the evidence and here can proceed with assurance but there with doubt and hesitation. All reasonable judgments, however, are made on evidence which does not exceed probability.

Having established the ground rules, Hume proceeds to apply these principles to the issue at hand: reasoning based on the testimony of others. "Evidence derived from witnesses and human testimony," says Hume,

> is regarded either as a *proof* or a *probability*, according as the conjunction between any particular kind of report and any kind of object has been found to be constant or variable. There are a number of circumstances to be taken into consideration . . . and the ultimate standard by which we determine all disputes that may arise concerning them is always derived from experience and observation.[43]

If the fact which the historical testimony endeavors to establish is "extraordinary and marvelous," the evidence will admit of a diminution "greater or less in proportion as the fact is more or less unusual." But if the fact which the witnesses affirm, instead of being marvelous, is actually miraculous and "the testimony, considered apart and in itself, amounts to an entire proof—in that case there is proof against proof, of which the strongest must prevail."[44] That is, according to Hume, a miracle is by definition a violation of the laws of nature, "and as a firm and unalterable experience has established these laws, the proof against a miracle, from the very nature of the fact, is as entire as any argument from experience can possibly be imagined."[45] For example, if a person in seeming good health should suddenly die, it would not be considered miraculous since, though unusual, such events are rather frequently observed. But if a dead person should come to life, it would be miraculous, for it has not been previously observed.

> There must, therefore, be a uniform experience against every miraculous act, otherwise the event would not merit that appellation. And as a uniform experience amounts to a proof, there is here a direct and full *proof,* from the nature of the fact, against the existence of any miracle.[46]

The plain consequence which Hume draws from the above is that "no testimony is sufficient to establish a miracle unless the testimony be of such a kind that its falsehood would be more miraculous than the fact which it endeavors to establish."[47] That fact is, then, that it appears that no testimony for any kind of miracle has ever amounted to a probability, much less a proof, "and therefore we may establish it as a maxim that no human testimony can have such force as to prove a miracle and make it a just foundation for any such system of religion."[48]

Hume wishes to make it clear that he has only established that "a miracle can never be proved so as to be the foundation of a system of religion." He does not categorically deny the possibility of miracles or violations of the *usual course* of nature. In cases of strong and general testimony concerning unusual events, one should be disposed not to doubt such occurrences in an unreasonable manner but rather to search out the causes of such prodigies.

> Suppose that all the historians who treat of England should agree that on the first of January 1600, Queen Elizabeth died; that both before and after her death she was seen by her physicians and the whole court . . . and that, after being interred for a month, she appeared again, resumed the throne and governed England for three years—I must confess that I should be surprised at the concurrence of so many odd circumstances but should not have the least inclination to believe so miraculous an event. I should not doubt her pretended death and of those other public circumstances that followed it. I should only assert it to have been pretended, and that it neither was, nor possibly could be, real. . . . I would still reply that the knavery and folly of men are such common phenomena that I should rather believe that most extraordinary events to arise from their concurrence than admit of so signal a violation of the laws of nature.[49]

Hume is arguing that unless one can assume a complete knowledge of the possibilities of natural occurrence so as to exclude from any event every possible natural cause, it is not possible to prove any particular event a miracle. Inexplicable as it may appear, it is always more reasonable to seek out some natural explanation of the phenomenon. Hume's conclusion is that the rational proof of religion from the testimony of miracle is entirely specious. In fact, religion is founded on faith, not reason. "I am the better pleased," concludes Hume,

> with the method of reasoning here delivered, as I think it may serve to confound those dangerous friends or disguised enemies of the *Christian religion* who have undertaken to defend it by the principles of human reason. Our most holy religion is founded on *faith,* not on reason; and it is a sure method of exposing it to put it to such a trial as it is by no means fitted to endure.[50]

How is this to be understood? Was Hume involved in a *volte-face* as A. E. Taylor claims,[51] or is this an example of Hume's derisive mockery? That Hume was being sardonic there is little doubt. Yet there is no reason why we should not take Hume's words here in a straightforward manner. Hume has shown that miracles are no proof of the Christian religion and will later demonstrate that reason is not able to prove the claims of Christianity. Yet Hume was well aware that for the faithful belief itself was a divinely conferred miracle. And so his concluding words, though not without irony, are stating what in fact was believed by many to be the case:

> Upon the whole we may conclude that the Christian religion . . . at this day cannot be believed by a reasonable person without [a miracle]. Mere reason is insufficient to convince us of its veracity. And whoever is moved by *faith* to assent to it is conscious of a continued miracle in his own person which subverts all the principles of his understanding and gives him a determination to believe what is most contrary to custom and experience.[52]

It must be remembered, however, that Hume is saying not only that reason is impotent to convince us of the claims of faith, but also that the rational man, who proportions his belief to the evidence, cannot take the way of faith. Here is the religious cul-de-sac that Hume alone appears to have grasped.

Section XI of the *Inquiry,* "Of a Providence and a Future State," was intended by Hume to be taken together with the section "Of Miracles." The latter, as we have seen, was to serve as a refutation of the proof from miracles; the former is an attempt to show that on the basis of the traditional argument from design, it is not possible to establish the kind of Deity that belief in a particular providence and a future state presuppose. The subjects of the title of Section XI are hardly touched on, the focus of Hume's analysis being the argument from design.[53] That Hume was aware of the explosive implications of this essay is evident in the fact that he resorts to a dialogue form by which his own views can be disguised in the words of an Epicurean friend "who loves skeptical paradoxes." Nevertheless, Hume is no longer willing to defer to the revered Bishop Butler who had confidently pronounced that "to an unprejudiced mind ten thousand instances of design cannot but prove a designer." Hume is now determined to attack the very citadel of rational theology.

Hume's "friend" observes that religious philosophers, rather than being satisfied with their traditions, indulge in rash curiosity in trying to prove religion by rational argument. "They paint in the most magnificent colors the order, beauty, and wise arrangement of the universe," claiming that such evidence points to a wise and benevolent Creator. They contend that the chief argument for a divine existence is found in the very order of nature. The "friend" continues:

> You allow that this is an argument drawn from effects to causes. From the order of the work you infer that there must have been project and forethought in the workman. If you cannot make out this point, you allow that your conclusion fails, and you pretend not to establish the conclusion in a greater latitude than the phenomena of nature will justify. These are your concessions. I desire you to mark the consequences.[54]

The consequences are twofold. First,

> when we infer any particular cause from an effect, we must proportion the one to the other and can never be allowed to ascribe to the cause any qualities but what are exactly sufficient to produce the effect. A body of ten ounces raised in any scale may serve as a proof that the counterbalancing weight exceeds ten ounces, but can never afford a reason that it exceeds a hundred.[55]

Second, it is not permissible to begin with an inferred cause and infer other effects than those already known.

> We can never be allowed to mount up from the universe, the effect, to Jupiter, the cause, and then descend downward to infer any new effect from that cause, as if the present effects alone were not entirely worthy of the glorious attributes which we ascribe to that deity.[56]

This was precisely Butler's procedure in the *Analogy.* From consideration of justice in our natural life, Butler infers a higher but analogous justice in some future state. He concludes from observation of this life that it is but a passage to something further— "a porch which leads to a greater and vastly different building." But let's take Butler's example of justice:

> *Are there any marks of distributive justice in the world?* If you answer in the affirmative, I conclude that, since justice here exerts itself, it is satisfied. If you reply in the negative, I conclude that you have then no reason to ascribe justice, in our sense of it, to the gods. If you hold a medium between affirmation and negation, by saying that the justice of the gods at present

exerts itself in part, but not in full extent, I answer that you have no reason to give it any particular extent, but only as far as you see it, *at present,* exert itself.[57]

At this point Hume asks his "friend" a question. If you observed a half finished building, surrounded by bricks and mortar, could you not properly infer that was a work of design and would it not be reasonable to infer that in time the building would be finished? Why, then, do you refuse to admit the same inferences with regard to the order of nature? The "friend's" answer is that the infinite difference of the subjects precludes such an analogy. In the case of human art, we can advance from effect to cause and then make new inferences concerning the effect because we already possess considerable knowledge concerning the capacities and practices of men. The case is not the same with our reasoning concerning the works of nature.

> The Deity is known to us only by his productions, and is a single being in the universe, *not comprehended under any species or genus,* from whose experienced attributes or qualities we can, by analogy, infer any attribute or quality in him. As the universe . . . shows a particular degree of perfections, we infer a particular degree of them, precisely adapted to the effect which we examine. But further attributes or further degrees of the same attributes, we can never be authorized to infer.[58] (Italics added.)

The supposition of further divine attributes is mere speculation. This is, Hume contends, exactly what occurs with the "religious hypothesis." But such ascribing of attributes to the Supreme Being "savors more of flattery and panegyric than of just reasoning." For "no new fact can ever be inferred from the religious hypothesis, no event foreseen or foretold, no reward or punishment expected or dreaded, beyond what is already known by practice and observation."[59]

The practical result of natural theology is, then, very slight. Certainly no reasonable inferences can be drawn from nature concerning such cornerstones of Christian belief as a wise and benevolent creator, a special providence, or future rewards and punishments. Epicurus's conclusion is that the religious inferences drawn from our experience of nature are

"uncertain and useless." Uncertain because we cannot legitimately draw any inferences from nature beyond what we already know; useless because we cannot make any additions to our common experience of nature from which we would derive principles of moral conduct. Despite Hume's opening disavowal, he ends convinced by Epicurus that the argument from design is religiously worthless.

The Dialogues Concerning Natural Religion

The fact that Hume recognized the argument from design to be the foundation of the rational theology of his day is evident in the central place he gives to analyzing it in his masterpiece, *The Dialogues Concerning Natural Religion.* The *Dialogues* were written during Hume's most productive period, 1751–1757. They were revised in 1761 and remained his chief preoccupation during the last months of his life. He was persuaded by friends, among them Adam Smith, not to publish the work during his lifetime, but he left definite instructions that if the *Dialogues* did not appear within two and a half years after his death, his nephew and heir should see to their publication. This request was carried out, without any revision of the text, in 1779.

The *Dialogues* are modeled after and are, in many ways, dependent on Cicero's *De Natura Deorum.* Hume presents his analysis of theology through the mouths of three protagonists. Like Butler, Cleanthes is the model of the eighteenth-century Christian apologist. Demea represents most often traditional orthodox fideism but, on occasion, the older a priori rationalism. Philo plays the gadfly and skeptic. Earlier studies of the *Dialogues,* taking Hume's words at their face value, claimed that Hume identified himself with Cleanthes. Such a verdict is based principally on the final words of the *Dialogues* where Hume concludes that "upon serious review of the whole, I cannot but think, that Philo's principles are more probable than Demea's; but that those of Cleanthes approach still nearer the truth." The identification of Hume with Cleanthes fails, however, to consider the import of Hume's whole argument in the *Inquiry* as well as the *Dialogues,* his use of irony and even ridicule, and his academical skepticism which caused him on occasion to concede ample place to historical convention and psychological need. Hume also desired to leave his readers free to judge for themselves rather than impose a dogmatical conclusion onto his analysis. The "bow" to Cleanthes leaves Hume's own view more ambiguous than would otherwise be the case.

More recently scholars have agreed with Kemp Smith's interpretation that Hume's own teaching is developed in and through the argument as a whole and that some of his own beliefs are put in the mouths of all three protagonists. Nevertheless,

> Philo, from start to finish represents Hume; Cleanthes can be regarded as Hume's mouthpiece only in those passages in which he is explicitly agreeing with Philo or . . . while refuting Demea, he is also being used to prepare the way for one or other of Philo's independent conclusions.[60]

The above view is correct, except that it does not give enough place to the very important agreements between Philo and Demea against the rationalist Cleanthes.

The central issue of the *Dialogues* is not the *existence* but the *nature* of God. Nevertheless, Hume's conclusions, which suggest that the *nature* of God is inaccessible to reason, raise the question as to what such an unknown God could possibly mean for religious faith. No summary of the argument of the *Dialogues* can begin to do justice to the richness and subtlety of the dialectical movement of the discussion. An account of the major arguments must, however, be attempted if we are to understand the nature and force of Hume's contribution.

The conversation turns on our knowledge of the nature of God. Demea affirms that due to our human weakness God remains unknown to our reason; further, that it is impious to seek to pry into his essence. Rather, as "finite, weak and blind creatures, we ought to humble ourselves in his august presence and . . . adore in silence his infinite perfections."[61] Philo concurs: "Our ideas," he affirms,

> reach no farther than our experience. We have no experience of divine attributes and operations. I need not conclude my syllogism. . . . And it is a pleasure to me that just reasoning and sound piety here concur in the same conclusion, and both of them establish the

adorably mysterious and incomprehensible nature of the Supreme Being.[62]

Cleanthes conceives the matter differently. He finds that the curious adapting of means to ends in nature resembles human art and that since these effects resemble each other, "we are led to infer, by all the rules of analogy, that the causes also resemble, and that the Author of nature is somewhat similar to the mind of man."[63] The issue is thus drawn. Philo now proceeds in his series of arguments with an Olympian calm. Cleanthes's views are countered one after another, and yet Hume maintains the dramatic interest by leading the reader to believe that Cleanthes is withholding the heavier weapons of his arsenal for the final engagements.

Philo first opposes Cleanthes with the argument offered previously in the *Inquiry*, namely, that Cleanthes is assuming that the universe may be taken as of the same species with houses and ships and furniture.

> Is a part of nature a rule for another part very wide of the former? Is it a rule for the whole? Is a very small part a rule for the universe. . .? And will any man tell me with a serious countenance that an orderly universe must arise from some thought and art like the human because we have experience of it? To ascertain this reasoning it were requisite that we had experience of the origin of worlds.[64]

Cleanthes does not reply to Philo's criticism but merely persists in his belief that the similarity of the works of art and of nature are "self-evident."

Philo's second major line of argument concerns Cleanthes's analogy between the human and divine minds. To claim that the plan of nature is derived from the mind of God as a building can be traced to a plan in the mind of an architect is to solve nothing. Whether we are considering a human or divine mind, there is no reason in considering questions of cause and effect to stop with ideas or mental causes, for "a mental world or universe of ideas requires a cause as much as does a material world or universe of objects."[65] That is,

> have we not the same reason to trace that ideal world into another ideal world or new intelligent principle?

But if we stop and go no farther, why go so far? Why not stop with the material world? How can we satisfy ourselves without going on *ad infinitum. . .*? If the material world rests upon a similar ideal world, this ideal world must rest on some other, and so on without end. It were better, therefore, never to look beyond the present material world. By supposing it to contain the principle of its order within itself, we really assert it to be God; and the sooner we arrive at that divine Being, so much the better.[66]

That is, if we claim that it is some *rational faculty* in the mind of the Creator that produces the order of the material world, we are merely making an *assertion,* and a similar claim could be as easily made for "the nature of material objects, and that they are all originally possessed of a *faculty* of order and proportion." Philo's conclusion is that neither hypothesis has any advantage over the other since "an ideal system, arranged of itself . . . is not a whit more explicable than a material one which attains its order in a like manner."[67]

The crux of Philo's argument comes in Part V of the *Dialogues.* Cleanthes persists in maintaining his analogy between the human and divine minds. Pressed by Philo, Cleanthes affirms that when considering the analogy between the divine and human minds, "the liker, the better." With an air of triumph, Philo now calls upon Cleanthes to mark the consequences.

> *First,* . . . you renounce all claim to infinity in any of the attributes of the Deity. For as the cause ought only to be proportioned to the effect, and the effect, so far as it falls under our cognisance, is not infinite; what pretensions have we . . . to ascribe that attribute to the divine Being. . .? *Secondly,* you have no reason, on your theory, for ascribing perfection to the Deity, or for supposing him free from every error. . . . At least you must acknowledge that it is impossible for us to tell, from our limited views, whether the system contains any great faults or deserves any considerable praise if compared to other possible and even real systems. . . . Many worlds might have been botched and bungled throughout an eternity, ere this system was struck out. . . . And what shadow of an argument, continued Philo, can you produce from your hypothesis to prove the unity of the Deity? A great number of men join in

building a house or ship, in rearing a city, in framing a common-wealth; why may not several deities combine in contriving and framing a world?[68]

If Cleanthes insists, in arguing by analogy, that the cause must be proportioned to the effect, then we have no grounds for ascribing to God such attributes as infinity, perfection, and unity.

To this point Cleanthes has maintained that a rational mind is needed to explain order in nature. He has continuously argued this point from the analogy of human art. Philo now questions Cleanthes's use of this particular analogy. If we look around us, we must acknowledge that the natural world bears a greater resemblance to "an animal or vegetable than it does a watch." The cause of the world, it is more probable, resembles the cause of the former rather than the latter. We know that the cause of animal or vegetable is generation or vegetation. Therefore, it is no "less intelligible or less conformable to experience to say that the world arose by vegetation, from a seed shed by another world, than to say that it arose from a divine reason or contrivance, according to the sense in which Cleanthes understands it."[69]

Here Demea raises an objection to Philo's speculation concerning the vegetative origin of the world by asking, "How can order spring from anything which perceives not that order which it bestows?"[70] Does not order presuppose the conscious mind of an orderer? To this Philo replies that our ordinary experience would lead to no such conclusion for "a tree bestows order and organization on that tree which springs from it, without knowing the order; an animal in the same manner on its offspring."[71] To hold that all order in nature proceeds ultimately from design, one would be required to prove a priori, "both that order is, from its nature, inseparably attached to thought and that it can never of itself or from unknown principles belong to matter."[72] *Experience alone* affords no justification for Cleanthes's view that mind is the only source of order. "Judging by our limited and imperfect experience, generation has some privileges above reason; for we see every day the latter arise from the former, never the former from the latter."[73]

At this point in the dialogue, Hume allows for a digression from Philo's relentless pursuance of the argument from design, in order to consider briefly the cogency of the a priori argument for the existence of God. The argument, put into the mouth of Demea, is a combination of the cosmological and ontological arguments used by Samuel Clarke in his *Discourse Concerning the Being and Attributes of God* (1704). The argument proceeds as follows. Whatever exists has a cause which precedes it. In going from effects to causes we must proceed in an infinite regression or have recourse to some cause that is *necessarily existent.* The question of why this particular succession of causes existed from eternity and not nothing requires reasonable explanation, since there is nothing absurd in *nothing* having existed from eternity. What was it, then, that determined *something* to exist rather than nothing? It could not be some *external cause,* for that would simply open the way for an infinite regress.

> *Chance* is a word without meaning. Was it *nothing?* But that can never produce anything. We must, therefore, have recourse to a **necessarily existent Being** who carries the *reason* of his existence in himself, and who cannot be supposed not to exist without express contradiction. There is, consequently, such a Being.[74]

Philo and Cleanthes agree that Demea's a priori demonstration has no force because matters of empirical fact cannot be proved by a priori arguments. Here is Cleanthes's refutation:

> Nothing is demonstrable unless the contrary implies a contradiction. Nothing that is distinctly conceivable implies a contradiction. Whatever we conceive as existent, we can also conceive as non-existent. *There is no Being, therefore, whose non-existence implies a contradiction. Consequently there is no Being whose existence is demonstrable.* . . . . The words, therefore, *necessary existence* have no meaning or, which is the same thing, none that is consistent.[75] (Italics added.)

Unable to answer Cleanthes's refutation, Demea shifts the discussion to the subject of evil—a topic more in line with his original position. He now declares that it is from "a consciousness of imbecility and misery rather than from any reasoning" that man is led to belief in a Being on whom all nature is dependent.

> The whole earth, believe me, Philo, is cursed and polluted. A perpetual war is kindled amongst all living creatures. Necessity, hunger, want, stimulate the strong and courageous: Fear, anxiety, terror agitate the weak and infirm.[76]

Philo agrees but points out that humans are not exempt from these evils which plague the lower animals: "Man is the greatest enemy of man. Oppression, injustice, contempt, contumely, violence, sedition, war, calumny, treachery, fraud; by these they mutually torment each other."[77] Having catalogued the sorrows and miseries of human life, Philo asks:

> And is it possible, Cleanthes, . . . that after all these reflections . . . you still persevere in your anthropomorphism, and assert the moral attributes of the Deity, his justice, benevolence, mercy, and rectitude, to be of the same nature with these virtues in human creatures? His power, we allow, is infinite; whatever he wills is executed; but neither man nor any animal is happy; therefore he does not will their happiness. His wisdom is infinite; he is never mistaken in choosing the means to any end; but the course of nature tends not to human or animal felicity; therefore, it is not established for that purpose. Through the whole compass of human knowledge there are no inferences more certain and infallible than these. In what respect, then, do his benevolence and mercy resemble the benevolence and mercy of men?[78]

Demea intervenes at this point to offer the "probation" or "porch" theory used earlier by Bishop Butler. This life of hardship is but a testing ground for the future life in eternity. At this point it is Cleanthes who counters Demea's argument, since, being committed to argument a posteriori, he cannot accept any inferences which are not consistent with the facts of actual experience. The only legitimate method of argument is, according to Cleanthes, to show that *in this life* "health is more common than sickness; pleasure than pain." To this Philo replies that Cleanthes has established the warrants for religion on a very frail base. For the belief that human health and happiness in this life exceed pain and misery is contrary to much human experience, and it is not possible, to compute, estimate, and compare all the pains and all the pleasures in the lives of all men and of all animals; and thus, by your resting the whole system of religion on a point which, from its very nature, must ever be uncertain, you tacitly confess that that system is equally uncertain. . . . Here, Cleanthes, I find myself at ease in my argument. Here I triumph.[79]

Cleanthes makes one last attempt to shore up the argument from analogy. To abandon all human analogy is unthinkable, for to do so is to abandon rationality in religion. But perhaps we can preserve the human analogy and conceive of "the Author of nature to be *finitely* perfect, though far exceeding mankind." Philo does not attempt here to present objections to Cleanthes's hypothesis of a finite God, for that is not the point at issue. The question is whether the ambiguous mixture of good and evil in the world justifies inferring to a God, *whether finite or infinite,* such moral attributes as justice and benevolence. If a person were brought into this world without any antecedent conviction concerning a supreme and benevolent intelligence but were

> left to gather such a belief from the appearances of things—this entirely alters the case, nor will he ever find any reason for such a conclusion. He may be fully convinced of the narrow limits of his understanding, but this will not help him in forming an inference concerning the goodness of superior powers, *since he must form that inference from what he knows,* not from what he is ignorant of.[80] (Italics added.)

As long as the goodness of the Deity cannot be established a priori and because such moral qualities must be inferred from experience, there can be no grounds for such inferences while the world is so full of evil.

> Look round this universe. What an immense profusion of beings. You admire this prodigious variety and fecundity. But inspect a little more narrowly these living existences. . . . How hostile and destructive to each other. . . . The whole presents nothing but the idea of a blind nature, impregnated by a great vivifying principle, and pouring forth from her lap, without discernment or parental care, her maimed and abortive children.[81]

Our experience, says Philo, would indicate that the first cause of things is benignly indifferent to our human judgments of good and evil.

With this, Philo's refutation of Cleanthes's argument from design comes to a conclusion. The force of the entire argument, as it reaches its climax in the depiction of humans in a blindly indifferent universe, appears irrefutable. Hume has not only countered the theistic proofs but left us with a feeling of existential abandonment. His concluding comment is that "to be a philosophical skeptic is, in a man of letters, the first and most essential step towards being a sound, believing Christian."[82] Hume was here again expressing his ironic attitude toward popular faith. There is, however, more in this and other similar statements than mere mordant irony. There is a very modern ring to these words, for in the almost two centuries since Hume, metaphysical skepticism and religious faith have often joined in a strange alliance. Hume's counsel certainly has been used to endorse Demea's views and to give philosophical support to many contemporary fideists of skeptical temperament. In this sense Hume anticipates several thinkers of the nineteenth and twentieth centuries, for example, Kierkegaard, as we will see.

It seems clear that Hume himself recognized the practical impossibility of Philo's skepticism and that he was sympathetic to Cleanthes's strictures against persisting in "total skepticism" and "philosophical melancholy." He certainly recognized that for the majority of mankind the skeptics' calm and leisurely negations are child's play in the face of life's practical needs. Where Hume joins with all the fideists of the modern period is in their common conviction that reason is impotent to either establish or falsify religious *beliefs.* This is one source of Hume's modernity and continuing importance in theological work. Hume, like many analytical philosophers and theologians in the twentieth century, did not consider religious beliefs to be factual assertions about the empirical world. For Hume religious convictions, like certain philosophical ideas, are what can be called *natural beliefs.* By this is meant beliefs that are not themselves factual inferences but instinctive and practical attitudes toward the world. Hume held that "there is a great difference between such opinions as we form after a calm and profound reflection, and such as we embrace by a kind of instinct or natural impulse on account of their suitability and conformity to the mind."[83] Among humanity's "natural beliefs" are the existence of the external world, the identity of the self, and such religious convictions as a particular providence and a future life. Hume thus held that there are these natural beliefs which are neither proven nor falsified by the experimental method, for the reason that such convictions are not to be confused with empirical assertions. Since religious belief does not involve factual assertions, the ground is cut from under the empirical skeptic. The price of such a victory for the theologian is very high, however, namely, the acknowledgment that religion does not claim to make metaphysical assertions about the world. As we will see, this issue posed by Hume is one of the most basic in the history of modern theology.[84]

Hume's modernity is also traceable to his candidly realistic view of human nature and history. There is in Hume's depiction of nature's "maimed and abortive children" a nihilism more chilling than that of any twentieth-century atheistic existentialist. Hume is no Dostoevskian "underground man," but the germ of a more militant skepticism is certainly present in the *Dialogues*. Strangely enough, Hume is even more modern than the strident nihilists of the nineteenth century. In spite of his skeptical pessimism, Hume is completely above the romantic storm and stress. He is able to descend into the skeptical abyss with Olympian calm. His indifference to the "religious hypothesis" is more typical of the healthy agnosticism of the modern secular person "come of age" described by Dietrich Bonhoeffer in his *Letters and Papers from Prison*. Hume is the modern secularist par excellence.

IMMANUEL KANT

Hume's importance in the history of theology has been essentially negative. He concluded his *Inquiry Concerning Human Understanding* by throwing down the following gauntlet:

> If we take in our hand any volume of divinity or school metaphysics, let us ask, *Does it contain any abstract reasoning concerning quantity or number?* No.

Does it contain any experimental reasoning concerning matters of fact and existence? No. Commit it then to the flames for it can contain nothing but sophistry and illusion.[85]

This has remained to the present a direct challenge to all philosophical theologians who wish to establish rational warrants for religious belief. It was Kant's own reading of Hume's critical analysis of the older metaphysics that first interrupted his "dogmatic slumber."[86] Kant came to recognize that the human mind finds itself in the peculiar situation of being burdened by certain metaphysical questions which it is unable to ignore but which also appear to transcend the mind's power to answer. Kant's importance for modern theology lies in the fact that he both extended Hume's critique of traditional natural theology *and* laid the theoretical groundwork for an entirely new approach to theology. Kant remarks in the Preface to *The Critique of Pure Reason* that he had "found it necessary to deny knowledge in order to make room for *faith*."[87] This sounds exactly like Hume in its denial of any relationship between religion and matters of empirical knowledge; but this is as far as the similarity goes. It is important to note that Kant is contrasting *faith* or *belief* (*Glaube*) with empirical *knowledge,* not faith and reason. Kant believed that there was a reasonable form of faith which a rational person would recognize as *implied* in an analysis of experience. Religious faith and knowledge are not radically opposed in Kant as in Hume, for they are two quite different, though equally necessary, aspects of reason. Kant's pivotal role in modern theology lies in the fact that he freed theology from the corrosion of classical empiricism while maintaining the rationality of religious belief.

Immanuel Kant (1724–1804) was born in Königsberg in East Prussia. Because both his parents were devout Pietists, Kant was nurtured in this form of Protestant piety, both at home and at the Collegium Fredericianum, where he studied from 1732 to 1740. Pietism placed great emphasis on ardent, personal religious experience, on God's grace in transforming the believer through conversion, and on strict moral integrity. The latter influence remained with Kant throughout his life and is basic to understanding his character and philosophy. Nevertheless, while Kant always remained respectful of the positive qualities of Pietism, the emotional fervor and hypocrisy which he encountered at the Collegium gave him a lifelong abhorrence of such "emotional" exercises as hymn singing and prayer.*

Kant lived his entire life in Königsberg where, as one writer noted, his life was like the most regular of regular verbs. He attended the University of Königsberg, became a tutor to a private family, and in 1755 returned to the University where he remained for the rest of his life. Despite his outwardly uneventful life, Kant was known to his students and friends as an eloquent, popular lecturer and charming host.

Kant began his career as a convinced disciple of the Leibnizian-Wolffian rationalism that reigned in the German universities. However, in the period between 1770 and 1781, he began to reject the Leibnitz-Wolff system and to work out his own philosophy. While Kant's mature thought reveals the influence of both his early Pietism and the rationalism of Wolff, it also reflects his reaction against them, as we will see. In 1781 *The Critique of Pure Reason* appeared and ushered in the Kantian "Copernican Revolution" in philosophy and theology. Once the first *Critique* appeared, a dozen or more additional works followed in quick succession for almost a quarter of a century, until his death in 1804. Kant's philosophical output after his fifty-seventh year is an unparalleled accomplishment.

What was Kant's "Copernican Revolution"? Among the British empiricists, from Locke to Hume, there was general agreement that the mind functions in a passive role. According to the empiricists, there are no innate ideas in the mind; rather, the mind at its beginning is an empty vessel, a *tabula rasa* receiving "impressions" from the exterior world. From these single impressions the mind somehow "collects" ideas, and thus all ideas come from empirical experience. Hume carried British empiricism to a skeptical blind alley by contending that belief in the simplicity or identity of the self or objects in the external world was simply the result of habit, since identity "is nothing really belonging to

these different perceptions and uniting them together; but it is merely a quality which we attribute to them because of the union of their ideas in the imagination."

Kant came to believe that it was the empiricists' passive and dualistic view of cognition, which conceived of the mind as simply a receptor of particular external sense impressions, that was inadequate and which led to Hume's skepticism. Kant suggested another hypothesis concerning the mind.

> Hitherto it has been assumed that all our knowledge must conform to objects. But all attempts to extend our knowledge of objects by establishing something in regard to them *a priori,* by means of concepts, have, on this assumption, ended in failure. We must therefore make trial whether we may not have more success in the tasks of metaphysics, if we suppose that objects must conform to our knowledge. This would agree better with what is desired, namely, that it should be possible to have knowledge of objects *a priori,* determining something in regard to them prior to their being given.[88]

Kant wished to begin with a new hypothesis: that the mind is active. That is, instead of beginning with the object as something already given to which the mind must conform, Kant reverses the order and conceives of the object as in some respects constituted by the a priori contributions of the knower. The mind imposes upon the material of experience its own forms of cognition, determined by the very structure of the human understanding. The raw material of experience is thus molded and shaped along certain definite lines according to the cognitive forms within the mind itself. These forms of the mind, such as space, time, causality, and substance, are the categories we use to "put things together." All experience presupposes these a priori categories which are not themselves observable.

It is important to notice that Kant meant that the cognitive forms of experience determine the possibility of objects of *knowledge.* That is, these categories of experience determine our knowledge of *phenomena.* If the word "object" were taken to refer to *things-in-themselves,* things apart from any relation to an experiencing and knowing subject, then we could not say they are *known by the human mind.*

---

*As an adult Kant attended church services only rarely and only to fulfill official responsibilities. It is told that when Kant became rector of the University, he duly led the academic procession to the cathedral for the customary service but deserted it at the door.

We cannot, then, according to Kant, *know noumena* or things-in-themselves, that is, supersensible objects, for we lack the necessary cognitive organ. The categories of human understanding are limited to the domain of empirical experience, of phenomena, and although the mind can conceive of a supersensible object, the mind cannot produce knowledge of such a transcendent being.

The Critique of Rational Theology and Metaphysics

Such was Kant's "Copernican Revolution." The implications of Kant's hypothesis are twofold. First, Kant has established the possibility of objective knowledge of the phenomenal world, since the synthetic function of the mind's a priori categories serves as a kind of universal law or structure of all possible experience and thereby makes a pure science of nature possible. To rehabilitate empiricism and establish the possibility of a pure science of nature was, however, only half of Kant's purpose. He also wished to show that such objective knowledge is thwarted when it is applied to a sphere which transcends that of space, time, and perception. That is, such metaphysical concepts as God's existence are not matters of experience and, if known at all, must be known in some other way.

In the section of the first *Critique* entitled the "Transcendental Analytic," Kant seeks to prove the validity of scientific knowledge. In the next section called the "Transcendental Dialectic," Kant seeks to extend Hume's refutation of rationalistic metaphysics. Because of its importance for philosophical theology, we must give some attention to the critique of theology as developed in the "Dialectic." Kant considers three areas of rationalistic speculation—the self, being in general, and God. We will limit our discussion to Kant's critique of speculative knowledge of God.

There are, Kant held, three possible ways of proving the existence of God by means of pure reason— the *ontological,* the *cosmological,* and the *physico-theological* (or argument from design). The ontological proof which was originally conceived by Anselm in the eleventh century was revived in the seventeenth century by Descartes and Leibnitz. The ontological argument proceeds from the very definition of God

as a perfect being. A perfect being must possess all perfections, for otherwise it would not be perfect. In the concept of a most perfect being, existence must be included; for if it were not, the concept would not be that of a most perfect being. Therefore, by definition such a being must necessarily exist.

Kant refutes the argument by demonstrating that "existence" is not a predicate and therefore cannot be a predicate of even a most perfect being. There is, he acknowledges, no difficulty in giving a verbal definition such as that there is something the nonexistence of which is impossible. But such a definition is

taken from *judgements,* not from *things* and their existence. But the unconditional necessity of judgements is not the same as an absolute necessity of things. . . . The [mathematical] proposition does not declare that three angles are absolutely necessary, but that, under the condition that there is a triangle [that is, that a triangle is given], three angles will necessarily be found in it. . . .

If in an identical proposition, I reject the predicate while retaining the subject, contradiction results; and I therefore say that the former belongs necessarily to the latter. But if we reject subject and predicate alike, there is no contradiction; for nothing is left that can be contradicted. To posit a triangle and yet to reject its three angles is self-contradictory; but there is no contradiction in rejecting the triangle together with its three angles. The same holds true of the concept of an absolutely necessary being. If its existence is rejected, we reject the thing itself with all its predicates; and no question of contradiction can then arise. . . .

If we admit, as every reasonable person must, that all existential propositions are synthetic how can we profess to maintain that the predicate of existence cannot be rejected without contradiction? This is a feature that is found only in analytic propositions, and is precisely what constitutes their analytic character. . . .

Being is obviously not a real predicate; that is, it is not a concept of something that could be added to the concept of a thing. . . . The proposition "God is omnipotent" contains two concepts, each of which has its object—God and omnipotence. The small word "is" adds no new predicate *in its relation* to the subject. If, now, we take the subject [God] with all its predicates, and say "God is," we attach no new predicate to the concept of God, but only posit the subject in itself with all its predicates. . . . A hundred real thalers do not contain the least coin more than hundred possible thalers. For as the latter signify the concept, and the former the object and the positing of the object, should the former contain more than the latter, my concept would not, in that case, express the whole object, and would not therefore be an adequate concept of it. My financial position is, however, affected very differently by a hundred real thalers than it is by the mere concept of them . . . ; yet the conceived hundred thalers are not themselves in the least increased through thus acquiring existence outside my concept.[89]

Kant's conclusion is that the attempt to establish the existence of God by means of the ontological argument is futile for "we can no more extend our stock of [theoretical] insight by mere ideas than a merchant can better his position by adding a few noughts to his cash account."[90] Since existence is not a predicate, if I deny God's existence, I am not denying a predicate of a subject; hence no logical contradiction is involved as the proponents of the argument contend.

From the ontological argument Kant turns to the two arguments which claim to be based on the facts of experience. The first of these is the cosmological proof. The argument runs thus:

> If anything exists, an absolutely necessary being must also exist. Now I, at least, exist. Therefore an absolutely necessary being exists. The minor premise contains an experience, the major premise the inference from there being any experience at all to the existence of the necessary.[91]

Kant finds at least two difficulties in this proof. First, this proof claims to take its stand on experience, but, says Kant,

> the cosmological proof uses this experience only for a single step in the argument, namely, to conclude the existence of a necessary being. What properties this being may have, the empirical premise cannot tell us. Reason therefore abandons experience altogether, and endeavours to discover by mere concepts what properties an absolutely necessary being must have. . . . Thus the so-called cosmological proof really owes any co-

gency which it may have to the ontological proof from mere concepts.[92]

The second difficulty with the cosmological proof is that the major premise ("an absolutely necessary being exists") rests on a "transcendent" use of the principle of causality, that is, a use of the principle of causality beyond the realm of sense experience when it cannot be legitimately used to transcend the world given in sense experience. Says Kant:

> The principle of causality has no meaning and no criterion for its application save only in the sensible world. But in the cosmological proof it is precisely in order to enable us to advance beyond the sensible world that it is employed.[93]

Kant considered the physico-theological proof (from design) to be "the oldest, the clearest and the most accordant with the common reason of mankind," and yet, Kant adds, "we cannot approve the claims which this mode of argument would fain advance." Like Hume before him, Kant found the argument from design logically inadequate. Since Kant's refutation resembles Hume's, we need not detail it here. Let it suffice to say that Kant concludes that the utmost the argument from design can prove

> is an *architect* of the world who is always very much hampered by the adaptability of the material in which he works, not a *creator* of the world to whose idea everything is subject. This, however, is altogether inadequate to the lofty purpose which we have before our eyes, namely, the proof of an all-sufficient primordial being. To prove the contingency of matter itself, we should have resort to a transcendental argument, and this is precisely what we have here set out to avoid.[94]

Kant defined natural theology as inferring "the properties and the existence of an Author of the world from the constitution, the order and unity, exhibited in the world."[95] For Kant the attempt of such a natural theology to prove the existence and attributes of God is completely fruitless. It must be noted, however, that Kant is carefully delimiting what he means by natural theology and that implied in his critique of metaphysics is the claim not only that God's existence cannot be theoretically proven but also that by pure reason alone neither can God's nonexistence be demonstrated. Kant's criticism of natural theology thus leaves the possibility open for another approach to and use of metaphysical concepts, or what Kant called "transcendental ideas."

Unlike Hume, Kant did not believe that such metaphysical concepts as self, world, and God were vain illusions. Kant had a deep respect for these persistent metaphysical impulses in humanity and believed that, while we are mistaken in conceiving of such transcendental ideas as the self, the world, and God as *objects of knowledge,* they are natural to reason and do have an important *regulative* use. That is, these ideas or concepts function as regulative maxims in guiding our scientific inquiry. Take, for example, the concept of a highest intelligence.

> Thus I say that the concept of a highest intelligence is a mere idea, not to be taken as consisting in its referring directly to an object. . . . It is only a schema . . . which serves only to secure the greatest possible systematic unity in the empirical employment of our reason. . . . We declare, for instance, that the things of the world must be viewed *as if* they received their existence from a highest intelligence. The idea is thus really only a heuristic, not an ostensive concept. It does not show us how an object is constituted, but how, under its guidance, we should *seek* to determine the constitution and connection of the objects of experience.[96]

The use of these regulative ideas is not, then, for the extension of our knowledge to objects beyond our normal experience but as a principle of systematization and unity. The idea of God as a supreme intelligence and cause of the world leads us to conceive of nature as a systematic, teleological whole, under the guidance of causal laws. Such a conception of the unity of nature is a spur to scientific investigation. The regulative use of the idea of God is thus both necessary and beneficial.

Here Kant is steering a kind of middle path between skepticism and dogmatism. He denies any knowledge of the attributes of God in himself and yet finds a legitimate function in the idea of a God of perfect intelligence, goodness, and justice "for us," that is, in the interests of furthering our knowledge of nature and its laws.

Kant's defense of a rational theism did not rest finally on his conception of the regulative use of the transcendental idea of God. The important problems raised by the third section of *The Critique of Pure Reason* were the prolegomena to Kant's fundamental concern, i.e., ethics and the primacy of moral faith. It is only in this context that we can understand Kant's statement that he "found it necessary to deny *knowledge* in order to make room for *faith.*" The first *Critique* paved the way for *The Critique of Practical Reason* (1788). It is in this latter work that Kant establishes theistic belief as a postulate of pure practical reason. In order to understand Kant's reconstruction of rational faith in God, we must understand something of the purpose and theory of this second great work.[97]

The Moral Foundation of Rational Faith

In the second *Critique* Kant sought to show that our relation to the world is not limited to scientific knowledge (fact), for the world is a stage upon which we must *act*—a realm of moral valuation. Kant's task in the second *Critique* is to demonstrate not only that there are a priori categories of our pure or scientific reason, by which scientific knowledge can be assured, but that the very limits of our empirical knowledge point to a pure reason operative in our practical life. That is, there are certain a priori propositions which constitute the moral order or realm of value. The most needful principles of our practical, moral life are, then, completely independent of our empirical experience and the principles of pure reason. Thus, according to Kant, we do not need to wait until the scientists determine the nature of the empirical world before we can know what we ought to do. Our knowledge of what we ought to do is prior to and more certain than any scientific findings.

Kant accepted as axiomatic that we are living in a moral world. We humans experience different moral obligations, but the experience of "oughtness" is universal. According to Kant, to act morally is not to act from inclination or even prudence but from a sense of duty. And dutiful action derives its warrant not from its consequences but from the conformity of such actions with some general law which can serve the will as a principle of action. Such a moral law is a "fact of reason" since it is not an empirical fact but announces itself as originally legislative. This originally legislative principle is the *categorical imperative,* namely, that one should "act only on that maxim whereby thou canst at the same time will that it should become a universal law."[98]

Kant held that we respect the moral law because it is a law which we as rational beings legislate for ourselves. The moral law is not something imposed from without but is that which we voluntarily obey. This is what Kant calls moral autonomy. Moral commands are not, then, derived from some source outside the self, such as the Bible or the Church. Kant thus denies any theological foundation for his ethical theory. Morality is not based on knowledge of God. Quite the contrary—knowledge of God is, for Kant, a postulate of moral reason. Whereas traditionally morals were grounded in theology, Kant reverses this order and attempts to demonstrate that the fundamental beliefs of religion are in need of the support of our moral reason. Thus Kant can say that "it is reason, by means of its moral principles, that can first produce the concept of God." This is Kant's "Copernican Revolution" in theology. Here Kant reveals his kinship with, and perhaps his dependence upon, Rousseau. Kant, like Rousseau, rejects speculative theology based on metaphysical proofs. For him the only way to knowledge of God is through the moral conscience; the only genuine theology is moral theology.

How is it that our moral conscience produces religious convictions? Kant's way of putting it is that our moral nature *demands* the reality of the objects of religious belief. They are moral *postulates,* that is, logically required by our acknowledgment of the implications of the moral law which is a "fact of reason." They are not sufficient "objectively" (knowledge), but they are so "subjectively." These moral postulates are not, however, mere "opinion," for they are justified by reasons that are universally valid. To deny them would lead to the overthrowing of the concept of moral law. They are, then, a "work of reason" or "a pure moral need." Religion is, for Kant, "trust in the promise of the moral law."

The way Kant establishes the religious postulates is as follows. What kind of world is required, Kant asks, if we are to make sense of the fact of the moral law? The only finally good thing is a good will, or virtue, what Kant called the supreme good (*supremum bonum*). Kant realized, however, that although virtue is an unconditional good, it does not follow that it is the perfect good (*summum bonum*), for the complete good includes both virtue (the "moral good") and happiness, (the "natural good"), that is, "the distribution of happiness is exact proportion to morality." The perfect accordance of the will with the moral law is the supreme good, and perfection would include an exact proportion of happiness. This state of affairs, our moral reason tells us, *ought* to obtain and "the ought implies the *can.*" Nevertheless, in spite of this moral demand, it is abundantly clear that no rational being is capable of attaining this supreme good within this allocated span of life. Yet

> since it is required as practically necessary (i.e., it is a state that ought to exist), it can only be found in a *progress in infinitum* towards that perfect accordance. . . . Now this endless progress is only possible on the supposition of an *endless* duration of the *existence* and personality of the same rational being. . . .[99]

Thus, Kant postulates the immortality of the soul.

Pursuing this same line of argument, Kant holds that our experience teaches us that in this life the morally virtuous people are not always the happiest. The possibility of a *summum bonum,* which our moral reason demands, leads to the supposition of a cause adequate to this effect; in other words, the postulate of a Supreme Being. Here is Kant's way of stating the proof:

> The *summum bonum* is possible in the world only on the supposition of a Supreme Being having a causality corresponding to moral character. Now a being that is capable of acting on the conception of laws is an *intelligence* (a rational being), and the causality of such a being according to this conception of laws is his *will;* therefore the supreme cause of nature, which must be presupposed as a condition of the *summum bonum* is a being which is the cause of nature by *intelligence* and *will,* consequently its author, that is God. . . . Now it was seen to be a duty for us to promote the *summum bonum;* consequently it is not merely allowable, but it is a necessity connected with duty as a req-

uisite, that we should presuppose the possibility of this *summum bonum;* and as it is possible only on condition of the existence of God, it inseparably connects the supposition of this with duty; that is, it is morally necessary to assume the existence of God.[100]

This is Kant's demonstration that "morality inevitably leads to religion" and that religion is founded on our moral faith. It is important to recognize that for Kant this moral necessity of theism is *subjective,* that is, a *want,* and not *objective,* that is, a *duty,* for there can be no moral duty to believe in the existence of anything. That concerns only the empirical employment of reason. Nevertheless, these theological beliefs are *rational postulates* and, being based on the requirements of practical reason, can best be considered as objects of pure *rational faith.*

Reason is compelled to admit such a supersensible object as God but "only so far as it is defined by such predicates as are necessarily connected with the pure practical purpose." We cannot know God as he exists in himself, only as he exists *for me.* Luther had maintained, similarly, that God could be known only "in his benefits." Luther had said that faith and God must be held together for "whatever thy heart clings to and relies upon, that is properly thy god." Kant, likewise, holds that knowledge of God is dependent upon faith, but in Kant's case it is a strictly moral faith. For Kant true religious faith is synonymous with "the recognition of all our duties as divine commands."

Kant's treatment of theology in the two *Critiques* reveals both his break and his continuity with the Enlightenment. Like Rousseau and Lessing, he is one of the great transitional figures between the Age of Reason and the nineteenth century. His critique of the metaphysical proofs of theism constituted an epochal break with the rationalistic theological pretensions of the eighteenth century. On the other hand, his conception of theology as a moral theology was certainly in keeping with the conception of religion in the Enlightenment. For Kant worshiping God was synonymous with obeying the moral law, and "everything which, apart from a moral way of life, man believes himself capable of doing to please God" was for Kant "mere religious delusion."

Rational Faith and Christianity

Of all the positive religions, Kant believed that Christianity, despite its historical imperfections, came closest to approaching the idea of a pure, rational, moral faith. Five years after the publication of *The Critique of Practical Reason,* Kant published his *Religion within the Limits of Reason Alone* (1793). His desire to write a book on Christianity was no doubt partly motivated by his Pietist upbringing. More important, certain "hard" facts of human experience forced him to pursue ethical issues left unresolved in the earlier works.

In *The Critique of Practical Reason* Kant had acknowledged that freedom includes not only moral autonomy but also spontaneity, involving the capacity to reject the moral law. Thus Kant faced the ethical problem of the power of free persons to misuse their freedom. It was largely this issue which led Kant to a philosophical analysis of the Christian faith in the *Religion.* The real fact of sin and evil, so central to the Christian conception of human nature, was, Kant recognized, at odds with his ethical doctrine. Yet Kant could not ignore the fact of moral evil; he considered it an incontestable element within experience and, therefore, made the fact of evil the starting-point for his analysis of Christianity.

The *Religion* sets out to demonstrate two things: (1) how the free will, though radically evil, can regenerate itself and (2) how Christianity, rationally interpreted, exemplifies this process of moral regeneration. The *Religion* opens, then, with a discussion of the radical evil in human nature. Kant rejects both the optimistic view of the *Aufklärung,* that mankind is naturally free from any evil propensity, and the opposite view of total depravity. Neither view accords with human experience. Human beings must be good. The propensity to evil could not be imputed to us if we did not conceive of some state of goodness from which we have fallen. At the same time we cannot ascribe our penchant for evil to a *natural* defect such as our finitude, for that would destroy moral responsibility. Nor can we conceive of our radical evil as an *inheritance,* such as an inherited disease (medicine), debt (law), or sin (theology). All these remove the responsibility of evil from ourselves and place it on our progenitors. The source of every actual sin is to be sought in intelligible acts of freedom, which Kant, like the biblical writers, does not attempt further to explain. The propensity to evil is of inscrutable origin. Kant does, however, find the usual motive of evil actions in self-love.

The question, then, is how this evil disposition can be converted to a good one—that is, how the moral imperative ("the ought") implies the ability ("the can") to overcome freely the evil propensity. Kant answers that such a recovery is not to be conceived of as a gradual reformation but a fundamental revolution of one's habits, a conversion tantamount to a new birth. "But," Kant asks, "if a man is corrupt in the very ground of his maxims, how can he possibly bring about this revolution by his own powers and of himself become a good man? Yet duty bids us do this and duty demands nothing of us which we cannot do."[101]

Here is the crux of Kant's problem. The *ought* implies the *can,* and yet the *radical* corruption of the will raises the question of how such an imperative is possible. Kant hints that divine cooperation is necessary.

> For despite the fall, the injunction that we *ought* to become better men resounds unabatedly in our souls; hence this must be within our power . . . *even though what we are able to do is in itself inadequate and though we thereby only render ourselves susceptible of higher and for us inscrutable assistance.*[102] (Italics added.)

Yet a few sentences earlier Kant had asserted that, granted the need for supernatural cooperation,

> man must first make himself worthy to receive it . . . that is, he must adopt this positive increase of power into his maxim, for only thus can good be imputed to him and he be known as good.[103]

Kant is saying that our radically evil disposition requires supernatural aid to overcome it and yet that it must be in our power to deserve such aid. Here Kant appears to founder on the religious concept of grace. Redemption from evil involves an *antinomy,* for redemption includes the two paradoxical realities of grace and freedom. It involves an enabling grace which is not within our power and the ability

to make ourselves worthy of such supernatural aid which is within our power. The difficulty is that while these are meant to be conjoined, we cannot conceive of them experientially except under the form of succession. Either grace begets a moral life or man freely makes himself worthy of enabling grace.

Kant recognized that this religious problem could not be resolved *theoretically.* Works of grace, like the means of grace (the sacraments, etc.) are *parergon,* i.e., subordinate or accessory works of religion within the limits of reason alone. Reason does not dispute the possibility of such operations, but it cannot include them within the province of knowledge since our use of the concept of cause and effect cannot be extended beyond matters of natural experience. When, however, we give *practical* consideration to this paradoxical matter, and for Kant this is the principal issue, the resolution is clear:

> But practically the question arises . . . where shall we start, i.e., with a faith in what God has done on our behalf, or with what we are to do to become worthy of God's assistance? In answering this question we cannot hesitate in deciding for the second alternative . . . we can certainly hope to partake in the appropriation of another's atoning merit, and so of salvation, only by qualifying for it through our own efforts to fulfill every human duty—and this obedience must be the effect of our own action and not, once again, of a foreign influence in the presence of whom we are passive.[104]

For Kant moral character must be determined by the exercise of individual free will. No person can be good for another, and each must bear the responsibility for his or her own actions. Kant thus faced a dilemma. He recognized the incompatibility of the imputation of forgiveness and autonomous freedom, and yet he was aware of humanity's radical evil and inescapable guilt. He sought to resolve this difficulty by insisting that grace implies that one has done all that one can. It is on this point that scholars disagree on whether Kant's solution breaks down, and either autonomous freedom or radical evil must be denied. For if the individual has done what is required to deserve grace, it would appear that he or she does not really need grace, for it is in the initial break with radical evil that enabling grace is needed. If grace is not operative until it is earned, is it not useless, for the will has within its own power the ability to choose the good.

Some argue that for Kant evil must be thought of as only superficial, not radical, and that Kant prefers to give up his conception of grace and radical evil rather than deny his conception of moral autonomy. Other scholars insist that Kant proposes divine grace as a *rational* belief. What he opposes is an irrational conception of grace, such as Kierkegaard's view of forgiveness as an "offense" to reason, or grace as an immoral leniency. Kant clearly states that we are never certain that we have done all in our power to do good, but that God knows this. It is perfectly rational, then, to believe that God, knowing our righteous *disposition,* may complement our effort with justifying grace. Kant writes:

> With all our strength we must strive after the holy disposition of a course of life well-pleasing to God, in order to believe that the love of God toward man (already assured us through reason), so far as man does endeavor with all his power to do the will of God, will make good, in consideration of his upright disposition, the deficiency of the deed, whatever this deficiency may be.[105]

It appears, these critics argue, that Kant does *not* hold that it is within our power to rid ourselves of the propensity to evil. What, for Kant, does lie within our power is the propensity to adopt a disposition to good. He believes that we rationally can trust that God will by grace forgive those previous imperfect efforts that can no longer be remedied. Allen W. Wood summarizes this interpretive position with regard to Kant's antinomy of autonomous freedom and divine grace:

> The doctrine of divine grace is necessary to Kant's resolution of the antinomy, and it must therefore be accorded, along with freedom, immortality, and God's moral governance of the world, the status of a *postulate of practical reason....* In faith the moral agent places his rational trust not only in God's benefiicence as world-creator and wise providence as world-ruler, but also in God's just forgiveness as the moral judge and the loving and merciful Father of mankind.[106]

Book One of the *Religion,* on the radical evil in human nature, is the most original and courageous of the whole treatise, in spite of the fact that Kant may fail, in the view of some, to resolve the antinomy of grace and freedom. Books Two through Four deal principally with Kant's conception of Christ and the Church. Both conceptions proved to be of considerable importance in subsequent developments in the nineteenth century. Nevertheless, in both cases Kant reveals a closer kinship with the Enlightenment than is true in his wrestling with the problem of evil.

Kant begins Book Two by asserting that "mankind in its complete moral perfection is that which alone can render a world the object of a divine decree and the end of creation."[107] According to Kant, the idea of humankind in its moral perfection eternally exists in God, essential to his nature, as his only-begotten Son, "and only in him and through the adoption of his disposition can we hope 'to become the sons of God.' "[108] "Now," says Kant,

> it is our universal duty as men to *elevate* ourselves to this ideal of moral perfection, that is, to the *archetype* of the moral disposition in all its purity—for this idea itself, which reason presents to us for our zealous emulation, can give us power. But just because we are not the authors of this idea, and because it has established itself in man without our comprehending how human nature could have been capable of receiving it, it is more appropriate to say that this archetype has *come down* to us from heaven and has assumed our humanity.... Such union with us may therefore be regarded as a state of *humiliation* of the Son of God.... For man can frame to himself no concept of the degree and strength of a force like that of a moral disposition except by picturing it as encompassed by obstacles, and yet, in the face of the fiercest onslaughts, victorious.[109]

Despite the fact that, due to our evil disposition, we must conceive of the Son of God as a heavenly ideal *come down* to earth, rather than as an earthly man become heavenly, every

> man may then hope to become acceptable to God (and so be saved) through *a practical faith in this Son of God.* ... In other words, he, and he alone, is entitled to look upon himself as an object not unworthy of divine ap-

proval who is conscious of such a moral disposition as enables him to have a well-grounded confidence in himself and to *believe* that under like temptations and afflictions, . . . he would be loyal unswervingly to the archetype of humanity and by faithful imitation, remain true to his exemplar.[110]

The important point here is Kant's emphasis on awakening the minds of individuals to the ideal of moral perfection, by which they can become the sons of God for which they were created. For this purpose a historical exemplar (such as Jesus) may be very effectual, for a person "in actual possession of this eminence . . . must attune our hearts to admiration, love and gratitude." Nevertheless, Kant insists that we need no historical example as our pattern.

> From the practical point of view this idea is completely real in its own right, for it resides in our morally-legislative reason. We *ought* to conform to it; consequently we must *be able* to do so. . . . We need, therefore, no empirical example to make the idea of a person well-pleasing to God our archetype; this idea as an archetype is already present in our reason. . . . According to the law, each man ought really to furnish an example of this idea in his own person; to this end does the archetype reside always in the reason: and this, just because no example in outer experience is adequate to it; for outer experience does not disclose the inner nature of the disposition but merely allows of an inference about it though not of strict certainty.[111]

Kant shares an eighteenth-century suspicion, even disregard, of history. Therefore, the question which so exercised Reimarus and theologians in the nineteenth century, i.e., whether the Gospel traditions give us the real, historical Jesus, was of no concern to Kant. The historical question neither can nor need be answered, for the real object of faith is the ideal of the Son of God well-pleasing to God. Whoever lets this ideal govern his or her actions may believe that they are justified in the sight of God; for the rightness of one's moral disposition covers or atones for the imperfection of one's previous evil deeds. This is how Kant conceives of the atoning *work* of the Son of God.

Kant felt as strongly as had Anselm that one must make satisfaction for the guilt incurred before one's conversion. He therefore took seriously the conception of Christ's vicarious atonement as a satisfaction for sinners. However, inasmuch as an actual substitution cannot take place between two persons without setting aside the moral law, the conception must be taken symbolically as a process within the heart of the individual believer, whereby in the daily discipline of obedience the new moral or *noumenal* person in us suffers vicariously for the old, *phenomenal* individual.

> The coming forth from the corrupted into the good disposition is, in itself (as "the death of the old man," "the crucifying of the flesh"), a sacrifice and an entrance upon a long train of life's ills. These the new man undertakes in the disposition of the Son of God, that is, merely for the good, though really they are due as punishments to another, namely, the old man (for indeed the old man is *morally* another).[112] (Italics added.)

The new person *in us* is our Redeemer who accepts the punishment of the old person's sins as a vicarious punishment.

Kant did think of Jesus Christ as the historical exemplification of the archetype of humanity well-pleasing to God, and no more. Living faith in this archetype is *in itself* a moral idea of reason and, therefore, not dependent upon the archetype in its phenomenal (historical) appearance. Hence, belief in Christ is, for Kant, belief in a moral example whereby one places in oneself confidence that one will "under like temptations and afflictions . . . be loyal to the archetype of humanity and, by faithful imitation, remain true to his exemplar."[113]

While Kant conceived of salvation as an inward experience of the individual, unlike many a fellow *Aufklärer* Kant gave considerable place to the role of the Church. He recognized that the rule of the good principle can only be assured by the upbuilding and maintaining of a society which makes the moral kingdom its end. Kant defined the Church as "an ethical commonwealth whose supreme lawgiver is God." The Church is distinguished from a civil theocracy by the fact that the Church's laws are "purely inward." The *invisible* Church is not an object of possible experience but, like the postulates, an ideal of moral reason. The *visible* Church is the actual union of people into a whole which harmonizes with that ideal. The true, visible Church is, then, that society which exhibits the moral kingdom of God on earth so far as it can be brought to pass by humans. Such a Church would be characterized by universality, purity, freedom, and unchangeableness, since it would be guided by universal principles of pure moral reason, accessible to every rational person. Kant's conception of morality is not individualistic. It is thoroughly social and communitarian. Every individual has the moral duty of furthering the good of others.

Kant was confident that the empirical Church-faith, though falling far short of the ideal archetype, nevertheless must and would be brought under the guidance of the principles of natural religion. The gradual transition from the statutory Church-faith to the faith of pure rational religion would constitute. "the approach of the Kingdom of God." Kant emphasized that God alone is the founder of his Kingdom but that individuals have a moral obligation to fit themselves to be citizens of this Commonwealth. And because the only divine service is the discharge of our moral duties, the only proper service in the visible Church will be directed toward the active dissolution of the visible, statutory, institutional Church—which has placed humanity under the tutelage, hence slavery, of priests—and loyalty to the pure religion within reason alone.

All "false worship" is, for Kant, that which puts the ecclesiastical and statutory in place of the pure, moral service of God. Kant acknowledged that originally special acts of ceremonial and special statutory regulations may have been useful in promoting a purer, moral faith but that these had now largely become hindrances to moral progress. Therefore, all that human beings think they can do, outside their moral duty, to become well-pleasing to God is "mere illusion and false worship." For Kant a "spirit of prayer" should pervade our entire life, and yet special acts of prayer are unnecessary. He regarded petitionary prayer as the "wheedling of God." So-called means of grace such as attending church services and partaking of the sacraments are usually followed, Kant believed, in order to evade the only

true "means of grace," i.e., a good life. Therefore, such ceremonials have value only insofar as they promote a good, moral disposition, and Kant acknowledged that such practices did frequently serve such a moral end.

We can recognize throughout Kant's discussion of the Church a sublime moral seriousness which is, nevertheless, almost totally lacking in appreciation of the place of sentiment and emotion in the religious life. For Kant moral reason remains supreme over all historical revelation, tradition, and practice, and Kant remained true to the spirit of the Enlightenment in his confidence that the consummation of such a rational faith was ensured.

> We have good reason to say that "the Kingdom of God is come unto us" once the principle of the gradual transition of ecclesiastical faith to the universal religion of reason . . . has become general and has gained somewhere a *public* foothold. . . . For since this principle contains the basis for a continual approach toward such a consummation, there lies in it (invisibly), as in a seed that is self-developing and in due time self-fertilizing, the whole, which one day is to illumine and rule the world.[114]

When we look at Kant's philosophical theology as a whole and from the vantage point of the late-twentieth century, it is true to say that Kant's contribution to modern Christian theology lies primarily in the far-reaching influence and use of his ideas rather than in the intrinsic worth of his own theological doctrines. Kant's influence on modern religious thought is immeasurable. No one, it can be argued, has had a greater influence. What Kant did was to sow the seeds of many tendencies of religious thought in the nineteenth century, tendencies which often took widely different directions. Kant's importance, then, lies in the wealth and suggestiveness of his ideas. *The Critique of Pure Reason* was the chief stimulus of modern religious agnosticism. Religious "illusionism" and "subjectivism" are often traced to Kant's "regulative" use of such ideas as God in Chapter III of the "Transcendental Dialectic." Religious pragmatism also is seen as originating in Kant's moral postulates for God and immortality. Kant's view of the a priori categories in the first *Critique* influenced Schleiermacher, and later others, in the search for the religious a priori, that is, for the uniquely religious category independent of both science and ethics. On the other hand, a number of important theologians, principally Albrecht Ritschl and his successors, took their lead from Kant's second *Critique* and, on the basis of Kant's separation of knowledge and moral faith, sought to construct an ethical theism. The catalogue of Kant's influence on subsequent theology could be extended. However, we must turn our attention briefly to those thinkers who, though influenced by Kant, nevertheless found his rational, moralistic, and unhistorical interpretation of religion unacceptable. These thinkers constitute what is often called the Counter-Enlightenment.

THE COUNTER-ENLIGHTENMENT

In the 1780s, in Germany, there erupted a movement in literature, expressive of a religious sensibility, that proved to be the harbinger of nineteenth-century Romanticism. This cultural ferment often is referred to as the *Sturm und Drang* (Storm and Stress), or more broadly the Counter-Enlightenment. It signaled a longstanding protest against, and opposition to, the Enlightenment's trust in autonomous reason, its confidence in the methods and progress of science—especially when applied to ethics, politics, and religion—as well as its suspicion, and often scornful dismissal, of tradition and the nonrational aspects of human feeling and emotion. In France this disaffection with the doctrines of the French *philosophes* and with the seeming anarchy and horrors loosed by the French Revolution and Terror took the form of Traditionalism—which saw itself as the enemy of a divisive, unbridled reason and the champion of a stabilizing authority in the form of the cohesive strength and wisdom of a great tradition, such as the collective experience of the Catholic Church. We will explore French Traditionalism and its importance for Christian thought in Chapter 6. Here we focus on aspects of the Counter-Enlightenment in Germany.

In the Germany of Wolff, Reimarus, and Lessing, the battles between the rationalists, the orthodox, and the *neologians* had to do with the prerogatives of

reason and revelation and their appropriate relationship. Reason had emerged the victor although, with Lessing and Kant, troubling questions were raised about reason's nature and limits. In the last years of the century, particularly in the literary movement *Sturm und Drang,* there arose a furious backlash against the Newtonian mechanistic interpretation of nature and its deadening effect on feeling and the life of the human spirit. In philosophy, the competency of analytical reason and the adequacy of Kant's critique of metaphysics and his reconstructed moral religion were now challenged. New thinkers, nurtured in the bosom of Pietism and the heritage of German Lutheranism, declared Newtonianism and Kantianism mistaken and subversive of authentic religion. Some found in Hume an ally who could be seen as upholding the right of faith over reason. The new thought came to be called *Glaubensphilosophie* or *Gefühlsphilosophie,* philosophy of faith or feeling. Prominent among these new thinkers were two independent, unsystematic, but influential writers: F. H. Jacobi and Johann Hamann.

F. H. Jacobi

Friedrich Heinrich Jacobi (1743–1819) was the son of a wealthy merchant and had been deeply influenced by Pietism as a child. Something of an amateur in philosophy, he never developed a coherent philosophical system. His early reflections were embodied in romances that he published in *Der Merkur* (*The Mercury*), a literary journal that he had cofounded. From 1807 to 1812 he served as president of the Munich Academy of Sciences. Jacobi is best known today for his criticisms of influential philosophers whom he considered to be subversive of authentic religion. These included Spinoza, Lessing, and Schelling, whom he charged with pantheism, and Kant, for his destructive critique of metaphysics.

Despite his criticism of Kant, Jacobi's mature "philosophy of Faith" reveals the deep impress of Kant's critical philosophy, as well as that of Hume. With Kant, Jacobi agreed that scientific reason is limited to the phenomenal world and cannot prove the existence of supersensible realities. But if we are confined to the world of phenomena, then we can, Jacobi believed, only pass from the conditioned to the conditioned, the result being a naturalistic determinism and monism such as Spinoza's, whose system Jacobi regarded as the perfect exemplification of demonstrative reason.

Jacobi considered Spinoza's determinism and pantheistic monism to be intolerable, for he believed they both led to moral nihilism and atheism. In letters written in 1785 having to do with Spinoza, Jacobi included the charge that Lessing was a pantheist. This embroiled him in a heated public controversy with the Jewish philosopher Moses Mendelssohn, Lessing's friend and collaborator.

Though Jacobi acknowledged that human freedom and God's existence are rationally undemonstrable, he felt both were confirmed in experience. And here Jacobi's interest in Hume is marked. To reply to charges that in his letters on Spinoza he was involved in "teaching a blind faith and deprecating reason," Jacobi published a dialogue, *David Hume on Belief,* in 1787. Hume had concluded that even though we cannot prove the existence of an external world, we accept its reality as a "natural belief." Likewise, so Jacobi contends, we have an intuitive feeling or faith in the certainty of supersensible realities. Just as we are endowed with sense perception, so, Jacobi argues, are we also invested with a "higher reason," a spiritual faculty that is natural to every person. At first Jacobi designated this spiritual faculty as *Glaube* or "Faith." Later, to indicate that he was not referring to the beliefs of the positive religions, he called this higher reason *Vernunft* or "Reason," which comes from the German *vernehmen,* "to apprehend." He contrasted *Vernunft* with *Verstand,* or "Understanding," which he identified with scientific reason.

Jacobi thus gives to reason a wholly new meaning. Reason is now conceived as that faculty which makes immediately present to us supersensible realities such as God—as immediately present as nature is to our sensory faculties. Like Kant, Jacobi divides reality into the noumenal and phenomenal but, unlike Kant, assumes a faculty by which noumenal realities can be immediately "perceived" or apprehended. Belief in God is not, then, a practical postulate as Kant would have it but a result of an inner illumination, of Reason or Faith. Both Reason (*Vernunft*) and Understanding (*Verstand*) give us

certain knowledge—one of supersensible reality, the other of the sensible phenomenal world:

> The reason . . . like the outward senses, is purely revelatory, making positive pronouncements. . . . As there is a sensible intuition, an *intuition* through *sense,* so there is also a rational intuition through *reason.* The two stand over against each other as actual sources of knowledge; the latter can just as little be derived from the former as the former from the latter. Likewise, each stands in the same relation to the intellect, and to this extent also to demonstration.[115]

Jacobi calls Reason belief since, like our sense perception of the physical world, it is immediate and revelatory. Both are what Hume calls natural beliefs; neither is demonstrative:

> There cannot be any demonstration of *sensible* intuition . . . as far as knowledge of nature is concerned, sensible intuition is first and last, the unconditionally valid, the absolute. For the same cause, there cannot be any demonstration of *rational intuition,* or the *intuition of reason,* which gives us knowledge of objects beyond nature. . . . If anyone says he knows, we rightly ask him how we know. He must then inevitably appeal in the end to one of these two: either sense perception or to spiritual feeling.[116]

Jacobi's importance lies in his effort to steer a way between the old rational theology based on demonstrable proofs and an irrational fideism, or "blind faith." And Jacobi is very modern in his claim that faith is the ground of all of our foundational convictions, whether they have to do with our confidence in the veracity of our sensory experience, the reality of our self or soul, or the existence of God.[117]

Johann Georg Hamann

Johann Georg Hamann (1730–1788) is best known as a minor figure in the *Sturm und Drang* movement in German literature and as a friend and critic of Kant. In the twentieth century, Hamann's influence on Kierkegaard (who called him "the Emperor") has increased interest in him; indeed, in Hamann one encounters many Kierkegaardian themes in embryonic form. Yet Hamann remains

Johann Georg Hamann

scarcely known in the English-speaking world. Despite this lack of recognition, the eminent intellectual historian Isaiah Berlin claims that Hamann is "one of the few wholly original critics of modern times," and that he remains "the forgotten source of a movement that in the end engulfed the whole of European culture."[118] Hamann was born in Königsberg in East Prussia. He matriculated at the university there at sixteen, but his studies were disorderly and ranged over many subjects; he never completed his degree. With friends he founded a literary weekly, *Daphne,* which continued publication for sixty years. However, Hamann moved from job to job. Then lonely and destitute, he underwent a conversion experience that reflected the deep Pietist spirituality of his upbringing. He was absorbed in reading the Bible, over and over, its stories and parables being understood by him as allegories of his own inner spiritual history—his pride, his wanderings in the wilderness, his idolatry, and his return and repentance. He arrived back in Königsberg a strikingly different man. His enlightened friends, however, saw him as a misguided, big-

oted, and irrational Christian and enlisted the help of Kant to draw him away from his "superstition" and "enthusiasm" and to restore him to his senses. Hamann responded to these bungling efforts with his *Socratic Memorabilia* (1759), ironically dedicated to his friends and benefactors, such as Kant. It is a manifesto of his "war upon the spirit of the age," presented in a highly personal style: aphoristic, obscure, fragmentary, but powerful. F. C. Moser called him— and Hamann enjoyed calling himself—the "Wise Man from the North," a reference to the journey of the wise men of the East who, like Hamann, saw the Star of Bethlehem when others saw nothing, or recoiled from such a dubious spiritual pilgrimage.

The new Hamann perceived Christianity to be profoundly opposed to the ideals of Enlightenment rationality. Against the *philosophes,* he calls upon the example of Socrates who told the sophists and the learned of his time, "I know nothing." Now the *lumières* of the eighteenth century, the modern sophists and the skeptics, feigned appeal to Socratic ignorance, but, as Hamann insists, there is a yawning abyss between Socrates's deep, existential sense of knowing nothing and the rationalists' skepticism, "greater than that between a living animal and its anatomical skeleton." Both

> the old and the new sceptics may wrap themselves as much as they please in the lion-skin of socratic ignorance, they still betray themselves. . . . If they know nothing, does the world need a learned proof of it? Their hypocrisy is ridiculous and shameless. But he who needs so much quickness and eloquence to convince himself of his own ignorance must have in his heart an immense opposition to the truth of his ignorance.[119]

Hamann reads the Enlightenment devotion to reason as *the* modern form of idolatry:

> Do not be against the truth with your vainglorious knowledge of God. . . . For all the propositions of your so-called general, healthy, and expert reason are lies— more incomprehensible, contradictory, and barren than all the mysteries, miracles and signs of the most holy faith. . . . The object of your reflections and devotion is not God, but a mere word-image, like your universal human reason, which by a more than poetic

license you deify as a real person . . . [so] that the grossest heathendom and blindest popery in comparison with your philosophical idolatry will be justified and perhaps acquitted on the day of judgment.[120]

Hamann's attack on the pretentions of rationalism is a crucial element in his new understanding of religious faith. And here Hume played a pivotal role. Hamann admitted to Jacobi that he was "full of Hume" when he wrote his critique of rationalism in the *Socratic Memorabilia,* and later he confessed to his friend and disciple, J. G. Herder: "Hume is always my man, because he at least honors the principle of belief and has taken it up into his system."[121] The echo of Hume's appeal to "natural belief" is unmistakable in Hamann's discourse on faith in the *Memorabilia:* "Our own being and the existence of all things outside us must be believed and cannot be established in any other way. . . . Faith is not a work of reason and therefore cannot succumb to any attack by reason; because believing happens as little by means of reason as tasting and seeing."[122]

In a letter to Kant the same year, Hamann tries to set his friend right about the Scottish philosopher:

> The Attic philosopher, Hume, needs faith when he eats an egg or when he drinks a glass of water. He says that Moses, the law of reason, to which the philosopher appeals, condemns him. Reason is not given to you in order that you may become wise, but that you may know your folly and ignorance; as the Mosaic law was not given to the Jews to make them righteous, but to make their sins more sinful to them.[123]

Hume correctly insisted that reason has a way of dissolving our common-sense view of the self and the world and brings us to ignorance. But for Hamann, Socratic ignorance did not imply, as it did for Hume, a resigned counsel to return to habitual belief. Hamann saw in ignorance a real and positive point of departure for faith. And for Hamann faith was intimately tied to the Christian virtue of humility. Our consciousness of the limits of reason engages our whole person, which issues in a new and vital awareness of our existential plight and thereby opens the way for an active faith. But, as R. G. Smith argues, faith for Hamann is not irrational, a blind leap. For while faith lies *beyond* reason, in the sense that faith comes to an awareness that our real existence is not merely an affair of *ratio,* it nevertheless engages our whole person. Just as faith needs reason, so reason also needs faith; they are, in Smith's reading of Hamann, dialectically related.[124]

Hamann drives home the point that God cannot be known in abstract formulas or by discursive reason—the latter can only prepare the way—but through our direct experience of the everyday realities of nature and of history. God does condescend to speak to us through our *senses,* through concrete, particular facts and images. God is not a mathematician; God is best understood as a writer, a poet. He speaks to us in sensuous images and symbols—couched in prophecy and poetry—as we perceive them in nature, history, and Scripture. Truth is always particular. These immediate, sensuous signs resonate in our own deepest being; they are revelatory. Kant was scandalized by appeal to the particular and singular. He had, Hamann tells us, "a gnostic hatred of matter." In a letter to Jacobi, Hamann advances a theme later developed by Herder, one that is central to contemporary Postmodernist criticism: the fundamental role of concrete language in our knowing. "The question is not so much," he tells Jacobi, "What is reason? as What is language?" Our sense world cannot be banished, for it is embedded in our language. Kant had sought to purify philosophy by rendering reason independent of both experience and tradition. What Kant failed to carry out was a metacritique of language, which is the fundamental source of all thinking and the link with human experience and tradition. "It is still a chief question," Hamann writes in the *Metacritique of the Purism of Reason,* "how the ability to think is possible—the ability to think right and left, before and without, with and beyond experience—then it needs no deduction to prove the genealogical priority of language and its heralding over the seven holy functions of logical propositions and inferences."[125]

Hamann continues on this theme:

> Existence is attached solely to things. No enjoyment arises from brooding, and all things . . . are for the enjoyment and not for speculation. The tree of knowledge has deprived us of the tree of life . . . and do we not want to become children, and like the new

Adam share in flesh and blood, and take the cross upon ourselves? All the terminology of metaphysics comes in the end to this historical fact, *sensus* is the principle of all *intellectus*.[126]

We can know and apprehend spiritual truth in and through the sensuous imagery and language of prophecy and poetry.

While in London, Hamann had discovered that revelation of truth through his reading of Scripture. In the Bible he found "all the indeterminate capacities, inexhaustible desires, endless needs and passions of our nature." God, he now believed, nowhere else has so condescended to empty himself and to reveal his word to humanity as in the incarnate flesh of Christ:

> This mustard-seed of anthropomorphosis and apotheosis, which is hidden in the heart and mouth of every religion, appears here in the greatness of a tree of knowledge and of a life in the midst of the garden—all philosophical contradictions and the whole historical riddle of our existence . . . are resolved by the primal message of the Word become flesh.[127]

Hamann's conception of faith or belief (*Glaube*) was rooted in a radically Augustinian conception of God's prevenient grace. Everything is a gift of God, and we must accept His gracious words and signs in nature and in the Bible with the humility of faith. And such a faith is, for Hamann, itself "a continued miracle" within one's own person—as Hume ironically had pointed out. Hume no doubt spoke scornfully of this miracle of grace that "subverts all the principles of understanding." Hamann simply witnesses to it; he does not attempt to clarify the mystery or the troubling question of why some persons are illumined by the signs of God's word in nature or Scripture and why others are not so gifted.

Hamann's favorite biblical passage was I Cor. 1:27: "God has chosen the foolish things of this world to confound the wise." And he concludes his *Thoughts about My Life* on this defiant note with regard to the terrible mystery and deep offense of God's Word: "The Holy Spirit set forth for us a book for his Word, wherein like a fool and a madman, like an unholy and impure spirit, he made for our proud reason childish stories and contemptible events into the history of heaven and God."[128]

Hamann may well be right that truth cannot be "created out of air" but must, as he says, be "dug out of the ground." He tells us that truth, "must be brought to light from earthly things, by metaphors and parables"—but only to those who, by grace, have eyes to see and ears to hear. Yet all too often his own words and images are obscured by impenetrable, occult references or by rapturous ejaculations. The question remains: Does Hamann, in his eagerness to confound and provoke the rationalists by his cryptic, obscure, highly personal use of language—which for him is the source and vehicle of knowledge—merely darken for others God's revelatory words in both nature and Scripture?

Johann Gottfried Herder

Johann Gottfried Herder (1744–1803) was born in a small town in East Prussia. He entered the University of Königsberg in 1762 to study medicine and then theology, but the two greatest influences on him while in Königsberg were Kant and Hamann. The latter's impression upon him proved to be the more enduring; and Herder became a far more influential critic of the Enlightenment than either Jacobi or Hamann. It is often remarked that Herder and his teacher, Kant, pioneered Modernity's two opposing and incompatible conceptions of reason and knowledge: the historical and the critical-analytical.

Herder's influence on the world of ideas has been extraordinary in its diversity. He not only was an eminent literary critic, poet, and translator but did pioneering work on language, on the study of the Bible, and on the interpretation of history. He is often referred to as the father of nationalism and the *Volksgeist,* ideas that have had fateful consequences in the twentieth century. Herder was ordained a Lutheran pastor in 1767 and, despite his enormous literary output, managed to serve as pastor of two of the largest churches in Riga, then part of Russia, as court preacher in Bückeburg, and as *Generalsuperintendent* of the church in the Grand Duchy of Weimar, an appointment that included numerous responsibilities.

Herder was foremost a literary scholar and writer, not a professional theologian, and many of his most important contributions to religious thought are found in his writings on language, literature, and history. Therefore we will not consider such matters as Herder's participation in the famous Spinoza controversy provoked by Jacobi or his distinctive interpretations of Spinoza and the conception of divine immanence; neither will we discuss Herder's writings on faith and Christian doctrine. For Herder's singular contributions to modern Christian thought lie in the implications for theology of his work on language and history.

It was Hamann's attention to language as the ground of knowledge and of human understanding that most influenced Herder. Yet in his treatise *On the Origin of Language* (1772), Herder rejects both the theory of the divine origin of language, as proposed by Hamann and other orthodox writers, and the theory, proposed by Rousseau and Condillac, that language is a human invention, originating in the imitation of animal sounds or by individuals seeking to cope with life's challenges. Herder rejected the divine origin, since it presupposed that language was given in the Garden of Eden fully developed and perfect. While Herder regards language as unique to humans, he also considers it a natural feature of the species. We humans are essentially linguistic creatures, language being the very foundation of human consciousness. Hence the development of imagination, reflection, reason, and culture are all rooted in language. Human reflective discernment is not, Herder asserts, rooted in animal instinct or perception but in the act of apperception, the mind's self-consciousness.

> Human beings exhibit reflection . . . when, from the fleeting dreams of images that pass before the senses, they can arouse themselves to a moment of alertness, concentrate deliberately on one image . . . and isolate some of its distinguishing marks so that it is identified as a specific object and no other. . . . This first act of apperception renders a clear concept: It is the first judgement of the soul. . . . This first distinguishing mark for consciousness was a word from the soul. With it, human language was invented.[129]

What is significant here is Herder's identification of the uniqueness of the species not only in the co-present working of language and reflective consciousness but in the social and historical implica-

tions of this unique gift. For Herder, consciousness *develops* with the development of language. We are, then, creatures of our language; our world is "created," ordered through our language. The circle of language and thought cannot be broken. As the twentieth-century philosopher Ludwig Wittgenstein would insist, our sense of reality and rationality is constituted by the "language-game," or linguistic rules and conventions we employ and that we assume as foundational. According to Herder, there is no single origin of language, for there develops in history distinct languages within diverse cultures and epochs to meet the special needs of particular times and places—a series of developing revelations or distinctive educations of the human race.

Herder connects language and thought and links them to the historical development and individuality of religions. Embedded in a particular culture, each religion is unique, individual. It is here that Herder's influence is most pronounced, namely in the field of historical hermeneutics or the interpretation and understanding of diverse peoples, cultures, and religions. Like nations and cultures, religions are singular, living organisms. "Who has noticed how *inexpressible* the *individuality* of one human being is. . . How different and particular all things are to an individual because they are seen by the eyes, measured by the soul, and felt by the heart of *that* individual?" And so it is with nations and religions. "As disparate as heat is from cold, and as one pole is from another, so diverse are the various religions."

One cannot hope, then, to capture the meaning of a nation or a religion without entering with empathy (*Einfühlen*) into their real life.

> For the instincts and actual accomplishments alone are the subjects at hand. In order to empathize with the soul's *entire nature,* which *reigns* in everything . . . which colors even the most trivial actions . . . enter the century, the region, the entire history, empathize with every part of it. . . . Only then will you give up imagining that "you are the sum of each and everything."[130]

Herder thus warns against the dangers of "present-mindedness," of the evaluation of another people or religion from one's own cultural and temporal vantage point, from our present standards of praise and blame. The Berlin Academy had foolishly asked, "Which is the happiest people in history?" But such comparisons are, for Herder, "disastrous." "Who can compare the Hebrew shepherd and patriarch with the [Egyptian] farmer and artist, the [Phoenician] sailor, the [Greek] runner, the [Roman] conqueror? . . . Each nation has its own *center* of happiness within itself, just as every sphere has its own center of gravity."[131] Each stage, each epoch of history is an end in itself.

It follows that Herder's "historicism," that is, his feeling for the value inherent in all cultures and the need to understand and judge them on their own terms, would cause him to cast a scornful eye on his own century's shallow notion of historical progress.

> The universal, philosophical, philanthropic tone of our century readily applies "our own ideal" of virtue and happiness to each distant nation, to each remote period in history. . . . In this way they invented the fiction of the "universal, progressive improvement of the world" which no one believed, at least not the true student of history and the human heart.[132]

Now the upshot of such a conception of historical diversity and value would appear to implicate Herder in an unqualified cultural relativism, one in which religions, like nations, are unique and incommensurate entities, resistant to any comparisons or evaluations. There is much in Herder's writings that suggests a relativist standpoint. And yet, it is apparent that he is thoroughly teleological. That is, he envisions a unity in the complex diversity and particularity of history. The unity is *in and through* the diversity and change. He writes:

> The Creator alone is the One who conceives the entire *unity* of one and all nations, conceiving them in all their *diversity* without losing sight of the *unity*. . . . Providence itself, you see, required no ideal. It wanted to achieve its aim only in change, in the process of tradition which takes place through the waking of new powers and dying of others.

"Nevertheless," Herder asserts, "a plan in this continual striving is evident. My great theme!"[133]

Herder envisions the historical process as "an *unending drama* with many scenes . . . a fable with a thousand variations replete with one great meaning!"—and yet without, it appears, a temporal, eschatological end-point. History is a vast drama without a *dénouement;* moreover, the purposes of history are "beyond the grasp of the human race." "Even if all of history were a labyrinth with hundreds of closed and open passages, the labyrinth would still be the 'palace of God,' created for God's purposes and perhaps for the pleasure of God's eye, but not yours!"[134]

For Herder, the labyrinth of history may not reveal a universal progress or a *telos*, but it does disclose the advance (*Fortgang*), or internal development, of myriad cultures, nations, and religions in achieving their own purposes and ends. This is what constitutes "the pleasure of God's eye," the continuous waking of new powers and potentialities.

The import of Herder's cultural pluralism for religion and for Christianity emerge in his *First Dialogue Concerning National Religions* (1802). The conversation between two friends turns to the pathos of one ancestral religion being forced upon a foreign people, with the consequence of the people not only losing their own religion but raising the question of the legitimacy of the universal claims of Christianity. "Would you be annoyed," the one friend asks, "if I hold Christianity to be the religion *of all religions*, of all peoples? "The second friend replies, "What distinguishes peoples?" Both have to agree that it is language and the shaping of a distinct physiognomy of the corporate soul. But, then, does it not follow that the language in which the heart of a people speaks most deeply from its soul and most lovingly of the gods must be the language of its own mother tongue, the language "in which we love, pray, and dream"?

Those who are ashamed of their nation and language destroy not only their religion but the bond that ties their people together. The dialogue ends with Herder's appeal for "national religions" of all the peoples of the earth, but he also answers the friend's question about Christianity's claim to be the religion of all peoples. Distinct ethnic and national religions

> further peace on earth and the development of every people out of its own trunk into its diverse branches.

In this way no foreign language or religion will tyrannize the language and character of another nation. No one will even think of a supreme shepherding nation of all the herds of humanity that does not understand their language and does not know their innermost needs. Every nation blossoms like a tree from its own roots. Christianity, that is, *the true conviction about God and human beings,* is nothing but the pure dew of heaven for all nations that, moreover, does not change any tree's character or type of fruit, and does not strip any human beings of their own nature. . . . Every religion would strive, according to and within its own context, to be better, no, the best of its kind without measuring and comparing itself to others. . . . I do not need to tell you that in this way the so-called propagation and expansion of Christianity would win a different character.[135]

It would appear that there is a deep ambiguity in Herder's understanding of Christianity's relation to other religions. He is a confirmed pluralist; religions reflect the deepest characteristics of a people; no religion should tyrannize over another; the measuring and comparing of religions is inadmissible—and, yet, "*Christianity is the true conviction about God and human beings.*" It is not apparent how Herder relates these judgments. Obviously, Christianity must not force itself on another culture and its religion. And he abhors the destruction of other cultures by Christian missionaries. Similar to Lessing, in *Nathan the Wise,* Herder calls for toleration, mutual respect, and understanding. But, unlike Lessing, he would appear to see Christianity as having a very special role in helping other religions to "purify" themselves, and, in so doing, helping all humans toward the ideal of *Humanität,* civilization. At the same time, Herder rejoices in a God who delights in his luxuriant, creative human diversity, a God who will enlighten each people in his own wise and providential way. For all of Herder's vagueness on these matters, there is little question of the attractiveness, both in his and our own age, of his appeal for understanding and toleration, his seeing great value in alien, including primitive, cultures and his advocacy of a form of cultural and religious pluralism. But it is also true that, like many champions of multiculturalism today, Herder leaves unaddressed very basic questions about truth, pluralism, and relativism,

especially as they relate to Christianity's claims to normativeness, as well as the possible liabilities, even dangers, of ethnic and religious particularism.

Herder's interest in language and history and his eminence as a literary critic lead us to our third theme: his contribution to biblical studies. Herder, as we have seen, received from Hamann his conviction that poetry is "the mother tongue of the human race," that poetry is not the exclusive interest of an elite group of intellectuals and artists. As he reiterated again and again, the spiritual genius of a whole people is found, not in its artificial productions, but in the natural, primal feeling and voice of its poetry. And so for Herder, the divine nobility of the Bible, too, is found in its real humanity. One must not, one cannot, read the Bible authentically either as the work of mechanical scribes recording God's dictation or as the accommodation of supernaturally gifted writers to the crude notions of their all-too-human readers.

Rather, as Herder insists in his *Letters Concerning the Study of Theology,* "the Bible must be read in a human [*menschliche*] way, for it is a book written by human beings for human beings; its language is human; it has been written and preserved by human means; finally, the mind whereby the Bible can be understood, every interpretive tool which elucidates it . . . are human."[136] Herder lays down a series of interpretive principles that steer a path between the orthodox belief in a divinely inerrant Bible and the rationalist reading of the Bible through modern preconceptions about what is and is not reasonable— for example, the ancient world's belief in miracle. In both cases, later presuppositions are imposed upon these vital, living books. With empathy and imagination, one must become "with the shepherds a shepherd, with the people of the sod a man of the land, with the ancients of the Orient an Easterner."

Herder wants to free the reader from both the hidden fears of the orthodox and the scorn of the rationalists as they encounter the real humanity of the Bible. In their different ways, each party asks, in effect,

> How can this book be a Word of God, a divine series of thoughts for human beings, where I perceive so much that is human? . . . Where so much pertains to trivial matters of a miserable people. . . . Where there is such a predominant tone of strange and undignified

images here, of confused regulations there, of unsupported promises. . . . One does not know where to begin or end to hear the voice of God.

Yet, these concerns of such readers disclose a lamentable failure to appreciate the fact that if God is to reveal himself to human beings, "How else would he do it but in a human language? That is not his language! These are not his words that drop from heaven! . . . . God has to explain himself to human beings . . . according to their nature and language . . . according to their weaknesses and within the limitations of their ideas." And the Bible happens to have been revealed to a people of the Ancient Near East, so it must carry traces of the life and culture of that ancient Eastern way of thinking. It is a language filled with bold images; it is what we would call a figurative, metaphorical, mythical way of thinking, although it was wholly realistic and historylike to the Hebrews. So, it is not extraordinary that the Bible's ancient images and modes of expression may be foreign to us now. Rationalists blunder when they chide the biblical writers for their scientific errors. The Bible is not a book of natural science.

> Perhaps Joshua did indeed believe that the sun stood still or sat in the sky. Why should this bother me? He was able to believe this in accordance with his own historical context; and God found it beneath his dignity . . . to prove himself to be a professor of astrology and to explain to Joshua whether the sun or the earth moved.[137]

Herder's historicism and his insistence on *Einfühlung,* on entering empathetically into the lifeworld of the Bible, place him in a modern position with regard to biblical interpretation. While he must share the life of the ancient Hebrews if he is truly to

understand them, he also knows that he engages their world from another, distant location. Herder must assume their figural, realistic, and historylike language, yet he knows that it is metaphor and myth, not literal statement. Herder was not troubled at all that the narrative of the Creation in Genesis is poetry, not science. As Hans Frei points out, Herder does not distinguish between historical fact and the factlike, realistic narrative of what we call biblical myth, legend, and prophetic typology. For him, they all convey historical *meaning* and have their place in the ongoing history of the human spirit. Frei writes of Herder's ambiguous use of the senses of history:

> He can affirm the factual truth of an account or its realistic character as writing, or both, and he can even stress the importance of both; and yet he can remain quite ambiguous as to whether the meaning of the account is the spatiotemporal occurrences to which it refers or the depiction it renders, or whether the meaning is the spirit or outlook that generated such a writing. And in the long run it is the latter that is more important.[138]

Despite Herder's lack of interpretive clarity, he prepared the way for a fresh approach to the study and appropriation of the Bible as a living book, free of the lifeless abstractions of orthodox verbal inspiration and the shallow present-mindedness of the rationalists. In the Bible one sees the paradoxical convergence of a developing divine revelation and providence within a truly natural, all-too-human historical narrative. Herder believed that neither the divine nor the human is compromised or subverted by this confluence. It was left, however, to later Romantic and Idealist thinkers to work out a more coherent doctrine of biblical inspiration.

NOTES

1. Lytton Strachey, *Books and Characters* (London, 1922), p. 174.
2. *The Creed of a Priest of Savoy,* trans. B. Foxley, in Jean Jacques Rousseau, *Emile,* Everyman ed. (London, 1961), p. 228.
3. Ibid., p. 260.
4. Ibid., p. 261.
5. Ibid., pp. 261–262.
6. Ibid., p. 263.
7. Ibid., pp. 270–271.
8. Ibid., p. 232.
9. See the work of E. H. Wright, *The Meaning of Rousseau* (New York, 1963); E. Cassirer, "Kant and Rousseau," in *Rousseau-Kant-Goethe* (Princeton,

1947), and *The Question of Jean-Jacques Rousseau* (New York, 1954); and C. Hendel, *Jean-Jacques Rousseau: Moralist* (New York, 1934).

10. Rousseau, op. cit., p. 237.
11. Ibid., p. 239.
12. Ibid.
13. Ibid., p. 272.
14. Ibid., pp. 275–276.
15. Ibid., p. 253.
16. Ibid., p. 254.
17. Cassirer, *Question of Jean-Jacques Rousseau,* pp. 117–118.
18. *Correspondence générale de J. J. Rousseau,* Vol. III, No. 490. Cited in Hendel, op. cit., 39–40.
19. William Law, *The Case of Reason,* Chap. 4. Quoted in J. M. Creed and J. S. Boys Smith, *Religious Thought in the 18th Century* (Cambridge, 1934), pp. 94–95.
20. Joseph Butler, *Works,* Vol. I, 6. References to Butler are to the W. E. Gladstone edition of 1896 unless otherwise cited. Volume I contains the *Analogy.*
21. Ibid., p. 9.
22. Ibid., p. 18.
23. Ibid., p. 22.
24. Ibid., p. 36. Butler simply overlooks the inordinate difference between the loss of an organ or limb and the loss of the brain and nervous system.
25. Ibid., pp. 42–43.
26. Ibid., pp. 54–55.
27. Ibid., p. 212.
28. Ibid.
29. Ibid., p. 247.
30. Ibid., pp. 247–248.
31. Ibid., pp. 248–249.
32. Ibid., p. 284.
33. Ibid., p. 188.
34. J. H. Randall, Jr., *Making of the Modern Mind* (New York, 1926), p. 299.
35. *Equity and Reasonableness of the Divine Conduct in Pardoning Sinners upon Their Repentance Exemplified . . . Occasioned by Dr. Butler's Late Book, Entitled The Analogy of Religion,* p. 35. Quoted in E. C. Mossner, *Bishop Butler and the Age of Reason* (New York, 1936), p. 101.
36. *Christianity Not Founded on Argument,* pp. 20–21. Quoted in Mossner, op. cit., p. 143.
37. *The Natural History of Religion,* H. E. Root ed. (Stanford, 1957), p. 75.
38. E. C. Mossner, *The Life of David Hume* (Austin, 1954), p. 485. For information on Hume's life and religious beliefs, the student should consult Mossner and N. K. Smith's "Introduction" to the Library of Liberal Arts edition of the *Dialogues Concerning Natural Religion.*

39. Smith, "Introduction," op. cit., p. 21.
40. *Private Papers of James Boswell,* Vol. XII (1931), 227–232. Quoted in Smith ,"Introduction," op. cit., p. 76ff.
41. For a thorough study of the centrality of the theological essays to the argument of the *Enquiry* and to Hume's philosophy as a whole and rejection of the contention that they are irrelevant insertions, see A. Flew, *Hume's Philosophy of Belief* (London, 1961).
42. Butler explicitly states this in the *Analogy,* pp. 302–303.
43. *An Inquiry Concerning Human Understanding,* C. H. Hendel ed. (New York, 1955), p. 120.
44. Ibid., p. 122.
45. Ibid.
46. Ibid., pp. 122–123.
47. Ibid., p. 123.
48. Ibid., p. 137.
49. Ibid., p. 138.
50. Ibid., pp. 139–140.
51. "David Hume and the Miraculous," in *Philosophical Studies* (London, 1934), p. 143.
52. *Inquiry,* pp. 140–141. N. K. Smith points out that Hume's conclusion, though mordant, "was the declared teaching of the Reformed Churches that Faith is impossible save with the aid of divinely conferred grace." Smith, "Introduction," op. cit., p. 47. A twentieth-century follower of the teachings of Karl Barth would find Hume's conclusion very congenial.
53. Hume's first choice for a title of this section was "Of the Practical Consequences of Natural Theology," which would have been a much more accurate indication of its content and intention.
54. *Inquiry,* p. 145.
55. Ibid., pp. 145–146.
56. Ibid., pp. 146–147.
57. Ibid., pp. 150–151.
58. Ibid., p. 153.
59. Ibid., p. 155.
60. Smith,"Introduction," op. cit., p. 59.
61. *Dialogues,* 2d ed., p. 141. All references to the *Dialogues* are to the Kemp Smith edition in the Library of Liberal Arts.
62. Ibid., pp. 142–143.
63. Ibid., p. 143.
64. Ibid., pp. 149–150.
65. Ibid., p. 160.
66. Ibid., pp. 161–162.
67. Ibid., p. 164.
68. Ibid., pp. 166–167.
69. Ibid., p. 178.
70. Ibid., p. 179.
71. Ibid.

72. Ibid.
73. Ibid., pp. 179–180.
74. Ibid., p. 189.
75. Ibid., pp. 189–190.
76. Ibid., p. 194.
77. Ibid., p. 195.
78. Ibid., p. 198.
79. Ibid., p. 201.
80. Ibid., p. 204.
81. Ibid., p. 211.
82. Ibid., p. 228.
83. *A Treatise of Human Nature,* Vol. I, ed. T. H. Green and T. H. Grose (London, 1874), 501.
84. Several British analytical philosophers have defended Christianity by conceding that religious beliefs do not claim to be *assertions* and, therefore, are neither verifiable nor falsifiable. According to these philosophers, religious statements are "bliks" or "feelings" similar to Hume's "natural beliefs." See the essays by R. M. Hare and T. McPherson, in A. Flew and A. MacIntyre, *New Essays in Philosophical Theology* (New York, 1955).
85. *Inquiry,* p. 173.
86. See Kant's comments on Hume's role in the development of his own critical philosophy in the *Prolegomena to Any Future Metaphysics* (New York, 1951), p. 5ff.
87. *Critique of Pure Reason,* 2d ed., trans. N. K. Smith (London, 1958), p. 29.
88. Ibid., p. 22.
89. Ibid., p. 501–505.
90. Ibid., p. 507. Some scholars contend that Kant's argument that "existence is not a predicate" misses the whole point of the ontological argument, the point being that on rational analysis existence is a predicate which belongs *necessarily* to the most perfect Being. Kant's insistence that existence is not a property of anything has also been extensively debated in philosophy. For the important texts and discussion of the ontological argument both before and since Kant, see A. Plantinga, ed., *The Ontological Argument* (New York, 1965).
91. Ibid., p. 508.
92. Ibid., pp. 509–510. Many philosophers and theologians dispute Kant's contention that the cosmological proof necessarily relapses into the ontological argument. For an example see F. Copleston, *History of Philosophy,* Vol. VI (London, 1960), 298–299.
93. Ibid., p. 511.
94. Ibid., p. 522.
95. Ibid., p. 526.
96. Ibid., p. 550.
97. We cannot attempt an examination of Kant's ethical theory but will sketch its important features as they relate to his philosophy of religion.
98. *Fundamental Principles of the Metaphysic of Morals,* in T. K. Abbott, *Kant's Theory of Ethics* (London, 1873), p. 38.
99. *The Critique of Practical Reason,* in Abbott, op. cit., p. 218.
100. Ibid., pp. 221–222.
101. I. Kant, *Religion within the Limits of Reason Alone* (New York, 1960), p. 43.
102. Ibid., pp. 40–41.
103. Ibid., p. 40.
104. Ibid., pp. 108–109.
105. Ibid., p. 110.
106. Allen W. Wood, *Kant's Moral Religion* (Ithaca, 1970), p. 248.
107. Ibid., p. 54.
108. Ibid.
109. Ibid., pp. 54–55.
110. Ibid., p. 55.
111. Ibid., pp. 55–57.
112. Ibid., p. 68.
113. Ibid., p. 55.
114. Ibid., p. 113.
115. F. H. Jacobi, *David Hume uber den Glauben,* in *Werke,* 2d ed., pp. 58–60. Trans. by B. A. Gerrish, in "Faith and Existence in the Philosophy of F. H. Jacobi," *Continuing the Reformation* (Chicago, 1993), p. 94.
116. Ibid., p. 95.
117. On this contribution of Jacobi, see Gerrish, op. cit. above.
118. Isaiah Berlin, "The Magus of the North," *New York Review of Books* (October 21, 1993), p. 64. While Berlin recognizes Hamann's historical importance and his creative genius, his estimation of this "Magus of the North" is essentially negative. He sees Hamann as perhaps the most original figure in the modern subversion of the Enlightenment values of order, rationality, and trust in the methods and results of scientific empiricism. In addition to the above, Berlin has written the following essays that touch on Hamann and his influence: "The Counter-Enlightenment" and "Hume and the Sources of German Anti-Rationalism," both in *Against the Current: Essays in the History of Ideas* (New York, 1980). Also, *Vico and Herder* (New York, 1977).
119. J. G. Hamann, "Socratic Memorabilia." Cited in Ronald Gregor Smith, *J. B. Hamann 1730–1788. A Study in Christian Existence* (London, 1960), p. 181. Smith's study includes selected writings in transla-

tion from the J. Nadler edition of Hamann's *Werke,* 6 vols. (Vienna, 1949–1957). All quotations from Hamann are from R. Smith's translation.

120. J. G. Hamann, "The Letter H By Itself." Cited in R. Smith, op. cit., pp. 203–204.

121. Letter to Jacobi, April 27, 1787, and to Herder, May 10, 1781. Cited in R. Smith, op. cit., pp. 53, 244.

122. Hamann, "Socratic Memorabilia." Cited in R. Smith, op. cit., pp. 181–82.

123. J. G. Hamann, Letter to I. Kant, July 27, 1759. Cited in R. Smith, op. cit., p. 241.

124. I believe R. Smith's position can be defended. Critics such as Isaiah Berlin dismiss too peremptorily Hamann's conception of faith as a radical "irrationalism" and "fideism." These terms require more careful elucidation or qualification. Berlin is, of course, correct that Hamann uses Hume's treatment of belief in the *Inquiry* for his own purposes, that Hamann had no illusions about Hume's agnosticism and his ironical appeal to faith at the conclusion of the *Dialogues,* or that Hume would have been horrified at Hamann's use of his writings. Furthermore, there are passages in Hamann that do flaunt the extravagances of the imagination, the exotic, and the irrational in the name of religion.

125. J. G. Hamann, *The Metacritique of the Purism of Reason.* Cited in R. Smith, op. cit., p. 216. Hamann overemphasizes Kant's a priorism here, but his insight into the role of language in cognition is important and points to Wittgenstein and contemporary linguistic philosophy.

126. J. G. Hamann, Letter of November 14, 1784. Cited in R. Smith, op. cit., p. 249.

127. J. G. Hamann, *Zweifel und Einfälle.* Cited in R. Smith, op. cit., p. 259.

128. J. G. Hamann, *Thoughts about My Life.* Cited in R. Smith, op. cit., pp. 156–157.

129. J. G. Herder, *On the Origin of Language,* in *Against Pure Reason: Writings on Religion, Language, and History,* trans. and ed. Marcia Bunge (Minneapolis, 1993), p. 72.

130. J. G. Herder, *Yet Another Philosophy of History.* Cited in Bunge, op. cit., pp. 38–39.

131. Ibid., p. 43.

132. Ibid., p. 44.

133. Ibid., pp. 41–42, 44.

134. Ibid., p. 47.

135. J. G. Herder, *First Dialogue Concerning National Religions.* Cited in Bunge, op. cit., pp. 102, 105–106.

136. J. G. Herder, *Letters Concerning the Study of Theology.* Cited in Bunge, op. cit., p. 218.

137. J. G. Herder, *Concerning the Divinity and Use of the Bible.* Cited in Bunge, op. cit., pp. 202, 204, 210.

138. Hans Frei, *The Eclipse of Biblical Narrative: A Study in Eighteenth and Nineteenth Century Hermeneutics* (New Haven, 1974), p. 191. Frei's nuanced account of Herder's biblical hermeneutics is the best analysis available. He believes, however, that Herder's twofold interpretive stance, for all its empathy, destroys the Bible's realistic narrative power.

SUGGESTIONS FOR FURTHER READING

The works of Cragg, Mossner, Stephen, and Creed and Boys Smith cited in the bibliography for Chapter 2 all deal with the breakdown of the Religion of Reason. Karl Barth, in *From Rousseau to Ritschl* (New York: Harper & Row, 1959) has some judicious, if not always balanced, things to say about Kant, Rousseau, Lessing, and Herder.

J. J. Rousseau

Cassirer, Ernst. *The Question of Jean-Jacques Rousseau,* trans. and ed. Peter Gay (New York: Columbia University Press, 1954).

———. "Kant and Rousseau." In *Rousseau-Kant-Goethe* (Princeton: Princeton University Press, 1947).

Crocker, Lester. *Jean Jacques Rousseau,* 2 vols. (New York: Macmillan, 1968–1973). One of the best biographical studies of Rousseau.

Grimsley, Ronald. *Rousseau and the Religious Quest* (Oxford: Oxford University Press, 1968).

Hendel, C. *Jean-Jacques Rousseau, Moralist* (New York: Oxford University Press, 1934). Especially Chapter 17 on "The Profession of Faith."

Wright, E. H. *The Meaning of Rousseau* (London: Oxford University Press, 1929). Especially Chapter 4 on "The Natural Religion."

Joseph Butler

Jeffner, Anders. *Butler and Hume on Religion: A Comparison* (Stockholm: Diakonistyrelsen, 1966).

Mossner, E. C. *Bishop Butler and the Age of Reason* (New York: Macmillan Co., 1936).

Norton, W. J., Jr. *Bishop Butler, Moralist and Divine* (New Brunswick, N.J.: Rutgers University Press, 1940).

Penelhum, Terence. *Butler* (London: Routledge and Kegan Paul, 1985). Part II contains an excellent critical analysis of Butler as religious apologist. Good bibliography of relevant studies.

David Hume

Flew, Antony. *Hume's Philosophy of Belief* (London: Routledge and Kegan Paul, 1961). Chapters 8 and 9 are particularly important for Hume's contribution to philosophical theology.

Gaskin, J. C. A. *Hume's Philosophy of Religion* (New York: Barnes and Noble, 1978). A comprehensive study of Hume's philosophy of religion.

Pike, Nelson, ed. *Hume: Dialogues Concerning Natural Religion* (Indianapolis: Bobbs-Merrill, 1970). Contains an excellent commentary and critique of Hume's argument and a bibliography of studies.

Smith, N. K. "Introduction" to David Hume, *Dialogues Concerning Natural Religion* (New York: Macmillan, Library of Liberal Arts, n.d.). Smith's introduction is the most thorough analysis available of Hume's personal views regarding religion, his general critique of religion, and the argument of the *Dialogues*.

Immanuel Kant

Fackenheim, E. L. "Immanuel Kant." In *Nineteenth Century Religious Thought in the West,* I, N. Smart et al. (Cambridge: Cambridge University Press, 1985).

Greene, T. M., and Silber, J. "Introduction" to *Religion within the Limits of Reason Alone* (New York: Harper, 1960). Green traces Kant's early religious training and the development of his philosophy of religion and analyzes the *Religion within the Limits of Reason Alone*.

Kroner, R. *Kant's Weltanschauung,* trans. J. E. Smith (Chicago: University of Chicago Press, 1956). Attempts to set forth in brief compass the basic perspective of Kant's philosophy as focusing on the primacy of moral faith and action over all speculation.

Rossi, Philip J., and Michael Wreen, eds. *Kant's Philosophy of Religion Reconsidered* (Bloomington: Indiana University Press, 1991). A valuable collection of recent studies on Kant's philosophy of religion and moral theology.

Silber, John. "The Ethical Significance of Kant's *Religion,*" "Introduction" to *Religion within the Limits of Reason Alone* (New York: Harper, 1960). Silber sees no solution to the conflict between autonomous freedom and divine grace in Kant's *Religion*. For an opposing view, see A. W. Wood, *Kant's Moral Religion*.

Webb, C. C. J. *Kant's Philosophy of Religion* (Oxford: Clarendon Press, 1926). An older but helpful study that traces the development of Kant's philosophy of religion and gives considerable attention to his treatment of Christianity in *Religion within the Limits of Reason Alone*.

Wood, Allen W. *Kant's Moral Religion* (Ithaca: Cornell University Press, 1970).

————. *Kant's Rational Theology* (Ithaca: Cornell University Press, 1978). The two studies by Wood complement one another and provide new insights into Kant's moral theology and philosophy of religion.

The Counter-Enlightenment

Beck, Lewis White. *Early German Philosophy* (Cambridge: Harvard University Press, 1969). Chapter 15 contains brief but interesting treatments of Jacobi, Hamann, and Herder.

Berlin, Isaiah. "The Counter-Enlightenment." In *Against the Current: Essays in the History of Ideas* (New York: Viking Press, 1980). Fine essay that indicates the historical significance of the movement.

Copelston, Frederick. *A History of Philosophy,* VI (London: Burns and Oates, 1960). Chapters 5–7 are lucid expositions of the thought of the major figures of the German Enlightenment and the Counter-Enlightenment.

Pascal, Roy. *The German Sturm und Drang* (New York: Philosophical Library, 1953). Very good on the literary-cultural movement but weak on the philosophical-theological aspects. Good for background.

F. H. Jacobi

There is little in English about Jacobi as a religious thinker. See Beck and Copleston above and the following:

Gerrish, B. A. "Faith and Existence in the Philosophy of F. H. Jacobi." In *Continuing the Reformation: Essays on Modern Religious Thought* (Chicago: University of Chicago Press, 1993). In this excellent essay Gerrish discusses Jacobi's interpreters, his dialogue with Hume, his concept of faith, and his current relevance. Includes references to the relatively small number of translations of and works on Jacobi in English.

J. G. Hamann

Alexander, W. M. *Hamann, Philosophy and Faith* (The Hague: Nijhoff, 1966). With Smith, below, one of the two full-length studies of Hamann in English.

Berlin, Isaiah. *The Magus of the North* (London: J. Murray, 1993); *Against the Current: Essays in the History of Ideas* (New York: Viking Press, 1980), pp. 162–187. Berlin's essays on Hamann are interesting but disapproving. He objects to Hamann's religious "irrationalism," as he sees it, and considers Hamann a crucial figure in the dark, Romantic protest against the Enlightenment.

German, Terence J. *Hamann on Language and Religion* (New York: Oxford University Press, 1981).

O'Flaherty, J. C. Trans. of Hamann's *Socratic Memorabilia* (Baltimore: Johns Hopkins Press, 1967). Includes an excellent introduction and notes to this important text.

Schmidt, James, ed. *What Is Enlightenment? Eighteenth Century Questions and Twentieth Century Answers* (Berkeley: University of California Press, 1996). Contains important material by and about Hamann.

Smith, Ronald Gregor. *J. G. Hamann, 1730–1788: A Study in Christian Existence* (London: Collins, 1960). A highly sympathetic, if slightly dated, study of Hamann as Christian existentialist. Smith does a commendable, if not wholly persuasive, job of rebutting the charges of irrationalism against Hamann.

J. G. Herder

There are numerous excellent studies in English of Herder's contribution to modern literary and historical studies but few on his contributions to religion. The following are among the best available:

Berlin, Isaiah. *Vico and Herder: Two Studies in the History of Ideas.* (New York: Viking Press, 1976). A rich and lucid essay on Herder's leading ideas that are significant in their bearing on religion.

Frei, Hans. *The Eclipse of Biblical Narrative: A Study in Eighteenth and Nineteenth Century Hermeneutics.* (New Haven: Yale University Press, 1974). The finest, brief, critical discussion of Herder's principles of biblical interpretation.

Herder, J. G. *Against Pure Reason: Writings on Religion, Language and History,* trans., ed., and with an introduction by Marcia Bunge. (Minneapolis: Fortress Press, 1993). The best collection of selections in English of Herder's wide-ranging writings on religion. Included is a helpful introduction and bibliography of texts, translations, and secondary studies.

Chapter 4
Christianity and Romanticism:
Protestant Thought

Friedrich Schleiermacher

INTRODUCTION

In Chapter 3 we have seen that eighteenth-century rational theology came under severe attack by thinkers who were themselves committed to the ideals and scientific methods of the Age of Reason. This is especially evident in the work of Hume and Kant. Toward the close of the eighteenth century in Europe, there came to prominence a generation of artists and thinkers who, though in many ways strikingly different, can nevertheless be grouped together as a single movement because of a spiritual kinship which clearly sets them apart from the ideals of eighteenth-century Classicism and Deism. We have encountered their forerunners in thinkers such as Hamann and Herder.

The artists and thinkers of this new generation have been called Romantics, and the revolution which they brought about is called the Romantic Movement. The first and purest phase of the Romantic Movement ran from 1780 to about 1830. Approximately during these fifty years Byron, Blake, Wordsworth, Coleridge, Beethoven, Goethe, Hölderlin, Novalis, and the theologian Schleiermacher, among many others, poured forth the fruits of their genius. Though of widely different temperaments and holding quite divergent convictions, they reflect certain beliefs and sympathies which make them spiritually akin and distinguish them in important ways from the spirit of the Enlightenment. It would be quite wrong, however, to envision the Romantic Movement as simply a repudiation of the Age of Reason. Rather, the Romantics strove to enlarge the vision of the eighteenth century and to return to a wider, more richly diversified tradition.

Romanticism did not merely oppose or overthrow the neoclassic "Reason" of the Age of Enlightenment but sought to enlarge its vision and fill out its lacks by a return to a wider tradition—national, popular, medieval, and primitive as well as modern, civilized and rational. At its fullest, Romanticism cherishes both experience and tradition, both emotion and reason, both the Greco-Roman and Medieval heritage, both religion and science, both formal strictness and the claims of substance, both the real and the ideal, both the individual and the group, both order and freedom, both man and nature.[1]

Furthermore, there was not a single Romanticism but several movements that shared certain vital things but were also distinct. French and German Romanticism, for example, differ, but they share a spirit and certain ideals. The very aim of Romanticism was *inclusiveness.* This involved an "openness to otherness," to the fragmented and mysterious dimensions of reality, and for that reason the Romantic spirit is difficult to define simply. However, there are certain convictions and values widely held by the Romantics which set the movement off as a transition from the age of Newton to the world in which we live today. First, the Romantics were unwilling to reduce experience either to an abstract rationalism or a narrow, scientific empiricism. Experience involved much that eluded both analytical reasoning and scientific experiment, including the power of imagination, feeling, and intuition.

> It was an emphasis on the less rational side of human nature, on everything that differentiates man from the coldly calculating thinking machine; and correspondingly a revolt against viewing the world as nothing but a vast mechanical order. It was the voicing of the conviction that life is broader than intelligence, and that the world is more than what physics can find in it. . . . Experience, in its infinite richness and color and warmth and complexity, is something greater than any intelligible formulation of it. . . .[2]

Wearied of the kind of rationalistic proofs put forward, for example, by William Paley in *Evidences of Christianity* (1794), the Romanticist was unashamed to declare: "My experience is my proof!"

Warrant for belief was now focused on the intensity of *experience,* whether it be personal or what is common to all. Individuality and free self-expression were given primacy over rules and conventions and rational demonstrability.

The Romantic appeal to personal experience was dependent in part on Kant's conception of the transcendental ego, interpreted, however, as a gloriously unlimited, creative personality that each individual must seek to develop and enjoy. Coupled with this emphasis on personal experience and expression was a new concern for the rich diversity of human life and the cultivation of a feeling for, or imaginative insight into, points of view, tastes, and values of others—even those experiences and tastes that might appear eccentric and even monstrous.[3]

The appeal to diversity was also expressive of a new and revolutionary conception of Nature and Nature's God. Nature was no longer conceived after the model of a great, cosmic machine (the purpose of which, as Spinoza suggested, being "to make men uniform, as children of a common mother,") but, rather, as an insatiably creative process of increasing diversification. The God of this creative process was conceived of, once again, as the Platonic Demiurge, the creative Eros who makes for the actualization of all creative potentials and who values creative diversity above all else. Life and art should, in turn, be a copy of Nature's insatiate creativity and the God who is the very soul of Nature's pulsing, multiform life. The Romantics were, in most instances, advocates of an unrestrained catholicity and a longing for the infinite.

> The Eternal Spirit knows that each man speaks the language which he has provided for him, that everyone expresses what is within him as he can and should. . . . [God] looks with satisfaction upon each and all, and rejoices in the variety of the mixture. . . . To him the Gothic church is as well-pleasing as the Grecian temple; and the rude war music of the savage is a sound as dear to him as religious anthems and choruses composed with richest art. Yet when I turn my gaze back from the Infinite to earth, and look about at my brothers—ah! how loudly must I lament that they so little strive to become like their great model in Heaven.[4]

To appeal to what is universally standard, uniform, and immutable is, as Schleiermacher remarked, to be guilty of "a radical lack of feeling for the fundamental characteristic of living Nature, which everywhere aims at diversity and individuality."[5]

This diversity is found not only in nature and art but in religion. The Deist search for a universal creed is pernicious, for variety is the very essence of religious experience. Schleiermacher calls upon the rationalists to

> abandon the vain and foolish wish that there should be only one religion; you must lay aside all repugnance to its multiplicity; as candidly as possible, you must approach everything that has ever, in the changing forms of humanity, been developed in its advancing career from the ever fruitful bosom of the spiritual life. . . . You are wrong therefore, with your universal religion that is to be natural to all; for no one will have his own true and right religion if it is the same for all. . . .[6]

The Romantics, while stressing individuality and variety, nevertheless shared a profound mystical sense of the elemental unity of Nature's dissimilitude. Humanity and Nature are not irreparably split into a Cartesian dualism of thought and extension. Human beings and Nature are fundamentally akin, for they are but variant manifestations of one infinite Whole. This sense of Nature's organic unity was experienced as an aesthetic wholeness—felt or intuited rather than comprehended rationally. Many Romantics found in humans' communion with Nature an artless wisdom that touches the very core of reality and that alone can give to the human spirit the understanding and repose which passes knowledge. Wordsworth expressed this feeling as simply and directly as any:

> Books! 'tis a dull and endless strife:
> Come, hear the woodland linnet,
> How sweet his music! on my life,
> There's more of wisdom in it.
>
> And hark! how blithe the throstle sings!
> He, too, is no mean preacher:
> Come forth into the light of things,
> Let Nature be your Teacher. . . .
>
> One impulse from a vernal wood
> May teach you more of man,
> Of moral evil and of good,
> Than all the sages can. . . .

> Enough of Science and of Art;
> Close up those barren leaves;
> Come forth and bring with you a heart
> That watches and receives.[7]

Common to the Romantics was the feeling that behind Nature some Spirit or Vital Force was at work. This Spirit in Nature, call it God if you will, was not the Deist watchmaker God, dispassionately transcendent over creation, but a vital Spirit immanent in all things, the creative Eros in which everything moves and has its being. The feeling for and longing to be in communion with this Infinite Spirit gave to Romanticism a distinctly religious sensibility. Typical, however, was Novalis's confession: "We *seek* the unconditioned everywhere, and always *find* only things."[8] Romantics *felt* themselves a part of a larger, spiritual reality, and in this the Romantics exemplify the quintessence of the *homo religiosus*.

The Romantic feeling for the Whole, though often acknowledged as a uniquely religious sentiment, was not, however, always equated with Christian belief. For many, including Friedrich Schlegel, all human striving for the infinite belongs to a peculiarly religious intuition. Typical of this rather vague and often deeply emotional feeling is Faust's response to Marguerite's question whether he believes in God:

> Sweet one! my meaning do not misconceive!
> Him who dare name
> And who proclaim,
> Him I believe?
> Who that can feel,
> His heart can steel,
> To say: I believe him not?
> The All-embracer,
> All-sustainer,
> Holds and sustains he not
> Thee, me, himself?
> Lifts not the Heaven its dome above?
> Doth not the firm-set earth beneath us lie?
> And beaming tenderly with looks of love,
> Climb not the everlasting stars on high?
> Do I not gaze into thine eyes?
> Nature's impenetrable agencies,
> Are they not thronging on my heart and
>   brain,

Viewless, or visible to mortal ken,
Around thee weaving their mysterious chain?
Fill thence thy heart, how large soe'er it be;
And in the feeling when thou utterly art blest,
Then call it, what thou wilt,—
Call it Bliss! Heart! Love! God!
I have no name for it!
'Tis feeling all;
Name is but sound and smoke
Shrouding the glow of heaven.[9] (Italics added.)

The feeling for the rich wholeness and infinite possibilities of life also expressed itself in a new enthusiasm for the past and especially for those periods which appeared superstitious and barbaric to the *philosophes.* The Middle Ages were admired because they represented chivalric romance and the Christian ideal of the unity of faith and culture. The new interest in the past, however, was not confined to the Middle Ages. It represented a more universal historical consciousness, the beginnings of which we have already seen in Lessing's *Education of the Human Race* and in the writings of Herder. Attacking the past now appeared childish, since every age, every culture has its own unique individuality and contribution to make to the richness and progress of humanity. This new interest in and appeal to history which flowered in the Romantic era proved later to be a two-edged sword for theology. It was responsible for a new appreciation of ancient tradition and led, for example, to renewed historical arguments for Catholic Christianity in the writings of Lamennais in France and John Henry Newman in England. At the same time, appeal to history and historical method ushered in a period of intensive investigation of the origins and development of Christianity, the results of which have not even yet been fully felt or assessed.

In short, the Romantics did nothing less than inaugurate a revolution in Western consciousness which, among other things, launched a new era in theology.

SAMUEL TAYLOR COLERIDGE

Samuel Taylor Coleridge (1772–1834) represents better than any other figure in England the Romantic protest against rationalism in the early decades of the nineteenth century. Coleridge was a poet, philosopher, literary critic, and theologian who directed all his energies against what he believed to be the deadening effect of a "mechanical philosophy" upon human life and culture. J. S. Mill, writing in 1838, saw in Jeremy Bentham and Coleridge the two seminal minds of his age in England. In Bentham, Mill saw the empirical and scientific heritage of the eighteenth century sustained. On the other hand, Coleridge's doctrine expressed to him the revolt of the human mind against the philosophy of the eighteenth century. Coleridge's doctrine was ontological because the eighteenth century was experimental; "conservative, because that was innovative; religious, because so much of that was infidel; concrete and historical, because that was abstract and metaphysical; poetical, because that was matter-of-fact and prosaic."[10]

More than any other individual, Coleridge was responsible for the rebirth of a vital English theology out of the cold and spare remains of late eighteenth-century orthodoxy and rationalism. Coleridge's own mind was catholic, and his influence on British theology in the decades after 1830 was not limited to any one school or party. John Henry Newman recognized Coleridge as one of the few people responsible for breathing new life into England's spiritual torpor, thereby giving impetus to the Catholic revival. Coleridge's influence on F. D. Maurice, perhaps the most influential Anglican theologian of the nineteenth century, is also well attested to in the Dedication of Maurice's *The Kingdom of Christ.*[11]

Coleridge did not begin his intellectual career as a critic of eighteenth-century rationalism and republicanism. As a student at Cambridge, he was an ardent supporter of Unitarian and republican views. For a while he even envisioned setting up, with the poet Robert Southey, a Utopian community modeled after the radical social theories of William Godwin. But Coleridge's social and religious liberalism was not deeply grounded, and by the time he left Cambridge he had already repudiated "Godwinism."

One of the major events of Coleridge's life was his meeting with the poet Wordsworth in 1795. Three years later, the two friends jointly published

Lyrical Ballads and then traveled together to Germany. While Wordsworth explored the countryside, Coleridge studied the German language, attended philosophical lectures, and purchased a considerable number of German philosophical works which he brought back with him to England. It is to a considerable extent through Coleridge that German Romantic and Idealistic philosophy were introduced into British intellectual life.

The maturing of Coleridge's own spiritual philosophy was largely the product of his discovery of the aesthetic principle of the Imagination in the poetry of his friend Wordsworth and the new conception of mind and experience which he found in his reading of Kant and German transcendental philosophy. The coincidence of what he found in Wordsworth and Kant with what he had been working out in his own mind served to confirm his ideas and set him on the way to articulating his own doctrine. A brief analysis of these influences will be helpful in understanding Coleridge's unique contribution to religion.

In his *Biographia Literaria* Coleridge relates how the reading of Wordsworth's poetry freed him from the narrow sensationalism that had dominated British thought since the time of Locke. What struck Coleridge in Wordsworth's poetry was "the union of deep feeling with profound thought: the fine balance of truth in observing, with the imaginative faculty in modifying the objects observed." Coleridge contrasted this "imaginative faculty" with what he called "fancy." Fancy is the mere juxtaposition of images in a deliberate and even contrived fashion. According to Coleridge, inferior poetry is the product of "fancy." Truly great poetry, such as Wordsworth's, is not a contrivance but a genuine creation. Such creation requires Imagination, for a poem is not an assemblage but a new whole, a spiritual unity. Artistic creation, then, is the fusion of mind and materials, or subject and object, into a spiritual unity through the faculty of Imagination.

The philosophical importance of Coleridge's discovery of the faculty of Imagination lies in the fact that he now conceives of the mind as active and not merely as a passive receptacle of sensations: "If the mind is not *passive,* if it be indeed made in God's Image, and that, too, in the sublimest sense, the

Image of the Creator, there is ground for suspicion that any system built on the passiveness of the mind must be false, as a system."[12]

Coleridge's discovery of the Imaginative faculty was confirmed in his reading of Kant. What Kant corroborated in Coleridge's mind was the belief that "the highest truths are those which lie beyond the limits of experience." Kant had affirmed that all our metaphysical truths are postulates of our practical reason—that is, of our *experience as moral beings,* not of our empirical or sensory knowledge. Like Kant, Coleridge taught that such metaphysical postulates as God, freedom, moral conscience, and immortality are derived from our moral convictions. "My metaphysics," he says, "are merely the referring of the mind to its own consciousness for truths indispensable to its own happiness."[13]

Reason, Understanding, and Faith

The creative activity of the mind, which Coleridge discovered in the faculty of Imagination and which was confirmed in his reading of Kant, served as the basis of his attack upon the sensationalism and mechanical philosophy of the eighteenth century. Coleridge found a counterpart for the aesthetic faculty of Imagination which he believed would save religion and morality from the fatal malady of materialism. That faculty he called Reason.

For Coleridge, Reason is the complement of Imagination. It is the "organ of the supersensuous." On the other hand, Fancy finds its counterpart in what Coleridge calls Understanding. Understanding is the "faculty of judging according to sense." Understanding is, then, the passive, receptive faculty, "the *vis receptiva* or recipient property of the soul, from the original constitution of which we perceive and imagine all things under the forms of space and time."[14] It is the empirical, synthetic faculty of Kant.

According to Coleridge, Europe was presently living under "the dynasty of the Understanding," the result being materialism, atheism, utilitarianism. This "imperialism" of the Understanding stood for everything Coleridge regarded as a threat to the human spirit. Reason implied everything that defined the unique spirituality of humanity. Basil

Willey sums up Coleridge's distinction in this striking way:

> Understanding is the faculty by which we generalize and arrange the phenomena of perception. Reason is "the knowledge of the laws of the whole considered as one"; Understanding is the "science of phenomena." Reason seeks ultimate ends; Understanding studies means. Reason is "the source and substance of truths above sense"; Understanding is the faculty which judges "according to sense." Reason is the eye of the spirit, the faculty whereby spiritual reality is spiritually discerned; Understanding is the mind of the flesh.[15]

Coleridge did not deny the value of the Understanding. In its own province he deemed it useful, even necessary. Yet the most important of truths—God, freedom, moral conscience—lie beyond its scope. Reason alone is concerned with moral and religious truth, for Reason alone is the instrument of spiritual apprehension, of those "truths above sense."

Coleridge never defined his conception of Reason systematically. Yet from his innumerable references to it we can discern much of what he meant by the term. First, Reason is unique to humans. Other creatures may possess the faculty of Understanding, if only in the form of instinct, but humans alone are rational animals. Second, Reason is a moral imperative, what Kant would call "want of reason."

> We (that is the human race) *live by faith.* Whatever we do or know that in kind is different from the brute creation has its origin in a determination of the reason to have faith and trust in itself. This, its first act of faith, is scarcely less than identical with its own being. . . . It is itself therefore the realizing principle, the spiritual *substratum* of the whole complex body of truths.[16]

Third, Reason should be thought of not as a separate faculty but, rather, as a *power,* an intuitive apprehension by which the total personality—senses, will, and emotions—acts as a whole. Apprehension of such supersensuous truth is the fruit of feeling and will in unity with sense and intellect; the heart acting upon and in union with the head. Reason, therefore, is that power by which the faculties are united and are enabled to experience an intuitive apprehension of the truth.

Whereas for Kant the ideas of the practical reason are merely regulative ideas, for Coleridge the ideas intuited by Reason are the objects of knowledge; they have real ontological status. Here Coleridge parts with Kant and reveals his affinity with Jacobi's philosophy and his dependence upon the Platonism of the seventeenth-century English divines. Human Reason serves as the unitive power by which all disparate experiences and truths are bound together and apprehended as a spiritual Whole, because Reason is grounded in the one Being (God) who "is the ground of all relations."

> It is the office, and as it were, the instinct of the reason, to bring a unity into all our conceptions and several knowledges. On this all system depends; and without this we could reflect connectedly neither on nature nor our own minds. *Now this is possible only on the assumption or hypothesis of a One as the ground and cause of the universe,* and which, in all succession and through all changes, is the subject neither of time nor change. . . .[17] (Italics added.)

Coleridge was especially fond of quoting the opening verse of the Gospel of John: "In the beginning was the Logos [Reason] and the Logos was with God and the Logos was God." Spiritual truths which transcend our sensory experience are real objects of knowledge because our human Reason is grounded in and is the image of the one infinite, eternal Reason—God.[18]

Especially significant in understanding Coleridge's concept of Reason is the importance he placed on the relation of Reason and Will. It is the Will which defines a person as a free, self-determining being rather than simply as a link in the natural chain of cause and effect. It is the Will which separates humans from Nature's necessity and the conditionedness of time and space. In *Aids to Reflection* (1825) Coleridge developed his concept of the Will in some detail, opposing his doctrine to that of the materialists and determinists. Coleridge sums up the distinction as follows:

Nature is a line in constant and continuous evolution. Its beginning is lost in the supernatural: and for our understanding therefore it must appear as a continuous line without beginning or end. But where there is no discontinuity there can be no origination, and every appearance of origination in nature is but a shadow of our own casting. It is a reflection from our own will or spirit. Herein, indeed, the will consists. This is the essential character by which Will is opposed to Nature, as spirit, and raised above nature as self-determining spirit—this namely, that it is a power of originating an act or state.[19]

For Coleridge, metaphysical truths are never discerned by the speculative or discursive reason alone but by the whole person, which includes deep feeling and willing.[20] The apprehension of spiritual truth involves the emancipation of the soul from the "debasing slavery to the outward senses" and the awakening of the mind "to the true *criteria* of reality, namely, permanence, power, *will manifested in act,* and *truth operating as life.*"[21] Thus Coleridge looked with particular horror on the many books purporting to "prove" Christianity by discursive reason alone.

I more than fear the prevailing taste for books of natural theology, physico-theology, demonstrations of God from Nature, evidences of Christianity, and the like. *Evidences of Christianity!* I am *weary of the word. Make a man feel the want of it; rouse him, if you can, to the self-knowledge of his need of it; and you may safely trust it to its own evidence* [italics added] remembering only the express declaration of Christ himself: *No man cometh to me, unless the Father leadeth him.*[22]

In Coleridge's view Christianity is not essentially a set of doctrines but a way of life. The proper approach to the honest doubter, then, is not to seek to resolve his or her speculative difficulties but to call upon the person to "Try it!"[23] The proof is found in the practice. In fact, for Coleridge theological dogmas are beyond apprehension unless grasped by the practical reason. This is where Coleridge leaves orthodoxy and, with Schleiermacher, founds modern theological apologetics on a new basis, i.e., human experience. According to orthodoxy and rationalism, theological dogmas are true without reference to any subjective judgment. Dogma is either evidenced positively in an authoritative book or is the product of rational demonstration. With Coleridge this conception of religious doctrine is left behind. Christian doctrines are vital, living truths of experience or are incomprehensible. Theologians have too long failed to realize this fact.

Too soon did the Doctors of the Church forget that the *heart,* the moral nature, was the beginning and the end; and that truth, knowledge, and insight were comprehended in its expansion. This was the true and first apostasy—when in council and synod the divine humanities of the Gospel gave way to speculative systems, and religion became a science of shadows under the name of theology. . . . without life or interest, alike inaccessible and unintelligible to the majority of Christians.[24]

Dogmas accepted by intellect or authority alone, and not evidenced by being lived in practice, are the very opposite of spiritual truths, for such truths are inextricably related to the moral Will. Coleridge thus makes an important distinction between objects of *faith* and objects of sight and demonstrative assent. Objects of religious faith are "the assurance of things hoped for, the conviction of things not seen," and are confirmed not by sight or logical persuasion but by experience and moral suasion. Coleridge thus advises initiates in the faith to

translate the theological terms into their moral equivalents; saying to themselves—This may not be *all* that was meant, but it *is* meant, and it is that portion of the meaning, which belongs to *me* in the present stage of my progress.[25]

Thus in speaking of the thorny doctrine of election, Coleridge commends the view of Leighton who "avoids all metaphysical views of Election, relatively to God, and confines himself to the doctrine in its relation to man."[26] He then adds:

The following may, I think, be taken as a safe and useful rule in religious inquiries. Ideas, that derive their origin and substance from the moral being, and to the reception of which as true objectively (that is, as corresponding to a reality out of the human mind) we are determined by a practical interest exclusively, may not, like theoretical positions, be pressed onward into all their logical consequences. The law of conscience, and not the canons of discursive reasoning, must decide in such cases. At least, the latter have no validity, which the single *veto* of the former is not sufficient to nullify. The most pious conclusion is here the most legitimate.[27]

Coleridge was so convinced of this rule in matters of spiritual truth that he could say, concerning the doctrine of God:

> It could not be intellectually more evident without becoming morally less effective; without counteracting its own end by sacrificing the *life* of faith to the cold mechanism of a worthless, because compulsory, assent.[28]

For Coleridge, faith and reason could not possibly be considered separately as two distinct modes of spiritual knowledge, since spiritual truth is apprehended only by the moral being, i.e., the individual conscience which is the union of Reason and Will. Coleridge, in fact, defines faith as *the act of conscience*, i.e., the act "by which we take upon ourselves an allegiance, and consequently the obligation of fealty." Here is Coleridge's fullest description of faith:

> Faith subsists in the synthesis of the reason and the individual will. By virtue of the latter therefore it must be an energy, and inasmuch as it relates to the whole moral man, it must be exerted in each and all of his constituents or incidents, faculties and tendencies;. . . . it must be a total, not a partial; a continuous, not a desultory or occasional energy. And by virtue of the former, that is, reason, faith must be a light, a form of knowing, a beholding of truth. In the incomparable words of the Evangelist, therefore—*faith must be a light originating in the Logos, or the substantial reason, which is coeternal and one with the Holy Will, and which light is at the same time the life of men.* Now as life is here the sum or collective of all moral and spiritual acts . . . so is faith the source and sum, the energy and principle of the fidelity of man to God, by the subordination of his human will, in all provinces of his nature to his reason, as the sum of spiritual truth, representing and manifesting the will Divine.[29]

Experience and the Interpretation of Scripture

Coleridge's conception of the moral and experiential apprehension of spiritual doctrine or truth is most thoroughly worked out in his thoughts on the interpretation of Scripture, which appeared in *Confessions of an Inquiring Spirit,* published posthumously in 1840. In the *Confessions* Coleridge finds himself opposed to both the orthodox view of scriptural inerrancy and the skeptical conclusions of the rationalists. Coleridge is among the first of that new breed of nineteenth- and twentieth-century Christian who desires to preserve the truths of orthodoxy while remaining committed to the findings of historical-critical research.

During the early decades of the nineteenth century, English theology was dominated by what Coleridge called *Bibliolatry,* i.e., the belief in the literal inerrancy of Scripture. The English divines had little knowledge of the critical scholarship on the Bible that had long been underway in Germany. Coleridge had been introduced to this new critical movement during his year on the Continent— especially through his reading of Lessing whose influence is evident in the *Confessions.* Coleridge recognized that the doctrine of biblical inerrancy is simply playing into the hands of the infidel skeptics, the likes of Tom Paine, who were having a field day demonstrating the contradictions and incongruities in the biblical texts. More than that, the inerrancy doctrine was forcing Christians to use all kinds of tortured and intellectually deceitful stratagems to seek to prove the Bible's infallibility. It was in this context that Coleridge wrote his *Letters on the Inspiration of the Scriptures* (published as the *Confessions*). The seven letters are addressed to a friend on the subject of whether it is "necessary, or expedient to insist on the belief of the divine origin and authority of all, and every part of the Canonical Books as the condition, or first principle, of Christian Faith?"[30] How, Coleridge asks, is it possible to accept biblical errancy and fallibility without at the same time falling into the "negative dogmatism" of those who regard the biblical texts as simply profane? How does one approach the Bible when one views it as neither inerrant nor merely profane?

Coleridge's answer is that the Bible should be taken up like "any other work" and that if it contains spiritual truth, those truths will "find me"—that is, the Bible will "bear witness for itself that it has proceeded from a Holy Spirit." What Coleridge means when he says that the Bible should be read like any other book is indicated in the analogy he draws with the reading of Shakespeare.

> In the course of my Lectures on Dramatic Poetry, I, in half a score instances, referred my auditors to the precious volume before me—Shakespeare—and spoke enthusiastically both in general and with detail of particular beauties, of the plays of Shakespeare, as in all their kinds, and in relation to the purposes of the writer, excellent. Would it have been fair, or according to the common usage and understanding of men, to have inferred an intention on my part to decide the question respecting Titus Andronicus, or the larger portion of the three parts of Henry VI? *Would not every genial mind understand by Shakespeare that unity or total impression comprising, and resulting from, the thousand-fold several and particular emotions of delight, admiration, gratitude excited by his works?*[31] (Italics added.)

The answer, of course, is that certainly this is what we mean by Shakespeare and that the appreciation of Shakespeare's incomparable literary merit is not called into question simply because his work includes *Titus Andronicus*. And so it is, says Coleridge, when we consider the Bible.

The reason for Coleridge's complaint is the faulty reasoning which holds that the spiritual truth of the Bible is dependent on its total and complete inerrancy. Coleridge, with Herder, argues that it is only in the *real humanity* of the biblical texts that its spiritual truth and power can be discerned. The Bible "finds me," says Coleridge, *only when it speaks to my human condition.*

> But let me once be persuaded that all these heart-awakening utterances of human hearts—of men of like faculties and passions with myself, mourning, rejoicing, suffering, triumphing—are but as a *Divina Commedia* of a superhuman—oh bear with me, if I say—Ventriloquist . . . that this *sweet Psalmist of Israel* was himself as mere an instrument as his harp, an *au-*

tomaton poet, mourner, and suppliant; all is gone—all sympathy, at least, and all example. I listen in awe and fear but likewise in perplexity and confusion of spirit.[32]

The doctrine of biblical inerrancy transforms the real-life persons of the Bible, with their "pathetic appeals," "their piercing outcries," "their hollow truisms," into the dead automatons of an infallible Intelligence. What has happened is that biblical authority has been logically confused with biblical infallibility, a doctrine *about* the Bible has been substituted for the inherent authority contained *within the spiritual experiences* of the biblical personalities—a confusion which "has the effect of substituting a barren acquiescence in the letter for the lively *faith that cometh by hearing.*"[33]

The proof of the Bible's spiritual authority, according to Coleridge, lies "in its fitness to our nature and our needs." He calls upon us to be only

> as orthodox a believer *as you would have abundant reason to be,* though from some accident of birth, country, or education the precious boon of the Bible, with its additional evidence, had up to this moment been concealed from you;—and then read its contents with only the same piety which you freely accord on other occasions to the writings of men, considered the best and wisest of their several ages! *What you find therein coincident with your preestablished convictions, you will of course recognize as the revealed Word,* while as you read the recorded workings of the Word and the Spirit in the minds, lives, and hearts of spiritual men, the influence of the same Spirit on your own being, and the conflicts of grace and infirmity in your own soul, will enable you to discern and to know in and by what spirit they spoke and acted—as far at least as shall be needful for you, and in the times of your need.[34] (Italics added.)

That the spiritual power and authority of the experience of the personalities of the Bible will "find you" in the depths of your own spiritual experience is no mere pious hope. It is historical fact.

> In every generation, and wherever the light of Revelation has shone, men of all ranks, conditions, and states of mind have found [the Bible] . . . a spiri-

tual World—spiritual, and yet at the same time outward and common to all. You in one place, I in another, all men somewhere or at some time, meet with an assurance that the hopes and fears, the thoughts and yearnings are not dreams or fleeting singularities [for] . . . the hungry have found food, the thirsty a living spring, the feeble a staff . . . and as long as each man asks on account of his wants, and asks what he wants, no man will discover aught amiss or deficient in this vast and many-chambered storehouse. . . . Good and holy men, and the best and wisest of mankind . . . have borne witness to its influences, have declared it to be beyond compare the most perfect instrument, the only adequate organ, of Humanity.[35]

Are we to say, in the light of our own experience and that of "the best and wisest of mankind," that these experiences are to lose their value and warrant because, in the case of the Bible, "a few parts may be discovered of less costly materials and of meaner workmanship?" Certainly not. Because contradictions, errors of judgment, moral weakness are found in the Bible, are we to say that

> the Apostle's and Nicene Creed is not credible, the Ten Commandments not to be obeyed, the clauses of the Lord's Prayer not to be desired, or the Sermon on the Mount not to be practised?—See how the logic would look. David cruelly tortured the inhabitants of Rabbah (2 Sam. XII, 31; Chron. XX, 3), and in several of the Psalms he invokes the bitterest curses on his enemies; *therefore* it is not to be believed that *the love of God toward us was manifested in sending his only begotten Son into the world, that we might live through Him* (I John IV, 9).[36]

The logic, of course, is foolish. It is based on the specious conjunction of two very different statements. To say that "the Bible contains the religion revealed by God" is not the same as saying, "Whatever is contained in the Bible is religion, and was revealed by God." One can hold to the former while rejecting the latter. According to Coleridge, the Bible contains all that is necessary for faith and for practice; it is "the appointed conservatory, an indispensable criterion, and a continual source and support of true belief. *But that the Bible is the sole source; that it not only contains but constitutes the*

Christian Religion,"[37] [italics added] is a doctrine that cannot be found in the Bible itself nor is it one that Christendom has widely held.

Coleridge advances the hermeneutical principle that the Bible can become "the living Word of God" only when it is read "in faith." By this he means that what in the Bible constitutes the indispensable kernel of the Christian faith requires some interpretive "master key." For Coleridge this key includes all that constitutes the Christian tradition—the confessions and doctrinal standards of the Church, the continued succession of the ministry, the spiritual experience of the whole communion of saints:

> Friend, it is my conviction that in all ordinary cases *the knowledge and belief of the Christian Religion should precede the study of the Hebrew Canon. Indeed, with regard to both Testaments, I consider oral and catechismal instruction as the preparative provided by Christ himself in the establishment of a visible Church.*[38] (Italics added.)

Thus Coleridge counsels that it is only where one sees a desire to believe, "a beginning of love of Christ" that one should then say

> there are likewise sacred Writings, which taken in connection with the institution and perpetuity of a visible Church, all believers revere as the most precious boon of God, next to Christianity itself. . . . In them you will find all the revealed truths which have been set forth and offered to you . . . in addition to these, examples of obedience and disobedience . . . the lives and actions of men eminent under each dispensation, their sentiments, maxims, hymns, prayers—their affections, emotions, conflicts; in all of which you will recognize the influence of the Holy Spirit, *with a conviction increasing with the growth of your own faith and spiritual experience.*[39] (Italics added.)

Unless one comes to the Bible "in faith" and instructed in the Christian religion, one will be prone to lay hold of an isolated text here or there and say, "of what spiritual use is this," which only proves "that nothing can be so trifling as to supply an evil heart with a pretext for unbelief."

Coleridge's biblical hermeneutic was clearly directed against the orthodox and rationalist view of the Bible and Christian belief as something objectively given and "wholly external, and like the objects of sense, common to all alike." It is sometimes charged that the Romantics, in abhorrence of rationalist objectivity, fell into the opposite error of subsuming the whole of faith within the receptive or subjective pole—thus reducing Christianity to subjective feeling or will. Such a charge certainly cannot be leveled at Coleridge. In several places he makes it clear that divine revelation is neither a wholly objective or subjective reality but requires both poles—objective fact and existential appropriation.

> I comprise and conclude the sum of my convictions in this one sentence. Revealed Religion is in its highest contemplation the unity, the identity or coinherence, of Subjective and Objective. It is in itself, at once inward Life and Truth, and outward Fact and Luminary. . . . no man, I say, can recognize his own inward experiences in such writings [the Scriptures], and not find an objectiveness, a confirming and assuring outwardness, and all the main characters of reality reflected therefrom on the spirit. . . . The unsubstantial, insulated Self passes away as a stream; but these are the shadows and reflections of the Rock of Ages, and of the Tree of Life.
>
> On the other hand, as much of reality, as much of objective truth, as the Scriptures communicate to the subjective experiences of the Believer, so much of present life, of living and effective import, do these experiences give to the letter of Scriptures.[40]

Coleridge does not subsume the objective side, the giveness of revelation, within the receptive pole of experience. Where he does part with the orthodox and the rationalists is in his awareness of the role of subjective experience in the discernment of spiritual truth. *Revelation occurs only at the convergence of objective reality and the subjective judgment of lived experience and need.* Spiritual truth is, then, partly dependent upon the subjective mode of experience—i.e., upon the imagination, will, and emotion—as well as the understanding.

Coleridge's principles of biblical interpretation had considerable influence, especially in certain university circles, during the mid-nineteenth century in Britain. The effect of the *Confessions* on the authors of *Essays and Reviews** (1860) was very great, although acknowledged in only one or two instances. It is safe to say that had Coleridge's *Confessions* had a wider reading, much of the furor and misunderstanding in the Victorian era over the interpretation of Scripture could have been avoided. Nevertheless, Coleridge, the man of catholic mind and romantic sensibility, had considerable effect on the renewal of Christian theology in Britain, both in the Anglo-Catholic and Broad Church movements. Among the Romantics there is perhaps only one man who surpasses Coleridge in establishing a new religious sensibility and in refashioning the whole conception of what constitutes Christian faith—that man is Friedrich Schleiermacher.

FRIEDRICH SCHLEIERMACHER

Friedrich Schleiermacher (1768–1834) is generally considered the most important Protestant theologian between John Calvin and Karl Barth. He carried out a "Copernican revolution" in theology as consequential as Kant's revolution in philosophy. Schleiermacher's conception of religion and the Christian faith has wide influence and appeal even today, which may be explained partly by the fact that we are still living in a later phase of that Romantic Movement inaugurated by Schleiermacher and his circle at the beginning of the nineteenth century.

Schleiermacher's theology is rightly acknowledged as the most impressive and systematic statement of the Romantic and liberal understanding of the Christian religion. For some this is enough to damn him without further notice. In the twentieth century Schleiermacher became the *bête noire* of the Neo-Orthodox Movement led by Karl Barth and Emil Brunner. The so-called dead end reached by liberal Protestant theology in the years just prior to World War I is traced by the Neo-Orthodox to what they consider the "false start" inaugurated by Schleiermacher one hundred years earlier. However one judges Barth's critique of Schleiermacher's theology, Barth is certainly correct in seeing Schleiermacher as *the* watershed of modern theology.

*See Chapter 10.

Schleiermacher's thoughts on religion emerge naturally out of his own personal history. He was born Friedrich Daniel Ernst Schleiermacher into the family of a Prussian army chaplain. In his teens he attended Moravian schools noted for their fervent Pietism. Although he later found the intellectual atmosphere of these schools too narrow, the experience of these early years was lasting. Later in life he could write:

> It was here that I awoke for the first time to the consciousness of the relation of man to a higher world. . . . Here it was that that mystic tendency developed itself, which has been of so much importance to me, and has supported and carried me through all the storms of skepticism. Then it was only germinating; now it has attained its full development, and I may say that after all I have passed through I have become a Moravian again, only of a higher order.[41]

In 1787 Schleiermacher entered the University of Halle—despite his father's protestations. Here he read Kant and Spinoza, and in the next few years his imagination was exposed to a whole new world completely foreign to the parochial Moravian piety. Schleiermacher's imaginative powers did not fully emerge, however, until he went to Berlin in 1796 and soon attached himself to a new literary society that included many writers who were soon to become the leaders of the German Romantic movement. Chief among these persons was Friedrich Schlegel. Schlegel and Henrietta Herz, whose salon Schleiermacher attended almost daily, recognized Schleiermacher's brilliance, tutored him in literature and the arts, and encouraged him to write. Schlegel's prodding and Schleiermacher's own religious unrest led to his first literary effort in 1799. In that year he published *On Religion: Speeches Addressed to Its Cultured Despisers.* It served as both an apology for his own religious views and vocation and as a critique of his cultured friends' conception of the religious life. The success of the book led to the publication of *The Soliloquies* the following year (1800). *The Soliloquies* is Schleiermacher's "Confession" and represents the quintessence of the Romantic spirit. In this book Schleiermacher calls upon people to accept their unique place in the sphere of humanity and to develop their own individual spirit to the full.

The early Berlin years ended, nevertheless, in anguish when Schleiermacher fell in love with Eleanor Grunow, wife of a Berlin clergyman. A strong sense of duty made Eleanor stay with the husband she did not love and renounce Schleiermacher forever. In 1804 he left Berlin and became a professor of theology at the University of Halle. For the next few years he poured his energies into lectures and writing—on almost every subject in the theological curriculum. In 1809 he was called back to Berlin as preacher at the Holy Trinity Church. That same year, at the age of forty, he married Henriette von Willich, the widow of an old friend.

In 1811 Schleiermacher was offered the chair of theology at the University of Berlin. This marked a new era in his life. He now began to give proof of his creative and organizing power as a theologian. The crowning achievement of these years was his theological masterpiece, *The Christian Faith,* appearing in two parts in 1821 and 1822 and in a revised second edition in 1830. His other lectures and prospective books were not published before his death in February 1834. Later, students and friends compiled his literary remains which today comprise over thirty volumes of books, lectures, sermons, and letters.

Schleiermacher's contribution to modern theology and his own theological development is best seen in his two greatest books, *On Religion,* the product of his youthful, Romantic period, and *The Christian Faith,* the crown of his maturity. In both of these works, Schleiermacher developed revolutionary interpretations—in the first work, a new conception of religion; in the second, a new interpretation of Christian theology.

The Speeches on Religion

Perhaps the foremost contribution of Romanticism to modern religious thought is its attempt to establish the nature and warrants of religious belief on an entirely new foundation. Chief among these attempts at reconstruction was that of Schleiermacher in his speeches *On Religion.* Schleiermacher wished to show the educated, the cultured, of his own time that what they despised and rejected in religion was not the essence of religion at all. What they considered religion was, for

Schleiermacher, the mere external and dispensable husk concealing the real essence of religion. The "externals" of religion are the product of what Coleridge and Schleiermacher would call "the handiwork of the calculating understanding." As Wordsworth was to complain, "our meddling intellect / Misshapes the beauteous forms of things;—/ We murder to dissect." This dissected corpse, this work of our "meddling intellect," is what we mistakenly identify as religion. Schleiermacher calls upon his friends to turn away from such an external, intellectual view.

> What else can they be, these systems of theology, these theories of the origin and the end of the world, these analyses of the nature of an incomprehensible Being, wherein everything runs to cold argufying . . . this is certainly not the character of religion. If you have only given attention to these dogmas and opinions, therefore, you do not yet know religion itself, and what you despise is not it. Why have you not penetrated deeper to find the kernel of this shell?[42]

Schleiermacher is astonished at the easy ignorance by which true religion is obscured because of the failure to penetrate beneath externals.

> Why do you not regard the religious life itself, the first of those pious exaltations of the mind in which all other known activities are set aside or almost suppressed and the whole soul is dissolved *in the immediate feeling of the Infinite and Eternal?* In such moments the disposition you pretend to despise reveals itself in primordial and visible form. He only who has studied and truly known man in these emotions can rediscover religion in those outward manifestations.[43] (Italics added.)

Schleiermacher also wishes to reject all attempts to define or defend religion on utilitarian or hedonistic grounds.

> Yet you need not fear that I shall betake myself in the end to that common device of representing how necessary religion is for maintaining justice and order in the world. Nor shall I remind you of an all-seeing eye, nor of the unspeakable short-sightedness of human management, nor the narrow bounds of human

power to render help. Nor shall I say how religion is a faithful friend and useful stay of morality, how it makes the struggle with self and the perfecting of goodness much easier for weak men. . . . To recommend religion by such means would only increase the contempt to which it is at present exposed.[44]

If religion cannot justify itself in terms of its own inherent value, then it is not worth bothering about, for "what is loved and honoured only on account of some extraneous advantage may be needful, but it is not in itself necessary."[45] But this is not Schleiermacher's view of the matter, for he contends that religion or piety is both a unique faculty and, in and of itself, of indispensable worth to the human spirit.

Having set the stage for his defense, Schleiermacher turns in the second Speech to define what he conceives to be the true nature of religion. Customarily we think of religion as either "a way of thinking, a faith, a peculiar way of contemplating the world" or as "a way of acting, a peculiar desire and love, a special kind of conduct and character." That is, we tend to think of religion from either the theoretical (metaphysical) or practical (ethical) point of view. The orthodox rationalists and Hegel, Schleiermacher's more famous colleague at Berlin, identified religion with theoretical knowledge; the Deists and Kant equated religion with morality. But this is to reduce religion to something else and therefore to make religion itself unnecessary. Religion "must be something different from a mixture of opinions about God and the world, and of precepts for one life or two." "*Piety,*" Schleiermacher retorts sharply, "*cannot be an instinct craving for a mess of metaphysical and ethical crumbs.*"[46] (Italics added.) Religion resigns at once all claims on anything that belongs either to theoretical science or morality. Take, for example, our scientific knowledge.

> However high you go; though you pass from the laws to the Universal Lawgiver, in whom is the unity of all things; though you allege that nature cannot be comprehended without God, *I would still maintain that religion has nothing to do with this knowledge, and that quite apart from it, its nature can be known. Quantity of knowledge is not quality of piety. Piety can gloriously display itself, both with originality and indi-*

viduality, in those to whom this kind of knowledge is not original.[47] (Italics added.)

If religion were really the highest knowledge, then reason or the scientific method would be the appropriate organ for its attainment. Religion or piety would be acquired by study, and the most knowledgeable would also be the most pious. Therefore, says Schleiermacher, "I cannot hold religion to be the highest knowledge, or indeed, knowledge at all."

Neither is religion to be confused with morality. In fact,

> *religion by itself does not urge men to activity at all.* If you could imagine it implanted in a man quite alone . . . the man, according to what we have said, would not act, *he would only feel.*[48] (Italics added.)

According to Schleiermacher, psychology teaches us that there are three essential elements in all mental life: perception, feeling, and activity. Perception issues in knowledge; activity in the conduct of the moral life; feeling is the peculiar faculty of the religious life. Hence, says Schleiermacher, "only when piety takes its place alongside of science and practice, as a necessary, an indispensable third, as their natural counterpart . . . will the common field be altogether occupied and human nature . . . complete."[49]

For Schleiermacher, feeling is the unique element of the religious life; religion is essentially *feeling*. What Schleiermacher means by feeling is not entirely clear, especially as he uses the term in his earlier writings. It is certain, however, that he is not speaking of feeling as a purely psychological emotion. As Paul Tillich has said in reference to Schleiermacher, feeling may be subjective, but it is also the impact of the universe upon us and the universe is not subjective! Schleiermacher states that feeling is, first of all, an "*immediate self-consciousness.*" This phrase bears some analysis.

By *immediate* Schleiermacher means that religious feeling is not derived, not the product of ratiocination—it is an immediate *intuition*. But it is also a special kind of intuition—that of the self present to the self as a unique, underived unity or identity. The feeling or intuition of immediate self-consciousness

which issues in the uniquely *religious feeling* is, furthermore, "the immediate consciousness of the universal existence of all finite things, *in and through the Infinite, and of all temporal things in and through the Eternal. . . . It is to have life and to know life in immediate feeling, only as such an existence in the Infinite and Eternal.*"[50] (Italics added.)

Schleiermacher, then, does not mean that all feeling is religious as such. It is the intuition of the self "in and through the Infinite"—as mysteriously posited and dependent: "The sum total of religion is to feel that, in its highest unity, all that moves us in feeling is one . . . to feel, that is to say, that our being and living is a being and living in and through God."[51] This does not mean that God must be present as a distinct concept or object. All healthy feelings are pious insofar as they are the result of the operation of God on us "by means of the operation of the world upon us." It is also important to keep in mind that by such a "feeling for the Infinite" Schleiermacher is not advocating a state of mystical absorption. The "Infinite," as Schleiermacher uses the term, simply means feeling the infinity of existence in the concrete world "upon us" and in relation to us. This feeling for the infinite through our experience of the world is the primordial means of God's operation upon us—whether or not this feeling issues in thought or action. It was only later, in *The Christian Faith,* that Schleiermacher was able to give greater clarity to his definition of religion by speaking of it as the feeling of absolute dependence.

> The common element in all diverse expressions of piety, by which these are conjointly distinguished from all other feelings, or in other words, the self-identical essence of piety is this: the consciousness of absolute dependence, or, which is the same thing, of being in relation with God.[52]

Having defined the essence of religion, Schleiermacher then turns to a discussion of how it is to be discovered and cultivated. First, one can discover and cultivate the peculiar feeling for the Infinite in nature "which is to many the first and only temple of the Godhead . . . the inmost sanctuary of religion." But emotions evoked by nature are ambiguous. Schleiermacher is not unmindful that nature is also, in Bertrand Russell's words, "the

trampling march of unconscious power." The sense
of the whole must then "be found chiefly within our
own minds, and from thence transferred to corpo-
real nature."[53]

One thing is clear—and that is that no person is
religious as a result of acquiring knowledge of doctrine or principles of action. Such individuals "have
memory and imitation," but they do not have religion. "They have no ideas of their own from which
formulas might be known, so they must learn them
by rote, and the feelings which they would have
accompanying them are copies."[54] True piety can
issue only from one's own original, indubitable feelings and not from the pale descriptions of the feelings of others.

If this is the true character and source of religion,
whence come those dogmas and doctrines that are
so widely considered the essence of religion? "They
are," Schleiermacher replies,

> the result of the contemplation of feeling. . . . The
> conceptions that underlie these propositions are noth-
> ing but general expressions for definite feelings. . . .
> They are not necessary for religion itself, scarcely even
> for communicating religion . . . but when feeling is
> made the subject of reflection and comparison they are
> absolutely unavoidable.[55]

Doctrines are the product of reflection on feelings, but just because one holds certain religious
ideas does not necessarily make one a religious person. Take, for example, the belief in an inspired
sacred book such as the Bible.

> Every sacred writing is in itself a glorious produc-
> tion, a speaking monument from the heroic time of re-
> ligion, but, through a servile reverence, it would be-
> come merely a mausoleum, a monument that a great
> spirit once was there, but is now no more. . . . Not
> every person has religion who believes in a sacred writ-
> ing, but only the man who has a lively and immediate
> understanding of it, *and who, therefore, so far as he him-
> self is concerned, could most easily do without it.*[56] (Italics
> added.)

The same is true of those first articles of any religious belief—God and immortality. The ideas of
God or immortality may, in the case of any individ-

ual, be badly or vaguely conceived. Some conceive
of God in grossly anthropomorphic fashion, while
those who seek to avoid such a conception often
tend toward a vague Pantheism.

> Nothing seems to me less fitting than for the ad-
> herents of the former view [the anthropomorphists] to
> charge with godlessness those who, in dread of this an-
> thropomorphism, take refuge in the other, or for the
> adherents of this latter view [the pantheists] to make
> the humanness of the idea of God a ground for charg-
> ing the adherents of the former with idolatry, or, for
> declaring their piety void.[57]

It doesn't matter what conceptions a person adheres
to, for piety may be, nay *is,* better than ideas. Ideas
are never the sign of a perfect or imperfect religion.
It is "the manner in which the Deity is present to a
man in feeling [that] is decisive of the worth of his
religion, not the manner, always inadequate, in
which it is copied in idea."[58]

A corollary of all this is that because religion has
to do with the manner of a person's innermost feelings, it cannot be taught.

> All that the activity and art of one man can do for
> another is to communicate conceptions to be the basis
> of thoughts. . . . Our opinions and doctrines we can
> indeed communicate, if we have words and our hear-
> ers have the comprehending power of the understand-
> ing. But we know very well that these things are only
> shadows of our religious emotions, and if our pupils
> do not share our emotions, even though they do un-
> derstand the thought, they have no possession that can
> truly repay their toil. This retreat into oneself, there to
> perceive oneself, cannot be taught.[59]

A person's engagement in the everyday world of
getting and spending, Coleridge's world of the
understanding, does not allow that person the calm
moments needed for "retreat into oneself" for
undisturbed contemplation. But it is only in such
moments of repose that the religious feelings can be
cultivated.

> A religious man must be reflective, his sense must
> be occupied in the contemplation of himself. Being
> occupied with the profoundest depths, he abandons

meanwhile all external things, intellectual as well as physical, leaving them to be the great aim of the researches of the people of understanding. . . . Hence it comes that, from of old, all truly religious characters have had a mystical trait, and that all imaginative natures . . . have at least some stirrings of piety.[60]

Here Schleiermacher touches the profoundly mystical and imaginative tendencies in Romanticism. Like Rousseau before him, Schleiermacher encourages each individual to give full rein to the development of his or her own individuality, to one's own imagination and feeling. And yet, like his fellow Romantics, Schleiermacher emphasizes our social nature. Deeply felt *individual* experience issues in a sense of common bond with all beings. Schleiermacher would concur with Wordsworth's sentiments, expressed in "Lines upon a seat . . . ,"

> that he who feels contempt
> For any living thing, hath faculties
> Which he has never used; that thought with
>   him
> Is in its infancy. The man whose eye
> Is ever on himself doth look on one,
> The least of Nature's works, one who might
>   move
> The wise man to that scorn which wisdom
>   holds
> Unlawful ever. O be wiser, thou!
> Instructed that true knowledge leads to love.[61]

For Schleiermacher, the deeper our personal life, the more we will "endeavor to become conscious of and to exhibit the true relation of our own life to the common nature of man."[62] Religion begins in the innermost recesses of the individual, but it is essentially social, for that is our nature. Each individual's deeply felt religious sentiments cry out to be shared.

Schleiermacher recommends, however, that the cultivation of religion in association with others not be attempted within too wide a circle but quickened in "the more familiar conversation of friendship or the dialogue of love, where glance and action are clearer than words."[63] There is, nevertheless, a place for the common worship of God where all peoples of like spirit can assemble. Schleiermacher depicts such a communion in language that reflects his own Moravian piety:

> Would that I could depict to you the rich, the superabundant life in this city of God, when the citizens assemble, each full of native force seeking liberty of utterance and full at the same time of holy desire to apprehend and appropriate what others offer. When one stands out before the others he is neither justified by office nor by compact. . . . It is the free impulse of his spirit, the feeling of heartfelt unanimity and completest equality. . . . He comes forward to present to the sympathetic contemplation of others his own heart as stirred by God, and, by leading them into the region of religion where he is at home, would infect them with his own feeling.[64]

In such a society the usual distinction between priest and layperson is transcended, for each is equally capable of expressing some rich experience of that religious feeling which is boundless in its individuality. For this very reason a communion of kindred spirits will always reflect diversity, but it will be a manifoldness within an organic whole. No individual or group, however, would seek to bring all others into some single, definite *form* of religion— none would adhere to that "awful watchword, 'No salvation save with us.' " There is, then, no proselytizing.

> The society of the pious . . . is occupied purely with mutual communication, and subsists only among persons already having religion of some kind. How can it be their business to change the minds of those who already profess to have a definite religion. . . . The religion of this society as such is simply the collective religion of all the pious. As each one sees it in others it is infinite and no single person can fully grasp it. . . . If any man, therefore, has any share in religion, it matters not what, would it not be a mad proceeding for the society to rend from him that which suits his nature? And how would they cultivate persons to whom religion generally is still strange?[65]

Schleiermacher is quite aware that the Church he is describing is the ideal Church, the Church triumphant. Nevertheless, it is the Church as it was meant to be and is whenever it is true to its real nature. The empirical and militant Church fails to be a true Church for many reasons. Chief among them, of course, is the fact that the Church does not reveal the "free inspiration that is proper to religion" but a "school-mastering, mechanical nature" which employs "creeds which are naturally last in religious communication, to stimulate what should properly precede them."[66] A further reason for the failure of the Church is its union with, and subservience to, the state. "As soon as a prince declared a church to be a community with special privileges, a distinguished member of the civil world, the corruption of that church was begun and almost irrevocably decided."[67] The state pollutes the pure spiritual fellowship of the Church by introducing its own special interests into the spiritual society.

Schleiermacher calls upon the Church to preserve its uniquely spiritual calling. He believed this could be done if it gave only a secondary role to creedal subscription, if it minimized the distinction between priest and laity, if it did not confuse unity with uniformity, and if it remained free of all external interests, which would be impossible in any union with the civil state.

In the final Speech Schleiermacher turns from a consideration of the Church as a pure spiritual fellowship to the question of the plurality of religions. Here he reveals himself once again as a true Romantic and a vigorous opponent of the rationalist conception of religion. He begins by affirming that, contrary to rationalist doctrine, the multiplicity of the positive religions is based upon the very nature of religion.

> The whole of religion is nothing but the sum of all relations of man to God, apprehended in all the possible ways in which any man can be immediately conscious in his life. In this sense there is but one religion. . . . Yet all men will not by any means apprehend them in the same way, but quite differently. Now this difference alone is felt and alone can be exhibited. . . . As long as we occupy a place there must be in these relations of man to the whole a nearer and a farther, which will necessarily determine each feeling differently in each life. Again, as long as we are individuals, every man has greater receptiveness for some religious experiences and feelings than for others.[68]

Religion always exhibits itself in some definite shape. There is no such thing as religion in general. Here Schleiermacher is critical of the abstract and unhistorical conception of religion held by the Deists. Such a natural religion "is usually so much refined away, and has such metaphysical and moral graces, that little of the peculiar character of religion appears."[69] Religion is by its very nature concrete and particular, and only those who "pitch their camp in some such positive form, have any fixed abode and . . . any well-earned right of citizenship in the religious world."

Schleiermacher does not mean that every religious person must affiliate with one of the existing sects or forms of religion. "It is only necessary that his religion be developed in himself characteristically and definitely"—that is, that it concretely reflect a religious sense suitable to the individual's own nature. However, most religious revelations reflect a feeling that is "great and common" and not merely idiosyncratic and personal. Thus "most men, following their nature, will belong to an existing form, and there will be only a few whom none suffices."

Those who advocate a universal natural religion and reproach the positive religions because their adherents abide by a certain sectarian uniformity have, in fact, a uniformity of their own—"the uniformity of indefiniteness." Schleiermacher observes that the resistance to "the positive and arbitrary" is nothing but resistance to "the definite and real."

> If a definite religion may not begin with an original fact, it cannot begin at all. There must be a common ground for selecting some one religious element and placing it at the center, and this ground can only be a fact. And if a religion is not to be definite, it is not a religion at all, for religion is not a name to be applied to loose, unconnected impulses.[70]

Schleiermacher counsels his readers:

> Go back, then, if you are in earnest about beholding religion in its definiteness, from this enlightened natural religion to those despised positive religions. There everything appears active, strong, and secure.[71]

At the conclusion of his discussion of the religions, Schleiermacher raises the question of

Christianity and its place in relation to the other positive religions. He considers Christianity to be a deeper, more sublime and universal religion than those positive religions that have preceded and followed it. The sublimity and power of Christianity is, for Schleiermacher, manifest in the peculiar role of its Founder. He sees the truly divine element in Jesus Christ neither in "the purity of his moral teachings," nor in "the individuality of his character," but in the glorious clearness with which the great idea of mediation between God and humanity came to expression in his person. Schleiermacher does not develop his conception of Christ's mediatorial role in any detail in this fifth Speech, but what he does make clear is that there is no evidence that Jesus conceived of himself as the sole mediator between God and humankind. What is central to the Gospels is not the uniqueness of Jesus's person but Jesus's profound *idea* of mediation:

> He [Jesus] never maintained He was the only mediator, the only one in whom His idea actualized itself. All who attach themselves to him and form His Church should also be mediators with Him and through Him. And He never made His school equivalent to His religion, as if His idea were to be accepted on account of His person, and not His person on account of His idea.[72]

A time may come when there is no need of a mediator, when God shall be all in all, but Schleiermacher believes that such a condition lies beyond this changing, corruptible existence. New mediators from God will be required in every new epoch. And even if there are always Christians, Christianity will never claim to be

> the sole type of religion, to rule alone in humanity. *It scorns this autocracy.* . . . As nothing is more irreligious than to demand general uniformity in mankind, so *nothing is more unchristian than to seek uniformity in religion.* . . . Varied types of religion are possible, both in proximity and in combination, and if it is necessary that every type be actualized at one time or another, it is to be desired that, at all times, there should be a dim sense of many religions.[73] (Italics added.)

Schleiermacher concludes *On Religion* with an appeal to all who experience the first traces of the religious feeling "to enter at once into the one indivisible fellowship of the saints, which embraces all religions and in which alone any can prosper."[74]

The historical significance of *On Religion* lies principally in the fact that Schleiermacher reversed the traditional method of proceeding religiously. Religion, according to Schleiermacher, does not emerge out of certain given institutions and doctrines. Rather, doctrines and institutions are the creations of a prior self-consciousness that is natural to human existence. Religion is a unique a priori form of self-consciousness that should not be confused with either moral or scientific knowledge. Related to this discovery of the religious feeling prior to all thought is Schleiermacher's sense of religion as a historical, social phenomenon which can best be described in terms of an empirical or experiential representation of a community's self-consciousness at a given time. Here we can see a similarity between Schleiermacher and Herder's historicist conception of religion. Such an experiential and historical conception of religion was something relatively new, and Schleiermacher sought to apply this approach systematically in his description of the Christian religion in his great work, *The Christian Faith*.

The Christian Religious Affections

Dogmatics, or the elucidation of "the Christian religious affections as set forth in speech," can never, according to Schleiermacher, be speculative and abstract. *Dogmatics is the formulation in language of the prior Christian feelings.* Hence it presupposes the Christian community, the Church, and is only meant for that Christian community which shares these common religious affections. Theology is thus conceived of as essentially confessional, not apologetic. It is principally an exercise in self-analysis on the part of the Christian community at a given time.

As we have learned, Schleiermacher believes that religion should be distinguished from all other human feelings by the consciousness of absolute dependence—and that the several religions have historically developed this consciousness in different ways. Schleiermacher defines the unique character of the Christian faith in the following way:

> Christianity is a monotheistic faith belonging to the teleological [moral] type of religion, and is essentially distinguished from other such faiths by the fact that in it everything is related to the redemption accomplished by Jesus of Nazareth.[75]

All Christian doctrines are determined by reference to the consciousness of redemption accomplished by Jesus. Thus, it is impossible for Christian theology to begin with natural reason or a speculative metaphysics, since it must begin with the Christian experience of redemption in Jesus. Schleiermacher's theology is then fundamentally Christo-centric in that the Christian's God-consciousness always comes to realization in the person of Jesus Christ as the Redeemer—as *Christus pro nobis*.

According to Schleiermacher, we can never know God as He is in Himself—but only as He is known in relation to us. God cannot possibly be known as an independent object, out there somewhere, but *only in relation to our own self-consciousness*. However, this is not to confuse self-consciousness and God, but only to say that

> any proclamation of God which is to be operative *upon and within us can only express God in His relation to us;* and this is not an infrahuman ignorance concerning God, but the essence of human limitedness in relation to Him.[76] (Italics added.)

All the attributes of God discussed in a Christian dogmatics will be those which express the various ways in which the Christian feeling of absolute dependence is referred to God.

When we consider the ways in which we feel our dependence on God, there are two primary modes of apprehending this dependence: First, God's being as felt in our experience of the totality of the world or nature; and, second, the divine attributes as related to our consciousness of sin and redemption. In the first instance, we can speak of God's eternity as "the absolutely timeless causality of God, which conditions not only all that is temporal, but time itself as well."[77] Likewise, the omnipresence of God

is understood as "the absolutely spaceless causality of God, which conditions not only all that is spatial but space itself."[78] In similar fashion Schleiermacher deals with such traditional attributes of God as omnipotence and omniscience.

Christians do not become conscious of the divine causality only, or primarily, in the apprehension of the natural world but principally in their sense of dependence on God in the experience of sin and redemption. The fact that Christians trace the annulment of sin by redemption to the divine causality is a fact that we may premise as given universally in the Christian consciousness.[79] The primary attributes of God which we relate to our consciousness of sin are God's holiness and justice. To speak of God as holy and just is to speak of that aspect of the divine causality which involves the activity of a person's conscience. Conscience simply apprehends God's relation to the world as morally legislative.

It is impossible to outline here Schleiermacher's whole systematic treatment of the Christian doctrine of God. Suffice it to say that each attribute is related to a feeling that is integral to the Christian experience of dependence. For this reason, Schleiermacher did not include any consideration of the doctrine of the Trinity in the main body of *The Christian Faith* but discussed it in an appendix as an addendum to the doctrine of God. The reason for this is that he did not consider the Trinity as immediately given in the Christian consciousness. This is not to say that he thought the doctrine unimportant. Schleiermacher recognized that behind the metaphysical abstraction lay a profound religious truth—namely, that the whole of Christianity is dependent upon the reality of the union of the divine with the human, both in the person of Jesus Christ and in the union of the Divine Spirit and the Church. Nevertheless, the Trinity is not immediately given in the Christian consciousness of dependence, hence is not of *primary* concern to faith.

At the center of Schleiermacher's reconception of the Christian faith is his understanding of human sin and the redemptive work of Jesus Christ. Therefore, some analysis of his conception of these matters is necessary. Knowledge of sin, according to Schleiermacher, is not derived from a reading of

Scripture but is intimately bound up with our consciousness. Specifically, we have consciousness of sin whenever our God-consciousness "determines our self-consciousness as pain." Sin is the experience of our innate God-consciousness being hindered by the conflict between our fleshly, sensuous nature and our higher spiritual nature.

> If in any particular moment under examination God has formed part of our self-consciousness, but this God-consciousness has not been able to permeate the other active elements therein . . . then sin and the consciousness of sin are simultaneous, and the sensuous self-consciousness by reason of its having been gratified is affected with pleasure, but the higher, owing to the impotence of the God-consciousness, with pain.[80]

Here Schleiermacher conceives of sin, much as does Augustine, as a disorder and confusion of our loves, whereby we place our love in that which is temporal and worldly rather than in God and the eternal.

Sin, then, is an arrestment of the God-consciousness due to the preponderance of the "flesh" over the "spirit" and is accompanied by a sense of discontent and instability for which Christians feel responsible. We are free to sin, and this very freedom implies responsibility, guilt, and misery. However, we are not free and able to overcome our sin. In fact, for Schleiermacher, it is Christ as Second Adam, as the true norm or archetype of human nature, who convicts us of our sin and makes us sensitive to how, through our sensuousness, we have obscured our God-consciousness.

The other side of the coin is that consciousness of sin, which comes into sharpest relief in the light of Christ, true humanity, has its antithesis in the grace and blessedness which proceeds from the person and work of this same Jesus Christ. Sin must always be seen, then, in relation to its antithesis, grace, for sin is nothing but the privation of true blessedness.

Though Schleiermacher stressed the point that we must always come to a personal consciousness of sin through individual experience, he was not unmindful of the social character of sin. We are communal beings, and our life is intimately bound up with the life of the community and race. Sin is always in a social matrix, being caused by the sins of others and in turn causing others to sin. However, Schleiermacher refuses to accept the ancient conception of sin as due to the curse placed upon the first man, Adam, because of his disobedience, and which has been transmitted through Adam to the generations of his progeny. Such a conception is unacceptable because, first, it would require that we conceive of human nature as very different before and after Adam's fall, a belief that destroys the unity of the race and its religious consciousness. Second, for Schleiermacher, it is unthinkable to hold that the action of a *single* individual could so completely change the whole human race.

In place of the old myth of Adam, Schleiermacher pictures the human race from the Creation as possessing a sinful propensity. Humanity's original perfection was not a static state of innocence; rather it was the latent human potentiality or predisposition in all to develop a full God-consciousness. However, concomitant with this latent perfection is the universal propensity of human nature to sin and thereby to fail to bring this God-consciousness to fruition. Humanity's latent perfection and disposition to sin are both equally "original." But the very fact that our original latent perfection and predisposition to sin are equal means, in Schleiermacher's view, that righteousness cannot *by itself* triumph, for

> from the concomitance and development of the two there could issue no active righteousness properly so called, but at best a vacillation between vitiated spiritual efforts and increasing and fully matured sin.[81]

Having discarded the mythical conception of an actual First Adam, Schleiermacher is faced with the question of how persons come to an acknowledgment of their sinful fallenness. Schleiermacher's answer is that the power to recognize our sin comes not from Adam but from Jesus Christ. As R. R. Niebuhr has commented,

> If we adhere in our reasoning to the logic of *The Christian Faith,* we not only *may* dispense with this mythical Adam as the mirror of true righteousness, but we *must* do so, for while each man's self-consciousness belongs indefeasibly to himself, the power which raises it toward the equilibrium of blessedness comes

not from the storehouse of the imagination alone but from the ever renewed historical communication of the life and light that originates in the preaching of Jesus of Nazareth.[82]

The work of redemption comes only from outside the individual, issuing from the person of Jesus Christ by means of the self-communication of his unique God-consciousness. Consistent with his method, Schleiermacher holds that Christ is known only through his benefits (his work) and that his effect upon us is the impress of the special dignity of his person, his unique God-consciousness. Christ's God-consciousness was perfectly realized in that, along with the growth of his natural powers, his God-consciousness gained perfect control of his entire person. In this sense we can speak of Jesus's perfection and sinlessness.

The only explanation of this historical realization of God-consciousness is that it was a *miraculous manifestation* of the ideal of humanity as the subject of a perfect God-consciousness. Hence, Jesus Christ is best understood as the full historical realization of archetypal humanity, the Second or true Adam. He embodies concretely the new human race and thus becomes for us the exemplar of God's will for us. Jesus Christ, therefore, is the mirror in which we see our true image and measure. But more than that, for Christ is not principally an example to be followed; he is the redeemer who gives a new impetus and power to humanity "in the flesh." It is wrong, therefore, to contend, as some have, that Schleiermacher's understanding of the work of Christ is reducible to a conception of Jesus as a moral example. Such a conception was unacceptable to Schleiermacher because it implied (1) the possibility that humanity could of itself establish such a conception of absolute perfection and (2) that humans have the power to deliver themselves from the control of sensuous affections.

Schleiermacher believed that the religious self-consciousness infected by sin could not of itself produce the exemplar of perfected humanity as it is given to us in the person of Jesus Christ. Here Schleiermacher takes exception to Kant's notion of the exemplary role of Christ set forth in *Religion Within the Limits of Reason Alone.* Schleiermacher wished to stress that humanity does not posit its own exemplar and yet that the Redeemer is exemplary (*Vorbildlichkeit*) in that he stands in a continuum with the rest of the human race—i.e., in solidarity with it, without which there could be no communication of redemption. Christ is the exemplar of perfect human nature in that he is the *medium* for the communication of God's redemptive power. However, the power itself lies beyond human nature and can be appropriated only as a gift. Christ, therefore, is both exemplar and Redeemer. R. R. Niebuhr sums up Schleiermacher's view of the person and work of Christ as exemplar and Redeemer in the following way:

> It is neither the naked power of God that Christ communicates, nor is it merely himself as teacher of a new doctrine about God that Christ proffers to others. What he gives are the power of God in the embodiment of his own ideal humanity and himself as the source from which men may receive that same power. These two aspects of Jesus, which Schleiermacher calls his *Urbildlichkeit* (ideality) and his *Vorbildlichkeit* (exemplarity), cannot be separated. By virtue of the former he is the redeemer; by virtue of the latter he communicates redemption. Therefore, while the *Vorbildlichkeit* or exemplary status of Jesus does not signify his life-giving power as the redeemer appointed eternally by God, it does signify his solidarity with the human race, apart from which there could be no communication of redemption.[83]

The work of Christ in redemption consists in the implanting of the God-consciousness as the dominant principle of life, thereby gaining the victory over the sensuous impulses and ordering human consciousness in such a way that pain and melancholy give way to a new sense of equilibrium and joy, a new attunement of the soul in its relation to God and the world.

For Schleiermacher it was quite natural that the power of Jesus's God-consciousness should result in the formation of a community around him. The Church is that community of persons whose personhood has been formed by the mind of Christ and whose vocation it is to communicate that unique Christian consciousness to those who come in contact with this community. If Schleiermacher's earlier writings reflect at times a too individualistic conception of the religious life, the writings of his maturity reflect a profound awareness of the place of community in the formation of self-consciousness. For Schleiermacher, a person's religious consciousness emerges out of the community life one shares, and therefore the Church is the historical medium of Christ's redemptive work.

It was Schleiermacher's awareness of the mediational role of the community that caused him to reject what he called a "magical" conception of redemption. A magical view is one that denies the necessary mediation of Christ's redemption through an empirical community. It is magical because it posits Jesus's influence as not presently mediated through anything historical and natural. Schleiermacher was responsible for producing a new awareness of the role of the Church in a Protestantism that had become highly individualistic and antiecclesiastical. He also gave new meaning to doctrines and practices, not by defending or reviving old institutional forms, but by showing that forms and doctrines are the natural fruit of a community's experience and life together.

Schleiermacher can justly be called the Kant of modern theology, both because of the new beginning which his work marks in the history of theology and because the issues which his theological reconstruction posed are issues that remain at the very center of theological discussion today. As was indicated earlier, the Neo-Orthodox theologians who came to prominence between the 1920s and 1950s believed that Protestant theology had reached a cul-de-sac due, in large measure, to the fact that it had followed the path mapped out by Schleiermacher in *The Christian Faith.* Karl Barth sees the distinctive character of Schleiermacher's work and its subsequent influence as grounded in his desire to be both a Christian *and* a modern man and that inevitably the emphasis on "human consciousness" and experience led Schleiermacher to take a position *above* Christianity. In other words, Schleiermacher approached his task in the serene confidence that he knew what Christianity was and that neither the Bible nor Church dogma could set any bounds to his freedom in the work of reconstruction.

Now it is true that with Schleiermacher theology undergoes a radical transformation in its notion of

theological authority. But it would be erroneous to say that for Schleiermacher the Bible and the Church no longer are theologically normative, for we know that Schleiermacher conceived of doctrine as the true expression of the Christian consciousness *in the Church* at a given time, and that such a consciousness must be a genuine expression of that piety which appears in the New Testament. Nevertheless, for Schleiermacher the real locus of authority does lie in the religious experience, for the religious person has his or her "self-consciousness" as the ultimate court of appeal. All external evidences and authorities are finally of no account if they are not confirmed experientially in the religious consciousness of the individual. But that consciousness is "a taste for the infinite," marked by a profound sense of dependence, need, and receptivity to the "other" that in the Christian consciousness is mediated through the Christian community. Therefore, it is questionable whether Barth is correct in saying that for Schleiermacher the reality of Christianity becomes imprisoned in a colossal self-consciousness. Schleiermacher has been charged by others besides Barth with fathering a form of religious subjectivism that finds its inevitable working-out in the psychological reduction of all religious beliefs—for example, in the writings of Ludwig Feuerbach. That is to say, with the study of humanity's own subjective aspirations, fears, and ideals as they become objectified in theological ideas and institutions.

Related to the charge of subjectivism is the further levy of agnosticism. Schleiermacher held that God is apprehended only in feeling and that we can never know God as he is *in himself.* Thus feeling serves Schleiermacher much the same way that the practical reason served Kant. All attempts at knowing God in himself by means of scientific or metaphysical analysis are doomed to failure. God is known only through a subjective "moral want" or, in the case of Schleiermacher, a feeling of absolute dependence—i.e., God in relation to our needs and feelings. Schleiermacher's awareness of the limits of our knowledge of God, like Kant's, may have played its part in the growth of a more thoroughgoing agnosticism later in the century, but it is quite misleading to refer to Schleiermacher as agnostic. That he denied access to knowledge of God as he is *in himself* is quite true, but he was, if anything, excessively confident that one can come to know God in his relation to us.

Schleiermacher's so-called subjectivism, therefore, needs careful qualification. For him the importance of the Christian community in the forming of self-consciousness has already been mentioned. For Schleiermacher there never was person-formation in a vacuum. It was always in the context of a community, through the mediation of other persons. Self-consciousness, then, is never entirely subjective, for it is always formed through the encounter with others who can serve both to illuminate and to check our own experience. Some would insist, all the same, that Schleiermacher gave too large a place to religious experience in his reconstruction of Christian doctrine, to the point of disregarding such other sources as biblical exegesis and doctrinal tradition.

That Schleiermacher's reconstruction of Christian faith left serious questions concerning the doctrine of God, sin, Christ, and redemption was widely acknowledged in his own time as well as today. What is more significant, however, is that Schleiermacher saw the necessity of theological reconstruction and had the courage and systematic power to carry it through. At the center of his reconstruction is the concentration on experience as the starting point for theology. After Schleiermacher, theology no longer felt obliged to vindicate itself at the court of science or of Kant's practical reason. Theology now had a new sense of its own self-authentication in experience, for, while it could no longer claim to be scientifically verified, its truth was now to be found in the symbolic rendering of the experiences of the life of feelings. Here Schleiermacher established a method followed to the present day by the liberal schools of "empirical" and "experiential" theology.

This radical change in the fundamental conception of theology and its foundation led to a more open and critical attitude toward the Bible and the creeds. It resulted in a deeper historical and psychological understanding of both Scripture and tradition but, at the same time, led to a purging of all doctrine and practice that failed to find any place in the Christian experience of redemption—e.g., the virgin birth, the Trinity, the second coming of Christ. Schleiermacher's experiential conception of

religion also gave considerable impetus to the comparative study of religions and to the scientific analysis and classification of religious phenomena—for example, in the work of the twentieth-century historians of religion, Ernst Troeltsch and Rudolf Otto.

Finally, Schleiermacher and his fellow Romantics played a significant role in the demise of the eighteenth-century Deistical conception of God and in overcoming the sharp separation between the natural and supernatural that was common to the eighteenth century. It was the Romantics' rediscovery of the immanence of God in the world of nature and history that made possible once again a more deeply felt personal experience of God. God was no longer banished from the world, remote and inaccessible, but was experienced as present in the most common, prosaic events of everyday life. All nature was once again revelatory of the divine, for

> Earth's crammed with heaven,
> And every common bush afire with God. . . .
> (Elizabeth Barrett Browning)

The development of the conception of divine immanence and its significance for a reinterpretation of traditional Christianity was, however, to be carried out much more rigorously and systematically by a colleague of Schleiermacher at Berlin—G. W. F. Hegel. It is to Hegel and the school of Christian Idealism that we will turn after examining Horace Bushnell, an important American theologian whose leading ideas also reflect the attraction of Romanticism.

HORACE BUSHNELL

European Romanticism's deepest influence on American religion was on New England Transcendentalism, seen most prominently in the writings of its leader, Ralph Waldo Emerson. Yet its effect was also felt on more traditional Christian theology, and this is best exemplified in the writings of the popular and revered Congregational minister Horace Bushnell (1802–1876).

The intellectual sources of Bushnell's theology are diverse, and they include New England Puritan theology and the impress of his teachers at Yale,

Josiah Gibbs and Nathaniel William Taylor, the latter a leader of the Second Great Awakening in New England. Bushnell was also influenced, however, whether directly or indirectly, by German Romantic writers, including Schleiermacher. But it is in Coleridge's *Aids to Reflection* that Bushnell found his deepest intellectual and spiritual kinship. In later life he was reported to have said that "he was more indebted to Coleridge than to any extra Scriptural author." And, as we will see, Coleridgean themes, even the echoes of his words, abound in Bushnell's most important writings.[84]

Horace Bushnell was born in rural Litchfield, Connecticut. His parents were members of the Congregational Church in New Preston, and in 1822 he joined that church. In 1823 he entered Yale College, graduating in 1827. He then tried teaching and journalism, only to return to Yale in 1829 to study law. By then Yale was aflame with a new religious awakening; and it was able even to vanquish young Bushnell's longstanding intellectual doubts about certain Christian doctrines. In words that were prophetic of a theme of his later theological writings, he is reported to have said in the midst of the revival:

> When the preacher touches the Trinity and when he shatters it to pieces, I am at all four winds. But I am glad I have a heart as well as a head. . . . My heart says the Bible has a Trinity for me, and I mean to hold by my heart. I am glad a man can do it when there is no other mooring.[85]

Now determined to follow a career of Christian service, Bushnell enrolled in Yale Divinity School in 1831. He then was called to what was to be his only pastorate, the North Congregational Church of Hartford, Connecticut, which he served from 1833 to 1859, when ill health forced him to relinquish his duties. In these years, during which he became a beloved pastor and popular preacher, Bushnell also was active in civic and political affairs, writing and speaking out on slavery, immigration, presidential politics, women's suffrage, and a variety of religious issues. In this period he also produced three of his most important works: *Discourses on Christian Nurture* (1847), *God in Christ* (1849), and *Nature and the Supernatural* (1858). After leaving North

Church, he remained active as a writer and in civic work, having achieved the stature of a revered elder wise man and public servant. The most significant theological accomplishment of Bushnell's later years was his reinterpretation of the classical Christian doctrine of the Atonement, which he published in two related books—*Vicarious Sacrifice* (1866) and *Forgiveness and Law* (1874).

The Nature of Language

The key that explains much of Bushnell's theology is found in his reflections on language. This interest can be traced both to the influence of his Yale tutor, Josiah Gibbs, and to his reading of Coleridge's *Aids to Reflection*. One commentator summarized Bushnell's view of language as follows:

> On the one hand, language was taken to be an appropriate image of the God-world relation. Nature was the "language" of God, the means by which He expresses Himself to other minds. On the other hand, the idea of nature as God's language was immediately borrowed back to provide a model for understanding the nature and limits of human language. As nature expresses God, but is by no means identical with Him, so human language expresses the spirit of man, but in metaphorical terms which are in no sense the literal equivalents of the inner states they express.[86]

Bushnell's fullest discussion of language as it bears on his theological method is found in his "Preliminary Dissertation on the Nature of Language," published as a long (117-page) preface to the addresses included in *God in Christ* (1849). There he describes language as taking two forms: the literal and the figurative or analogical. Literal words are only names that we assign to physical things; figurative language includes all of the words that we use in the world of human thought and spirit. They, too, are the "signs of thoughts to be expressed" and do not literally convey a thought from one mind to another, as we normally assume. "They are," Bushnell explains, "only hints or images, held up before the mind of another, to put *him* on generating or reproducing the same thought." But this could be a facsimile only if the other mind were to contain the same personal contents. This is never possible, however, "hence there will be different measures of understanding and misunderstanding, according to the capacity or incapacity, the ingeniousness or moral obliquity of the receiving party."[87]

It is important to Bushnell that words used in our moral or intellectual discourse never lose their indeterminate character, never settle into a sense "so perfectly unambiguous, that they are to be regarded as literal names." And this is especially critical in theology where it is assumed that words like hope, fear, love, or sin have settled, agreed-upon meanings. Take, for example, the word "sin." Most persons imagine that it names a fixed act or state. Yet

> no two minds ever had the same impression of it. The whole personal history of every man, his acts, his temptations, wants, and repentances; his opinions of God, of law, and of personal freedom; his theory of virtue . . . in fact his whole theology and life will enter into his impression of this word *sin,* to change the quality, and modify the relations of that which it signifies.[88]

The interminable disputes of the theologians are, of course, incontestable proof that, simple as the word "sin" may appear, there is little agreement as to its meaning. And so it is with all the great words associated with theology: God, grace, forgiveness, incarnation, trinity, atonement. They all take on meanings that are deeply embedded in the life-experiences of individuals, their spiritual struggles and their prepossessions, so that each person sees these words "under a color peculiar to himself."[89]

Moreover, words that express our thought and our spiritual being are not only inexact, "they always affirm something which is false, or contrary to the truth intended." Theology, Bushnell reminds us, is naturally conveyed in earthen vessels, yet it offers its "mere pottery as being the truth itself." Theological disputes thus arise because the disputants fail to separate the spiritual kernels of truth from the forms, the husks, in which they are clothed and even fail "to see how the essential truth may clothe itself under forms that are repugnant."[90]

Bushnell further urges consideration of how forms—terms, images, metaphors—must change with changing times and contexts and holds that various verbal and rhetorical forms—poetic, dialectical, definitional, paradoxical, symbolic—must be used to attempt to express the truth, since all representation of our spiritual thought and experience is inexact and inadequate. "Language," he writes,

> will be ever trying to mend its own deficiencies, by multiplying its forms of representation . . . to multiply words or figures, and thus to present the subject on opposite sides or many sides. Thus as form battles form, and one form neutralizes another, all the insufficiencies of words are filled out. . . . Accordingly, we never come so near to a truly well-rounded view of any truth, as when it is offered paradoxically; that is, under contradictions.[91]

Just as the poet often is required to express his or her most inexpressible thoughts and feelings by means of paradox, so the great Christian mysteries of the Incarnation and Trinity often are conveyed in seemingly repugnant and contradictory language.

Bushnell appeals to the genius of the poet Goethe, who spoke in clashing contradictions only to bring out the deep unity and truth in the world's vast multifariousness. How weak and ineffectual Goethe would have been "had he been willing to stay under some one figure, and draw himself out into formal consistency, throwing off none of those bold antagonisms." "What, then," asks Bushnell, "shall we say of Christ and the Gospel of John? If it requires such an array of antagonisms to set forth the true idea of poetry, what does it require to set forth God and redemption?" What should we or the theologians do, for example, "with the trinity, the atonement, the bondage and freedom of sin?" In words reminiscent of Coleridge, Bushnell replies:

> Shall we say, with the infidel, this is all a medley of contradiction—mere nonsense, fit only to be rejected? Shall we take up these bold antagonisms, as many orthodox believers have done, seize upon some one symbol as the real form of the truth, and compel all the others to submit to it; making, thus, as many sects as there are symbols . . . ? Or shall we endeavor, with the Unitarians, to decoct the whole mass of symbol, and draw off the extract into pitchers of our own; fine, consistent, nicely rounded pitchers, which, so far from set-

ting out anywhere toward infinity, we can carry at pleasure by the handle, and definitely measure by the eye? What critic ever thought of handling Goethe in the methods just named? We neither scout his inconsistency, nor drill him into some one of his forms, nor decoct him into forms of our own. But we call him the many-sided great man, we let him stand in his own chosen symbols . . . and do him the greater honor because of the complexity and the magnificent profusion of his creations.[92]

Bushnell's doctrine of language is the groundwork of his understanding of the Bible and its interpretation. The Bible is like Goethe's *oeuvre*. No other book, Bushnell acknowledges, has "so many repugnances, or antagonistic forms of assertion." Yet, whoever truly wants to receive all truth would find in the Bible "the truth-world overhung him as an empyrean of stars, complex, multitudinous, striving antagonistically." Such a person would find his or her "nature flooded with senses, vastnesses, and powers of truth. . . . God's own lawgivers, heroes, poets, historians, prophets, and preachers and doers of righeousness, will bring him their company," giving to the seeker "the most complete and manifold view possible of every truth."[93]

Bushnell's doctrine of language necessarily demands a different view of the Bible and its reading than do the ways of rationalism, whether it be that of the skeptic, the orthodox, or the unitarian. "The scriptures will be more studied than they have been in a different manner—not as a magazine of propositions and mere dialectic entities, but as inspirations and poetic forms of life; requiring also, divine inbreathings and exaltations to us, that we may ascend into their meaning."[94] Christian truth is God coming to expression through language, by his Word—God's love, justice, and compassion. And if it is difficult to reduce a poet of humanity, like Goethe, to a few short formulas, how much more difficult "to transfer the grand poem of salvation, that which expresses God, into a few dull propositions." It ought not to be necessary, then, to "remind the reader of the bible, that religion has a natural and profound alliance with poetry."[95] "Poets are the true metaphysicians, and if there be any complete science of man to come, they must bring it."[96] Christ's teachings, likewise, do not consist of argu-

ments but of living images or parables that "*find us*," as Coleridge truly expressed it.

Doctrines and Creeds

Bushnell's conception of language has obvious implications for his understanding not only of the Bible but of dogma and creeds. In mental science and religion it is contrary to the very nature of language to be dogmatic, since "no such exactness is possible." Due to its proximate and relative character, our language cannot claim the definite status of an algebra or a geometry. The same is true of creeds and catechisms which, though serving a role in the religious life, suffer from the standpoint occupied by their authors. As we pass from age to age, we are naturally brought to a different point, and we see things in a different light. "It is not that truth changes, but that we change. . . . We are different men, living as parts in a different system of things . . . and as our contents and antagonisms are different, we cannot see the same truths in the same forms. It may even be necessary to change the forms, to hold us to the same truths."[97]

Bushnell observes how the phrases used in the older New England Calvinism were now "waxing old" and how they demanded restatement. In the course of time and repetition, the living figure dies out; it settles into a dead literality. And if the language of doctrine or the creed continues in such a condition, it, too, becomes an assent to what is untrue. Therefore, "all formulas of doctrine should be held in a certain spirit of accommodation." Taken in such a spirit, a person then can sincerely assent to most creeds, distinguishing what belongs to the antique form of the truth and the interior spiritual truth itself. For this reason Bushnell was unsympathetic to the Unitarian antipathy against creeds and was quite prepared to accept a great many creedal formulations.

> For when they are subjected to the deepest chemistry of thought, that which descends to the point of relationship between the form of the truth and its interior formless nature, they become, thereupon, so elastic and run so freely into each other, that one seldom need have any difficulty in accepting as many as are offered him.[98]

Because of the inherent difficulties presented by creedal formulas, the best solution is to use one, such as the Apostles' Creed, "that stays by the concrete most faithfully, and carries its doctrine, as far as possible, in a vehicle of fact and of real life." Otherwise, if creeds and systematic dogma must be used, the next best arrangement would be "to allow assent to a great number of such creeds at once; letting them qualify, assist, and mitigate each other," serving as complementary forces and thus keeping us "in the fullest, liveliest, and most many-sided apprehension of the Christian truth."[99] It should be pointed out that Bushnell is not advocating a doctrinal relativism or a pluralism indifferent to the claims of truth. As he says, these various doctrinal formulations serve as "complementary forces"; and out of struggle and analysis can come the more adequate and comprehensive, because multisided, apprehension of the Christian truth.

Christian Comprehensiveness

Bushnell's irenic approach to theology can, using his own term, be called the method of "Christian Comprehensiveness," the title of a critically important essay published in 1848. Bushnell recognized, of course, that every Christian group is liable to error in the expression of its belief; but neither was he an advocate of an easy compromise. What he sought to oppose is the dogmatist and extremist who claims that he or she alone possesses the truth. "A want of catholicity, or comprehensiveness," he writes, "is itself error." For "to see anything partially, or at one pole, is to see it insufficiently, thus in defective forms and proportions." The extreme sectarian is, moreover, "instigated, in part, by evil passions and blinded by false prejudices."[100]

Bushnell, the ecumenist, dwells nevertheless only fleetingly on the exclusive side of sectarianism, since "we may lay it down as true, in general, that all the Christian sects, in their manifold repugnances of doctrine, are only concerned to exhibit the great elemental truths of Christianity . . . some form of truth to maintain."[101] And so we almost never see a dogma, "however monstrous," advanced by any body which, "if it were dissolved and viewed in its contents historically, would not yield some important truth."[102] What is required, then, is to show

that all Christian truths, as humanly expressed, stand in repugnant opposites or extremes and are in need of a deeper comprehension:

> There rises up now a man, or a few men, who looking again at the extreme schools [such as the Unitarians and the confessional Calvinists], begin to ask whether it is not possible to comprehend them. . . . The very thought gives compass or enlargement to the soul in which it is conceived. . . . In this effort to comprehend extremes, it offers no disrespect, but the highest respect, rather, to the great and earnest spirits that have stood for the truth and fought her battles. . . . It is in fact a disciple of the extremes, taking lessons of both, and ceasing not till it has gotten whatever good and whatever truth made their opinions sacred to themselves.[103]

The goal of this great effort is not, then, the achievement of a smooth synthesis; it is the discovery of the kernel of truth that is seeking to be expressed in each and every limited form.

Bushnell conceived the effort of comprehensiveness, in seeking to find the truth embedded in the antagonisms of human thought and religion, "to be the highest and most ingenuous that a human soul can propose." It is a goal that only God, of course, can perfectly realize, and the person who undertakes it "gives some evidence therein of a resemblance to God." Indeed, "a comprehensive character is, in fact, the only really great character possible among men,"[104] the one who is especially cherished by God.

Nature and the Supernatural: Religious Experience

Bushnell's suspicions about religious language and dogma did not cast him in the role of skeptic or Deistical critic of these instruments of the religious life. As a Romantic, he had a firm conviction about religious knowledge, even about the truth of doctrine, for he believed they were grounded in spiritual experience. Acknowledging that his views of language "unquestionably" mitigated "the dogmatic tendencies in religion" and any confidence in "the speculative theologer," he nevertheless called upon the Church to turn the industry of its teachers to "giving a more esthetic character to their studies and theories, and drawing them as much closer to the practical life of religion." The rationalistic theology of New England had declared against the ability of the natural person to understand spiritual things. "It has not been held, as a practical, positive, and earnest Christian truth, that there is a *PERCEP-TIVE POWER* in spiritual life, an unction of the Holy One, which is itself a kind of inspiration—*an immediate, experimental knowledge of God.*"[105] (Italics added.) Here Bushnell is one with Schleiermacher and Coleridge in refusing to separate sharply nature and God or the supernatural. They constitute one, organic spiritual order or system which, for Coleridge and Bushnell especially, is neither Deistical nor Pantheistic. In *Aids to Reflection*, Coleridge had written:

> Nature is the term in which we comprehend all things that are representable in the forms of time and space, and subjected to the relations of cause and effect; and the cause of the existence of which, therefore, is to be sought for perpetually in something antecedent. . . . *It follows, therefore, that whatever originates in its own acts, or in any sense contains in itself the cause of its own state, must be spiritual, and consequently supernatural.*[106] (Italics added.)

In *Nature and the Supernatural*, Bushnell sought to demonstrate the inadequacy of a religion established on purely naturalistic premises, as in the Transcendentalism of the American preacher Theodore Parker. Bushnell endeavors to do so, however, by showing the very unity of nature and the supernatural in the "one system" of God. His object is, as he writes, "to obtain a solid, intellectual footing for the supernatural, evincing not only the compatibility, but the essential complementary relation of nature and the supernatural, as terms included, *ab origine,* in the unity of God's plan." To reverse the terms appropriate to the Romanticism of a Goethe or a Wordsworth, Bushnell's theology can properly be called a "supernatural naturalism."

Christianity is not an historical afterthought of God. Christianity, Bushnell insists,

> even antedates the world of nature, and is "before all things." . . . Instead of coming into the world, as being

no part of the system, or to interrupt and violate the system of things, they all *consist,* come together into a system in Christ, as the center of unity and the head of the universal plan. . . . All which is beautifully and even sublimely expressed in the single word *"con-sist,"* a word that literally signifies *standing together.*[107]

Consistent with the *organic* nature of God's plan and truth, there exists then in the heart of every person an intuitive and aesthetic sense of God's immediacy and reality as a vital power. "We shall delight in truth," writes Bushnell, "more as a concrete, vital nature, incarnated in all fact and symbol round us—a vast, mysterious, incomprehensible power which best we know, when most we love."

Bushnell recognized that his appeal to the aesthetic and experiential grounds of knowledge of God would elicit the charge of mysticism from his orthodox critics. But he patiently reminded them that such censures sadly fail to comprehend the true and essential nature of mysticism itself:

> A mystic is one who finds a secret meaning, both in words and in things back of their common or accepted meaning—some agency of *LIFE,* or *LIVING THOUGHT,* hid under the forms of words and institutions and historical events. . . . Man is designed, in his very nature, to be a partially mystic being; the world to be looked upon as a mystic world. Christ himself revealed a decidedly mystic element in his teaching.[108]

Christian Nurture

Bushnell's doctrine of the unity of nature and the supernatural and his experiential method in theology leads directly to his social and organic conception of both human sin and redemption, or what he calls Christian nurture. God's truth in Christ is not conveyed by occasional divine interruptions but, as Bushnell writes, is "incarnated in all fact and symbol round us"—and especially through the ordinary human channels of words and gestures. This is true of our spiritual nurture whether it be for evil or for good, for sin or for growth in Christ's spirit.

Bushnell's doctrine of the organic solidarity of sin and redemption was occasioned by another controversy between New England orthodoxy and Unitarianism, and it resulted in his first important work, *Discourses on Christian Nurture* (1847), later published in an expanded edition entitled *Christian Nurture* (1861). Many of Bushnell's orthodox colleagues held that to be redeemed before God one had to undergo a rather dramatic conversion experience after one had reached the age of discretion. Sin was conceived as a "total depravity," physically passed on from the First, fallen Adam to his progeny. The Unitarians, on the other hand, considered the notion of a natural depravity to be immoral; in its place they taught a doctrine of the natural goodness of human nature. Bushnell thought both views too abstract and individualistic. They also ran counter to our real experience and the observations of social psychology. Both sin and virtue, Bushnell asserts, are communicated through our ordinary interpersonal relations, especially within the intimate social intercourse of the family, and then in ever-widening circles of human association.

To be "born," for example, is not simply an independent physical act, nor is "re-birth" simply an isolated deliberative act. They are, Bushnell argues, gradual processes of formation that take place in the organic unity of the family, or in the larger family, the Church or Body of Christ. Neither sin nor moral virtue is the result of the child's, or even of the adult's, autonomous choice. In the case of the former, the family's power over the infant's character "is not properly called influence," for that would imply a "persuasive power" exerted purposively with conscious design. But parental power over children is exerted not only when "they teach, encourage, persuade, and govern, but without any purposed control whatever . . . unconsciously and undesignedly—they must do it. Their character, feelings, spirit, and principles must propagate themselves whether they will or not."[109] All such acts of parental control which have metaphysical priority over any deliberative choice by either parent or child Bushnell refers to as "*organic* causes"—which take effect as if they "accrued under the law of simple contagion." "So, too," Bushnell insists, "when the child performs acts of will under parental direction that involve results of character, without knowing or considering that they do, these must be classed in the same manner."[110]

Bushnell uses to advantage his doctrine of "organic causes" to counter the individualistic and abstractly theoretical doctrines of both the "total depravity" and the "essential goodness" of human nature and, in their place, provides a natural, social, and experiential explanation for the onset of both infantile sin and moral virtue. Both moral dispositions are nurtured in the bosom of our nascent social relations and emergent social self. Here the true insights of both the Calvinist predestinarians and the Unitarian defenders of "free moral agency" are taken into account.

Bushnell's *Christian Nurture* was the most influential of his books, and it exerted a profound influence on the theory and practice of religious education over the next century. The essential feature of Bushnell's doctrine is the insight—now a commonplace of educational psychology—that a true and abiding nurture is a gradual and continuous process and is indispensably social in character. It is what Bushnell called the "law of organic connection as regards character," that is, the conviction that the character of one, especially the parent, is "actually included in that of the other, as a seed is formed in its capsule; and being there nurtured, by a nutriment derived from the stem, is gradually separated from it."[111] Not only does the child, after physical birth, undergo the process of spiritual birth for many years within the matrix of the family, but this process of nurture and formation of the self remains a continuous social process. Moreover, it is characteristically an unpremeditated, intuitive formation.

> At first the child is held as a mere passive lump in the arms, and he opens into conscious life under the soul of the parent streaming into his eyes and ears, through the manners and tones of the nursery. . . . A smile awakens a smile; any kind of sentiment or passion, playing in the face of the parent, wakens a responsive sentiment or passion.[112]

It is only later that parents begin to govern their children "by appeals to the will, expressed by commands." It is at this point that they "appoint his school, choose his books, regulate his company, decide what form of religion, and what religious opinions he shall be taught."[113] It is the will and character of the parents and associates that are then the matrix of the child's emerging will and character. But this is not a foreign infringement; rather, it is the natural context of a growing human individuality and responsibility. It is, therefore, a wholly false notion that the child "becomes, at some certain moment, a complete moral agent, which a moment before he was not. . . . And this is the very idea of Christian education, that it begins with nurture and cultivation."[114]

Bushnell proceeds to extend his theory of spiritual nurture beyond the domestic sphere of the family and to point to its universal cultural import. "All society" he concludes, "is organic—the church, the state, the school, the family; and there is a spirit in each of these organisms, peculiar to itself and more or less hostile, more or less favorable to religious character, and to some extent, at least sovereign over the individual man. . . . We possess only a mixed individuality all our life long. A pure, separate, individual man living *wholly* from within and from himself is a mere fiction."[115]

This insight into the deeply organic, social character of human life was one of the foremost contributions of Romantic sensibility to our modern consciousness. It has had a profound influence not only on theology, especially as it is developed in later forms of Speculative and Personal Idealism, but also on education, psychology, and cultural anthropology.

Bushnell's *Christian Nurture* often is associated with the avowedly liberal movement of progressive religious education, but his theory is, in fact, profoundly conservative both in its character and in its social implications. Bushnell's attention to the social framework of the educative process, to what social theorists call "patterns of prestige," as the basis of behavior and character formation, is the conservative foundation of many ancient religious traditions, including Chinese Confucianism, where spiritual nurture is essentially the social process of an imitation and transmission of traditional values and patterns of behavior. Responding in a truly conservative *spirit* to the controversies of his time, Bushnell can be said to have substantially reconceived but thereby also to have reclaimed the truths of many time-worn forms of the Christian tradition and to have made these truths comprehensible and attractive to a modern audience. Therefore, by an influence unforeseen, the "critical orthodoxy" of Horace Bushnell also gives him claim to the title of "father of American liberal theology."

NOTES

1. Jacques Barzun, *Berlioz and the Romantic Century* (Boston, 1950), I, 379.
2. J. H. Randall, Jr., *The Making of the Modern Mind* (New York, 1926), p. 395.
3. For an excellent account of the new discovery in Romanticism of the value of diversity, see A. O. Lovejoy, "Romanticism and Plenitude," in *The Great Chain of Being* (Cambridge, 1936).
4. W. H. Wackenroder, *Herzensergiessungen* (1797), as cited in Lovejoy, op. cit., p. 305.
5. F. Schleiermacher, *On Religion*, trans. John Oman (New York, 1958).
6. Ibid., pp. 214, 217.
7. "The Tables Turned," in *The Complete Poetical Works of William Wordsworth* (London, 1928), p. 85.
8. *Athenaeum: Eine Zeitschrift*, I, ed. A. W. Schlegel and F. Schlegel (Berlin, 1798), 70.
9. J. W. von Goethe, *Faust*, trans. Anna Swanwick (New York, n.d.).
10. J. S. Mill, *Dissertations and Discussions* (London, 1867), I, 403.
11. F. D. Maurice says: "I am sure that I should not have had courage to differ from them or him [Coleridge] if he had not assisted me to believe that truth is above both, most of all above myself and my own petty notions and apprehensions, that it is worthy to be sought after and loved above all things, and that he who is truth, is ready, if we will obey him, to guide us into it." *The Kingdom of Christ*, (London, 1958), II, 364.
12. S. T. Coleridge, *Letters*, ed. E. H. Coleridge (1895), I, 352.
13. *The Friend*, Bohn ed. (1865), p. 67.
14. *The Friend*, Shedd ed. (New York, 1853), II, 164n.
15. *Nineteenth Century Studies* (New York, 1966), p. 29.

16. *The Statesman's Manual,* Shedd ed. (1853), I, 430.
17. *Aids to Reflection,* Shedd ed., (1853), I, 210–211.
18. Coleridge's philosophical handling of the doctrine of God has often been considered "Pantheistic." That Coleridge sought to avoid Pantheism is evident, but whether he entirely succeeded is still debated. See J. D. Boulger, *Coleridge as Religious Thinker* (Yale, 1961), Chap. 4.
19. *Aids to Reflection,* p. 272.
20. Coleridge wrote in one letter: "And this I believe not because I understand it; but because I *feel* that is not only suitable to, but needful for my nature, and because I find it clearly revealed." *Unpublished Letters,* ed. E. L. Griggs, I, 203.
21. *Aids to Reflection,* p. 363.
22. Ibid. Elsewhere Coleridge wrote that spiritual truths were "substantiated for us by their correspondence to the wants, cravings, and interests of the moral being. . . . For some of the faithful these truths have, I doubt not, an evidence of reason; but for the whole household of faith their certainty is in their working." *Literary Remains* I (New York, 1967), p. 366.
23. *Aids to Reflection,* p. 233.
24. Ibid., p. 226.
25. Ibid., p. 150.
26. Ibid., p. 209.
27. Ibid., pp. 209–210.
28. *Biographia Literaria,* Showcross ed., I, 135–136.
29. *Essay on Faith,* Shedd ed., V, 565.
30. S. T. Coleridge, *Confessions of an Inquiring Spirit,* ed. H. St. J. Hart (Stanford, 1956), p. 38.
31. Ibid., p. 49. Again: "I demand for the Bible only the justice which you grant other books of grave authority, and to other proved and acknowledged benefactors of mankind. Will you deny a spirit of wisdom in Lord Bacon, because in particular facts he did not possess perfect science . . . ?" Ibid., p. 62.
32. Ibid., p. 53.
33. Ibid., p. 66.
34. Ibid., pp. 64–65.
35. Ibid., pp. 68–70.
36. Ibid., p. 74.
37. Ibid., p. 60.
38. Ibid., pp. 65–66.
39. Ibid., p. 67.
40. Ibid., pp. 79–80.
41. *Aus Schleiermachers Leben in Briefen,* ed. W. Dilthey, I, 308; *Letters,* trans. F. Rowan (London, 1860), I, 283.
42. *On Religion: Speeches to Its Cultured Despisers,* trans. John Oman (New York, 1958), p. 15. We are citing the Oman translation of the final (1831) edition of the *Speeches.* For a sense of Schleiermacher's

Romantic feeling in 1799, see the Crouter translation listed in the "Suggested Readings."
43. Ibid., pp. 15–16.
44. Ibid., pp. 18–19.
45. Ibid., p. 21.
46. Ibid., p. 31.
47. Ibid., p. 35.
48. Ibid., p. 57.
49. Ibid., pp. 37–38.
50. Ibid., p. 36.
51. Ibid., pp. 49–50.
52. *The Christian Faith,* ed. H. R. Mackintosh and J. S. Stewart (Edinburgh, 1948), p. 12.
53. *On Religion,* p. 71.
54. Ibid., p. 48.
55. Ibid., pp. 87–88.
56. Ibid., p. 91.
57. Ibid., p. 95.
58. Ibid., p. 97.
59. Ibid., p. 122.
60. Ibid., pp. 132–133.
61. Wordsworth, op. cit., p. 34.
62. *On Religion,* p. 149.
63. Ibid., p. 150.
64. Ibid., p. 151.
65. Ibid., p. 155.
66. Ibid., p. 161.
67. Ibid., p. 167.
68. Ibid., pp. 217–218.
69. Ibid., p. 214.
70. Ibid., p. 234.
71. Ibid.
72. Ibid., p. 248.
73. Ibid., pp. 251–252.
74. Ibid., p. 253.
75. *The Christian Faith,* p. 52.
76. Ibid.
77. Ibid., p. 203. See the whole of Schleiermacher's discussion of the eternity of God in *The Christian Faith,* op. cit., p. 203ff.
78. Ibid., p. 206.
79. Ibid., p. 325.
80. Ibid., p. 271.
81. Ibid., p. 303.
82. R. R. Niebuhr, *Schleiermacher on Christ and Religion* (New York, 1964), p. 208. The account given in this chapter of Schleiermacher's understanding of sin and the work of Christ draws heavily on Neibuhr's excellent analysis in Chaps. 4 and 5 of the above book.
83. Ibid., p. 226.
84. Mary B. Cheney, *Life and Letters of Horace Bushnell* (New York, 1880; rpt. 1969), p. 499. For a fine,

brief discussion of Coleridge's themes in Bushnell's writing, see David L. Smith, ed., *Horace Bushnell: Selected Writings on Language, Religion, and American Culture* (Chico, Calif., 1984), pp. 10–11.

85. Quoted in Cheney, *Life and Letters,* p. 56. I am indebted to David L. Smith for this reference.

86. Smith, *Horace Bushnell: Selected Writings,* p. 10.

87. Horace Bushnell, "Preliminary Dissertation on the Nature of Language as Related to Thought and Spirit," *God in Christ,* 3d ed. (Hartford, 1852), p. 46.

88. Ibid., p. 47.

89. Ibid., p. 48.

90. Ibid., pp. 48–49.

91. Ibid., p. 55.

92. Ibid., pp. 68–69.

93. Ibid., p. 70.

94. Ibid., p. 90.

95. Ibid., p. 74.

96. Ibid., p. 73.

97. Ibid., p. 80.

98. Ibid., p. 82.

99. Ibid., pp. 83–84.

100. Horace Bushnell, "Christian Comprehensiveness," *New Englander* VI (1848). Quotations from *Horace Bushnell,* ed. H. Shelton Smith (New York, 1965), pp. 117–118.

101. Bushnell, "Preliminary Dissertation," p. 123.

102. Ibid., p. 118.

103. Ibid., p. 115.

104. Ibid., pp. 116–117.

105. Ibid., pp. 92, 93.

106. S. T. Coleridge, "Aids to Reflection," *Complete Works of Samuel Taylor Coleridge,* I, ed., W. G. T. Shedd, p. 263.

107. Horace Bushnell, *Nature and the Supernatural* [1858] (New York, 1876), pp. 32, 31.

108. Bushnell, "Preliminary Dissertation," pp. 94–95.

109. Horace Bushnell, *Christian Nurture* [1861] (New Haven, 1947), p. 76.

110. Ibid., p. 77.

111. Ibid., p. 18.

112. Ibid., pp. 19–20.

113. Ibid.

114. Ibid., p. 21.

115. Ibid., p. 22.

SUGGESTIONS FOR FURTHER READING

ROMANTICISM

Abrams, M. H. *Natural Supernaturalism* (New York: W. W. Norton and Co., 1971). A rich study of the central theme of the title in the works of leading Romantics.

Barzun, Jacques. *Classic, Romantic, and Modern* (New York: Doubleday Anchor Books, 1961). An excellent study of Romantic art and life and the phases of Romanticism by a foremost cultural historian.

Lovejoy, A. O. "Romanticism and the Principle of Plentitude," *The Great Chain of Being* (Cambridge: Harvard University Press, 1936).

Randall, J. H., Jr. *The Career of Philosophy,* II, *From the German Enlightenment to the Age of Darwin* (New York: Columbia University Press, 1965). Chapters 4, 10–12 are good on German Romanticism.

SAMUEL TAYLOR COLERIDGE

Barth, J. R. *Coleridge and Christian Doctrine* (Cambridge: Harvard University Press, 1969).

Boulger, James D. *Coleridge as Religious Thinker* (New Haven: Yale University Press, 1961).

Sanders, Charles R. *Coleridge and the Broad Church Movement* (Durham: Duke University Press, 1942). A description of Coleridge's influence on a number of important English religious writers.

Welch, Claude, "Samuel Taylor Coleridge." In *Nineteenth Century Religious Thought in the West,* II, ed. Ninian Smart (Cambridge: Cambridge University Press, 1985). A fine brief account with a good bibliography.

Willey, Basil. *Nineteenth Century Studies,* Chap. 1 (New York: Harper Torchbook, 1966). An excellent brief study of Coleridge as religious thinker.

FRIEDRICH SCHLEIERMACHER

Barth, Karl. *Protestant Thought from Rousseau to Ritschl* (New York: Harper & Brothers, 1959). Barth's essay on Schleiermacher is provocative and must be read critically.

Brandt, Richard R. *The Philosophy of Schleiermacher* (Westport: Greenwood Press, 1968).

Clement, Keith W. *Friedrich Schleiermacher: Pioneer of Modern Theology* (Minneapolis: Fortress Press, 1991). A collection of selections from Schleiermacher's writings on key themes, with a long and helpful introduction.

Crouter, Richard, ed. Friedrich Schleiermacher, *On Religion* (Cambridge: Cambridge University Press,

1988). This English translation of the first (1799) edition of Schleiermacher's text includes a valuable introduction on the background, milieu, and argument of this Romantic classic.

Forstmann, Jack. *A Romantic Triangle: Schleiermacher and Early German Romanticism* (Missoula: Scholars Press, 1977). Valuable discussion of the Romanticism of Novalis and Schlegel in relation to that of Schleiermacher.

Gerrish, B. A. *A Prince of the Church: Schleiermacher and the Beginnings of Modern Theology* (Philadelphia: Fortress Press, 1984).

————. "Friedrich Schleiermacher." In *Nineteenth Century Religious Thought in the West,* I, ed. Ninian Smart (Cambridge: Cambridge University Press, 1985). Gerrish's monograph and essay offer valuable insights on Schleiermacher.

Niebuhr, Richard R. *Schleiermacher on Christ and Religion* (New York: Charles Scribner's Sons, 1964). An important study and reinterpretation of certain themes in Schleiermacher's thought.

Redeker, Martin. *Schleiermacher: Life and Thought,* trans. J. Wallhauser (Philadelphia: Fortress Press, 1973). Though brief, the best introduction in English to both Schleiermacher's life and thought.

HORACE BUSHNELL

Cross, Barbara, *Horace Bushnell: Minister to a Changing America* (Chicago: University of Chicago Press, 1958). An informative biographical study.

Duke, James O. *Horace Bushnell: On the Vitality of Biblical Language* (Chico, Calif.: Scholars Press). A monograph study of a little-explored aspect of Bushnell. Excellent bibliography of Bushnell's books, articles, and addresses.

Smith, David L. *Symbolism and Growth: The Religious Thought of Horace Bushnell* (Chico, Calif.: Scholars Press, 1981).

————. *Horace Bushnell: Selected Writings on Language, Religion, and American Culture* (Chico, Calif.: Scholars Press, 1984). A fine monograph study and a valuable selection of Bushnell's writings with a good introduction.

Smith, H. Shelton. *Horace Bushnell* (New York: Oxford University Press, 1965). A good selection from Bushnell's writings with valuable introductions to their theological contexts.

Chapter 5
Christianity and Speculative Idealism

G. W. F. Hegel

Few periods in history have been as rich in intellectual activity as the years immediately preceding and following 1800 in Germany. During this time Kant, Goethe, Fichte, Schelling, Schleiermacher, and Hegel wrote some of their most important works. Those of Kant, Schleiermacher, and Hegel alone determined the course of theology for the next century and beyond. We have examined the ways in which Kant and Schleiermacher sought to reconstruct Christianity; we must look now at the philosophy of Hegel which is perhaps the most audacious attempt yet devised to resolve the issues between Christianity and philosophical analysis.

Hegel was consumed by the problem of the reconciliation of religion and culture from the very earliest period of his career, and his philosophic reinterpretation of Christianity had a wide appeal in the

universities and seminaries first in Germany and then in England and the United States. At Oxford, Hegelianism was the reigning philosophy from the 1870s to the turn of the century. In America, Emerson and the Transcendentalists were deeply indebted to German Idealism, and Josiah Royce "taught scores of Harvard students how to sublimate Calvinism into what Santayana called the 'genteel tradition' of religious Idealism. . . . Hegelianism was the philosophy introduced into the colleges during the 1890s to save the students' faith."[1]

With the discovery of the Danish philosopher Kierkegaard and the emergence of Neo-Orthodoxy in the 1920s, Idealism came under severe criticism, and the union of theology and philosophical speculation was widely repudiated. Nevertheless, Hegel was a dominant influence in Christian theology for almost a century. His rich influence is still present, though often unrecognized. We shall examine Hegel's own conception of Christianity, look at a few major examples of Hegelianism in later nineteenth-century theology, and then conclude with a brief assessment of the enduring influence and importance of Hegel for modern Christianity.

G. W. F. HEGEL

Georg Wilhelm Friedrich Hegel (1770–1831) is the greatest of the German Idealists and one of the most fertile minds in the history of Western thought. He was born at the waning of the Enlightenment and came to maturity during the birth of Romanticism. He was influenced by both of these movements and yet was satisfied with neither. His philosophy is, in one sense, a bringing together of the insights of both into a grand synthesis.

In 1788 Hegel entered the Protestant theological seminary at Tübingen where he formed close friendships with the poet Hölderlin and the philosopher Schelling. The spirit at Tübingen was still that of enlightened rationalism, and such an atmosphere did not speak to the young Hegel who was beginning to discover the values of emotion and imagination espoused by the young Romanticists. When Hegel left the university in 1793, his academic record was unexceptional. He worked as a family tutor in Berne and Frankfurt between 1793 and 1800. These would appear to be uneventful years, but we now know that this was an extremely important period in Hegel's intellectual development. It was during this period that Hegel wrote his first essays on religion and Christianity.[2] These essays furnish important insights into his early theological speculation as well as into the beginnings of the dialectical method which so controls his later thought.

In 1801 Hegel was offered a teaching position at the University of Jena but was deprived of his job when the university was closed after the battle of Jena. For several years he served as rector of the Gymnasium at Nuremberg, during which time he produced his *Science of Logic* which inaugurated his mature period, that best known to English language

scholars. In 1818 Hegel was invited to the chair of philosophy at the University of Berlin, a position he occupied until his death in 1831. During this Berlin period Hegel rose to unrivaled prominence in the German philosophical world. His popularity among Berliners who attended his lectures had to be shared, nevertheless, with a colleague in the chair of theology by the name of Schleiermacher. The two men had little in common and never could appreciate one another's teaching. Hegel apparently felt only contempt for Schleiermacher's conception of religion as intuition and feeling and called the author of the *Speeches* a "virtuoso of edification and enthusiasm." Hegel is said to have remarked that if the essence of religion consists in the feeling of an absolute dependence, "then the dog would be the best Christian." For Hegel during his Berlin years, religion is not principally a feeling of the divine presence or even a doing of God's will. Religion means to *know* God, and theology is, in its final phase, philosophic knowledge—a going beyond the images of positive religion to a knowledge of their universal conceptual significance.

Hegel's Early Theological Writings

Hegel's early theological writings did not share this antipathy to Romanticism. In fact, the earliest fragments, collected by Nohl under the title *Volksreligion and Christentum,* reveal the profound influence of Greek culture on the young Hegel—as interpreted, nevertheless, through Romanticist eyes. At this time Hegel made a sharp distinction between an objective religion of the understanding and a subjective religion of the heart.

> Objective religion can be arranged in one's head, can be brought into a system, set forth in a book. . . . subjective religion expresses itself only in attitudes and actions. When I say of a man that he is religious I do not mean that he has a knowledge of it, but that his heart feels the activity, the awe and presence of the Godhead . . . he bows before Him, utters thanks and praise.[3]

What the young Hegel found lacking in Christianity was that, unlike the *Volksreligion* of the

Greeks, it did not reflect the spirit and genius of a people. Christianity appeared to the young Hegel as something imposed and alien, lacking a sense of beauty and joy. In these earliest fragments one can already see the beginnings of the Hegelian theme of estrangement—what Hegel was later to call the "contrite consciousness."

It was during his stay in Berne in 1794 that Hegel undertook an intensive reexamination of Kant's moral philosophy. The writings of 1794–1796 are inspired almost entirely by Kant's *Religion within the Limits of Reason Alone*. Kant had suggested in that book that it was necessary to attempt to harmonize the teachings of Jesus with the dictates of reason. Hegel set himself this task in 1795 by writing a *Life of Jesus*—again not for publication but principally to clarify his own thinking.[4] In this essay Hegel simply interpreted the life and teachings of Jesus in the spirit and, indeed, even the letter of Kant. He has Jesus advise persons to "act on the maxim which you can at the same time will to be a universal law among men." According to Hegel, Jesus was forced to emphasize the uniqueness of his mission only because the Jews were accustomed to thinking of all truth as coming from a special revelation given by a messenger of God.

Hegel recognized that while there is a unity between Kant's rational ethics and Jesus's teachings, there is also a wide gulf between Kant's ethics and the later ecclesiology and dogma of the Church. How is it that the teachings of Jesus, so much in agreement with Kant's principles of moral reason, could develop into the objective law of the Church—what Kant had called "statutory religion," which is not rational but "positive" and imposed from without? Hegel sought to answer this question in *The Positivity of the Christian Religion* (1795–1796). He found the displacement of the Greek autonomous religion, which developed neither dogma nor ecclesiastical institutions, by a Christian positive religion largely in the social and political changes which brought the ancient world to a close.

> The Greek and Roman religion was a religion only for a free people and with the loss of their freedom, the meaning, the power and the suitability of their religion must also have been lost. The prime reason for this loss

of freedom is economic and political; wars and the increase of wealth and luxury lead to aristocracy and to inner decay. Loyalty and freedom, the joyous participation in a common life all disappeared. . . . All activity, all purposes were now referred to individuals; no more was there an activity for the sake of a totality, for an Idea.[5]

The center of gravity of man's life was no longer found in the Polis: "Cato turned to Plato's *Phaedo* only after what had been for him the supreme order of things, his world, his republic was destroyed; then he took refuge in another world."[6]

Positive Christianity won out, according to Hegel, because it was adapted to the exigencies of the time since its ideal, its center of gravity, was the remote, the transcendent. The world was estranged from itself, and this explains the reception of the Christian conception of God as a transcendent being.

> The despotism of the Roman emperors had driven the spirit of man from the earth, the loss of freedom compelled him to rescue his eternal, his absolute, by taking refuge in the deity; and the spread of misery forced him to seek and expect blessedness in heaven. The objectification of the deity went hand in hand with the slavery of man.[7]

Hegel believed that Jesus was thus compelled by circumstances to describe his message as the will of God, as if its sanction consisted in its derivation from some foreign, supernatural authority. So destitute of genuine moral autonomy were Jesus's followers that in no other way could they be made to listen to his message. As a result, the "Christians have come to just the place where the Jews were—slaves under the law."[8]

Hegel's break with Kant is clearly evidenced in the series of writings completed during the last two years of the decade. These essays have been grouped together by Nohl under the title, *The Spirit of Christianity and Its Fate*. Once again Hegel tried to develop a conception of the true religion—this time, however, not against the background of the "positivity" of Christianity, but in reaction to the "estrangement" he had come to find epitomized in Hebrew religion and Kant's moral philosophy.

The Hebrew religion is interpreted by Hegel as the religion of a people in conflict with themselves and with nature, of a people not at home in their universe. The first recorded act of Abraham was an act of estrangement, the leaving of his fatherland.

> The first act which made Abraham the progenitor of a nation is a disseverance which snaps the bonds of communal life and love. The entirety of the relationship in which he had hitherto lived with men and nature . . . he spurned. Cadmus, Danaus, etc., had forsaken their fatherland too, but they forsook it in battle; they went in quest of a soil where they would be free and they sought it that they might love. Abraham wanted *not* to love, wanted to be free by not loving . . . while the others by their gentle arts and manners won over the less civilized aborigines and intermingled with them to form a happy and gregarious people.[9]

Even the one love Abraham had, love for his son, he was willing to sacrifice.

> The whole world Abraham regarded as simply his opposite; if he did not take it to be a nullity, he looked on it as sustained by the God who was alien to it. Nothing in nature was supposed to have any part in God; everything was simply under God's mastery.[10]

The successive misfortunes of the Jewish people simply are the consequence of their complete estrangement from nature and their slavish dependence upon their alien God. It is quite clear that here Hegel is teaching us by parable. The Hebrews are his symbol of the estranged and contrite human consciousness.

Hegel's dissatisfaction with Kant is now also evident in his new portrayal of Jesus. Jesus is now pictured as having "made undetermined subjectivity, character, a totally different sphere, one which was to have nothing in common with the punctilious following of objective [rational] commands."[11] The spirit of Jesus is a spirit raised above morality.

> The Sermon does not teach reverence for the laws; on the contrary, it exhibits that which fulfils the law but annuls it as law and so is something higher than obedience to law and makes law superfluous. Since the commands of duty presuppose a cleavage [between

reason and inclination] and since the domination of the concept declares itself in a "thou shalt," that which is raised above this cleavage is by contrast an "is," a modification of life.[12]

This modification of life is a quality of life in which reason and inclination are in harmony. Kant had reduced the command "love God first and then your neighbor" to the categorical imperative, unmindful that the whole point of Jesus's message is that love cannot be commanded, that it is beyond the law and represents an "is" rather than an "ought," that it is a synthesis of law (reason) and inclination. This "is," which is the confluence, the mutual sharing of the universal and the particular, of law and inclination, is difficult to conceptualize, but Hegel calls it Life (*Leben*). The dynamic relationship of different elements in life (*Leben*) is Love. Hegel characterizes love as a feeling for the whole—a unity of self and world.

Hegel now turns to the question of how an Abraham, estranged from the wholeness of Life, might once again be reconciled to Life. He finds that in the concept of Fate such a reconciliation can be effected. When punishment comes as the act of Fate and not as the retribution of an alien Law, it does not stand forever above and against the individual. Since all Life is one and is a totality, the wrong-doer comes to see that through the wrong he or she has really injured his or her own life and not merely violated an external law. The person has introduced a separation within his or her own real life. Hegel develops his idea of reconciliation in an important passage which we will quote at length:

> The wrong-doer supposed that it was but an external foreign thing that his sin affected; really he has but torn asunder his own life. For no life is separate from Life, because all life is divine and of God. The wrongdoer has in his wantonness, to be sure, done damage—but it is the friendliness of Life which he has injured; he has made it an enemy. . . . Thus his punishment, regarded as his fate, is the return of his own deed, a force which he himself has set in motion, an enemy of his own making. . . . It seems far more hopeless to expect a reconciliation with this Fate, than with the Law; for in order to become reconciled with Fate, it would appear necessary that the injury itself should disappear. But

Fate has the advantage over an external Law, because with Fate, the entire process goes on within *Leben*. A wrong-doing in the Kantian realm of law is in the realm of irreconcilable opposites, both of which are fixed realities. There is no possibility here of transcending the punishment or of allowing the consciousness of having done wrong disappear. The law is a power, to which all *Leben* is a slave, and to which there is nothing superior, for God himself is but the giver of the law. . . . *Leben* can heal its wounds, can bring back to itself that sundered, hostile life which the wrong-doing caused to split-off; can atone for and sublate the bungling work of the wrong-doer, the law and the punishment. From just the moment when the wrong-doer feels the wounding of his own life [suffers punishment] or is conscious of his own life as sundered and bruised [in remorse], then the working of Fate has commenced and the consciousness of the wounded life must also be a longing for its restoration. The lost life is now appreciated as his own, as that which should now be his but which is not. This gap, this void, is not a mere nothing, but is actively known and felt as the lack of life. . . . Opposition is the possibility of reunification, and the extent to which in affliction life is felt as an opposite is also the extent of the possibility of resuming it again. . . . This sensing of life, a sensing which finds itself again, is love, and in love fate is reconciled.[13]

Hegel identifies this healing of fate through love with the teaching of Jesus. It is necessary, however, to understand what he means by love, for it is not the meaning which has traditionally been given to Christian love. For Hegel, love means wholeness—a union of reason, sense, feeling, and will. It is a harmony in which reason and inclinations are no longer at war with one another.

Love itself pronounces no imperative. It is no universal opposed to the particular. . . . To love God is to feel oneself in the "all" of life, with no restrictions, in the infinite. In this feeling of *harmony* there is no universality, since in a harmony the particular is not in discord but in concord.[14]

Professor Kroner[15] has called this period of Hegel's philosophy a "Pantheism of Love." Jesus is depicted as restoring humanity's estranged existence to its original unity through the love which heals the split between duty and inclination. In *The Spirit of Christianity* one can discern many themes that Hegel later was to develop with great logical power. One sees, for example, his opposition to a one-sided rationalism but also his revulsion to excessive emotionalism and his concern to reconcile dialectically the opposites of experience into a higher unity. Nevertheless, *The Spirit of Christianity* proved a failure for Hegel. He came to recognize that love is a kind of "holy innocence," an unconscious, undeveloped unity—only one (the subjective) side of mature consciousness. Hegel realized that if estrangement is the emergence of intellect from the level of natural immediacy to the consciousness of one's particular selfhood, then reconciliation cannot be thought of in terms of a simple return to immediacy. Hegel now sees the necessity of a third stage—a synthesis of subjective immediacy and objective form in what he calls *religion*.

Love is a divine spirit but it falls short of religion. To become religion, it must manifest itself in an objective form. A feeling, something subjective, it must be fused with the universal, with something represented in idea. . . . The need to unite subject with object, to unite feeling and feeling's demand for objects, with the intellect, to unite them in something beautiful, in a god, by means of fancy, is the supreme need of the human spirit and the urge to religion.[16]

Hegel was certain, in any case, that Christianity failed to embody this religious synthesis of subjective feeling and objective form. The fate of Christianity is to extract the spirit of unitive love from the contents of its consciousness and submit to that which is positive and intellectualistic. His conclusion is that it is the fate of Christianity "that church and state, worship and life, piety and virtue, spiritual and worldly action, can never dissolve into one."[17]

As is evidenced in these early essays, the young Hegel was consumed by the problem of finding a thought form that could encompass the dynamic polarities of experience. From his obsession with religion and Christianity, it would appear that he was convinced that religious experience, as expressed in such concepts as estrangement, incarnation, love, and reconciliation, could afford him a clue to such a form of thought. However, the early theological writings did not satisfy Hegel's search. The closest he came was the following statement from *The Spirit of Christianity:* "What is religious is the pleroma ['fulfillment'] of love; it is reflection and love united, bound together in thought."[18]

The writings of the 1790s indicate that Hegel was convinced that the dynamic polarities of experience, subject and object, finite and infinite, the one and the many, could not be united by conceptual thought. Thought tends either to deny the distinction or to dissect reality into discrete parts. Christianity also failed to achieve such a stage of synthesis, for it remained hopelessly positive. The search for a *religious stage* which would be capable of restoring humanity to wholeness was thus given up after 1800.

The years between 1800 and 1807 mark Hegel's effort to find a *philosophical form* which could express his ideal synthesis of emotion and intellect, life and thought—that is, a new form of logic which could conceptualize the unity of reality without denying multiplicity and individuality. These years reveal Hegel's metamorphosis from a theologian, or antitheologian, to a logician and philosopher. However, his attitude toward Christianity is no longer negative, satirical, and shrill. It is as if Hegel's wrestling with Christianity and rejection of its traditional form freed him to see it in a new way. In terms of his new dialectic, Hegel's conception of Christianity had to be *aufgehoben.** This new attitude toward the Christianity he had scathingly denounced is indicated as early as 1800 in comments he makes about his plans for rewriting "The Positivity of Christianity." He writes that

> The following essay does not have the purpose of inquiring whether there are positive doctrines and commandments in the Christian religion. . . . The horrible blabbering in this vein with its endless extent and inward emptiness has become too boring and has altogether lost interest. . . . *Rather, one would have to deduce this now repudiated dogmatics out of what we now consider the needs of human nature and thus show its naturalness and its necessity. Such an attempt would

*The German verb *aufheben* conveys the double meaning of having "done away with" and at the same time "preserved" on a higher level.

presuppose the faith that the convictions of many centuries—that which the millions, who during these centuries lived by them and died for them, considered their duty and holy truth—were not bare nonsense or immorality.*[19] (Italics added.)

Hegel recognized that his earlier view of Christianity was too narrow and negative and needed to be transcended. He now developed a more historical orientation to philosophy and recognized that the faith held by millions for centuries could not simply be dismissed as "bare nonsense." The positive, historical, dogmatic medium of Christianity needed to be *aufgehoben* so that its truth could be more adequately seen and attested to in philosophy. Historical Christianity had grasped the truth in representational form, but philosophy grasps this same truth in its rational necessity. Nevertheless, truth is now not something abstract and ahistorical for Hegel. "The universal must pass into actuality through the particular" and only then can it be seen in its rational necessity. The truth of Christianity, therefore, is not to be reduced to certain abstract principles but seen in the historical actualization of the unity of the divine and human and the coming into being of the Absolute Spirit. This is what it means to say that God is revealed in history:

> In the Christian religion God has revealed himself, *i.e.,* he has given men to understand what he is, so that he is no longer a concealment, a secret. This possibility to know God lays upon us the duty to do so; and the development of thinking Spirit which has proceeded from this basis, from the revelation of the divine Being, must finally proceed *to grasp in thought that which has at first been exhibited to Spirit in feeling and representation.* Whether the time has come to comprehend depends upon whether that which is the final purpose of the world has at last passed into actuality in a universally valid and conscious way.
>
> Now what distinguishes the Christian religion is that with it this time has come; this constitutes the *absolute epoch* in world history. . . . So we know as Christians what God is; now God is no longer unknown: if we still say that, we are not Christians. The Christian religion demands the humility . . . to apprehend God, not on its own terms, but on the terms of

God's own knowledge and apprehension. Christians are initiated into the mysteries of God and so the key to world history is also given to us. Here is given a definite apprehension of providence and its plan.[20] (Italics added.)

In the historical events of Christianity's origin, "the final purpose of the world" has been actualized, or has made explicit what was only implicit before. What is now called for is that what has been mediated through historical representation (revelation) now be "grasped in thought."

Hegel's Conception of Christianity

The Fall of Man. According to Hegel, humanity's actual history on this earth is a chronicle of misery and suffering. This condition is largely attributable to humanity's self-alienation and longing for a reconciliation of the ceaseless contradictions between spirit and flesh, between infinite, free selfhood and slavish finitude. This conflict and estrangement within self-consciousness is what Hegel calls the "Unhappy Consciousness,"[21] history being the sorry panorama of the successive forms of this human self-alienation. Hegel finds the world historical importance of Israel in the fact that it was the Jewish people who brought this sense of alienation to absolute self-consciousness. This feeling

> we find expressed most purely and beautifully in the Psalms of David, and in the Prophets; the chief burden of whose utterances is the thirst of the soul after God, its profound sorrow for its transgressions, and the desire for righteousness and holiness.[22]

Humanity's contrite or unhappy consciousness is, of course, most powerfully depicted in mythopoetic form in the biblical story of the Fall of Adam. Hegel finds this poetic representation of human estrangement rich in significance and totally lost to the rationalism of the Enlightenment. When grasped in thought, the story of the Fall of Adam expresses the conceptual truth of our human condition.

> Man, created in the image of God, lost, it is said, his state of absolute contentment, by eating of the Tree of the Knowledge of Good and Evil. Sin consists here only in Knowledge: this is the sinful element, and by it man is stated to have trifled away his Natural happiness. *This is a deep truth, that evil lies in consciousness: for the brutes are neither evil nor good* [italics added]; the merely Natural Man quite as little. Consciousness occasions the separation of the Ego, in its boundless freedom as arbitrary choice, from the pure essence of the Will—*i.e.,* from the Good. Knowledge, as the disannulling of the unity of mere Nature, is the "Fall," which is no casual conception, but the eternal history of Spirit. For the state of innocence, the paradisaical condition, is that of the brute. Paradise is a park, where only brutes, not men can remain. For the brute is one with God only *implicitly* (not consciously). Only Man's Spirit has a self-cognizant existence. This existence for self, this consciousness, is at the same time separation from the Universal and Divine Spirit. If I hold to *my* abstract Freedom, in contraposition to the Good, I adopt the standpoint of Evil. The Fall is therefore the Mythus of Man—in fact, the very transition by which he becomes man. Persistence in this standpoint is, however, Evil, and the feeling of pain at such a condition and of longing to transcend it, we find in David, when he says: "Lord create for me a pure heart, a new *steadfast* Spirit." This feeling we observe even in the account of the Fall; though an announcement of Reconciliation is not made there, but rather one of continuance in misery. Yet we have in this narrative the *prediction* of reconciliation . . . profoundly expressed where it is stated that when God saw that Adam had eaten of that tree he said, "Behold Adam is become as one of us, knowing Good and Evil." God confirms the words of the Serpent.[23]

It is evident that in Hegel's view the Fall of humankind is to be interpreted in a quite different manner from the traditional exegesis. He believes the Fall is a necessary movement from innocence to self-consciousness. If we speak of it as a "fall," we must remember that it is a "necessary" and fortunate movement toward making *explicit* humanity's *implicit* unity with God. The estrangement that results from the Fall is evil, of course, but it is also a positive advance beyond innocence. To Hegel, life in Paradise is a "dreaming innocence" which is lacking in the knowledge of good and evil, lacking in self-consciousness and deliberate choice. "Innocence means to be without a will—without indeed being evil, but also at the same time without being good."[24] It is just this sinless state of innocence that Hegel believes must be "judged and condemned," for it is knowledge that makes humans conscious of their independence and which separates them from the animals and plants.

Nevertheless, knowledge is evil since it leads to separation and estrangement.

> It is said, then, that human beings have eaten of this tree. . . . What it really means is that humanity has elevated itself to the knowledge of good and evil; and this cognition, this distinction, is the source of evil, is evil itself. . . . For cognition or consciousness means in general a judging or dividing, a self-distinguishing within the self. . . . The cleavage, however, is what is evil. . . . Only in this cleavage is evil contained, and hence is itself evil."[25]

The Fall, the movement from innocence to knowledge, is evil because it implies alienation, but it is also the necessary step toward reconciliation. Adam and Eve, in yielding to the temptations of the Devil, are in reality making the necessary move toward realizing the highest nature of the Spirit.

Moreover, the serpent says that by eating the fruit of the tree Adam and Eve will become like God, and this appeals to human pride. God later communes with himself, saying, " 'Behold, Adam has become like one of us' [Gen. 3:22]. So the serpent did not lie, for God confirms what it said."[26]

Much confusion has resulted from this biblical declaration by God that "Adam has become like one of us." Some have given these words an ironical interpretation, but "the higher explanation," Hegel declares, "is that by this 'Adam' the Second Adam, or Christ, is understood."[27] The knowledge which comes with the Fall involves the promise and certainty of attaining once more the state of reconciliation.[28]

Fallen humanity is historical humanity—no longer innocent and yet estranged and painfully cognizant of its separation from God. But this disunion is not permanent; our yearning for "a new steadfast Spirit" will be answered "in the fullness of time." This *kairos,* or right time, was heralded by the Jewish people. In Israel the opposition between God and humanity, subject and object, finite and infinite, comes to consciousness; the time is now ripe for reconciliation:

> From that unrest of infinite sorrow—in which the two sides of the antithesis stand related to each other—is developed the unity of God with Reality. . . . The recognition of the identity of the Subject and God was introduced into the World when *the fulness of Time was come:* the consciousness of this identity is the recognition of God in his true essence. . . . The nature of God as pure *Spirit* is manifested to man *in the Christian Religion.*[29]

The Incarnation.   The *implicit* unity of God and humanity is made *explicit* in Christianity in that the foundation of Christianity is laid on *the historical fact* of the Incarnation. In Jesus Christ the God-man unity is realized in a concrete temporal event. Hegel maintains that Christ is divine because he is the embodiment of the Truth, the incarnation of God in himself (*an sich*), God manifest in the world. As speculative idea, the God-man unity is only implicit. Hence Christ's uniqueness lies not principally in his teachings but in the fact that he *is* God manifest in the world. Nevertheless, this fact cannot be established by historical-critical research.

> Considered only in respect of his talents, character and morality—as a Teacher and so forth—we place him [Jesus] in the same category with Socrates and others. . . . But excellence of character, morality, etc.—all this is not the *ne plus ultra* in the requirements of Spirit. . . . If Christ is to be looked upon only as an excellent, even impeccable individual, and nothing more, the conception of . . . Absolute Truth is ignored. But this is the desideratum, the point from which we have to start. Make of Christ what you will, exegetically, critically, historically—demonstrate as you please, how the doctrines of the Church were established by Councils, attained currency as the result of this or that episcopal interest or passion—let all such circumstances have been what they might—the only concerning question is: What is the Idea or the Truth in and for itself?[30]

Christ's unique God-manhood, Hegel believes, is posited upon the speculative Idea, upon Hegel's conception of Absolute Truth. This very Idea demands that the implicit truth be historically manifest.

> This implicit unity exists in the first place only for the thinking speculative consciousness; but it must also exist for the sensuous, representative consciousness—it must become an object for the World—it *must appear,* and that in the sensuous form appropriate to Spirit which is the human. *Christ has appeared*—a Man who is God—God who is Man; and thereby peace and reconciliation have accrued to the World. . . . The appearance of the Christian God involves further its being *unique* in its kind; it can occur only once, for God is realized as Subject, and as manifested Subjectivity is exclusively One individual.[31]

The Idea demands the unique historical appearance of the God-man union in human form but, as has been indicated, such an historical occurrence is immune to any historical-critical test.[32] It is clear, as many critics of Hegel have shown, that Hegel is more interested in the symbolic truth in the doctrine of the divine-human union in Christ than in the historical life of Jesus of Nazareth. Nevertheless, Hegel does emphasize the historical reality and uniqueness of the Incarnation, the concrete actualization of the universal in a particular historical individual. Christ is not simply symbolic of the divine presence in every human, *for with Jesus Christ the history of both God and humankind has actually changed.* God has passed from abstract idea into historical individuality and *only in so doing attains full reality.* The history of Jesus Christ is the history of *both* God and humanity.

Hegel points out that the appearance of the God-man must be viewed from two perspectives simultaneously. The incarnation demands a real and singular, but ordinary, historical appearance in accord with normal human circumstances. This is the nonreligious view of Christ as an ordinary human. But Christ also appears in the perspective of the Spirit which penetrates to the truth concerning the God-man. Christ is not to be viewed, then, only in the same light as a Socrates. Christ's teaching, seen from the perspective of the Spirit, "is a matter of the consciousness of absolute reconciliation, one finds here a new consciousness of humanity, a new religion." In Christ's teaching "a new world is thereby constituted, a new actuality, a different world-condition." Christ's teaching affirms the universal and, as such, represents "a revolutionary doctrine, which partially sets aside all that is established and in part nullifies and overthrows it. . . . This kingdom of God, the new religion, thus contains within itself the characteristic of negation vis-à-vis what presently exists."[33] This radical teaching leads to Christ's suffering and death.

Central to the Incarnation, of course, is the passion and death of the Christ. For Hegel the conceptual truth of the crucifixion is to be found in the fact that when Spirit becomes united with the finite, it must take on radical finitude, which includes estrangement and death. Otherwise, God is not fully manifested in finite existence. The most radical sign of finitude is death, for in death our temporality is fully revealed.

> The pinnacle of finitude is not actual life in its temporal course, but rather death, the anguish of death; death is the pinnacle of negation . . . the limit, finitude in its highest extreme. The temporal and complete existence of the divine idea in the present is envisaged only in [Christ's] death.[34]

The death of Christ symbolizes the destruction of finitude, so that in the crucifixion we see in sensible form the yielding up of all that is peculiar to the individual, all those interests and personal ends with which the natural will can occupy itself.[35] Absolute Spirit must, in other words, lose its life before it can fully realize itself. Understood conceptually, Spirit must not only undergo the negation of its finitude. *Spirit or God must die!* But what God's death on the cross symbolizes is that God's finitude is only a transitional moment in the emergence of Absolute Spirit. What dies is the existence of God as an individual standing over against us; the personal transcendent God of traditional theism. "Death then ceases to signify what it means directly—the nonexistence of *this* individual [God]—and becomes transfigured into the universality of spirit which lives in its own communion."[36]

The death of the God-man, however, is only one aspect of a single event. The cross is followed by the resurrection and ascension. The conceptual understanding of this event does not, then, terminate with God's death, for God is maintained in this process. Hence God's death is really the death of death, the negation of finite negativity. The resurrection and ascension into Heaven is the pictorial representation of the truth that Spirit sacrifices its particular embodiment and thereby initiates the advent of Absolute Spirit, the coming of the Holy or Universal Spirit.

For Hegel, consciousness of the spiritual significance of Christ's death as including his resurrection and ascension is consciousness of the fact that God's death is merely the transitional stage in the emergence of Christ as Spirit or the actualization of the Spiritual Community.

> The sensuous existence in which Spirit is embodied is only a transitional phase. Christ dies; only as dead is he exalted to Heaven and sits at the right hand of God; only thus is he Spirit. He himself says: "When I am no longer with you, the Spirit will guide you into all truth." Not till the Feast of Pentecost were the Apostles filled with the Holy Ghost. To the Apostles, Christ as living was not that which he was to them subsequently as the Spirit of the Church, in which he became to them for the first time an object for their truly spiritual consciousness.[37]

The inauguration of the Kingdom of the Spirit represents the universal reconciliation of the divine and human that was implicit from the beginning. As Christ overcame sin and death, so we, as heirs of the Spirit, must strip ourselves of our finite point of view.

> It has already been remarked that only after the death of Christ could the Spirit come upon his friends; that only then they were able to conceive the true idea of God, viz., that in Christ man is redeemed and reconciled; for in him the idea of eternal truth is recognized, *the essence of man acknowledged to be Spirit, and the fact proclaimed that only by stripping himself of his finiteness and surrendering himself to pure self-consciousness does he attain the truth.* Christ—man as man—in whom the unity of God and man has appeared, has in

his death, and his history generally, himself presented the eternal history of Spirit—*a history which every man has to accomplish in himself, in order to exist as Spirit, or to become a child of God,* a citizen of his kingdom. The followers of Christ, who combine on this principle and live in the spiritual life as their aim, form the Church, which is the Kingdom of God.[38] (Italics added.)

The reconciliation accomplished in Christ is passed on to his followers for their appropriation. "[The] kingdom of God *is* the Spirit. Thus subjects are implicated in the process. The divine Idea, which exists for them as infinite love in infinite anguish, is within these subjects precisely in this perception: they [are] the community of Spirit." And the community "has given up all external distinctions in this infinite value, distinctions of mastery, power, position, even of sex and wealth. Before God all persons are equal." Herein lies the root of a truly universal justice and the actualization of freedom.[39]

The Kingdom of the Spirit and Christianity as the Absolute Religion. The Kingdom of the Spirit, as Hegel understands it, is the goal of the entire process of history and is that moment which inaugurates the Absolute or Consummate Religion. Christianity is the Consummate Religion, for in Christianity alone do we see the actual dialectical process by which Spirit (God) works itself out to full expression in history. God is Spirit, but to Hegel this means something very different from what most Christians mean by the term. For him Spirit is *the process of life itself,* "it is life, movement" whose nature it is "to differentiate itself, to give itself a definite character, to determine itself."

According to Hegel, Absolute Spirit develops and realizes itself according to a dialectical process that must be comprehended under three determinations. The idea goes forth into nature and actualizes itself as Spirit. It is for this reason that universal Spirit has found its adequate sensuous representation in the Christian religion under the name of the Holy Trinity. The divine Trinity, as Hegel sees it, is the sensuous representation of the dialectical process of the Absolute Spirit, and in the Kingdom of the Spirit (the Synthesis of the Logic) the truths contained in the Kingdoms of the Father and the Son are reconciled and overcome. It can be said, then, that for Hegel God only comes to *full historical actu-*

alization in the Kingdom of the Spirit. The Holy Spirit is the only member of the Trinity in which the *reality* of God is explicitly manifest. This is why Christianity is rightly called *the* "revealed" religion, for in the Kingdom of the Spirit God is no longer an object "out there" or "back then" but is a God who is not only revealed but has come to consciousness in and through the finite world. Thus, for Hegel, without the world God is not God.

The Kingdom of the Spirit *is* the Church or "the Spiritual Community" (*Die Gemeinde*). God, as fully actualized Spirit, is realizable only in a community of finite human minds, for, as Hegel maintains, Spirit achieves consciousness only through finite particularization or concretion. Since it is only through finite consciousness in its manifold forms that Absolute Spirit realizes itself, God as Father and as Son does not enjoy such perfection of consciousness. And if it is the case that God comes to explicit historical realization in and through the Spiritual Community of finite consciousness, then the naïve conception of God as *a person* must be left behind. Spirit actualized in a community of finite minds may have the unity of a personality but certainly cannot be *a person* in our limited sense.[40]

Christianity, according to Hegel, must give up its traditional theistic view, for such a view still conceives of God as a transcendent Being "out there." It has not yet made the dialectical move from the Kingdom of the Son to that of Absolute Spirit; it still persists in retaining the theistic gulf between humanity and God and fails to realize that "pure knowledge . . . is not merely intuition of God Himself" in finite consciousness. In other words, the absolute religion is the one in which humanity knows God insofar as God is known in humanity. God's knowledge of humanity is also humanity's knowledge of God.

Christianity's Aufhebung *into Philosophy*. Christianity, *the* Revealed Religion, is the Absolute or Consummate Religion in that for the first time religion realizes the *notion* of religion—i.e., of being the self-revelation of Absolute Spirit. And yet, for Hegel, Christianity has not yet risen to the level of speculative truth, to Absolute Knowledge in its scientific form. Religion, even the Absolute Religion, apparently never can rise above the external and objective mode of imaginative, pictorial presentation to pure conceptual thought. The spiritual content of religion is not itself to be confused with pure truth, for it is only the presentation of truth in the form of art, which is that of "feeling" (*Gefühl*), and "representation" (*Vorstellung*). Therefore, religion, or spiritual content in the form of sensuous representation, is a kind of exoteric metaphysics for Hegel which is needful for those who cannot rise to pure conceptual universality. Nevertheless, such religious representations must finally be *aufgehoben* into the forms of pure thought (*Begriff*), for there clings to such *Vorstellungen* something of the historically accidental and contingent and, therefore, leaves them open to rational attack. The transcending of the point of view of religious representation into forms of pure thought does not mean moving to the level of formal abstraction. It means, rather, that the truth represented in finite experience is raised to the level of rational universality without sacrificing its concreteness. Spirit achieves its concrete fulfillment only in conceptual thought, for only in this moment does it overcome both individuality and abstraction by becoming the concrete universal—the perfect union of content and form. Contrary to general opinion, the transformation of religion into philosophy does not, according to Hegel, destroy the content of religion; rather it elevates it from the level of imagination to that of conceptual universality.

For Hegel it was the very "translation" of Christianity into philosophy which *justified* the Christian religion. It appears clear to Hegel that refusal to carry out such an *Aufhebung* would result in a rational and historical critique of Christianity that would culminate in its dissolution. Thus many post-Hegelian thinkers have believed that Hegel's claim that Christianity is justified only in its conceptual transformation led him to substitute a "philosophical surrogate for Christianity, a figurative way of using dogmatic terms to express his own systematic concepts."[41]

It would appear, however, that Hegel's own attitude toward Christianity is ambiguous, and this very ambiguity led his contemporaries and later thinkers to see in him both the archcritic of Christianity and its modern philosophic savior. The historical significance of Hegel's attempted justification of Christianity in philosophy is well stated by Karl Löwith:

The distinction, and the consequent exaltation, of religion out of the form of feeling and imagination into that of the notion, are the means by which Hegel accomplishes his positive justification of the Christian religion, and at the same time his criticism of it. The ambiguity of this distinction forms the background for all post-Hegelian criticism of religion; it even produced the breakdown of the Hegelian school into a left and right wing. . . . Ecclesiastical orthodoxy declared Hegel's translation to be non-Christian because it destroyed the positive content of the faith; the Young Hegelians, on the contrary, were offended by Hegel's retention of dogmatic Christianity even in the *form* of his concept.[42]

The division of the Hegelian school into a right and a left wing is one of the most interesting and important intellectual developments in the nineteenth century. There were many philosophers and theologians in the latter decades of the nineteenth century who found in Hegel's philosophy the most adequate scientific tool for reconstructing Christianity in terms acceptable to modern experience. Those theologians in Germany who used Hegel, entirely or in part, in their reconstruction of Christianity were known generally as the Right-Wing or Center Hegelians. In Britain they were called the Neo-Hegelians. The Right-Wing movement in Germany included such important theologians as Philipp Marheineke (1780–1846), Karl Daub (1765–1836), and A. E. Biedermann (1819–1885). In Britain, Hegelian categories dominated the theological writings and reinterpretation of Christianity in John and Edward Caird.

From our present position at the end of the twentieth century, the more influential of the Hegelian movements appears to be the radical or Left-Wing Hegelian school. These "Young Hegelians," as they were also known, were in most cases not interested in using Hegel's ideas as a bulwark for preserving Christianity. On the contrary, the more radical members of the group saw in Hegel's philosophy the possibility of overcoming the Christian tradition. Among these "Young Hegelians" were D. F. Strauss, Bruno Bauer, Ludwig Feuerbach, and Karl Marx. Their critique of the Christian religion was so radical and historically so significant for an understanding of Christianity in the last century that we will

postpone our account of this movement for a later chapter.

However, before leaving Hegel, some indication of his constructive influence will give a more balanced view of his immense contribution to nineteenth-century religious thought. It will also set the stage for the later radical critique of the Left-Wing Hegelians. Three examples of his influence on German and English Hegelianism will suffice for our purposes.

F. C. BAUR

Our first example of the influence of Hegelianism must be a highly qualified one since Ferdinand Christian Baur (1792–1860), the great biblical scholar and church historian, developed many of his ideas before he felt the influence of Hegel (Schleiermacher was also crucial), and some of his most important theological contributions arose out of his reaction against Hegel. Nevertheless, his view of the historical process and of the relation of God and the world reflect Hegel's influence, and it is appropriate to introduce this important theologian in this Hegelian context. More will be said of Baur's influence on biblical scholarship in a later chapter.

F. C. Baur is widely considered the most important historical theologian of the nineteenth century, at least until the work of Adolf von Harnack later in the century. Baur's greatest work, *The History of the Christian Church,* appeared in five volumes between 1853 and 1863. He also wrote *The Epochs of Church Historiography* (1852), in which he sets forth his understanding of the writing of church history and dogma as a critical discipline; important multivolume works on the history of dogma from the early church to modern times; and monographs on the New Testament that challenged received views concerning the Gospels and the writings of Paul. His prodigious output was equivalent to the writing of a four-hundred-page book every year for forty years. Here we will sketch the Hegelian influences on his historical and theological work that are especially evident after about 1835.

Baur was born near Stuttgart, Germany, in 1792 and was educated at the Blaubeuren seminary and at Tübingen University. From 1817 to 1826 he taught at the seminary but then moved back to Tübingen where he remained until his death. He was recognized as the leader of the Protestant "Tübingen school" that was identified with, and criticized for, its association with Hegelian speculative theology. Baur clearly was influenced by Hegel's profound insight into the *historical* character of Christianity, e.g., that the Christian Church and its doctrine have a history, that they must be understood in relation to universal history, and that there can be no separation of ecclesiastical and secular history. Following Hegel, Baur also saw the process of historical development as the temporal working out of the Idea or the Divine Spirit to full expression or self-manifestation. He further saw this historical movement of Spirit, which is not simply the process of abstract thought, as developing in a Hegelian-like dialectic of opposing movements. He interpreted both the development of early Catholicism—as the synthesis of Jewish and Gentile Christianity in the primitive Christian community—and the great doctrinal controversies of the early centuries in terms of such a dialectical process of opposing tendencies.

Baur also took what, at the time, were radical positions on the New Testament, such as denying the authenticity of the Pastoral Epistles, but he defended his use of historical criticism against the unhistorical approach of both the rationalist theology of the time and that of orthodoxy. He argued that it was just such historical investigation as his that could safeguard Christianity from illusion and establish it on a sound basis. What the critical study of Church history and doctrine can do, according to Baur, is bring to light the true course of divine history. The work of the historical theologian is not, then, a destructive one—as it became in the case of David Friedrich Strauss—but rather a positive effort to recover the true development of the dogmatic tradition and one that could withstand critical investigation.

Baur insists that the historian is not simply a pedant who collects myriad facts; the historical theologian must understand the theological significance of the facts and must penetrate to the theological Idea. This involves a speculative endeavor, and it is evident in Baur's historical treatment of the development of the doctrines of the Trinity and the Incarnation. In both of these doctrines he sees, in

Hegelian fashion, the movement and manifestation of the Idea of God-manhood or the reconciliation of God and humankind working itself out in the course of the historical dialectic within Christianity.

Baur describes this critical and speculative task of the historical theologian in unmistakably Hegelian terms:

> Whether one calls the speculative method "Hegelianism" or something else, the nature of speculation is and remains the reasoning consideration of the object with which one is concerned; it is the posture of the consciousness in relation to the object, in which the object appears as that which it really is. . . . Without speculation, every historical investigation. . . is a mere tarrying on the superfluous and external side of the subject matter. The more important and comprehensive the object is with which historical investigation is concerned . . . the more such investigation approaches not merely reproducing in itself what the individual thought and did but a rethinking in itself of the eternal thoughts of the eternal Spirit, whose work history is.[43]

Thus for Baur theology is an historical discipline, but that means that the theologian must not only engage in the task of empirical historical research but also penetrate the "thoughts of the eternal Spirit" as they are manifest in the movements of Christian history, which is itself the self-revelation of the divine reconciliation, that is, the life of Spirit or God. Only by so joining historical research and a philosophy of history can theology avoid the subjectivism that Baur found in Schleiermacher's theology. It was his concern with the historical objectivity of Christianity that led Baur to find not only Schleiermacher's Christology inadequate but also that of his student, David Friedrich Strauss, as well as Hegel's lack of interest in the historical Jesus. In each of these cases , the historical Jesus is either minimized or disregarded in favor of an archetypal Christ (Schleiermacher) or the Christ-idea (Hegel and Strauss), in the latter case involving a too-abrupt move from history (*Vorstellung*) to speculative philosophy (*Begriff*), that is, to an abstract idea of the unity of the human and divine.

Baur's treatment of christology is distinctive. He refuses to allow a complete disjunction between the

Jesus of history and the Christ of faith or to identify the latter alone with the Hegelian idea of God-man-hood. His criticism of Hegel on this point is clear. For Hegel,

> The historically factual objective reality which lies behind faith made it possible for a merely external historical view to become faith, [but this] remains veiled in a mystery into which we should not penetrate, because the question is not whether Christ himself was the Godman in his objective historical appearance. All that matters is that he became the Godman for faith.[44]

Yet Baur the philosophical theologian agrees that Hegel was correct that the Christ of faith cannot *simply* be identified with the Jesus of history since the Christ of faith is the absolute or infinite idea which enters human consciousness *through* Jesus, though it is not wholly or perfectly realized in him. Here Baur is one with Hegelian Idealism. And yet, for Baur, Jesus the historical *founder* of Christianity and the Christ of faith must be integrally linked, since Jesus must be seen as unique in relation to other people in his actions and teachings. "How could faith in the Godman arise," Baur asks,

> unless he was in some way also objectively what faith took him to be? The necessary presupposition is in every case that the self-subsisting truth, the unity of the divine and human nature, first became in Christ a concrete truth, a self-conscious knowledge, and was expressed and taught by him as truth.[45]

It was this insistence on the continuity between the historical founder of Christianity and the Christ of the Christian community's faith that drove Baur to examine the historical sources from a purely historical perspective and to refuse to appeal to the purely dogmatic and supernatural interpretations of the historical Jesus assumed by the orthodox theologians. In this he proved to be one of the preeminent modern theologians whose work presupposes the inadequacy of the earlier theological work of both the orthodox supernaturalists and the Enlightenment rationalists. He also saw the necessity to move beyond Schleiermacher and to ground Christian faith on a truly objective, historical foundation.

A. E. BIEDERMANN

One of the last important representatives of German Hegelian theology was Alois Biedermann (1819–1885) who was a student of Marheineke and served as professor of dogmatics at Zurich from 1860 to his death in 1885. Biedermann was not dependent solely on Hegel for his philosophical ideas—he drew also from Kant and Schleiermacher—but the dominant influence on his thought and language in his *Christliche Dogmatik* is that of Hegel. Biedermann's importance lies, in part, in his attempt to answer the negative critique of theology of D. F. Strauss and the other radical "Young Hegelians" by offering a speculative reconstruction of theology through the use of categories that were essentially Hegelian. He also corrects certain difficulties in Hegel's own reconstruction of Christianity, especially the latter's Christology, and therefore represents an Hegelian theology more consistent with the Church's creedal traditions.[46]

Biedermann was convinced that the Left-Wing Hegelian critique of Christianity often was correct as far as it went but that it did not go beyond a negative criticism of historical representation to the purification of the historical in conceptual thought. But for Biedermann, as for Baur, this did not mean a final disinterest in the representational form of religion as it did for Hegel and some of his followers. For Biedermann the natural language of religion is the sensuous or representational, and the conceptual form is not so much an *aufhebung* of the historical as it is the clarification of the real meaning of the representational form.

Biedermann's handling of the difficult question of the "personality" of God illustrates his general interest in preserving the representational form of religion while clarifying its conceptual meaning. He argues that "personality" is actually the definition of *finite* spirit. When we speak of a personal subject, we think not only of a spirit but a *finite* spirit, "spirit with a sensuous, natural presupposition in itself," a natural, individual corporeality. But when we *think* of God or Absolute Spirit as having a personality, we run into difficulties:

> When we identify absolute spirit with absolute personality, we either actually think it as personality—but

then not as truly absolute or we think it as only absolute—but then personality is present only as an image. We *think* absolute spirit; we have an absolute personality only in *representation, i.e.,* we view the purely spiritual in an abstract sensuous way, but this sensuousness we have abstracted from human personality, to the essence of which it belongs. . . .[47]

Does this mean that the personality of God is an illicit conception? Not at all, if it is properly understood.

> Permission to *represent* God as personality, and to speak of him in expressions that are taken from human personality, remains. Now for the first time . . . it finds its psychological foundation and therein its justification. We can only think absolute spirit, and only represent absolute personality. And the two indeed coincide: absolute spirit as conception and absolute personality as representation. . . . [But only] in thinking of God as absolute do we know that, and why, we must also represent him to ourselves as personality. Yes—if we would represent him to ourselves at all! But that is already sufficiently cared for by the psychological nature of our spirit. All our thinking is first thinking in representations, and our thinking as pure thinking is only scientific reworking of our representations. . . . However scientifically concerned for pure thought, we lead our conscious life, before as after, in representation, we seek only to make ourselves aware, intellectually certain, of the truth of our representations, when we abrogate and absorb representations in their conceptions and no longer forthwith identify our subjective representational form with the objective truth dwelling in the representation. . . . Only man as finite spirit is personality; God as absolute spirit is not. Yet the religious intercourse is always a personal one, and indeed not merely in subjective representation but in objective truth, because it goes on between the infinite and finite spirit within the finite human spiritual life and thus must take place throughout in the form of the latter.[48]

Biedermann's concern to show the conceptual content appropriate to the ecclesiastical, representational form is best seen in his discussion of Christology. What is basic to all the traditional Christological formulae is what Biedermann calls

"the Christian principle" and how this principle is related to the historical person of Jesus. According to Biedermann, Hegel was quite right in his emphasis on the principle or *Idée* of the Incarnation; but where Hegel failed, in part, and Strauss certainly failed, was in relating the principle adequately to the person of Jesus.

First, Biedermann holds that it is quite wrong to conceive of the "Christian principle" as an abstraction, "a kind of subjective idea first generated by our thought or abstracted from actuality," as did some of the Young Hegelians. The Christian principle

> first entered the actuality of history, in the actual event of Jesus' religious self-consciousness and of faith in him. The definition of its content is therefore not to be understood as if the content has also been realized *eo ipso* in human history before and apart from that fact.[49]

Having said this, however, it is important not to confuse the "idea newly appearing in human history in his [Jesus's] person" with "a personal definition of the single person Jesus."

> The principle shows itself as the actualization of the true relation between God and man, and thereby as the principle of salvation for the natural humanity which through sin stands in contradiction to God and its own divine destiny. Its content must therefore still be identified as intrinsically contained in the full actualization of what is contained therein.[50]

If this latter conception is not taken with utter seriousness, "then the Christian principle is not understood as truly human and as the truly human religious principle, but as something supernatural in the bad supernaturalistic sense of the word."[51] The "Christian principle" first entered into history factually in the person of Jesus, "but *intrinsically* it is eternally contained in the essence of God and man as their true religious relationship."[52] Whereas the Church's dogma personified the principle and identified it immediately with the person bearing the revelation of the principle—hence calling him the God-man—the proper designation should be God-manhood which in Jesus became a religious actuality in human spiritual life. What the Church represented in mythological form as the God-man is in actuality the definition of the true relation between God and humanity, the absolute and the finite spirit, or what Biedermann calls the "absolute religious self-consciousness." This is the new principle of religious consciousness which entered history with Jesus and which can be appropriated in faith. What Jesus actualized in human history is intrinsically immanent in human spiritual life. Biedermann's way of stating this reveals his indebtedness to Hegel.

> Thus wherever a human ego achieves the actualization of its true being as man, *viz.* as finite spirit, there the being of God, of absolute spirit, is revealed in it and proved in it to be the active power of its subjective spirituality. . . . Now if that which accordingly is intrinsically immanent in every human spiritual life as the active principle lying at its basis, *i.e.,* the absoluteness of spirit as such in its pure being-in-self, is actualized in a human person as the actual content of its own subjective spiritual life . . . then this humanly personal self-consciousness of the absoluteness of spirit is the factual union of the divine and the human essences as the unity of personal spiritual life, or thus the entrance of the principle of God-manhood (which is intrinsically immanent in man as finite spirit) into the actuality of the life of humanity.[53]

God-manhood, which is intrinsically immanent in finite human spirit, has first been historically actualized in Jesus. However, the question of *the actual historical form* of this source of Christianity is the subject of historical research and not dogmatics. Dogmatics is concerned "to bring the essence of this religious self-consciousness (historically primitive in Jesus) to its pure conceptual expression."[54] Nevertheless, Biedermann is concerned that the relation between the historical Jesus and the Christian principle not be considered as "external and accidental" as it was considered by Strauss and other Left-Wing Hegelians:

> It would be accidental and external either if that principle had merely consisted in a doctrine newly delivered by Jesus or if its emergence in history had merely indirectly received impetus from the person of Jesus. But Jesus' personal religious life was the first self-

actualization of that principle as a world-historical figure, and it is the source and efficacy of this principle in history: Jesus is the historical redeemer as the historical revelation of the principle of salvation.[55]

The purpose of dogmatics, for Biedermann, is to bring to conceptual expression the essence of Jesus's religious self-consciousness. The creedal definitions point to conceptual truths but, as such, "wear themselves out in pure contradictions." Dogmatics, then, must trace out the intention which came to expression in representational, creedal form. Only then can its historical legitimacy be shown. What happened historically was that the original relation of the man Jesus to God "was elevated by the believing consciousness, as it sought to give account of the essentially new therein, into the view of a metaphysical relation of the preexistent ego of Christ to God."[56] This was the necessary and "correct expression of the fundamental truth that it is not the historical person as such but a principle entering human life in this person which is the actual ground of the new religious relation of divine childhood disclosed to humanity in this person."[57]

In the latter part of the *Dogmatik,* in a section entitled "The Rational Nucleus of the Christian Faith," Biedermann sets forth the conceptual bases of the Christological formulae. Here is a brief sampling of his conceptual understanding of the Church's positive dogma:

> §820. That the metaphysical divine sonship was pressed to the full homoousia ["of one substance"] was the necessary expression of the truth that the absoluteness of spirit that discloses itself in the self-consciousness of divine childhood [Jesus] is the revelation of the essence of absolute spirit itself.
>
> §821. That the church's doctrine also demanded time and full humanity for its God-man was the expression of the truth that the absolute religious self-consciousness of divine childhood is at the same time nothing other than the true and full actualization of the human essence, in which the sensuous natural presupposition in man also achieves the fulfillment of its destiny as the medium for man's absolute destiny.
>
> §822. The Chalcedonian definition of the equally inseparable and unmixed unity of the two natures in

the God-man was the necessary expression in the Church's doctrine of the truth that in the absolute religious self-consciousness the absoluteness of spirit and the creaturely finitude of the ego constitute the two elements, surely logically to be distinguished but in actuality undivided, of the *one* personal life-process of this self-consciousness.

§825. The pre-worldly eternal being of the Son with the Father is the representational and therefore mythologizing expression of the truth that in the essence of absolute spirit its self-revelation in finite spirit is already co-posited in itself.[58]

Like Hegel, Biedermann found in the Christian dogma of the Trinity the representational form in which the truth of Absolute Spirit has come to historical expression. The Trinity is the highest and most sublime of all representations of God:

> If the true concept of God is the concept of absolute spirit and that of the Christian principle is the absoluteness of spirit in the religious self-consciousness of finite spirit, then the core of the doctrine of the Trinity, or the Christian trinitarian concept of God, is this: The absoluteness of spirit which proves itself in finite spirit to be the power of annulling finite spirit's self-contradiction and discord, is an element of the *actus purus* of absolute spirit itself; and what is more, in the actual entrance of this principle into history God is first actually manifest in humanity as absolute spirit.[59]

Biedermann, like a number of other mid-nineteenth-century speculative and mediating theologians, sought a middle way between the old supernaturalism and the new naturalism and materialism of the radical Hegelians. Like Schleiermacher, he regarded the religious self-consciousness as something intrinsic and enduring which could never be replaced by any higher form of knowledge, such as philosophy. Philosophy can purify our religious modes of conceiving reality, but it can never replace religious faith itself. Thus Biedermann rejected Hegel's *Aufhebung* of Christianity into a philosophy. Nevertheless, Biedermann held that the old supernaturalism was quite unable to explain the proper relation between God and the world, and he found in Hegel a conceptual framework which would delineate this relationship in a way more consonant with experience and philosophical reflection—and which would, at the same time, point to the real intention behind the Church's creedal representations.

BRITISH HEGELIANISM: JOHN AND EDWARD CAIRD

Neo-Hegelianism in theology became dominant in Britain in the last decades of the nineteenth century primarily through the writings of the Scottish brothers Caird. Both Cairds possessed rare gifts as writers and public speakers and thus exercised considerable influence on a generation of university students. Edward Caird (1835–1908) was successively Fellow of Merton College, Oxford, Professor of Moral Philosophy at the University of Glasgow (1866–1893), and Master of Balliol College, Oxford. He wrote important studies of Kant and Hegel, and in 1893 his Gifford Lectures, entitled *The Evolution of Religion,* were published in two volumes.

John Caird (1820–1898) was a Presbyterian clergyman and was appointed to an academic post, as Professor of Theology at Glasgow, only in his middle years. From 1873 until his death in 1898, he served as Principal of Glasgow University. His two important works on religion, *Introduction to the Philosophy of Religion* (1880) and his Gifford Lectures, published posthumously in 1899 as *The Fundamental Ideas of Christianity,* show the indelible stamp of Hegel. Yet the Cairds were not slavish disciples of their German master, but took from him the general lines of the Hegelian system and adapted it, especially in the case of John Caird, to a form of piety and theological style unique to Scottish divines.

In his book *The Evolution of Religion,* Edward Caird approaches both the doctrine of God and the history of humanity's religions from the perspective of the Hegelian dialectic. According to Caird, it is humanity's natural religious consciousness which drives it to seek an underlying unity and ground of self and world or subject and object. Our uniqueness lies in the fact that our experience of the finite causes us to seek after the Infinite. And if we consider the general nature of our conscious life, we find that that life is circumscribed by *three ideas* which are indissolubly connected:

> These are the idea of the object or not-self, the idea of the subject or self, and the idea of the unity which is presupposed in the difference of the self and the not-self and within which they act and react on each other: in other words the idea of God. . . . The *object* is the general name under which we include the external world and all the things and beings in it, all that we know and all that we act on, the whole environment, which conditions the activity of the ego. . . . There is only one thing which stands over against this complex whole of existence and refuses to be regarded *simply* as part of the system; and that is the ego, the self, the *subject* for which it exists. For the primary condition of the existence of this subject is that it should distinguish itself from the object as such. . . . All our life, then, moves between these two terms which are essentially distinct from, and opposed to, each other.[60]

Our consciousness recognizes that these two ideas are indivisible but also necessarily opposed, else the one could be subsumed within the other as a mere phase. Such an awareness forces us

> to seek the secret of their being in *a higher principle, of whose unity they in their action and reaction are the manifestation, which they presuppose as their beginning and to which they point as their end*. . . . To put it more directly, the idea of an absolute unity, which transcends all the oppositions of finitude, and especially the last opposition which includes all others—the opposition of subject and object—*is the ultimate presupposition of our consciousness*. . . . Every creature who is capable of the consciousness of an objective world and of the consciousness of a self, is capable also of the consciousness of God. Or, to sum up the whole matter in one word, *every rational being as such is a religious being*.[61] (Italics added.)

For Caird, apart from God nothing can be known, for God is the unitary ground of all being and knowing. This does not mean that all humans are aware of God as this unitary ground. In fact, the history of religion is the history of the successive stages of humanity's developing rational conscious-

ness—or, put another way, "history is just religion progressively *defining itself*." If we study the history of religious (rational) consciousness, Caird believes that we will note that it has passed through three distinct stages in which each of the three ideas predominates.

> Hence we can distinguish three stages in the development of man, in which the form of his consciousness is successively determined by the ideas of the object, of the subject and of God as the principle of unity in both; and each of these stages brings with it a special modification of the religious consciousness.[62]

Caird describes the first or objective stage of religious consciousness in much the way that Hegel described Greco-Roman religion.

> The earliest life of man is one in which the objective consciousness rules and determines all his thoughts, or that in this stage both his consciousness of himself and his consciousness of God are forced to take an objective form. Man at first looks outward and not inward: he can form no idea of anything to which he cannot give a "local habitation and name," which he cannot body forth as an existence in space and time. . . . God necessarily at this time must be represented as an object among other objects.[63]

The second stage of religious consciousness is that in which the subjective element predominates. This is best exemplified in the inner, prophetic religion of later Judaism, which prepared the way for the third stage, Christianity. The second period is one in which

> the *form of self-consciousness* prevails and determines both the consciousness of objects and that of God. In such a period, the interest of life becomes predominantly moral, or at least subjective and the outward world loses its power over the human spirit. . . . His mind, his inner life, is now "his kingdom". . . . He is freed from the superstitious dread of outward things . . . the poetic halo vanishes from nature. A glory has passed away from the earth, and "great Pan is dead". . . . The manifestation of the divine is no longer found in nature but in man. . . . Man alone is supposed to be made in the image of God. . . .[64]

The third stage, or synthesis, which is exemplified in Christianity, is that in which

the object and the self appear, each in its proper form, as distinct yet in essential relation, and, therefore, as subordinated to the consciousness of God, which is recognized as at once the presupposition and as the end of both. Here, for the first time the religious consciousness takes its true place in relation to the secular consciousness, and God is known in the *true form of His idea*. . . . This is the only form which religion can take for the modern world. It is impossible for any one who has breathed the spirit of modern science . . . to believe in a purely objective God: to worship any power of nature or even any individualized outward image such as those of Apollo or Athene. . . . Again, though our own religion is developed out of Judaism, it is impossible for moderns to recall the attitude of the pure Monotheist, to whom God was only a subject among other subjects, though lifted high above all the rest. We cannot think of the infinite Being as a will which is external to that which it has made. We cannot, indeed, think of Him as external to anything, least of all to the spiritual beings who, as such, "live and move and have their being in Him." This idea of the immanence of God underlies the Christian conception; and . . . we can see that it is an idea involved in all modern philosophy and theology.[65]

Edward Caird, like most Hegelian theologians, conceived of Christianity as the final or absolute religion in that it was the historial synthesis of the philosophically antithetical objective and subjective consciousness—the absolute religion in which God is known not as external object or highest subject but as the immanent unitary ground of all knowing and being, of subject and object.

John Caird took up the task where his brother's *The Evolution of Religion* left off, namely, with Christianity established as the absolute religion. In his *Fundamental Ideas of Christianity,* John Caird proceeds, like Hegel, to attempt to demonstrate that the seeming contradictions of positive Christian revelation are transcended when advanced to the level of speculative idea and that the Christian *idea* is congruent with the highest philosophical analysis of experience. Take, for example, the difficult question of God's relation to the world. Caird, like Hegel,

finds in the Christian conception of God's revelation and Incarnation a representational expression of the truth of the God-world relationship. Neither Pantheism nor Deism has been able to give an adequate view of the relation of God to the world, "Pantheism by the annulling of the finite world or its absorption in the Infinite, Deism by reducing God to a finite anthropomorphic personality." The human mind cannot rest, according to John Caird, in the idea of a God who is all only by obliterating the finite world.

The pantheistic notion of the unreality and illusoriness of the finite world involves a self-contradiction. For even *as* a mere semblance or illusion it needs to be accounted for; and that it is more than an illusion the capacity to detect its illusoriness is the unconscious witness. The mind that can look on the world from the point of view of the Infinite virtually asserts for itself something more than a negative relation to the Infinite. The contradiction thus involved in its thought forces it onwards in quest of an Infinite which contains and accounts for the finite instead of annulling it.[66]

Likewise, Deism is not rationally satisfying.

In finding a place for the finite in the presence of the Infinite, Deism satisfies the consciousness of freedom, but it does so only by rending in twain the system of the universe. It lends a false elevation to its anthropomorphic God, by placing Him in hard, transcendent opposition to the world, and it leaves in nature, and still more in the finite spirit, elements which are in no inner and essential relation to Him. The gulf between the infinite and the finite remains unbridged.[67]

Caird finds in the Christian idea of God an understanding of God's relation to the world which neither Pantheism nor Deism can satisfy. The Christian doctrine of God as Infinite, Self-revealing Spirit or Mind contains all the elements necessary for an adequate theology. It shows:

1. That it is Infinite Mind or Intelligence which constitutes the reality of the world, not simply as its external Creator, but as the inward Spirit in and through which all things live and move and have their being;

2. That by its very nature, Infinite Mind or Spirit has in it a principle of self-revelation—a necessity of self-manifestation to and in a world of finite beings; and

3. That the infinitude of God, conceived of as Infinite Spirit, so far from involving the negation or suppression of the finite world, is rather the principle of the individuality and independence of nature and man.[68]

Theology had long conceived of God as the first cause and creative source or ground of the world. What is new in Hegel and, in turn, in Caird is the idea that God's being and the world are interdependent and that this insight is rooted in the Christian doctrine of God's triune nature. Caird develops a doctrine of God similar in ways to that of twentieth-century Panentheism.*

> Not only is it true that the finite world can be understood only in the light of the idea of God, but there is a sense in which that idea [God] involves the existence of a finite world. In the nature of God as self-revealing Spirit, there is contained, so to speak, the necessity of His self-manifestation in and to a world of finite beings, and especially in and to a world of finite beings, and especially in and to a world of finite intelligences made in His own image. If it be true that without the idea of God, nature and man would be unintelligible, there is a sense in which it is also true that without nature and man God would be unintelligible.[69]

For Caird, as for Hegel, God fulfills and realizes His own nature in the temporal existence of the world and above all in the spiritual life of humanity:

> When we say that the plant is related to the root or germ, not arbitrarily, but by an inward and essential necessity of nature, so that the former could not be

*Contemporary Panentheists, as distinguished from Pantheists and Deists, hold that God and the world are interdependent. While God does not limit the real freedom of the world, nor the world exhaust God's being and creativity, nevertheless, the one is unthinkable without the other. God influences the world, and the world influences God. Since there is real freedom, the future is open for both the world and God. Hence, God is, in some sense, temporal. This view is most systematically developed by A. N. Whitehead and Charles Hartshorne.

what it is without the latter, we imply conversely that the root or germ has in it something which seeks its realization in the plant, and without the latter would remain unfulfilled and incomplete. So, when we say that, in its whole spiritual nature—its intelligence, its moral and religious life, the finite spirit rests on and is rooted in the Infinite, what we imply is that in the Infinite there is that which involves the existence of the finite spirit. If there be a divine element in man, *there must be a human element in God, of which the whole spiritual life and history of the world is the manifestation.*[70] (Italics added.)

For Caird, the idea of the self-manifestation of Spirit, or God, in the history of the world is formulated in the language of Scripture in the expression that humanity is "made in the image of God." That is, human nature, though in one view only a finite existence, is nevertheless differentiated from all other existences in that it is in a special sense a manifestation of the Infinite. Part of the difficulty with such a conception lies, Caird believes, in a mistaken reading of the biblical text. Theologians have suffered from the mistaken notion that only what is perfect can have come from the hand of God or constitute God's self-manifestation. Hence theologians have indulged in imaginary pictures of the original, paradisaical perfection of humanity, picturing

> the first representatives of mankind . . . [as] full-fledged specimens of humanity, equipped with the wisdom of the sage, the exalted virtue of the hero, the piety and holiness of the saint.[71]

This is to fail to realize that what the *imago Dei* "points to is not the *initial* or *original,* but the *ideal* perfection of man's nature . . . what it is capable of becoming."[72] Caird's reading of the biblical teaching concerning the image of God in humanity is essentially Hegelian.

> It is not to man as originally created that likeness to God is exclusively ascribed in the Old and New Testament Scriptures. However we are to conceive of the paradisaical state, it is represented as prior to that "knowledge of good and evil," without which moral action cannot really exist and goodness can, at most, be only the unconscious innocence of childhood.

Though, again, the act of disobedience by which this knowledge comes is depicted as a retrogression, it is, on the other hand, described as an advance; though it loses one kind of likeness to God, it marks the rise of another: "*Ye shall be as gods,* knowing good and evil." And finally, the highest form of Godlikeness, according to the Scripture representation, is neither man's primitive state nor the restoration of that state. A return to forfeited innocence, a recovery of the unconscious harmony of nature which sin has broken up is impossible. . . . But the discord which sin has introduced is but the transition step to a more glorious harmony. Out of the death of nature rises a higher and nobler life. On the soul that has passed through the terrible experience of evil and, through the redemptive power of the Christian faith, has triumphed over it, there begins to be impressed a likeness to God far surpassing in spiritual beauty the lost image of Paradise. . . . It is of the very essence of a spiritual nature that its ideal perfection cannot be an immediate gift of nature, but must be wrought out by its own conscious activity.[73]

John Caird's Christology is much more orthodox than Hegel's, but even here his Hegelianism is ever present. This is especially the case in his attitude toward the historical Jesus where his Idealism is pronounced. Speaking of Christ, Caird remarks that

it is not the facts of His individual history, but the ideas that underlie it, that constitute the true value of his life. A true idea is true independently of the facts and events that first suggested it. There are many universal ideas which are their own evidence, apart from the superficial phenomena or the historic events that were the particular occasion of their discovery. The latter— the empirical, historic, element—may be disputed, may be difficult to ascertain, may even turn out to be more or less fictitious. . . . The principle remains true, whatever becomes of the facts. The life of Christ has been the source of ideas concerning God and man, and relations of human nature to the divine, transcending in originality and importance the contributions made to our knowledge of spiritual things by all other teachers. But, even if many of the details of Christ's life and teaching should fail to stand the test of scientific criticism . . . still the ideas and doctrines . . . which had their historic origin in that life, would be recognized as true in them-

selves, and as having an indestructible evidence in the reason and conscience of man.[74]

Because it is the *idea* which Christ represents rather than the historical occasion of Jesus as the Christ which is paramount for Caird, he can, with Hegel, give greater place to the Kingdom of the Spirit than the Kingdom of the Son. Thus, according to Caird, those who were in direct, personal contact with Jesus could only form vague and imperfect conceptions of his spiritual greatness. It was St. Paul, with his *idea* of the organic unity of all believers in Christ as their living Spirit or Head, who first saw the true import of the Christological idea. According to Caird's interpretation of Paul, no division is possible between Christ and the Church; both must be seen as a living, interdependent organism. Hence, for Caird, Christ is not fully actualized when considered in isolation from the community of believers.

And if the members live and fulfil themselves only in union with the universal principle, so, on the other hand, *does it fulfil or realize itself in them.* Apart from its members or organs, the principle of life is only an abstraction. It is, at most, not a reality, but only an unrealized possibility. . . . As an individual person He [Christ] has long passed away from the world; but He lives forever, as the ever-present, ever-active principle of its highest life.[75]

The dispensation of the Spirit is depicted pictorially in the New Testament in a variety of ways— in terms of Christ's ascension, his exaltation, the sending of the Holy Spirit at Pentecost—but underlying all these pictorial representations is the *idea* that

the divine principle which manifested itself in the human person and life of Christ, never did or can pass away from the world; and that, now and forever, it manifests itself in the life of every individual believer and in the universal or corporate life of the Church, in which "dwelleth all the fulness of the Godhead bodily."[76]

Life in the Kingdom of Absolute Spirit is described by Caird in language at once authentically Christian and markedly Hegelian:

What this absolute principle . . . demands of every human spirit is the sacrifice, the surrender, the abnegation of our private, particular self—its limited ends and interests; that we cease to think our own thoughts, to gratify our own desires, to do our own will, but rejoice to let this absolute, all-comprehending will reign in us and over us.

Yet, on the other hand, it is also the experience of the religious life that, in thus losing and abnegating, we truly gain ourselves: that our true will is not the will of this particular and private self, but a will that is in harmony with the absolute will . . . when we lose all sense of anything that divides our own self-consciousness from the consciousness of God.[77]

CONCLUSION

The Hegelianism of men like John and Edward Caird can be viewed as a kind of "third force" in the nineteenth-century defense of Christianity. First, there were the Kantians and especially the followers of Albrecht Ritschl (of whom we have yet to speak in Chapter 11) and the Romantics, represented by Schleiermacher. Of the three major movements, Hegelianism is in certain respects the most important, although Hegel's own direct influence was shortest lived. Hegelian theology suffered the general fate of German Idealism after the middle of the century—that is, it was abandoned as the result of philosophical analysis. Yet the apparent rejection of Hegelian categories and ideas is deceptive; his influence lives on indirectly. Many of the issues at the center of contemporary theology find their origin in Hegel.

Part of the difficulty in assessing the present significance of Hegel lies in the ambiguity of his own position, which led to the wide-ranging interpretation of his thought by his disciples. In 1821 Hegel had spoken pessimistically of the decadence of Christendom and the "passing away of the community." This has contributed to the opposing interpretations of Hegel's vision of Christianity's future. And as a result in many ways it is easier to trace the more radical and negative influences of Hegel on theological speculation—for example, on Feuerbach's reduction of theology to anthropology,

on Marx, and on twentieth-century theologies of the "death of God." Of all this we shall have more to say later.

Theologians who today acknowledge Hegel's enduring importance, and their indebtedness to him, also recognize the limitations of his kind of speculative system in the cultural context of the late twentieth century. Despite the brilliance of his speculation, there is a fundamental suspicion of the intellectual pretention in Hegel's grand philosophical setting aside and preservation of Christianity. We are dubious of his working out such a world-historical teleology in his own head. Furthermore, Hegel appears to drain evil of its reality and its horror by incorporating it into a necessary moment of his dialectic. His philosophical grasp of the Absolute Spirit also strikes one as involving a certain blindness to the reality of God's mystery and awesome otherness, of what Rudolf Otto called the sense of God as the *mysterium tremendum et fascinans.*[78]

Hegel's importance for Christian thought lies not, however, in his speculative *system* but in the richness of the ideas that underlie that system. We can mention only a few that have had such a profound influence on theology to the present day. First, and perhaps foremost, is Hegel's deep understanding that nature, history, *and* God, Reality-itself, must be understood in terms of interdependence and process. For Hegel, time and history are not the accidents but the essential constituents of reality. Hegel's contribution to this revolutionary shift in human consciousness is incalculable. Specifically, his influence here can be observed in three crucial areas of Christian thought. First, Hegel gave powerful impetus to our understanding of the *historical development* of Christian doctrine and institutions and to the implications of this discovery for claims regarding the continuity of the Christian tradition. We will see the importance of this question in the work of the Tübingen theologians and J. H. Newman, discussed in Chapter 8.

A second area of Christian reflection influenced by Hegel's historical orientation is his sense of the historical sweep and totality of human spiritual life. Hegel's brilliant phenomenology of the human spirit envisioned the human race passing through successive stages of religious life, each one reflecting a necessary moment in the development of spiritual consciousness and adding to a deeper, fuller comprehension of the truth. Hegel's phenomenology proved therefore to be of critical importance for the scientific and phenomenological study of religion that emerged in the latter decades of the nineteenth century.

Finally, Hegel's understanding of God's or Spirit's *actualization through immanent manifestation in and dependence on the world* provoked a wholly new discussion of Christianity's understanding of the relation of God and the world. The orthodox theologians charged Hegel with *Pantheism,* but it is clear that Hegel's *intention,* whether or not successful, was to move beyond both a dualistic *Deism,* which conceived of God as "alien" and "beyond" the world, and a *Pantheistic monism,* either in its *atheistic* or *acosmic* forms. Many of the Left-Wing Hegelians, for example Feuerbach, conceived of the finite world itself to be Spirit or God. Others, following Spinoza's acosmism, denied the finite world its distinct reality in differentiation from God and conceived of God alone as the one Reality. Many commentators today would argue that Hegel was successful in avoiding either form of Pantheism. His true position is what we earlier called *Panentheism,* although the term was not Hegel's. Panentheism denies that God and the world are identical (Pantheism) *or* that God and the world are separate (Deism). It proposes, rather, that the world is included in God's being, although it does not exhaust God's being. God and the world are interdependent, which means that God changes in some sense in experiencing the world. This was a radical challenge to traditional Christian theism, for it appeared to deny such classical concepts as God's

impassibility or changelessness and the divine omniscience. Nevertheless, it also opened up new ways of thinking about such questions as finite freedom, divine love, the incarnation, and theodicy. Hegel thus profoundly altered the way theologians were to think about the relation of God and the world.

Closely related to the above was, of course, Hegel's role in altering thinking about Christology and the Trinity. The elaborate trinitarian structure of Hegel's system, with its three fundamental moments that constitute reality itself, renewed interest in the doctrine of the Trinity and the possibilities of a new theological understanding of its meaning. Hegel's conception of the self-actualization of Spirit in the historical figure of Jesus also raised a host of issues having to do with Christology. For one thing, it gave philosophical support to more traditional doctrinal formulations of the Divine-human unity. But it also sharpened the issues surrounding the historical figure of Jesus. While insisting on the real historical and particular nature of the Incarnation, Hegel also appears to minimize the issues posed by the actual historical effort to recover the man Jesus, as if it were a secondary matter. It is the *meaning* of the historical Incarnation, the second moment in the actualization of Spirit, that is significant for Hegel. And so, Hegel's discussion of the Incarnation heightened the debate provoked by the emerging quest of the historical Jesus and the relationship between the "Jesus of history" and the "Christ of faith."

While Hegel's system is today often repudiated, it is clear why his seminal ideas continue to inform and illumine contemporary theological discussion. This is underlined by the fact that there has been a lively revival of interest in Hegel studies in the latter decades of the twentieth century.

NOTES

1. John H. Randall, Jr., *The Career of Philosophy,* II (New York, 1962), 343.
2. The essays written between 1793 and 1800 were published for the first time in 1907 by Herman Nohl, who entitled the collection *Hegel's Early Theological Writings.* Because Hegel scholarship went into eclipse in the English-speaking world about the time these essays were published, Hegel's early religious writings were not widely considered in English studies of his thought. Acknowledging the great importance of Hegel's early writings, Walter Kaufmann (*Philosophical Review,* Jan. 1954) nevertheless finds Nohl's title misleading. Kaufmann considers these writings antitheological. Kaufmann may be right if we mean by *theological* that which is creedal or orthodox. However, a deep religious interest and conviction runs through all these writings.

3. Herman Nohl, *Hegels theologische Jugendschriften* (Tübingen, 1907), p. 6.

4. There is considerable disagreement as to just what were Hegel's intentions in writing *Das Leben Jesu*. Richard Kroner ("Introduction," *On Christianity: Early Theological Writings*, ed. T. M. Knox [1961]) and Kaufmann (*Hegel* [1965]) agree that Hegel did not intend it for publication. Kroner, however, believes Hegel did not commit himself to the book's interpretation, whereas Kaufmann holds that it "is plainly Hegel's attempt to write a scripture for such a folk religion as he had envisaged" and that "it may have been at least partly the grotesqueness of this effort that persuaded him once and for all that man could *not* be restored in his totality and harmony by religion." T. M. Knox ("Hegel's Attitude toward Kant's Ethics," *Kant-Studien*, Vol. 49, No. 1) contends that Hegel was seriously under the influence of Kant at this time and discharged his duty of writing a life of Jesus in harmony with his master's spirit but that this very duty "eventually helped to convince him that there was something wrong with the enterprise."

5. Nohl, op. cit., pp. 221–223.

6. Ibid., p. 222.

7. Ibid., p. 227. The similarity of this statement to those made by the later Left-Wing Hegelian critics of Christianity, such as Feuerbach and Marx, is striking.

8. Ibid., p. 208.

9. "The Spirit of Christianity and Its Fate," in T. M. Knox, ed., *Hegel's Early Theological Writings* (1961), p. 185.

10. Ibid., p. 187.

11. Ibid., p. 209.

12. Ibid., p. 212.

13. Nohl, op. cit., pp. 280–283.

14. "The Spirit of Christianity," p. 247.

15. *On Christianity*, p. 11.

16. Ibid., p. 289.

17. Ibid., p. 301.

18. Ibid., p. 253.

19. Nohl, op. cit., as cited in Kaufmann, op. cit., pp. 65–66.

20. Friedrich Hegel, *Vorlesungen uber die Philosophie der Weltgeschichte*, I, 45, ed. J. Hoffmeister (Hamburg, 1955); cited by Stephen Crites, "The Gospel According to Hegel," *Journal of Religion*, XLVI (April 1966), 248. Crites's article is an excellent, brief summary of the mature Hegel's understanding of Christianity and was of considerable help to this writer in grasping an overview of Hegel's interpretation of Christianity.

21. Hegel deals with the "Unhappy Consciousness" at considerable length in *The Phenomenology of Spirit*, where he identifies it especially with the religious life of the Middle Ages under the dominion of the Roman Catholic Church and feudalism.

22. *The Philosophy of History*, trans. J. Sibree (New York, 1944), p. 321.

23. Ibid., pp. 321–322. Hegel was fond of explicating the text from Genesis concerning Adam's Fall; and discussions of it can be found, in addition to the above, in *History of Philosophy*, trans. Haldane, III, 8–10; *Lectures on the Philosophy of Religion* (1827), ed. Peter C. Hodgson (Berkeley, 1988), pp. 215–217, 442–446; *Lectures* III, ed. P. C. Hodgson (Berkeley, 1985), pp. 101–108, 207–211, 300–304; and, in an earlier form, in *The Phenomenology of Spirit*, trans. J. B. Baillie, pp. 770–772.

24. *Lectures on Philosophy of Religion*, III, ed. Peter C. Hodgson (Berkeley, 1985) p. 298.

25. Ibid., p. 301.

26. Ibid., p. 207.

27. Ibid.

28. Ibid.

29. *Philosophy of History*, p. 323.

30. Ibid., pp. 325–326.

31. Ibid., pp. 324–325.

32. Here Hegel's Christology has much in common with the views of Paul Tillich. See James Livingston, "Tillich's Christology and Historical Research," in *Religion in Life* (Winter 1966).

33. *The Christian Religion*, ed. Peter Hodgson (1979), pp. 194–195.

34. *Lectures on Philosophy of Religion*, III, p. 124–125.

35. Ibid., p. 128.

36. *Phenomenology of Spirit*, p. 780.

37. *Philosophy of History*, p. 325.

38. Ibid., p. 328.

39. *The Christian Religion*, pp. 238, 235.

40. See J. M. E. McTaggart's comments on the personality of God in Hegel's theology in *Studies in Hegelian Cosmology* (Cambridge, 1918), pp. 205f.

41. James Collins, *God in Modern Philosophy* (Chicago, 1959), p. 235. For a different view of Hegel's demand that Christianity be *aufgehoben* into philosophy, see the article by Crites, op. cit.

42. Karl Lowith, *From Hegel to Nietzsche* (New York, 1964), p. 333.

43. F. C. Baur, *Die christliche Lehre von der Dreieinigkeit und Menschwerdung Gottes in ihrer geschichtlichen Entwicklung*, I (Tübingen, 1841) pp. XVIII–XIX. As cited in Peter Hodgson, *The Formation of Historical Theology: A Study of Ferdinand Christian Baur* (New York, 1966), p. 164.

44. F. C. Baur, *Die christliche Gnosis* (Darmstadt, 1967) p. 712ff. As cited in Robert Morgan, "Ferdinand

Christian Baur," in Ninian Smart, ed., *Nineteenth Century Religious Thought in the West,* I (Cambridge, 1985), p. 279. I am especially dependent on Morgan's fine analysis of Baur's Christology in relation to Hegel and Strauss.

45. Baur, *Die christliche Gnosis,* cited in Morgan, op. cit., p. 279.

46. It is interesting to note that Karl Barth has positive things to say about Biedermann's program: "The task of free theological study [for Biedermann] was just to study Christian doctrine, as it developed in accordance with its inner necessity, and illuminate it by considering the question of its real meaning . . . in other words, to raise it from the level of intuition to that of pure concept. . . . It was, in the sense in which he [Biedermann] understood it, a good programme, and a most promising legacy. And if I were a liberal theologian I should ask myself if it might not be salutary, even at the cost of having to go a good way along with Hegel, to take it up fresh in its entirety." (*Hibbert Journal,* LIX [April 1961], p. 215).

47. A. E. Biedermann, *Christian Dogmatics,* p. 716, n. 6, as translated by Claude Welch, ed., *God and Incarnation in Mid-Nineteenth Century German Theology* (New York, 1965), p. 363.

48. Ibid., pp. 363–364.

49. Ibid., p. 367.

50. Ibid.

51. Ibid.

52. Ibid.

53. Ibid., pp. 368–369.

54. Ibid., p. 374.

55. Ibid., p. 375.

56. Ibid., pp. 375–376.

57. Ibid., p. 376.

58. Ibid., pp. 376–379.

59. Ibid., p. 381.

60. Edward Caird, *The Evolution of Religion* (New York, 1893), I, 64–65.

61. Ibid., pp. 67–68.

62. Ibid., pp. 188–189.

63. Ibid., p. 189.

64. Ibid., pp. 191–192.

65. Ibid., pp. 195–196.

66. John Caird, *The Fundamental Ideas of Christianity* (Glasgow, 1915), I, 140–141.

67. Ibid., p. 142.

68. Ibid., pp. 143–144.

69. Ibid., p. 154.

70. Ibid., pp. 155–156.

71. Ibid., pp. 170–171.

72. Ibid., p. 169.

73. Ibid., pp. 171–172.

74. Ibid., II, 241–242.

75. Ibid., pp. 245–246.

76. Ibid., p. 247.

77. Ibid., pp. 249–250.

78. P. Hodgson, "Georg Wilhelm Friedrich Hegel," in Ninian Smart, ed., *Nineteenth Century Religious Thought in the West* (Cambridge, 1985). On these and other criticisms, see "Suggestions for Further Reading" below.

SUGGESTIONS FOR FURTHER READING

I. Overviews of Hegel's Philosophy

Copleston, Frederick. *A History of Philosophy,* VII. *From Fichte to Nietzsche* (Westminster, Md.: Newman Press, 1963). Chapters 9–11 are a clear and accurate overview.

Taylor, Charles. *Hegel* (Cambridge: Cambridge University Press, 1975). Widely considered to be the best thorough presentation of Hegel's thought in English.

II. Hegel's Philosophy of Religion and Christianity

On the Early Theological Writings:

Kaufmann, Walter. *Hegel: A Reevaluation* (New York: Doubleday, 1965); and "The Young Hegel and Religion," *From Shakespeare to Existentialism* (New York: Doubleday, 1960).

Kroner, Richard. "Introduction" to *On Christianity: Early Theological Writings,* ed. T. M. Knox (New York: Harper, 1961).

Kaufmann and Kroner offer very different interpretations of Hegel's early religious writings.

On the Mature Philosophy of Religion:

For brief, lucid overviews, with valuable comments on Hegel's limits and legacy, see the following:

Crites, Stephen. "The Gospel According to Hegel," *Journal of Religion,* XLVI (April 1966).

Hodgson, Peter. "Georg Wilhelm Friedrich Hegel," *Nineteenth Century Religious Thought in the West,* I, ed. Ninian Smart et al. (Cambridge: Cambridge University Press, 1985). Very helpful bibliography.

Also see Hodgson's "Commentary" appended to his ed. and trans. of Part III of the *Lectures on the Philosophy of Religion,* entitled *The Christian Religion* (Missoula, Mont., 1979). This essay is a more extended commentary on Hegel's treatment of Christianity in the *Lectures.*

Welch, Claude. *Protestant Thought in the Nineteenth Century,* I (New Haven: Yale University Press, 1972), Chap. 4.

For more extended and specialized studies, the following are recommended:

Crites, Stephen. *In the Twilight of Christendom: Hegel vs. Kierkegaard on Faith and History* (Chambersburg, Penn.: American Academy of Religion, 1972). A striking essay on Hegel and Kierkegaard on the problem of faith and history.

Fackenheim, Emil. *The Religious Dimension of Hegel's Thought* (Chicago: University of Chicago Press, 1982). A sympathetic and discerning account by a noted Jewish philosopher who shares neither Hegel's philosophy nor his religious views.

Lauer, Quentin. *Hegel's Concept of God* (Albany: State University of New York Press, 1982).

Williamson, Raymond Keith. *Introduction to Hegel's Philosophy of Religion* (Albany: State University of New York Press, 1984). Valuable in its comprehensive treatment of the early writings on religion, the mature philosophy of religion, and the various interpretations of Hegel's concept of God.

Yerkes, James. *The Christology of Hegel* (Albany: State University of New York Press, 1983).

Chapter 6
Romanticism and French Catholic
Thought: Traditionalism and Fideism

Félicité Robert de Lamennais

The significance of Jean Jacques Rousseau's ideas for modern Christian thought is varied and rather Janus-faced, as was pointed out in Chapter 3. He infused reason with deep feeling and moral sentiment, one of the wellsprings of both the Romantic Enlightenment and Liberal Protestantism. But paradoxically his ideas also were found useful by a generation of French writers who emerged after 1800 as powerful defenders of traditional Roman Catholicism. During the Revolution and the Napoleonic era, there were gathering signs in France of disillusionment with the illiberal rationalism of the freethinking *philosophes*. Robespierre's abstract cult of the Supreme Being proved to have little appeal. Rousseau's religious *sentiment* was closer to the hearts of these French intellectuals, although it often was held in a precarious balance with their skepticism.

Many intellectuals came to see the rationalism of the eighteenth century as the poisonous seedbed of radical individualism and a dissolving skepticism, the fruits of which were plain to see in the policies of the revolutionary Jacobins and the horrors of the Reign of Terror of 1793. Across Europe many poets and writers, such as Edmund Burke in England, recoiled from this radicalism and what they perceived to be its divisive and anarchistic consequences. They yearned nostalgically, if fancifully, for the peace and unity which they viewed as characteristic of the Middle Ages, a time when religion and culture were a seamless whole. What was needed, they were certain, were the authority and the cohesive strength of the wisdom of the past, handed down in the form of an awe-inspiring tradition. The most ancient and sublime of traditions was, to their minds, the enduring yet creative and developing experience of the Catholic Church.

This Romantic vision was given fresh life by Pope Pius VII's courageous stand against Napoleon's usurpation of church prerogatives. The Pope's resistance to the demands of the French emperor, which included his suffering the humiliation of five years' imprisonment in Paris and Fontainbleau, won the admiration of Catholic Europe. The Papacy had regained its lost moral authority and the Church was experiencing spiritual renewal. Especially striking was the large number of conversions to Catholicism of leading intellectuals, including the German Protestant Romantic writers Friedrich Schlegel (1772–1829) and Adam Müller (1779–1829), and the young, popular author and skeptic, François René, Vicomte de Chateaubriand (1768–1848). These writers, and others, emerged as apologists for a lost tradition, for authority, and for the restoration of an organic, idealized feudalism: corporate, Catholic, and hierarchical. The watchword was "restoration," and the new defenders of Traditionalism, as it came to be called, were known as the "Prophets of the Past." This first wave of Romantic reaction against the Enlightenment and political liberalism was to last from the restoration of the Bourbon King Louis XVIII in 1815 to the revolutions of 1848.

FRANÇOIS RENÉ de CHATEAUBRIAND

In 1802, shortly after the signing of the Concordat, or agreement between the Vatican and the French government, the after-effects of which had stiffened Pius VII's resolve not to bend his knee to Napoleon, a work was published entitled *Le Génie du Christianisme*, (*The Genius of Christianity*), an apology for Catholic Christianity. It was a large success and signaled the new Catholic revival. Its author was the Vicomte de Chateaubriand, a Breton from St. Malo and son of an aristocratic family. As a boy, Chateaubriand's Romantic feeling for religion had been nourished by the medieval enchantments that were still vivid in Brittany. As a young man he journeyed to America and on his return found the revolution in the control of the Jacobins. He joined the

François René de Chateaubriand

émigré army, was wounded, and sought refuge in London, where he lived in poverty for several years.

Chateaubriand's first book, *Essai Historique sur les Révolutions* (Historical Essay on the Revolutions) (1797), continued to reflect the influence of eighteenth-century French skepticism. However, while in London he learned not only of his mother's and sister's deaths but of the grief that his *Essai* had caused them. Deeply troubled, Chateaubriand resolved to expiate this deed by writing a religious work. That work was *The Genius of Christianity*, and in the preface he gives an account of the origin of this act of expiation: "These two voices proceeding from the tomb," he wrote, "overwhelmed me. I became a Christian. I did not yield, I admit, to any mighty supernatural illumination. My conviction came out of my heart. I wept and I believed."[1]

The question often has been asked whether Chateaubriand's return to Catholicism was sincere. The judgment of the great critic Sainte-Beuve is, perhaps, not wholly unjust. He wrote that the author of *The Genius of Christianity* was "an Epicurean with a Catholic imagination, sensual in life and at bottom skeptical in heart."[2] And yet the single thing that Chateaubriand may have truly believed in was religion, by which he meant Catholicism. "Obstinate Catholic as I am," he wrote, "there is no Christian so believing and no man so unbelieving as I."[3]

Whatever disagreements there may be over Chateaubriand's sincerity, there is no dispute regarding the power and influence of his apology for Christianity. He considered the rationalistic arguments of the seventeenth and eighteenth centuries—regarding such matters as revelation, miracles, and God—to be exhausted and useless. The defender of Catholicism must begin afresh, attending not to abstract argument but to the particular, evocative evidences of history and tradition. "*No longer to prove that Christianity is excellent because it comes from God but that it comes from God because it is excellent.*"[4] Chateaubriand attempts to demonstrate the truth of Christianity by showing that the beauty and the glories of Western civilization owe their very life to Christianity and the Catholic Church. It is, perhaps, the first modern attempt to defend Catholicism on the grounds of its historical and social utility.

The French public had been seduced by the unbelieving *philosophes* when told that Christianity "was the offspring of barbarism, the enemy of the arts and sciences . . . a religion whose only tendency was to encourage bloodshed . . . and to retard the progress of the human understanding."[5] It was essential to prove, on the contrary, that

the Christian religion, of all the religions that ever existed, is the most humane, the most favorable to liberty and to the arts and sciences; that the world is indebted to it for every improvement, from agriculture to the abstract sciences—from the hospitals for the reception of the unfortunate to the temples reared by the Michelangelos and embellished by the Raphaels. It was necessary to prove that nothing is more divine than its tenets, its doctrine, and its worship; that it encourages genius, corrects the taste, develops the virtuous passions . . . that there is no disgrace in being believers with Newton and Bossuet, with Pascal and Racine. In a word, it was necessary to summon all the charms of the imagination and all the interests of the heart to the assistance of that religion against which they had been set in array.[6]

After hearing such a hymn of praise, one might ask if there is not some danger in defending religion from a merely human point of view. "Why so?" asks Chateaubriand. "Does our religion shrink from the light? Surely one great proof of its divine origin is that it will bear the test of the fullest and severest scrutiny of reason. . . . Will Christianity be the less true for appearing the more beautiful?"[7] But, again, one asks: Does Chateaubriand not grasp the distinction between a truth-claim and an aesthetic judgment? In our own era of pluralism and multicultural awareness, Chateaubriand's apologetic would likely appear naive. And to the rationalist unbeliever it remained wholly unpersuasive. But it carried force in the yearning hearts and imaginations of untold disillusioned French citizens. And for certain temperaments, the grandeur of such a cumulative historical appeal to the benefits of Christianity remains compelling, especially in periods of apparent cultural dissolution.

The Genius of Christianity attracted Napoleon. He recognized that the extremists of the revolution had divided France into two irreconcilable factions and that the future of France required internal peace. But domestic harmony demanded a rapprochement with the Catholic Church, not only in France but in Europe—and that meant with the Pope. The emperor's motives were, of course, entirely political. Religion alone, he had come to believe, could give the nation a strong and enduring political foundation. "If there were no pope," he declared, "it would have been necessary to invent one." After Napoleon's Concordat with the Vatican, he dispatched Chateaubriand to Rome as secretary to the French ambassador. The aristocratic vicomte soon, however, turned against Napoleon when he recognized that the emperor, while saving a new France, was undermining the very foundations of old France. When the Napoleonic Empire fell, Chateaubriand championed the restoration of the Bourbon monarchy. He later served the Bourbon court as minister to Berlin and ambassador to London and to Rome. His influence on French literature and on the French religious imagination in the nineteenth century was great. He was the "herald" of Catholic Traditionalism.

JOSEPH de MAISTRE

The extraordinary ideas and the importance of the French writer Joseph de Maistre (1753–1821) continue to be debated today. That he represents the passionate complexity of European Romanticism has long been recognized, but his meaning and his enduring significance are disputed. Liberal commentators have portrayed him as representing the last despairing effort of feudalism to resist the march of modern progress. The French writer Émile Faguet characterizes Maistre as "a fierce absolutist, a furious theocrat, an intransigent legitimist, apostle of a monstrous trinity composed of Pope, King, and Hangman . . . part learned doctor, part inquisitor, part executioner."[8] Clearly, a monster. Some critics respond similarly but add that we can be thankful that Maistre's outrageous views, though perhaps historically of interest, are now anachronistic and obsolete. This view has become routine in popular accounts of Maistre, but it fails to plumb the depths of his radicalism and his paradoxical modernity. Addressing this latter dimension of Maistre are interpreters who see in his historicism, that is, his historical relativism and pessimism, and in his pragmatism, the harbingers of developments in contemporary social theory. More recently, Isaiah Berlin has attended to Maistre's preoccupation with the instinctive, the irrational, and the mysterious attractions of blood and soil, that is, to Maistre as forerunner of twentieth-century Fascism and its fanatical demands for a social mythology and a collective obedience. In this view, Maistre's ideas—no matter how abhorrent—reveal terrifying truths about our own century, truths denied or repressed by more liberal and sanguine minds.[9]

Joseph de Maistre was born in 1753 in Chambéry in Savoy. His father was president of the Senate of the dukedom of Savoy. He was raised in a pious home and studied with the Jesuits. He then studied law in Turin and returned to Chambéry to a post as public prosecutor in the Senate of Savoy. The young magistrate showed signs of being influenced by liberal political views, but these quickly disappeared when the new French Republican army invaded Savoy in 1792. Maistre fled to Lausanne, where he wrote his countrymen warning against the horrors of the revolution. Here began his career as a political and religious writer. He remained in exile for the next twenty-five years, separated from his wife and children and often living in miserable financial straits. In 1802 Victor Immanuel I, the Italian king of Sardinia, appointed Maistre ambassador to St. Petersburg, where he lived for fifteen years. While in Russia he wrote many of his influential books, including *Du pape* (*The Pope*) (1819), the charter of the new Ultramontanism, the movement in support of Papal supremacy and infallibility. He returned to Turin in 1817 and died there in 1821.

At the heart of Maistre's doctrine is his belief in the necessity of social order in a world peopled by sinful, egoistic human beings. The human lust for power is, he wrote, unquenchable:

> Man is insatiable for power; he is infinite in his desires and, always discontented with what he has, loves only what he has not. People complain of the despotism of princes; they ought to complain of the despotism of *man*. We are all born despots, from the most absolute monarch of Asia to the infant that smothers a bird with its hand for the pleasure of seeing that there exists in the world a being weaker than itself.[10]

The paradox of human existence is that, while egoistic and sinful, human beings are by nature *social.* Maistre finds Rousseau's talk about an original "state of nature" or a "natural man" absurd. "Thus properly speaking, there never has been a time previous to society for *man,* because, before the formations of political societies, man was not a complete man." How odd that Rousseau could overlook the fact that "if the social order derives from nature, there is no social compact." Following Edmund Burke, Maistre insists that "art is man's nature." "Man with all his affections, all his knowledge, all his arts is the true *natural man.* . . . Man's *natural state* is therefore what he is today and what he has always been, that is to say, *sociable.*"[11]

We humans are social, true, but people will abuse their power if they are given the chance. The *philosophes* tell us to study nature. Let us do so, and what a nightmare we will behold. Few writers have described the spectacle in more frightening terms than has Maistre:

In the whole vast dome of living nature there reigns an open violence, a kind of prescriptive fury which arms all the creatures to their common doom: as soon as you leave the inanimate kingdom you find the decree of violent death inscribed on the very frontiers of life. You feel it already in the vegetable kingdom: from the great catalpa to the humblest herb, how many plants *die* and how many are *killed;* but, from the moment you enter the animal kingdom, this law is suddenly in the most dreadful evidence. A power, a violence, at once hidden and palpable . . . has in each species appointed a certain number of animals to devour the others. . . . And who [in this general carnage] exterminates him who will exterminate all others? Himself. It is man who is charged with the slaughter of man. . . . The whole earth, perpetually steeped in blood, is nothing but a vast altar upon which all that is living must be sacrificed without end, without measure, without pause, until the consummation of things, until evil is extinct, until the death of death.[12]

The human condition has been in a war of all against all since the fateful Fall of Adam and the human inheritance of Original sin. It is "Original sin," Maistre declares, "which explains everything and without which nothing can be explained." Because of Original sin our freedom has been poisoned; our wills are perverse. Our freedom thus constitutes our grandeur but also our devilish misery. "Man in harmony with his Creator is sublime and his actions are creative; equally, once he separates himself from God and acts alone, he does not cease to be powerful, since that is a privilege of his nature, but his acts are negative and lead only to destruction."[13]

The source of all human problems is, then, fallen freedom, exercised in all of its forms—political, intellectual, religious. Humans are not fit to be trusted with liberty, or they will only misuse it. Human life and happiness therefore depend on our being governed. The free exercise of reason, history shows, leads to disbelief and anarchy. Left to its own devices human reason can neither create nor conserve any real political or religious society. What human beings need, then, are beliefs, not questions and problems. "His cradle should be surrounded by dogmas, and when his reason awakes, all his opinions should be given. . . . Nothing is more vital to him than *prejudices.*"[14] By prejudices, Maistre does not mean ideas that are groundless or held in disregard of the facts; rather, they are beliefs that have been adopted without personal examination.

The source of genuine knowledge and social stability is not, Maistre contends, to be found in our individual discursive reason but in our communal, intuitive, habitual sense of what is true and right. "A man's primary need is that his nascent reason should be curbed . . . and it should lose itself in the national mind, so that it changes its individual existence for another communal existence." Human happiness lies in obeying this "national mind." When the fabric of a cultural tradition and its moral habits is rent, the community is threatened. No generation can rediscover or relearn by trial and error what it needs to know.

The divine will is not, however, only revealed in communal traditions and sentiments. It often is disclosed by a great hero or genius who embodies the "national mind" and whose instincts are "well-nigh infallible." Maistre shared with writers such as Fichte, Hegel, and Thomas Carlyle a Romantic belief in the role of the hero in history. It is from a single great man that a nation forms its distinctive character.

> Gifted with an extraordinary penetration or, what is more probable, with an infallible instinct, he divines those hidden powers and qualities which shape a nation's character. . . . He is never seen writing or debating; his mode of acting derives from inspiration; and if sometimes he takes up the pen, it is not to argue but to command.[15]

Maistre was scornful of the idea of the sovereignty of the people. A society is not an aggregate of individuals but an organism; therefore, no government can be the work of deliberation and modification by an assembly of individuals. God provides a people with a government in one of two ways.

> Most often he reserves to himself its formation more directly by making it grow, as it were, imperceptibly like a plant, through the conjunction of a multitude of those circumstances we call fortuitous. But when he wants to lay quickly the foundations of a political structure . . . he confides his power to rare men, the true Elect.[16]

In either case, sovereignty resides in God's hands, and to coincide with the two sides of human nature—body and soul—God has established two kinds of sovereignty, a temporal and a spiritual.

While Maistre did not argue that the divine right of kings was the only possible form of temporal sovereignty, he thought it practically the best form, less susceptible to power struggles and constant social change. The single sovereign's authority is absolute and can better represent the will of God to the people. But as the body is inferior to the soul, so is the spiritual authority above the temporal which must give way to it in cases of disagreement. The Pope, Maistre argues, is the apex of the entire social order, answerable to God alone.

The Pope is Maistre's fullest defense of papal supremacy and infallibility. Though suspect in Rome, the book had a prominent role in the growth of the Ultramontanist Movement that won its foremost victory at the First Vatican Council in 1870 when the council defined the dogma of papal infallibility. Such an elevated Ultramontane conception of papal authority had not been typical in Catholic Europe in the early modern era; indeed, in the period prior to the nineteenth century the papacy often was weak and threatened.

Despite the political nature of his argument in *The Pope,* Maistre never works out a clear doctrine of the relationship between the Church and the state. He does not, for instance, advocate theocracy; rather, he appears to prefer a delicate balance between the temporal monarchy and the spiritual power of the Church, that is, the papacy. But what if the monarch abuses his or her power? Since Maistre conceived every established temporal sovereignty as invested with divine right, he was loath to allow any resistance to temporal sovereignty, even in cases of tyranny. He was willing to allow the monarch, no matter how evil his or her power, to remain sovereign and to wait upon the operations of time and nature to set things straight. Ironically, in this as in other matters, Maistre was not in accord with the traditional teaching of the Catholic Church. It long had affirmed that a people had a right to active resistance when a government became tyrannical and acted against the common good.

What was crucial, however, to Maistre's argument was his conviction that sovereignty in the temporal order led directly and logically to an acknowledgment of papal sovereignty and infallibility, that is, to a supreme spiritual authority. It is in this regard that his apology for papal supremacy and infallibility represents something distinctive and new. It is fundamentally a political and not a theological argument. He insists, for example, that "theological truths are not other than general truths manifested and divinized within the sphere of religion, and in such a manner that it is impossible to attack the one without attacking a law of the world." According to Maistre, the Church is infallible *because* it follows that it must be the highest sovereignty as the final court of appeal. The Church's claim to infallibility is not, then, demanded as some unique privilege; it merely claims what it must enjoy as common to all sovereignties in their proper order of jurisdiction. If any government is resisted under the claim that it is in error or unjust, it no longer exists. To Maistre, infallibility inheres in the concept of supremacy. If one can tell the Church, i.e., the Pope, that it is mistaken, one no longer owes it allegiance and therefore destroys its very unity and sovereignty.

For Maistre, a republican church—such as the Congregationalist or Presbyterian polities—is a contradiction in terms. "For as soon as there is no longer a centre or common government there can be no unity, nor consequently a *universal* or *Catholic Church.*" "Once admit appeal from [the Pope's] decrees, and there is no longer government, unity, or a visible Church."

The Catholic Conciliarists, who place the authority of the Church in the periodic meeting of councils of bishops, are as mistaken as the republican Protestant sects. These "ecumenical councils are nothing else than *the parliament or states-general of the Church, assembled by the authority and under the presidency of the Sovereign.* Wherever there is a Sovereign, and in the Catholic economy his existence is undeniable, there can be no legitimate national assemblies with him." Maistre offers a temporal analogy. Suppose that during an interval there were no king of France, and that the states-general were divided in their opinion and actually dispersed. Where would be the kingdom of France? The same question can be asked of the Church. "Remove the *Queen bee,* you still have bees in abundance; but a hive, never." Maistre was convinced that the Pope could provide much better than a general council for the extraordinary needs of the Church in the modern age. He believed that councils, after the great Council of Trent of the sixteenth century, were dispensable. They "seem only," he writes, "to have been intended for the youth of Christianity."[17]

Maistre's Ultramontanist vision of the Church, assuming his first principles, followed a kind of inexorable logic, but his logic, he believed, was supported by his empirical analysis of the failed governments, schisms in the Church, insurrections, and revolutions that had violently dismantled the social structure of Europe since the Middle Ages. He was certain that it all proved his contention that there can be no society without a state; no state without legitimate sovereignty; no sovereignty without an incontestable infallibility; hence no infallibility without divine sanction. Since the Pope is God's regent on earth, all legitimate authority is, finally, derived from him.

Isaiah Berlin has correctly perceived that Maistre's dark vision of human depravity and its need for a higher authority has more in common with the sinister ideologies of the twentieth century than with his own time. For Maistre saw society

as an inextricable network of weak, sinful, helpless human beings, torn by contradictory desires, driven hither and thither by forces too violent for their control, too destructive to be justified by any comfortable rationalist formula. All achievement is painful, and likely to fail, and could be accomplished, if at all, only under the guidance of a hierarchy of beings of great wisdom and strong will, who, being the repositories of the forces of history, laid down their lives in performing their task of organization, repression, and preservation of the divinely ordained order.[18]

HUGHES-FÉLICITÉ ROBERT de LAMENNAIS

The writings of Maistre and of his contemporary, the philosophical writer Viscount Louis de Bonald (1754–1840), inspired a generation of younger Catholic writers. Some writers of this next generation, however, represent a very different but equally complex temper of mind. Most notable among this group is Félicité de Lamennais (1782–1854), an enigmatic personality who was at once a traditionalist and a liberal. His friend, the composer Franz Liszt, saw in him all of the complexities of Christianity in the nineteenth century. He was a passionate man but a reluctant priest, for whom the Pope intended a cardinal's hat, but he ended his life an apostate. At the height of his early fame, after the writing of his acclaimed *Essai sur l'indifférence en matière de religion* (*Essay on Indifference in Matters of Religion*) (1817–1823), it is said that Pope Leo XII had set up on a wall, on either side of the crucifix, the image of the Holy Virgin and the portrait of Lamennais.[19]

Félicité Lamennais was born on June 29, 1782, at St. Malo on the same street where Chateaubriand was born. His father was a wealthy Breton businessman. His mother died when he was five, and some claim that his subsequent isolation and his moody, melancholy nature can be traced, in part, to his mother's early death. Lamennais spent lonely childhood hours reading in his uncle's library and as a young man was capable of reading six languages. After a period of deep depression, followed by a spiritual crisis, he came under the influence of his brother Jean Marie, a priest, and committed himself to the task of restoring Catholicism in France. The first result of this labor was an anonymously published work entitled *Reflexions sur l'état de l'Eglise en France* (*Reflections on the State of the Church in France*) (1809), which sets out many of the themes of his later writings devoted to a revived Catholicism—most notably on the need for a central authority, on freedom for the Church, and on what he would call "indifference" in religion.

Lamennais's journalistic work for the royalist press found him at odds with Napoleon on the latter's return from exile. As a result, he was required to flee to England. There, under the influence of an *émigré* Breton priest and after great misgivings, he decided to become a priest. He was ordained in 1816. Shortly thereafter—and to seek distraction from his unhappiness in carrying out his priestly duties—he began work on his first great book, the *Essai sur l'indifférence,* the first volume of which appeared at the end of 1817. It was eloquent and an enormous success, and for the next decade

Lamennais became the *enfant terrible* of the reactionary press. He was hailed as another Pascal and Bossuet.

Lamennais and Traditionalism

Lamennais's *Essai* is essentially a continuation of the Traditionalist argument of Maistre and Bonald, that is, directed against the self-sufficiency of individual reason and in defense of the principle of religion, namely, humanity's dependence on a Higher Power. Central to his task was Lamennais's Romantic conviction—shared with Coleridge and Chateaubriand—that the older rationalistic apologetic ("Evidence theology") was wholly inadequate to the task of addressing religious doubt and unbelief—realities which he knew from personal experience.

It is important to understand what Lamennais meant by indifference, for it has nothing to do with laxity toward religion. Rather, it addresses the assumption that there is no necessary relationship between personal and public morality and one's beliefs or doctrines. The strength of Lamennais's apology is his deep sense of the sociological significance of religion, of the role of belief in sustaining the health of the body politic—a point not lost on Auguste Comte and Emile Durkheim. "Everything," he writes, "proceeds from doctrines: morals, literature, constitutions, laws . . . civilization, barbarism, and those terrible crises which destroy whole peoples or renew them."[20] The first half of volume one of the *Essai* is devoted to an analysis of three kinds of "indifference" present in the modern era. They represent the "indifference" of the atheist, the Deist, and the heretical Protestant.

The atheist *philosophe,* while an unbeliever, finds religion socially useful for the masses. It provides them with moral interdictions and restrains them from engaging in antisocial behavior, such as Voltaire's servants slitting their master's throat! This form of "indifference" is attractive to some unbelieving neo-conservative intellectuals even today. The second form of modern "indifference" is characteristic of the Deists. While they recognize the need for natural religion and belief in the Divine, the Deists—for example, Rousseau—deny revelation. Deism, not surprisingly, is not found any-where, since it cannot be identified with any of the positive religions. Doctrines are viewed as basically harmful to religion. The third form of "indifference" is associated with Protestants. They look to Scripture, but when asked by Catholics what fundamental doctrines are to be found in the Bible, the several Protestant sects cannot agree, since the Scriptures are to be interpreted according to each person's reason or spiritual judgment. "Who," Lamennais writes, "does not see that the authority of Scripture becomes the authority of reason alone. . . . everyone ought to believe what his reason clearly shows him to be true, which is precisely the principle of the deist and the atheist."[21]

Lamennais's critique of the various forms of religious "indifferentism" was only preparatory to his constructive point: how persons do, in fact, arrive at certitude about anything. First, it is clear that we human beings are not left alone to discover truth by our unaided reason; we are essentially social beings. The *individual* person cannot by logic or by discursive reason alone come to any certitude about anything. The philosophers Descartes and Hume have shown definitively that such a path leads to skepticism. Yet our skepticism is continually contradicted and overridden by the common reason of the race. "All men, without exception, believe invincibly thousands of truths which are the necessary bond of society and the foundation of human life."[22]

Nature, Lamennais contends, would not permit anarchistic skepticism; faith is our natural human condition:

> Man is in a state of natural impotence to demonstrate any truth fully, and an equal impotence to refuse to admit certain truths . . . all the truths necessary to our conservation, all the truths whereon the ordinary intercourse of life and the practice of the indispensable arts and crafts are founded. We believe invincibly that there exist bodies endowed with certain properties, that the sun will rise tomorrow. . . .[23]

According to Lamennais, belief is inherent in humanity, rooted in the fact that we all are born equipped with a knowledge of certain primal truths. And we can distinguish these truths from falsehoods by a universal criterion, what he calls the *sensus communis* or a common consent. Such beliefs are the common reason and possession of the race. And the foremost truth that the *sensus communis* teaches us with virtual unanimity is the existence of God. Moreover, it is upon that belief that all other beliefs are anchored. For God would not have left humanity bereft of a knowledge of those truths necessary for the fulfillment of both personal needs and social life. What God attests or reveals must, then, be *certain.* It follows that those religious truths which humans are united in believing, the *sensus communis,* have the weight of supernatural authority.

Having established how humans attain certitude in general, Lamennais turns to the matter of how they can come to certitude regarding the *true religion.* What of the claims of Christianity and of Catholicism? His argument is similar in many respects to that of the Deists, except that the ultimate appeal is to a revealed authority rather than to a common-denominator natural religion discoverable by unaided reason. According to Lamennais, it follows from the very definition of religion that there can be but one true religion. And God's primal revelation to the human race, history demonstrates, includes such universal beliefs as the existence of one God; prayer, worship, and acts of sacrifice; a fall or separation from God and the need for redemption; the hope of immortality; and future rewards and punishments. With some boldness, he claims that all the religions of humankind testify to these beliefs in one or another form. However, to explain their differences, and the unique authority of the Catholic Church, Lamennais appeals to a then-popular theory of degeneration. After the Fall there was a corruption of the original divine revelation given to the race. To counter this degeneration God offered a second revelation, this one to the people of Israel. It communicated to this chosen people a clear knowledge of monotheism, a positive divine law, and a prophetic hope for the coming of a Redeemer. A third revelation, the Gospel of Christ, was necessary, however, to reveal God's perfect will for humanity. And therefore Christ came as the fulfillment of all that had come before; and he established his Church as the visible embodiment and instrument of his redemptive work.

> Since Jesus Christ, what authority dare anyone compare to that of the Catholic Church, the heir of all

primordial traditions, of the first revelation and the Mosaic revelation, of all the truths known in antiquity of which its teaching is only the development? Going back as it does to the origin of the world, it reunites in its authority all the authorities.[24]

Lamennais argued that Catholic Christianity had existed in an inchoate form in all the religions since the beginning of human history; indeed, it is the epitome of the history of religions. Catholicism alone by its antiquity, perpetuity, universality, and unity has thus proven to be the true embodiment and fulfillment of the spiritual testimony of the entire human race. And that universal religious *sensus communis* now speaks infallibly through the Pope.

As will become apparent, Lamennais's defense of both Catholicism and Ultramontanism, or the movement that appealed to the unique authority of the Pope, was open to a quite different reading— one that years later he himself would champion. If authority rests in the universal human reason or *sensus communis,* is it not the case that not only kings but also prelates, even popes, may be disputed when they are in conflict with the common consent? The Royalist Gallicans in Paris, who defended the religious rights of the monarch, sensed the danger in Lamennais's apology for tradition on these very grounds. But his *Essai* was warmly received by Pope Leo XII, and he had a prolonged interview with the Pope in 1824. Lamennais's Ultramontane argument was nicely summarized at the time: no Pope, no Church; no Church, no Christianity; no Christianity, no religion; no religion, no society; so that the very life of nations has its source in papal authority.

Lamennais and Liberal Catholicism

Lamennais believed that an Ultramontane form of Catholicism was crucial to the social and political regeneration of both France and Europe and that the sovereign authority of the Pope was essential to the unity and perseverance of Catholic Christianity. The social renaissance of Europe required that the grounds of certitude and social cohesion be so established. But Lamennais was no ordinary Ultramontanist, and it was to become clear in his writings between 1825 and 1830 that what he sought was a European society that joined Catholic social stability and order *with civil liberty* in a setting in which the Church would be entirely free to fulfill its mission unfettered by the state. What he sought then was neither a return to the reactionary order of the *ancien regime* nor to the secular republican liberalism of the French Jacobins.

It is not surprising that Lamennais's emerging program was to make enemies of three powerful groups in France: the Royalists, the ecclesiastical Gallicans, and the secular Liberals. The Royalists were threatened by his insistence that the Church be separated from its longstanding alliance with the throne and its political agenda. The Gallican clergy feared his rejection of the sovereignty of the French bishops and their claim that the Pope's authority was subservient to that of general councils. Lamennais insisted that to weaken the Church's allegiance to Rome would destroy its unity and make it captive to the objectives of the several European governments. And Lamennais rejected secular Liberalism since he held that a supreme and invariable spiritual authority was incompatible with a secular sovereignty based on individual reason that varied continuously, an *anarchie des esprits*. While the state and the Church each exercises its distinctive sovereignty, in principle the temporal is subordinate to the spiritual. In the last resort, it must be the spiritual sovereign, the Pope, who interprets the divine law for humanity. The people therefore have a right and duty to resist any temporal authority that is in defiance of the Church or of God's law. And so it is that the Pope is "the supreme defender of justice and the rights of humanity." What Lamennais and his circle of friends now perceived was an Ultramontanism in the service of liberty; a Pope, characterized by benevolence and liberality, serving as guarantor of true freedom. Here was the charter of a new social movement in the Church that was to be called Liberal Catholicism.

In 1829 Lamennais published a book entitled *Des Progrès de la révolution et de la guerre contre l'Eglise* (*The Progress of the Revolution and the War against the Church*) which outlined his view of a new Christian social order. He demanded that the Catholic Church be granted the same freedom from the state that now was guaranteed to all other religions in France, such as Protestantism and Judaism.

Furthermore, he called for freedom of conscience, of the press, and of education—since true Catholicism could flourish only under conditions of liberty. The July Revolution of the next year (1830) brought the abdication of King Charles X. The time now was opportune to carry forward the new Catholic renaissance. Central to that task was the launching of a new daily newspaper, called *L'Avenir* (*The Future*), first published in October 1830. Its motto was "*Dieu et la liberté,*" and its views were to be both authentically Catholic and avowedly liberal. In the first issue it called for the separation of Church and state as the necessary precondition of true liberty and for the Pope to cut the Church's ties with the old order and "baptize" the principles of the revolution, since the future rested with democracy. A new alliance was to be formed between Catholicism and the forces of political democracy.

Lamennais gathered round him a brilliant and talented group of like-minded men. They included the theologian Abbé P. O. Gerbet (1798–1864), later Bishop of Perpignan; Père Henri Lacordaire (1802–1861), whose sermons at the Cathedral of Notre Dame in Paris brought him fame; and the young nobleman Charles de Montalembert (1810–1870), an Ultramontane who, however, opposed the doctrine of papal infallibility prior to the meeting of the First Vatican Council (1870). With the support of these men, Lamennais initiated his program. The first task was to free the French Church from the state whose ministers were largely indifferent to the real mission of the Church. *L'Avenir* called for the Church and its clergy to refuse the financial support of the state, as well as its privileges, which bound them in a spiritual servitude. And so, as the Mennasian movement developed, the earlier Traditionalist hopes for an alliance of throne and altar in the creation of a Christian society dissolved. Christianity now was to be linked with liberty as a moral and spiritual end in itself. Political liberty was an essential component of that liberty for which Christ had come to make humanity free.

In an article in *L'Avenir*, Lamennais summarized the liberal Catholic program under six themes:

1. *Liberty of conscience and religion.* This entailed total separation of Church and state, including the annulment of all concordats. All religions should be

assured freedom of belief and practice and none should be privileged.

2. *Freedom of education.* Parents should have complete freedom to allow their children to be educated as they choose, and laws restricting the educational freedom of schools and colleges should be repealed.

3. *Freedom of the press.* This included not only print media but freedom of speech and the cessation of censorship, for example, of stage plays.

4. *Liberty of association.* The right of groups to meet freely and to express themselves is essential if tyranny is to be held in check.

5. *Universal suffrage.* All citizens should have a voice in government; therefore the vote should not be the exclusive privilege of the wealthy.

6. *Decentralization of government.* Tyrants thrive on centralized power. Local autonomy and self-government therefore should be maximized.

To advance this program, now under surveillance and attack, Lamennais founded in 1830 the General Agency for the Defense of Religious Liberty, a sort of religious civil liberties union to secure legal redress against any infractions of religious liberty. However, the growing hostility of the government toward *L'Avenir* and the agency, and fear that they would be shut down, emboldened Lamennais and his friends Lacordaire and Montalembert to take their case to the new Pope, Gregory XVI. The three "pilgrims of God and liberty" set out for Rome confident of the Pontiff's support. However, their hopes soon were dashed. They had to wait several months for an audience with the Pope and then were able to see him only briefly. Disillusioned, Lacordaire and Montalembert left for Munich. When Lamennais joined them there in August 1831, a copy of Gregory XVI's encyclical *Mirari vos* was awaiting him.

Mirari vos mentioned neither Lamennais nor *L'Avenir,* but the program of liberal Catholicism was brutally condemned. Ironically, Lamennais and his companions were charged with "indifferentism." The encyclical read: "Now from this evil-smelling spring of indifferentism flows the erroneous and absurd opinion—or rather, derangement—that freedom of conscience must be asserted and vindicated for everyone. This most pestilential error

opens the door to the complete and immoderate liberty of opinions, which works with such widespread harm both in Church and state." *Mirari vos* also condemned separation of Church and state, freedom of the press, and the right of peoples to revolt against their unjust princes.

The Pope's rejection of liberalism could not have been more absolute, but as a Catholic Lamennais submitted in 1832. *L'Avenir* was suspended, and the agency was dissolved. Lamennais agreed to submit to the Pope in all matters regarding faith and morals, although he did not say he would cease to write about political issues. Despite the submission, the action of Gregory XVI had undermined Lamennais's Ultramontane Catholicism, though he remained a theist. His ever-present melancholic and apocalyptic temper of mind deepened. He now despaired of the Church's role in the transformation of society. He felt that humanity alone could do something to change it and came to perceive his silence as cowardice. To a friend he wrote: "What is going on in France and in Europe, the abominable system of despotism which is developing everywhere with such hateful shamelessness, so revolts me. . . . Consequently, I have resolved at all costs to save my conscience and my honor, by making a protest with all the force I have."[25] The result was *Paroles d'un Croyant* (*Words of a Believer*) (1834) which produced another sensation. Written with the inspired passion and power of a Hebrew prophet, the book attacked the cowardice and the corrupt power of kings and priests. It later was described as a lyrical version of the Communist Manifesto—"l'apocalypse de Satan." Lamennais was called "Robespierre in a surplice," among other epithets. While *Words of a Believer* was widely viewed as exclusively dominated by politics, it was more truly a Romantic, utopian, but Christianly inspired vision of a world of social justice and equality.

Lamennais did not believe that the book included anything that could be condemned on doctrinal grounds, but he was mistaken. In June 1834 *Words of a Believer*—described by Rome as a book "small in size but immense in its perversity"—was condemned by Gregory XVI in the encyclical *Singulari nos.* This time Lamennais refused to submit; indeed he treated the condemnation with contempt. While he was not formally excommunicated, he had already ceased to carry out his priestly duties, and he slowly drifted from the Church. His friends Gerbet and Montalembert broke with him publicly on the issue and submitted to the condemnation. By 1841 Lamennais had given up the essentials of doctrinal Christianity. He continued to insist that "what one rejects is not authentic Christianity, but a certain sterile and material system that has taken its name and disgraces it."[26] However, what in fact remained was an unorthodox theism infused with deep Christian moral feeling. Christianity was now seen as the forerunner of a new religious faith. "In the present mood," he wrote to a friend, "when the old faith, enfeebled and almost extinct, is undergoing profound modifications, there is a great need for . . . a faith in harmony with the undying instincts of man. I have no doubt that it will have its roots in Christianity, of which it will mark a new phase." Yet, he confessed, "until it emerges, Catholicism is, I believe, the Christian communion that beyond all comparison has best preserved the essential spirit of the institution of Jesus Christ."[27]

At the time of the Revolution of 1848, Lamennais took his place as an elected deputy in the National Assembly, representing the extreme Left, the Comité Démocratique Socialiste. He died refusing the rites of the Church in 1854. He was a typical Romantic— passionate, melancholic, a solitary man who become a magnetic leader, a traditionalist, and a liberal—a bundle of seeming contradictions. His contributions to modern Catholicism are many, although not always easy to credit directly. He helped to alter—as did John Henry Newman in a different way—the method of Christian apologetics and, unintentionally, certain fideistic tendencies in Catholic philosophy. He strengthened the case for Ultramontanism, although, again, not in the form that was to triumph in 1870. He clearly was a force in the decline of French Gallicanism and indirectly influenced the emergence of both political and social Catholicism in the nineteenth century and beyond.

LOUIS BAUTAIN

The French Traditionalist rejection of individual reason and its resort to faith in a primal divine revelation to humanity found another, though quite dif-

ferent, champion in the Abbé Louis Bautain (1796–1867). But the popularity of the Traditionalist apologetic had already reached its crest by the early 1830s; and it was to decline in favor after its official proscription by Church authorities. The year 1834 was decisive. Pope Gregory XVI's encyclical *Singulari nos,* condemning Lamennais, was followed within a few months by an *Advertissement* addressed to his clergy and to the Holy See by the Bishop of Strasbourg attacking Louis Bautain's unorthodox views on faith and reason. Bautain was a thinker whose influence was substantial in his own day, and it can be detected in later French thought, although his work has been largely passed over by historians of theology.

Louis-Eugène-Marie Bautain was born in Paris and was raised a Catholic. He studied at the École Normale under the philosopher Victor Cousin, lost his faith, and "took pride in becoming a freethinker." His subsequent philosophical reflections led him, however, to reject both rationalist individualism and materialism. Philosophical skepticism convinced him of the need for a faith grounded in some form of common-sense or intuition. At the conclusion of his thesis on the existence of the self, defended in 1816, Bautain revealed his attraction to Pascal and his own emergent Traditionalist temper:

But this observation, so laborious and so difficult— what does it reveal to us? Judgments, notions, opinions of our mind, natural prejudices whereby we are compelled to believe in the existence of that which we cannot see. I certainly know that I exist. But who am I? What is my nature? . . . For what purpose was I born? Whence came I; where am I; whither am I being whirled away? Experience has no answers to these questions, which nevertheless incessantly tempt and trouble the human mind. . . . Strange indeed is the condition of men, who forever seek to know what it is not given them to know, and who have the firmest faith in those things of which they are necessarily ignorant.[28]

On graduation from the École Normale in 1816, Bautain was appointed to teach philosophy at the Collège Royal in Strasbourg. Immediately he proved to be a powerful and attractive teacher. After a trip to Germany, he took up the study of post-Kantian Idealism, especially the work of the German philosopher J. G. Fichte. After his reconversion to Catholicism, however, it was this philosophy that he was to oppose with his own form of Traditionalism. The German "Promethean" phase of Bautain's Romanticism ended in 1819 when he suffered a severe mental and spiritual breakdown. His career may have ended in suicide had he not met at Baden a remarkable fifty-four-year-old woman named Louise Humann. She was knowledgeable in German philosophy and deeply religious, and she and Bautain developed an enduring companionship. Not only was she instrumental in restoring him to health, but she guided his thinking along new channels and was largely responsible for his return to Catholicism.

It is clear that Bautain's period of nervous exhaustion and melancholy had undermined his confidence in reason and in the Fichtean glorification of the autonomous will. Bautain undertook a new study of Kant, now more deeply convinced of the impotence of pure reason alone to plumb the ultimate questions. For him this meant a repudiation of speculative Idealism as well as Scholastic philosophy and its rationalistic arguments for the existence of God. Bautain resumed his lecturing in 1821, but his views were now those of a complete *philosophical* skeptic. The educational authorities were alarmed and temporarily suspended him from his teaching duties.

During this period, and under Mlle. Humann's gentle tutelege, his scorn for Christian doctrine dissolved, and he began to prepare for the priesthood. He later wrote that he slowly had "acquired the conviction that Christian doctrine is philosophy's crown, or, if you will, her last word."[29] The government's effort to suppress Bautain actually caused a backlash, and his influence both spread and deepened among a circle of admirers. As W. M. Horton has noted, Bautain now took on the Romantic role of the inspired genius and prophet. "Nowhere was there a more worshipful band than this which gathered about Louis Bautain and Mlle. Humann—St. Augustine and his mother Monica, as many called them."[30] The Bishop of Strasbourg—who later condemned his writings—recognized Bautain's exceptional qualities and exempted him from seminary

training. He was ordained a priest in 1828 and was at the height of his fame and influence. He became known as the leader of the "Strasbourg School," and the letters that were to comprise his *La Philosophie du Christianisme* (1835) were something of a compendium of the doctrines of the school. It is one of the most important works of Catholic apologetics in the nineteenth century.

Bautain was certain that his apology for Christianity would have wide effect on the present spiritual condition of France, but he had no illusions about the Church's response to his attack upon the rationalism of Scholastic theology now thriving in Strasbourg. He wrote: "When I entered her [the Church's] doors, I was not ignorant of all that lay ahead of me there: I knew that the narrowest Rationalism was devastating her and drying up her vital sap. . . . I was going to combat it by all the means God gave me, because I am firmly convinced that it is the greatest plague of ecclesiastical instruction."[31]

Initially, the Bishop of Strasbourg had every confidence in Bautain's educational mission and gave him complete control of the *Petit Séminaire,* the preparatory school for aspirants to the priesthood. Bautain reorganized the school; French, not Latin, was the language of instruction, the older Scholastic textbooks were not used, and the former methods of logical disputation were abandoned. It was not long, though, before complaints about the teaching at the *Petit Séminaire* were circulating. The most powerful attack came from the *Grand Séminaire* in Strasbourg, now a center of the Neo-Scholastic revival. But to understand the hostility toward Bautain we can best turn to a summary of his leading themes and doctrines.

Bautain's Philosophy of Faith

Reason and Faith.   We have noted that it was Bautain's reading of Kant that convinced him that discursive reason, either that of deduction or of induction, was incapable of giving a person knowledge of metaphysical realities. In a letter of 1822 defending himself against the charge of skepticism, Bautain laid down some of the leading themes of his later Christian philosophy and apologetic. First, he addressed his critic's question about what remained if the older rational bases of the Catholic faith were removed. "I do not think," Bautain replied,

> that a passionate or wretched man can be calmed or consoled by arguments. Syllogisms have no power against the soul's distress and the heart's agitations. Something loftier and deeper is needed: faith in God, the feeling of His activity within us and His providence over us, surrender to the higher Will—none of the things that reasoning will ever give.[32]

For Bautain the critical philosophy was to play an indispensable but only preliminary role. It closes out one (the rationalist) road to God. Reason, or what Jacobi called *Verstand,* discursive reason, is but one of the powers of the mind. Bautain agreed with Jacobi that the mind also possesses an intuitive reason—what Jacobi called *Vernunft.* Bautain agreed: Kant's reason cannot transcend sensible reality. Only *Vernunft,* Jacobi's intuitive act of "faith," is capable of grasping metaphysical truths; it is, like Coleridge's Reason, the organ of spiritual apprehension. Thus, God can be known only by "faith," by the immediate intuition of the intelligence or *Vernunft.* God is not an object of demonstration; rather, God is revealed, for the human intelligence is fundamentally a receptive faculty. Therefore, the unfolding of any spiritual truth requires receptivity and the active cooperation of the self's will and intelligence.

Bautain's doctrine was labeled and condemned as "Fideism." The word is appropriate, but only if what Bautain means by "faith" is correctly understood. Contrary to some of his detractors, Bautain does not mean blind faith or a *fides implicita.* Faith, for Bautain, implies three things: a willingness to make assumptions, receptivity, and the dawning perception of truth.[33] It has something in common with St. Augustine's doctrine of the mind's movement from faith to understanding through the activity of divine illumination. First, faith precedes reason logically since all first principles of reason are axioms or premises which themselves do not admit of proof. Faith is, then, our primordial willingness to begin with assumptions and reason from them. Second, faith is a vital act of receptivity in which we expose ourselves to the influence of some other person or object. This, too, is psychologically primal. It is

absurd, for example, to expect a child, or an adult for that matter, not to respond in most instances in a believing and trustful way before acting. Faith and trust are the preconditions of much knowing. "To believe in the most general sense, " writes Bautain, "is simply to let in the truth, and react freely toward it; to believe is the essentially vital act of the human creature in his present state." And so it is "that knowledge is born of belief, and never precedes it. . . . nothing is more absurd, more contrary to the law of your mind, than the pretention to know, to judge, to reason before believing."[34]

Faith is not, however, merely the precondition of knowledge; it is also a form of knowledge, though a dim and confused perception seeking greater light. It is "felt rather than seen." Bautain writes of its noetic character:

> The superior light which must produce it, descends into the depths of the soul and it is absorbed there; and thus cannot be reflected in the intelligence, still insufficiently developed, and therefore incapable of conceiving the idea and embracing knowledge. There results what is called *faith,* which is the root of the idea. . . . But let one not be deceived: faith, as obscure as it is on account of its depth, is intelligent; *it is an intelligence penetrated by the action of the truth, but which is not yet conscious of itself and that which penetrates it; it is an unreflected and hence less brilliant light.*[35]

Bautain's "Fideism" often is equated with the doctrines of those later nineteenth-century movements known as Voluntarism and Pragmatism, with, for example, William James's "will to believe." And, indeed, Bautain often sounds like Pascal or James, as in this passage: "It is therefore not from the reason, properly speaking, but from the center of the human being, from that which is profoundest, most mysterious in man, that judgments come. . . . It is his will which pronounces the *yes* or the *no;* it alone exercises the sacred function of separator, judge, sacrificer."[36]

For Bautain the will does decide, not because the conditions require a blind leap or a Pascalian wager, but because the will is informed by intelligence. Faith and the will are connected but are not identical. "Thus," writes Bautain, "although there is no faith without a certain adhesion of the will, the will is nevertheless not the mistress of faith; it can neither create it for itself nor stimulate the sentiments which accompany it, any more than it can root it out or destroy it."[37] If faith is not identical with the will, neither is it an act of cognition. Faith is a distinct faculty, although it includes volitional, cognitive, and emotional aspects. As Bautain insists, it is a movement of the whole person.

Faith and Revelation.
Bautain's conception of faith was integrally related to two central themes of French Traditionalism: the idea of a primordial divine revelation and that of an organic society as the foundation of tradition. Both ideas counter an Enlightenment confidence in individual autonomous reason. Faith is grounded in an objective, historically revealed and communicated deposit of knowledge. Society must be seen after the analogue of the child. Phylogeny "recapitulates" ontogeny. Just as a child must come to knowledge through time and with the help of more mature persons, so the human race undergoes an intellectual and moral development, and if it is cut off from its human traditions it will return to barbarism. The ego simply cannot derive knowledge of the first principles of metaphysics from itself. Another intelligence must communicate these realities before the individual intelligence can think and act. So the human mind must first receive divine truth by an act of divine self-revelation received through "faith." Bautain writes:

> If there exists, as we are told, a world superior to that which we inhabit, there has to have been an envoy from this world to proclaim its existence to us and to inform us about the relationship in which we stand to it; if there be supernatural truths there has to have been supernatural speech, akin to those truths, in order to teach them to us; and if we are interested in knowing that speech, insofar as it is not addressed immediately to us, it is necessary that it be transmitted to us by a succession and guaranteed by a visible and permanent authority—an authority instituted by this speech itself—which it is necessary to believe.[38]

The unaided reason can never discover those metaphysical concepts or truths by itself, yet they are ever present in human thought. And Bautain insists that their presence requires a revealer, an "envoy" from the transcendental world. In typical Romantic fashion, Bautain's doctrine of revelation appeals to the inspiration of the genius and prophet. "It is by the men of genius," he writes, "prophets, poets, apostles, as one will have to call them by reason of their more or less pure participation in the spirit of God, that the life of heaven has been communicated to humanity since the beginning, and that his communication is maintained and renewed across the centuries."[39]

Bautain sees humanity as divided into two classes. First, there are *les hommes du fini,* those who constitute the much larger class and who lack all feeling for the infinite. They are earth-bound and focused on the world of sense, self-interest, and calculation. The other, a small and elite class, are those souls of genius whom Bautain celebrates in exemplary, Romantic rhetoric, and who

> obediently follow the celestial instincts which urge them, [and] are called to do great things among men; for they are like reservoirs in which the divine influence is stored, into which the life of heaven flows. They are mirrors reflecting the eternal Light. . . . Humanity advances to its goal only by virtue of suffering and by a path of blood; genius and charity incessantly furnish victims for the great expiatory sacrifice which is to reconcile earth with heaven.[40]

For Bautain there is a difference, however, between the genius as poet and the genius as prophet and apostle. The latter is the bearer of revelation, the Divine Word.

> From the beginning and throughout the course of the ages, God has manifested himself to men. He has enlightened some of them with a supernatural light. . . . These men have thus been prophets and apostles; and, like the men of genius who have been able to seize certain of these truths by intellectual intuition, they have said simply, positively, dogmatically, what they have seen or heard.[41]

In his discussion of revelation, Bautain makes the further distinction between Light and Word. Revelation, as it is made present in the mind of the prophet, is Divine Light, or inspiration. But for revelation to be conveyed to the minds of others, it must take the form of language and tradition. Here, as Horton observes, there appears to be a rupture in Bautain's concept of divine revelation. A Platonic "illuminism" informs his understanding of the inspiration of the genius and prophet who are infused with the immediate perception of the idea. But his conception of revelation as conveyed in the external form as Word, in the shape of tradition and an external authority, appears to reflect the influence of the Traditionalism of Maistre and Bonald, rather than that of Plato and St. Augustine. Yet Bautain, like Bonald, assumes that the development of revealed Truth in the human race "recapitulates" that of the individual. And as no person is born a fully formed genius or prophet, so the first prophets also must have assimilated the truth handed down by the Word. "It must have been so, for the divine Word is the first condition of the intellectual and moral development of mankind. Hence the first man had to have a teacher; he had to be spoken to, that he might speak; it is God, says the Scriptures, who first spoke to Adam."[42]

It appears that the relations of individual divine illumination and authoritative tradition are now reversed; tradition precedes inspiration. Bautain never clarifies this ambiguity satisfactorily. However, it is also clear that he never perceived divine revelation as being a purely external, verbal communication based on authority alone. He believed that every individual has an innate capacity—no matter how badly impaired by the Fall—to recognize the truth, or to have a dim sense of it when it is presented. Yet some see the truth immediately and believe the Word of the prophet and apostle; others find the truth through practice, by "tasting" it; but others never comprehend it. Unlike Lamennais, Bautain did not believe that all persons possessed an equal spiritual capacity. Thus for him the Church cannot be guided by Lamennais's criterion of a *sensus communis*. Neither, however, is a purely external authority adequate. Bautain's apology is directed at those who are willing to "taste and see," at those who "wish evidence and not authority, who wish to see the truth for themselves and not receive it on the testimony of another."[43]

According to Bautain, a primal divine revelation and ongoing tradition are necessary for two reasons. First, because we are social beings; our ideas are conveyed to us communally through language; our capacities are developed slowly through social intercourse. Second, the reason (*Vernunft*) possessed by each individual does not develop equally or at the same pace; most humans are dependent on the insight of the genius and prophet. God in his infinite love provided humanity with his revealed Word:

If in our present state we had been able by the sole strength of our mind and by using our natural lights to elevate ourselves to these pure and sublime ideas, revelation would not have been necessary. If after the fall of the first man and in the total ignorance of the true God into which the greater part of his descendants had fallen, no one could any longer awaken in himself the sense of truth . . . If for this effect was required . . . an immediate revelation made to the people most capable of receiving it, it is clear that to participate in this immense benefit it is necessary to have recourse to the Mosaic word, the prophetic word, the evangelical word; it is necessary to listen to the church, which is the depository of this word and which has received the authority to teach it. Certitude of the existence of God presupposes the idea of God, and that idea can be obtained not by speculation, by abstraction, but only by faith in God, which is born of hearing and word.[44]

Bautain's Apologetic. Bautain's apology for Christianity is in large measure a modern formulation of St. Augustine's *credo ut intelligam,* I believe in order to understand. It begins with the human need to believe and then appeals to the test of religious experience. It opposes a purely rational theology that claims to be able to compel belief. Bautain recognized that unaided, discursive reason is incapable of coming to a knowledge of the *Christian* God. Human reason must first become "Christianized," open and receptive to the Divine Word. Thus, the Christian apologist must never comply with the unbeliever's demand for an ironclad proof. Rational theology

forgets her dignity and her celestial origin, she degrades herself, every time she enters the lists and combats with the reason. "Can you believe?"—that is her first condition, and not "Can you understand, discuss, argue." . . . "We announce to you," says the Apostle—not "We prove to you," but—"We announce to you the Word of Life."[45]

If no light of the Word penetrates the heart and mind of the unbeliever, it is impossible, Bautain insists, for the apologist to proceed. It simply is illusory to think that there is some infallible means of convincing persons; we know that humans often resist the most evident of truths. For this reason the apologist's traditional appeal to natural theology for proofs of God's existence is futile. At best one can prove the existence of a great First Cause, but a Cause devoid of all the attributes of the Christian God. Neither the cosmological nor the teleological argument is intellectually compelling to the doubting mind. One cannot conclude anything about the infinite by appeals from the finite. Nor can one draw analogies from the properties of the natural world to those attributes of a transcendent God. Nature reveals itself as amoral, not benevolent. Therefore, one must already believe in God before one can perceive divine design and purpose in creation. Furthermore, the conscientious unbeliever will be repelled by such proofs. And for the Christian, God can never be known *in abstracto;* for "the Christian believes that God, the principle of all that exists, is the unfathomable abyss, the devouring fire, the jealous God whom no creature can approach, whom no intelligence can contemplate, and of whom no one can form either an idea or an image."[46]

For Bautain, God is known only through self-revelation, and even that indirectly through the Word. The great evil in theology, he contends, has been the influence of Aristotle's rationalism, the result of which is a pagan deism, not a Christian theism. At the beginning of his correspondence with his Jewish disciples, included in *Philsophie du Christianisme,* Bautain writes:

O my friends, do you realize that between a true Israelite and a deist there is the same difference as between a civilized man and a child growing up in savagery? The god of the deist is force, nature, fate, destiny; it is a general cause, assumed to exist because the reason demands a cause . . . or else . . . a rational entity, an abstraction, an idol of the mind. . . . And that is what you would substitute for the God of Israel and of Moses, the living God who created man in his image, animated him with his spirit, and preserves him with his Providence.[47]

During the early 1830s Bautain's career reached its zenith. He and his "School of Strasbourg " were considered the vanguard of a reawakened progressive Catholicism. However, his attacks on almost every other school of thought brought severe counterattacks, and within a remarkably brief time he found himself in wholesale disfavor. The Church authorities were hostile because of Bautain's attack, even ridicule, of the new, resurgent Scholastic philosophy and theology. The new coadjutor Bishop of Strasbourg was Andreas Raess, a leader of the Neo-Scholastic Movement. His *Advertissement* attacking the heresies in Bautain's teachings soon followed, and a long controversy ensued. The Tübingen faculty in Germany, led by J. A. Möhler, supported Bautain and conferred on him a doctorate in theology. However, as opposition to Bautain gained strength, Henri Lacordaire advised him to go to Rome and personally explain his teachings to the Roman authorities. He was received amicably by the Pope, but months passed and no decision was reached. Bautain's contact during this time with the great Roman Jesuit theologian Giovanni Perrone appears to have convinced him of the extreme character of his views. And Pope Gregory XVI informed him, after a friendly interview, that he sinned "by too much faith." Bautain returned to Strasbourg shaken and uncertain of his position. On September 8, 1840, he signed a sweeping recantation of his views, a disavowal prepared by Bishop Raess. Characteristic of the six propositions to which Bautain assented was one in which he had to agree with the statement that "In these various questions reason precedes faith, and should lead us to it."

As indicated earlier, Bautain's "fideism" or "voluntarism," if properly understood, did not repudiate reason, if by reason one means Jacobi's *Vernunft,* the intuitive grasp of metaphysical truths. Yet Bautain was never able to persuade the authorities of this. He felt strongly that it was a Christian's duty to defer to competent authority and that his teaching had, in fact, crossed the threshold into anti-intellectualism. Later in life, preaching before a Parisian audience, he confessed his error: "In order to give a wider range to the Word of God," he acknowledged, "I was led to weaken the validity of the human reason; and, to make an end of rationalism at a stroke, I menaced the very life of reason, like those imprudent physicians who risk killing the patient by attacking the disease too violently."[48]

By the late 1830s interest in Bautain's philosophy was rapidly waning. He and some of his disciples left Strasbourg in 1841 to carry out their educational work at the College of Juilly, near Paris. The scheme soon failed, due to defections by members of the group. In the latter years of his life, Bautain lectured on moral theology at the Sorbonne, but the fire and originality of his earlier writings were now dampened in the service of a conventional orthodoxy. Nevertheless, his books of sermons, meditations, and spiritual counsel gained some popularity. Despite the failure of his Christian philosophy to gain acceptance by the Catholic authorities during his lifetime, he died spiritually at peace and in the service of his Church.

Louis Bautain is the most important representative of French moderate Traditionalism. Aspects of this moderate Traditionalism were to persist in French thought, especially in its distinctly post-Kantian form as characterized by the themes that dominated Bautain's philosophy. These would include recourse to the idea of a primal revelation; the importance of the role of an organic society in the spiritual education of the human race; believing as the starting point of knowledge, and of the response to the tradition mediated and passed on by society; and the rejection of analytical reason as a possible means to metaphysical truth.

This form of Traditionalism continued in an uneasy relationship with Thomism until 1879, when Pope Leo XIII declared Thomism to be the official philosophy of the Catholic Church. Thereafter, post-Kantian philosophy and the Aristotelianism of the Neo-Thomists were locked in an irreconcilable battle. Nevertheless, Bautain's influence, though largely unavowed, can be detected in the Catholic Tübingen School in Germany, and more especially in the intuitionist and voluntaristic tendencies that one finds in the philosophy of Léon Ollé-Laprune, professor at the École Normale, and in the "Philosophy of Action" of his disciple Maurice Blondel, author of *L'Action* (1893), as well as in the apologetic work of Abbé Lucien Laberthonnière, editor of *Annales de Philosophie Chrétienne*. One can also hear the resonances of Bautain's "voluntarism" in the Catholic Modernist philosopher Édouard Le Roy's *Dogma et Critique,* and parallels, though not an influence, in John Henry Newman, as we will see. These strains of French Neo-Augustinianism and Romanticism will be further explored in Chapter 14.

NOTES

1. Quoted in C. S. Phillips, *The Church in France 1789–1848* (New York, 1966), p. 48.
2. Quoted in Bernard Reardon, *Liberalism and Tradition: Aspects of Catholic Thought in the Nineteenth Century* (Cambridge, 1975), p. 6.
3. Quoted in Phillips, op. cit., pp. 49–50.
4. Viscount de Chateaubriand, *The Genius of Christianity,* trans. Charles I. White (Baltimore, 1856; New York, 1976), p. 48.
5. Ibid., p. 48.
6. Ibid., pp. 48–49.
7. Ibid., p. 49.
8. Émile Faguet, *Politiques et morals du dix-neuvième siècle,* 1st series (Paris, 1899), p. 1.
9. Isaiah Berlin, "Joseph de Maistre and the Origins of Fascism," *The Crooked Timber of Humanity* (New York, 1991), pp. 91–174.
10. Joseph de Maistre, "Study on Sovereignty," in *The Works of Joseph de Maistre,* ed. Jack Lively (New York, 1965), p. 118.
11. Ibid., pp. 96–98.
12. Joseph de Maistre, *The St. Petersburg Diaries,* quoted in Berlin, op. cit., p. 111.
13. Joseph de Maistre, "The Generative Principle of Political Constitutions," in *The Works of Joseph de Maistre,* ed. Jack Lively (New York, 1965), p. 170.
14. Maistre, "Study on Sovereignty," p. 108.
15. Maistre, Ibid., pp. 109, 102.

16. Maistre, Ibid., p. 103.
17. Maistre, *The Pope* (New York, 1975; 1850 English ed., trans. Aeness McD. Dawson), pp. 4, 6, 11, 17, 21.
18. Berlin, op. cit., pp. 173–74.
19. Walter Marshall Horton, *The Philosophy of the Abbé Bautain* (New York, 1926), p. 17.
20. Hughes-Félicité Robert de Lamennais, *Essai,* I, ed. Garnier, p. 30. Cited in Reardon, *Liberalism and Tradition* (1975), p. 68.
21. Ibid., p. 176.
22. Lamennais, *Essai,* II, ed. Garnier, p. 93.
23. Ibid., p. 83. Cited in Horton, op. cit., p. 19.
24. Ibid., p. 283.
25. Auguste Laveille, *Un Lamennais inconnu* (1898). Cited in Alec Vidler, *Prophecy and Papacy: A Study of Lamennais, the Church and the Revolution* (New York, 1954), p. 242.
26. Lamennais, *Affaires de Rome,* ed. Garnier, p. 336. Cited in Vidler, op. cit., p. 262.
27. Ibid., p. 266.
28. Louis Bautain. Cited in Horton, op. cit., p. 58. I am especially indebted to Horton for his exposition of Bautain. Horton's study remains among the finest studies of Bautain and certainly is the best in English.
29. Abbé E. de Regny, *L'Abbé Bautain: sa vie et ses oeuvres* (Paris, 1884), pp. 60–61. Cited in Horton, op. cit., p. 67.
30. Cited in Horton, op. cit., p. 80.
31. L. Bautain, *Cahiers,* II, p. 18. Cited in Horton, op. cit., p. 84.
32. L. Bautain, *Fonds Bautain,* 9. Unpublished, Cited in Horton, op. cit., p. 76.
33. See Horton, op. cit., pp. 168–176.
34. L. Bautain, *Philosophie du christianisme,* I (Paris, 1835), pp. 293–295, 296–297. Cited in Horton, op. cit., p. 169.
35. L. Bautain, *Psychologie expérimentale,* II (Paris, 1839), pp. 376–377. Cited in Horton, op. cit., pp. 170–171.
36. L. Bautain, *Variétés philosophiques* (Strasbourg, 1823), p. 41. Cited in Horton, op. cit., p. 172.
37. L. Bautain, *Philosophie morale,* I (Paris, 1842), pp. 494–495. Cited in Horton, op. cit., p. 172.
38. L. Bautain, *Philosophie du christianisme* (Paris, 1835). Trans. by Joseph Fitzer, in *Romance and the Rock: Nineteenth-Century Catholics on Faith and Reason* (Minneapolis, 1989), p. 161.
39. Bautain, *Psychologie expérimentale,* II, p. 406. Cited in Horton, op. cit., p. 177.
40. Ibid., pp. 406–407. Cited in Horton, op. cit., pp. 181–182.
41. Ibid., pp. 102–103. Cited in Horton, op. cit., p. 182.
42. L. Bautain, *Résumé des conférences faites au cercle catholique* (Paris, 1843), pp. 46–47. Cited in Horton, op. cit., p. 185.
43. L. Bautain, *De l'enseignement de la philosophie en France au XIX siècle* (Paris, 1833), p. lxii. Cited in Horton, op. cit., p. 187.
44. Bautain, *Philosophie du christianisme.* Cited in Fitzer, op. cit., p. 163.
45. L. Bautain, *Fonds Bautain,* 10. Unpublished. Cited in Horton, op. cit., p. 223.
46. Bautain, *Philosophie du christianisme.* Cited in Fitzer, op. cit., p. 156.
47. Bautain, *Philosophie du christianisme,* I, pp. 19–21. Cited in Horton, op. cit., p. 249.
48. de Regny, op. cit., p. 381. Cited in Horton, op. cit., p. 96.

SUGGESTIONS FOR FURTHER READING

I

There is no thorough study in English of French Traditionalism as a complex movement of the nineteenth century. One must consult French studies, such as Edgar Hocédez, *Histoire de la Theologie au XIXe siècle,* 3 vols (Paris: Desclée, 1948). The best brief accounts in English are Walter Marshall Horton, *The Philosophy of the Abbé Bautain* (New York: New York University Press, 1926), Chaps. 1–3; Bernard Reardon, *Liberalism and Tradition: Aspects of Catholic Thought in Nineteenth-Century France* (Cambridge: Cambridge University Press, 1975), Chaps. 1–6; and Gerald A. McCool, *Catholic Theology in the Nineteenth Century* (New York: Seabury Press, 1977), Chap. 2.

There is a rich literature in French on each of the four writers below. Only the best studies in English are cited. Translations of excerpts from some works of Chateaubriand, Maistre, and Bautain may be found in *Romance and the Rock,* ed. Joseph Fitzer (Minneapolis: Fortress Press, 1989).

Brief notices of many Catholic authors and movements of this period can be found in *The Harper Collins Encyclopedia of Catholicism* (1995).

François-René de Chateaubriand

Maurois, André. *Chateaubriand,* trans. Vera Fraser (New York: Harper and Row, 1938).

Painter, George D. *Chateaubriand: A Biography, I, The Longed-For Tempests, 1768–1793* (New York: Alfred A. Knopf, 1978).

Joseph de Maistre

In addition to Chapter 2 in Reardon above, see the following:

Berlin, Isaiah. *The Crooked Timbers of Humanity* (London: J. Murray, 1990).

Lebrun, Richard Allen. *Throne and Altar: The Political and Religious Thought of Joseph de Maistre* (Ottawa: University of Ottawa Press, 1965).

Lively, Jack, ed. *The Works of Joseph de Maistre* (New York: Macmillan, 1965). This fine collection of selected passages includes a good introduction to Maistre.

Hughes-Félicité Robert de Lamennais

B. M. G. Reardon's study listed above includes two excellent chapters on Lamennais, and his *Religion in the Age of Romanticism* (Cambridge: Cambridge University Press, 1985) also includes a chapter that focuses on Lamennais's career just before and after his condemnation.

Vidler, Alec R. *Prophecy and Papacy: A Study of Lamennais, the Church, and the Revolution* (New York: Charles Scribner and Sons, 1954). The best study in English on Lamennais and one that brings him vividly to life.

Louis Bautain

Reardon's *Liberalism and Tradition* includes a good chapter on Bautain, as does McCool's Chapter 2 of *Catholic Theology in the Nineteenth Century.*

Horton, Walter Marshall. *The Philosophy of the Abbé Bautain* (New York: New York University Press, 1926). One of the best studies of Bautain and the only thorough account in English of his thought and influence.

Chapter 7
Romanticism and Anglo-Catholicism: The Oxford Movement

John Henry Newman

Viewed from our present vantage point, the Oxford Movement can be seen as an aspect of that larger spiritual and cultural movement which reacted against the Age of Reason and is known as Romanticism. It can also be seen as an effort at recovery and conservation. The individuals of the Oxford or Tractarian Movement* reflect much that characterized the Romantic poets and novelists. They abhorred what they considered the presumptuous usurpation by "reason alone" of all claims to truth. They looked upon "private judgment" as evidence of a shallow sense of history and as politically and religiously divisive. They possessed a deep but

often uncritical admiration of ancient ways, looking to the glory of unified Christendom in the Middle Ages or the ascetic purity of the primitive martyrs with a certain sentimental wistfulness. They loved mystery, sometimes reveling in their paradoxes to the point of unintelligibility—and thereby closing themselves off from those outside their party. They possessed a deep mystical feeling and were essentially poetic spirits concerned with restoring a sense of humble obedience before the holy mysteries—in a church shorn of the *mysterium tremendum*.

The Oxford Movement was not only, nor even principally, a movement of religious *thought*. Like all movements of restoration, it had deep social and political currents. But it was, first of all, a movement of religious devotion and discipline. However, this revival of a more Catholic piety was accompanied by historical and theological investigations of ancient

---

*Also referred to as the Anglo-Catholic Revival, the Anglican "Counter Reformation," and, by contemporaries of the movement, as "Puseyism," after Dr. E. B. Pusey, one of the Oxford leaders.

thought and practice, and these studies gave theological warrant for the Church's religious renewal. The writings of the Tractarians—Keble, Newman, Pusey—lacked, for the most part, the originality of the German theologians. By their learning and prolific writing, however, these Oxford writers were able to make not only the Church of England but much of non-Roman Christendom aware of the riches of her pre- Reformation heritage. This effect was not immediate. Resistance to the Oxford revival was very great within the Anglican Church itself and no more so than among her bishops. Nevertheless, the Oxford Movement has had a slow and almost imperceptible influence on aspects of European and American Christianity. Outwardly that influence can easily be seen in the areas of spiritual discipline and liturgy, but, in turn, this revival of the religious life and worship has had a significant, though less observable, influence on theology, on the renewal of mission, on social thought, and on ecumenism.

THE BEGINNINGS OF THE ANGLO-CATHOLIC REVIVAL

Before turning to the characteristic *thought* of the Oxford Tractarians, something must be said of the beginnings and development of the movement itself. Much can be learned about the character of the Oxford Movement by looking closely at the political and social situation existing in Europe in the first decades of the nineteenth century. As we have seen, both on the Continent and in England there was a reaction against the excesses of the French Revolution and the Terror. Originally drawn to the Revolution by its heroic denunciation of despotism, many Romantics found the outcome of radical republicanism, in the likes of Tom Paine, horrifying. We have seen how in France the reaction took a strongly political turn in the Catholic traditionalism of Bonald and Maistre, who combined royalism and papalism. In England the distrust of the new liberalism was epitomized in Edmund Burke's *Reflections on the Revolution in France* (1790).

French radicalism helped to effect a conservative reaction in England to such a degree that, in the words of the historian Froude, it "frightened all classes out of advanced ways of thinking, and soci-

ety in town and country [became] Tory in politics, and determined to allow no innovations upon the inherited faith."[1] In the early decades of the nineteenth century, the Tory party became increasingly reactionary but, under the pressure of dissent, had been required in 1828 to repeal the old Test and Corporation Acts which had excluded Dissenters from Parliament and other public office. A year later came Catholic Emancipation. The old High Church Anglican ideal of the union of Church and state was in jeopardy. Then, in 1830 the Whigs came to power, and in two years the famous Reform Bill was passed. The alliance of Whigs, Dissenters, and emancipated Catholics marked evil days ahead for the Established Church. Thomas Arnold wrote at the time that "the Church, as it now stands, no human power can save."

In 1833 the Whig administration introduced the Church Temporalities Bill into Parliament. The measure sought to reform the Irish Church by reducing the number of bishoprics and redistributing the rich, ecclesiastical incomes. The Irish Church had long needed reorganization, but the conservative bishops were opposed to change. The Whig Irish Church Temporalities Bill of 1833 was in fact a moderate and reasonable measure. Nevertheless, after the victories of the Reform Bill, it was interpreted as one more defeat for the Church in its struggle with the growing tide of secular power. The High Church party saw a growing Erastianism—the authority of the state over Church matters—slowly weakening the hold of the Church of England over the lives of the people and, moreover, transforming the Church into a dutiful servant of the secular state. The Oxford Movement, can, in part, be seen as a *political* reaction to the growth of this political liberalism. One historian has written that the Tractarian Movement "was the English equivalent of the French traditionalism of de Maistre, de Bonald and Lamennais . . . conservative reactions to the reforming tendencies of liberalism in Church and State."[2] There is much truth in this view, but it may not do justice to the essence of the Oxford counter-revolution. Erastianism was one element of a larger danger, i.e., the pretensions of reason and science to solve all of humanity's difficulties, thus calling into question the need for any supernatural religion at all. The more insidious enemy of the Tractarians was Benthamism and a growing scientific positivism. E. R. Fairweather may underplay the social and political factors, but he does point to the very real theological issues at stake:

> The Oxford Movement was unquestionably an affirmation of the Church's God-given authority and inherent power, but this affirmation was part of an attempted renewal of the Church in the interests of supernatural religion. Over against the aridities of empiricist philosophy and Utilitarian ethics, the Tractarians sought a renewed awareness of transcendent mystery and a renewed sense of human life as guided by a transcendent power to a transcendent goal. If they insisted on the authority of the Church they did so because they saw in the Church an indispensable witness to the grace and truth that came by Jesus Christ—not because they looked to it as one more bulwark of a threatened social order.[3]

According to its own leaders, the Oxford Movement began with a sermon preached by John Keble before His Majesty's Judges of Assize at Oxford on July 14, 1833.* The immediate cause of the sermon was the Church Temporalities Bill and the suppression of the ten Irish bishoprics, in defiance of the Church's opinion. What alarmed Keble and others was the fact that the state had taken upon itself, without the Church's consent, to determine episcopal authority, even episcopal existence. Keble entitled his sermon "National Apostasy." In the Advertisement to the First Edition he wrote:

> The legislature of England and Ireland (*the members of which are not even bound to profess belief in the atonement*), this body has virtually usurped the commission of those whom our Saviour entrusted with *at least one voice* in making ecclesiastical laws, on matters wholly or partly spiritual. The same legislature has also ratified, to its full extent, this principle—that the apostolical Church in this realm is henceforth only to stand, in the eye of the state as *one sect among many*, depending, for any preeminence she may still appear to retain, merely upon the accident of her having a strong party in the country.[4]

*Years later J. H. Newman wrote: "I have ever considered and kept the day as the start of the religious Movement of 1833."

Keble counted such action a "profane intrusion" into the realm of divine authority. He called upon church people to treat such an intrusion as they would treat any other "tyranny"; "deprecate and adjure it." The cause of this situation was the growing indifference of people toward the supernatural realities of religion, disguised in the garb of toleration. Keble called such a condition *Apostasy:*

> Under the guise of charity and toleration we are come almost to this that no difference, in matters of faith, is to disqualify for our approbation and confidence, whether in public or domestic life. Can we conceal it from ourselves, that every year the practice is becoming more common, of trusting men unreservedly in the most delicate and important matters, without serious inquiry, whether they do not hold principles which make it impossible for them to be loyal to their Creator, Redeemer and Sanctifier? . . . The point really to be considered is, whether, according to the coolest estimate, the fashionable liberality of this generation be not ascribable, in a great measure, to the same temper which led the Jews voluntarily to set about degrading themselves to a level with the idolatrous Gentiles. And, if it be true anywhere, that such enactments are forced on the legislature by public opinion, is APOSTASY too hard a word to describe the temper of that nation?[5]

Keble's sermon summed up the sentiments of many of the younger clergy who were distressed and angered by the Church's acquiescence to secularism. The sermon served as a call to action. Between the 25th and 29th of July 1833, a small meeting was held in Hugh James Rose's rectory at Hadleigh to consider what might be done. Those joining Rose were Hurrell Froude, Arthur Perceval, and William Palmer, all of Oxford. John Henry Newman and John Keble did not attend but were kept informed of the plans. It was agreed that an Association of Friends of the Church should be formed and that certain petitions and addresses to the Archbishop of Canterbury and others should be drawn up. Not a great deal came of these plans, but they did prepare the way for the famous *Tracts for the Times* which contained the fundamental principles of the movement.

The series of tracts began to appear in the early autumn of 1833. The first one, only four pages in length, was written by Newman. It was entitled *Thoughts on the Ministerial Commission Respectfully Addressed to the Clergy*. Its urgency and confidence served as a keynote for the series. Its theme was *apostolic succession* since it was this, and this alone, Newman argued, to which the clergy must look for their authority. If the state were to deprive the Church of its temporal benefits, on what, Newman asked the clergy, would they establish their office?

> Should the government and the country so far forget their God as to cast off the Church, to deprive it of its temporal honours and substance, *on what* will you rest the claim of respect and attention which you make upon your flocks? Hitherto you have been upheld by your birth, your education, your wealth, your connexions; should these secular advantages cease, on what must Christ's ministers depend . . . *on what* are we to rest our authority when the state deserts us?
>
> Christ has not left his Church without claim of its own upon the attention of men. Surely not. Hard Master he cannot be, to bid us oppose the world, yet give us no credentials for so doing. There are some who rest their divine mission on their own unsupported assertion; others, who rest it on their popularity; others on their success; and others, who rest it upon their temporal distinctions. This last case has, perhaps, been too much our own; I fear we have neglected the real ground on which our authority is built—OUR APOSTOLICAL DESCENT.
>
> We have been born not of blood, nor of the will of the flesh, nor of the will of man, but of God (Jn. 1:13). The Lord Jesus Christ gave his Spirit to his apostles (cf. Jn. 20:22); they in turn laid their hands on those who should succeed them; and these again on others; and so the sacred gift has been handed down to our present bishops, who have appointed us as their assistants, and in some sense representatives.[6]

The notion had gone abroad that the state could deprive the clergy of their power by confiscating the Church's property. A confusion had been made between the divine commission of the priestly office and the temporal power of the Church. Newman concludes Tract I with an appeal to the clergy to enlighten their flocks on this matter and with the following challenge:

> If you will not adopt my view of the subject, which I offer to you, not doubtingly, yet (I hope) respectfully, at all events, CHOOSE YOUR SIDE. To remain neutral much longer will be itself to take a part. *Choose* your side; since side you shortly must, with one or other party, even though you do nothing. Fear to be of those whose line is decided for them by chance circumstances, and who may perchance find themselves with the enemies of Christ, while they think but to remove themselves from worldly politics. Such abstinence is impossible in troublous times, HE THAT IS NOT WITH ME IS AGAINST ME, AND HE THAT GATHERETH NOT WITH ME SCATTERETH ABROAD (Mt. 12:30).[7]

The early tracts and Newman's sermons at St. Mary's Church, Oxford, incited a movement, and soon new recruits were joining the cause—among them the young statesman Gladstone. The most important of these new adherents was Edward B. Pusey, Regius Professor of Hebrew at Oxford and a man of vast influence in the university and in the world outside clerical Oxford. Pusey's accession to the movement was signaled by the appearance of Tract 18 on fasting, which appeared over his initials in 1837. The next year he published three tracts (67, 68, 69) on baptism which grew into a treatise of four hundred pages. It was a learned work, summing up the theology and spirit of the Anglo-Catholic party. It also proved to be a turning point in the movement's history, in that it gave to it a theological erudition and responsibility which it had not yet entirely achieved. Looking back at the movement years later, Newman commented on the significance of Pusey's entrance into the cause.

> Dr. Pusey's influence was felt at once. He saw that there ought to be more sobriety, more gravity, more careful pains, more sense of responsibility in the Tracts and in the whole Movement. It was through him that the character of the Tracts was changed. . . . I suspect it was Dr. Pusey's influence and example which set me, and made me set others, on the larger and more careful works in defence of the principles of the Movement which followed in a course of years.[8]

By 1835 the movement was a power to be reckoned with. It continued to grow in numbers and influence for the next several years. There were some setbacks, however. In 1836 Hurrell Froude died, and his letters and papers were published by Newman and Keble two years later. The anti-Protestant sentiments expressed in Froude's journals incensed many and scared others away.* In 1839 the suspicions raised by Froude's papers were deepened by the publication of Tract 80, written by Isaac Williams and titled *On Reserve in Communicating Religious Knowledge.* Williams objected to the Evangelicals' careless use of sacred language and appealed to the whole tradition of the Church as a corrective to the Evangelical practice of focusing almost exclusively on the doctrine of the Atonement. Nevertheless, it was attacked widely as exemplifying the worst evils of Romanism.

> The word "Reserve" was enough. It meant that the Tract-writers avowed the principle of keeping back part of the counsel of God. It meant, further, that the real spirit of the party was disclosed; its love of secret and crooked methods . . . its deliberate concealments, its holding doctrines and its pursuit of aims which it dared not avow, its *disciplina arcani,* its conspiracies, its Jesuitical spirit.[9]

Such was the state of mind in which Tract 80 was received by the opponents of the Revival—a suspiciousness which was never again allayed.

Despite these and other reversals, the movement reached its zenith between 1836 and 1838. In the latter year over 60,000 tracts were sold, Newman's published sermons were widely read, and the *British Critic,* the organ of the party edited by Newman, was flourishing. However, outward appearances were deceptive. Between 1840 and 1845 the movement was about to move into a second phase, which was marked by doubts and divisions, caused partly by the influx of new, often extreme people whose tendency was clearly Roman-ward. The breakup of the Oxford Movement and its dispersion during these years can be observed in a series of events, especially in John Henry Newman's own changing

course. First, there was a series of defeats and humiliations for the Tractarians at the hands of their Oxford opponents. In August 1838 the Bishop of Oxford, in a charge to his clergy, had accused the Tractarians of Romanish practices. This was especially bitter for Newman because of his deep sense of obedience to his episcopal superior. During the same year a proposal was introduced for the raising of a subscription for an Oxford memorial to the Reformation martyrs Cranmer, Ridley, and Latimer. This was clearly a move directed against the High Church party. Newman and Keble would have nothing to do with it, but the subscription was a success, and the Martyrs' Memorial was built.

In 1841 a proposal was made, and accepted by men in high authority, for the establishment of an Anglo-Prussian Protestant Bishop of Jerusalem. The bishop was to be nominated alternately by England and Prussia and consecrated by English Bishops for jurisdiction over English and German Protestants in Palestine. The idea that the English Church, which was out of communion with both the Roman and the Eastern Church, could enter lightly into communion with Protestant heretics was against all that the Oxford party was fighting for. Newman protested bitterly and later acknowledged that this was one of the blows that led to his final disillusionment with the *Via Media* of the English Church.

During the same period a controversy over the Poetry Professorship at Oxford increased the rift between the parties. Isaac Williams, a loyal Tractarian and fine poet, was thought to be the natural choice for the chair, but because of his Tractarian affiliation he was opposed and defeated. In the next years the Tractarians suffered two additional humiliations which, while revealing the fear and even panic of their Oxford opponents, also made clear the serious differences between the Catholic party and the majority within the English Church. In 1844 Dr. Pusey was suspended for two years from preaching in the university. The suspension was the result of a sermon Pusey had preached on "The Holy Eucharist, a Comfort to the Penitent." He was accused of teaching transubstantiation and other heretical doctrines and, without a hearing or trial, was found guilty by a board of six professors, all of whom opposed "Puseyism."

---

*Froude had written such things as: "Really I hate the Reformation and the Reformers more and more," and "The Reformation was a limb badly set; it must be broken again to be righted."

A year later William G. Ward, a zealous new-comer to the Catholic cause, was censured and stripped of his university degrees for statements published in a book entitled *The Ideal of a Christian Church.* The book actually does reveal how Romanized the movement had become, at least among some of the younger leaders. Ward could find nothing excellent in the English Church. At the same time he looked uncritically to the Roman Communion as the historical exhibition of his "Ideal." He also exulted in the fact that he found "the whole cycle of Roman doctrine gradually possessing numbers of English Churchmen" and boasted that he still retained his Oxford fellowship after having publicly stated "that in subscribing the Articles I renounce not one Roman doctrine." It is no wonder that his book was condemned, but the punishment of reducing Ward to the status of an undergraduate was a ridiculous act, only making plain the bitter strife of the time.

All of these events had their effects in demoralizing and dividing the movement during the early 1840s, but none was as important in the movement's decline as the unsettlement of Newman's own mind and his final secession from the Church of England. Newman's religious pilgrimage during these years cannot be detailed here; only a few of the most important factors can be sketched.*

While becoming increasingly assured that the Anglican Church, though differing from Rome, should on the whole be more like it, Newman did not question his claim that the Church of England represented the Church's genuine antiquity until the summer of 1839. Then his confidence was shaken. He had been absorbed in reading about the Monophysite heresy of the fifth century C.E. and saw in this fifth-century controversy an analogy to his own times. He perceived the English Church to be like the Monophysites, a small, unsteady island broken away from the firm, majestic mainland. At this very moment of uncertainty, Newman records that he received "the first real hit from Romanism." A

friend had put into his hands an article written by the English Roman Catholic Bishop Nicholas Wiseman. The article compared the isolation of the Anglican *Via Media* with the Donatist sect which had seceded from Rome in the fourth century. What struck Newman was not the parallel between the Donatists and the English Church but Wiseman's citation of a phrase from St. Augustine—*securus judicat orbis terrarum*—against the Donatists. The phrase, "the wide world is secure in its judgment," made Newman conscious that the English Church, like the heretical sects of the fourth and fifth centuries, was a small, prideful communion, glorying in its separation from the great universal Church. Not only did the Anglican Church lack Catholicity; in Newman's eyes it no longer could appeal to Antiquity. The significance of this occasion is recorded by Newman:

> What a light was hereby thrown upon every controversy in the Church! . . . *The deliberate judgement, in which the whole Church at length rests and acquiesces, is an infallible prescription and a final sentence against such portions of it as protest and secede. . . .* For a mere sentence, the words of St. Augustine, struck me with a power which I had never felt from any words before. . . . *Securus judicat orbis terrarum! By those great words of the ancient Father, the theory of the Via Media was absolutely pulverized.*[10] (Italics added.)

For Newman, as well as for Ward and others, Rome now possessed the true marks of the Church. Yet Newman was not yet ready to give up his apologetic for the Church of England. If Rome possessed the notes of the true Church, it was necessary to show that Anglicanism was actually compatible with Rome. The stumbling block, of course, was the Thirty-Nine Articles. Could it be shown that these articles were compatible with the doctrine of the Old Church? In 1841 (in the famous Tract 90, entitled *Remarks on Certain Passages in the Thirty-Nine Articles*) Newman undertook to show that this was, indeed, possible. He put down as the first principle of interpreting the articles the following rule:

> It is a duty which we owe both to the Catholic Church and to our own, to take our reformed confessions in the most Catholic sense they will admit: We have no duties towards their framers.[11]

---

*This is a fascinating history and can be found in Newman's own spiritual autobiography, *Apologia Pro Vita Sua.* Also, there is a lively account of these years in Geoffrey Faber's *Oxford Apostles.* For a detailed, sympathetic account see Ian Ker, *John Henry Newman: A Biography.*

This principle led many to claim, with considerable warrant, that Newman's allegiance was already to Rome. The tortured, ingenious, and often seemingly inconsistent arguments of the tract also did not allow for any greater confidence, outside the Roman-ward party, in Newman's position. One example of his procedure will suffice. Article XXI states that forasmuch as General Councils are assemblies of humans, "they may err and sometimes have erred in things pertaining to God. Wherefor things ordained of them as necessary to salvation have neither strength nor authority, unless it may be declared that they are taken out of Holy Scripture." Newman adds the gloss that "General Council, then, may err, *as such*—may err, *unless* in any case it is promised, as a matter of supernatural privilege, that they shall *not* err; a case which lies beyond the scope of this Article, or at any rate beside its determination."[12]

Newman's motives for writing Tract 90 will never be completely known. Was he simply hoping to remove the barrier of the Thirty-Nine Articles for those extreme Romanizers in the party, such as William G. Ward? Or, like Ward, was he wishing to put the final challenge to the Church of England? In any case, Tract 90 produced a storm of protest, and in March 1841 the Heads of Houses at Oxford condemned the tract, claiming it to be dishonest and incompatible with the university statutes. Things grew steadily worse for the Catholic party in Oxford; the High Church group was discriminated against in numerous ways. In February 1842 Newman retired to the village of Littlemore. It was now only a matter of waiting for the ties with the past to be broken and the new conviction to gain assurance before he would be received into the Roman Church. During the evening of October 8, 1845, in the same year as the condemnation of Ward's *The Ideal of the Christian Church,* Newman fell on his knees before the Passionist Father Dominic and begged to be received "into the Church of Christ."

Newman's secession was a severe blow to the Anglo-Catholic Movement. After Newman the movement continued to influence the life of the Church, but it never again achieved the spiritual power, depth, and brilliance of the movement of the 1830s and early 1840s. Some individuals like J. A. Froude and Mark Pattison were cast adrift by Newman's action and ended up as skeptics. Others like Ward, Faber, Manning, and Robert Wilberforce sooner or later joined Newman in the Roman Church. Others like Keble and Pusey remained in the English Church and continued their labors in the cause of Anglo-Catholicism. In 1855 Pusey published his book entitled *The Real Presence* and in 1857 Keble's *On Eucharistic Adoration* appeared. Both works were characteristic of the continuing work of the Anglo-Catholic party within the Anglican Communion. The leadership of the movement soon passed into the hands of able, younger people such as H. P. Liddon and R. W. Church and, at the end of the century, was taken up by those of a more liberal Catholic mind, such as Scott Holland and Charles Gore, who were associated with *Lux Mundi.* However, what is most distinctive about the movement between 1850 and 1890 is the revival of ritualism and ceremonial, the growth of monastic communities, and missions in the urban slums. Our chief concern remains the characteristic *thought* of the early Oxford Movement, and to that we now turn.

THE THOUGHT OF THE OXFORD MOVEMENT: KEBLE, NEWMAN, WILLIAMS, AND PUSEY

The Oxford Movement was a revival of Catholic piety, and the leaders, therefore, considered themselves restorers of the ancient faith and practice. They abhorred the idea of being *innovators* and distrusted novelty. Liberal change appeared to the Tractarians as nothing but apostasy. However, the movement was not a mere repetition of the theology of the Fathers; it was, most clearly in the case of Newman, a creative restatement of the ancient verities.

To understand the thought of the Tractarians it is first necessary to grasp the peculiar spirituality of men like Keble, Newman, Pusey, and Isaac Williams. In their feeling for the fresh beauty of nature, for the mystery of medievalism, and in the awe and thrill with which they approached the heritage of the past, they were Romantics. The unique piety which marks them all can, perhaps, best be seen in their genuine feeling for supernatural mystery, in their sense of humble reserve, and in the attention they gave to self-denying obedience. An understanding of these spiritual qualities is indispensable to an appreciation of Tractarian thought.

In an age of growing immanentism (Schleiermacher and Hegel), what is most striking about the Tractarians is their feeling for the actuality of the supernatural and the invisible heavenly world of angels and spirits. This is especially true of Newman and Pusey (referred to by Brilioth as the *doctor mysticus* of the movement), for whom the visible world is but an appearance, at best symbolizing but more often veiling the reality of the invisible. Newman expresses this in his sermon on "The Invisible World."

> Even when it [the earth] is gayest, with all its blossom on, and shows most touchingly what lies hid in it, yet it is not enough. We know much more lies hid in it than what we see. A world of Saints and Angels, a glorious world, the palace of God, the mountain of the Lord of Hosts, the Heavenly Jerusalem, the throne of God and Christ, all these wonders lie hid in what we see. . . . We know that what we see is as a screen hiding from us God and Christ, and his Saints and Angels. And we earnestly desire and pray for the dissolution of all that we see, from our longing after that which we do not see. . . .[13]

For the Tractarians our sense experience and our ideas are but pale expressions of the spiritual truths which they feebly attempt to approximate. But the Christian can let go of these visible things, for he or she understands the transience of this world. Because the world is a veil hiding the vast mysteries of the invisible world, the Christian will not fear to believe what seems credulous in the eyes of the world, for the religious mind will always appear superstitious to the worldly-wise. But when one considers how baffling Nature is, is it any wonder that the supernatural should be ineffably mysterious? "It would be strange indeed," says Newman, "if any doctrine concerning God's infinite and eternal Nature were not mysterious." It is understandable, then, that the Trinity and the Incarnation, being the highest mysteries of the faith, are not rationally explicable. They are to be approached in reverent awe:

No earthly images can come up to the awful and gracious truth, that God became the Son of Man—the Word became Flesh, and was born of a woman. This ineffable mystery surpasses human words.[14]

Think but for a moment of the awful mystery of the Passion:

> Now I bid you consider that that Face, so ruthlessly smitten, was the Face of God Himself; the Brows bloody with the thorns, the Sacred Body exposed to view and lacerated with the scourge, the Hands nailed to the Cross. . . . it was the Blood, and the Sacred Flesh, and the Hands and the Temples, and the Side, and the Feet of God Himself, which the frenzied multitude then gazed upon. This is so fearful a thought, that when the mind first masters it, surely it will be difficult to think of anything else; so that while we think of it, we must pray to God to temper it to us, and to give us strength to think of it lightly, lest it be too much for us.[15]

According to the Tractarians, religious truth is so sublime as to require that it be approached in wonder, fear, and reserve—in the spirit of the Greek *Cherubikon*: "Let all mortal flesh keep silence and with fear and trembling stand." It was, therefore, a first principle of the Tractarians that a person's soul must be spiritually prepared to receive and understand the mysteries of the faith. One feeds milk, not strong meat, to spiritual babes. The Tractarians found support for this view in the practice of the *disciplina arcana* in the ancient Fathers. This secret discipline taught that the Creed should be declared to the catechumens only as they became morally and spiritually prepared to receive it and that the holy rites and mysteries should be kept from being profaned by unbelievers. The Tractarians considered Evangelical preaching irreverent, for it exposed the most sacred mysteries to the indifference and mockery of the crowd.

This sense of reserve in communicating religious knowledge is especially evident in the personality and writings of John Keble and in the poems of Isaac Williams. In Williams's poem "The Cathedral" the church's choir screen serves as the symbol of the *disciplina arcana,* but the whole poem is expressive of this feeling.

When out of Sion God appear'd
   For perfect beauty fear'd,
The darkness was His Chariot,
   And clouds were all about.
Hiding His dread sublimity,
   When Jesus walked nigh,
He threw around His works of good
   A holier solitude,
Ris'n from the grave appear'd to view,
   But to a faithful few.

Alone e'en now, as then of old,
   The pure of heart behold
The soul-restoring miracles
   Wherein His mercy dwells;
New marvels unto them reveal'd,
   But from the whole concealed.
Then pause, and fear—when thus allowed
   We enter the dark cloud,
Lord, keep our hearts, that soul and eye
   Unharm'd may Thee descry.[16]

Spiritually akin to this reverential reserve before the supernatural is a certain self-abasement and quality of humble obedience. This is again expressed by Williams in his tract "On Reserve in Communicating Religious Knowledge," one of the most characteristic treatises of the movement. In addressing himself to the danger of private judgment in religious matters, Williams writes:

> Surely we know not what we do when we venture to make a scheme and system of our own respecting the revelations of God. His ways are so vast and mysterious that there may be some great presumption in our taking one truth, and forming around it a scheme from notions of our own. . . . The very idea of forming such a scheme arises from a want of a due sense of the depth and vastness of the divine counsels, as if we could comprehend them. . . . Religious doctrines and articles of faith can only be received according to certain dispositions of the heart; these dispositions can only be formed by a repetition of certain actions. And therefore a certain course of action can alone dispose us to receive certain doctrines. . . . For instance, charitable works alone will make a man charitable, and the more anyone does charitable works, the more charitable will he become; that is to say, the more will he love his neighbour and love God. . . . Or again, he only will

be humble in heart who does humble actions, and no action is (morally speaking) an humble action but such as proceeds from the spirit of humility; and he who does humble actions most will be most humble; and he who is most humble will be most emptied of self-righteousness, and therefore will most of all value the Cross of Christ, being least of all sensible of his own good deeds: and the more he does these works, the more will the Holy Spirit dwell with him, according to the promises of Scripture, and the more fully will he come to the knowledge of that mystery which is hid in Christ.[17]

The Tractarians felt that only such a sense of awe before the holy mysteries of God could lead to a condition of humility. And only in humility are we able to cast ourselves on God, in obedience to whom alone lies a knowledge of His Truth. For the Tractarians a humble obedience was not only a sign of one's awareness of the vast mystery of God's dealings but also a check on personal pride and vanity. Obedience to the teachings of the Church provided a way of witnessing to both of these deeply felt sentiments.

> Much might be said on that mode of witnessing Christ which consists in conforming to His Church. He who simply did what the Church bids him do (if he did no more) would witness a good confession to the world, and one which cannot be hid; and at the same time, with very little, if any, personal display. He does only what he is told to do; he takes no responsibility on himself. The Apostles and Martyrs who founded the Church, the saints in all ages who have adorned it, the Heads of it now alive, all these take from him the weight of his profession, and bear the blame (so to call it) of seeming ostentations. I do not say that irreligious men will not call such a one boastful, or austere, or a hypocrite; that is not the question. The question is, whether in God's judgement he deserves the censure; whether he is not as Christ would have him, really and truly (whatever the world may say) feigning humility to a bold outward profession; whether he is not, in thus acting, preaching Christ without hurting his own pureness, gentleness and modesty of character. If indeed a man stands forth on his own ground, declaring himself as an individual, a witness for Christ, then indeed he is grieving and dis-

turbing the calm spirit given us by God. But God's merciful providence has saved us this temptation, and forbidden us to admit it. He bids us unite together in one, and to shelter our personal profession under the authority of the general body. Thus we show ourselves as lights to the world far more effectively . . . at the same time we do so with far greater secrecy and humility.[18]

The spiritual disposition just described—the awesome sense of divine mystery, the reserve and obedience—was a necessary climate for the development of the most fundamental of the Anglo-Catholic doctrines: the authority of the Church.

The Authority of the Church

The question of authority is the touchstone of any religious system or school . It is the first principle, implied or explicitly acknowledged, on which all else hangs. We have already seen what principle of final authority grounded and shaped the doctrines of several earlier movements, and we will see how prominent the issue is in such movements as Catholic Neo-Thomism and the Princeton Theology. For the Tractarians the seat of authority is to be found in the ancient traditions and corporate teachings of the Church.

The reasons why the Oxford leaders looked to *tradition* for their authority are many. The novels of Sir Walter Scott and others contributed to a Romantic idealizing of the past. But far more important was the awareness that an unshakable breakwater was required against the inundation of liberal individualism. Yet appeal could no longer be made to "Scripture alone"—the Bible was the cause, not the cure, of sectarian division. Hume and Bentham were enough to convince Newman of the corrosive, skeptical tendencies of reason. There was additional need of a firm base on which to take a stand against the secular state and Erastianism in the Church. All of these feelings and needs found their answer in an appeal to the ancient Church and, more specifically, to the principle of apostolic succession. This is not to say that the Tractarians were desperately searching for such a foundation and happily fell upon this principle. The High Church party had always looked to the traditions of the

Fathers as uniquely authoritative. Hooker, Lancelot Andrewes, and, in the Tractarians' own age, John Jebb, all had stressed the importance of apostolic succession. It was what they considered the undeniable truth of the principle, and not its utility, that led the Tractarians to give such preeminence to the doctrine. In any case, it became the *first principle* of the movement. The encouragement, calm hope, and romance which it gave to the Tractarians' cause in those early years is captured in one of Newman's sermons:

> The royal dynasty of the Apostles is far older than all the kingly families which are now on the earth. Every Bishop of the Church whom we now behold is a lineal descendant of St. Peter and St. Paul after the order of a spiritual birth. . . . He, Christ, has continued the line of His apostles onwards through every age, and all troubles and perils of the world. Here then surely is somewhat of encouragement for us amid our loneliness and weakness. The presence of every Bishop suggests a long history of conflicts and trials, sufferings and victories, hopes and fears, through many centuries. His presence at this day is the fruit of them all. He is the living monument of those who are dead. He is the promise of a bold fight and a good confession and a cheerful martyrdom now, if needful, as was instanced in those of olden time. We see their figures on our walls, and their tombs are under our feet; and we trust, nay we are sure, that God will be to us in our day what He was to them.[19]

The theme of apostolic succession runs like a continuous thread through the early tracts. The arguments are presented with great confidence. It was felt that history clearly demonstrated apostolic succession to be a fact which scarcely could be questioned. And does not our own experience as well as the testimony of Scripture argue strongly for such a succession as the base of authority?

> Consider how *natural* is the doctrine of a Succession. When an individual comes to me, claiming to speak in the name of the Most High, it is natural to ask him for his authority. . . . In the case of the Catholic Church, the person referred to, *i.e.,* the Bishop, has received it from a predecessor, and he from another, and so on, till we arrive at the Apostles

themselves, and thence Our Lord and Saviour. . . . Lastly, the *argument from Scripture* is surely quite clear to those who honestly wish direction from *practice*. Christ promised He should be with His Apostles always, as ministers of His religion, even unto the end of the world. In one sense the Apostles were to be alive till He came again; but they all died at the natural time. Does it not follow that there are those now alive who represent them? Now, who were the most probable representatives of them in the generation next their death?[20]

Succession did not constitute the only argument for the authority of the Church. In the sermons and later writings, a wider and deeper base is found for the Church's claims in the *tradition* of the ancient and undivided Church, particularly the teachings of the Fathers. Of course, the appeal to the ancient traditions of the Fathers was not new with the Tractarians. Those traditions had long been appealed to by the old High Church party, and among Roman Catholics they were basic to Gallican apologists like Jacques Bénigne Bossuet (1627–1704). The most important statement of the Tractarian position, vis-à-vis Protestantism and Rome, is found in Newman's *Lectures on the Prophetical Office of the Church, Viewed Relatively to Romanism and Popular Protestantism,* published in 1837. Newman's thesis is that both the Protestant appeal to the "Bible alone" and the Roman claim to infallibility are historically untenable. Newman did not deny that the Bible, as the Articles state, contains all things necessary to salvation but, rather, that the individual unaided reason is able to interpret the Bible properly. Here, in striking resemblance to the Roman Catholic traditionists, he argued that private judgment concerning Scripture is no ground of authority; it is an invitation to chaos.

> The Bible is a small book; anyone may possess it; and everyone, unless he is very humble, will think he is able to understand it. And therefore, I say, controversy is *easier* among Protestants, because anyone can controvert; easier but not shorter; because though all sects agree together as to the *standard* of faith, viz. the Bible, yet no two agree as to the *interpreter* of the Bible, but each person makes himself the interpreter, so that what seemed at first sight a means of peace, turns out

to be a chief occasion or cause of discord. . . . Accordingly acute men among them see that the very elementary notion which they have adopted . . . is a self-destructive principle.[21]

The Tractarians rightly observed that the Scriptures were not originally written as systematic essays on doctrine but were received by Christian communities which had already appropriated the common, unwritten faith of the Church. Newman did not deny the Protestant principle of responsible, personal judgment concerning the teachings of Scripture. Rather, the deeper question was what are the means which are to direct our choice of interpretations. In addition to the internal means such as natural experience and reason, there are external means of equal place: "The existing Church, Tradition, Catholicity, Learning, Antiquity, and the National Faith." According to Newman, since Scripture was not written "to instruct in doctrine," but

> with intimations and implications of the faith, the qualifications for rightly apprehending it are so rare and high, that a prudent man, to say nothing of piety, will not risk his salvation on the chance of his having them; but will read it with the aid of those subsidiary guides which have ever been supplied as if to meet our need. I would not deny as an abstract proposition that a Christian may gain the whole truth from the Scriptures, but would maintain that the chances are very seriously against a given individual. I would not deny but rather maintain, that a religious, wise and intellectually gifted man will succeed; but who answers to this description but the collective Church? There, indeed, such qualifications might be supposed to exist; what is wanting in one member being supplied by another, and the contrary errors of individuals eliminated by their combination. The Catholic Church may truly be said almost infallibly to interpret Scripture.[22]

All the Tractarians taught that the ancient tradition was the indispensable guide to interpreting Scripture. The Church prepares the mind of the individual for the proper reading of the Bible. In fact, it is clearly demonstrable that before the canon of the New Testament was established, the unwritten tradition actually served as a test for the apostles' own writings. Tradition was, in the words of Keble, "divinely appointed in the Church as the touchstone of canonical Scripture itself." The Tractarians agreed with the Romanists that authority rested in Scripture *and* the ancient traditions of the Church. But how, after all, is such a general concept as ancient tradition to be understood? Newman sums up the Tractarian view in *The Prophetical Office* as follows:

> Let us understand what is meant by saying that antiquity is of authority in religious questions. Both Romanists and ourselves maintain as follows: That whatever doctrine the primitive ages unanimously attest, whether by consent of Fathers, or by Councils, or by the events of history, or by controversies, or in whatever way, whatever may fairly and reasonably be considered to be the universal belief of those ages is to be received as coming from the apostles. . . . The rule or canon which I have been explaining is best known as expressed in the words of Vincentius of Lérins in his celebrated treatise upon the tests of heresy and error; viz., that that is to be received as apostolic which has been taught "always, everywhere, and by all."* Catholicity, antiquity, and consent of the Fathers is the proper evidence of the fidelity or apostolicity of a professed tradition. Infant baptism, for instance, must have been appointed by the apostles or we should not find it received so early, so generally, with such a silence concerning its introduction. . . . The washing of feet enjoined in the thirteenth chapter of St. John is not a necessary rite or a sacrament because it has never been so observed—did Christ or his apostles intend otherwise, it would follow (which is surely impossible) that a new and erroneous view of our Lord's words arose even in the apostles' lifetime, and was from the first everywhere substituted for the true. . . . The sabbatical rest is changed from the Sabbath to the Lord's Day because it has never been otherwise since Christianity was a religion.[23]

The confidence with which the Tractarians asserted the canon of antiquity as the foundation of their doctrine of authority is somewhat astonishing to an age sensitive to the findings of modern historical-critical research. For the Tractarians there

*"quod semper, quod ubique, quod ab omnibus."

appears to be little problem concerning the purity or unity of the apostolic traditions. Part of their assurance was due to an inference drawn from a conviction agreed upon by all Christians alike—that is, that there was an original revelation which has not been superseded and which was given as *the* means of salvation. If one believes in such a supernatural gift of God, can one easily doubt the truth of a belief or practice that has been held by God's Church from the beginning, everywhere, and at all times? William Palmer reflects the characteristic fervor and assurance with which this argument was proposed:

> If any given doctrine was universally believed by those Christians who had been instructed by the apostles and the disciples of the apostles; if this doctrine was received by all succeeding generations as sacred and divine, and strictly conformable to those scriptures which were read and expounded in every church; this belief, one and uniform, received by all churches, delivered through the ages, triumphing over novel and contradictory doctrines which attempt to pollute it, guarded with jealous care . . . and after a lapse of eighteen hundred years believed in firmly by the overwhelming mass of Christians among all nations as when it was first promulgated; *such a doctrine must be a truth of revelation. It rests on evidence not inferior to that which attests the truth of Christianity. Is it possible that the infinite majority of Christians in all ages can have mistaken or adulterated their own religion? . . . If so, then they may have been equally deceived as to the authenticity of Scripture, as to the truth of the mission of our Saviour; and the whole fabric of revelation totters to its base. Hence I maintain that Christians cannot possibly admit that any doctrine established by universal tradition can be otherwise than DIVINELY, INFALLIBLY, TRUE.*[24] (Italics added.)

The Tractarians were certain that the unwritten, authoritative tradition of the apostolic Church could be established as *historical fact* with the same kind of tools of research that one would apply to any historical question. If the testimony of the Fathers, the Councils, and the ancient customs are rejected as uncertain, then *eo ipso* all human testimony is uncertain, and there can be no facts of history. But, they believed, there is no good reason for such radical skepticism. The authentic documents give us clear evidence of the primitive tradition, and it is here that the Tractarians built their case against Rome. The question was naturally raised as to how in fact the Anglican doctrine of authority differed from that of Rome. Did they not both appeal to the ancient tradition as the true interpreter of Scripture and guide in faith and practice? Yes, but in the Roman system there is another canon which supersedes even that of Vincent of Lérins, namely:

> They profess to appeal to primitive Christianity; we honestly take their ground, as holding it ourselves; but when the controversy grows animated, and descends into details, they suddenly leave it and desire to finish the dispute on some other field. . . . In truth there is a tenet in their theology which assumes quite a new position in relation to the rest, when we pass from the abstract and quiescent theory to the practical workings of the system. The infallibility of the existing Church is then found to be its first principle. . . . Whatever principles they profess in theory . . . yet when they come to particulars, when they have to prove this or that article of their creed, they supersede the appeal to Scripture and antiquity by the pretence of the infallibility of the Church, thus solving the whole question by a summary and final interpretation both of antiquity and of Scripture.[25]

Newman points out that the Vincentian canon, to which the Roman theologians frequently appealed, is altogether silent on the subject of the Church's infallibility, let alone the Pope's supreme authority. He challenges the Romanists to prove their doctrines apostolic. Newman asserts that they are not continuous with antiquity but "innovations," human traditions. For the Tractarians the departures of the post-Tridentine Roman Catholic Church brought it far from the pure stream of antiquity, the Church of England alone having preserved the true, apostolic marks of the undivided Church. Today when one reads the Tractarians on the authority of the Church, one senses a naive smugness reflecting an extraordinarily insular view of the history of the Church. This is especially pronounced in Isaac Williams's "The Church in England," though the poem is not atypical of Tractarian apologetic.

> When the infatuate Council named of Trent
> Clogg'd up the Catholic course of the true
>   Faith,
> Troubling the stream of pure antiquity,
> And the wide channel in its bosom took
> Crude novelties, scarce known as that of old;
> Then many a schism overleaped the banks,
> Genevese, Lutheran, Scotch diversities.
> Our Church, though straiten'd sore 'tween
>   craggy walls,
> Kept her true course, unchanging and the
>   same,
> Known by that ancient clearness, pure and
>   free,
> With which she sprung from neath the Throne
>   of God.[26]

The Tractarian doctrine of authority was founded on an appeal to history. Yet, except for Newman, its view of the historical was primitivist and static, just at the time when Europe was beginning to think of history in organic and evolutionary categories. It was the period of Hegelian ascendancy on the Continent, but the Oxford leaders did not read the Hegelian theologians, not even the Catholic Johann Adam Möhler. Brilioth has rightly concluded that the Tractarian appeal to antiquity "was no result of a learned inquiry" but "a bold postulate," "profoundly unhistorical and doomed to failure." The reason was that the Oxford school never clearly defined what it meant by Christian antiquity, when it ended, or how the diverse developments of Christian experience in the early centuries represented a discernible unity of faith and practice. The Vincentian canon appealed to a standard that was, if not unreal, at least historically elusive. The strength of the Tractarian conception of the Church was in its appeal to apostolicity. Yet it was an appeal made with zeal and deep feeling but fraught with difficulties. More significantly, it was an appeal made at the expense of Catholicity and Unity. Newman came to realize this in the summer of 1839 while working on the history of the Monophysite controversy. It forced him to rethink not only his concept of the Church but also his view of history. As we will see, the result was his essay on *The Development of Christian Doctrine*, the rejection of the static, Tractarian concept of history, and a bold new apologetic for an organic, evolutionary theory of doctrinal development. It also paved the way for his entrance into the Roman Catholic Church.

The Doctrine of Faith

Faith and Reason. As one would expect, there is a close relationship between the Tractarian doctrine of authority and its view of faith and reason. Behind both is the deep sense of the mystery of divine revelation, that this truth is a gift of grace and requires moral submission. In the Tractarian writings on faith, there is a clear distrust of the traditional "evidences" of Christianity. Most of the Tractarians had a strong element of metaphysical skepticism in them. This was due in part to their own piety, which found the rational demonstrations of Paley arid and cold, and to the influence of Bishop Butler and Coleridge.* Newman in particular has been called a philosophical skeptic, who, surrendering to the authority of the Church, was able to revel in the irrational and credulous. T. H. Huxley declared that if he were writing a primer of infidelity, he would draw generously from the writings of Newman! The skeptical element is there, but to refer to the Tractarians as such is inexcusably misleading. The Tractarian view of faith and reason, with Newman's doctrine representing its most subtle expression, was profound and influential.

It is important to appreciate what the Tractarians meant by reason and its role in human life. By reason they meant "mere" reason, demonstration, or proof—what Coleridge called the Understanding or "the mind of the flesh." Such reason has its vital role in human life, but it is not the sole guide or rule; especially it is not the root or final warrant of faith, as maintained by the rationalists. But such it had become; reason, since the seventeenth century, had been increasingly ascendant, encroaching on and judging all other provinces of life. In the eyes of the Tractarians, it had become the sole arbiter of truth.

Newman addressed himself to this situation in an early sermon of 1831, "The Usurpations of Reason."

*Butler's influence on the Tractarians, especially on Newman, is pronounced. Coleridge influenced many of the Oxford people, although Newman did not read him until 1835. Nevertheless, Newman acknowledged that he found Coleridge's views congenial.

Newman's theme is that while reason is but one faculty of human life—moral sense, feeling, and imagination being others—it has been made unduly "judge of those truths which are subjected to another part of our nature." The fact of the case is that reason alone is peculiarly unsuited to make such judgments in morality and religion, for example. It is clearly taught throughout Scripture "that there is no necessary connexion between the intellectual and moral principles of our nature; that on religious subjects we may prove anything or overthrow anything, and can arrive at truth but accidentally, if we merely investigate what is commonly called reason."[27] On this matter Scripture is supported by common experience. Why should Christians be desirous of disguising the fact that many persons of intellectual brilliance are indifferent to revealed religion, unless Christians have been falsely led to believe that there is a necessary connection between reason and one's religious sense?

> Yet is it not a fact . . . when the humblest village may show us that those persons who turn out badly—are commonly the very men who have received more than the ordinary share of intellectual gifts? . . . Thus much it seems to show us, that the powers of the intellect . . . do not necessarily lead us in the direction of our moral instincts, or confirm them; but if the agreement between the two be but a matter of accident, what testimony do we gain from the mere reason to the truths of religion?[28]

What Newman found repellent in theological rationalists like Paley was the attempt to prove Christianity independently of the grace of faith. Rationalistic apologetic is wrong because it

> draws men away from the true view of Christianity and leads them to think that Faith is mainly the result of arguments, that religious Truth is a legitimate matter of disputation. . . . For is not this error, the common and fatal error, of the world, to think itself a Judge of Religious Truth without preparation of heart?[29]

What disturbed Newman was the rationalist assumption that any persons, mentally endowed, could rightfully discuss religion and enter into disputes about the most sacred mysteries "in a careless frame of mind, in their hours of recreation, over the wine cup." "Is it wonderful," Newman asks, "that they so frequently end in becoming Indifferentists?"[30]

Not only do the rationalists fail to take account of faith as the necessary foundation of religious knowledge; they overlook the fact that the so-called natural "evidences" are compelling only to those who already believe—but "when men have not already recognized God's voice within them, ineffective." Indeed, says Newman, "It is a great question whether Atheism is not as philosophically consistent with the phenomena of the physical world, taken by themselves, as the doctrine of a creative and governing Power."[31]

According to Newman, religious faith and truth may on occasion be justified by reason, but reason never can *produce* faith. Religious knowledge arises from *moral obedience,* out of the hunger and thirst after righteousness. Faith is essentially a moral principle. Pusey states the Tractarian view as follows:

> Scripture gives us but one rule, one test, one way of attaining the truth, *i.e.,* whether we are keeping God's commandments or not, whether we are conformed to this world, or whether we are, by the renewing of our minds, being transformed into His image. . . . The knowledge is not in our own power to attain. It is the gift of God, vouchsafed or withheld by Him, and each more or less according as man becomes conformed to the world and things earthly or to God and things divine. . . . It is in vain that people will even strive to retain a belief in high and holy things, while their life is wrong. They will strive to convince themselves, but it is in vain; they study but it is of no use. . . . As their thoughts are more and more occupied with the world, holy truth becomes fainter and fainter. . . .[32]

What distinguishes the evidences of reason from the assurances of faith is what today we would call the existential factor—what the Tractarians called the moral sense. The proofs of reason are impersonal. An individual does not make the proofs; they exist independently of him or her and require but a hearing to elicit acceptance. There is no room for choice. But a person is responsible for his or her faith, because, as Newman asserts, "he is responsible for his likings and dislikings, his hopes and his opinions, on all of which his faith depends." In other words, faith has to do with those things which cannot be measured, demonstrated, proved but which require an act of moral judgment.

> Faith is created in the mind, not so much by facts, as by probabilities; and since probabilities have no definite ascertained value, and are reducible to no scientific standard, what are such to each individual, depends on his moral temperament. A good man and a bad man will think very different things probable. In the judgement of a rightly disposed mind, objects are desirable and obtainable, which irreligious men will consider to be fancies.[33]

Newman acknowledges that faith does not require evidence as strong as is demanded by reason. Why?

> For this reason, because it is swayed by antecedent considerations. . . . Faith is influenced by previous notices, prepossessions, and (in the good sense of the word) prejudices; but Reason, by direct and definite proof. The mind that believes is acted upon by its own hopes, fears and existing opinions. . . . Faith is a principle of action, and action does not allow time for minute and finished investigations.[34]

The disparity between assent of faith and that of reason may not actually be as great as some might think. Newman had read Hume, and did Hume not convince us that even our most assured empirical knowledge is grounded in habit and at best probable?

> However full and however precise our producible grounds may be, however systematic our method, however clear and tangible our evidence, yet when our argument is traced down to its simple elements, there must be something assumed ultimately which is incapable of proof. . . . For instance, we trust our senses, and that in spite of their often deceiving us. They even contradict each other at times, yet we trust them. But even were they ever consistent, never unfaithful, yet their fidelity would not thereby be proved. We consider that there is so strong an antecedent probability that they are faithful, that we dispense with proof. We take the point for granted; or if we have grounds for it,

these lie in our secret belief in the stability of nature, or in the preserving presence and uniformity of Divine Providence—which, again, are points assumed . . . so it need not be weakness or rashness, if upon a certain presentiment of mind we trust to the fidelity of testimony offered for a revelation. . . . Nothing, then, which Scripture says about Faith, however startling it may be at first sight, is inconsistent with the state in which we find ourselves by nature with reference to the acquisition of knowledge generally—a state in which we must assume something to prove anything, and can gain nothing without a venture.[35]

If the assent of reason is not free of assumptions, its probabilities are, nevertheless, based on a stricter and more exacting evidence than the rather vague and slender evidence of faith. Newman acknowledged this. What, then, is to safeguard faith from all manner of prejudice, bigotry, credulity, and superstition? "Antecedent probabilities may be equally available for what is true, and what pretends to be true, for a revelation and its counterfeit, for Paganism, or Mohametanism, or Christianity." Newman felt the difficulty, but he rejected the rationalists' ready answer, "Cultivate the reason." Reason alone is no safeguard of true faith; the true safeguard is love.

> The safeguard of Faith is a right state of heart. This it is that gives it birth; it also disciplines it. This is what protects it from bigotry, credulity and fanaticism. It is holiness or dutifulness, or the new creation, or the spiritual mind, however we word it, which is the quickening and illuminating principle of true Faith. . . . It is Love which forms it out of the rude chaos into an image of Christ; or in scholastic language, justifying Faith, whether in Pagan, Jew or Christian, is *fides formata charitate*.[36]

For the Tractarians a faith which is safeguarded by a holy and obedient life is an intellectual act, a form of knowledge, justified as reasonable and open to the scrutiny of reason, though not solely dependent on reason. Newman summarized the Tractarian view as follows:

> Such, then, under all circumstances is real Faith; a presumption, yet not a mere chance conjecture—a reaching forward, yet not of excitement or of passion

—a moving forward in the twilight, yet not without clue or direction; a movement from something known to something unknown, kept in the narrow path of truth by the Law of dutifulness which inhabits it, the Light of heaven which animates and guides it. . . . It is itself an intellectual act, and takes its character from the moral state of the agent. It is perfected not by mental cultivation but by obedience. It does not change its nature or its function, when thus perfected. It remains what it is in itself, an initial principle of action; but it becomes changed in its quality, as being made spiritual. It is, as before, a presumption, but the presumption of a serious, sober, thoughtful, pure, affectionate and devout mind. It acts because it is Faith; but the direction, consistency, and precision of its acts, it gains from Love.[37]

Faith and Sanctification. The important place that the Tractarians gave to moral obedience as the ground of true faith made them extremely suspicious of the Protestant doctrine of "justification by faith *alone*." The Tractarians interpreted Luther as teaching that justification was simply a "declaring" righteous, a gift of grace which was to be understood as distinct from a holy or sanctified life itself. They believed such a doctrine contributed to an antinomian disregard of good works and was therefore a dangerous threat to the religious life. For the Tractarians, Justification and Sanctification are one, inseparable gift.

The Tractarian doctrine finds its definitive statement in Newman's *Lectures on Justification* of 1838. The lectures represent the best theological work of the movement and are a classic example of the Anglican *Via Media*. Newman attempts to show that the Protestant emphasis on justification by faith alone and the Roman emphasis on justification by obedience are both defective. The issue had been put as follows:

> One side says that the righteousness in which God accepts us is *inherent,* wrought in us by the grace flowing from Christ's Atonement; the other says that it is *external,* reputed, nominal, being Christ's own sacred and most perfect obedience on earth, viewed by a merciful God *as if* it were ours. And issue is joined on the following question, whether justification means in Scripture *counting* us righteous, or *making* us righteous.[38] (Italics added.)

For Newman this way of putting the issue is mistaken. No one, he asserts, denies that justification is a free act of divine mercy, but neither is it possible to believe that God's grace leaves the soul in the unregenerate state in which it was found. It stands to reason that a soul that is justified is not in the same state as if it had not been justified. "Surely it is a strange paradox to say that . . . the glory of His pronouncing us righteous lies in His leaving us unrighteous." What, then, is the state of the justified person? It is not enough, Newman contends, to assert with Luther that "a state of justification consists in the foregiveness of sins, or in acceptance, or in adoption," for all these things are God's acts.

> When faith is said to be the inward principle of acceptance, the question rises, what gives to faith its acceptableness? Why is faith more acceptable than unbelief? Cannot we give any reason at all for it, or can we conceive unbelief being appointed the instrument of justification? Surely not; faith is acceptable as having something in it which unbelief has not; that something, what is it? It must be God's grace if God's grace acts *in* the soul and not merely externally. . . . If it acts in us . . . then the having that grace or that presence, and faith, which is its result, must be the real token, the real state of a justified man.[39]

In Newman's opinion Justification is not only "counting" righteous but the actual "making" righteous, the imparting to the soul of a supernatural quality of grace. It is the actual indwelling of the divine: "I mean the *habitation* in us of God the Father and the Word Incarnate through the Holy Ghost. . . . *This* is to be justified, to receive the divine presence within us and be made a temple of the Holy Ghost."[40] Salvation, therefore, does not consist only of being forgiven our sins but in a life of *holiness*. Newman can even say that if a person "is justified and accepted, *he has ceased to be a sinner. The Gospel only knows of justified saints; if a saint sins, he ceases to be justified and becomes a con-demned* sinner."[41] Here we see that strain of moralism that many commentators have found at the very heart of Tractarian piety. A person cannot tell that he or she has faith by feeling himself or herself a sinner, or by consciousness of dependence on God, or even

by praising God and resolving to live according to His will. Why?

> Because there is an immeasurable distance between feeling right and doing right. A man may have all these good thoughts and emotions, yet (if he has not yet hazarded them to the experiment of practice), he cannot promise himself that he has any sound and permanent principle at all. Though a man spoke like an angel, I would not believe him on the mere ground of his speaking. . . . Do fervent thoughts make faith *living?* St. James tells us otherwise. He tells us *works,* deeds of obedience, are the life of faith.[42]

The Tractarians believed that righteousness, being maintained and enlarged by the faithful use of God's grace in works of obedience, admits of more and less.

> When we compare the various orders of just and acceptable beings with one another, we see that though they all are in God's favour, some may be more "pleasant," "acceptable," "righteous," than others, that is, may have more of the light of God's countenance shed on them; as a glorious saint is more acceptable than one still in the flesh. In this sense, then, *justification does admit of increase and of degree; and whether we say justification depends on faith or on obedience, in the same degree that faith or obedience grows so does justification.* And again, if justification is conveyed peculiarly through the sacraments . . . so must [they] be the instrument of a higher justification. On the other hand, those who are declining in their obedience, as they are quenching the light within them, so are they diminishing their justification.[43] (Italics added.)

Here we are at the center of the Tractarian doctrine. Justification/Sanctification is an intrinsic quality or substance of the soul whose presence is witnessed by a holy and obedient life—the sacraments being the special means of imparting this very presence of Christ in the soul. True faith, then, is the actual indwelling of divine grace, confirmed in a life of good works, especially through sacramental obedience. What distinguishes the Tractarian doctrine of faith is its stress on the objectivity of sanctifying grace transmitted through the outward and visible sacraments and ordinances of the Church. These sacramental means are efficacious in their operation independent of subjective feeling or moods. The Church is not a voluntary fellowship of like-minded believers; it is *the* divinely appointed means of grace.

The Sacramental Principle

The Tractarians were not exceptional in looking to the Incarnation as the mysterious foundation of redemption. They did, however, give special attention to one aspect of the doctrine. As the Incarnation is the perfect indwelling of the divine in the human, it is the precondition of the divine nature being imparted to our human nature. Christ, therefore, is the firstborn of a new human creation: deified humanity. Following St. Athanasius's words, "He became man that we might be made divine." Pusey writes, "He came to Deify our nature by His own indwelling in us."

For the Tractarians this sanctifying or deifying of our fallen human nature is most often spoken of in relation to the ministration of the Sacraments. And they are not averse to referring to the sacramental elements as "the Food of Immortality," since grace is conceived as the infusion of an objective reality in the most substantial sense. This high, mystical doctrine of the sacramental imputation and indwelling of the divine is especially prominent in Pusey's sermons. Since holiness is the actual presence of Christ's virtues in the soul, Pusey can speak of the Sacraments as "the channels whereby . . . He conveys these Exceeding Gifts to us. . . All of which we have, we have in Him, by being made members of Him. And members of Him we are made and preserved through His Sacraments."[44]

The essentiality and objectivity of the Sacraments is exemplified in the Tractarian writings on baptismal regeneration, especially in Pusey's Tract 67, "Scriptural Views of Holy Baptism." Throughout the tract Pusey stresses the theme that infant baptism is a pledge that God's forgiveness and regeneration do not depend on the faith of the recipient, since the infant is unable to respond in faith. The child receives God's grace by virtue of the Church's faith. And in no way other than baptism can there be a complete washing away of sin.

We are not said, namely, to be born again *of* faith, or love, or prayer, or any grace which God worketh in us, but to be "born *of* water and the Spirit (Jn. 3:5). . . . Our life in Christ is, throughout, represented as commencing when we are by baptism made members of Christ and Children of God. That life may through our negligence afterwards decay, or be choked, or smothered, or well-nigh extinguished . . . but a *commencement* of life in Christ *after* baptism, a death unto sin and a new birth unto righteousness at any other period than at that one first introduction into God's covenant, is as little consonant with the general representations of Holy Scripture as a commencement of physical life long after our natural birth is with the order of his providence.[45]

Because the Tractarians held such a high conception of baptism, it being the only means of losing the blight of original sin, they also took a very serious view of post-baptismal sin. The reason was that receiving the gift of baptismal grace in no way in itself ensured the recipient against losing it. As Robert Wilberforce was to comment, "it is sometimes forgotten that baptism does not determine what *shall be* men's future state, but what *is* their present position."[46] Every sin committed after baptism, the Tractarians believed, weakens the effect of baptismal grace. This explains in part the Tractarian introspection and scrupulous concern for daily devotions, penitence, and good works—all of which were integral to its piety. It also partially explains the central place of the Sacrament of the Eucharist, for if baptism gives the soul its spiritual birth, the Eucharist is the spiritual food which sustains the soul during its earthly pilgrimage, keeping it unstained from the world. It is *the* Sacrament through which the soul is continually renewed and maintained. The sacramental principle made it quite natural for the Tractarians to speak of the elements of the Eucharist as a "heavenly feast," a "spiritual food" and to equate failure in receiving the Sacrament with "the starvation and death of the soul." John Keble describes the receiving of Christ in the Sacrament by just such an image.

Now the gift of the Holy Eucharist is Christ himself. . . . And how can we conceive even Power Almighty to bring it more closely and more directly home to each one of us, than when his Word commands and his Spirit enables us to receive him as it were spiritual meat and drink? entering into and penetrating thoroughly the whole being of the renewed man, somewhat in the same way as the virtue of wholesome meat and drink diffuses itself through a healthful body. . . .[47]

This indwelling of Christ in which He becomes "one with us, and we with Him," is the literal infusion and presence of God's grace and power in the soul, the closest possible union of God and the individual. The Tractarians were one in affirming the *real presence* of Christ in the Eucharist—that we receive, really and spiritually, the flesh and blood of the Incarnate Son which are present beneath the natural elements of bread and wine. Yet their writings lack any precise definition as to what they meant by Christ's real presence. They clearly denied the Roman doctrine of transubstantiation and the Zwinglian conception of the elements as symbolic "memorials"— but they resisted any attempt to give a dogmatic or metaphysical explanation of what they felt was a most holy and supernatural mystery. Pusey's most explicit statement is typical in its vagueness.

> The presence of which our Lord speaks has been termed sacramental, supernatural, mystical, ineffable, as opposed *not* to what is real, but to what is natural. The word has been chosen to express, not our knowledge, but our ignorance. . . . We know not the manner of his presence, save that it is not according to the natural presence of our Lord's human flesh. But it is a presence without us, not only within us. . . . It is not a presence simply in the soul of the receiver. . . . But while the consecrated elements remain in their natural substances, still, since the Lord says, "This is my body," "This is my blood," the Church of England believes that "under the form of bread and wine," so consecrated, we "receive the body and blood of our Saviour Christ."[48]

What was important to the Tractarians was not the mode of the real presence but its *reality.* And because the Sacrament was conceived as the spiritual food, indispensable to the health of the soul, Tractarian sacramental piety was marked by frequent Communion. Since the Eucharist has as its end the infusion of divine grace, "the cleansing of our sins, the refining of our corruptions, the repairing of our decays," is it any wonder, Pusey asks, that where the Eucharist is forgotten, "love should have waxed cold and corruptions abound?" Is it strange that "the Divine life becomes so rare, all higher instances of it so few and faint when 'the stay and staff,' the strength of that life is willingly forfeited? How should there be the fulness of the Divine life, amid all but a month-long fast from our 'daily Bread'?"[49]

According to the sacramental principle, the sacraments and ordinances of the Church are the divinely appointed means of growth in devotion and holiness. Frequent Communion not only sustains us but teaches us a deeper discipline and a reverence for the outward and visible signs through which the spiritual grace is made known. While the Tractarians were generally conservative as regards ritual and ceremonial, their high doctrine of the Sacraments led naturally to a greater appreciation of the forms of worship and their role in inciting a greater spirituality. According to the sacramental principle, the whole of nature shows forth symbolically the glory of God. The things of sense—water, bread, color, movement—are to be used to make known and bear witness to the great acts of God's providence and mercy. Ritual, ceremonial, the adornment of churches, spiritual disciplines, the so-called forms of religion are not to be scorned; they serve as the natural vehicles "to make the beauty of holiness visible," thereby encouraging a more reverent worship and tutoring us in a deeper spirituality. The Tractarians realized that these symbols and forms could teach religious truths and mold Christian character unconsciously, as it were, where more prosaic, didactic methods fail. Faith must receive the assent of the whole person, not only the intellect.

> These symbols have I gazed on long and oft,
> Threading their morals and their mysteries,
> And thence beguiled to deeper, holier,
>   thoughts.
> And surely heart-expanding Charity,
> If ought she finds that ministers to good,
> To others would like instruments supply.
> For objects pleading through the usual sense

Are stronger than discourses to the ear
More powerfully they reach and move the soul.

The Church 'tis thought, is wakening through
   the land
And seeking vent for the o'erloaded hearts
Which she has kindled—pours her forth
   anew—
Breathes life in ancient worship—from their
   graves
Summons the slumbering Arts to wait on her,
Music, and Architecture, varied forms
Of Painting, Sculpture, and of Poetry;
These are allied to sense, but soul and sense
Must both alike find wing and rise to Heaven;
Both soul and body took the Son of man,
Both soul and body must in Him serve God.[50]

The sacramental principle not only encouraged the use of sacramental forms, thereby inculcating a profound devotion and a greater reverence for the Church, but required a view of the Church as itself the visible, divinely appointed channel of God's grace. It conceived of the Church as God's own earthly Tabernacle, the very Body of Christ. For does the Incarnation not teach that the Word became flesh? It therefore follows that "where His Flesh is, there He is, and we receiving It receive Him, and receiving Him, are joined on to Him through His Flesh to the Father, and He dwelling in us, dwell in Him, and with Him in God."[51]

Such a sacramental view of the Church as Christ's mystical Body prepared the way for a conception of the Church as *the extension of the Incarnation.** One discovers at the heart of Tractarian faith an incarnational theology which joins inseparably the Incarnation, the Sacraments, the Church, and the holy life. As E. R. Fairweather has remarked:

> To their minds it was no less clearly a part of the Christian message that the saving person and work of the Mediator were effectually "re-presented" in the Church by means of certain sacramental "extensions of the Incarnation." It was, they insisted, supremely fit-

*For an early development in this direction, see, for example, Robert Wilberforce's important *The Doctrine of the Incarnation* (1848).

ting that the life-giving flesh and blood of God's Eternal Son who was made man should be communicated through fleshly signs wrought by human hands. Indeed, they were prepared to argue that the failure to recognize the "extensions of the Incarnation" stemmed from a feeble apprehension of the two-fold truth of the Incarnation itself—on the one hand, that man's salvation comes from God alone; on the other, that God's saving action really penetrates and transforms man's world and man's life.[52]

When viewed in its fullness and richness, the thought of the Oxford Movement is in essentials remarkably uniform and consistent. Their conception of the Christian life, their view of the sacraments, their concern for the integrity of the Church and its ministry, and their doctrine of authority are all strikingly interdependent—this despite the fact that the Tractarians were not systematic theologians.

The movement which had its beginnings in Oxford in the 1830s came to an end by 1845, but by that time its influence was already felt throughout the English Church and beyond. The ideals and principles of the early Tractarians were carried on by Keble and Pusey and taken up by younger men, such as Church and Lidden. Anglo-Catholicism did not remain static but grew and changed. Yet these later developments cannot be understood without Keble, Newman, and Pusey. The long-term theological influence of the Oxford Movement is difficult to trace because many of its results are indirect and have been unconsciously appropriated in later years by very different traditions. It is true that a good many of the Tractarian doctrines and interpretations were repudiated or proven historically indefensible within a generation of their publication. Yet many influences are felt even today. The Tractarian view of faith as having its ground in moral judgment is perhaps the most significant contribution of the movement to modern philosophy of religion. In the realm of biblical studies, no modern theologian can now overlook the role of tradition in the development of a hermeneutical theory or in considering the question of biblical authority. The Tractarians thus contributed in no small way to the rejection of a naive doctrine of *sola Scriptura*. The Tractarian concern for apostolicity, catholicity, and unity compelled them to take with utmost seriousness the question of the One, Undivided Church. This concern contributed to the beginnings of the modern ecumenical discussion and the search for reunion not only with Rome but with all Christians in one visible Church. All of these results are there but are difficult to trace out concretely.

The Tractarian influence on worship and religious discipline is much easier to document. The role of the Oxford revival in the introduction into services, not only Anglican but Reformed and Free Church as well, of such practices as regular Communion, liturgical music, and increased ceremonial is well attested. The movement also had a lasting influence upon the devotional life of the Church, as reflected in the increase in daily services, Lenten observance, private confession, and in the opening of many communities for the "religious" in the English Church in the last half of the nineteenth century. In all this, the movement contributed to a renewed and deepened awareness of the holy; to a vivid sense of the awesome mystery of the divine; and the peace and joy that comes from obedient service.

If the more strictly theological doctrines of the Tractarians failed to have a wide or lasting influence, it was largely due to the fact that the Oxford leaders had insulated themselves from the new movements in science and history that were just appearing and would not be put down. The Tractarians and some of their followers of the next generation were not prepared to tackle the enormous questions that the new theories of Darwin and the German biblical critics were beginning to pose. As a result, many of their doctrines were merely anachronistic by 1860.

Frederick Denison Maurice, a contemporary of the movement, who was at first attracted and then repelled by its doctrine, aptly remarked that the tragic weakness of the Tractarians consisted "in opposing to the spirit of the present age the spirit of a former age, instead of the ever-living and active Spirit of God." It was not until the last years of the century that a group of Anglican theologians of Catholic mind were able to reconcile their Catholicism, with the new science and the new criticism. Out of this convergence of tradition and criticism emerged the movement known as *Liberal Catholicism.* Only then was Tractarian theology again tenable, but only because it was developed and clothed in quite new modes of thought. Anglo-Catholicism at the turn of the century had, in the words of Owen Chadwick.,

> abandoned most of the positions characteristic of Dr. Pusey upon the authority of the Church. They had accepted a far looser idea of Biblical inspiration. They had rejected the belief that the ancient and undivided Church was inerrant. But in their sweeping revolution they sought to preserve what they believed to be of essential value in the position which Newman, Keble, and Pusey had taken up.... They [the Tractarians] provided for the liberal movement in England a ballast which helped it not to be swept along by the excesses of evolutionary theology and philosophy.[53]

Before examining later developments, we must first turn to a movement in Roman Catholicism that also reflects the ethos of Romanticism.

NOTES

1. J. A. Froude, *Short Studies on Great Subjects* (1886), IV, 239.
2. J. H. Nichols, *Romanticism in American Theology* (Chicago, 1961), p. 78.
3. *The Oxford Movement,* ed. Eugene R. Fairweather, Library of Protestant Thought (New York, 1964), p. 5.
4. Ibid., p. 48.
5. Ibid., pp. 41–42.
6. Ibid., pp. 55–56.
7. Ibid., p. 59.
8. John Henry Newman, *Apologia pro Vita Sua* (London, 1965), pp. 142–143.
9. R. W. Church, *The Oxford Movement 1833–1845* (London, 1892), pp. 264–265.
10. Newman, op. cit., pp. 184–185.
11. Ibid., p. 197.
12. *Oxford Movement,* p. 153.
13. *Parochial Sermons* (London, 1839), Vol. IV, 239.
14. Ibid., Vol. I, 233f.

15. Ibid., Vol. VI, 80–81.
16. Isaac Williams, *The Cathedral* (1838), pp. 210–211.
17. *Oxford Movement*, pp. 263–266.
18. *Parochial Sermons,* Vol. I, 176f.
19. Ibid., Vol. III, 272f.
20. *Tracts for the Times* (London, 1834), Vol. I, Tract Seven, "The Episcopal Church Apostolical," p. 3.
21. *Oxford Movement*, pp. 114–115.
22. *The Prophetical Office* (1838), p. 193.
23. Ibid., pp. 62–65. Cf. Keble in the sermon on "Primitive Tradition": "The paramount authority of the successors of the apostles in Church government; the three-fold order established from the beginning; the virtue of the blessed Eucharist as a commemorative sacrifice; infant baptism; and above all, the Catholic doctrine of the most Holy Trinity, as contained in the Nicene Creed. All these, however surely confirmed from Scripture, are yet ascertainable parts of the primitive, unwritten system, of which we yet enjoy the benefit. If anyone asks how we ascertain them, we answer, by application of the well-known rule, *Quod semper, quod ubique, quod ab omnibus*— Antiquity, Universality, Catholicity. . . ."
24. W. Palmer, *A Treatise on the Church of Christ,* 3d ed.(1842), II, 35–36.
25. *Prophetical Office.*
26. I. Williams, *Thoughts in Past Years* (Oxford, 1838), p. 263.
27. *Oxford Movement*, p. 22.
28. Ibid., p. 25.
29. J. .H. Newman, *Sermons, Chiefly on the Theory of Religious Belief* (London, 1843), pp. 189–190.
30. Ibid., pp. 190–191.
31. J. H. Newman, *Fifteen Sermons Preached before the University of Oxford* (London, 1872), p. 194.

32. E. B. Pusey, *Parochial Sermons* (1878), III, 202–203.
33. *Sermons, on the Theory of Religious Belief,* pp. 182–183.
34. Ibid., p. 179.
35. Ibid., pp. 205–207.
36. Ibid., pp. 227–228. Many of Newman's contemporaries found this aspect of his argument as unconvincing as we do today.
37. Ibid., pp. 243–244.
38. *Oxford Movement*, p. 218.
39. Ibid., p. 222.
40. Ibid., p. 227.
41. *Parochial Sermons,* Vol. V, 217.
42. Ibid., I, 197. Orthodox Lutherans would have found subjective feeling as the ground of justification as repellent as Newman found it.
43. *Oxford Movement*, p. 232.
44. E. B. Pusey, *Sermons during the Season from Advent to Whitsuntide* (Oxford, 1848), p. 220.
45. *Oxford Movement*, pp. 209–211.
46. Ibid., pp. 353–354.
47. Ibid., pp. 381–382.
48. Ibid., p. 374.
49. E. B. Pusey, *Sermons Preached before the University of Oxford* (1879), pp. 28–29.
50. Isaac Williams, *The Baptistry* (1842–1844), pp. IX–X.
51. E. B. Pusey, *A Sermon Preached before the University in the Cathedral Church of Christ* (Oxford, 1841), p. 14. This was the sermon that brought about Pusey's condemnation in Oxford.
52. *Oxford Movement*, p. 11.
53. O. Chadwick, *The Mind of the Oxford Movement* (Stanford, 1967), p. 60.

SUGGESTIONS FOR FURTHER READING

There are two excellent books of selections from the writings of the Tractarians:

Chadwick, Owen, ed. *The Mind of the Oxford Movement* (Stanford: Stanford University Press, 1967). A broad, judicious selection of short passages, with a masterful introductory essay on the Oxford Movement. The essay is included in Chadwick's *The Spirit of the Oxford Movement* (Cambridge: Cambridge University Press, 1990).

Fairweather, Eugene R., ed. *The Oxford Movement,* Library of Protestant Thought (New York: Oxford University Press, 1964). An excellent selection of materials from most of the important Tractarian writings, with helpful introductions.

Among the numerous studies of the Oxford Movement, the following are especially recommended:

Brilioth, Yngve. *The Anglican Revival: Studies in the Oxford Movement* (London: Longmans, Green, 1925). Still among the best studies of Tractarian piety and thought.

Cameron, J. M. "John Henry Newman and the Tractarian Movement," in N. Smart, et al., *Nineteenth Century Religious Thought in the West,* II (Cambridge: Cambridge University Press, 1985).

Chadwick, Owen. *Newman* (Oxford: Oxford University Press, 1983). A contribution to the excellent Past Masters series, this is a pithy, highly readable account of Newman the spiritual man and thinker.

Church, R. W. *The Oxford Movement: Twelve Years, 1833–1845* (Hamden, Conn.: Archon Books, 1966). A new edition (1980) edited by G. F. A. Best. A beautifully written, sympathetic, firsthand story of the movement, still highly praised for its historical balance.

Faber, Geoffrey. *Oxford Apostles: A Character Study of the Oxford Movement* (Baltimore: Penguin Books, 1954). A lively, absorbing, heavily psychological account of the movement and the personalities connected with it. Especially interesting on Newman.

O'Connell, Marvin R. *The Oxford Conspirators: A History of the Oxford Movement* (New York: Macmillan Co., 1969). A good account of the movement by a Roman Catholic historian.

Rowell, Geoffrey. *The Vision Glorious: Themes and Personalities of the Catholic Revival in Anglicanism* (Oxford: Oxford University Press, 1983). An account of the major figures with emphasis on their spiritual ideas.

Newman

The number of studies of J. H. Newman is staggering. The following are among the best:

Dessain, C. S. *John Henry Newman,* 3d ed. (Oxford: Oxford University Press, 1980). A fine, brief biography by the editor of Newman's letters and diaries.

Gilley, Sheridan. *Newman and His Age* (London: Darton, Longman and Todd, 1990). Excellent full-scale biography, with attention to the historical and intellectual contexts within which Newman moved.

Ker, Ian. *John Henry Newman: A Biography* (Oxford: Clarendon Press, 1988). The fullest, most up-to-date chronicle of Newman's life and writings, making extensive use of the correspondence. An invaluable study of man and thinker, though lacking critical distance.

Trevor, Meriol, *Newman.* Vol. I, *The Pillar and the Cloud.* Vol. II, *Light in Winter* (Garden City, N.Y.: Doubleday, 1962–1963). A well-written, absorbing, though highly partisan, biography.

Keble and Pusey

Some of the best accounts are found in the above studies on the movement as a whole. Also consult:

Battiscombe, Georgina. *John Keble: A Study in Limitations* (New York: Knopf, 1964).

Butler, Perry, ed. *Pusey Rediscovered* (London: S.P.C.K., 1985).

Chapter 8
Catholic Thought in Germany and England:
The Tübingen School
and John Henry Newman

Johann Adam Möhler

A prominent feature of the Romantic Movement is its rediscovery of and enthusiasm for history in all of its multitudinous variety and mystery and for the organic process of history itself. In both the Oxford Movement and French Traditionalism, we see not only a new respect for historical tradition but new arguments for a return to the "primordial Catholic tradition." Yet this interest in historical tradition and organic process posed crucial questions for those theologians imbued with the Romantic spirit: What is the link or unifying principle or immanent spirit that binds the "primordial tradition" of earliest Christianity to the present-day Catholic Church in all of its complex dogmatic and institutional forms? Can one speak of a uniform and continuous

dogmatic development of tradition in light of what we know about the diversity of present-day Christianity? Must not we speak of multiple "traditions" of Christianity, but does this not relativize church doctrine and practice? Theologians now recognized that there had been an undeniable *development* of doctrine and ecclesial forms. The apologetic appeal to history could, therefore, prove dangerous: It could bolster confidence in ancient authority, but it could also undermine it. The issue now was, how does one account for the continuity of religious truth within the process of historical development, even change? First the Catholic Tübingen theologians, and then J. H. Newman, would take up that question as a central preoccupation.

THE CATHOLIC TÜBINGEN SCHOOL

The Romantic Movement was a European phenomenon, but nowhere was it so deeply embedded in the culture and in various fields of humanistic endeavor as in Germany. We need only to be reminded of Goethe, Novalis, Schiller, Hölderlin, and Schlegel in literature; Fichte, Jacobi, Hamann, Schelling, and Hegel in philosophy; Schleiermacher and the Hegelian theologians Philipp Marheineke in Berlin and Karl Daub in Heidelberg among the Protestants; the Catholic religious writers Franz von Baader and Johann Joseph Görres in Munich; and the theologians Johann Sebastian Drey and Johann Adam Möhler in Tübingen.

We noted that the German *Aufklärung* was not infected with the skepticism, atheism, or materialism of the French Enlightenment, of a Voltaire or d'Holbach, or with the radical politics of the Parisian *libertins*. Furthermore, the Romantic renaissance of German Catholicism was, unlike that in France, largely associated with university circles in Munich, Tübingen, Münster, Jena, and Berlin. Many of these intellectual centers of Romanticism were dominated by Protestant thinkers. The Catholic thinkers in these universities not only read and were influenced by the philosophers Kant, Fichte, Schelling, and Hegel but also conversed, argued with, and learned from theologians such as Schleiermacher, Neander, and Baur. These German Catholic writers and theologians also were more progressive and open to the new transcendental philosophy and its turn to subjective consciousness, and they were more familiar with historical criticism than were their Catholic colleagues elsewhere in Europe. The German Romantic *sense of history* is particularly important in understanding the impulse, the methods, and the aims of the Catholic Tübingen School. Concerning this context, one historian has commented:

> At Tübingen the young Catholic professors found themselves face to face with established Protestant theologians there. The consequent debate . . . forced the Catholics to present their faith in terms which Protestants could respect. It seemed above all essential to meet the Protestant criticism that Catholic authority nullified genuine research by ordering the re-

search worker to produce a determined answer. . . . And if they claimed liberty of inquiry, they must also allow that some of the Protestants' historical conclusions upon the growth of Catholic dogma were accurate. . . . Perhaps for the first time Catholic theologians were having to frame a doctrine of authority and tradition which allowed the partial justice of Protestant historical criticism while it denied any theological deductions which the Protestants sought to draw from it.[1]

We will see, in the work of the theologians J. S. Drey and J. A. Möhler, how very different were the Catholic conclusions regarding history from those of Protestants such as Herder or Baur. Yet all of these aspects of German Romantic Catholicism set it apart from its French counterpart. Chateaubriand, Bonald, and Maistre all were laymen, essentially ignorant of the technicalities of research in Christian origins and historical theology. Neither Lamennais nor Bautain was a professional theologian. The religious interests of the French Traditionalists were sociological and political, and they were principally occupied, because of the French political situation during and after the revolution, with the problem of authority.

The Catholic theologians in Germany in the first third of the nineteenth century also faced a very different political, ecclesiastical, and institutional context. A form of state-church Gallicanism (in the German-speaking lands it was called Josephism or Febronianism), which limited the authority of the papacy while emphasizing the autonomy of the territorial bishops, was influential in the German states. In Württemberg, site of the university city of Tübingen, as in other jurisdictions, the Gallican doctrine was dominant. Powerful ecclesiastical rights were exercised by secular rulers over the local Church authorities. Some bishops even sympathized with the idea of a national Church free of the authority of Rome. In 1812 the king of Württemberg established a small Catholic seminary in the town of Ellwangen. However, in reorganizing the University of Tübingen in 1817, King Wilhelm transferred the Ellwangen seminary to Tübingen as the nucleus of a new Catholic faculty of theology, alongside the famous Protestant theological faculty. The leader of these Ellwangen theologians was the forty-year-old J. S. Drey, and he was joined in Tübingen in 1823 by his student at Ellwangen, J. A. Möhler.

What is distinctive about these young Tübingen theologians was their interest and special training in history. They were knowledgeable about the early Christian Church and about the historical developments of Church doctrine. This made them wary of the historical naiveté and simplifications, as well as the abstractness, which they found in the out-of-date forms of Catholic theology of their own training. As young seminary teachers, they took stands and published monographs that were looked upon with suspicion in Rome. However, the Roman ecclesiastical authorities did not intervene directly, due in large measure to the independent tradition of the Württemberg church authorities. These young scholars openly criticized the use of relics and pilgrimages; some even opposed clerical celibacy. Johann Hirscher (1788–1865) suggested reforms of the Mass, including the use of the vernacular. His book was put on the Index. Karl Joseph Hefele, who taught at Tübingen from 1840 to 1869, when he was consecrated bishop of the local diocese of Rottenburg, was a leader of the opposition to papal infallibility at the First Vatican Council (1870), offering trenchant historical arguments against the doctrine. His colleague, Drey's successor Johannes von Kuhn, never published another word after an investigation in 1868 by the Roman Inquisition.

J. S. Drey wrote a book in which he demonstrated that private confession of sins to a priest was not practiced in the early centuries in the Church and therefore was not apostolic. His purpose, however, was to argue that this lack of antiquity did not weigh against its later and current practice. All the same, as a result of his book Drey's nomination to the bishopric of Rottenburg by the Württemberg government was blocked by Rome in 1823. While they were hardly trusted in Rome, the Tübingen theologians nevertheless enjoyed relative freedom in their inquiries and were respected by the local authorities. Their methods and the themes of their theological work were to prove influential and enduring, but only after a hiatus of almost a century, due to the opposition engendered by the Neo-Thomistic revival.

Johann Sebastian von Drey

Johann Sebastian von Drey (1777–1853) was the founder of the Catholic Tübingen School and the initiator of many of its distinctive ideas. He was born the son of a village shepherd in the hamlet of Killingen near Ellwangen. Taken in by a local priest after his father's death, Drey was able to attend the local *gymnasium* through the priest's financial help. At school he developed interests in both the natural sciences and theology. After four years of seminary training in the diocese of Augsburg, he was ordained a priest in 1801. For the next five years he served as a parish priest under his earlier benefactor in his home parish. During these years he was able to read the leading German philosophers of the time, including Kant, Fichte, and Schelling, who had a profound influence on his thinking. From 1806 to 1812 he taught mathematics, physics, and philosophy of religion at the *lyceum* in Rottweil. In 1812 he returned to Ellwangen to serve as professor of dogmatics, the history of dogma, and apologetics at this small, newly established theological faculty. In 1817 the three Ellwangen theologians were transferred to Tübingen to constitute the Catholic theological fac-

Johann Sebastian von Drey

ulty at this venerable old center of learning. Here, as we have noted, Catholic theology was brought into direct contact with the most learned and progressive Protestant scholarship and the rich intellectual life of the university.

In 1819 Drey helped establish the *Tübinger Theologische Quartalschrift,* the oldest continuous Catholic theological journal. Its purpose was specifically to bring Catholic theology into conversation with modern knowledge. Drey set the agenda for the journal and was a major contributor even into his retirement. Drey also wrote two important works in 1819. The first, "On the Spirit and Nature of Catholicism," set forth some of his most characteristic ideas; the second, *Short Introduction to the Study of Theology,* outlined his views on the appropriate method and subject matter of theology emphasizing the essential role of historical background and perspective as the starting point of any constructive theology. In 1837 Drey reduced his heavy teaching responsibilities because of a severe illness, and in 1847 he retired at the age of sixty-nine. On that occasion he was publicly honored by the king. Though he lectured on dogmatic theology throughout his teaching career, his *Dogmatics* was never published. His major published work is his three-volume *Apologetik,* which appeared between 1838 and 1847. He died in 1853.

Drey had considerable influence on the renewal of Catholic thought in the first half of the nineteenth century. He was largely responsible for initiating the historical study of dogma in Catholic theological training and for making history a constitutive component of theological method. His historical-cultural approach to apologetics was in bold contrast to both the older rationalism of Enlightenment Catholicism and the new Scholasticism which was about to be initiated by the Roman Jesuits and which was to prove triumphant for almost a century. Drey is important also as the influential teacher of several young theologians who went on to distinguished careers of their own. These include Franz Anton Staudenmaier (1800–1857), Professor of Theology at Giessen; Johannes Evangelist von Kuhn (1806–1887), who succeeded Drey as Professor of Dogmatic Theology at Tübingen from 1837 to 1882; Karl Joseph Hefele (1810–1893), Professor of Church History at

Tübingen for thirty years and later Bishop of Rottenberg; and Johann Adam Möhler, Professor of Church History at Tübingen from 1822 to 1835.

On Theological Method.   Steeped in the ethos of the Romantic movement, Drey looked back to the Middle Ages as the last authentic expression of the Catholic ideal of the organic unity of society and culture. He saw the decline of Scholastic theology after the twelfth century, the onset of the Protestant revolution, and then seventeenth- and eighteenth-century rationalism as all being related, a sign of the loss of a mystical spirituality and the degeneration of theology into a heretical subjectivism. Reason and revelation became separated, as did God and the world, the final result being rationalistic Deism.

The declining spirituality that accompanied the collapse of medieval Scholasticism was temporarily countered, Drey believed, by the early Protestant reformers who made genuine spiritual demands on the faithful. But a prideful individualism soon won out.

> Heresy proceeded not from irreligion but from error, and this error is one of the byways into which mysticism can go astray when pride overtakes it, that is, pride inclines mysticism to take its inner, subjective perceptions as objectively, universally valid, to oppose them to a universal faith.

While Protestant spirituality sought an objective basis in Scripture, its subjectivism led to the science of exegesis, disputes over interpretation, and a breakdown of the spiritual organism.

> Now it came about that knowledge of those ancient languages, the art of research into and interpretations of ancient foreign customs and modes of expression . . . the collecting of manuscripts, fragments, and variants, in short, the whole *apparatus eruditionis,* as torn apart and scattered as all the things in the world, now became the indispensable condition of a genuine theology.

With the rise of modern science and the dominance of an empirical method and spirit, mysticism, the soul of Christianity, was eclipsed. "With the disappearance of mysticism there vanished also the exalted conception of Christianity as a great divine decree encompassing the whole history of mankind. Also lost was the conception of the church as the infinitely progressive realization of this decree." Empiricism ended in naturalism and rationalism. History itself was thereby secularized, and Christianity was interpreted as the product of contingent natural, historical forces. That is, undermined by the very rationalism that they had appealed to for support, the theologians turned their apologetics to history itself. But, as Lessing and Kant had taught, history is the realm of the phenomenal and contingent.

> The defenders of theology had forgotten that they themselves had annihilated history in the only sense that would be of use in refuting the naturalists, for they recognized in history not the work of eternal necessitation which the religious man calls providence, but the work of subjective freedom and therefore the work of chance. . . . These Christian theologians were themselves naturalists, except that they knew it not.[2]

Drey recognized that theology no longer could join forces with a rationalism that issued in either materialism or, at best, Deism or Pantheism. Drey's solution was not to abandon history but, with the help of Lessing and especially the young Tübingen philosopher F. W. J. Schelling, to appropriate the social, organic, developmental, and unitive vision of history that had captured the imagination of the Romantic writers. He would make this his own thought-world in the service of a revitalized Catholicism, that is, Catholicism as a living, divine, developing organism. God's revelation to humanity and the providential unfolding of his purposes are not to be known by abstract reason but rather by a religious interpretation of the "divine positivity," that is, in and through the concreteness, the positive "givenness," of the empirical-historical. Drey states that "the whole of Christianity as a given and positive reality—in history and doctrine—can be initially known only empirically and historically; and historical knowledge of it certainly must precede scientific knowledge."[3] By "scientific" Drey means a "necessary" knowledge of Christianity; the former is the material basis of the latter.

The starting point for a renewed and engaged theology is history, not abstract reason. But neither is it the autonomous, wholly contingent history that had separated God from the ongoing world process. Drey sees the divine activity not only in original creation, as did the Deists, but in the continuous becoming of world history. "All faith and all knowledge," he writes, "rests on the dimly felt or clearly perceived presupposition that every existing finite reality has not only emerged from an eternal and absolute ground but that its temporal being and life remain rooted in that ground and dependent upon it."[4]

This feeling of the divine immanence not only is true of God's ongoing creative relation to the natural order but is also felt as intrinsic to human subjectivity and history. Both the rationalists and supernaturalists have erred when they separate reason and revelation and consider "natural religion" as originating in the autonomous reason alone or, in the case of the supernaturalists, when they claim revelation as a necessary but extrinsic supplement. In both cases God is conceived as an external agent. But since the entire world is grounded in God— "man becomes aware of God, as he becomes aware of himself"—our being is uniquely determined by our primal consciousness of the Other, of God, of ourself as a distinct subject in relation to the immanent Other.

This innate feeling of God in the human *Gemüt,* the heart or soul, reveals Drey's Romantic affinity with Schleiermacher. They both see religion as "natural" to humanity though not an autonomous "natural religion," since every human being is grounded in and comes to consciousness through its encounter with the Other, the Ground of all Being. This primal sense of the divine ground, of God, is the basis of all positive religion, that is religion as it moves from the obscure, mystical sense of the divine to its articulate expression in ritual and doctrine. Positive religion emerges, then, by God's ever-present revelatory action as it is mediated through the objects and events of the world. Therefore, religion as we know it is thoroughly historical-cultural, taking its specific content from those finite objects and experiences that serve as the expressive mediators and vehicles, the "outward perceptions," of our innate religious sensibility.

All religion necessarily takes on a particular, positive character, shaped by our perceptions of objects in the world. The work of "scientific" theology is to examine and to interpret these spiritual concretions in history and to understand what expressions mediate that which is intrinsically related to human nature, that is, what is "necessary" in contrast to what is merely contingent and accidental. The former is what Drey calls *revelation*. Genuine divine *revelation* is that which is intrinsically related to and required by the human spirit and, though understood by reason, *is other than reason.*

> The necessity of revelation . . . can only be demonstrated if one shows that reason could not—either in the beginning or afterwards—develop without those external appearances which we call the revelations of God in the history of mankind. Only in this way does revelation appear no longer as something merely accidental, which is added on to reason as an afterthought, but rather as something which is posited simultaneously with reason and is always posited, and yet is different from reason.[5]

Revelation as the Education of the Human Race. Following Lessing, Drey believes that "revelation . . . is for the whole of mankind what education is for the individual."[6] But even the individual requires "another" on whom he or she is dependent both to instruct and to awaken knowledge. Here Drey sounds a theme that is also central to French Traditionalism. The specific purpose of revelation is to awaken humanity to religion in its ever-developing service to reason, since everything from God can only be through and for reason. And certain unique, God-inspired individuals—Christ being the supreme case—are called to serve as God's instruments in initiating and expanding a religious community and its revelatory message.

Drey envisions the successive revelatory dispensations in world history as the great divine plan for the education of humanity. This education reaches its culmination in the revelation in Christ and the ongoing community, the Church, which embodies his truth and which is meant to include all humanity. It is Drey's apologetic purpose, and that of the Tübingen School generally, to seek to demonstrate *historically* that the so-called mysteries of

Christianity best illuminate those divine feelings and ideas that lie deep within the self and that constitute the primal revelation present to each member of the race. Here again, Drey is in accord with a theme of the French Traditionalists. While the ultimate goal of the revelatory occasions of history is a *knowledge* of the content of this revelation—its "necessity"—the content of revelation is not self-evidently manifest. The critical beginning must be the receptive attitude of believing. Just as in education, learning begins with trust in the teacher, so in revelation faith in God is essential. Our reason, in other words, is presented with truths in the form of "mysteries" that we are not yet fully able to grasp. "A certain taking-captive of reason," Drey writes, "under the obedience of faith follows from the essential concept of a revelation." And it is from this "faithful exercise of reason in the service of faith that knowledge grows."

Revelation supposes certain historical facts that are meant to be understood. But only as the mind embraces these realities with love and seeks to cultivate an understanding of them can the mind "succeed in penetrating its object and produce a science of religion." Such a "scientific" knowledge is, in Drey's terms, a recognition of the "necessity and inner truth of the ideas" of revelation. What was at first believed on the testimony of God "now appears to reason as a nexus of doctrines which bear in themselves their truth and necessity; the mystery passes over into the idea, and the truths of revelation pass over into the truths of reason."[7]

According to Drey, God is making known to human minds those divine ideas that are the spiritual content of God's revelatory history, especially the history of the Church. Revelation does not cease, however, with Scripture, as many Protestants would claim. If that were the case, all theology would be limited to exegesis. "But if (along with Scripture) there exists a living objective reality which is generally recognized as the continuence of the originating event and therefore as its most authentic tradition, then the historical witness is found in and through it. This reality is the Church."[8] This leads to Drey's conception of the development of doctrine.

The Development of Doctrine. This living, objective phenomenon, the Church, is not a fixed and unchanging entity; it is a body in the process of development, a living tradition. Drey and his colleagues perceived the life of the Church after the analogy of the life of the individual. Both retain an essential self-identity through time that ensures the survival of the self-same nature, yet both develop through successive stages. Using Schelling's concept of the dialectic of opposites, Drey posits a dynamic view of Church development as involving genuine freedom and conflict. Thus the history of the emergence of the Church's "necessary ideas" involves the real engagement and struggle with discord and opposition and with incompatibilities that lead to "heresy." The latter is separatist, represents the misuse of freedom, and introduces "false possibilities" that are contested by the communal *Geist* or Spirit in the Church. Through this dialectical engagement, the Church brings out or realizes those true ideas that are consonant with that Spirit in the Church since its beginning.

Heresy is therefore characterized by its partiality or novelty. And the test of later developments is not whether they are present in the earliest Church, but whether they protect and serve the Spirit in its living, developing tradition. God's Spirit lives on in the community and is continuously active. Drey's own research on the sacrament of penance, for example, convinced him of the truth of private confession of sins to a priest, an observance that had not existed in the earliest centuries of the Church. God's revelation is not, then, confined to its beginnings but unfolds ceaselessly throughout history.

How is the truth or error of development to be judged? According to Drey, it is the work of the historian to provide the theologian with the full documented history of the development of doctrine and practice. It is the Church theologian's task, in turn, to judge whether a doctrine or practice expresses the authentic "idea" of Christianity, the truth of its "inner history" or Spirit. In other words, Drey appears to leave the decision to the Church's teaching authority. But, in fact, his apologetic appeals to the criterion of history itself, to something similar to what John Henry Newman later called the test of "chronic vigour." For Drey, of course, such a practical test, conjoined with others, is not a coercive proof; but it can be, and has proven to be, compelling to the receptive and trusting soul. The Church's very durability, adaptability, and unity—

joined with its ability to satisfy the spiritual needs of vastly dissimilar souls—vindicate its claim to be God's revelatory means of educating the human race.

For the Tübingen theologians, history is not to be conceived as a series of arbitrarily organized periods or epochs. History is the organic growth and outworking of the Divine Spirit's self-expression. That is, history reveals an all-inclusive purpose, "God's eternal design manifesting itself in time." And the study of history is the attempt to interpret God's revelation in terms of a fundamental "Idea" that summarizes the eternal divine plan. For Drey that master "idea" is the *Reich Gottes,* the kingdom of God. History is moving toward the realization of the reign of God. The plan is apparent first in Creation and then in the earliest earthly hopes for the coming of a political Messianic age, but this "Idea" is purified in Christ's preaching of a universal, moral kingdom of God. The various phases of human history can then be seen as the successive developments of the *Reich Gottes*—disturbed by the Fall and humanity's refusal of God's purposes—toward a greater realization of human spiritual freedom and relatedness to God.

As revealed by Christ, the *Reich Gottes* essentially is a social reality, a body of persons, that transcends nation and race.

> It is . . . a purely spiritual and ethical Kingdom, which recognizes no other Lord than God and His Son, whom he has sent and destined not to destroy the kingdoms of this world but to ennoble them through his religious and ethical spirit, and not to subjugate the peoples of the earth to one nation, but rather to unite them under the dominion of the Father of men and the King of Kings.[9]

For Drey the Church is the continuing bodily presence in human history of God's revelatory "Idea" and plan. Ruled by the Holy Spirit, it is the guardian and mediator of the means of human salvation and the essential agency for the realization of God's "Idea," the *Reich Gottes* as the dominion of love, the putting behind of a selfish egoism and surrender to the communion of the Church and to God's rule. The visible Church thus plays an absolutely crucial role in Drey's theology.

We must leave the analysis of Drey's theology here and turn to the thought of his most eminent student, J. A. Möhler. It is Möhler who pursues further Drey's ideas of the Church, especially with the apologetic intention of defending the Catholic idea of Tradition and the Church against the several Protestant confessions.

Johann Adam Möhler

It has been asserted, perhaps correctly, that Drey was the most original of the Tübingen theologians. While the others were extraordinarily gifted, and several were more prolific and influential, on the whole they built on the fundamental method and the themes laid down by Drey. However, Drey's student Möhler is far better known. His books not only had great influence in their own time but have been a source of Catholic theological renewal in the twentieth century.

Johann Adam Möhler (1796–1838) was born in the village of Igersheim near Würzburg in 1796, the son of a successful innkeeper. In 1813 he entered the Catholic seminary at Ellwangen and then Tübingen in preparation for the priesthood and was ordained in 1819. After a year of parish work, he returned to Tübingen to prepare for an academic career, studying classical philology. In 1822 Möhler was appointed a private teacher in Church history, a step toward higher appointment. With an additional stipend from the government, he was able to visit several of the great universities and libraries of Germany. His visit to the University of Berlin proved to be one of the formative experiences of his professional life. In Berlin he attended the lectures of Schleiermacher, Marheineke, and the church historian Neander. The latter's great learning and Romantic sense of history's organic wholeness especially impressed the young Möhler.

Back in Tübingen, Möhler began teaching church history, patristics, and canon law. In 1825 he published the first of his two most influential works, *The Unity of the Church, or the Principles of Catholicism Expounded in the Spirit of the Fathers of the Church of the First Three Centuries.* As one commentator has aptly remarked: "One might suggest that what Möhler did was to discover the theology of Drey in the writings of the fathers. . . . in any case, the fathers are pressed into service . . . as witnesses to

the truth of what Möhler learned from Drey."[10] We will return to *The Unity of the Church* shortly.

Möhler taught at Tübingen for twelve years, until 1835, when he left to accept the chair of New Testament exegesis at the University of Munich in Bavaria. Sadly, he fell seriously ill in 1836 and was able to resume teaching only early in 1838. He died in April of that year, shortly before the King intended to appoint him as Dean of Würzburg cathedral. Möhler's professional career lasted only a dozen years, but they were rich in accomplishment. He contributed numerous valuable and provocative articles to the *Tübinger Theologische Quartalschrift* on such subjects as papal authority and the idea of Church history. He wrote studies of Athanasius and Anselm, and in 1830 he began lecturing on the subject of *symbolics,* or the comparative study of Church confessions; these lectures resulted in the publication in 1832 of his best-known work, *Symbolics, or Presentation of the Dogmatic Differences of Catholics and Protestants.*

Spirit-Church-Tradition. Möhler approached theology from both his historical researches and his religious reflections on history. His historical perspective, therefore, was twofold. First, he was committed to an investigation of the original sources, especially the early Church Fathers, and later the medieval scholars and the reformers. Yet, with his mentor Drey, Möhler used these historical researches as the groundwork and departure for the defense of certain theological ideas and for his polemical forays with scholars both within and outside his Church.

What distinguishes Möhler's theology is that he begins neither with defined doctrines nor with the religious consciousness of the individual, but with the presence of the Holy Spirit in the Christian community. The living Church is the fundamental datum of theology. This demands both candid historical inquiry into the actual life of the Church and a historical vision to distinguish the true Church, that is, the true development of the spiritual community, from false and heretical ones.

In *The Unity of the Church* Möhler seeks to show that the Church is a bond of unity in Christ gifted to the community by the Holy Spirit. It is a community that finds its embodied expression, its historical forms, in a tradition that includes Scriptures, doctrine, liturgy, and hierarchy. He writes: "The Church is the external, visible form of a holy, living power of love, which the Holy Spirit imparts. The Church is the body belonging to the spirit of believers, *a spirit that forms itself from inward out.*" (Italics added.)[11] Here we can perhaps see the influence of Schleiermacher. Later, however, in his work on Athanasius and in his *Symbolics,* Möhler criticizes—whether fairly or not—Schleiermacher's subjectivism and his divine immanentism, that is, his failure to emphasize properly the transcendence of God and genuine human freedom. Nonetheless, Möhler's starting point in *The Unity of the Church* is the inner spiritual life of the community—the work of the Spirit in believers "that forms itself from inward out." Doctrine, liturgy, polity—all the forms of the external Church—are expressions of the spiritual needs and convictions of the Christian community. Christianity, in Möhler's definition, "consists of life, a life that is immediately and always moved by the divine Spirit, a life that maintains itself and progresses *through* the reciprocal love of the faithful."[12]

Möhler's use of the term "divine Spirit," or *Geist* in German, is ambiguous, since it can convey both the sense of the "Spirit of God" who, though immanent in the community, also transcends it and the *Geist* of the community itself, as often found in the German Romantic appeal to the *Volksgeist,* or the spirit of the German people and nation. Möhler uses the word analogously, yet later he will repudiate any tendency to a thorough divine immanentism and will stress the objective, historical revelation in Christ. It is in this earlier mystical conception of the Church, however, that Möhler draws heavily on German Romantic Idealism, a source that is crucial to his organic doctrine of the Church and to his conception of the development of ecclesial tradition.

Möhler's ecclesiology is, then, influenced by the Romantic conception of an organic, evolving, living tradition and a united and unbroken community consciousness that is guided by the Divine Spirit, *in and through which alone* the individual person can understand and appropriate the mysteries of Christian life and belief. This latter conviction was, of course, crucial to Möhler's theology and to his apology against the Protestants and all sectarians.

The authentic Christian consciousness belongs not only to the solitary *homo religiosus,* no matter how deep and fervent his or her piety; the Christian consciousness is fundamentally collective and communal, the *sensus communis* of the faithful. And so the test of an individual's faith is "the identity of Christian consciousness of the individual . . . with the consciousness of the whole Church."[13] The very nature of this latter consciousness is to unfold in history and to take bodily form under the direction of the Holy Spirit. And it is this embodied, developing consciousness that Möhler and the Tübingen theologians mean by *tradition.*

The given, *objective* character of the Christian tradition is, however, assumed in *The Unity of the Church.* Möhler writes that "this vital, spiritual force *which we inherit from our fathers* and which is perpetuated in the Church, is interior tradition." (Italics added.)[14] In *Symbolics,* Möhler emphasizes that this interior, spiritual tradition is formed by the exterior tradition, that is, by Scripture, doctrine, and liturgy, and is sealed and safeguarded by the hierarchy. It is this exterior tradition that thereby protects the faithful from isolation, egoism, and a false individual judgment.

Möhler's understanding of the unity of the interior and exterior aspects of the one living, developing tradition can best be observed in his discussion of Scripture and tradition. Here he develops a position that is distinct not only from the Protestant principle of *sola Scriptura,* Scripture alone, but also from the position taken by the sixteenth-century Catholic bishops at the Council of Trent. The Tridentine documents allow for a separation of Scripture and tradition into two distinct and parallel sources.

For Möhler tradition is not formulated statically, for instance in written form in a book. Tradition is, rather, the Gospel living continuously in the Church. Thus the New Testament is the first *written* document of the tradition, of the ever-living work of the Holy Spirit:

> Tradition is the expression of that Holy Spirit who enlivens the community of believers—an expression that courses through all ages, living at every moment, but always finding embodiment. The Scriptures are the expression of the Holy Spirit, embodied at the beginning of Christianity through the special grace given

to the apostles. The Scriptures are in that respect the first component of written tradition.[15]

Christ's Spirit was, of course, present to the Church before the letter of Scripture. Yet Scripture has its essential place in the work of the Spirit—but always in relation to tradition.

> Without sacred Scripture as the most ancient embodiment of the gospel, Christian teaching would not have been preserved in its purity and simplicity. . . . However, without an ongoing tradition we would lack an overview of Scripture, for without any links connecting it and us, we could perceive no continuity. . . . Without Scripture we would not be able to project an integral image of the Redeemer. . . . Without tradition we would have no Scripture. . . . In short, all belongs together, for in God's wisdom and grace it was given to us as inseparable.[16]

In *Symbolics,* Möhler presses the question of Scriptural interpretation against the Protestants. How, he asks, does the individual "obtain a clear knowledge of the institute of salvation proferred in Christ Jesus?" The Protestant replies, "By searching Holy Writ, which is infallible." But the Catholic must protest that it is "by the Church, in which a man arrives at the true understanding of Holy Writ."[17] What the Protestant fails to recognize is that after Christ's gospel was preached and he departed, even the evangelists were required to choose and to arrange the oral and written materials. In order to be passed on, the message was translated and shaped into new idioms and forms, for example, by the Gospel writers and by St. Paul and St. John. Once the Scripture canon was determined and delimited by the Church, it was necessary to ensure that these various documents were rightly interpreted. Möhler reminds Protestants that, as with Christ, so with his Word: The Word *did become flesh.* In an important passage Möhler articulates his conception of the Catholic position.

> Thus the scripture is God's unerring word, *but however the predicate of inerrability may belong to it, we ourselves are not exempt from error.* . . . In this reception of the word, human activity, which is fallible, has necessarily a part. But in order that in this transit of the

divine contents of the Sacred Scriptures into possession of the human intellect no gross illusion or general misrepresentation may occur, it is taught that the Divine Spirit to which are entrusted the guidance and vivification of the Church becomes, in its union with the human spirit in the Church, a peculiarly Christian tact, a deep, sure-guiding feeling, which, as it abideth in truth, leads also into all truth. By a confiding attachment to the perpetuated Apostleship, by education in the Church, by hearing, learning, and living within her pale, by the reception of the higher principle which renders her eternally fruitful, a deep interior sense is formed that alone is fitted for the perception and acceptance of the written Word. . . . *Nay, when instruction through the apostleship, and the ecclesiastical education in the way described, takes place in the individual the Sacred Scriptures are not even necessary for our acquisition of their general contents.*[18] (Italics added.)

Möhler's phrase about the Sacred Scriptures being "not even necessary" may appear to separate Scripture and tradition, but that would overlook his insistence that the written Scriptures are necessary in preserving the purity of the earliest Christian teaching. But it is the "general sense"—that of the Christian community—that must judge the truth of Scripture against "particular opinion." Christ, Möhler insists, "dwells in the community; all his promises, all his gifts are bequeathed to the community—but to no individual, as such, since the time of the apostles."[19] And it is this "general sense," this ecclesial consciousness, that Möhler calls *tradition.* It is a consciousness that is never detached from its primal subject matter, i.e., Christ's gospel. Nevertheless,

> Tradition is the living word, perpetuated in the hearts of believers. . . . The declaration which it pronounces on any controverted subject is the judgment of the Church, and therefore the Church is judge in matters of faith. Tradition, in the objective sense, is the general faith of the Church through all ages, manifested by outward historical testimonies; in this sense tradition is usually termed the *norma*—the standard of Scriptural interpretation—the rule of faith.[20]

Church-Authority-Hierarchy. We have seen that Möhler's conception of the Church evolved from the Romantic, mainly spiritual, view in *The Unity of the Church* to that in *Symbolics*. The former attends to the internal communal Christian consciousness from which derives the external notes of the Church, such as doctrine and hierarchy. In the latter, the Church is perceived more objectively as the real bodily presence of Christ that serves to guarantee and to pass on the inner spiritual truth. In an important sense the visible Church is, for Möhler, the extension of Christ's body, his work and Word. The Church is Christ carrying on his work of salvation:

> A living, visible association of the faithful sprang up . . . Christ's institution, wherein he continues to live, his spirit continues to work, and the word uttered by him eternally resounds. Thus, the visible Church . . . is the Son of God himself among men in a human form . . . the permanent incarnation of the same, as in Holy Writ, even the faithful are called "the body of Christ."[21]

Möhler rejects the notion, common in some Protestant ecclesiology, of a too-sharp distinction between the "invisible" and "visible" Church. The Church is one, undivided. As with Christ, the human and divine can be distinguished but are bound in unity. So, too, the Church is at once human *and* divine in an indivisible union. God did not speak through an incorporeal Spirit and thus produce only an internal, invisible spiritual Church. The Divine Word became *incarnate,* taking the form of a servant—an outward, perceptible, and human presence. The Church, likewise, "is the Christian religion in its objective form." The Word of God, therefore, never can be separated from the Church, nor the Church from God's Word.

The union of the divine and the human in the Church has crucial implications for a doctrine of authority:

> We can never arrive at an external authority, like Christ, by *purely spiritual* means. The attempt would involve a contradiction, which could only be disposed of in one of two ways; either we must renounce the idea, that in Christ God manifested himself in history . . . or we must learn the fact through a living, definite, and vouching fact. Thus authority must have authority for its medium. As Christ wished to be the ade-

quate authority for all ages, he created, by virtue of his power . . . something *attesting* and *representing* the same, eternally destined to bring his authority before all generations of men.[22]

Because the visible Church is a divinely appointed institution, its teaching is guided by the Holy Spirit. There cannot, then, be some incorporeal, inerrant spiritual authority separate from the visible ecclesial authority:

> If the divine—the living Christ and his spirit—constitute undoubtedly that which is infallible, and externally inerrable in the Church; so also the human is infallible and inerrable in the same way, because the divine without the human has no existence for us: yet the human is not inerrable in itself, but only as the organ, and as the manifestation of the divine.[23]

What distinguishes the Catholic faith from that of Protestants, in Möhler's analysis, is that Catholics trust that the visible Church cannot fail in preserving and passing on Christ's eternal Word. That is, the Catholic believes the Church is divinely gifted with *infallibility.* By giving him or herself up to the guidance of the Church, the believer must trust that he or she is secure against error and delusion—that the Church is *inerrable.* And to no individual can such an infallibility be claimed by the Catholic Christian. This, in Möhler's estimation, is one, if not the key difference, between Catholicism and Protestantism. Protestants, he argues, must find it difficult, if not impossible, to distinguish between dogma and opinion, since authority is vested, ultimately, in the individual consciousness as it encounters Scripture alone. Luther, not surprisingly, is for Möhler the prototype Protestant, for it was he who embodied "the inordinate pretension of an individuality which wished to constitute itself the arbitrary centre round which all should gather."

Möhler insists that every positive religion, if it is to have a decisive and permanent influence on humanity, "must be ever imparted to successive generations, through the medium of an authority." Christian truth is mediated through historical embodiment, and in the crosscurrents of history the truth is found and is maintained through contest and struggle. The history of Christianity in its battle with heresy and schism is the test case to that fact. And such contention "explains the necessity of a living, visible authority. . . . Otherwise, we should have *only* the variable—the disputed—and at last Nihilism itself."[24] What such an interpretive havoc and complacency entail is the conclusion that since Scripture includes untold possible senses, it consequently has none!

Now Luther's, and by extension the Protestant, idea of the Church is not false, only dangerously one-sided. Luther's emphasis on the spiritual inwardness of citizenship in the Church is commendable, since no one can belong only outwardly to the Church. Where Luther erred is in his failure to recognize that the revelation of Christ is external, the Word of God become visible, and that the warranty of faith needs to be external. Here we observe Möhler reproving not only Luther but his own spiritual one-sidedness in *The Unity of the Church.*

The prominence that Protestantism gives to the invisible Church makes it impossible, Möhler argues, for Protestantism to believe that the Church was given a visible hierarchy and head. Möhler wrote, however, before the meeting of the First Vatican Council of 1870, and his own conception of the Church's hierarchy is not wholly congruent with the dogma of papal infallibility as it was defined at the Vatican Council. Indeed, in an early article in the *Theologische Quartalschrift* (1823), Möhler had attacked what he called the "papal system"; and his attitude toward papal infallibility was especially hostile. His early position was essentially that of the Conciliarists of the fifteenth century, in that he maintained that the Pope can err in matters of faith and morals and can be corrected by an ecumenical council of bishops. Doctrines, to be Catholic, i.e., universal, must be approved by an ecumenical council of bishops. Hence, a doctrine cannot become more Catholic by the action of the Pope; his approval is neither more nor less required than that of any other bishops. The Pope's primacy symbolizes the unity of the church, and the Pope's distinctive role is to execute the decisions of the Church. Möhler reasoned that the move to centralize power in the Roman bishop is to be explained *historically* by the fact that the contentions among powerful bishops and the threat of heresy and schism argued

practically for Roman primacy. At the time, Möhler believed that papal infallibility implied that a doctrine was Catholic only when it was approved by a single individual, that is, by the Pope.

In *The Unity of the Church* Möhler undertakes to explain the evolution of hierarchical authority not only in practical terms but dynamically and spiritually as the work of the Holy Spirit. Through the Spirit the members of the Christian community see the personification of the community's love and unity in the person of their bishop. But the bishop is actually the effectuation of the community through the work of the Holy Spirit and all should share in his election. That is, the bishop's ordination is essentially the community's recognition of the bishop's special ministerial gift. "Ordination consists in nothing else than this: the Church testifies that the Spirit is present in this member of the faithful and makes him capable of representing the love of a certain number of believers. . . . In ordination, then, the Holy Spirit is not conferred so much as recognized."[25]

Here Möhler appears to champion a form of *episcopalianism* as well as possibly *presbyterianism,* in that the bishop (*episcopus*), like the *presbyter,* is elected by the community of the faithful. While stressing the divine origin of the hierarchy (the episcopate), Möhler nevertheless sees the hierarchy as emerging "from below," out of the life of the faithful, the interior spirit engendering the exterior authority. In *Symbolics* this interior one-sidedness is corrected by an emphasis on the visible Church—its teaching authority and its life and liturgy—that engenders and sustains the "invisible" interior spiritual life of the individual and the community.

In his discussion of the hierarchy and the papacy in *Symbolics,* Möhler reverts to his critical idea of the internal and the external or visible aspects of the Church cohering in one body. As he now writes of priestly ordination and the sacramental life of the Church, "the heavenly and earthly unction become one and the same." Not every individual who declares that he or she has received the call to the priesthood can be approved by the Church. "On the contrary, as he must previously be carefully and strictly bred up, and instructed in the divine dogmas of the Church . . . so he receives through the

Church, through her external consecration, the inward consecration from God ... through the imposition of the hands of *the bishops,* the Holy Spirit."[26] Here Möhler stresses that the visibility and stability of the Church require such external consecration, since Christ originated the unbroken succession of apostolic witness through his appointment of apostles who, in turn, instituted bishops who appointed their successors. It is this ministerial succession, Möhler now argues, that is the outward work and guarantor of the true Church as founded by Christ.

The episcopate, as the continuation of the apostles, is a divine institution and, Möhler continues, "not less so, the Pope, who is the center of unity and the head of the episcopate."[27] It is on the subject of the nature and authority of the papacy that we can recognize a development in Möhler's own ecclesiology in *Symbolics.* Having demonstrated the need for an outward, visible institution that can protect and perpetuate Christ's message and work, Möhler now gives special attention to the fact that the essential unity required by such a visible institution demands a "center" by which all can be firmly united. Möhler writes:

> Had not the universal Church possessed a head instituted by Christ and had not this head *by acknowledged rights and obligations* been enabled to exert an influence over each of its parts, those parts, abandoned to themselves, would soon have taken a course of development contrary to each other and absolutely determined by local relations—a course which would have led to the dissolution of the whole body.[28]

Without a visible head—which now, for Möhler, demands acknowledged *rights and influence* over the many national and distinctive parts of the universal Church—the Church would splinter and disintegrate. For example, if the Pope had no decisive influence over the right to confirm and appoint bishops to their dioceses, certain civil or ecclesiastical leaders would inevitably seek to raise to the office of bishop persons whose interests would be opposed to those of the universal Church. The same would be the case if the Supreme Pontiff did not have authority to remove priests from their

duties. A visible head *with inalienable rights was essential and divinely ordained.*

Through the turmoils of history, the revolutions and contentions of various times, two systems of authority emerged in the Catholic Church: the episcopal and the papal system. Möhler's judgment on this parallel development is of special interest. Rather than seeing the two systems as inevitably divisive and a threat to the peace of the Church, he declares such

> an opposition very beneficial to ecclesiastical life, so that, by their counter-action, the peculiar free development of the several parts was on the one hand preserved, and the union of these in one living, indivisible whole was on the other hand maintained. The dogmatic decrees of the episcopate, united with the general head and centre are infallible; for it represents the universal Church.[29]

Möhler's mature and balanced conception of the organic, living Church succeeded in showing its interior and visible unity, as well as the need for a hierarchy and its distinctive authority. It is generally agreed that Möhler bequeathed to modern Catholicism a conception of the Church that avoided the extremes of both the static and juridical notions of the Counter-Reformation as well as the dominantly mystical and purely spiritual conceptions of an invisible Church. Because of this, Möhler did not commit himself on the *personal* infallibility of the Pope, certainly not as it was to be defined in 1870. It is now clear, however, that his last writings on the hierarchy proved to be an inspiration to Catholic theologians in the twentieth century, for example, Henri de Lubac and Yves Congar, who have sought to develop an organic conception of the Church and tradition that would do justice to the Church's mystical and institutional reality. The doctrine of the "collegiality" of Pope and bishops, as articulated in the dogmatic constitution *Lumen Gentium* of the Second Vatican Council (1962–1965), is a decisive development in the understanding of the relations of the Pope and the bishops, and it largely reiterates Möhler's language and ideas as expressed in the later editions of *Symbolics.*

The theology of the Tübingen School came into conflict with the Roman-supported Neo-Thomist revival in the decades after 1840. The methods and spirit of the two movements were, as we will see, in many respects profoundly opposed. Tübingen was deeply rooted in history and historical inquiry, in the study of Christian origins and patristics, and in the work of the German Romantic and Idealist thinkers. Neo-Thomism had little interest in historical studies. It was suspicious of German Idealism and looked to Aristotle for its philosophy. The Neo-Thomists believed that the Tübingen theologians, due to their historical and speculative methods, had failed to deal adequately with such matters as the relation of faith and reason and the external and immutable aspects of the Church, its teachings and authority. The Tübingen theologians' views of the development of doctrine, living tradition, and the Spirit in the Church were considered highly suspect and unsafe.

Between the encyclical *Aeterni Patris* (1879), in which Pope Leo XIII declared the theology of St. Thomas Aquinas as normative for Catholic teaching, and the appearance of the "new theology" in France in the 1930s, the theology of Drey, Möhler, and their Tübingen colleagues remained under a cloud of suspicion. It was only the revival of interest in the Tübingen School by German scholars and by French theologians just before World War II that brought to light the creative and orthodox ideas of the Tübingen group, especially on such matters as tradition, the development of doctrine, the Church, and the liturgy. Most important was the rediscovery of its historical approach to theology. There is today an effort by Catholic theologians to use the insights of the Tübingen School, especially its historical orientation, to develop an authentic Catholic theology for the late twentieth century, one that would offer an alternative, with regard to method, epistemology, and metaphysics, to twentieth-century Neo-Thomism. Many distinguished Catholic theologians today believe that the tradition of Neo-Thomistic theology is not capable of dealing adequately with the strongly exegetical, historical, and even philosophical commitments that now inform so much theological activity. In any case, it appears that the Tübingen theology is now

recognized as a legitimate and valuable source of inspiration for Catholic theology in the years ahead. The echo of Tübingen themes in some of the dogmatic constitutions of the Second Vatican Council would signify that that has, in fact, been the case for some time.

ENGLISH ROMAN CATHOLICISM

Since the reign of Henry VIII in the mid-sixteenth century, the Catholic Church and its people had suffered intolerance and civil exclusion in England. Because of papal opposition to his divorce from Catherine of Aragon and his marriage to Anne Boleyn (mother of Elizabeth I), Henry broke with papal jurisdiction over the English Church and declared himself to be the supreme head of the Church of England. Later events completed the separation. In 1559 the Elizabethan Settlement required an oath of all bishops in support of the monarch as "supreme governor" of the English Church. This caused the resignation of the Catholic bishops; as a result, Rome rejected the legitimacy of the newly consecrated Archbishop of Canterbury. The Test Act (1563) further estranged the churches by condemning anyone upholding papal jurisdiction and barring Catholics from the House of Commons. For three hundred years the condition of Roman Catholics in England hardly improved. The English fear of "Popery" and suspicion of the civil loyalty of Catholics persisted. The growing population of immigrant working-class Irish in England felt themselves to be foreigners, and the old aristocratic Catholic families increasingly remained aloof from public affairs. There was little creative work done in the field of Catholic scholarship and theology.

This condition of the Catholic Church in England changed significantly in the nineteenth century.[30] First, the Catholic population grew rapidly in the 1830s and 1840s through Irish immigration and then increased steadily during the rest of the century. However, far more critical to its changed fortunes and its character were two events. The first was Catholic Emancipation achieved through a Relief Act passed by Parliament in April 1829. The act did include some traditional oaths, for example, a denial of the Pope's deposing power and civil jurisdiction in the United Kingdom, as well as an oath in which Catholics were to disavow "any intention to subvert the present Church Establishment as settled by law." Now Catholics were, however, by law able to hold most offices under the Crown and were given the franchise. The first Catholic to take his seat in the House of Commons did so in May 1829. Nicholas Cardinal Wiseman later was to say that "the year 1829 was to us what the egress from the catacombs was to the early Christians."[31] Over the next decades Catholics assumed positions of leadership in English institutions, though Pope Pius IX's *Syllabus of Errors* and the militant Ultramontanism of Roman converts such as Edward Cardinal Manning and W. G. Ward continued to feed suspicion of "Popery" among the English.

The second event that prepared the way for a renewal, even a refashioning, of English Catholicism was the Oxford Movement itself. The Catholic revival in the Church of England produced varied responses but, except for the excesses of some of the High Anglican ritualists, prepared the way for wider acceptance of Catholic ways by members of the Established Church and beyond it. Especially significant was the fact that many of the leaders of the Tractarian cause were to follow John Henry Newman into the Roman Catholic Church after 1845 and to take leadership roles in their new Church. William George Ward, whose book *The Ideal of a Christian Church* was condemned for its "Roman" sympathies by the convocation of Oxford University in 1845, became, after his conversion, the editor of the *Dublin Review*. Under his direction the review was the trumpet of extreme Ultramontanism during the crucial decade of the 1860s. Frederick William Faber, an Anglican parish priest and zealous defender of the Catholic movement in the Anglican Church, followed Newman to Rome. He was a writer of extremely popular devotional books and hymns and has been called "the guiding spirit of Victorian popular Catholicism."[32] Henry and Robert Isaac Wilberforce, both Tractarians and brothers of Samuel Wilberforce (who later was Anglican Bishop of Oxford), joined the Roman Church in 1850 and in 1854. Robert

was perhaps the finest theologian among the Oxford leaders. He died in 1857 while preparing for the Catholic priesthood in Rome.

More significant even than Newman for the immediate life and direction of the English Catholic Church was the conversion in 1851 of Henry Manning, Anglican archdeacon of Chichester. A few months after his conversion, Manning was ordained a Catholic priest by Cardinal Wiseman. Then, after study in Rome, he returned to England as a priest in the diocese of Westminster, was soon appointed Provost of the Chapter at Westminster, and, at Cardinal Wiseman's death in 1865, was named Archbishop of Westminster by Pope Pius IX, over the recommendations of the Westminster Chapter. He immediately became the leading spokesman of English Ultramontanism and defender of papal infallibility. He declared that the voice of the Roman Church was the voice of God, that is, infallible, and if the Church is infallible, so must be its head, the Pope.

Newman and Manning became identified as the leaders, or at least the symbols, of the two movements of European Catholicism: Liberal Catholicism and Ultramontanism, despite the fact that Newman rejected the former label. The two emerged into the public limelight at roughly the same time: with Manning's elevation to archbishop in 1865 and with the appearance in 1864 of Newman's *Apologia,* the defense of his Anglican position and his conversion to Rome but also his depiction of a Catholicism that was not Ultramontane. The two men distrusted one another, and they differed on many issues over the years, including the matter of papal infallibility. We will not pursue this latter question here, but we will return to Manning, Ultramontanism, and the consolidation of papal authority in Chapter 13. Our purpose here is to examine the foremost contributions of John Henry Newman to Christian thought in the nineteenth century, ideas that endure to the present day. These, as we will see, are also more in accord with the Romantic cast of mind of the Tübingen theologians and with aspects of French Traditionalism than with the contemporary developments of Catholic Neo-Thomism on the Continent. But neither can

Newman be identified simply as a Liberal Catholic—in the form assumed by either Lamennais or the historian Lord Acton.

John Henry Newman

In Chapter 7 we traced some of the events and factors that led John Henry Newman (1801–1890) to be received into the Roman Catholic Church in 1845. His reading and reflection on the early Christian heretical movements increasingly bore in on him a sense of the historical isolation of the Church of England. The great words of St. Augustine—*securus judicat orbis terrarum* (secure in the judgment of the world)—were finally decisive. "By these great words," he wrote in the *Apologia*, "the theory of the *Via Media* was absolutely pulverized." His defense of Anglicanism had fallen apart. The issue centered on authority and the Church's indefectibility, that is, its unity and preservation in the truth. It is important to emphasize, however, that Newman's conversion was the outcome of a long intellectual and spiritual process. He simply came to see the Catholic Church, not the Church of England, as the preserver of Christian truth. This is important, because, as Edward Norman has pointed out, Newman did not radically change, and he remained something of an independent mind within his new spiritual home. This helps to explain his isolation as a Catholic, as well as the cloud of suspicion under which he worked until almost the last decade of his long life.[33]

After his conversion Newman studied in Rome, was ordained a priest, and entered the Congregation of the Oratory, a community that allowed him more opportunity to pursue his work and interests. On his return to England, he served as Superior of the English Oratory and established an oratory in London and then in Birmingham, where he remained until his death. In the years immediately after his period in Rome, he published *Loss and Gain, the Story of a Convert* (1848); *Lectures on Certain Difficulties Felt by Anglicans in Submitting to the Catholic Church* (1850); and *Lectures on the Present Position of Catholics in England* (1851). He was appointed Rector of the Catholic University of Dublin in 1851, but he was deeply frustrated in achieving his goals for this new institution.

Nevertheless, the enduring result of this venture was Newman's discourses and lectures on education which were published as *Idea of a University* (1873), one of the great books on the subject.

In 1859 Newman served briefly as editor of *The Rambler,* a lay Catholic magazine headed by the liberal Catholic historian Sir John Acton. *The Rambler* was embroiled in controversy with Church authorities, but Newman accepted the editorship—though he thought these amateur lay theologians were in a false position in opposing Church theology—because he felt strongly about the voice of the laity in the educational life of the Church. Ironically, Newman's own famous essay, "On Consulting the Faithful in Matters of Doctrine," was published in *The Rambler* and was submitted to Rome for its opinion by an English bishop. Newman resigned as editor. Once again, he had found himself between two opposing sides in the Church. Newman's position and authority in Church matters greatly improved after favorable response to the publication of his *Apologia,* yet his attempt to found a Catholic college in Oxford in 1865 was rejected by Rome through the intervention of H. E. Manning.

Newman's *Essay in Aid of a Grammar of Assent,* his finest work in philosophy, appeared in 1870 and sparked a long and lively debate in the intellectual periodicals. It remains a seminal work. Newman's election to the first honorary fellowship of Trinity College, his undergraduate, alma mater at Oxford, proved that he was by now no longer suspect but admired by his old university. In 1879 Newman was created a cardinal by Pope Leo XIII in one of the new Pope's first acts.

The Development of Doctrine. Newman is one of the great English prose writers. It is said that he was incapable of writing a boring letter, and his collected letters encompass over a score of large printed volumes. He wrote poetry, novels, and autobiography. Some of his most important work was that of an apologist and controversialist, for example, his Anglican *Tracts for the Times* and his *Letter to the Duke of Norfolk,* a response to the former prime minister W. E. Gladstone's attack on the loyalty of Catholic citizens. Newman's sermons, published in many volumes, are beautiful and powerful and remain persuasive reading. Some of his theological treatises have not stood the test of time, but the ideas explored in two of them continue to be of critical importance in theological discussion today. One is *The Essay on the Development of Christian Doctrine.* A leading contemporary authority on the history of Christian doctrine has called the *Essay* "the almost inevitable starting point for an investigation of development of doctrine."[34]

Newman begins his essay by conceding what he calls the "principle of dogma." By this he means the belief that supernatural truths are given definitively and irrevocably, even if they are given in human language that requires continuous, developed forms of expression and explication. Against this principle he opposed two things which he identified as central to religious "liberalism." One was the modern belief that there are no irrevocable, supernatural truths; the second was the growing conviction that divine revelation is ever changing and progressing. Newman opposed both claims, but, as he saw his Anglican foundations crumbling and was increasingly drawn toward Catholicism, he was perplexed as to how to reconcile the Roman claim to being apostolic with the fact that its developed doctrine was not apostolic. How could he be sure that the Roman Catholic Church had not added "corrupting doctrines" to the apostolic deposit of faith—especially as that faith was defined by the great ecumenical councils of Nicea and Constantinople?

As an Anglican, Newman had based his faith on *antiquity,* on the Church Fathers and the early councils. But his historical researches on the first six centuries of the Church forced him to recognize that the Council of Nicea already was the outcome of a long process of development. Why should the process of development come to a halt? Why should the Council of Trent be less divinely guided than the Council of Nicea of Chalcedon? By what criteria, by what principles, can a true development be distinguished from a corruption?

These questions were, first and foremost, highly personal to Newman, but they were, of course, part of the intellectual ethos of Europe at the time and central to the question of how one can make claims about "irrevocable truths" in view of the ceaseless historical process of flux and change. This question forced Newman to seek an answer by writing the *Essay on Development.* But his inspiration and

sources were not German Romantic Idealism, not Schelling or Hegel; neither were they to be found in Möhler and Tübingen. As Owen Chadwick has shown, Newman's sources were patristic, not modern, and his mode of argument was his own. Newman was familiar with Möhler's early work, largely through W. G. Ward, but it was not a decisive influence. Furthermore, and unlike the Tübingen theologians, Newman was deeply averse to immanentist doctrines and to ideas of progress.[35]

Newman proposed the *Essay* as "an hypothesis to account for a difficulty."[36] The difficulty was the Roman Catholic claim of an *historical identity* of the present with the past apostolic Church. Newman's purpose was relatively modest. He did not offer a *positive* argument for Catholicism; rather, he proposed a negative case in which he openly assumed that there *is* an historical identity of the present and past Church. He then answered objections by way of offering a theory of development that, he trusted, would be more compelling than those of previous apologists.

The first theory that Newman opposes is one favored by many Protestants. The latter tend to find the doctrines and practices of Christianity to be so variously represented that they give up as useless any effort to seek *in history* the revealed truth of Christianity vouchsafed to humanity. "They cannot," Newman asserts, "be historical Christians if they would . . . [for] they are forced, whether they will or not, to fall back upon the Bible as the sole expounder of its doctrine."[37] For Newman one thing is clear: "Whatever history teaches . . . whatever it says or unsays, at least the Christianity of history is not Protestantism. . . . to be deep in history is to cease to be a Protestant."[38] This is evident by the fact that most Protestants date Christian apostasy as early as the second or third century. And radical Protestant spiritualists, such as the Reformer Sebastian Franck, teach that immediately after the death of the apostles the Church was assumed directly into heaven. All Church history thereafter is looked upon as a corruption of the apostolic witness. Some liberal Protestants, on the other hand, side with Herder and acknowledge that Christianity has always changed from the earliest years and has accommodated itself to various times and places. But it is difficult, Newman replies, "to understand how such a view is compatible with the special idea of a revealed truth."[39]

A second hypothesis, favored by some Catholics and by High Church Anglican divines, is that set forth by St. Vincent of Lérins. It claims that history does show that a pure Christianity existed in the early centuries and that it was then corrupted by heresies. But a line can be drawn between pure and apostolic doctrine and later corruptions by the application of St. Vincent's canon, "*quod semper, quod ubique, quod ab omnibus,*" (apostolic Christianity is that which has been held "always, everywhere, and by all"). Newman recognized that such a rule had guided the Anglican *Via Media* between Protestantism and Romanism. But Newman's historical researches had exploded the Vincentian hypothesis, for it fails when applied to particular crucial cases. For example, "What is meant by being 'taught *always*'? Does it mean in every century, or every year, or every month? Does 'everywhere' mean in every country, or in every diocese? And does 'the Consent of the Fathers,'" Newman asks, "require us to produce the direct testimony of every one of them?"[40] It is a test that can never be fully satisfied.

Against the Vincentian rule, Newman takes as his prime example the doctrine of the Trinity. In the years before the Council of Nicea, the Christian creeds "make no mention in their letter of the Catholic doctrine [of the Trinity] at all. They make mention indeed of a Three; but that there is any mystery in the doctrine, that the Three is One, that they are coequal, coeternal, all increate, all omnipotent, all incomprehensible, is not stated, and never could be gathered from them."[41] Many of the great bishops of the early Church were, by Nicene standards, guilty of one or another Trinitarian heresy. Newman was struck by the fact that in the early centuries some Church Fathers had spoken of Christ's relation to God in a sense that implied his subordination, not his coequality with the Father.

A third hypothesis that was proposed to account for the seeming lack of continuity between the early Church and its later aspects was appeal to a *disciplina arcana,* or secret discipline. The theory held that doctrines which we associate with later periods of Church history, say the Immaculate Conception of the Virgin Mary, were really and explicitly held by the early Church, but that they were not publicly taught. Many reasons might exist for this, for example, the belief that doctrines might not be fully or properly understood by new catechumens, or that they might be profaned, and so on. Reserve and time are often required for a doctrine's full elucidation and publicity. Newman concedes that the *disciplina arcana* does account for some variations and for the growth of some doctrines, "yet it does not explain the whole, since the variations continue beyond the time when it is conceivable that the [secret] discipline was in force,"[42] and doctrines manifest themselves not abruptly but by a slow but visible growth which gives little sign of coming to an end. None of the above hypotheses appeared to Newman as capable of accounting for the *historical identity* of the Church through the ages.

Newman came to believe that the true test of doctrine was neither immutability nor antiquity but "life and growth." The great truths of the Christian faith had been shaped in the mind of the Church by a gradual process of development. We must, he wrote, take the view

that, from the nature of the human mind, time is necessary for the full comprehension and perfection of great ideas; and that the highest and most wonderful truths, though communicated to the world once for all by inspired teachers, could not be comprehended all at once by the recipients but, as being received and transmitted by minds not inspired and through media which were human, have required only the longer time and deeper thought for their full elucidation. This may be called the *Theory of the Development of Doctrine.*[43]

Newman faced squarely a fact that so struck the Romantic writers: the deep impression made by the distinctive characteristics of the life of cultures, of time and place, on human thought and institutions. Religion, too, is modified and shaped by the environment which surrounds it. Its growth is "interrupted, regarded, mutilated, distorted"; "it may be absorbed by counter energetic ideas"; "it may be coloured by the received tone of thought into which it comes."[44] It may even be destroyed by the development of some foreign or heretical fault that has taken hold of it. But true ideas can absorb, and change, and take on new forms and yet endure. In a passage that has become famous, Newman describes the dynamic process which characterizes living and abiding ideas:

> Whatever the risk of corruption from intercourse with the world around, such a risk must be encountered if a great idea is duly to be understood, and much more if it is to be fully exhibited. It is elicited and expanded by trial, and battles into perfection and supremacy. . . . It is indeed sometimes said that the stream is clearest near the spring. Whatever use may be fairly made of this image, it does not apply to the history of a philosophy or belief, which on the contrary is more equable, and purer, and stronger, when its bed has become deep, and broad, and full. It necessarily rises out of an existing state of things, and for a time savours of the soil. Its vital element needs disengaging from what is foreign and temporary, and is employed in efforts after freedom which become more vigorous and hopeful as years increase. Its beginnings are no measure of its capabilities, nor of its scope. At first no one knows what it is, or what it is worth. . . . From time to time it makes essays which fail, and are in consequence abandoned. It seems in suspense which way to go; it wavers, and at length strikes out in a definite direction. In time it enters upon strange territory. . . . parties rise and fall around it; dangers and hopes appear in new relations; and old principles reappear under new forms. It changes with them in order to remain the same. In a higher world it would be otherwise, but here below to live is to change, and to be perfect is to have changed often.[45]

Newman proceeds to argue that if such a process of development is rejected, the Nicene Creed cannot be justified. But if the hypothesis of development is recognized, then why accept the definitions of the Council of Nicea and reject the Council of Trent? The bishops at Trent, just as at Nicea, shaped new forms of doctrine to protect and to elucidate ancient truths. And what often may appear to be doctrinal "additions" are really organic components of a family of doctrines. They may confirm, suggest, correlate, or illustrate one another. One can furnish evidence for another. If one doctrine is proved, then correlative doctrines may be probable. Take the Incarnation as an exam-

ple. The Incarnation is the antecedent and the archetype of the Sacramental principle. From the Sacraments come "the unity of the Church, and the Holy See as its type and centre; the authority of Councils; the sanctity of rites." The sacrament of baptism develops "into Confirmation on the one hand; into Penance, Purgatory, and Indulgences on the other." Newman stresses how these doctrines, rites, and usages are parts of one whole, how they grow together and sustain one another. He insists that one "must accept the whole or reject the whole; attenuation does but enfeeble, and amputation mutilate."[46]

Now this development of doctrine over time is not essentially one of "logical explication" as taught by the Scholastics, that is, an activity of reasoning in the sense of a highly conscious rational operation, although a logical sequence often can be discerned in retrospect. It is, rather, like an individual's coming to belief and certitude, a spontaneous convergence of factors.

> The question may be asked whether a development can be other in any case than a logical operation; but, if by this is meant a conscious reasoning from premises to conclusion, of course the answer must be in the negative. An idea under one or another of its aspects grows in the mind by remaining there; it becomes familiar and distinct, and is viewed in its relations; it leads to other aspects, and these again to others, subtle, recondite, original. . . . and thus a body of thought is gradually formed without his recognizing what is going on within him.[47]

While Newman rejects "logical explication," his doctrine of development is not to be confused with the modern idea of a "continuing revelation." Newman believed that God's revelation was given to the apostles once and for all, although its full meaning may initially be only implicit and unconscious. An explicit form of a doctrine is not essential to its genuineness or its perfection. As Newman earlier had written in his Oxford University sermon on "The Theory of Developments in Religious Doctrine," "A peasant may have such a true impression, yet be unable to give any intelligible account of it. . . . It is no proof that persons are not possessed, because they are not conscious of an idea."[48]

The first part of Newman's *Essay* is concerned with the nature of organic development. In the second part he attempts to provide the reader with a series of "notes" or criteria that, taken together, might help one to see how it is possible to recognize, indeed to establish, that modern Roman Catholicism is the natural and necessary development of the doctrine of the early Church. By employing biological analogies, Newman suggests seven such "notes"—others might be added—that he finds illustrate and embody an uncorrupted or healthy life. These notes make clear how a person can differentiate the healthy development of an idea from one marked by corruption or dissolution. It is important to stress the suggestiveness (the "varying cogency") of Newman's seven tests and their force when taken as a whole, for it is evident that few persons, not already receptive, were or are persuaded by Newman's criteria. We will mention all of the tests suggested by Newman but exemplify only a few in detail.

The first test of a true development is *preservation of type*. It was important to Newman that there be historical evidence that the Church of the later centuries possessed the distinctive individual features (the "type") of the early Church. To deviate from the type is to become something else. Newman believed that there was evidence that the characteristic features of the early Church were absent in the non-Roman communions but that they were prominent in the Church of Rome.

The second test is *continuity of principles*. By "principles" Newman means "first principles," those beliefs that do not themselves develop but are the laws or governing moral and practical principles which doctrines embody in their development. They are similar to the laws and forms of nature recognized by the physical scientist. Newman says that before the early Church had grown into the full measure of its doctrines, it was rooted in its principles. He expands on ten such principles out of many that he finds govern Catholic Christianity throughout its life and that have assured its continuity. Among these are the principles of *dogma; faith,* as internal assent in contrast to sight or reason; *theology,* or the place of inquiry or science in religion; *the sacramental principle;* the *mystical sense,* for example, in reading Scripture in more than a literal sense; and the principle of *development* itself.

The third criterion is *assimilative power*. A healthy body "grows by taking into its own substance external materials," which then come to enter into its unity. But such assimilation does not distort or corrupt the body; indeed, it perfects it through this strong assimilative potential. No Church has shown this power to borrow from non-Christian sources and rites, and to adapt them to an "evangelical use," as has the Church of Rome. As we shall see, for Protestant historians such as Adolf von Harnack such assimilative power is not always a sign of health but rather a corrupting syncretism.

The fourth criterion is *logical sequence*. Newman uses the term "logical" here not in its formal, inferential sense, but rather in the sense that, in retrospect, one can look back and see how one doctrine leads to another, so that the whole displays a real logical coherence. Newman shows, for example, how the doctrine of Purgatory later developed over the question of how post-baptismal sin could be diminished. Similarly, the decision at Nicea that Christ is *homoousios* (of the same substance) with the Father opens the way logically to the decision, at the Council of Ephesus, that the Virgin Mary is *Theotokos* (Mother of God).

The fifth note of a genuine development is *anticipation of its future*. A living and influential idea often will show or foreshadow itself in earlier as well as later times. Specimens of later teachings can usually be discerned in earlier manifestations. The medieval celibate ideal is anticipated in the early Church's high estimation of the virtue of virginity as found in the writings of the early or ante-Nicene Church Fathers. This anticipation of future development is seen especially, Newman believes, in the New Testament portent of the future Marian doctrines.

The sixth test used by Newman is what he calls *conservative action upon the past* or *preservative additions*. The development of new doctrines can conserve essential doctrines, such as the Incarnation, that had been established in the past. But just as a child may not be wholly recognizable in the grown person, so early doctrines may be conserved in later developments but in ways that may not be instantly obvious. Hence a doctrinal addition may be "in one sense real and perceptible" without distorting or losing what came before; rather, it may be "protective and confirmatory of it." Protestants have said that the devotions paid to Mary have weakened the faithful's devotion to Christ. In response, Newman again reverts to the action of the Fathers at Ephesus in sanctioning the honor of *Theotokos* as a title for Mary. The action was taken "to protect the doctrine of the Incarnation, and to preserve the faith of Catholics from a specious Humanitarianism."[49] Newman contends that it is those very communions that denounce devotion to Mary, and not Catholicism, that have ceased to worship Jesus Christ as God.

Newman's seventh and final note of true development is *chronic vigour.* The Catholic Church, like other institutions, is subject to various perils and attacks, but like a healthy body it has survived these threats, the tests of "fire and water," and thrives—a sign of its genuine development. "She pauses in her course, and almost suspends her functions; she rises again, and she is herself once more. . . . Indeed, it is one of the most popular charges against the Catholic Church . . . that she is 'incorrigible.'"[50] Protestant historians, of course, were to read the Roman Church's "incorrigibility" differently. For them it meant not health but, ironically, a stubborn failure to truly adapt to historical conditions in order that Christianity might retain its authentic witness in the modern world.

Until the very end of the nineteenth century, Newman's *Essay* had little impact on Catholic theology. When it was consulted, it often was interpreted in the terms of the official Neo-Scholastic theology. It frequently was viewed as supporting a rather abstract idea of the "homogeneous evolution" of doctrine, taking Newman's organic analogies much too literally and systematically. At the turn of the century, the Catholic Modernists were drawn to Newman's *Essay,* but, as we will see, they either developed it in a direction that would have horrified Newman or they broke with Newman's organic analogy entirely.

Many Catholic theologians today would argue that, for all of Newman's profound sensitivity to history, his theory seriously underestimates the historically conditioned nature of doctrines and the possibility of their being "reversed." The twentieth-century Catholic theologian Karl Rahner is one who, for example, appears to break with any purely

organic, "homogeneous" conception of doctrinal evolution. He makes use of the concept of the Church's "memory." In its long history, the Church "stores up" in memory many doctrines and practices. But it also "stores up" more than it can always remember or use at any particular moment. Thus, there may also be "forgotten truths" that served their time and purpose. Other theologians use concepts such as "pruning." If one were to use the organic analogy of a developing plant, it would be appropriate to speak of the necessity of "pruning" in order to retain the plant's health and life. Development might then be achieved by pruning away rather than by further expansion. Different times and circumstances may require quite different forms of "development."[51]

It is widely conceded that Newman's apology in the *Essay* is *a priori* and circular, in that it is the Roman Church's developments that are presupposed to be the true ones, providentially guided. That is, Roman doctrinal standards, used as the historical measure, allow Newman to reject Protestant developments out of hand, since they do not issue in Roman Catholicism. In fact, Newman knew little of modern Protestant theology, and most of his concrete examples of identity come from the period up to the sixth century, while he purports to be testing the identity of the *present* Church with that of the earliest. Despite these and other problems, Newman's *Essay* retains a power which is present in his sense of the rich movement of history—a sense which he shared, despite their profound differences, with writers such as Chateaubriand, Herder, Hegel, and Möhler. For all its limitations, Newman's apologetic for Catholic Christianity is *historical.* Western society had awakened to the flux and change wrought by the historical process, and Newman sensed it and openly faced its implications for Christianity. In commenting on the abiding import of Newman's *Essay,* Owen Chadwick may be correct when he concludes: "The idea of development was the most important single idea which Newman contributed to the thought of the Christian Church. . . . In the long view the *Essay* was more weighty than one man's introspection of his predicament. That predicament happened to be only a single case to illustrate the predicament of Christendom."[52]

Faith and Reason: "The Grammar of Assent."

Newman did, indeed, address aspects of the predicament posed for Christian belief by the new attention to history. Yet some, including his compatriot Sir John Acton, believed that Newman also was too quick to dismiss the claims of historical science when they appeared to injure religious interest. Newman's contribution to philosophical theology, it can be argued, certainly has been as influential as his contribution to historical theology. His reflections on the various modes of human reasoning, on inference, assent, and belief, have a very contemporary ring. The question that occupied Newman during his most productive years from the 1830s to the 1870s had to do with the relations of faith and reason as they bear on the question of religious belief.

The nineteenth century in Britain witnessed a longstanding debate over issues posed by the competing claims of science and religion. The controversy is symbolized by, and to a considerable degree traceable to, the influence of two seminal minds: Jeremy Bentham and S. T. Coleridge. The tradition of Benthamite empiricism traces its descent through James Mill and his son, John Stuart Mill, to a host of the latter's disciples, including such influential writers as T. H. Huxley and John Morley. The empiricists came to look to J. S. Mill's *System of Logic* (1843) as a kind of sacred book. It stood in opposition to all "intuitionism" represented, in the minds of the scientific empiricists, by the writings of Coleridge. The empiricists stood by a method of inquiry that claimed to yield truth by reasoning inductively from the facts of experience to an inference or conclusion. Scientific induction alone was the method of progress toward the sifting of fact from opinion. Since belief in this method was crucial to the overcoming of error and superstition, it was a matter of the deepest ethical import. Beliefs are not merely personal matters, since they are that upon which a person is prepared to act. They have social consequences.

In the middle decades of the nineteenth century in Britain, Newman represented, in the minds of the scientific empiricists, the "intuitionist" tradition that was traceable to Coleridge, whose ideas do find echoes in Newman's *Grammar of Assent.* This is especially evident in Newman's conception of the act of assent by means of a natural intuitive inference which he called the "illative sense." Newman's epistemological distinction between "implicit" and "explicit" reason, that is, between the personal and scientific modes of knowing, was worked out in his Oxford University sermons, preached between 1826 and 1846. They embody, in brief, many of the themes that he was to develop more systematically in the *Grammar of Assent.*

In an early sermon, "The Usurpations of Reason," Newman had criticized the eighteenth-century reliance on the rationalistic "Evidences of Christianity." Such a mode of scientific reasoning may be ideal for certain purposes, for example, in cases strictly amenable to logical inference or direct proof. But human belief, Newman insisted, often is swayed by what he calls "antecedent considerations": "previous notices," "prepossessions," and, in the good sense of the word, "prejudices." Such belief or faith is not opposed to reason but is, rather, a particular mode of reasoning based on those antecedent prepossessions that are not always capable of being explicitly exhibited; for "much lies in the character of the mind itself, in the general view of things, its estimate of the probable and the improbable," and so on. While belief cannot be grounded on direct, undisputed proof, it must nevertheless have grounds. But if such a direct proof were required, it would be necessary that "every child, every peasant, must be a theologian." Faith does have grounds, "but it does not follow that all who have faith should recognize, and be able to state what they believe and why."

Several of Newman's ideas about belief, for example regarding assent and the nature of certitude, are not developed in the *Sermons,* but the seeds of his later reflections on these questions are sown in these early discourses. Central to the whole argument about faith in the *Sermons* is Newman's compelling analysis of the pervasive character of the personal, or what today we would call the *existential,* nature of both reasoning and belief:

> Who shall analyze the assemblage of opinions in this or that mind, which occasions it almost instinctively to reject or accept . . . these and similar posi-

tions? Far be it from me to seem to insinuate that they are *but* opinions, neither true nor false, and approving themselves or not, according to the humour or prejudice of the individual: so far from it, that I would maintain that the recondite reasons which lead each person to take or decline them, are just the most important portion of the considerations on which his convictions depends.[53]

Newman's journal reveals that between 1846 and 1866 he tried nineteen times to begin the work that was to be published as *An Essay in Aid of a Grammar of Assent* in 1870. He finally recognized that he should begin the book by an analysis of the contrast between assent and inference, for this, he believed, was the key to the idea that he had been struggling to develop. The analysis of this issue focused, he believed, on the crucial difference between himself and other heirs of John Locke's empiricism. Newman had read Locke as an undergraduate and was drawn to his strong empirical bent. But Newman disagreed with Locke's demand that assent be directly proportioned to evidence. Locke had written that there was one unerring mark of the lover of truth, namely, not to entertain "any proposition with greater assurance than the proofs it is built upon will warrant." "Whoever," Locke continued, "goes beyond this measure of assent, it is plain . . . loves not truth for truth's sake but for some other end."[54]

Locke's Victorian disciples had translated his standard of proof into a new and demanding ethic of belief. And it was directed against the "intuitionists" such as Newman who, they charged, assented to religious beliefs on mere authority or for their practical or spiritual use. Newman was stung by these charges of credulity and a lack of moral rectitude, of wishing to believe on insufficient evidence. He wrote the *Grammar of Assent* in large measure to convince such critics—as he wrote to his scientific friend William Froude—that one can honestly "believe what you cannot absolutely prove."[55]

By 1866 Newman was convinced that it was wrong to focus exclusively on the questions of proof and certitude when inquiring into the nature of human believing. For certitude is only one kind of assent. One should begin, rather, by contrasting assent and inference. Locke had claimed that assent should be proportioned to the evidence. But it follows from this, Newman responds, "that assent becomes a kind of necessary shadow, following upon inference. . . . it is never without an alloy of doubt, because inference in the concrete never reaches more than probability." According to Locke and his followers, assent in matters of fact must always be conditional. For them assent and inference are the same mental activity. And since in matters of fact there can be only degrees of assent, probabilities should never lead to certitude.

Newman thought Locke's assertion about assent to be a "pretentious axiom," unrelated to what we actually experience and do in the real world. There are many truths, for example, that cannot be irrefutably proven yet that we unconditionally accept. Newman points out that when Locke considers the real practices of human beings, his candor requires that he qualify his rigorous standard of proof. In his chapter "On Probability" in the *Essay on Human Understanding,* Locke writes that "most of the propositions we think, reason, discourse, nay act upon, are such as we cannot have undoubted knowledge of their truth; yet some of them *border so near* upon certainty that we *make* no doubt at all about them, but *assent* to them as firmly . . . as if they were infallibly demonstrated."[56]

It is important to note that when Newman speaks of inference he limits his use of the term to considerations of matters of fact, not to the necessary truths of formal logic. Inference is, simply, the giving of reasons for making an assertion of fact, for example, that it will rain tomorrow based on the fall of the barometer, the appearance of dark, low clouds, and so on. But, Newman insists, inference and assent are not the same. Why? First, because the one can be present when the other is absent. Often we continue to assent to a proposition when we have forgotten and can no longer marshall the evidence—for example, the reasons for assenting to a particular complex political position. Second, inference and assent do not vary concomitantly or proportionately. For example, an assent, once given, may cease while the reasons for it are still forcefully present in our minds. Or good arguments may be recognized as good as far as they go, yet they may not be strong enough to command assent. More importantly for Newman, assent is distinct because it is unreserved and unconditional. His study of the actual concrete practices of human beings convinced him of the numberless cases where a person does not assent at all, but none in which assent is evidently conditional. Newman gives many examples of the latter, such as our belief that we exist, that we assent to our memory of what happened this morning, or to the claim that Great Britain is an island.

Logical sequence is not, according to Newman, the method employed by individuals that enables them to gain certitude in such concrete matters. In such cases conditional inferences *can* and *do* move to an unconditional assent through an informal inferential process that involves the accumulation and convergence of probabilities "too fine to avail separately, too subtle and circuitous to be convertible into syllogisms, too numerous and various for such conversion."[57] None of these separate factors may admit of demonstration, but each carries with it "independent probable arguments, sufficient, when united, for a reasonable conclusion."[58] A person might, for example, draw a conclusion to which he or she assents on the basis of a convergence of probabilities derived from historical events, the words of a trusted authority, compelling exemplars, reasonable doctrines or ideas, and personal experience. From the convergence of these factors, a person can achieve a reasonable certitude.

The characteristics of such an informal inferential process are that (1) while it does not supersede logical inference, it moves beyond the purely abstract and is carried out in the untidy world of everyday life that requires judgment and belief; (2) it is an implicit form of reasoning and is not capable of a complete analysis of the motives that carry one to a conclusion, so that the whole is not equal or reducible to the sum of its parts; and (3) such a cumulation of probabilities is a highly individual activity, and it will follow that what to one intellect is a proof is not so to another. Informal inference is our ordinary and natural mode of human reasoning, and Newman gives numerous examples of such "natural inference." The latter often is an uncultivated faculty, similar to a "gift." It often is observed in the untutored person or in the genius, "in those who know nothing of intel-

lectual aids and rules, and those who care nothing of them."[59] The weather-wise farmer exemplifies the first type. In his judgment about the weather, "his mind does not proceed step by step, but he feels all at once and together the force of various combined phenomena, though he is not conscious of them."[60] What is true here about reasoning is also true with regard to taste. The connoisseur often can make a true judgment about the origin of a painting or the authorship of a book when the individual factors taken singly may not be compelling.

What is striking, especially in the case of reasoning, is that the genius in one quarter may prove to be a poor or worthless judge of other matters. "We should betake ourselves to Newton for physical, not for theological conclusions, and to Wellington for his military experience, not for his statesmanship."[61] Newman calls this special power of judging and concluding in *concrete reasoning* the *illative sense*. It is a *personal* certitude, in that it assumes certain first principles or preconceptions, it selects out of the rich complex of concrete experience a point of view, it chooses and discards various testimony, and so on. Because it is personal certitude, Newman recognized that what is reasonable or a proof to one person may be wholly unconvincing to another. Therefore, it is as absurd to attempt to coerce a person by strict logical argument as it would be to torture that person into believing. Here Newman sounds very contemporary in his awareness of the variety of modes of human rationality and in his claim that when individuals understand each other's *meaning* "they see, for the most part, that controversy is either superfluous or hopeless."

Newman was, of course, proposing his philosophy of belief as a defense of religious belief, in which truth and certitude are reached by a different path than would be the case in the sciences. Newman's epistemology, as it bears on concrete reasoning, could, however, be viewed as relativistic because of his insistence on the *personal* nature of such knowledge and certitude. And, in a certain sense, the word "relative" is, perhaps, accurate. But it invites misunderstanding of Newman's position. There are, indeed, a variety of specific modes of reasoning appropriate to the artist, the physicist, and the religious believer, but if one is open and receptive to the understandings of the believer—to those convergent though probable reasons that have led the believer to assent with certitude—there is nothing that would constitute an insurmountable barrier to the nonbeliever's also finding these reasons compelling. It was just such a receptivity to a certain point of view and preconceptions that brought Newman to the position to assent to the truth-claims of the Roman Catholic Church. In the last analysis, however, it was a personal process of informal reasoning, a personal judgment, and a personal certitude.

When the *Grammar of Assent* first appeared, it was received enthusiastically in some circles. Catholic Thomistic and Ultramontane theologians were generally critical or wary, seeing "subjectivist" or "fideistic" tendencies in the book. Yet the English Ultramontane W. G. Ward praised the *Grammar* for its "genius and power" and saw it as serving a critical apologetic role in countering the arguments against Christianity advanced by the scientific empiricists.[62] The most telling criticism of the *Grammar,* voiced by many, was that Newman had produced a brilliant essay on the psychology or phenomenology of belief, but that he had failed to address the laws of *right* or *true* belief. This was the view taken by Leslie Stephen, who complained that Newman had written an account "of the methods by which men are convinced, not the method by which doctrines are proved."[63] Stephen concedes that what one person may consider to be congruous another person will perceive to be incongruous. But this does not establish objective certainty, only subjective conviction. Stephen assumed, however, that certain rules of formal logic and scientific evidence were the true and only measure of reasonable belief and that they always should be given greater weight than the judgments of the "illative sense." Regarding Newman's example of the expert or connoisseur, Stephen points out that such a person's informal inferences can never be considered as conclusive proof for anyone else. And we know that experts are often too peremptory in their judgments and are found to be wrong.

This line of criticism of Newman was pursued not only by the scientific empiricists. Theologians argued similarly. F. D. Maurice, a Coleridgean whom many regard as the most important theologian in mid-Victorian Britain, criticized Newman's failure to recognize some crucial distinctions. Is it not essential, Maurice asked, to distinguish "between faith in the general character of the speaker, which years may have deepened instead of weakening, and assent to a certain proposition depending on evidences with which he may have been imperfectly acquainted?"[64] Critics also disagreed with Newman's claim that assent does not admit of degrees, that it is unconditional and will not allow any alloy of doubt, since a conditional assent cannot be a firm guide to thought or action. Against Newman, one could argue, in the manner of the philosopher William James, that half a loaf is better than nothing when assent to a belief is living, that is, a genuine option and crucially important to us, and when it is forced, in the sense that there is no escaping assent either to the belief or its opposite.

Newman's understanding of unconditional assent may, however, be misunderstood. He certainly agrees that in matters of fact a belief can be based on less than conclusive evidence. But for him the alternatives are neither an agnostic suspension of belief, a mere "wait and see," nor a blind, willful "leap of faith" involving a radical discontinuity. For Newman, belief is an intellectual act, though it does engage the whole person. The "illative sense" leads to an intellectual judgment when the reasons or evidence become compelling. That is, a person does not *leap* to a conviction but, rather, *grows into it,* although the actual assent may be sudden.[65] Newman's understanding of certitude as "a state of mind definite and complete" may be clarified by the use of the concept of a "critical threshold." Newman actually alludes to this idea in his use of the example of boiling water. Water gets hotter and hotter, but it does not come to a boil until it reaches a critical threshold. Once that threshold is reached, however, a decisive, qualitative change takes place, and any increase in temperature after that point is superfluous to the achievement of that qualitative change. M. Jaime Ferreira has employed this idea in illuminating Newman's conception of assent and certitude:

One of the distinctive features of a critical threshold is that there is continuity at the same time as there is discontinuity. The transition achieved in reaching certitude is a qualitative transition: it is an all-or-nothing kind of movement. Although there is not a quantitative cumulation by degrees, it is nevertheless anchored in what preceded it. Evidence, like heat, can be registered during a process, even though the qualitative transition only occurs after the critical threshold is reached.[66]

The Grammar of Assent, we have noted, met with a mixed response. But it provoked a long and lively intellectual debate in the 1870s and beyond. It was the subject of an impressive and protracted debate among the leading British intellectuals in the meetings of the Metaphysical Society, and it incited a similar high-level discussion in the leading British periodicals over several years. Yet the *Grammar,* like the *Essay on Development,* fell into disfavor in many Catholic circles in the latter years of the nineteenth century. This was due in large part to the dominance, even militancy, of the Roman-supported Neo-Scholastic revival and to the perceived threat to the Church by the phe-

nomenon that came to be called Roman Catholic Modernism. While critical of some of Newman's ideas, many of the leaders of both English and French Modernism were also indebted to Newman and wrote favorably about him. When Modernism was condemned by the Vatican in the encyclical *Pascendi gregis* (1907), Newman's writings were placed under a cloud of suspicion, only to come into prominence again in Catholic theology after 1945. Today, Newman's writings are once again influential, and this is especially true of the *Grammar of Assent.* It is now recognized that in both his *Oxford University Sermons* and in the *Grammar,* Newman had subtly explored issues in epistemology and belief that are central to philosophical and theological discussion in the late twentieth century. This renewed interest is especially evident in the scores of articles and books on Newman's present significance which were the outcome of the centenary commemoration of his death in 1990.

NOTES

1. Owen Chadwick, *From Bossuet to Newman: The Idea of Doctrinal Development,* 2d ed. (Cambridge, 1987), p. 103.

2. J. S. Drey, "Revision des gegenwartigen Zustandes der Theologie" ("Toward the Revision of the Present State of Theology" [1812]). The trans. are found in Joseph Fitzer, *Romance and the Rock: Nineteenth-Century Catholics on Faith and Reason* (Minneapolis, 1989), pp. 69, 68, 69, 70–71.

3. J. S. Drey, *Kurze Einleitung in das Studium der Theologie* (*Brief Introduction to the Study of Theology*) (1819), para. 64, p. 27. Cited in Michael J. Himes, trans., *Brief Introduction to the Study of Theology* (Notre Dame, 1994). The translations used here from Drey's two published books—*Die Apologetik,* 3 vols. (1838–1847) and the *Kurze Einleitung*—are those of Himes and of Wayne L. Fehr, *The Birth of the Catholog Tübingen School: The Dogmatics of Johann Sebastian Drey* (Chico, Calif., 1981). The *Apologetic* remains untranslated and is difficult to find. The first German editions of both books were reissued in photographic reprints by Minerva (Frankfort/Mainz) in 1967 and 1966 respectively.

4. Drey, *Kurze Einleitung,* para. 1, p. 1. Cited in Himes, op. cit. I am especially indebted to Fehr's clear exposition of the themes of Drey's theology for this elucidation of his thought.

5. J. S. Drey, *Tübinger Theologische Quartalschrift,* 10 (1828), p. 686. Cited in Fehr, op. cit., p. 57.

6. J. S. Drey, *Theologische Quartalschrift,* 8 (1826), p. 206. Cited in Fehr, op. cit., p. 58.

7. J. S. Drey, *Die Apologetik,* I (1838), para. 35, pp. 303, 306, 305. Cited in Fehr, op. cit., pp. 67, 69, 71.

8. J. S. Drey, *Kurze Einleitung,* para. 47, p. 20. Cited in Himes, op. cit.

9. J. S. Drey, *Die Apologetik,* II (1843) para. 56, p. 212. Cited in Fehr, op. cit., p. 205.

10. Joseph Fitzer, *Möhler and Baur in Controversy, 1832–38: Romantic-Idealist Assessment of the Reformation and Counter-Reformation* (Tallahassee, Fla., 1974). This monograph is not only an excellent study of Möhler's controversy with his Tübingen colleague, the Protestant New Testament scholar and Church historian Ferdinand Christian Baur, but also a useful introduction to the study of Möhler's leading themes.

11. J. A. Möhler, *Unity of the Church* (Mainz, 1825), p. 9.
12. Ibid., sec. 7, p. 21.
13. Ibid., sec. 12, p. 39.
14. Ibid., sec. 3, p. 11.
15. J. A. Möhler, *Unity* (Tübingen, 1825), p. 56. Cited in James T. Burtchaell, *Catholic Theories of Biblical Inspiration* (Cambridge, 1969), p. 18.
16. Ibid., pp. 60–61. Cited in Burtchaell, op. cit., pp. 19–20.
17. J. A. Möhler, *Symbolism, or Exposition of the Doctrinal Differences between Catholics and Protestants as Evidenced by their Symbolical Writings,* trans. James Burton Robertson (New York, 1844 [1832]), pp. 349–350.
18. Ibid., p. 350.
19. Ibid., p. 351.
20. Ibid., p. 352.
21. Ibid., p. 333.
22. Ibid., p. 340.
23. Ibid., pp. 333–334.
24. Ibid., p. 100.
25. Möhler, *Unity of the Church,* p. 168.
26. Möhler, *Symbolism,* p. 376.
27. Ibid., p. 377.
28. Ibid.
29. Ibid., p. 379.
30. A fine account of this subject can be found in Edward Norman, *The English Catholic Church in the Nineteenth Century* (Oxford, 1984).
31. Cardinal Nicholas Wiseman, *The Religious and Social Position of the Catholics in England* (London, 1864), p. 9.
32. Sheridan Gilley, "Vulgar Piety and the Brompton Oratory, 1850–1860," *Durham University Journal,* XLIII (1981), 15.
33. Norman, *English Catholic Church,* p. 312ff.
34. Jaroslav Pelikan, *Development of Christian Doctrine: Some Historical Prolegomena* (New Haven, 1969). p. 3.
35. On these questions of sources and influences on Newman's *Essay,* see Owen Chadwick, op. cit., especially Chap. 5.
36. J. H. Newman, *An Essay on the Development of Christian Doctrine* [1878] (Notre Dame, 1989), p. 30. Unless otherwise indicated, the quotations cited are from this recent reprint of the *Essay* in its third and final edition.
37. Ibid., pp. 6.
38. Ibid., pp. 7–8.
39. Ibid., p. 10.
40. Ibid., p. 12.
41. Ibid., pp. 15–16.
42. Ibid., p. 29.
43. Ibid., pp. 29–30.
44. Ibid., p. 39.
45. Ibid., pp. 39–40.
46. Ibid., p. 94.
47. Ibid., pp. 179–180.
48. John Henry Newman, *Fifteen Sermons Preached before the University of Oxford* (London, 1892), pp. 320–321.
49. Newman, *Essay,* p. 426.
50. Ibid., p. 444.
51. On the reception, interpretations, and limitations of Newman's conception of the development of doctrine, see Nicholas Lash, *Newman on Development* (Shepherdstown, W.V., 1975), esp. Chap. 7; and *Change in Focus* (London, 1973), Ch. 9 and passim.
52. Owen Chadwick, *Newman* (Oxford, 1983), p. 48.
53. Newman, *Fifteen Sermons,* pp. 54ff, 187, 218, 254, 272.
54. John Locke, *Essay Concerning Human Understanding,* II (Oxford, 1894), pp. 428–429.
55. G. H. Harper, *Cardinal Newman and William Froude* (Baltimore, 1933), p. 120.
56. Locke, op. cit., p. 364; J. H. Newman, *Grammar of Assent,* Longman's ed. (1947), p. 121.
57. Newman, *Grammar of Assent,* p. 288.
58. Ibid., p. 291.
59. Ibid., p. 331.
60. Ibid., p. 332.
61. Ibid., p. 341.
62. For an account of the reactions to Newman's *Grammar,* see *An Essay in Aid of a Grammar of Assent,,* ed. I. T. Ker (Oxford, 1985), Introduction, "The Critics"; and James C. Livingston, *The Ethics of Belief: An Essay on the Victorian Religious Conscience* (Tallahasse, Fla., 1974).
63. Leslie Stephen, "Newman's Theory of Belief," *Fortnightly Review* (Nov., 1877), p. 209. This paper was later reprinted in Stephen's *An Agnostic's Apology* (London, 1893).
64. F. D. Maurice, "Dr. Newman's Grammar of Assent," *Contemporary Review,* 14 (1870), p. 156.
65. On this point see, Nicholas Lash, "Introduction," *An Essay in Aid of a Grammar of Assent* (Notre Dame, 1979), p. 12ff.
66. M. Jaime Ferreira, "The Grammar of the Heart: Newman on Faith and Imagination," in Gerard Magill, ed., *Discourse and Context: An Interdisciplinary Study of John Henry Newman* (Carbondale, Ill., 1993), p. 137.

SUGGESTIONS FOR FURTHER READING

I. THE TÜBINGEN THEOLOGY

The best studies of the Tübingen School and its members are in German. Most of the studies in English are brief overviews and essays, some of which are listed below. The twentieth-century Tübingen scholar Josef Rupert Geiselmann put the spotlight on Möhler, Drey, and Kuhn and *"Die Katholische Tübinger Schule."* See his monograph in English, *The Meaning of Tradition* (London: Burns and Oates, 1966). Part II includes a discussion of Drey and Möhler on this important theme. More recent scholars have criticized Geiselmann's too-schematic effort to portray the Tübingen School as an orthodox *alternative* to Neo-Thomism.

The Background of German Theology

Dru, Alexander. *The Contribution of German Catholicism* (New York: Hawthorn Books, 1963). A helpful survey of German Catholic thought from the late eighteenth century to 1918.

McCool, Gerald A. *Catholic Theology in the Nineteenth Century: The Quest for a Unitary Method* (New York: Seabury Press, 1977). A good survey focusing on the theologians of the Neo-Scholastic revival, but with treatments of Hermes, Günther, Italian Ontologism, and Drey and Möhler.

O'Meara, Thomas F. *Romantic Idealism and Roman Catholicism: Schelling and the Theologians* (Notre Dame: Notre Dame University Press, 1982). A study of the influence of Schelling on Catholic thought, but with helpful commentaries on numerous German Catholic thinkers, including Drey, Möhler, Kuhn, and Staudenmaier.

Reardon, Bernard. *Religion in the Age of Romanticism* (Cambridge: Cambridge University Press, 1985). Excellent accounts in Chapters 1, 4, and 5 of Romanticism, Schelling, and German Catholic theology in the Romantic era. Brief but lucid accounts of Drey and Möhler.

Schoof, Mark. *A Survey of Catholic Theology 1800–1970* (New York: Paulist Press, 1970). An account of attempts to integrate historical thinking into Catholic theology. Treats Tübingen scholars and Newman.

Johann Sebastian Drey

In addition to the works of McCool, O'Meara, and Reardon above, see the following:

Burtchaell, James T. "Drey, Möhler, and the Catholic School of Tübingen," in Ninian Smart, et al., *Nineteenth Century Religious Thought in the West,* II (Cambridge: Cambridge University Press, 1985). Brief overview, including Drey, with an excellent bibliography.

——. *Catholic Theories of Biblical Inspiration since 1810* (Cambridge: Cambridge University Press, 1969). The chapter on the "Tübingen School" is an excellent account of Drey, Möhler, Staudenmaier, and Kuhn on the Bible, inspiration, and tradition.

Fehr, Wayne L. *The Birth of the Catholic Tübingen School: The Dogmatics of Johann Sebastian Drey* (Chico, Calif.: Scholars Press, 1981). The most extensive and best treatment of Drey in English. Good bibliography.

Himes, Michael J. "Introduction", J. S. Drey, *Brief Introduction to the Study of Theology* (Notre Dame: University of Notre Dame Press, 1994). Includes helpful bibliography.

Hinze, Bradford E. *Narrating History, Developing Doctrine: Friedrich Schleiermacher and Johann Sebastian Drey* (Atlanta, Ga.: Scholars Press, 1993).

Johann Adam Möhler

In addition to the works of Burtchaell, Geiselmann, McCool, O'Meara, and Reardon above, consult the following:

Fitzer, Joseph. *Möhler and Baur in Controversy, 1832–38: Romantic-Idealist Assessment of the Reformation and Counter-Reformation* (Tallahassee: Scholars Press, 1974). A fine account of Möhler's controversy with the Protestant Tübingen theologian F. C. Baur, with a good exposition and analysis of Möhler's *Symbolik.*

Möhler, J. A. *Unity in the Church,* ed. and tran. with an introduction by Peter C. Erb (Washington, D.C.: Catholic University of America Press, 1995).

Savon, Hervé. *Johann Adam Möhler: The Father of Modern Theology* (Glen Rock, N.J.: Paulist Press, 1966). A brief introductory book, but the only one in English that attempts to deal with Möhler's life as well as his major writings.

II. JOHN HENRY NEWMAN

See the biographies of Newman listed at the end of Chapter 7.

General Studies of Newman's Philosophical Ideas and Theology

Boekraad, A. J. *The Personal Conquest of Truth* (Louvain: Editions Nauwelaerts, 1955).

Ferreira, M. Jaime. *Doubt and Religious Commitment: The Role of the Will in Newman's Thought* (Oxford: Clarendon Press, 1990).

Ker, Ian, and Alan G. Hill, eds. *Newman after a Hundred Years* (Oxford: Clarendon Press, 1990). Over a score of important essays on the whole range of Newman's work and ideas and on Newman the writer.

Magill, Gerard, ed. *Discourse and Context: An Interdisciplinary Study of John Henry Newman* (Carbondale: Southern Illinois University Press, 1993). A dozen essays, most of which explore Newman in wider, including contemporary, contexts.

Vargish, Thomas. *The Contemplation of Mind* (Oxford: Oxford University Press, 1970).

Some of the above studies give critical attention to Newman's *Development of Doctrine* and *A Grammar of Assent*. For specialized studies see:

Chadwick, Owen. *From Bossuet to Newman: The Idea of Doctrinal Development* (Cambridge: Cambridge University Press, 1987). Explores Newman's *Essay* in relation to its earlier context, Newman's theory, and the Roman response.

Ker, I. T., ed. *An Essay in Aid of a Grammar of Assent* (Oxford: Clarendon Press, 1985). This recent critical edition includes an introduction that deals with the development of Newman's ideas, the composition and history of the text, and the critics.

Lash, Nicholas. *Newman on Development* (Shepherdstown, W.V.: Patmos Press, 1975). An analysis of Newman's aim, method of argument, and major ideas and themes in the *Essay*.

Price, H. H. *Belief* (London: Allen and Unwin, 1969). Includes an interesting account of Newman's ideas on belief as developed in the *Grammar*.

Chapter 9
The Post-Hegelian Critique of Christianity in Germany

David Friedrich Strauss

Each in his own way, Kant, Schleiermacher, and Hegel had attempted to reestablish positive Christianity on a new philosophical basis. Beginning in the 1830s, these grand syntheses began to break down. From Hegel to Nietzsche, German thought was characterized in one respect by its relentless philosophical criticism of Christianity. The 1830s and 1840s were dominated philosophically by the students of Hegel, whose system, we have learned, had left considerable room for dispute. This was especially true of two fundamental issues of the time: theism and social philosophy. As mentioned in Chapter 5, these issues divided the Hegelians into two parties, the Right and Left Wing. The Right Wing believed that Hegel's Speculative Idealism was the perfect instrument for interpreting the truths of historic Christianity. The Left Wing, or "Young Hegelians," were convinced that Hegel's "preservation" represented a dissolution of historical Christianity and the emergence of a new humanistic religion.

Among the radical "Young Hegelians" were David Friedrich Strauss, Ludwig Feuerbach, Bruno Bauer, and Karl Marx. These men reveal much in common. All were radical Hegelians; all were activists, and their writings were characterized by a polemical, programmatic spirit; all were ruthlessly logical and honest and, as a result of their writings, were outcasts who suffered from the loss of teaching positions and withdrawal from society. Each contributed to perhaps the most far-reaching historical and metaphysical critique Christianity has yet had to face. An understanding of the writings of these men will therefore illuminate considerably the issues which dominate much of later nineteenth- and twentieth-century theology.

DAVID FRIEDRICH STRAUSS

Karl Barth has said that D. F. Strauss (1808–1874) signifies the bad conscience of modern theology, for he "confronted theology with a series of questions upon which it has not, right down to the present day, perhaps, adequately declared itself."[1] The questions which Strauss raised in a radical way were the historical questions concerning Christianity's origins—questions which, as Barth suggests, more recent theologians have often bypassed. Strauss is not read anymore, and his influence on academic theology was not as considerable as one might expect, even in his own day. However, there probably was no theologian of the nineteenth century who was better known and had a greater influence on intellectual circles outside the Church in both Germany and England than D. F. Strauss.*

D. F. Strauss was born at Ludwigsburg in Germany and from 1821 to 1825 attended the theological seminary at Blaubeuren, where he was a student of the historian F. C. Baur. In 1825 he went to Tübingen, where he came under the influence of the writings of Hegel. He served briefly as an assistant pastor at Klein-Ingersheim near Ludwigsburg and then, in 1831, went to Berlin to attend the lectures of Schleiermacher and Hegel. A few months after his arrival Hegel died of cholera, and Strauss soon lost sympathy with Schleiermacher's teachings. In the spring of 1832, Strauss returned to Tübingen to take up the position of assistant lecturer in the theological college. This offered him an opportunity to lecture on philosophy, and he did so as a zealous disciple of Hegel. At this point in his career, he could write:

> In my theology philosophy occupies such a predominant position that my theological views can only be worked out to completeness by means of a more thorough study of philosophy, and this course of study I am now going to prosecute uninterruptedly and without concerning myself whether it leads me back to theology or not.[2]

Strauss had already come to realize that his theological views were an offense to his colleagues, so he

---

*The influence of Strauss on mid-Victorian English religious thought will be indicated in the next chapter.

refused to deliver lectures on theology. Nevertheless, it was during this period that he wrote his *Das Leben Jesu, kritisch bearbeitet (The Life of Jesus, a Critical Treatment)* which was first published in two volumes in 1835. This book propelled Strauss into the limelight and made him at once the most controversial theologian in Germany. It also destroyed any opportunities for further advancement in either the university or Church. J. C. F. Steudal, the conservative president of the theological college, succeeded in having Strauss removed from his post as lecturer.

Strauss's academic career thus came to an abrupt end. He returned to Stuttgart, where he lived for many years and busied himself with writing to his critics and preparing new editions of the *Leben Jesu*. In 1838–1839 Strauss issued a third edition of the book which was irenical in spirit and conceded many points to his critics. That same year he published a series of monologues entitled "Transient and Permanent Elements in Christianity" which was reissued the following year as "Leaves of Peace." It appeared that these actions might bring about Strauss's reinstatement in the academic world, and in January 1839 he was appointed professor of dogmatics at Zurich. However, conservative opposition prevailed; the government revoked the appointment, and Strauss was pensioned off. This, and his own coming into financial independence at the death of his father, gave Strauss a new sense of freedom and turned him, once and for all, against all attempts at compromise.

In 1840–1841 he published *Die christliche Glaubenslehre (The Christian Doctrine of Faith)* in which he sought to show how Christian doctrine grew out of its ancient environment and became harmonized with later philosophical speculation. The book concludes by advocating the dissolution of traditional supernaturalism, replacing it with a purely secular, Hegelian theology of Absolute Spirit.

From the early 1840s to 1864, Strauss removed himself from theological debate. During this time he served as a journalist, wrote biographies of Ulrich von Hutten and H. S. Reimarus, and entered politics. Strauss reentered the theological arena once again in 1864 with his second life of Jesus, this one entitled *A Life of Jesus for the German People (Das Leben Jesu, für das deutsche Volk bearbeitet)*. It is totally different from the first *Leben Jesu*. Whereas the first book questioned the very possibility of reconstructing a life of Jesus, the book of 1864 is hardly a notch better than the common, garden-variety lives of Jesus that became so popular in the latter decades of the nineteenth century. Strauss tried to write a life of Jesus for the German people as Ernst Renan had done for his fellow Frenchmen. Whereas Renan succeeded in presenting a portrait of Jesus which was, though fanciful, full of life and popular appeal, Strauss failed. The new life of Jesus was stiff and sober, devoid of movement and feeling.

Strauss's last book, *The Old Faith and the New, (Der alte vnd der neue Glaube),* appeared in 1872. This final work reveals no Promethean anti-Christ but, rather, the ideals of an intellectual bourgeois without, as Barth remarks, "the slightest notion of all the true heights and depths of life, the bourgeois quality in its specific national German form at the sunset hour of the age of Goethe."[3]

Indeed, the Strauss of the *Leben Jesu* of 1864 and of *The Old Faith and the New* is a pale, almost unrecognizable reflection of the author of the first *Leben Jesu.* Although these later books went through several editions, they were scorned by the theologians who now declared Strauss intellectually bankrupt. Strauss suffered all his life from rebuffs but never so painfully as in these last years. Not a year after the publication of *The Old Faith and the New,* Strauss was stricken with an internal ulcer which he suffered from for several months until his death in February 1874. The great enemy of Christianity was now dead—dead but not overcome, for the questions which he raised in the *Leben Jesu* of 1835 remain even today. It is, therefore, to the *Leben Jesu* of 1835 that we must turn to learn of the real challenge put to Christian theology by D. F. Strauss.

The *Leben Jesu* of 1835

Albert Schweitzer goes so far as to say of Strauss's first *Life of Jesus* that it "is one of the most perfect things in the whole range of learned literature." The book is provocative and programmatic. Strauss was convinced that the study of the New Testament was impaled on "the antiquated systems of supranaturalism and naturalism" and that the new interpretive key to the New Testament, and especially to the study of the Gospel accounts of Jesus, was the *mythical.*

Strauss acknowledged that this interpretive key was not new but that it had not to his own time been applied to the New Testament in a radically consistent manner. Biblical interpretation had from ancient times been either *supernaturalist* or *rationalist.*

> The exegesis of the ancient church set out from the double presupposition: first, that the gospels contain a history, and secondly, that this history was a supernatural one. Rationalism rejected the latter of these presuppositions, but only to cling the more tenaciously to the former, maintaining that these books present unadulterated, though only natural history. Science cannot rest satisfied with this half measure: the other presupposition must also be relinquished, and the inquiry must first be made whether in fact, and to what extent, the ground on which we stand in the gospels is historical.[4]

This is Strauss's program: to test *the historical claims* of the New Testament concerning Jesus. Strauss felt that most theologians of his day were lacking in the one requirement needed for the pursuit of this task, "namely, the internal liberation of the feelings and intellect from certain religious and dogmatical presuppositions,"[5] the freedom which Strauss felt he had achieved by means of his philosophical studies. Strauss, the disciple of Hegel, concludes his Preface to the first edition with the following claim that could only amaze and shock theologians and historians standing outside the Idealist camp:

> The author is aware that the essence of the Christian faith is perfectly independent of his criticism. The supernatural birth of Christ, his miracles, his resurrection and ascension, remain eternal truths, whatever doubts may be cast on their reality as historical facts . . . that the dogmatic significance of the life of Jesus remains inviolate: in the meantime let the calmness and insensibility with which, in the course of it, criticism undertakes apparently dangerous operations, be explained solely by the security of the author's conviction that no injury is threatened to the Christian faith.[6]

The long introduction to the book consists of an analysis of the development of biblical interpretation to Strauss's own time, the threshold of the mythical point of view, and a consideration as to the reasons why the mythical viewpoint was so long opposed. The basic reasons why the concept of myth was not readily adapted to the study of the New Testament was the long association of the term with the study of pagan religion and the false idea that myth was found principally in primitive cultures in which written records of events were not common. Strauss points out that since the investigations of Bauer, Gabler, and Eichhorn it is clear that, while the New Testament history is by no means altogether mythical, the history is woven through with mythical materials.

Another reason why theologians failed to apply the concept of myth to the New Testament was the supposition that the Gospel events were written by eyewitnesses.

> But this alleged ocular testimony, or proximity in point of time of the sacred historians to the events recorded, is mere assumption, an assumption originating from the titles which the biblical books bear in the Canon. . . . But that little reliance can be placed on the headings of ancient manuscripts, and of sacred records more especially, is evident, and in reference to biblical books has long since been proved. . . . It is an incontrovertible position of modern criticism that the titles of the biblical books represent nothing more than the design of their author or the opinion of Jewish or Christian antiquity respecting their origin.[7]

The fact was that by Strauss's time historians seriously questioned the notion that the Gospel writers were eyewitnesses, and even if only a single generation separated Jesus from these writers, that was more than enough time to allow for mythical elaboration.

Finally, some brave souls had conceded that myth can be found in the traditions concerning the origin and final destiny of Jesus, the birth and ascension traditions, but extended their application of the mythical theory no further.

> Thus the two extremities were cut off by the pruning knife of criticism, whilst the essential body of the history, the period from the baptism to the resurrection, remained as yet unassailed: the entrance to the

gospel history was through the decorated portal of mythus and the exit was similar to it, whilst the intermediate space was traversed by the crooked and toilsome paths of natural interpretation.[8]

Strauss finds no scientific justification for such a limited application of myth as an interpretive key.

> The proceedings of these Eclectics is most arbitrary, since they decide respecting what belongs to the history and to the mythus almost entirely upon subjective grounds. Such distinctions are equally foreign to the evangelists, to logical reasoning and to historical criticism. In consistency with these opinions, this writer applies the notion of the mythus to the entire history of the life of Jesus; recognizes mythi or mythical embellishments in every portion, and ranges under the category of mythus not merely the miraculous occurrences during the infancy of Jesus, but those also of his public life; not merely miracles operated on Jesus, but those wrought by him.[9]

That Strauss overestimates the place of mythical material in the Gospels is generally acknowledged today. However, this should not obscure the significance of Strauss's *historical* discovery, namely that the supernaturalists and rationalists were reading their own presuppositions into the thought forms of primitive Christianity. Quite aware that the Palestinian Jews of Jesus's day lacked an historical consciousness, Strauss assumes, in part rightly, that they thought in mythopoetic terms.

To be unable to conceive of the Jews of Jesus's day thinking mythically is indicative of the failure of the theologians to think historically. Myth, for Strauss, is the natural mode of perception in the prescientific, prehistorical mind. Unmindful of this, or refusing to accept such a view, the supernaturalists are forced to exempt the events of biblical history from the laws of general experience, whereas the rationalists are forced to admit that the witnesses misinterpreted what they saw or that the writers were misinformed. In any case, unconscious or conscious deception is at work. For Strauss no such tortured arguments are required. Myth is the natural language of religion.

> If religion be defined as the perception of truth, not in the form of an idea, which is the philosophic

perception, but invested with imagery, it is easy to see that the mythical element can be wanting only when religion either falls short of it, or goes beyond its peculiar province, and that in the proper religious sphere it must necessarily exist.[10]

According to Strauss, the Gospel writers were generally not guilty of fraudulent intention. The myths with which Jesus's life and works were invested were not inventions but simply lay at hand in the Jewish expectations of a coming Messiah.

> The expectation of a Messiah had grown up amongst the Israelitish people long before the time of Jesus and just then had ripened to full maturity. . . . thus many of the legends respecting him (Jesus) had not to be newly invented; they already existed in the popular hope of the Messiah . . . and had merely to be transferred to Jesus and accommodated to his character and doctrines. In no case could it be easier for the person who first added any new feature to the description of Jesus, to believe himself its genuineness, since his argument would be: Such and such things must have happened to the Messiah; Jesus was the Messiah; therefore such and such things happened to him.[11]

Thus it was that very few new myths were actually formed by the early Christian community; there remained only the necessity of transferring to Jesus the living Messianic legends, already formed, with very few alterations.

Having shown the possible existence of myth as a natural phenomenon in the New Testament, Strauss turns next to the question of how, in particular cases, the presence of myth can be determined, i.e., the criteria for distinguishing the mythical and the historical in the Gospels. Strauss recognizes both negative and positive criteria for determining the presence of mythical material. One can be relatively certain that an event could not have taken place as described, i.e., could not be historical, if the following conditions are present:

I. *Negative. First.* When the narration is irreconcilable with the known and universal laws which govern the course of events. Now according to these laws, agreeing with all just philosophical conceptions and all credible experience, the absolute cause never disturbs the chain of secondary causes by single, arbitrary acts of interposition, but rather manifests itself in the production of the aggregate of finite causalities, and their reciprocal action. When therefore we meet with an account of certain phenomena or events of which it is either expressly stated or implied that they were produced immediately by God himself (divine apparitions—voices from heaven and the like), or by human beings possessed of supernatural powers (miracles, prophecies), such an account is *in so far* to be considered as not historical.

Another law which controls the course of events is the law of succession, in accordance with which all occurrences, not excepting the most violent convulsions and the most rapid changes, follow in a certain order of sequence of increase and decrease. If therefore we are told of a celebrated individual that he attracted already at his birth and during his childhood that attention which he excited in his manhood; that his followers at a single glance recognized him as being all that he actually was; if the transition from the deepest despondency to the most ardent enthusiasm after his death is represented as the work of a single hour; we must feel more than doubtful whether it is a real history which lies before us. Lastly, all those psychological laws, which render it improbable that a human being should feel, think and act in a manner directly opposed to his own habitual mode and that of men in general, must be taken into consideration. As for example, when the Jewish Sanhedrin are represented as believing the declaration of the watch at the grave that Jesus was risen, and instead of accusing them of having suffered the body to be stolen away whilst they were asleep, bribing them to give currency to such a report. By the same rule it is contrary to all the laws belonging to the human faculty of memory that long discourses, such as those of Jesus given in the fourth Gospel, could have been faithfully recollected and reproduced. . . .

Secondly. An account which shall be regarded as historically valid must neither be inconsistent with itself, nor in contradiction with other accounts. The most decided case falling under this rule, amounting to a positive contradiction, is when one account affirms what another denies. Thus, one gospel represents the first appearance of Jesus in Galilee as subsequent to the imprisonment of John the Baptist, whilst another Gospel remarks, long after Jesus had preached both in Galilee and in Judea, that "John was not yet cast into prison. . . ."

Sometimes an occurrence is represented in two or more ways, of which only one can be consistent with reality; as when in one account Jesus calls his first disciples from their nets while fishing on the sea of Galilee, and in the other meets them in Judea on his way to Galilee. We may class under the same head instances where events or discourses are represented as having occurred on two distinct occasions, whilst they are so similar that it is impossible to resist the conclusion that both the narratives refer to the same event or discourse.

II. *Positive.* The positive characters of legend and fiction are to be recognized sometimes in the form, sometimes in the substance of a narrative.

If the *form* be poetical, if the actors converse in hymns, and in a more diffuse and elevated strain than might be expected from their training and situations, such discourses, at all events, are not to be regarded as historical. The absence of these marks of the unhistorical do not however, prove the historical validity of the narration, since the mythus often wears the most simple and apparently historical form; in which case the proof lies in the substance.

If the *contents* of a narrative strikingly accord with certain ideas existing and prevailing within the circle from which the narrative proceeded, which ideas themselves seem to be the product of preconceived opinions rather than of practical experience, it is more or less probable . . . that such a narrative is of mythical origin. The knowledge of the fact that the Jews were fond of representing their great men as the children of parents who had long been childless, cannot but make us doubtful of the historical truth of the statement that this was the case with John the Baptist; knowing also that the Jews saw predictions everywhere in the writings of the prophets and poets, and discovered types of Messiah in all the lives of holy men recorded in their Scriptures; when we find details of the life of Jesus evidently sketched after the pattern of these prophecies and prototypes, we cannot but suspect that they are rather mythical than historical.[12]

Equipped with these rules of historical criticism, Strauss turned to the Gospel accounts of the life of Jesus and painstakingly examined each separate pericope. Each incident is carefully considered, first as it was traditionally explained according to supernaturalism and then according to the accounts of rationalism. Strauss plays the one type of interpretation off against the other, thus opening up the possibility of a mythical explanation of many of the events and discourses of Jesus's career. However, it would be quite wrong to say, as has been done, that Strauss dissolved the life of Jesus into myth. Because of his systematic application of the mythical theory and his isolated approach to each pericope, it is true that Strauss saw far less historical material in the New Testament than most critical historians working on the Gospel traditions today. Nevertheless, he acknowledged that many incidents have an histori-

cal core—including, for example, Jesus's baptism, the cleansing of the Temple, and even Jesus's Messianic consciousness. Strauss also makes it clear that the real facts of the case often cannot be determined, and he wishes especially to guard himself in those instances where he declares "he knows not what happened, from the imputation of asserting that he knows that nothing happened."[13]

Despite the fact that Strauss saw more myth in the Gospels than is warranted, his work on the life of Jesus, in Schweitzer's words, "marked out the ground which is now occupied by modern critical study."[14] We can be fairly certain that those who are still confident of reconstructing the life of Jesus without taking into account the considerable amount of mythical tradition in the Gospels have not taken the trouble to read Strauss. Some indication of the assumptions concerning life-of-Jesus research before Strauss will make clearer the historical significance of his critical work. Until the appearance of Strauss's *Leben Jesu,* it was widely assumed that the Gospel traditions were historical sources for the life of Jesus in the very same sense that Roman histories of Livy could be used as sources for the life of the emperors; also, that the historical Jesus could be easily distinguished from the sources themselves, as the kernel can be extracted from its husk; even more, that Jesus as an historical personality, including his development and his own self-consciousness, were accessible to historical research.

Strauss questioned all of these assumptions. He did not deny that many of the sources had an historical core but emphasized instead that these traditions are fundamentally mythical-religious ideas couched in poetic imagery. Peel away the mythical material, and there is some history, here and there, but exceedingly little—certainly not enough to reconstruct a life of the man Jesus so that he might become accessible as a human personality. For Strauss the only Jesus who is accessible in the sources, i.e., the apostolic testimonies, is the superhuman God-man, the mythical Messianic figure prophesied in the Jewish literature.

"Jesus held and expressed the conviction that he was the Messiah; this is an indisputable fact." Furthermore, Strauss saw Jesus's Messianic vocation as being a temporal and national hope that would be brought about by supernatural, miraculous intervention and Jesus's second advent on the clouds of heaven. Strauss adds: "They who shrink from this view, merely because they conceive that it makes Jesus an enthusiast, will do well to reflect how closely such hopes corresponded with the long cherished messianic idea of the Jews."[15] One notes how similar Strauss's depiction of Jesus's eschatological vocation is to that of Reimarus, although Strauss rejects the latter's conception of Jesus's Messiahship as that of a political revolutionary.

Albert Schweitzer has pointed out that during Strauss's own time his *Life of Jesus* meant "an end of miracle as a matter of historical fact," but for our time it has a more positive historical significance, namely, that Jesus emerges "from the mist of myth" as a Jewish Messiah "whose world of thought is purely eschatological."[16] The judgment of New Testament scholarship in the late twentieth century is less certain of Strauss's picture of Jesus's Messianic consciousness and of Schweitzer's interpretation of Jesus's eschatology. As Hans Frei has written, "the consistent eschatological view set forth by Reimarus, Strauss and Schweitzer, the view of Jesus as a great deluded man, has found a smaller latter-day echo than one might have expected." And yet, as Frei readily acknowledges, the gulf between the Jesus of history and the Christ of the Church's faith left by Strauss's *Life of Jesus* led to a succession of fanciful portraits of Jesus in the nineteenth century. And so Strauss's and Schweitzer's "picture of an eschatological hero and a genius strange to ordinary expectations" has proven to be "a powerful antidote" to those imaginary and sentimental so-called "Lives of Jesus" that followed in the wake of Strauss's negative yield.[17]

It was Strauss then who first raised, in such a radical way, the question of the historical accessibility of Jesus. His importance as a theologian is assured if for no other reason than for posing this historical question, for it has remained at the center of theological discussion to the present day. An indication of Strauss's significance here is seen in his response to his early master, Hegel. The latter had mediated the relationship of dogma and the positivity or particularity of history by means of his speculative dialectic which claimed that positive history and philosophy have, in fact, the same content—that is, that philosophy somehow can establish or save the historical by

demonstrating the latter's "necessity." It is this Hegelian claim that Strauss repudiates. The judgment about historical facts must, he insists, be separated from a priori philosophical or theological claims. In his *Defense of My Life of Jesus against the Hegelians,* Strauss writes:

> My whole critique of the life of Jesus grew out of Hegel's thesis that religion and philosophy have the same content, the first in representational [*Vorstellung*] the second in conceptual [*Begriff*] form. Here is how Hegel's school understood their master's words: The historical credibility of the gospel accounts is demonstrated by the fact that they convey, in representational form, true philosophical ideas. The actuality of history is understood to be derived from the truth of ideas. The whole critical part of my *Life of Jesus* was directed against this position. . . . From the truths of ideas, said I, nothing can be derived concerning historical reliability. The latter must be judged solely in the light of its own laws, in accordance with the rules of events and the nature of the accounts."[18]

Strauss put the *historical* warrants for Christian faith on an uncertain foundation, and all those who take Christianity seriously as an historical religion have had to come to terms with Strauss's questions. If Strauss remains, as Barth claims, the bad conscience of modern theology, it is perhaps because too many theologians since his time have avoided and bypassed his question. Chief among these "avoiders" of Strauss, one can argue, are Karl Barth himself and the theologians of the Dialectical movement in the twentieth century. It is significant that Barth, who claims to love the questions which Strauss raised, at the same time has said that "proper theology begins just at the point where the difficulties disclosed by Strauss are seen *and then laughed at.*" (Italics added.) However, it will take considerably more than laughter to silence D. F. Strauss.

Strauss's work, it was soon shown, had many serious faults.[19] Like many innovators, he carried his discovery too far. The historical material in the New Testament is more extensive than Strauss was wont to admit, and his rather narrow concern with the question of "What really happened" blinded him to other important historical questions such as the *meaning* of the mythical narratives.[20] Nevertheless, these limitations do not minimize Strauss's real significance, which was to demonstrate more dramatically than previous critics that as an historical religion Christianity could not escape the scrutiny of historical-critical research and that this very inquiry raised the vexing question of whether and just how the claims of theology and the findings of critical historical research could be held together. More particularly, he altered the scholarly perception of the character of the New Testament sources.

As if this were not enough, having confronted the historical question in Strauss, Christian theology soon faced an attack of equally serious proportions on its metaphysical flank in the person of Ludwig Feuerbach.

LUDWIG FEUERBACH

Unlike Strauss, Ludwig Feuerbach (1804–1872) was not only a follower of Hegel but studied for two years under the master in Berlin. Son of a Bavarian lawyer, Feuerbach began his academic career in theology at Heidelberg as a student of the rationalist H. E. G. Paulus (who was criticized by Strauss in his *Leben Jesu*) and the Hegelian Karl Daub. Feuerbach was as little impressed by Paulus as was Strauss, calling the former's teachings "a spider web of sophistries." Feuerbach moved to Berlin in 1824 to hear Schleiermacher, Marheineke, and Neander but was drawn to Hegel and soon devoted himself entirely to philosophy. He concluded his studies under Hegel with a dissertation in 1828 and was appointed a Privatdozent in philosophy at Erlangen. There he gave a controversial lecture, "Thoughts on Death and Immortality," which destroyed his chances for any further academic advancement. As a result, Feuerbach gave up his academic career and became a private scholar, living for some time in a small Bavarian village. There he wrote a *History of Modern Philosophy* as far as Spinoza, studies on Leibnitz and Pierre Bayle, and, in 1839, a critique of Hegel's philosophy. Between 1841 and 1848 Feuerbach produced three of his most important works on philosophy and religion, *The Essence of Christianity* (1841), *The Philosophy of the Future* (1843), and *The Essence of Religion,* delivered as lectures in Heidelberg in 1848 but not published until

Ludwig Feuerbach

1851. At the time of his death in 1872, he was living as a private scholar near Nuremberg.

The Critique of Hegel

Although Feuerbach was deeply influenced by Hegel, even as a student he was resolved not to become simply a Hegelian. His dissertation revealed an early move away from Hegel's Idealism toward a more sensuous and materialistic dialectic. In fact, Feuerbach has been referred to as "Hegel's fate," in that his thought represents the complete antithesis of Hegel's, while at the same time having required and been prepared for by the Hegelian system.

Feuerbach found Hegel's philosophy especially deficient in its understanding of the role of sense-experience in knowledge. While he agreed with Hegel that philosophy starts with Being, for Feuerbach Being is not to be equated with Thought but with Nature; and Nature is the ground of all human consciousness and thought, not the reverse. For Feuerbach philosophy must not begin with abstract thought but with the many determinate things which are immediately given to us in sensory experience. Philosophers since Descartes have disregarded sense experience and have been like men "who have torn their eyes out of their heads in order to think more clearly." This is due in part to the fact that modern philosophy has been in bondage to theology. This is especially true of Hegel. Idealism is, in fact, nothing but a new form of Neoplatonism, and, for Feuerbach, Hegel is the last of a long line of Christian apologists.

> Hegelian philosophy is the last refuge, the last rationalistic support of theology. Just as once the Catholic theologians became *de facto* Aristotelians in order to combat Protestantism, so now the Protestant theologians must become *de jure* Hegelians in order to combat atheism. . . . Hegelian philosophy is the last ambitious attempt to reestablish lost, defeated Christianity by means of philosophy, by following the universal modern procedure and identifying the negation of Christianity with Christianity itself. The much lauded speculative identity of spirit and material, infinite and finite, divine and human, is nothing more than the accursed paradox of the modern age: the identity of belief and unbelief, theology and philosophy, religion and atheism, Christianity and paganism, at the very summit, the summit of metaphysics. Hegel conceals this contradiction by making of atheism, the negation, an objective component of God—God as a process, and atheism as one component of this process.[21]

Feuerbach rejects such speculative theology and the various surrogates for God that philosophy has devised. He calls for the first principle of philosophy to be "a *real* being , the true *Ens realissimum—man.*"[22] If one looks deeply within the Hegelian speculative theology, one can discern this true *Ens realissimum,* for Hegel's metaphysics is, Feuerbach contends, in truth "an esoteric psychology." If one pierces behind the outward form of Hegel's metaphysical nonsense, one discovers profound psychological and anthropological truths. What Hegel's religious speculations reveal essentially is the psychological fact of human self-alienation reflected in the religious consciousness of God. Hegel unconsciously has brought to light the fact that religion is the revelation of a self-alienated humanity.

For Hegel the human subject is conceived as God in his self-alienation; for Feuerbach the exact opposite is the truth, i.e., *God is the human subject in self-*

alienation. Thus to understand the truth of Hegel, one must carry out what Feuerbach calls "transformational criticism."

> It suffices to put the predicate in place of the subject everywhere, *i.e., to turn speculative theology upside down,* and we arrive at the truth in its unconcealed, pure, manifest form.[23]

Hegel would state his doctrine of God as follows:

> Man is the revealed God: in man divine essence first realizes itself and unfolds itself. In the creation of Nature God goes outside of himself, he has relation to what is other than himself, but in man he returns into himself:—man knows God, because in him God finds and knows himself, feels himself as God.[24]

For Feuerbach this is the truth turned on its head; God is the revealed human subject:

> If it is only in human feelings and wants that the divine "nothing" becomes something, obtains qualities, then the being of man is alone the real being of God—man is the real God. And if in the consciousness which man has of God first arises the self-consciousness of God, then the human consciousness is, *per se,* the divine consciousness. Why then dost thou alienate man's consciousness from him, and make it the self-consciousness of a being distinct from man, of that which is an object to him? . . . The true statement is this: man's knowledge of God is man's knowledge of himself, of his own nature. . . . Where the consciousness of God is, there is the being of God—in man, therefore; in the being of God it is only thy own being which is an object to thee, and what presents itself *before* thy consciousness is simply what lies *behind* it. If the divine qualities are human, the human qualities are divine.[25]

Turned upside down, Hegel's "speculative theology" gives us the key to the secret about humanity, for the secret of theology is anthropology. In theology humans project their own being into objectivity (God), and hence a person's religion is the self and activity externalized and objectified. "God is, *per se,* his (a person's) relinquished self."[26]

The Reduction of Christianity to Anthropology

Feuerbach originally intended to entitle *The Essence of Christianity* "Know Thyself," for the essence of religion was humanity's own alienated self. Feuerbach thought of himself as a second Luther, for just as Luther had given birth to a new form of Christianity out of the old, so Feuerbach saw himself bringing to birth a new religion of humanity. It was Luther, "the German St. Paul," who taught that faith is "all-powerful," can make possible things that are impossible. "But," writes Feuerbach, "this power of faith or God, unhampered by the laws of nature, is precisely the power of the [human] imagination, to which nothing is impossible." To label Feuerbach an atheist is to fail to appreciate the deeply religious motivation of his work. His religion of humanity is, he claimed, badly misunderstood when simply labeled "atheism."

> He who says no more of me than that I am an atheist, says and knows *nothing* of me. The question as to the existence or non-existence of God, the opposition between theism and atheism, belongs to the sixteenth and seventeenth centuries but not to the nineteenth. I deny God. But that means for me that I deny the negation of man. . . . The question concerning the existence or non-existence of God is for me nothing but the question concerning the existence or non-existence of man.[27]

Feuerbach believed that his critics could rightly accuse him neither of negative motives nor of wishing to destroy religion.

> The reproach that according to my book religion is an absurdity, a nullity, a pure illusion, would be well-founded only if, according to it, that into which I resolve religion, which I prove to be its true object and substance, namely, *man—anthropology,* were an absurdity, a nullity, a pure illusion. . . . I, on the contrary, while reducing theology to anthropology, exalt anthropology into theology, very much as Christianity, while lowering God into man, made man into God. . . .[28]

Feuerbach proceeds to examine Christianity, as the perfect paradigm of religion, according to a strict anthropological method. That is, traced genetically to their human source, Christian beliefs and practices reveal humanity's own deepest self-consciousness—its needs, its fears, and its fondest hopes. "Religion," says Feuerbach, "is the dream of the human mind." But he adds,

> even in dreams we do not find ourselves in emptiness or in heaven, but on earth, in the realm of reality; we only see things in the entrancing splendour of imagination and caprice.[29]

What needs to be done, then, is to "change the object as it is in the imagination into the object as it is in reality."

Religion is actually the revelation of humanity's uniqueness. For only human beings are *homines religiosi,* only in humans is religion identical with self-consciousness, with the consciousness that one has of his or her own unique nature.

> Religion, expressed generally, is consciousness of the infinite; thus it is and can be nothing else than the consciousness which man has of his own—not finite and limited, but infinite nature. A really finite being has not even the faintest adumbration, still less consciousness, of an infinite being, for the limit of the nature is also the limit of the consciousness. The consciousness of the caterpillar, whose life is confined to a particular species of plant, does not extend itself beyond this narrow domain. . . . A consciousness so limited we do not call consciousness, but instinct. Consciousness, in the strict or proper sense, is identical with consciousness of the infinite; a limited consciousness is no consciousness; consciousness is essentially infinite in its nature. The consciousness of the infinite is nothing else than the consciousness of the infinity of the consciousness; or, in the consciousness of the infinite, the conscious subject has for his object the infinity of his own nature.[30]

In Feuerbach's opinion, God is the objectification or projection of humankind's own infinite self-consciousness. Human beings are always projecting great models for emulation, but these models or objects are nothing else but the subject's own, although objectified, nature. Religious consciousness of an object is synonymous with self-consciousness.

> The object of any subject is nothing else than the subject's own nature taken objectively. Such as are a man's thought and dispositions, such is his God; so much worth as a man has, so much and no more has his God. Consciousness of God is self-consciousness, knowledge of God is self-knowledge. By his God thou knowest the man, and by the man his God; the two are identical. Whatever is God to a man, that is his heart and soul; and conversely, God is the manifested inward nature, the expressed self of a man—religion the solemn unveiling of a man's hidden treasures, the revelation of his intimate thoughts. . . .[31]

God is "nothing else than the human being, or, rather, the human nature purified, freed from the limits of the individual man, made objective—*i.e.,* contemplated and revered as another, a distinct being."[32]

This projection of idealized human nature as a distinct divine being to be revered and worshiped is an unconscious process. Ignorance of it is fundamental to the religious consciousness. Religious consciousness is, in fact, the historical sign of humanity's unconscious self-estrangement. Here Feuerbach develops an idea of far-reaching significance, namely, that religion is the principal sign of a person's self-alienation. In religion we see the human being as a divided self. On the one hand, unconsciously the individual is his or her own projected perfection objectified as a deity; on the other hand, the individual sees the self, in comparison with the projected self, as an imperfect, contemptible being. Feuerbach thus says:

> Religion is the disuniting of man from himself; he sets God before him as the antithesis of himself. God is not what man is—man is not what God is. God is the infinite, man the finite being; God is perfect, man imperfect; God eternal, man temporal; God almighty, man weak: God holy, man sinful. God and man are extremes: God is the absolutely positive, the sum of all realities; man the absolute negative, comprehending all negations.[33]

The specific nature of the self-alienation and repression is revealed in the nature of the deity revered and worshiped. Feuerbach contends that in those religions where the differences between God and humans are great, or where the identity of the divine and human is denied, human nature is especially depreciated. "To enrich God, man must become poor; that God may be all, man must be nothing."[34]

The person's depreciation of him or herself is not a loss of the self but only a sign of the self's alienation and repression. What one denies oneself, one enjoys vicariously in God. In a passage which augurs of Freud, Feuerbach explains the psychological process at work.

> He desires to be nothing in himself, because what he takes from himself is not lost to him, since it is preserved in God. Man has his being in God; why then should he have it in himself? . . . What man withdraws from himself, what he renounces in himself, he only enjoys in an incomparably higher and fuller measure in God.
>
> The monks made a vow of chastity to God; they mortified the sexual passion in themselves, but therefore they had in heaven, in the Virgin Mary, the image of woman—an image of love. They could all the more easily dispense with real women in proportion as an ideal woman was an object of love to them. The greater the importance they attached to the denial of sensuality, the greater the importance of the heavenly virgin for them: she was to them in the place of Christ, in the stead of God. The more the sensual tendencies are renounced, the more sensual is the God to whom they are sacrificed.[35]

A person's projection of his or her desires and ideal self in God is not only a sign of self-alienation but also of the fact that this alienated consciousness is what Hegel would call the unhappy or "contrite consciousness." God is the ideal which the individual recognizes he or she *ought* to be. The very disparity between the human empirical and latent self leads to a condition of self-depreciation and suffering. Such a condition could not exist, however, if there were not a genuine identity between the two divided selves.

The inherent necessity of this proof is at once apparent from this—that if the divine nature . . . were really different from the nature of man, a division, a disunion could not take place. If God is really a different being from myself, why should his perfection trouble me?[36]

Humanity's self-alienation reflects our disposition to *project* our own being into God to the extent that his real life is bereft of value and meaning. However, humans also use this contemplation of the self in God as a *compensation* for the poverty of their own empirical life. Here Feuerbach reminds us not only of Freud but of Marx. The human vision of God becomes a surrogate (or opiate) for a real life on earth.

Feuerbach's analysis of the various ways in which human self-alienation finds compensation in religious consciousness is exhaustive and had considerable influence on Marx and later Marxist theories of human alienation. A particularly striking example of a Feuerbachian idea that was a forerunner of Marxist theory is the notion of our alienation from our own creative activity.

The idea of activity, of making, of creation, is in itself a divine idea; it is therefore unhesitatingly applied to God. In activity man feels himself free, unlimited, happy; in passivity, limited, oppressed, unhappy. Activity is the positive side of one's personality. . . . And the happiest, the most blissful activity is that which is productive. . . . Hence this attribute of the species—productive activity—is assigned to God; that is, realized and made objective as divine activity.[37]

In projecting creativity in God, humans fail to live up to their own productive potential. We simply experience creativity vicariously in our imaginative vision of God as Eternal Creator. Such is the nature of our self-alienation. However, to recognize that religion is at the root of the human problem does not mean that the beliefs and practices of religion must be rooted out and destroyed. Rather, it means that what, in the childhood of the race, was thought to be objective must now be recognized as subjective; "what was formerly contemplated and worshiped as God is now perceived to be something *human*."

From an objective point of view, the Christian doctrines and sacraments are nothing but fantasy and illusion, but, understood subjectively, they are expressions of profound human truths. At the time that he wrote *The Essence of Christianity,* Feuerbach agreed with Hegel that Christianity was the most advanced or consummate religion—the religion that is best suited to his transformative analysis in revealing humanity's true nature. Feuerbach, therefore, proceeds to examine each Christian doctrine—Incarnation, the Trinity, Holy Spirit, Prayer, Baptism, the Lord's Supper—to demonstrate how it reflects natural human hopes and ideals, these being the true, anthropological essence of religion. Two examples of Feuerbach's analysis—the Resurrection and the Trinity—will make plain his psychogenetic method.

What lies at the basis of the Christian belief in the mystery of Christ's resurrection? According to Feuerbach's method, the answer should not be hard to determine as follows:

Man, at least in a state of ordinary well-being, has the wish not to die. This wish is originally identical with the instinct of self-preservation. Whatever lives seeks to maintain itself, to continue alive, and consequently not to die. Subsequently, when reflection and feeling are developed under the urgency of life, especially of social and political life, this primary negative wish becomes the positive wish for a life, and that a better life, after death. But this wish involves the further wish for the certainty of its fulfillment. Reason can afford no such certainty. It has therefore been said that all proofs of immortality are insufficient, and even that unassisted reason is not capable of apprehending it, still less of proving it. . . . Such a certainty requires an immediate personal assurance, a practical demonstration. This can only be given me by the fact of a dead person, whose death has been previously certified, rising again from the grave; and he must be no indifferent person, but, on the contrary, the type and representative of all others, so that his resurrection also may be the type, the guarantee of theirs. The resurrection of Christ is therefore the satisfied desire of man for an immediate certainty of his personal existence after death—personal immortality as a sensible, indubitable fact.[38]

Such is Feuerbach's analysis of the "true or anthropological" explanation of belief in the resurrection of Jesus. This belief has something naturally human about it, whereas the Greek concept of the immortality of the soul is far too abstract and bloodless. According to Feuerbach, a belief in bodily resurrection could alone fully gratify human feelings; therefore, the resurrection of the body "is the highest triumph of Christianity" over the "sublime but abstract spirituality of the ancients."

The paradoxical mystery of the Trinity is, likewise, just an objective or alienated reflection of a beautiful human truth. A person can only be satisfied as a whole person, not as disunited and limited. Thus "man's consciousness of himself in his totality is the consciousness of the Trinity."[39] And the reason for this is that human self-consciousness is never an empty, solitary consciousness; it is always a consciousness of self and other, of *I and thou* in separation and participation. So it must be, therefore, with God. Full self-consciousness in God is consciousness of unity in participation.

> From a solitary God the essential need of duality, of love, of community, of the real, completed self-consciousness, of the *alter ego,* is excluded. This want is therefore satisfied by religion thus: in the still solitude of the Divine Being is placed another, a second, different from God as to personality, but identical with him in essence—God the Son, in distinction from God the Father. God the Father is *I,* God the Son *Thou.* . . . Participated life is alone, true, self-satisfying, divine life—this simple thought, this truth, natural, immanent in man, is the secret, the supernatural mystery of the Trinity. But religion expresses this truth as it does every other, in an indirect manner, *i.e.,* inversely, for it here makes a general truth into a particular one, the true subject into a predicate when it says: God is a participated life, a life of love and friendship. The third Person of the Trinity expresses nothing further than the love of the two divine Persons toward each other, the unity of the Son and the Father, the idea of community. . . .[40]

What Christians have done is to substitute for the natural love and real bond of family life this purely religious idea of love and unity. Thus, in compensation for a lost or rejected human love and family fellowship, the Christians have a Father and Son in God. And so the Trinity continues to be an object of wonder and reverence "because here the satisfaction of those profoundest human wants which in reality, in life, they denied, became to them an object of contemplation in God."[41] What is uniquely powerful about Feuerbach's critique of Christianity is that he does not simply reject it as superstition. His is a "hermeneutics of suspicion." from *within* Christianity, offering an alternative reading of its meaning. Christianity is full of meaning, not about God but about human nature and the human heart.

When humanity recognizes the "latent" truth in Christian belief, it no longer needs to objectify these beliefs in a being outside humanity but can perceive them as fully human. Only then can humanity achieve authentic self-realization, or what Feuerbach would call "realized Christianity." Such a humanized religion has at its core the love of neighbor; not the love of an illusory God but of a real human being. Authentic religion is found only in true human communion.

> The being of man is given only in communion, in the unity of man with man, a unity resting on the reality of the distinction between the I and the Thou. . . . Man for himself is man in the ordinary sense; man in communion with man, the unity of the I and Thou, is God.[42]

According to Feuerbach, a social unity based on such a religion of love can alone effect true community, for political unity is always a unity of force or power. Not only is love the basis of true community, but it is also the root of a purposeful life. The real atheist, the person devoid of genuine religious sensibility, is one who has no goal in life.

> Every man must place before himself a God, *i.e.,* an aim, a purpose. The aim is the conscious, voluntary, essential impulse of life. . . . He who has no aim, has no home, no sanctuary; aimlessness is the greatest unhappiness. . . . He who has an aim, an aim which is in itself true and essential, has, *eo ipso,* a religion, if not in the narrow sense of common pietism, yet—and this is the only point to be considered—in the sense of reason, in the sense of the universal, the only true love.[43]

Here, as J. H. Randall has noted,[44] Feuerbach identifies religion with the current existentialist theme of an "ultimate concern" which alone can overcome the threat of meaninglessness.

Feuerbach closes *The Essence of Christianity* with a call for making sacred the most profane of everyday activities. Eating and drinking should be approached, for example, as religious acts.

> Think, therefore, with every morsel of bread which relieves thee from the pain of hunger, with every draught of wine that cheers thy heart, of the God who confers these beneficent gifts upon thee—think of man! But in thy gratitude toward man forget not gratitude toward holy Nature! . . . Forget not the gratitude which thou owest to the natural qualities of bread and wine! . . . Hunger and thirst destroy not only the physical but also the mental and moral powers of man; they rob him of his humanity. . . . It needs only that the ordinary course of things be interrupted in order to vindicate to common things an uncommon significance, *to life, as such, a religious import.* Therefore let bread be sacred for us, let wine be sacred, and also let water be sacred! Amen.[45]

Such, in brief, was Feuerbach's psychogenetic critique of Christianity and his own humanistic philosophy of religion.

While our concern here is Feuerbach's specific critique of Christianity, it is important to note that *The Essence of Christianity* was not Feuerbach's last word on religion. Indeed, he returned to the subject on numerous occasions after 1841 in an effort to formulate a more adequate theory of religion in general, one that would go beyond his critique and interpretation of the Christian religion itself.[46] Most important in these efforts are three books: *The Essence of Religion* (1845), *Lectures on the Essence of Religion* (1848), and *Theogonie* (1857). In these works Feuerbach addresses the criticisms made of *The Essence of Christianity,* especially the fact that it is a theory of Christianity, not of religion as such, for example, that it does not account for primal nature religions or the nontheistic Asian religions.

In these later studies Feuerbach gives much more attention to the human dependence on physical nature in all of its rich diversity, and he does not sharply separate human self-consciousness or the human spirit from nature generally. He points out that in primal and archaic societies human beings feel a dependence on specific objects in nature, such as on animals or plants, and that this issues in ambivalent feelings of fear, awe, and attraction as well as acts of worship, propitiation, and sacrifice. Furthermore, this primal sense of dependence on nature expresses itself in human *egoism,* in the sense that the human imagination not only endows nature with anthropomorphic qualities but expresses itself in human wishes and hopes. The very projection of these spiritual powers and gods is reflective of this imaginative egoism or wishful thinking.

This shift away from the remnants of Hegelianism in his analysis of religion and his earlier emphasis on the humanistic liberation of self-consciousness in a "realized Christianity" also allows the later Feuerbach to break with the notion that Christianity is the most advanced form of religion. In fact, he now sees Christianity, even in its humanistic "realized" form, as inferior to pagan nature worship. The reason is that Christianity, or its humanistic surrogate, attempts to exceed the limits of natural life either in an afterlife or in some abstract notion of the perfection of the species. In the *Lectures* Feuerbach writes that Christianity "tries to make more of man than he should be, and consequently makes less of him than he could be; it tries to make him into an angel and consequently, given the opportunity, makes him into a true devil."[47]

In *Theogonie* Feuerbach develops a new but related ground of religion, not in egoism per se, but in the human drive for happiness. The spirits or gods he now sees as rooted in our primal wish to be happy, which is thwarted by the fear of death and nothingness. The gods alone are not subject to failure and annihilation, and their wishes are always realized. Furthermore, they alone can grant our human wishes, hence the role of prayer and sacrifice. The variety of religions are, then, reflective of the variety of human fears, hopes, and wishes. Here in *Theogonie* we encounter a theme—wish-fulfillment—that will be a central motif in Sigmund Freud's psychoanalytic theory of religion. But we also recognize a thesis that will prove to be critical to Nietzsche's critique of Christianity, for Feuerbach develops the idea that in Christianity the drive for happiness finds resolution only on the other side of the grave, only in an afterlife or a belief in immortality. All the Christian doctrines can be read, then, as supporting this one overriding wish. The result is that Christianity is a religion that devalues this natural finite world in its obsession with an otherworld. Feuerbach thus sees Christianity as a "naysaying," world-renouncing religion, as does Nietzsche. In one of his letters, Feuerbach writes: "There is only one true reasonable religion. It is the joy of life; the delight, which will not permit itself to be interrupted, in whatever is positive in life."[48]

What are we to make of Feuerbach's critique? First, it must be conceded that, with the other Left-Wing Hegelians and with Nietzsche, Feuerbach points to many—what might well be called heretical—*tendencies* that are apparent in historical Christianity. Among these would be an antinomian quietism and other-worldliness; a gnostic denial of the goodness of the natural creation; and an ideological use of its teachings to support injustice, discrimination, and privilege, as well as war and torture. One senses, however, an overreaching here, a lack of balance in Feuerbach's portrayal of real or historical Christianity. Certainly, Christianity provides opportunity for a crippling self-alienation. But can one look at the great Christian artists, poets, philosophers, and scientific geniuses, or at untold ordinary believers, and seriously say that belief in a Creator God arrested their creative potential, so that they could only experience creativity vicariously? Can one truly say that Christianity abstracts humans from nature and makes them wholly preoccupied with a life beyond the grave, or that Christianity sees all bodily instincts and needs as evil? To say that these are intrinsic or normative to Christianity is to see Christianity from a highly selective viewpoint and also, it would appear, with prejudice and malice.

Feuerbach makes much, in the second part of *The Essence of Christianity,* of the contradictions in Christian theism, many of which are derived from the effort to join personalistic or anthropomorphic attributes of God with abstract concepts such as eternality, impassibility, omnipotence, and so on. Yet Feuerbach views the crude anthropomorphism as normative and wants it to remain unmodified—an easy target for psychogenetic reduction. As an authority on Feuerbach comments:

He [Feuerbach] insisted that it was precisely the literal anthropomorphism of theism that reveals its true origins and that constitutes its appeal. This may, perhaps, be the case, but it is not self-evidently so and if accepted without any question puts the theologian in an unfair position: insofar as the theologian attempts to modify the idea of God, he or she is accused of not dealing with real religion; if, on the other hand, the theologian accepts anthropomorphism, he or she is ridiculed.[49]

This, unfortunately, is not an uncommon strategy of modern critics of theism.

Finally, another common criticism of Feuerbach merits mention. It has to do with the irony that Feuerbach, the materialist and nominalist, engages in the most egregious abstraction in his discussion of human beings, an abstraction that leads him into a sentimental and idolatrous humanism. Feuerbach discusses individual human beings in terms of what he calls "species man" or the "consciousness of the species." In speaking of individual humans in this interchangeable way, he appears to attribute divinity to the individual human. In any case, it is clear that his transformative analysis of God issues in the ascent of the species humanity to a point where it culminates in the actual apotheosis or deification of humanity itself. Had he started from a truly existential point of view, Feuerbach would have begun with individual human beings, not humans in general. And had he done so, as Karl Barth suggests, "he might perhaps have seen the fictitious nature of the concept generalized man. He would then perhaps have refrained from identifying God with man, the real man, that is, who remains when the element of abstraction has been stripped from him."[50]

Feuerbach's influence on modern thought far exceeds that of thinkers of much greater reputation and popularity. Many of Feuerbach's themes foreshadow ideas that became commonplace in twentieth-century Existentialism. Kierkegaard, Nietzsche, Heidegger, and Sartre are all deeply influenced by Feuerbach's work. Contemporary social psychology, especially the work of Freud and Erich Fromm on religion, is difficult to conceive without Feuerbach, and Martin Buber's philosophy of I-Thou is profoundly indebted to Feuerbach's view of persons in community. But most significant of all is

Feuerbach's role in the development of the social theories of Karl Marx and Friedrich Engels. Early Marxism is unthinkable without Feuerbach, and Marx's mature thought was built on the foundation of his early writings. Feuerbach, therefore, served as *the* bridge between Hegel and Marxism. It was Feuerbach's *The Essence of Christianity* which both liberated the young Marx from Hegel and also made him aware of the profound truth latent in Hegel's thought. Marx's first reaction to the appearance of *The Essence of Christianity* was to advise all speculative theologians that "there is no other road to truth and freedom for you than through the 'brook of fire' (Feuerbach). Feuerbach is the *purgatory* of our time."[51] Friedrich Engels was also to write later about the "liberating effect" that Feuerbach's book had on the Young Hegelians and how they "all became disciples overnight."

Feuerbach's influence on Marx and Engels is especially important for our purposes, for, while his effect on these men was far-ranging, it was of particular significance in the development of their critique of Christianity—a critique that has prevailed in large parts of the world in the twentieth century. The Hegelian critique of Christianity finds its historical consummation in the socioeconomic theories of Karl Marx and his later disciples.

KARL MARX

Karl Marx (1818–1883) was born into the family of a Westphalian lawyer. His father, Herschel Marx, was of Jewish descent, politically liberal and philosophically rationalist, being an admirer of Voltaire and Kant. Herschel Marx, nevertheless, was baptized a Protestant Christian in 1816, although his new religious confession apparently was lukewarm and motivated largely by prudential considerations. Young Karl was baptized in 1824. At seventeen Karl entered the University of Bonn to study law but transferred the next year to Berlin. In Berlin he joined the circle of Young Hegelians called the Doctors Club. Here Marx came under the influence of Strauss, Bauer, and Feuerbach. However, Berlin proved too conservative for this radical new Hegelian, and he moved on to the University of Jena, where he received his doctor's degree in 1841.

The following year Marx began his long and stormy career as a journalist. He joined the staff of the newly founded *Rheinische Zeitung,* a daily paper of which he soon became editor-in-chief. In 1843 the Prussian government suppressed the paper, and Marx went to Paris, where he joined a group of fellow radicals, including Arnold Ruge, in the publication of the *Deutsch-Französische Jahrbücher.* In the first and only issue that appeared, Marx wrote an article entitled "Introduction to the Criticism of the Hegelian Philosophy" in which he set forth his first critical thoughts on religion. As we shall see, at this point Marx still reflects the influence of Feuerbach.

It was during this Paris period that Marx met his future friend and collaborator, Friedrich Engels. Engels was the son of a wealthy industrialist but had come under the influence of both the radical Hegelians in Germany and the English socialists. He had just come to Paris from Manchester where, while working for his father's firm, he had written a study of the situation of the working classes in England.

Early in 1845 Marx and his collaborators were expelled from France. He moved to Brussels, and there he wrote eleven "Theses on Feuerbach," which were discovered and published by Engels forty years later. The "Theses" and "The German Ideology," written with Engels in 1845–1846, signal Marx's break with Feuerbach and the emergence of his own socioeconomic critique of religion.

In 1847 Marx joined the International Communist League and was commissioned with Engels to write a declaration of aims for the league's Congress held in London. The result was *The Communist Manifesto.*

In 1864 Marx founded the International Working Men's Association, or First International, and in 1867 the first volume of *Das Kapital,* "the Bible of the working class" as it was called, was published in Hamburg. The second and third volumes were published posthumously by Engels in 1885 and 1894.

Marx's naturalistic critique of religion is found in his earliest writings. In the preface to his doctoral dissertation, he wrote:

> Philosophy makes no secret of it. Prometheus' admission: "In sooth all gods I hate" is its own admission,

its own motto against all gods, heavenly and earthly, who do not acknowledge the consciousness of man as the supreme divinity.[52]

What Marx had early received from Feuerbach was a naturalistic humanism freed from the abstruse speculations of Hegelian theology. Between 1841 and 1844 Marx remained a true Feuerbachian, and his comments on religion during this period reflect Feuerbach's influence. Read carefully, however, they indicate the beginning of a movement away from Feuerbach's rather abstract discussion of humanity's self-alienation in religion to a more concrete analysis of the historical factors producing such an alienated consciousness. In the Introduction to *The Critique of Hegel's Philosophy of Right* of 1844, Marx says, in Feuerbachian fashion, that humans have searched for a superman in some heavenly realm but have found nothing but their own alienated reflection. The basis of all criticism of religion must, therefore, be that

> *Man makes religion,* religion does not make man. In other words, religion is the self-consciousness and self-feeling of man who has either not yet found himself or has already lost himself. But *man* is no abstract being squatting outside the world. Man is *the world of man,* the state, society. This state, this society, produce religion, *a reversed world-consciousness* because they are *a reversed world.* [Religion] is . . . *the fantastic realization* of the human essence because the *human essence* has no true reality. The struggle against religion is therefore mediately the fight against *the other world,* of which religion is the spiritual *aroma.* . . . Religion is only the illusory sun which revolves around man as long as he does not revolve round himself.[53]

Marx goes on, however, to indicate more exactly than Feuerbach the sociopolitical source of humanity's distress.

> Religious distress is at the same time the *expression* of real distress and the *protest* against real distress. Religion is the sigh of the oppressed creature, the heart of a heartless world. . . . It is the opium of the people. . . . The abolition of religion as the *illusory* happiness of the people is required for their *real* happiness.

The demand to give up the illusions about its condition is the *demand to give up a condition which needs illusions.* . . . Thus the criticism of heaven turns into the criticism of the earth . . . the *criticism of theology* into the *criticism of politics.*[54]

The criticism of religion does not end, then, with a general psychogenetic analysis of alienation; it proceeds to an analysis *and* overthrow of all social and economic relations that so debase and enslave humans that they require the solace of religious illusions. Take away the social conditions that produce illusions about another world, and the religious need for such otherworldly illusions will wither away. Here is the revolutionary imperative in Marx which was lacking in Feuerbach's humanism. It is stated with classic succinctness by Marx in his eleventh thesis on Feuerbach: "The philosophers," says Marx, "have only *interpreted* the world, in various ways; the point, however, is to *change* it."[55]

Marx's break with Feuerbach and the development of an historically "realized" humanism is indicated in the "Theses on Feuerbach" written a year after the critique of Hegel but not published until 1886. Feuerbach's theory of religious self-alienation is inadequate, according to Marx, because it fails to explain concretely what historical conditions produced certain kinds of illusory beliefs. Feuerbach's theory is deficient, therefore, in its exclusive concentration on individual psychology. For Marx the real source of alienation is rooted in humanity's social life and not in personal alienation from some abstract essence. This is expressed as follows in Marx's fourth thesis:

> Feuerbach starts out from the fact of religious self-alienation, the duplication of the world into a religious, imaginary world and a real one. His work consists in the dissolution of the religious world into its secular basis. He overlooks the fact that after this work is completed the chief thing still remains to be done. For the fact that the secular foundation detaches itself from itself and establishes itself in the clouds as an independent realm is really only to be explained by the self-cleavage and self-contradictoriness of this secular basis. The latter must itself, therefore, first be understood in its contradiction, and then revolutionized in

practice by the removal of the contradiction. Thus, for instance, once the earthly family is discovered to be the secret of the holy family, the former must then itself be criticized in theory and revolutionized in practice.[56]

Self-alienation is not found by turning inward on the self but outward on the realities of the social life of human beings.

> Feuerbach resolves the religious essence into the *human* essence. But human essence is no abstraction inherent in each single individual. In its reality it is the ensemble of the social relations. . . . Feuerbach, consequently, does not see that the "religious sentiment" is itself a *social product,* and that the abstract individual whom he analyzes belongs in reality to a particular form of society.[57]

For Marx the nature of a religion can be learned by examining the concrete social conditions that produced it. Therefore, there is no single essence of religion such as Schleiermacher's reduction of religion to the feeling of absolute dependence. Religion is always a cultural product, and thus each religion reflects the unique social conflicts of its particular culture. Remove the social conflicts, and you remove the religious illusions required by the conflicts.

In *The German Ideology,* written with Engels in 1845–1846, Marx developed for the first time his theory of the relationship between religion and "ideology." In this work Marx contends that consciousness, including humanity's religious ideas, is the product of society. Humanity's primordial consciousness was rather limited, consisting principally of a consciousness of the immediate sensuous surroundings. But as human social life evolved, consciousness became more and more determined by other, social factors, principally by the division of labor and attendant economic changes. This was, of course, evident to other sensitive observers during the "Iron Age" of the Industrial Revolution—the period during which Marx wrote. However, for Marx the *determinative* shapers of human consciousness were the economic conditions which separated persons into classes and which perpetuated socially stratified conditions by means of a "ruling class" ideology. Ideology, according to Marx, is any

social idea—legal, philosophic, religious—which is used by the class in political and economic power to maintain its own class interests. Marx remarked that "the ruling ideas of each age have always been the ideas of its ruling class."[58] It therefore follows that the religion of a particular culture not only reflects the conflicts inherent in that culture's social structure but also reveals the religious ideology or system that perpetuates the interests of the ruling class. However, we should not think that every ruling class ideology is a cynical form of brainwashing. Most often it is an unconscious and sublimated product of the material conditions producing the particular socioeconomic structure. But that such ideological consciousness is the product of material life-processes is unquestionable. In *The Communist Manifesto* written in 1847–1848, two years after *The German Ideology,* Marx asks:

> Does it require deep intuition to comprehend that man's ideas, views and conceptions, in one word, man's consciousness, changes with every change in the conditions of his material existence, in his social relations and in his social life? What else does the history of ideas prove, than that intellectual production changes its character in proportion as material production is changed? . . . When people speak of ideas that revolutionize society, they do but express the fact that within the old society the elements of a new one have been created, and that the dissolution of the old ideas keeps even pace with the dissolution of the old conditions of existence.[59]

During the early 1840s both Marx and Engels came under the influence of another Left-Wing Hegelian named Moses Hess. Hess had transformed Feuerbach's conception of religious self-alienation into a theory of economic alienation. According to Hess, the essential attribute of humans is creativity or productive activity. However, this original creativity has been perverted by egoistical individuals who exploit human productivity for their own selfish gain. They exploit human labor in order to amass private property or money. Hence, for Hess, money is the symbol of the alienation of humans from one another. "Money," says Hess, "is the product of mutually alienated men; *it is externalized man."*[60] He saw an analogy between Feuerbach's interpretation of human self-alienation in Christianity and the social alienation in capitalist societies. In fact, he interpreted both Christianity and capitalism as different expressions of the same egoistic religious phenomenon. Money and God are both forms of externalized humanity and *human* alienation. In the one case humans externalize themselves psychologically in God; in the other they externalize themselves materially in money. Hess thus contended that the "essence of the modern world of exchange, of money, is the realized essence of Christianity. The commercial state . . . is the promised kingdom of heaven, as, conversely, God is only idealized capital."[61] Hess called upon humans to give up their worship of both God and worldly acquisitions.

> You have been told that you cannot serve two masters at once—God and Mammon. But we tell you that you cannot serve either one of them, if you think and feel like a *human* being. Love one another, unite in spirit, and your hearts will be filled with that blessedness which you have so vainly sought for outside of yourselves, in God. *Organize,* unite in the real world, and by your deeds and works you will possess all wealth, which you have so vainly sought in *money.*[62]

Marx was profoundly influenced by Hess's economic transformation of Feuerbach's doctrine of alienation, and one can observe in the writings of the mid-1840s and later Marx's joining together the themes of economic alienation and religious ideology. The influence of Hess is most pronounced in a concluding section of Marx's essay "On the Jewish Question." Following Hess, Marx sees a parallel between the alienation produced by the capitalist religion of money-worship and the self-alienation produced by Christianity. However, Marx called this practical religion of money "Judaism," probably because the word in German (*Judentum*) connoted "commerce," as well as the religion of the Jewish people. For Marx, "Judaism" is the worship of money:

> What is the world cult of the Jew? *Huckstering.* Who is his worldly god? *Money.* . . . Money is the jealous one God of Israel, beside which no other God may

stand. Money dethrones all the gods of man and turns them into a commodity. Money is the universal, independently constituted value of all things. It has, therefore, deprived the whole world, both the world of man and nature, of its own value. Money is the alienated essence of man's work and his being. This alienated being rules over him and he worships it.[63]

In Marx's view, Christianity and "Judaism" (capitalism) are the theoretical and practical forms of humanity's egoistic alienation. Marx believed that historical evidence showed that Christianity served as a theoretical or "ideological" superstructure and justification for capitalism. Just as belief in God is a surrogate for a genuine personal life, so a person's work in capitalist society is no longer his or her own but belongs to another. In *Capital* Marx indicates that Christianity and capitalism go hand in hand.

> The religious world is but the reflex of the real world. And for a society based upon the production of commodities, in which the producers in general enter into social relations with one another by treating their products as commodities and values, whereby they reduce their individual private labour to the standard of homogeneous human labour—for such a society, Christianity with its *cultus* of abstract man . . . is the most fitting form of religion.[64]

Marx, of course, did not contend that Christianity is the *cause* of human alienation. Christianity is merely one of the evil, attendant effects of the socioeconomic system. Thus Marx was not basically concerned with attacking religion,* for he was confident that a revolutionary change in the socioeconomic order which made such a religion possible would lead to the withering away of Christianity. Where the

---

*Nor did Marx make a careful study of the origins of any of the world's religions on the basis of dialectical materialism, as Freud did with his discovery of the Oedipus complex and infantile projection. And what Marx wrote was historically ill-informed. However, later Marxists, including Engels, did apply Marxist principles to the interpretation of movements in the history of Christianity. Engels wrote a Marxist interpretation of Early Christianity and of the Peasants' Revolt at the time of the Reformation. For a classic example of the application of Marxist principles to the study of the origins of Christianity, see Karl Kautsky, *Foundations of Christianity* (New York, 1953).

conditions of alienation no longer exist, there will be no need for the religious hypothesis—religion will be "transcended." Marx prophesied that such a stage of human history would come with the proletarian revolution and the abolition of private property, the source of human alienation. Communism would, therefore, be the *definitive* resolution of the conflict between humans. It is, Marx said, "the solution of the riddle of history."

The question of whether Marx's "solution" to the riddle of history, as set forth in *Capital,* should be viewed as in the tradition of empirical science or imaginative vision is much debated. One can legitimately view Marx's writings as a great mythical drama of secular redemption or as a vast apocalyptical prophecy.[65] Marx has his own concept of the *imago Dei* in human creativity or productivity; he has his fall and expulsion from Paradise, occasioned by humanity's egoistic greed and resulting in estrangement from oneself and one's fellow humans. Marx also has his Anti-Christ (the Capitalists), his Armageddon and Last Judgment (the Proletarian Revolution and defeat of the Capitalists), and his New Jerusalem (the classless society). Louis Halle, for example, sees Marx as a Messianic herald of a new religion for our secular, industrial age.

> We understand Marx best as a visionary who was overcome by a great dramatic vision. . . . We understand him best as the maker of a myth. . . . He was a man of vast literary imagination who had a mythic vision that, in the circumstances of the industrial revolution, was destined to move men with the power of a new religion. At a time when factories were mushrooming in England and on the Continent, when millions of people were losing their ancient independence and becoming wage-slaves to the owners of the new machines—at such a time, what could have greater appeal than this drama in which the oppressed proletarian, suddenly in the last act, overthrows the capitalist tyrant, bringing into being the Kingdom of Heaven on Earth?
>
> Jesus had spoken to shepherds in pastoral terms, not to factory workers in the terms of industrial society. . . . Marxism met the city man's need for a new body of belief. It met the need for a religion of the industrial age.[66]

It is not difficult to point out the serious limitations in Marx's critique of Christianity. He sees it in entirely "Idealist" and other worldly terms. He appears to have no sense of the prophetic and subversive, in contrast to the legitimating, role of Christianity in history—or its "protest against real suffering" that he finds in his own prophecy. The naiveté of his own religious vision of an overthrow of the capitalists and the emergence of the classless paradise is often remarked. It takes some credulity to believe that a change in economic systems will bring about a race of selfless, peaceful, and just human beings. Marx's prophetic attack on the dehumanizing structures of nineteenth-century industrial society, though admirable, lacks any sense of prophetic self-criticism of communist society itself. As Paul Tillich has pointed out, one of the tragedies of Marxism is the fact that the victorious Communist party was never able to apply criticism against itself.[67]

Marx's contention that religious beliefs and sentiments would wither away with a change in humanity's socioeconomic condition also lacks historical and empirical support. Social science has demonstrated, nevertheless, that there is a close relationship between socioeconomic class and the *form* of religious belief and practice *and* that socioeconomic structures are frequently supported by religious ideologies. Marx's recognition of the relationship between religious belief and social ideology is a genuinely positive contribution to the study of religion, and contemporary sociologists of religion are greatly in his debt.

The world-historical influence of Marx's ideas are epochal, of course, and it is not predictable what the final effect of Marxist thought will be on Christianity. Its effect on the institutional Church in Russia, China, and parts of Europe and Africa in the twentieth century has been immense, though Christianity is reviving in many of those previously Communist-dominated countries. Nevertheless, Marx's materialist doctrine has been perhaps the most serious challenge that Christianity has yet suffered in the modern world. In volume two of this work, attention will be given to the Marxist-Christian dialogue and to the relationship between Marxism and Liberation theology in the latter decades of the twentieth century.

NOTES

1. Karl Barth, *Protestant Thought: From Rousseau to Ritschl* (New York, 1959), p. 386.
2. *Deutsche Revue,* June 1905, p. 343ff.. Quoted in Albert Schweitzer, *The Quest of the Historical Jesus* (New York, 1961), pp. 70–71.
3. Barth, op. cit., p. 370.
4. D. F. Strauss, *The Life of Jesus Critically Examined,* trans. from 4th German ed. by George Eliot (London, 1906), p. xxix.
5. Ibid., p. xxx.
6. Ibid.
7. Ibid., p. 70.
8. Ibid., p. 64.
9. Ibid., pp. 64–65.
10. Ibid., p. 80.
11. Ibid., pp. 83–84.
12. Ibid., pp. 87–89.
13. Ibid., p. 92.
14. Schweitzer, op. cit., p. 84.
15. Strauss, op. cit., pp. 284, 296.
16. Schweitzer, op. cit., p. 95.
17. "David Friedrich Strauss," in N. Smart, ed. *Nineteenth Century Religious Thought in the West,* I (Cambridge, 1985), 243.
18. Hans W. Frei, *The Eclipse of Biblical Narrative: A Study in Eighteenth and Nineteenth Century Hermeneutics* (New Haven, 1973), p. 336.
19. Strauss's own contemporary, F. C. Baur, while recognizing the genuine importance of the *Leben Jesu,* offered some trenchant criticisms of Strauss's handling of the Gospel sources and his extreme negativity toward some of the New Testament data. See P. Hodgson, *The Formation of Historical Theology: A Study of Ferdinand Christian Baur* (New York, 1966), pp. 73–84.
20. On this point see the criticism of Van A. Harvey, "D. F. Strauss' *Life of Jesus* Revisited," *Church History,* Vol. 30 (June 1961), 191ff. Also, Frei, op. cit., p. 242.
21. L. Feuerbach, "Zur Kritik der Hegelschen Philosophie," *Sämtliche Werke,* II (Jodl ed., 1959), 277.
22. L. Feuerbach, *The Essence of Christianity,* trans. George Eliot (New York, 1959), p. xxxv.
23. L. Feuerbach, *Kleine Philosophische Schriften,* ed. Max Gustav Lange (Leipzig, 1950), p. 56.
24. Feuerbach, *Essence of Christianity,* p. 228.
25. Ibid., p. 230.
26. Ibid., p. 31.
27. *Sämtliche Werke* (Stuttgart, 1903), I, xiv–xv. Cited in Sidney Hook, *From Hegel to Marx* (New York, 1950), pp. 222–223.
28. Feuerbach, *Essence of Christianity,* p. xxxviii.
29. Ibid., p. xxxix.
30. Ibid., pp. 2–3.
31. Ibid., pp. 12–13.
32. Ibid., p. 14.
33. Ibid., p. 33.
34. Ibid., p. 26. Again: "The more empty life is, the fuller, the more concrete is God. The impoverishing of the real world and the enriching of God is one act. Only the poor man has a rich God" (p. 73).
35. Ibid., p. 26.
36. Ibid., p. 33.
37. Ibid., pp. 217–218. For this reference and its significance for Marx, as elsewhere in this chapter, the author is dependent on Robert Tucker's excellent discussion of Feuerbach and Marx in Chapters 5 and 6 of *Philosophy and Myth in Karl Marx* (Cambridge, 1961).
38. Ibid., p. 135.
39. Ibid., p. 65.
40. Ibid., p. 67.
41. Ibid., p. 70.
42. Feuerbach, *Kleine Philosophische Schriften,* p. 169. Cited in Tucker, op. cit., p. 91.
43. Feuerbach, *Essence of Christianity,* p. 64.
44. J. H. Randall, Jr., *The Career of Philosophy,* II, 374.
45. Feuerbach, *Essence of Christianity,* pp. 277–278.
46. On Feuerbach's later critique of religion, see Van A. Harvey, "Ludwig Feuerbach and Karl Marx," in Smart, op. cit., Chap. 9.
47. Ludwig Feuerbach, *Lectures on the Essence of Religion,* trans. Ralph Manheim (New York, 1967), p. 302.
48. Karl Grun, *Ludwig Feuerbach in seinen Briefwechsel,* I, 316. Cited in Harvey, op. cit., p. 320.
49. Harvey, op. cit., p. 300.
50. Barth, op. cit., p. 361.
51. K. Marx and F. Engels, *Historische-Kritische Gesamtausgabe, erste Abteilung,* I, 1, 175. Cited in Tucker, op. cit., p. 81.
52. Karl Marx, *On Religion* (Moscow, n.d.), p. 15.
53. Ibid., pp. 41–42.
54. Ibid., p. 42.
55. Ibid., p. 72.
56. Ibid., p. 70.
57. Ibid., p. 71; Theses VI and VII.
58. Ibid., p. 88.
59. Ibid.
60. Hess, *Sozialistische Aufsätze,* 1841–1847 (Berlin, 1920), p. 167. Cited in Tucker, op. cit., p. 110.
61. Ibid., p. 170. Cited in Tucker, op. cit., p. 110.

62. Hess, p. 149. Cited in Hook, op. cit., p. 198.
63. Marx and Engels, *Historische-Kritische Gesamtausgabe,* I, 1, 601, 603. Cited in Tucker, op. cit., p. 111.
64. Marx, *On Religion,* p. 135.
65. The "antireligious" religion of Marx has often been commented on. Reinhold Niebuhr, Robert Tucker, Louis Halle (see bibliography), and many others have interpreted Marx as a secular religious visionary and mythmaker.
66. Louis J. Halle, "Marx's Religious Drama," *Encounter* (October 1965), p. 37.
67. Paul Tillich, *Perspectives on 19th and 20th Century Protestant Theology* (New York, 1967), p. 191.

SUGGESTIONS FOR FURTHER READING

THE LEFT-WING HEGELIANS AND THE POST-HEGELIAN CRITIQUE OF CHRISTIANITY IN GENERAL

Brazill, William J. *The Young Hegelians* (New Haven: Yale University Press, 1970).

Hook, Sydney. *From Hegel to Marx* (Ann Arbor: University of Michigan Press, 1962).

Löwith, Karl. *From Hegel to Nietzsche* (New York: Holt, Rinehart and Winston, 1964).

Marcuse, Herbert. *Reason and Revolution: Hegel and the Rise of Social Theory,* 2d ed. (Boston: Beacon Press, 1960).

Thielicke, Helmut. *Modern Faith and Thought* (Grand Rapids: Eerdmans Publishing Company, 1990). Chapter 14 deals with the critiques of Strauss, Feuerbach, and Marx.

Toews, John Edward. *Hegelianism: The Path toward Dialectical Humanism 1805–1841* (Cambridge: Cambridge University Press, 1980). Good study of Hegel's project and its appropriation by Strauss, Bauer, and Feuerbach.

David Friedrich Strauss

Barth, Karl. *Protestant Thought: From Rousseau to Ritschl* (New York: Harper, 1959). An interesting appraisal of Strauss and his significance for theology.

Frei, Hans. "David Friedrich Strauss." In *Nineteenth Century Religious Thought in the West,* I, ed. Ninian Smart (Cambridge: Cambridge University Press, 1985). Important short study that focuses on the place of Strauss in the early nineteenth-century discussion of Christology and the problems posed by historical science.

Harris, Horton. *David Friedrich Strauss and His Theology* (Cambridge: Cambridge University Press, 1973). The best theological biography of Strauss in English that makes available valuable material in translation.

Harvey, Van A. "D. F. Strauss' *Life of Jesus Revisited,*" *Church History,* Vol. 30 (June 1961). A fine analysis of the strengths and weaknesses of Strauss's historical work.

Hodgson, Peter C. "Introduction" to D. F. Strauss, *The Life of Jesus Critically Examined* (Philadelphia: Fortress Press, 1973). A valuable essay on Strauss's theological development from 1825 to 1841.

Massey, Marilyn Chapin. *Christ Unmasked: The Meaning of "The Life of Jesus" in German Politics* (Chapel Hill: University of North Carolina Press, 1983). An important study of the social context of Strauss's *Life of Jesus.*

———. "Introduction" to D. F. Strauss, *In Defense of My Life of Jesus against the Hegelians,* trans. and ed. Marilyn Chapin Massey (Hamden, Conn.: Archon Books, 1983). This introduction to Strauss's defense of his *Life of Jesus,* and the defense itself, illuminate the theological issues between Hegel, the Right-Wing Hegelians, and Strauss on the issue of Christology and history.

Schweitzer, Albert. *The Quest of the Historical Jesus* (New York: Macmillan, 1961). Chapters 7–9 represent a classic study of Strauss and his significance, emphasizing the theme of "consistent eschatology," but are weak on other aspects of Strauss's work.

Ludwig Feuerbach

The works of Barth, Brazill, Hook, Löwith, Marcuse, and Toews cited above all contain interesting accounts of Feuerbach's philosophy and critique of Christianity. In addition, the following studies are recommended:

Barth, Karl. "Introduction" to Ludwig Feuerbach, *The Essence of Christianity* (New York: Harper Torchbook, 1958).

Harvey, Van A. "Ludwig Feuerbach and Karl Marx." In *Nineteenth Century Religious Thought in the West,* I, ed. Ninian Smart (Cambridge: Cambridge University Press, 1985). A valuable essay that traces Feuerbach's effort to develop a theory of religion well beyond the publication of *The Essence of Christianity.*

———. *Feuerbach and the Interpretation of Religion* (Cambridge: Cambridge University Press, 1995). The best study of the subject.

Kamenka, Eugene. *The Philosophy of Ludwig Feuerbach* (London: Routledge and Kegan Paul, 1970). A highly readable, thematic study of Feuerbach's philosophy including his critique of religion.

Tucker, Robert C. *Philosophy and Myth in Karl Marx* (Cambridge: Cambridge University Press, 1961). Chapters 5 and 6 of this book give a good analysis of Feuerbach's philosophy and his influence on Marx.

Wartofsky, Marx. *Feuerbach* (Cambridge: Cambridge University Press, 1977). An important, full-length study of Feuerbach's philosophical development up to 1843 but with little attention to what Feuerbach wrote about religion after that date.

Karl Marx

The works of Harvey, Hook, Löwith, Marcuse, Thielicke, and Tucker, cited above, all contain worthwhile accounts of Marx's critique of religion. The following studies are recommended:

Kee, Alistair. *Marx and the Failure of Liberation Theology* (London: SCM Press, 1990). Good exposition and analysis of Marx on religion.

Lash, Nicholas. *A Matter of Hope. A Theologian's Reflections on the Thought of Karl Marx* (Notre Dame: University of Notre Dame Press, 1982). Contains valuable critical insights on Marx's critique of religion but also is an effort to reflect on Marx's positive doctrines from a theological perspective.

McLellan, David. *Karl Marx, His Life and Thought* (New York: Harper and Row, 1973). Among the many biographies of Marx available in English this is perhaps the best.

———. *The Thought of Karl Marx: An Introduction* (New York: Harper and Row, 1971). Useful chronological and thematic study for the initiate.

Plamenatz, John. *Karl Marx's Philosophy of Man* (Oxford: Oxford University Press, 1975). A critical analysis by a foremost scholar of political thought.

Schaff, Adam. *Marxism and the Human Individual* (New York: McGraw Hill, 1970). A good introduction to the humanistic interpretation of Marx.

Chapter 10
The Encounter Between Science and Theology:
_____ Biblical Criticism and Darwinism _____

Charles Darwin

In Chapter 9 we reviewed aspects of Christianity's encounter with modern thought in Germany in the first half of the nineteenth century. It was there that the so-called modern hermeneutics of suspicion emerged in the thought of the post-Hegelians—Strauss, Feuerbach, and Marx. It is worth noting, however, that Germany did not initiate the encounter of Christianity with modern critical thought. Germany actually came late to the discussion, only in the last decades of the eighteenth century. The influence of English critical thought was more impressive as well as influential in Europe in the late seventeenth and eighteenth centuries, influencing both the French and the German Enlightenment. Continental thinkers were greatly indebted to Locke and to Newton, to the English Deists—John Toland, Matthew Tindal, Anthony Collins, and Conyers Middleton—and, of course, to David Hume. The great German orientalist J. G. Eichhorn (1752–1827), who pioneered the literary-critical study of the Old Testament, conceded that the Germans had built on the ideas initially imported from England: "Now," he wrote, "the sons of the Britons' grateful German pupils can give back to the Britons the light which was kindled for their fathers—and give it back stronger, purified, and clarified."[1] Indeed, what the Germans received from the English they raised to the heights of a great science. German biblical scholarship in the nineteenth century is one of the supreme achievements of humanistic learning. And the English interest in the scholarly pursuit of biblical criticism coincidentally declined in the last years of the eighteenth century and did not revive until the 1860s. In the latter decades of the nineteenth century, however, a group of learned British scholars were able to match German biblical scholarship and to correct the extravagance and speculative tendencies of some German scholarship. In this chapter we will explore the challenges to Christian theology posed specifically by the historical-literary criticism of the Bible and by the sciences of geology and biology as these resulted in the movement known as Darwinism. We will begin with an analysis of the impact of biblical criticism. Because the laurels go to the Germans, we will trace briefly some of the highlights of German biblical scholarship, beyond the contributions of Semler, Reimarus, Herder, and Strauss, whom we already have met. We will give greater attention to the interesting story of the response in England to the advances in biblical criticism at mid-century. We will then focus on the challenges to Christianity posed by the natural sciences after 1840 and on the responses to Darwinism, specifically by a variety of Anglo-American Christian thinkers.

ADVANCES IN THE STUDY OF THE BIBLE

Since its beginnings, Christianity has claimed to be an historical religion—that is, has claimed that the crucial biblical events having to do with its origin and development are historically reliable. These events—even those understood to be miraculous and supernatural—purport to describe what actually happened in the world of space and time. At least this was the view of the Bible that was held until late in the eighteenth century. With the advent of the Enlightenment, miraculous biblical events, though frequently recognized to be historical, were now often given natural interpretations and explanations. This type of criticism was carried out by the English Deists and by writers like H. E. G. Paulus and Reimarus in Germany. With Herder and the Romantics a new interpretive principle emerged: The Bible must no longer be viewed through the

dogmatic lenses of the Church's confessions and theology but must be read like any other book, just as the Greek and Roman classics were being read. That is, the Bible must be read *historically,* but this means in its own temporal, cultural, and linguistic context. The scholar must ask of the Bible the same historical-literary questions that one puts to Homer or Hesiod: Do we possess the original text? Is the author the one claimed by tradition? Is it a single or a composite work? What sources are used by the author? Does internal evidence confirm or challenge the time and place of composition? What social or other factors are evident in the shaping or modifying of the text and its purpose? And what is the literary genre or form of the text: Is it poetry, legend or tale, myth, history, or something else?

It was the German Old Testament scholars J. G. Eichhorn (1752–1827), J. P. Gabler (1753–1826), and W. M. L. de Wette (1780–1849) who systematically raised these kinds of historical and literary questions about the Old Testament, questions that had not previously been so explored. Eichhorn, along with Herder, saw the Old Testament as a collection of oriental literary texts, written by different authors, each with its own style, idiom, and context. He recognized that the primeval history in Genesis was largely mythological in nature, and he observed, from internal evidence, that the Book of Isaiah was written by several authors living in different historical periods. De Wette raised serious questions about the Mosaic authorship of the Pentateuch, or the first five books of the Old Testament, by showing that the book of Deuteronomy was closely related to the book discovered in the Jerusalem temple during King Josiah's reign in 621 B.C.E. Subsequently, the Mosaic authorship of the Pentateuch was questioned by many scholars, and various sources and hypotheses began to be proposed.

Reimarus and Strauss had, of course, raised similar questions regarding the New Testament, especially about the value of certain documents in reconstructing what could be known historically about the figure of Jesus. The most influential German scholar in this regard was F. C. Baur whom we met in Chapter 5 as representing a qualified endorsement of an Idealist speculative theology. Baur's importance as a New Testament scholar rests in the fact that he did not separate the New Testament canon from its historical context but saw the canonical texts as reflecting their historical situation. Furthermore, he saw Church doctrine as not emerging after the New Testament but as being worked out in and through the conflicts of various parties and points of view regarding Jesus and his teaching present in the New Testament itself. This insight resulted in Baur's famous theory of an original antithesis between Jewish and Gentile Christianity that slowly became synthesized, through the threats of the Gnostic heresy and division, into the unity of early Catholicism.

This too-schematized view of how primitive Christianity developed led Baur to search for the distinct "tendency" in each document and to a chronology of the New Testament writings that required that he date some "Catholic" writings very late in the second century C.E. Baur rightly saw that the Epistles of St. Paul were the earliest Christian documents, but he was led to conclude that only four of Paul's Epistles—Romans, I and II Corinthians, and Galatians—were unquestionably authentic. First Corinthians and Galatians reveal a struggle between parties, which Baur saw as the Jewish party devoted to Cephus (Peter) and the Gentile party represented by Paul and his break with the Jewish law. According to Baur, it was not until the middle of the second century that a genuine reconciliation took place in the emerging Catholic Church. Thus he dated the Catholic Epistles late.

Baur rightly saw that the Gospel of John is different from the Synoptic Gospels; he dated it about 170 C.E., asserting that it represented Jesus in such a way as to reflect the overcoming of the opposition between the earlier Jewish and Pauline Christianity in the later post-apostolic period. Baur's theory of the development of early Catholic Christianity and his consequent chronology and dating of the New Testament writings was soundly criticized later in the century by New Testament critics, such as the learned English scholar J. B. Lightfoot (1828–1889), and today many of Baur's specific literary judgments are rejected. What he accomplished, however, was to set a standard of historical-critical scholarship and to insist on the contextualization of the New Testament documents in their historical environment, and these remain prerequisites for any serious study of the New Testament to this day.

What all of these new historical-literary inquiries did, of course, was to raise questions about the genuineness and trustworthiness of, for example, Genesis or the Gospel of John as *historical* sources— that is, whether or not a text was meant to be read as history, or as myth, story, or wisdom, and whether it had been edited, or even falsified or corrupted. Now these kinds of questions received little public airing in England between 1800 and 1860. The works of the great German biblical scholars were not translated into English until after mid-century, and only a few English biblical scholars studied in Germany or were influenced by German critical work. One of the exceptions was Henry Hart Milman (1791–1868), Dean of St. Paul's Cathedral in London from 1849 to 1868. He was well versed in German biblical criticism, and in his *History of the Jews* (1829), first published anonymously, he sought to portray the ancient Hebrews as a people of their own time and culture. Furthermore, he was willing to suggest natural interpretations of many supernatural events and viewed the story in Joshua of the sun standing still as poetic license and not as historical fact. He referred to Abraham as an oriental "Emir" and to Joseph as a "Vizier." While falling short of the critical erudition of the Germans, Milman's study of the Jews and his history of early Christianity prepared the way for the acceptance of biblical criticism in England by demonstrating that such criticism was not simply negative or hostile to belief.

Another Englishman who was familiar with German thought was Connop Thirlwall (1797–1875), the Bishop of St. David's for thirty-four years. Early in his career he had published a translation of Schleiermacher's *Critical Essay on St. Luke* (1825) with a favorable introduction, chiding the Oxford scholars for their ignorance of German and their suspicion of German scholarship. He also collaborated with his friend Julius Hare in the translation of the great German historian G. B. Niebuhr's *History of Rome* (1828–1832). Niebuhr's history applied the most recent methods of historical criticism to the Roman documents and, in passing, made critical comments on the received view of Genesis. The orthodox in England charged Niebuhr with unbelief, and Thirlwall came to his defense. Thereafter,

Thirlwall and Hare were accused of "Schleiermachery" and with destroying the divine inspiration and authority of Scripture. The courage of clergymen like Milman, Thirlwall, and Thomas Arnold in commending the methods of recent German criticism cost them support in high places and put them under a cloud of suspicion.

What troubled many progressive English clergy and theologians was the unethical position taken by their superiors on the question of biblical criticism. Many, like Bishop Samuel Wilberforce of Oxford, acknowledged the nonhistorical character of the early chapters of Genesis but at the same time held that such views could not be allowed to be admitted publicly by clergy holding office in the Church of England. The progressives saw this for what it was: an uncandid hypocrisy. The protest against it by John William Colenso, Bishop of Natal in South Africa, is interesting. His entry into the field of biblical scholarship was motivated by a deep moral revulsion against the attitude of deceitfulness and bad faith regarding the Bible and modern criticism that he encountered among the clergy. He saw biblical criticism as liberating believers from having to accept every passage of Scripture literally or the entire text as the Word of God. In Part I of *The Pentateuch and Joshua Critically Examined* (1862), Colenso makes this point. "How thankful we must be," he writes,

> that we no longer are obliged to believe, as a matter of fact, of vital consequence to our eternal hope, the story related in N[umbers] XXXI, where we are told that a force of 12,000 Israelites slew all the males of Midian . . . and then, by command of Moses, butchered in cold blood all the women and children. The tragedy of Cawnpore [the Indian massacre of English women and children in 1857], where 300 were butchered, would sink into nothing compared with such a massacre, if, indeed, we were required to believe it.[2]

The consciences of many clergy and laity were profoundly shaken and shaped by this moral issue. Much of the religious turmoil among the educated in early and mid-Victorian England is explained by it.

If English thought was out of touch with intellectual movements on the Continent in the early decades of the nineteenth century, the isolation could not last. The Oxford Movement was able to delay the full airing of critical questions in the Church; and its failure to see anything but "Infidelity" in the work of scientific criticism was, in part, responsible for the uncertainty and the loss of faith that gripped so many of the ablest young minds in England during the 1840s and 1850s. Keble's advice to Thomas Arnold "to pause in his inquiries and to pray earnestly for help and light from above," sincere as it was, did not meet the challenge of persistent intellectual questioning which sensitive young persons were unable to put aside. Liberal views were beginning to have a wider exposure in the universities. In 1846 George Eliot's translation of Strauss's *Life of Jesus* was published and had a very large sale. Strauss's critical principles and mythical theories were also introduced to the public by his English disciple, Charles Hennell, whose *Inquiry Concerning the Origin of Christianity* appeared in 1838.

It was not only the new biblical criticism that created uneasiness; the growing interest in the new discoveries and theories of natural science also caused religious unrest. In the period between 1830 and 1860, England saw a rapid rise of popular interest in science and the appearance of numerous popular books on natural history. Especially significant was Robert Chambers's *Vestiges of the Natural History of Creation,* a book that acquainted the English public with the idea of evolution. This flood of new ideas, complex and not easily assimilated, brought on a variety of response and ushered in an age of doubt and perplexity.* Some responded to the new knowledge by ignoring it or, like Pusey, by convincing themselves that it would eventually be proven wrong. Others, like Frederick Harrison, hastily and often uncritically accepted the new science and

---

*Many factors were responsible for the Victorian crisis of belief and the growth of skepticism and agnosticism. Biblical criticism and science were major causes, but the apparent cruelty implied in such Christian doctrines as predestination and eternal damnation was also a significant factor in turning sensitive spirits like Francis Newman and J. A. Froude away from orthodoxy. See H. R. Murphy, "The Ethical Revolt against Christian Orthodoxy in Early Victorian England," *American Historical Review* (LX, 1955).

became apostles of Auguste Comte and Positivism. For most, however, there was no easy victory but a long and often indecisive battle between the recognition of the undeniable findings of science and the deep convictions of a sensitive religious spirit.* Many hoped against hope that the old religious views could be preserved, but, as the great New Testament scholar B. F. Westcott observed at the time, "The broad stream of events could not be stayed." The question was whether theology could be "guided along fertilizing channels" or whether it would be allowed to follow a reactionary course.

The encounter between theology and the new sciences is a major chapter in the intellectual history of the second half of the nineteenth century. Not all of the controversies can be chronicled here. But the two mentioned earlier—occurring almost simultaneously in the 1860s—stand out as especially significant, both in their effects and because they raised some of the most fundamental issues theology has yet found itself faced with in an age of unprecedented scientific advance. In the case of each dispute, we will attempt to clarify what were the real issues by giving a brief account of the conflict itself. Then we will illustrate how a few representative theologians responded to the scientific challenge and something of the present significance of this chapter of history.

ESSAYS AND REVIEWS

In February 1860 a collection of seven essays was published under the title *Essays and Reviews*. At first the book was taken little account of, but it soon became the center of one of the most bitter religious controversies of the century. The significance of *Essays and Reviews* was two fold. Scientifically, it was a landmark in the acceptance of the historical-critical study of the Bible in the English-speaking world.

*The spiritual conflicts and pilgrimages of many of the eminent Victorians is a fascinating and moving story. For an introductory account of Victorian belief and unbelief, see Basil Willey, *More Nineteenth Century Studies: A Group of Honest Doubters;* and A. O. J. Cockshut, *The Unbelievers;* and Frank M. Turner, *Between Science and Religion: The Reaction to Scientific Naturalism in Late Victorian England.*

Popularly, it helped to introduce theological issues to the educated public and to make for a more liberal attitude toward differences of religious conviction. Of this latter effect the historian W. E. H. Lecky has written:

> No change in English life during the latter half of the nineteenth century is more conspicuous than the great enlargement of the range of permissible opinions on religious subjects. Opinions and arguments which not many years ago were confined to small circles and would have drawn down grave social penalties, have become the common-place of the drawingroom and the boudoir. The first very marked change in this respect followed, I think, the publication in 1860 of the "Essays and Reviews."[3]

The publication of such a book of essays was first proposed by Henry Bristow Wilson (1803–1888), a country vicar and graduate of St. John's College, Oxford. Wilson had long been a champion of theological freedom and was one of the liberal opponents of the Tractarians. He asked Benjamin Jowett, then Regius Professor of Greek at Oxford, to contribute an essay to the volume. The invitation appealed to Jowett, since it offered him the opportunity of publishing an article on the critical study of Scripture on which he had been at work for a decade. Jowett's essay proved to be the most important, if not the most controversial, of the seven that were printed. All of the essays were concerned with theological freedom; three had to do specifically with freedom to examine Scripture in the light of current discoveries in the historical and natural sciences. What was especially significant, and shocking to some, was the fact that all but one of the essayists were ordained clergymen. Three (Jowett, Frederick Temple, and Mark Pattison) were also distinguished educators and Oxford men of high reputation.

What all of the essayists felt deeply was that, because of its fear of scholarly criticism, Christianity was losing the best minds of the generation. As Jowett remarked: "In a few years there will be no religion in Oxford among intellectual young men, unless religion is shown to be consistent with criticism."[4] Many recognized this and yet feared that an open statement of the problems facing Christian belief would be too negative and might upset or even destroy the faith of the less mature. While sensitive to this possibility, Jowett felt the situation made silence morally reprehensible.

> We do not wish to do anything rash or irritating to the public or the University, but we are determined not to submit to this abominable system of terrorism, which prevents the statement of the plainest facts, and makes true theology or theological education impossible. . . .[5]

Most of what the essayists wrote would be considered fairly commonplace today. One or two of the essays were slightly contentious and, in retrospect, needlessly provocative. Professor Baden Powell's "On the Study of the Evidences of Christianity" smacks of a too-confident rationalism, and some statements of Temple and Jowett cause us to smile at their optimism and Victorian moralism. Nevertheless, the significant critical principles for which these writers sought recognition are considered indispensable today to the serious biblical scholar.

What concerned most of the essayists were the dogmatic constraints which had been placed upon the interpretation of the Bible—especially the concept of inspiration which conceived of divine revelation as coextensive with the written Scripture itself. The term "Word of God" was particularly mischievous, for it is

> a phrase which begs many questions when applied to the canonised books of the Old and New Testaments, a phrase which is never applied to them by any of the Scriptural authors, and which, according to Protestant principles, never could be applied to them by any of sufficient authority from without. In that which may be considered the pivot Article of the Church this expression does not occur, but only "Holy Scripture," "Canonised Books," "Old and New Testaments." It contains no declaration of the Bible being throughout supernaturally suggested, nor any intimation as to which portions of it were owing to a special divine illumination, nor the slightest attempts at defining inspiration . . . nor the least hint of the relation between the divine and human elements in the composition of the biblical books. . . .[6]

The essayists wished to free theology of a crude biblicism which was making it increasingly difficult to be both a Christian and a thinking person. What was needed was an openness to the findings of modern science and a widening of the ideas of inspiration and revelation. In Rowland Williams's essay on "Bunsen's Biblical Researches," a concern to acknowledge the results of the literary and historical study of the Bible is the predominant theme, while in C. W. Goodwin's "On the Mosaic Cosmogony" the desperate attempt to salvage the scientific veracity of Genesis is shown to be doomed to failure. The two essays reflect the two major threats to the old biblicism: critical historiography and natural science.

The Essays of Williams and Goodwin

Williams's essay is an enthusiastic review of the biblical researches of Baron von Bunsen, a learned Prussian diplomat whose popular works on the Bible showed the influence of the most up-to-date German scholarship. Williams uses his review of Bunsen as a means of commending the methods and findings of historical criticism and to suggest a more acceptable view of revelation. He begins with the hermeneutical principle affirmed by most of the essayists: The Bible must be read like any other book. "We cannot," Williams contends, "encourage a remorseless criticism of Gentile histories and escape its contagion when we approach Hebrew annals; nor acknowledge a Providence in Jewry without owning that it may have comprehended sanctities elsewhere."[7] If the Bible is studied like other texts, much that was taken before as only fantastic can now be seen in its natural light.

> Our deluge takes its place among geological phenomena, no longer a disturbance of law from which science shrinks, but a prolonged play of the forces of fire and water, rendering the primeval regions of North Asia uninhabitable, and urging the nations to new abodes.[8]

Nor should the critic blink at what the science of literary analysis tells us about many cherished Christian beliefs concerning prophecy.

Fresh from the services of Christmas, he may sincerely exclaim, *Unto us a Child is born;* but he knows that the Hebrew translated *Mighty God,* is at least disputable, that perhaps it means only Strong and Mighty One, Father of an Age; and he can never listen to anyone who pretends that the Maiden's Child of Isaiah VII, 16, was not to be born in the reign of Ahaz, as a sign against the Kings Pekah and Rezin.[9]

To recognize the natural and therefore fallible character of the biblical writings does not require the denial of the spiritual preeminence of Scripture; it does, however, demand that we change our way of reading the Bible. It is childish to think that "apart from omniscience belonging to the Jews, the proper conclusion of reason is atheism." Revelation does not require inerrancy.

> It is not inconsistent with the idea that Almighty God has been pleased to educate men and nations, employing imagination no less than conscience, and suffering His lessons to play freely within the limits of humanity and its shortcomings.[10]

According to Williams, the critical approach to the Bible requires a wider conception of revelation which, while recognizing God's hand in the history of Jewry, also sees God's spirit as a perpetual presence in human history. Like Coleridge, Williams holds that the Bible is inspired only as, through the Spirit, it "finds" him. It was such a view that brought charges against Williams in the ecclesiastical courts. He had been bold to say that "if such a Spirit did not dwell in the Church the Bible would not be inspired, for the Bible is, before all things, the written voice of the congregation."[11] Williams contended that such a conception of inspiration was held by the early Church and was the only one which the facts of Scripture would allow:

> The sacred writers acknowledge themselves men of like passions with ourselves, and we are promised illumination from the Spirit which dwelt in them. . . . Instead of objecting that everyone of us is infallible, we should define inspiration consistently with the facts of Scripture, and of human nature. These would neither

exclude the idea of fallibility among Israelites of old, nor teach us to quench the Spirit in true hearts for ever.[12]

Williams's criticism of the static, inerrant view of inspiration is forceful. However, he was ambiguous on whether there was to be any distinction between biblical inspiration and the inspiration of a Milton and, if so, exactly what it would be. The question of general and special revelation is not discussed. It is clear, however, that Williams does not wish to maintain any radical distinction between natural and revealed religion.

Williams emphasized, as did Coleridge before and Matthew Arnold after him, the importance of distinguishing the language of image and metaphor from the language of science. What the biblical authors often meant as metaphors or poetic vision has been misread as literal fact. We must not, Williams urged, be forced into a position which demands that we equate the truths of Scripture with a scientific literalism. Literalism is a modern aberration which has turned "symbol and poetry into materialism."

Williams's own "demythologizing" of Scripture is often ingenious and rationalistic. What does stand, however, is his appeal for freedom of criticism and his recognition that Christian faith could not long survive when blatant falsehoods continued to be taught concerning the foundation of the faith.

Charles Goodwin says much the same concerning the relations between theology and natural science in his essay "On the Mosaic Cosmogony." The difficulties in which theology finds itself are due not only to its rejection of science but to its pathetic attempts to harmonize the Bible with the new science. It is a losing battle that, after each new defeat, only makes Christian belief less tenable in the minds of thinking persons.

Goodwin sees the situation in the nineteenth century as similar to that of the sixteenth century. As the earlier period was shaken by Copernicus, so now is belief challenged by geology. The school books now teach that the earth moves but still assure the child that it is less than six thousand years old—at a time when geologists of firm religious faith are agreed that the earth has existed for millions of years. This situation forced the theologians to attempt once again to reconcile the Mosaic narrative with the new scientific facts. Goodwin views this attempt as disastrous for scientific honesty and for a true reading of Scripture. His thesis is that if the value of the Bible is to be maintained,

> it must not be by striving to prove it scientifically exact, at the expense of every sound principle of interpretation, and in defiance of common sense, but by a frank recognition of the erroneous views of nature which it contains.[13]

Goodwin skillfully demonstrates that the popular attempts to harmonize Genesis and geology cancel one another and in each case do violence to the clear meaning of the Hebrew text. There were at the time two principal approaches to the reconciliation of the Mosaic narrative and geology. The one was best represented by the eminent Oxford geologist William Buckland in his *Bridgewater Treatise*. It held that most geological ages evolved between "the beginning" and the "first day":

> It is nowhere affirmed that God created the heaven and the earth in the *first day*, but in the *beginning;* this beginning may have been an epoch at an unmeasured distance. . . . No information is given to events which may have occurred upon this earth, unconnected with its history of man, between the creation of its component matter recorded in the first verse, and the era at which its history is resumed in the second verse; nor is any limit fixed to the time during which these intermediate events may have been going on: millions of millions of years may have occupied the interval between the beginning in which God created the heaven and the earth and the evening or commencement of the first day of the Mosaic narrative.[14]

For Buckland it was not necessary to maintain that "the substance of the sun and moon was first called into existence on the fourth day," for otherwise how could life be maintained? "The fact of their creation had been stated before in the first verse."[15] Nevertheless, this did require that Buckland account for the narrative of the fourth day. This he did by describing the primeval darkness of the first day as

a temporary darkness, produced by an accumulation of dense vapours upon the face of the deep. . . . An incipient dispersion of these vapours may have readmitted light to the earth, upon the first day, while the existing cause of light was obscured; and the further purification of the atmosphere upon the fourth day may have caused the sun and the moon and the stars to reappear in the firmament of heaven. . . .[16]

Goodwin's caustic reply to Buckland's theory is typical of his refutation:

> The violence done to the great and simple words of the Hebrew writer must strike every mind. "And God said Let there be light—and there was light—and God saw the light that it was good. And God divided the light from the darkness, and God called the light day, and the darkness called he night; and the evening and the morning were the fourth day." Can anyone sensible of the value of words suppose that nothing more is here described, or intended to be described, than the partial clearing away of fog? Can such a manifestation of light be dignified by the appellation of day?[17]

It is clear that Buckland's zeal has forced him to torture a meaning out of the text that is quite foreign to its intention.

A second approach to the conciliation of Genesis and geology is typified in the works of the famous Scottish naturalist Hugh Miller. Miller refuted Buckland's hypothesis of a great geological age between "the beginning" and the "first day" and the latter's view of the six subsequent days as natural days of twenty-four hours. Miller held to the biblical order of creation but considered each of the six days to be vast periods of time. Goodwin finds two principal difficulties in Miller's view. They concern the biblical order of creation and Miller's use of the concept "day." To be sure, there is a certain vague resemblance between the Hebrew poet's order of Creation and the findings of geology. But, when pressed very far, the resemblance vanishes.

> The agreement is far from exact, as according to geological evidence, reptiles would appear to have existed ages before birds and mammals, whereas here the creation of birds is attributed to the fifth day, that of reptiles to the sixth. There remains, moreover, the in-

superable difficulty of the plants and trees being represented as made on the third day—that is, more than an age before fishes and birds, which is clearly not the case.[18]

Likewise there are problems in the use of the word "day":

It is evident that the bare theory that a "day" means an age of immense geological period might be made to yield some strange results. What becomes of the evening and the morning of which day is said to have consisted? Was each geologic age divided into two long intervals, one all darkness, and the other all light? And if so what becomes of the plants and trees created in the third day or period, when the evening of the fourth day (the evenings, be it observed, precede the mornings) set in? They must have passed through half a seculum of total darkness, not even cheered by that dim light which the sun, not yet completely manifested, supplied on the morning of the third day. Such an ordeal would have completely destroyed the whole vegetable creation, and yet we find that it survived. . . .[19]

Such a labored interpretation of the biblical texts would be unnecessary if only the theologians would admit that the Mosaic cosmogony is not science but Hebrew poetry. "The spectacle," writes Goodwin, "of able, and we doubt not, conscientious writers engaged in attempting the impossible is painful and humiliating." It was not the object of the divine revelation to instruct humankind in physical science, for humans were given natural facilities for such knowledge. If we admit that physical science is not what the Hebrew writers profess to convey, "Why," Goodwin asks, "should we hesitate to recognize their fallibility on this head?"[20]

Jowett's "On the Interpretation of Scripture"

Jowett's long essay appeared last in the book and was a fitting conclusion to the whole. Though the essay discusses issues touched on earlier, Jowett gives to the problems of biblical interpretation his own scholarly experience and moral earnestness. The essay rounds out the volume with a moving paean of praise to the life of scholarship and the love of truth.

Distinguished scholars had long called for silence on the difficulties of scriptural interpretation on two grounds: one, that the problems were of an esoteric sort, having no real impact on the ordinary layperson, and, second, that the issues were still indecisive, making any statement premature. Jowett contends that the difficulties referred to are very well known; "they force themselves on the attention of every intelligent reader of the New Testament." But because no one dares break through the veil of silence, there is abroad "a sort of smoldering scepticism." Nor is it possible any longer to ignore the results of criticism. "The Christian religion is in a false position when all the tendencies of knowledge are opposed to it."[21] A terrible mischief has come upon the Church when intelligent criticisms are automatically ascribed to atheism! "It would be a strange and almost incredible thing," Jowett muses, "that the Gospel, which at first made war only on the vices of mankind, should now be opposed to one of the highest and rarest of human virtues, the love of truth."[22]

The fundamental cause of this mischief lies in the fact that the Bible is not read like any other book. It is overladen with a priori notions concerning its origin and nature. The reasons for this are several. There is a natural conservatism in the religious community which dislikes challenging the critical canons of former ages. Chief among those canons is the rather modern identification of the written Scriptures with the inerrant "Word of God." The result is that the blatant discrepancies in the books of Kings and Chronicles, for example, must be considered as somehow only apparent. There is also the desire to adapt the words of Scripture to the doctrines of the Church's Creeds and, especially among modern apologists, to conform the statements of the Bible to the language and practice of the present age. An example of the former procedure is seen in the way St. Paul is made to agree with the abstract formulas of the Nicene and Athanasian Creeds:

Absorbed as St. Paul was in the person of Christ with an intensity of faith and love . . . high as he raised the dignity of his Lord above all things in heaven and earth—looking to Him as the Creator of all things . . . he does not speak of Him as "equal to the Father" or "of one substance with the Father."[23]

A priori notions are not, however, the possession only of the orthodox. The liberals also have their rules of faith by which they distort the natural sense of biblical texts. All parties are guilty of extracting selected verses from the Bible which are then "eagerly appealed to and made too much use of," being "forced into the service of received opinion and beliefs," while other texts "have been either unnoticed or explained away." Our "favorite verses shine like stars, while the rest of the page is thrown into the shade."[24]

So much for the mischievous principles that guide the interpretation of most divines. Against this Jowett set his own critical canons of interpretation. Most people considered them outrageous at the time. They were and are open to serious criticism but stand, nevertheless, as a kind of charter for critical biblical scholarship even today.

Jowett's basic principle is what most shocked his contemporaries. His hermeneutics is but an expansion of one canon: "*Interpret the Scripture like any other book.*" For Jowett this meant that the biblical scholar is to bring no special notions to the study of Scripture that he or she would not also expect to apply to the texts of Plato or Shakespeare. The purpose of the author—the meaning of the text—remains as it was first produced. It is not the function of the critic to find other meanings.

> The book itself remains as at the first unchanged amid the changing interpretations of it. The office of the interpreter is not to add another, but to recover the original one: the meaning, that is, of the words as they struck on the ears or flashed before the eyes of those who first heard and read them. He has to transfer himself to another age to imagine that he is a disciple of Christ or Paul; to disengage himself from all that follows. The history of Christendom is nothing to him. . . . All the after thoughts of theology are nothing to him. . . . The greater part of his learning is a knowledge of the text itself; he has no delight in the voluminous literature which has overgrown it.[25]

The science of hermeneutics must be an inductive one, based on the thoughts and narratives of the writers themselves. The critic begins with only a few common-sense rules of thumb. The first, as we have seen, is that Scripture has one meaning. To recon-

struct the inner and outer life of Jesus and His contemporaries is no easy task. But the alternative is not to intrude into this problem certain a priori solutions. This means that the scholar will often have to choose the more inconclusive or difficult interpretation "and refuse the one more in agreement with received opinions." This will not increase the scholar's popularity. To the charge that the scholar is merely making the reading of the Bible "difficult and perplexing," he or she can only answer: "That may very well be—it is a fact." One thing is clear: admitting the problems of interpretation does not mean that the scholar is "willing to admit to hidden or mysterious meaning."

> In the same way we recognize the wonders and complexity of the laws of nature to be far beyond what eye has seen or knowledge reached, yet it is not therefore to be supposed that we acknowledge the existence of some other laws different in kind from those we know which are incapable of philosophical analysis. In like manner we have no reason to attribute to the Prophet or Evangelist any second or hidden sense different from that which appears on the surface.[26]

Jowett's second precept is an application of the general rule, "Interpret Scripture from itself." This simply means that, since little other contemporary literature survives, one passage of Scripture must be interpreted in the light of other similar passages. This must, of course, be done with great care, since all parts of the Bible are not to be regarded as "an indistinguishable mass." The Old Testament is not to be identified with the New, nor the Gospels with the Epistles. It is therefore necessary that this rule

> should be confined to the writings of the same age and the same authors, except where the writings of different ages or persons offer obvious similarities. It may be said further that illustrations should be chiefly derived not only from the same author, but from the same writing, or from one of the same period of his life.[27]

What Jowett found especially pernicious was the common practice of indiscriminately using seemingly parallel passages from one part of Scripture and applying them to other very different biblical texts.

Jowett goes on to contend that a critical hermeneutics would also require a quite different view of inspiration than was current in his day, for example, in the Princeton Theology. It would demand that the supernatural doctrine of inerrant inspiration be refuted. The critical canons enunciated by Jowett would not allow that there is any foundation for such a doctrine in the New Testament writings themselves.

> There is no appearance in their writings that the Evangelists or Apostles had any inward gift, or were subject to any power external to them different from that of preaching or teaching . . . nor do they anywhere lead us to suppose that they were free from error or infirmity. St. Paul . . . exhibits all the emotions and vicissitudes of human feeling, speaking, indeed, with authority, but hesitating in difficult cases and more than once correcting himself, corrected, too, by the course of events in his expectation of the coming of Christ.[28]

In Jowett's opinion the nature of inspiration can be known only from a study of Scripture itself. "To the question, 'What is Inspiration?' the first answer is 'The idea of Inspiration which we gather from a knowledge of Scripture.' " If we examine the Bible, we must acknowledge that it is a book embracing beliefs and practices of a widely different nature—a mixture of the monstrous and the sublime, the true and the false. And such should be expected, unless we come to the Bible with some preconceived ideas as to what it must contain. A study of the Bible leads us, Jowett argues, to some conception of *progressive revelation* or progressive inspiration.

> For what is progressive is necessarily imperfect in its earlier stages, and even erring to those who come after. . . . Scripture itself points the way to answer the moral objections to Scripture.[29]

Such a principle is of value to the interpreter, since it allows him or her to be faithful to the whole of Scripture while free to distinguish clearly the several parts.

> It leaves him room enough to admit all the facts of the case. No longer is he required to defend, or to ex-

plain away, David's imprecations against his enemies. . . . Still, the sense of the increasing purpose which through the ages ran is present to him, nowhere else continuously discernible or ending in divine perfection.[30]

Jowett nowhere reflects the mid-Victorian *Zeitgeist* more than in his conception of progressive revelation. Like Lessing, he compares the history of God's people to a kind of progress from childhood to adulthood.

> In the child there is an anticipation of truth; his reason is latent in the form of feeling. . . . he is led by temporal promises, believing that it is good to be happy always; he is pleased by marvels and has vague terrors. . . . he imagines God to be like a human father only greater and more awful. . . . As he grows older he mixes more with others. . . . At length the world opens upon him; another work of education begins; and he learns to discern more truly the meaning of things. . . . And as he arrives at manhood he reflects on his former years . . . and he now understands that all this was but a preparation for another state of being. And . . . looking back on the entire past, which he reads anew, perceiving that the events of life had a purpose or result which was not seen all the time.[31]

If a critical study of Scripture requires some such concept of progressive revelation, it also demands another rule disapproved of and neglected by most writers.

> It is this—that any true doctrine of inspiration must conform to all well-ascertained facts of history or of science. The same fact cannot be true and untrue any more than the same words can have two opposite meanings. The same fact cannot be true in religion . . . and untrue in science when looked at through the medium of evidence or experiment.[32]

Jowett felt that there was no need to reconcile religion with science; "they reconcile themselves the moment any scientific truth is distinctly ascertained." If this canon appears now to be oversimple and Jowett too zealous in embracing the "certainties" of science, we must keep in mind the times in which he wrote as well as the many reckless and dishonest efforts to discount the advances in scientific knowledge.

Jowett did not fear the scientific study of the Bible because he possessed a deep assurance that while the Bible is like any other book, it is also unique. When examined with the canons of criticism

> the Bible will still remain unlike any other book; its beauty will be freshly seen, as of a picture that has been restored after many ages to its original state; it will create a new interest and make for itself a new kind of authority by the life that was in it.[33]

The "life" that Jowett found afresh in the Bible was essentially the life patterned after the moral example of Christ. It was this which became for him the hermeneutical key to the Bible. Late in life Jowett recorded his musings on the future of Christian belief. He asked himself, "What is the possible limit of changes in the Christian religion?" He acknowledged that belief in miracles may be abandoned, that the personality of God may be given up, and that "doctrines may become unmeaning words." Yet the essence of religion would remain. And for Jowett that meant the life and death of Christ, that is,

> *the life and death of Christ in the soul, the imitation of Christ*—the inspiration of Christ—the sacrifice of self—the being in the world and not of it, the union with God and the will of God such as Christ had.[34]

The Book's Reception

At first *Essays and Reviews* received little notice.[35] The storm broke after the appearance of an article in the *Westminster Review* by Frederick Harrison entitled "Neo-Christianity." Harrison had been a High Church Anglican who had lost his faith through exposure to the new science and had become a disciple of Auguste Comte. Harrison took pleasure in pointing out the unorthodox notions of the essayists and the fact that these leading church scholars now agreed with many of the findings of the Positivists.

Harrison's article provoked another response from Bishop Samuel Wilberforce, the famous evangelical leader who had recently entered the lists against Darwinism. Wilberforce's denunciation of *Essays and Reviews* produced alarm and panic among orthodox persons of both the High Church and Evangelical parties and united them against their new common enemy. Petitions and protests against the book urged the bishops to do something. They met and, under the leadership of Wilberforce, issued a letter expressing their horror that such opinions could be held by the clergy of the Church and promising that the question of the book's condemnation was under consideration. The book was now widely attacked by prelates and village curates who never even took the time to read it. The seven authors were labeled *Septum Contra Christum,* the seven against Christ.

The book was discussed in both Houses of Convocation, resulting in a decision by the bishops to prosecute the essayists in the church courts. As it happened, only Williams and Wilson could be tried in this way. Their cases were brought before the Court of Arches, and they were condemned on five of thirty-two charges, the principal accusation being a denial of the inspiration of Scripture. The two men appealed to the Privy Council which overruled the previous decisions on the grounds that the Thirty-Nine Articles simply did not define inspiration. The orthodox parties found the decision demoralizing, for once again the Church courts allowed the silence of the Articles to condone views that they believed stood contrary to the long traditions of the Church.

But the storm was not over. Dr. Pusey, in alliance with the Evangelicals, circulated a petition which was signed by 11,000 clergy and 137,000 laypersons protesting the Privy Council's decision and declaring their

> firm belief that the Church of England and Ireland, in common with the whole Catholic Church, maintains without reserve or qualification, the Inspiration and the Divine Authority of the whole Canonical Scriptures, as not only containing but being the Word of God. . . .[36]

When the Convocation of Canterbury met in April 1864, Wilberforce moved that the bishops condemn the book. After a few months of heated debate and committee study, Wilberforce prevailed and the book was condemned by a large majority in both Houses of Bishops.

The essayists, of course, must not only be condemned but also be refuted. Thus, each of the orthodox parties produced a volume of essays in 1861 countering the opinions of the "seven against Christ." *Replies to Essays and Reviews* was edited by Bishop Wilberforce who, in his preface, frankly admitted that he had never read *Essays and Reviews!* Excepting one or two essays, the *Replies* make plain the rather poor state of orthodox biblical scholarship. Christopher Wordsworth, later Bishop of Lincoln, and J. W. Burgon, Dean of Chichester, both attacked Jowett's view of inspiration by defending the infallibility of the biblical text.

The essays in *Aids to Faith* were, on the whole, more balanced and reasonable. Yet even the more liberal of these defenses were marred by claims and evidences that would not stand up to historical-critical scrutiny. The literal account of creation in Genesis, the Mosaic authorship of the Pentateuch, and the predictive gift of prophecy were all defended. The essay on "Inspiration" by Harold Browne, the Norrisian Professor of Divinity in Cambridge, was the most advanced and irenic. Unlike most of his collaborators, Browne acknowledged that the Church cannot claim that the Bible is inerrant in matters of history and science. He recognized the real human element in Scripture and acknowledged that it is just this element that makes any theory of biblical inspiration extremely difficult. Nevertheless, Browne rejects a view such as Coleridge's as hopelessly subjective and falls back upon the assurance that what we have is "*an infallible* depository of religious truth."[37] This, he insists, follows from our assurance that God did appoint special messengers to communicate His will to mankind and that "it is surely proof enough that they would never be permitted to mislead us in questions of faith."[38]

The replies to *Essays and Reviews* reveal that both ignorance and fear of scientific advances were to be found in the highest places in the Church. The whole effort is based on precritical assumptions. It is regrettable that scholars dedicated to critical standards, and yet of a more orthodox faith, did not come forth with a modifying position somewhere between Pusey and Jowett. The authors of *Essays*

and Reviews, correct as they were in their defense of the critical method, were not possessed of profound theological minds. They were persons of learning whose conception of religion was largely rationalistic and moral. "What is wanted," Bishop Tait wrote at the time, "is a deeply religious liberal party, and almost all who might have formed it have, in the alarm deserted. . . . The great evil is that the liberals are deficient in religion and the religious are deficient in liberality."[39]

Among those "deeply religious" liberals who might have served as a mediating force, and whose work later did perform this function, were the Cambridge New Testament scholars, Joseph Lightfoot, B. F. Westcott, and F. J. A. Hort. Hort had originally been invited to contribute to *Essays and Reviews.* In declining he expressed his agreement with the essayists "in maintaining absolute freedom of criticism" but wrote that he had

> a deeply-rooted agreement with High-Churchmen as to the Church, Ministry, Sacraments and, above all, Creeds, though by no means acquiescing in their unhistorical and unphilosophical treatment of theology.[40]

After the appearance of *Essays and Reviews,* Hort expressed even greater sympathy with the aims of the contributors. When his friend Westcott, concerned about the injury the book might cause, suggested the preparation of a volume of mediating essays, Hort demurred. However, the fact that *Essays and Reviews* was causing some to give up their faith and forcing others into uncritical traditionalism finally induced Hort to agree to such a volume.[41] As it turned out, the project came to nothing when Lightfoot declined the proposal because of the press of other work. Nevertheless, in the next decade the important commentaries, critical studies, and textual work of Lightfoot, Westcott, and Hort did seriously challenge the more radical theories of the liberal critics and gave warrant, on critical grounds, for the historical reliability of portions of the New Testament previously dismissed. However, in the 1860s and 1870s there was little to choose from between the Traditionalists and the Modernists.

Though their work appeared largely negative, the authors of *Essays and Reviews* made an invaluable contribution to the progress of Christian thought in an age of scientific revolution. They played the commanding role in the renewal of scholarly freedom in the Church at a time when that freedom had suffered an eclipse. If their work was too destructive, it can be argued that such weapons were required to shatter the false foundations on which the faith had been lately constructed. It would be left to others to build anew in time on "deeper foundations." Speaking in general of the contribution of nineteenth-century biblical scholars, Leonard Hodgson states well Christianity's debt to the authors of *Essays and Reviews:*

> When in the nineteenth century [the pre-critical] way of accepting the Bible was challenged by the progress of scientific and historical enquiries, the challenge had to be met, and the only honest way in which the Church could meet it was by encouraging its theologians themselves to subject the Bible to the most rigorous criticism. This had to be done, and we today owe a debt of gratitude to those of our forefathers who had faith enough to do it. . . . We should think of those scholars as men upon whom the circumstance of their time laid the intolerable strain of finding that what they had taken to be the foundation of their faith was full of quick sands, as men who had faith and courage enough to dig and sift until they reached the solid ground on which they could and we can stand. For the time being this digging and sifting was a whole time job. If they could not be expounding the Bible as the Word of God, that was because they were occupied in making it possible for us to do so.[42]

THE DARWINIAN CONTROVERSY

The Situation before Darwin

The change in world view that occurred in England in the less than sixty years between Paley's *Natural Theology* (1802) and Darwin's *Origin of Species* (1859) is a fascinating chapter in the history of ideas.[43] Paley's book represented the eighteenth-century argument from design in its quintessential form. "There cannot be design without a designer," Paley wrote. "Arrangement, disposition of parts, subserviency of means to an end, relation of instru-

ments to a use, imply the presence of intelligence and mind."[44] The world is like a great machine, made of infinitely complex parts, each working for the well-being of the whole. And such a vast design requires the existence of an eternal, omniscient Designer, for, according to Paley, such a magnificent world could not have been the result of blind, unthinking chance. It is in the very intricate choices and adaptations of small organisms that the proof of a creative, providential Intelligence is most clearly demonstrated.

Paley's world is Newtonian, based on a static mechanical model of nature. It was a world of design, not of development, concerned with the order of nature, not the history of nature. The Newtonian world was especially suitable for natural theology, for this theology was itself traceable to the static, immutable categories of Greek metaphysics. In the eighteenth century, science was the handmaid, not the enemy, of Theism, or at least Deism. This alliance between theology and natural science continued well into the nineteenth century in England. Darwin read Paley while at Cambridge and had commented that he had "hardly ever admired a book more than Paley's *Natural Theology.*"[45] And yet, after the discovery of the mechanism of natural selection not many years later, Darwin considered Paleyism overthrown, the belief in a Providential design in nature inadmissible on the evidence.

The change in the world-view that occurred within those decades is illustrated by comparing Paley's perception of nature with Tennyson's very different view in *In Memoriam.* In 1802 Paley wrote:

> It is a happy world after all. The air, the earth, the water, teem with delighted existence. In a spring noon or a summer evening, on whichever side I turn my eyes, myriads of happy beings crowd upon my view. "The insect youth are on the wing." Swarms of new-born flies are trying their pinions in the air. Their sportive motions, testify their joy and the exultation which they feel in their lately discovered faculties.[46]

Tennyson, in 1850, had a quite different perception of nature. It was a "Nature red in tooth and claw."

LV

Are God and Nature then at strife,
That Nature lends such evil dreams?
So careful of the type she seems,
So careless of the single life;

That I, considering, everywhere
Her secret meaning in her deeds,
And finding that of fifty seeds
She often brings but one to bear,

I falter where I firmly trod. . . .

LVI

So careful of the type? but no.
From scorped cliff and quarried stone
She cries, "A thousand types are gone:
I care for nothing, all shall go."

Tennyson's grimly pessimistic view of nature was due in large part to the fact that he looked at the natural world through the eyes of contemporary science. He had read Charles Lyell's *Principles of Geology* (1830–1833), Robert Chambers's *The Vestiges of Creation* (1844), and other scientific works of the time. He no longer saw nature proclaiming the glory of God but witnessing to a blind, inexorable development, heedless of human values, destroying everything that could not compete in the unending struggle for life. This change in worldview is largely attributable to the evolutionary theories current in the first half of the century.

Only in the late eighteenth century did natural scientists in France—Buffon, LaPlace, and Lamarck—challenge the biblical account of Creation. Among the first works in England to raise doubts about Genesis was James Hutton's *Theory of the Earth* (1795). Hutton never mentioned Genesis, nor did he attempt to give any account of the earth's origin. He confined his attention to what he was able to observe and deduce from the present condition of the earth. Nevertheless, his findings forced him to conclude that the earth had existed for an indefinitely long time. This, of course, challenged a literal reading of the biblical account of Creation which, if accepted, required that the earth has existed for only six thousand years. Furthermore, while Hutton maintained a teleological view of purpose in nature, his teleology did not require a theological base.

Most geologists at the time of Hutton held that the earth had undergone a sequence of periodic revolutions which explained its geological strata. The theory could rather easily be reconciled with the six days of Genesis since the theory's time scheme was vague and did imply that the forces which had produced the periodic changes were no longer at work. Many believed that the earth had now achieved its divine design, a rather stable place for human habitation. Recognizing the earth's age to be vastly more than six thousand years old, other theorists postulated a series of creations divided by periodic geologic upheavals. Often these creations or epochs were represented as the six days of Genesis which were now to be read not as literal days but as periods of indefinite length. Such was the view of William Buckland, as we have seen. It is clear that these theories were compromises between religious tradition and scientific advance. They recognized periodic change but no continuity of development. Among those advocating one or another form of this position was Adam Sedgwick, Darwin's teacher.

Other natural scientists advocated a theory of uniform development that did not require periodic catastrophes followed by new creations. This was called "Uniformitarianism," a theory not widely accepted until Charles Lyell published his *Principles of Geology*. Lyell convinced the scientific world of Uniformitarianism by amassing an immense amount of evidence to discount the need for a theory of world catastrophes. Lyell challenged the theory by asserting that

> when we are unable to explain the moments of past change, it is always more probable that the difference arises from our ignorance of all the existing agents, or all their possible effects in an indefinite lapse of time, than that some cause was formerly in operation which has ceased to operate.[47]

Lyell further maintained that the natural history of the earth can be understood only when it is accepted

> that all former changes of the organic and inorganic creation are referrable to one uninterrupted succession of physical events governed by the laws now in operation.[48]

When Lyell wrote *Principles of Geology,* he was not a believer in transformism, but, as G. S. Carter has remarked,

> the result of his book was to establish a picture of the history of the world which gave a possible background in geology for evolution if on other grounds it was shown to have occurred. Indeed, more than this can be said. If the living world was not destroyed by a catastrophe at the end of each epoch, it must have given rise to the life of the next epoch which could be shown by study of the fossils to be different. Change of form, and therefore evolution, must have taken place.[49]

While Lyell paved the way for acceptance of evolutionary transformism among the scientists, the appearance of *The Vestiges of the Natural History of Creation* in 1844 did much to prepare the public for Darwin's own theory. *Vestiges* was published anonymously but later was shown to be the work of Robert Chambers, an amateur naturalist and prolific writer on a wide range of subjects. The book was an immediate success and went through eleven editions by 1860. It represents the last of Paleyism and a decisive step toward the thoroughgoing naturalism of Darwin. Chambers saw in the uniform law of natural development the very expression of God's mind and plan.

> We have seen powerful evidence that the construction of this globe and its associates . . . was the result, not of any immediate or personal exertions on the part of the Deity, but of natural laws which are the expression of His will. What is to hinder our supposing that the organic creation is also a result of natural laws, which are in like manner an expression of His will?[50]

Chambers connected the idea of Creation according to natural law with the idea of continuous evolutionary development.

> The idea which I form (of the progress of organic life) is, *that the simplest and most primitive types, under a law to which that of like production is subordinate, gave birth to the type superior to it . . . that this again produced the next higher, and so on to the highest, the advance being in all cases small.*[51]

Chambers saw dimly some of the theories which would soon be established on a sound scientific basis by Darwin. He spoke, for instance, of organic structures modifying in accordance with external circumstances such as food and habitat, thus foreshadowing Darwin's theory of adaptation. He also saw humans as a species continuous with the whole organic creation and recognized the fact that the individual is thrown into the great, amoral struggle for existence. Chambers wrote:

> It is clear from the whole scope of the natural laws, that the individual, as far as the present sphere of being is concerned, is to the Author of Nature a consideration of inferior moment. Everywhere we see the arrangements for the species perfect; the individual is left, as it were, to take his chance amidst the melee of the various laws affecting him.[52]

Chambers even foresaw the possible emergence of a higher species than the present type of humanity.

> It is startling to find an appearance of imperfection in the circle to which man belongs, and the ideas which rise in consequence are no less startling. Is our race but the initial of the grand crowning type? Are there yet to be species superior to us in organization, purer in feeling, more powerful in device and act who shall take a rule over us?[53]

If Chambers presaged much that was to be established by Darwin, *Vestiges* was not a book of scientific distinction. It was soon demolished by the professional naturalists. Nevertheless, it did influence popular opinion and helped prepare the way for 1859. Darwin wrote that in his opinion the book had "done excellent service in calling in this country attention to the subject, and in removing prejudice."[54] It must be kept in mind, however, that the *Vestiges of Creation* was accepted by the public despite the book's advocacy of evolution only because Chambers saw himself as serving the cause of religion.

> When all is seen as the result of law, the idea of the Almighty Author becomes irresistible, for the creation of a law for an endless series of phenomena—an act of

intelligence above all else that we can conceive—could have no other imaginable source.[55]

Astute minds recognized, however, that Chambers's evolutionary Uniformitarianism was, in fact, a grave threat to the idea of a providential control of nature. A special Providence appeared to many to find its last sure ground in the immutability of species, and it was this that Chambers was willing to give up. Chambers was simply saying that Providence is what is. In such a view, Providence was nothing more than a name for order. But why, then, appeal to some extranatural agency to explain the orderly process of nature? Only because the creation of new species remained unaccountable on natural grounds? If so, then one only need find a natural explanation, and the belief in a governing Providence would no longer be required.

Such a mechanism was discovered by Darwin in natural selection. Darwin argued that natural selection provides a more reasonable account of the evolutionary process than the idea of an intervening Providence, for a continuous Providence is not intelligible in light of our knowledge of variations in species. Darwin expressed this view in a letter to his friend Lyell who, at the time, continued to believe in a Providential control over the course of natural evolution.

> If you say that God ordained that at some time and place a dozen slight variations should arise, and that one of them alone should be preserved in the struggle for life and the other eleven should perish in the first or few generations, then the saying seems to me to be verbiage. It comes to merely saying that everything that is, is ordained. . . . Why should you or I speak of variation as having been ordained and guided, more than does an astronomer in discussing the fall of a meteoric stone? . . . Would you have him say that its fall at some particular place and time was "ordained and guided without doubt by an intelligent cause on a preconceived and definite plan"? Would you not call this theological pedantry or display?[56]

With the discovery of natural selection, the last support of Paleyism seemed to Darwin to be removed.

> The old argument of design in nature, as given by Paley, which formerly seemed to me so conclusive, fails now that the law of natural selection has been discovered. We can no longer argue that, for instance, the beautiful hinge of a bivalve shell must have been made by an intelligent being, like the hinge of a door by man. There seems to be no more design in the variability of organic beings, and in the action of natural selection, than in the course which the wind blows.[57]

Darwin's theory did not deny the possibility of an original Creator, but his conception of nature did exclude the idea of a superintending Providence. If there is a God, at best God is a radically remote and impersonal deity.

Darwin's Theory

The traditional theological view held that each species was created directly by God. This ensured the distinctiveness of each species and agreed with the account of Genesis. Catastrophic theories of the earth's history had given additional support for a theory of discontinuous organic change. As we have seen, Lyell and the Uniformitarians challenged this traditional theory. Darwin accepted the Uniformitarian view of natural development but was unable to give an adequate natural explanation of the continuous development of species from one or a few descendants, from the lower to the higher animals.

In 1838 Darwin read Malthus's *Essay on Population* "for amusement." Malthus had put forward the thesis that because "population increases in a geometrical, food in an arithmetical ratio," population will inevitably outrun the food supply unless other factors are introduced to check the population explosion. It was Malthus's essay that suggested to Darwin the idea of natural selection as an explanation of the origin of species.

> Being well prepared to appreciate the struggle for existence which everywhere goes on from long-continued observation of the habits of animals and plants, it at once struck me that under these circumstances favorable variations would tend to be preserved, and unfavorable ones to be destroyed. The result of this would be the formulation of new species.[58]

For the next twenty years Darwin amassed an astounding amount of evidence in support of this theory. He was planning to write a multivolume defense of his thesis when, in the summer of 1858, he received an essay from the biologist A. R. Wallace. The essay expressed ideas about natural selection very similar to Darwin's own. Darwin was shaken and sought the counsel of his friends Lyell and Joseph Hooker. They persuaded him to allow a summary of his views, given in an unpublished essay of 1844, to be read before the Linnaean Society and to be published with Wallace's essay in the society's *Journal*. Darwin was now stirred to action. He gave up the idea of a massive work and, late in 1859, published *On the Origin of Species by Means of Natural Selection, or the Preservation of Favored Races in the Struggle for Life*. The essentials of Darwin's theory in the *Origin*, which he defended with a wealth of evidence, are summarized in a single passage:

It is interesting to contemplate a tangled bank, clothed with many plants of many kinds, with birds singing on the bushes, with various insects flitting about, and with worms crawling through the damp earth, and to reflect that these elaborately constructed forms, so different from each other, and dependent upon each other in so complex a manner, have all been produced by laws acting around us. These laws, taken in the largest sense, being Growth and Reproduction; Inheritance which is almost implied by reproduction; Variability from the indirect and direct action of the conditions of life, and from use and disuse; a Ratio of Increase so high as to lead to a struggle for life, and as a consequence to Natural Selection, entailing Divergence of Character and Extinction of less-improved forms. Thus from the war of nature, from famine and death, the most exalted object which we are capable of conceiving, namely the production of higher animals, directly follows.[59]

What disturbed Darwin's contemporaries was the inference, not elaborated in the *Origin*, that humans were not different in kind from other members of the animal class. Even biologists like Wallace, who accepted the theory of natural selection in general, held that humanity's unique qualities could not be fully explained by this law. Darwin feared that just such arguments for unique moral and intellec-

tual faculties would ultimately undermine the theory of natural selection itself. Darwin did not deny the extraordinary difference between humans and the brutes, but, from his long and intimate study of animal behavior, he was convinced that the differences were of degree, not kind, and that such differences could be explained as the result of evolution over a long course of time. As J. C. Greene has written:

He (Darwin) who had seen the naked Fuegians gathering limpets and mussels in the cold rain or squatting in their wretched shelters "conversing" in hoarse grunts, he who had seen one of their chiefs dash his own child against the rocks for dropping a basket of sea urchins, would not be inclined to exaggerate the difference between the lowest man and the highest animals or reject as preposterous the suggestion that both might be descended from common ancestors.[60]

Darwin determined to write *The Descent of Man* specifically to make plain his views on the place of the human race in natural history. The book appeared in 1871. As most people feared, Darwin traced human descent back through the Old World monkeys and their progenitors.

In the class of mammals the steps are not difficult to conceive which led from the ancient Mono-tremata to the ancient Marsupials; and from these to the early progenitors of the placental mammals. We may thus ascend to the Lemuridae; and from these to the Simiadae. The Simiadae then branched off into two great stems, the New World and the Old World monkeys; and from the latter, at a remote period, Man the wonder and glory of the Universe proceeded.

Thus *we have given to man a pedigree of prodigious length, but not, it may be said, of noble quality.* The world, it has often been remarked, appears as if it had long been preparing for the advent of man: and this in one sense is strictly true, for he owes his birth to a long line of progenitors. *If any single link in this chain had never existed, man would not have been exactly what he is now.* Unless we willfully close our eyes, we may, with our present knowledge, approximately recognize our patronage; nor need we feel ashamed of it. The most humble organism is something much higher than the inorganic dust under our feet; and no one with an unbiased mind can study any living creature, however humble, without being struck with enthusiasm at its marvelous structure and properties.[61] (Italics added.)

Darwin's last sentence above was small comfort to his contemporaries, for what stuck in their minds were the sentences we have set off in italics as well as others which were written with such apparent serenity. Those sentences appeared to challenge the very foundations of Christian belief. Darwin's interpretation of nature was infinitely more damaging to a Christian vision of the world than the revolutions of either Copernicus or Newton. If the theories of these earlier scientists forced certain readjustments in the Christian's conception of humanity's place in nature, they did not essentially threaten the Christian drama of Creation, Fall, and Redemption. Darwinism challenged the entire biblical account of the human race's unique creation, fall, and need for redemption. The doctrine that humanity was the product of a long evolutionary process from lower to higher species appeared incompatible with the traditional interpretation of the Fall in Genesis. In Darwin's opinion humankind had risen from a species of dumb animal, not fallen from a state of angelic perfection. How could one impute a sinful fall to a creature so superior to his brutish ancestors in intellect and morals? And if humanity is the *chance* product of natural variation, what sense does it make to say that we are the crown of God's plan, created in the very image of the Creator?

Darwin came at the end of a long development in which the classical metaphysics, which had persisted since Plato, was giving way to a new worldview which stressed the qualities of process, change, and diversity. The static, hierarchical universe of Greek metaphysics was breaking up. *The Origin of Species* provoked a violent response because, coming when it did, it symbolized the final death blow to orthodox metaphysics. More particularly, it appeared to destroy the argument from design by showing that the creation of species, including humans, required no rational plan but originated by chance, fortuitous events. This demise of the older metaphysics had one crucial result for theology: It appeared to remove God's providential hand from the whole of natural history. Evolutionism

appeared to many as another step by which God was being pushed out of the created order. In the Newtonian world it was still possible to relate God the Creator to the world machine. . . . In the geological and biological theories which followed there was no apparent need for the God hypothesis. It was not that he could be excluded. No one could prove that. But for all practical purposes, he seemed unnecessary; and that was most damaging. Moreover, it was difficult to relate God to a process of such endless duration and such apparently chaotic and unstructured development. . . . Every need for God as a necessary source of explanation had disappeared.[62]

The Reception of Darwin's Theory

Considering the revolution in humanity's understanding of itself and its world wrought by evolution, it is little wonder that it caused such a heated response. The enormity of the issues ought to make us rather more sympathetic toward those who now appear to have reacted so unreasonably. We must also keep in mind that it was not simply a contest between the scientists and the theologians. Most of the biologists of the time opposed *The Origin of Species*. T. H. Huxley wrote that, besides himself, only two or three noted biologists accepted Darwin's view of evolution immediately after the publication of *The Origin of Species.* The theologians were clearly encouraged in their opposition by the support of eminent natural scientists. It is known, for example, that Sir Richard Owen, England's leading anatomist, assisted Bishop Samuel Wilberforce in his critical review of Darwin's book which appeared in the *Quarterly Review.* It should be further remarked that it was not only the religionists who reacted in ignorance and with violence. A scientist has reminded us that "It is perhaps through the spirit of the age that we remember the arrogance of conservative theologians rather than of revolutionary Darwinists."[63]

The controversy was ignited by the encounter of two celebrated but pugnacious men, Bishop Samuel Wilberforce and T. H. Huxley. Both seemed to thrive on controversy, and the occasion presented itself quite unexpectedly at the meeting of the British Association for the Advancement of Science in Oxford in June 1860. The previous February,

Huxley had given a provocative lecture on Darwin's theory at the Royal Institution. He goaded the clergy by claiming that in every battle with the theologians since the time of Galileo, the former had been "crushed" and that the future salvation of England rested with the professional scientists. He concluded by suggesting that "man might be a transmuted ape." Wilberforce's attack on *The Origin of Species* was equally disdainful of the scientists.

In the spring of 1860, the attacks and counterattacks increased apace. Characteristically, Darwin did not attend the potentially contentious meeting at Oxford in June. He was grateful for Huxley's support but had no desire to face his pugnacious opponents at such a crowded meeting. The story of the encounter between Wilberforce and Huxley has grown into a legend, and the many versions wildly exaggerate the facts. The skirmish was, in fact, unpremeditated. There was no set debate on Darwinism. It was incited by a talk by the American scientist John William Draper on Darwin and social progress. Wilberforce was provoked to reply and did so in a boring, two-hour speech. Attempting to interject some humor, Wilberforce turned to Huxley and, appealing to the Victorian sentimental idealization of women, asked whether Huxley would be willing to trace his descent from an ape to his grandmother's side.

The legend has it that Huxley devastated Wilberforce by retorting that if it were put to him either to have a miserable ape for a grandfather or a man of Wilberforce's station and influence, yet who employed himself "for the mere purpose of introducing ridicule into a grave scientific discussion," he would unhesitatingly affirm his preference for the ape. According to Huxley's report, his riposte elicited "inextinguishable laughter," and he carried the day. Others, however, including Darwin's friend and colleague Joseph Hooker, reported that Huxley could not be heard and therefore could not command the audience and that it was he, Hooker, who had silenced Wilberforce by demonstrating his ignorance of science. Upon leaving the field after a four-hour battle, both scientists thought they had secured the victory for Darwin's cause. However, many others in the audience judged the confrontation to have ended in a draw. In any case, it was not exactly the victory that the young, beleaguered

Darwinists claimed; nevertheless, the wide publicity that the event received in the press signaled the beginning of the controversy that was to occupy British intellectual life for the next three decades.[64]

Most of the scientists opposed to Darwin were motivated by strongly scientific questions, especially concerning the theory of natural selection. Some of the theories set forth in *The Origin of Species* have now been rejected; others have been modified and extended, while the answers to some of those original questions continue unresolved to this day. Nevertheless, the main lines of Darwin's theories concerning evolution and its mechanism (natural selection) are now generally agreed upon by natural scientists. There were scientists, on the other hand, with deeply felt religious convictions who did oppose Darwin largely on moral and religious grounds. Darwin's views did not accord with their religious beliefs. The story of these men—the naturalist Philip Gosse, for example—is often painful and pathetic. Gosse held that the world was created in six days, as Genesis records, and was only a few thousand years old. In order that his knowledge of geology might conform to these religious beliefs, Gosse theorized about a pre-Creation world which was fashioned into the present biblical one, with certain species fully evolved and even extinct. In this ingenious way he explained the existence of fossils in rocks.

A number of scientists attacked Darwinism because of its denial of a divine teleology. For example, Adam Sedgwick, upon receiving a copy of *The Origin of Species,* expressed indignation at learning of his former pupil's denial of supernatural design.

> Tis the crown and glory of organic science that it *does,* through *final cause,* link material to moral. . . . You (Darwin) have ignored this link; and, if I do not mistake your meaning, you have done your best. . . . to break it. Were it possible (which, thank God, it is not) to break it, humanity, in my mind, would suffer a damage that might brutalize it, and sink the human race into a lower grade of degradation than any into which it has fallen since its written records tell us of its history.[65]

Even Asa Gray, the American botanist and Darwin's friend and defender, was disturbed by the

Englishman's rejection of design. Writing on the import of the theory of natural selection, Gray asked:

> Will such a mind, under such circumstances, infer the existence of the designer—God—when he can, at the same time, satisfactorily account for the thing produced, by the operation of this natural selection? It seems to me perfectly evident that the substitution of natural selection, by necessity, for design in the formation of the organic world, is a step decidedly atheistical.[66]

These scientists and the conservative theologians were agreed in their conviction that, at present, there was little alternative between a literal biblicism and a rather vague, theistic teleology. Philip Gosse remained committed to a biblical fundamentalism, while Asa Gray and other scientists developed a spiritual conception of evolution that often had very little in common with traditional Christianity.

The reaction to Darwin outside the scientific community was extremely varied. There were those whose religious beliefs continued, as in the past, blissfully free from any intellectual problems. There were others who claimed to have lost their faith as a result of reading Darwin. In most of these instances, as in the case of the agnostic Leslie Stephen, their faith had already been weakened through a gradual process of doubt. A third group sought to exorcize the Darwin specter by scorn or by ignoring it. Such was the response of the writers Carlyle, Samuel Butler, and George Bernard Shaw. Carlyle replied that if Darwin's theory was true, "it was nothing to be proud of, but rather a humiliating discovery, and the less said about it the better."[67] There were still others who responded by dividing science and faith into two radically different spheres, advancements in science being considered quite irrelevant to the truths of faith. This, as we shall see, was the response of some Ritschlian theologians.

While the challenge of Darwinism to faith should not be exaggerated, there were many thoughtful laypersons and theologians who saw the revolutionary implications of Darwinism and knew that these problems had to be faced. It is this direct response to Darwin's ideas and the attempts to come to some resolution of the real issues between evolu-

tion and the theological tradition that will occupy us for the remainder of this chapter.

Christian Darwinism: Aubrey Moore

First, there were a number of theologians who, while holding orthodox beliefs, acknowledged the force of Darwin's conclusions. In England many of them were of the Broad Church party or of the Cambridge school. In 1860 Hort wrote to Westcott: "Have you read Darwin? . . . In spite of the difficulties, I am inclined to think it unanswerable."[68] Charles Kingsley sent sympathetic letters to both Darwin and Huxley. He informed Darwin that he had now come to reject the permanence of species and the idea that a Christian doctrine of God required belief in His special acts of creation. Kingsley wrote:

> I have gradually learnt to see that it is just as noble a conception of Deity to believe that He created primal forms capable of self-development into all forms needful *pro tempore* and *pro loco*, as to believe that He required a fresh act of intervention to supply the *lacunas* which He Himself had made.[69]

Even John Henry Newman recognized the weight of Darwin's findings and entered the following in a private notebook in 1863:

> It is strange that monkeys should be so like man with no historical connection between them. . . . I will either go the whole hog with Darwin or, dispensing with time and history altogether, hold not only the theory of distinct species but also of the creation of fossil-bearing rocks.[70]

The openness of many orthodox theologians toward Darwinism is perhaps best exemplified in the writings of Aubrey Moore, a theological tutor at Oxford and a contributor to *Lux Mundi*. He can be properly referred to as a Christian Darwinist.[71] Moore was disturbed by the religious apologetics of his time, for, while accepting the general idea of evolution, most theologians continued to place great stock in the argument from design and for special creations, particularly in contending for the unique status of the human species. Moore perceived that these arguments were essentially Deistical and contrary to the Christian understanding of God's relation to the world. Moore even found this Deistical tendency in Frederick Temple's very progressive Bampton lectures on *The Relations between Religion and Science* (1884). Temple, one of the contributors to *Essays and Reviews,* had rejected the idea of special creation but, in defending a wider conception of teleology, had written:

> God did not make the things we may say; no, but He made them make themselves. And surely this rather adds than withdraws force from the great argument. It seems in itself something more than majestic, something more befitting Him . . . thus to impress His will *once for all* on His Creation, and provide for all its countless variety by His *one original impress,* than by special acts of creation to be perpetually modifying what He had previously made.[72]

Moore saw in Temple's argument the influence of Hume which, he remarks,

> might be none the worse for that if it were not that, in the words we have italicized, Hume's Deism reappears. It is one thing to speak of God as "declaring the end from the beginning," it is another to use language which seems to imply . . . that God withdraws Himself from His Creation and leaves it evolve itself.[73]

Moore agreed with Darwin that he had "done good service in overthrowing the dogma of separate creations." Separate creation implies gaps in nature and a primitive conception of an absentee God who intervenes supernaturally in the natural world from time to time. Moore found such a conception neither in the Bible, nor the Church Fathers, nor the Medieval Schoolmen. It had its origin, Moore believed, in Milton's *Paradise Lost.* For Moore the doctrine of "special creation" was not only opposed to the scientific evidence but was theologically indefensible. Evolution,

> *as a theory* is infinitely more Christian than the theory of "Special Creation." For it implies the immanence of God in nature, and the omnipresence of his creative power. Those who opposed the doctrine of evolution

in defense of "a continued intervention" of God seem to have failed to notice that *a theory of occasional intervention implies as its correlative a theory of ordinary absence.* . . . Anything more opposed to the language of the Bible and the Fathers can hardly be imagined. . . . Cataclysmal geology and special creation are the scientific analogue of Deism. Order, development, law, are the analogue of the Christian view of God.[74]

Moore also considered the argument from design poor apologetic. He believed that for Christian theism the argument had received its death blow from Kant. The old *couleur de rose* view of nature was no longer possible. "Destruction is the rule; life is the exception." The Christian now, as in Paley's day, trusts that God is omnipotent and loving and that there is design and purpose everywhere.

> But he is not bound to know, or to say that he knows what that purpose is, or to show that marks of beneficence are everywhere apparent. Still less is he bound to assert, as the old teleology did, that he can demonstrate the wisdom and goodness of God from nature alone.[75]

The scientist and the Christian both start with certain "acts of faith," one being "that everything is rational, even that which is at present irreducible to law" and the other "that God is good," despite the obvious suffering in the world.

The attempt of Christian apologists to ensure a unique place for humanity in nature also produced some strange heresies. The theory of A. R. Wallace is a good example. Wallace accepted Darwin's theory of natural selection but only as it applied to subhuman life. He held that natural selection would have given human beings a brain a little superior to that of an ape and since humans are greatly superior, a "higher intelligence" must have supervened and *used* the law of natural selection to produce humanity. Wallace called his theory his scientific "heresy." To this Moore responded:

> Whether, from the scientific side, this is rightly called a "heresy" or not, it is not necessary to decide; but certainly from the religious side, it has a strangely unorthodox look. If, as a Christian believes, the "higher intelligence" who used these laws for the cre-

ation of man was the same God who works in and by these same laws in creating the lower forms of life, Mr. Wallace's distinction as a distinction of cause disappears; and if it was not the same God, we contradict the first article of the Creed. Whatever be the line which Christianity draws between man and the rest of the visible creation, it certainly does not claim man as "the work of God," and leave the rest to "unaided nature."[76]

What disturbed many Christians was Darwin's low view of the human species. They called Darwinism a "gospel of dirt." As a label of rebuke, Moore found it peculiarly inappropriate coming from the mouths of Christians.

> If such a charge had come from a representative of those nations which held the descent of man from gods or demigods, it would have been intelligible enough, but it sounds strange in the mouth of those who believe that "the Lord God formed man of the dust of the ground."[77]

Far from degrading humanity, Darwinism traces its rise from the lowest of origins to its role as vicegerent over the earth, having dominion over all other species. But what of the soul? Is the soul also a product of evolution, or did it require a "special creation"? Moore contends that, like original creation, the origin of the soul lies in the realm of mystery. Nevertheless, two things can be said. First, science must remain silent on the subject of the soul, since it lies outside its province. Theologically we can say that "the soul cannot be a 'special' creation whether in Adam or his children," for "there is no species of soul. We may call it, if we will, an 'individual' creation but is not all creation 'individual' creation from the religious point of view?"[78]

Moore takes the position that the Christian theologian is not bound to any *theory* of the origin of the soul. What the theologian is alone required to uphold is "the *fact* that, by God's creative act, man's relation to Himself is unique among created beings, and that this unique relationship of man to God is ... represented invariably as a relation of likeness."[79] Moore perceived that Christians were guilty of the "genetic fallacy" of judging a thing by its origin. What Christians have to contend for is the present reality of human moral and spiritual life. What humanity came from and how are not the important issues and in no way determine our present stature.

> When Darwin, in all the wealth of his scientific experience, and all the strength of his disciplined reason, gives us his matured judgment on the processes of nature, who would dream of saying "How can I trust the conclusions of a man who was once a baby?" We trust him for what he *is*, not what he *was*. And man is man, whatever he came from.[80]

Moore was confident that two fundamental doctrines of Christianity considered vulnerable to Darwinism in fact remained untouched by it. For that reason, Christians had nothing to fear from a completely open attitude toward evolution.

> The original creation of the world by God, as against any theory of emanation, is a matter of faith! The existence of the soul—i.e., the conscious relation of man with God—lies at the root of all religion. Guard those two points—and they are both strictly beyond the range of inductive science—and for the rest, we are bound to concede to those who are spending their lives in reading for us God's revelation of Himself in nature, absolute freedom in the search, knowing that truth is mighty and must in the end prevail.[81]

Anti-Darwinism: Charles Hodge

There were many theologians, of orthodox or conservative views, whose response to Darwinism was radically different from Moore's. They saw Darwinism as a serious threat to Christian belief and approached it as a theory to be refuted. The principal weapons of these Anti-Darwinists were the lacunae and contradictions in the scientific evidence then available, which they compiled with great energy and care. The most learned and indomitable of these conservatives was the American Presbyterian Charles Hodge (1797–1878), professor of Theology at Princeton Theological Seminary, whom we will meet again in Chapter 12. Unlike his contemporary, Albrecht Ritschl (see Chapter 11), Hodge would not separate science and theology into two distinct spheres of fact and value. For Hodge science and the Bible were reconcilable. Conflicts could only be apparent and would be shown to be so when either the facts were better known or the truth of the Bible more clearly discerned. As a conservative, Hodge naturally was cautious in accepting new theories. His defense of the Bible against Darwinism often consisted of citations of bits and pieces of scientific information which appeared to contradict Darwin's theory. Reading Hodge today makes one aware of the danger of a theological apologetic based on the "gaps" in scientific knowledge.

Hodge's critique of Darwinism appears in both his monumental three-volume *Systematic Theology* (1872) (which is still used in some conservative Protestant seminaries) and in a more popular book entitled *What is Darwinism?* (1874). One of Hodge's basic criticisms of Darwinism is that it is a fantastic hypothesis lacking full factual evidence. Second, and most importantly, he feels it must be rejected theologically because of its unjustified denial of both the uniqueness of humanity and God's providential design.

> The first objection to the theory is its *prima facie* incredibility. . . . Darwin wants us to believe that all living things, from the lowly violet to the giant redwoods of California, from the microscopic animalcule to the Mastodon, the Dinatherium—monsters the very description of which fill us with horror . . . came one and all from the same primordial germ.[82]

It is, Hodge insists, an incredible hypothesis and can claim to be no more. Hodge makes much of Darwin's own candor in admitting the tentativeness of his own theories. "There is," Hodge writes, "no pretence that the theory can be proved. Mr. Darwin does not pretend to prove it. . . . All he claims for the theory is that it is possible. . . ."[83] Yet the facts can be accounted for in other ways. Darwinists have generally failed to make important distinctions between facts and the theories deduced from them and have expected theologians to swallow some rather far-fetched interpretations.

> No sound-minded man disputes any scientific fact. Religious men believe with Agassiz that facts are sacred. They are revelations from God. Christians sac-

rifice to them, when duly authenticated, their most cherished convictions. . . . Religious men admit all the facts connected with our solar system; all the facts of geology, and of comparative anatomy and of biology. Ought not this to satisfy scientific men? Must we also admit their explanations and influences? If we admit that the human embryo passes through various phases, must we admit that man was once a fish, then a bird, then a dog, then an ape, and finally what he is now? . . . It is to be remembered that the facts are from God, the explanations from men; and the two are often as far apart as Heaven and its antipode.[84]

Hodge was, of course, only partly correct in his distinction between fact and interpretation. Facts and interpretations are interdependent. When the facts are few or vague, honesty should demand very tentative interpretations. More and clearer facts eliminate some theories and make others more or less probable. Hodge could emphasize the distinction because at the time when he wrote the factual evidence in support of Darwin's theories was, in important instances, imprecise and partial. Hodge thus based his critique, in part, on what he considered the paucity of the facts and that they did not appear to support uniformly any single explanation, for example, the mechanism of inheritance. But the facts in support of Darwin's hypothesis at the time were neither as wanting nor as ambiguous as Hodge made them out to be, and as time passed new facts gave greater weight to Darwin's theories. However, Hodge could justifiably claim at the time that Darwin himself had acknowledged "many facts for which his theory will not account."[85]

Hodge did his homework well. He was able to marshal a considerable amount of information which appeared to argue, for example, against the antiquity of the human species and the modification of the species. Yet much of this ammunition consists of citations of overhasty conclusions drawn by geologists and archaeologists concerning human antiquity. A piece of pottery discovered at the mouth of the Nile was claimed to have come from the prehistoric period—until it was proved that it came from the Roman period. Lake-dwellings discovered in Switzerland and dated in the Stone Age later revealed bones of species of living, domesticated animals, and so on. Fossil remains of creatures mixed together, though of widely different periods, are explained by open fissures in the earth into which the more recent species had fallen. Human bones found deeply buried and mingled with extinct animals are accounted for by "sudden catastrophes" such as earthquakes.[86] And so Hodge's argument proceeds. It is not even necessary, he concedes, to accept Archbishop Usher's calculation that the world was created only four thousand years before Christ. Usher adopted the Hebrew text as his guide and assumed that in the genealogical tables each name marked but one generation. But most biblical scholars adopt the Septuagint chronology "so that instead of four thousand years from the creation to the birth of Christ we have nearly six thousand years." And considering the fact that probably more than one generation was designated by each name, the facts of science and history might "make it necessary to admit that eight or ten thousand years have elapsed since the creation of man."[87] Nothing in the Bible, Hodge grants, would stand in the way of such a concession.

Hodge opposed Darwinism, not the possibility of theistic evolution per se, as long as the development of species was under divine control. What Hodge could not concede was natural selection and the chance evolution of new species, for these theories conflicted with the clear teaching of Scripture concerning providential guidance. According to Hodge's reading of the Bible,

> each species was specially created, not *ex nihilo,* nor without the intervention of secondary causes, but nevertheless originally, or not derived, evolved, or developed from preexisting species. These distinct species . . . separately originated, are permanent. They never pass from one into the other. . . . if at any time since the original creation new species have appeared on the earth, they owe their existence to the immediate intervention of God.[88]

Hodge's arguments for the fixity of species may have been plausible at the time, but the study of members of single species geographically separated over long periods, as well as advances in genetics, prove Hodge's arguments wrong. Hodge argued, for example, that members of species geographically separated remain fixed in their original forms and

therefore would be able to breed successfully if reunited. Evidence now shows that this is not true and that, because the hybrid offspring of such unions are at a disadvantage, natural selection will favor the development of barriers to such breeding and in time, through separation, the two forms will evolve into different species.

Fundamental, of course, to Hodge's doctrine of the fixity of species was his protest against the view that humans were developed apes. This ran counter to belief in the *special* creation of humans in a state of original perfection. When Hodge wrote, the oldest known human skull was the "Engis" found in Belgium. One scientist had commented at the time that it was comparable to the skull of an American Indian which, according to Hodge, only went "to show that the earliest men were better developed than any extant races."[89] Again, Hodge cannot be faulted for having written this before the discovery of *Pithecanthropus erectus,* but the precariousness of his method, of picking an isolated statement from a scientist here and appealing to a scientific "gap" there, is evident enough.

In one form or another the teleological argument had remained the basic argument in the arsenal of natural theology. Hodge was aware, from statements of Darwin and Huxley and others, that the Darwinian denial of design implied atheism, though did not demand it. The focus of Hodge's critique of Darwin was directed toward exposing this implication. *For Hodge the peculiar character and danger of Darwinism was neither in its advocacy of evolution, or even natural selection, but in its rejection of teleology, of providential guidance.* Darwin's theory was not only ateleological, it was antiteleological.

> The conclusion of the whole matter is that the denial of design in nature is virtually the denial of God. Mr. Darwin's theory does deny all design in nature, therefore his theory is virtually atheistical; his theory, not he himself. He believes in a Creator. But when that Creator, millions on millions of ages ago, did something—called matter and living germ into existence,—and then abandoned the universe to itself to be controlled by chance and necessity, without any purpose on his part as to the result, or any intervention or guidance, then He is virtually consigned, so far as we are concerned, to non-existence. . . . Mr. Darwin's

admirers adopt and laud his theory, for the special reason that it banishes God from the world.[90]

Hodge believed that, despite some inadequacies, the teleological argument was compelling. For example, he thought preposterous Darwin's suggestion that the eye was the product of the unintended action of blind physical forces: "To any ordinarily constituted mind, it is absolutely impossible to believe that it is not the work of design."[91] Nevertheless, Hodge did not appeal to the teleological argument, as did the American Asa Gray and other evolutionary theists. Hodge believed in design *because* of Christianity's belief in providential guidance. Hodge's argument was not *from* design in nature to God (a largely modern argument of natural theology) but *to* design. That is, presuming a providential God, all things must be designed. Darwinism denied that living species, including the human, are providentially designed. Therefore, in Hodge's judgment, Darwinism is atheistical. In Christianity, God's existence simply entails belief in divine purpose and design.[92]

Hodge further discerned that, as far as a Christian vision of things is concerned, a vague theistic doctrine was not much of an improvement on atheism. Except for belief in a Creator, most orthodox Christian doctrines were irrelevant to an evolutionary theistic teleology. Such a theism is frequently nothing but Deism.

> The second method of accounting for contrivances in nature admits that they are foreseen and purposed by God, and that he endowed matter with forces which He foresaw and intended should produce such results. But here his agency stops. He never interferes to guide the operation of physical causes. He does nothing to control the course of nature or the events of history. . . .[93]

Hodge considered this banishing of God from the world intolerable. Such a God is sub-Christian, is utterly different from the God revealed in the Bible, and would render irrational such Christian practices as prayer.

Hodge sensed better than the liberals of his day the real threat of Darwinism, and his refusal to recast Christian belief in the form of a general evolutionary theism can be viewed as salutary. Where Hodge, and most conservatives like him, failed in meeting the challenge of evolution was in the attempt to deny the factual evidence for the antiquity of the human species, the mutability of species, and other scientific theories by rather desperate appeals to scraps of evidence which could be read in other ingenious ways. It was a hazardous apologetic, since it rested on the slender hope that more definite evidence would not be forthcoming. It was based on the belief that science would never close the "gap" on such questions as the creation of life or the link between the higher apes and rational humans. Since Hodge's position was that biblical teaching never conflicted with scientific fact, he demanded that one respond to new scientific evidence by either denying its validity or by defending the infallibility of Scripture by tortured and ingenious methods of interpretation. Though contrary to Hodge's intention, this was to be the policy of Fundamentalism to the present day.

Christian Darwinisticism: Lyman Abbott

Hodge represented the Christian anti-Darwinian response to Darwin. At the other pole were many theological liberals, the proponents of a Christian Darwinisticism that mixed a pseudo-Darwinism with a progressive evolutionary theism. Their accommodation to evolutionary theories frequently represented a severe reduction in the substance of Christian belief. Some of these writers began as orthodox and evangelical believers but, largely through the influence of evolution, became liberal—even humanistic—in their religious views. In England the accommodation of theology to evolutionary views is best represented in the writings of Henry Drummond (1851–1897). Drummond was a scientist and amateur theologian whose own piety was strongly evangelical. He remained a close friend of conservative theologians and evangelists all his life. Yet his own interpretation of Christianity was far from orthodox. It was an optimistic, evolutionary theism based on the thought of Herbert Spencer, not on Darwin. It ignored the profound enigmas and paradoxes of Christian faith.

In *The Ascent of Man* (1894) Drummond proposed that, contrary to Darwin, all living things exhibit two functions: "Nutrition," the basis of the "Struggle for Life," and "Reproduction," which he associates with the "Struggle for the Life of Others." Drummond proceeds to justify the struggle for life, since its "vigorous mood" has weeded out the imperfect, without which world progress and "the steady advance of the final type" would have been impossible. In Drummond's theodicy the "Struggle for the Life of Others" is, however, steadily advancing over the "Struggle for Life," and the coming Kingdom of Love is a certain prophecy of science itself. "The path of progress," he writes, "and the path of Altruism are one. Evolution is nothing but the Involution of Love, the revelation of Infinite Spirit, the Eternal Life returning to Itself."[94]

The liberal Christian accommodation to evolution was more sweeping in America than in England or on the Continent. Among the earliest and most important of the American reconcilers of evolution and theism was John Fiske (1842–1901). His views were formulated in *Outlines of Cosmic Philosophy* (1874). Fiske's religious speculations had very little relation to Christian theology, but he did exert a strong influence on Unitarian and liberal Trinitarian theologians. Another influential work was *Evolution and its Relation to Religious Thought* (1888) by Joseph LeConte. The first prominent American preacher to join the evolutionists was Henry Ward Beecher (1813–1887) who, in *Evolution and Religion* (1885), declared that science was "the deciphering of God's thought as revealed in the structure of the world."

One of the most thoroughgoing and influential Christian evolutionists was Lyman Abbott (1835–1922), the successor to Beecher in the pulpit of the Plymouth Church in Brooklyn. Abbott was not an original thinker, but few religious writers exerted a greater influence on the American public between 1865 and 1920 than Lyman Abbott. He was a popularizer of new ideas and, at the time of his death, was something of a national patriarch.[95] Once converted to an evolutionary view, Abbott saw in it the intellectual framework within which Christianity could again be made meaningful to thinking persons. Abbott spoke of himself as an evolutionist and not a Darwinist, for he identified the latter with the struggle for existence and the survival of the fittest—that is, with laissez-faire social Darwinism, which he considered unchristian. He adopted LeConte's definition of evolution ("continuous progressive change, according to certain laws and by means of resident forces") as his own and gave it a theological interpretation.

> God's work, we evolutionists believe, is the work of progressive change—a change from a lower to a higher condition; from a simpler to a more complex condition. It is a change wrought according to certain laws which are capable of study. It is never arbitrary. Finally the process of growth is produced by forces that lie within the phenomena themselves. . . . God dwells in nature fashioning it according to His will by vital processes from within, not by mechanical processes from without.[96]

For Abbott the evolutionary laws discovered from a study of nature were identical with the laws of the spiritual life, and he came to believe that the latter were only adequately understood when viewed as analogous to the former. This meant that the older theology, based on a hierarchical feudal model, had to be set aside. It had assumed a God apart from the Universe, ruling over it like a Roman emperor and governing His domain by a series of interventions. The New Theology, as Abbott called it, conceived of God's relation to the world in immanentist and evolutionary categories. It taught that

> God has but one way of doing things . . . the way of growth or development, or evolution; that He resides in the world of nature and in the world of men; that there are no laws of nature which are not the laws of God's own being; that there are no forces of nature, that there is only one divine infinite force, always proceeding from, always subject to the will of God; that there are not occasional or exceptional theophanies, but that all nature and all life is one great theophany; that there are not occasional interventions in the order of life which bear witness to the presence of God, but that life is itself a perpetual witness to His presence.[97]

Abbott used a few basic evolutionary categories to interpret anew the beliefs and institutions of Christianity. Everything is now seen in terms of change, development, and progress. In the Bible we do not see a complete and perfect revelation but "men gradually receiving God's revelation of Himself." The Bible is the "history of the growth of man's consciousness of God."[98] Abbott even spoke of the development of Semitic religion as witnessed to in the Bible as a "process of natural selection."[99]

Abbott's firm belief in historical progress demanded that he reject the traditional view of humanity as having fallen from a state of original perfection. He faced the issue squarely.

> The doctrine of the Fall and of redemption (as traditionally stated) is inconsistent with the doctrine of evolution. It is impossible to reconcile the two. Evolution declares that all life begins at a lower stage and issues through gradual development into a higher.[100]

This means that mankind has progressed from a bestial position to a higher and higher spiritual condition. Sin, for Abbott, is thus described as a relapse caused by the persistence of those depraved elements that lie in the older nature. Sin is the ever-present human experience of partial retrogression. Abbott's definition is similar to Schleiermacher's.

> (The) fall is not an historic act of disobedience by the parents of our race in some prehistoric age, through which a sinful nature has descended. . . . It is the conscious and deliberate descent of the individual soul from the vantage ground of a higher life to the life of the animal from which he had been uplifted.[101]

Spiritual progress is not easy, but Abbott saw too many evidences of moral growth to doubt that it was an historical fact. Society has progressed naturally, or providentially if you prefer, under the impetus of that one "resident force," God. The goal of spiritual evolution was, for Abbott, the full incarnating of Christ in humanity. Christ came not only to exhibit divinity to us "but to evolve the latent divinity which he has implanted in us." Christ is to be seen as "the type and pattern of that which will be wrought in universal humanity when spiritual evolution is consummated."[102]

Abbott envisioned human history as the progressive evolving of divinity out of humanity, and his use of the categories of process and immanent spiritual law led him to stress the continuity and likeness between the divine and humanity. He wrote that "the difference between God and man is a difference not in essential nature" and argued that the Bible taught that "in their essential nature they are the same."[103] An evolutionist, Abbott maintained, could view the divinity of Christ as different only in degree from that of every other human.

> There are differences in degree so great that they became equivalent to a difference in kind; but, with this qualification, I answer unreservedly, the difference is in degree and not in kind. There are not two kinds of divinity. . . . The divinity of man is not different in kind from the divinity of Christ, because it is not different in kind from the divinity of God.[104]

Abbott surveyed human history and saw in it a continuous progressive change from animal instinct to moral virtue, moving according to certain spiritual laws and by means of the force of God. He did not see this process as a grim and ultimately futile struggle for existence but, rather, as a slow but certain victory of Christian love, freedom, and fraternal democracy over selfish individualism and paternalism. History, as Abbott saw it, was the story of a spiritual pilgrimage depicting "the life of God in the soul of man, recreating the individual; through the individual constituting a church; and by the church transforming human society into a kingdom of God."[105]

Abbott's optimistic theology was hailed by liberals as the best restatement of Christianity yet made in the United States. Conservatives attacked him severely for his views on the Bible and for robbing Christ of a unique divinity. It is fairly obvious that Abbott's adjustment of Christianity to evolution was paid for at the price of Christian substance. Abbott played fast and loose with the biblical texts. His talk about the evolutionary unfolding of humanity's latent divinity is close to Pantheism. His view of sin was superficial and his doctrine of redemption naively voluntaristic. The weakness of Abbott's evolutionary theism lay in the fact that he lacked a profound knowledge of theology and knew very little about the technical aspects of evolutionary theory. His correlation, therefore, was lax and superficial, plumbing the depths of neither doctrine.

Yet Abbott hit upon certain aspects raised by evolution which today continue to find a place at the center of philosophical theology. For example, Abbott was concerned with the question of how God was related to the natural order and whether God is the chief metaphysical exemplification of that order, or whether God is to be thought of as apart from and foreign to the world. He was concerned to restate the divine-human natures of Christ in such a way as to make sense of the continuity of Christ's humanity with our own. These are issues presently at the forefront of discussion by process theologians, using the organic and evolutionary categories of A. N. Whitehead. Abbott's theism is different from that of Whitehead, but it is clear that the language and categories of both men are traceable to the evolutionary ideas current since Darwin.

Because of the public utterances of writers such as Moore and Kingsley in England and Beecher and Abbott in the United States, it was frequently reported in the press during the 1880s and 1890s that the quarrel between Darwinism and theology had passed. For Abbott this was true. But the conservatives continued to fight. In the United States the Darwinian controversy did not reach its most bitter and notorious stage until the famous Scopes "Monkey" trial in Tennessee in 1920. In America Darwinism was always close to the center of the Fundamentalist-Modernist battle throughout the first third of the twentieth century. Impervious to the evidence as were the conservatives and the fundamentalists, they did recognize the depths of the challenge of Darwinism of which the liberals were too frequently unaware. The liberal compromises with the Christian theological tradition were indeed great. Huxley, the great "smiter" of the theologians, expressed the annoyance of religious conservatives and skeptics alike when he protested: "There must be some position from which the reconcilers of science and Genesis will not retreat."[106]

It was true that Darwinism did not exclude theism from its view, but it did require a more radical reconception of the doctrine of God than statements like "Evolution is God's way of doing things" appeared to require. Assuming Darwin's doctrines, God appeared to many thoughtful people to be either a rather remote First Cause or a God not assuredly in control. "They asked how an omni-scient mind which knows precisely what is wanted can set Nature *groping* her way forward as if she were blind to find the path of least resistance."[107] Darwinism did not settle the theistic issue by dressing it in evolutionary terms, as Abbott and others had hoped. What Darwinism did was to set the theistic question in an entirely new context. Accepting Darwinian evolution meant a change in world-view, hence a new understanding of God and God's relation to the world. Would, then, the old attributes of God still apply? For instance, is God's omnipotence and omniscience believable in Darwin's radically fortuitous world of natural selection? These questions could no longer be settled by appeal to a pre-Darwinian cosmology.

The conservative theologians also recognized Darwin's challenge to traditional Christian anthropology. They saw how fatal to certain Christian values was natural selection and the survival of the fittest. Again, Abbott's rosy vision of progress simply ignored this whole dimension of Darwinism. For Darwin survival was a brute fact. In no way did it imply the victory of moral values. Survival of the fittest was not equivalent to the survival of goodness or beauty. Huxley understood this better than most evolutionists. "Let us understand once and for all," he wrote, "that the ethical progress of society depends, not on imitating the cosmic process, still less in running away from it, but in combating it."[108] The biblical picture of humanity was perhaps true after all, despite its deception. Is not humanity that unique species found at the crossroads of nature and spirit, a creature of evolution who at the same time finds itself reluctant master of the evolutionary process itself?

The profound moral ambiguities of human nature and history, made more rather than less acute by Darwinism, were seldom plumbed by the liberal theologians, or the scientists. The times, of course, lent support to a progressive, optimistic vision of human history. Events of the twentieth century would prove grim reminders of other dimensions of the human spirit. Neo-Orthodox and Existentialist theology would find much in Darwin, as in Freud, that would support the Bible's realistic portrayal of the human condition. They would also find in the Bible dimensions of human existence and spiritual resources ignored by positivism and naturalism.

The challenge of Darwinism to Christian thought was very great. It called into question age-old interpretations of the Bible; challenged traditional conceptions of God and humanity's place in nature; and forced theology to reconceive its doctrines in new metaphysical categories. If the immediate threat was frequently traumatic, the long-term effect may be salutary. Christian thought was forced to give up much that was untenable and which stood in the way of an honest profession of faith. If some Christian substance was lost in the process of accommodation, more recent history has shown that the fundamental substance of Christian belief has survived. But, contrary to common opinion, the conflict between Darwinism and Christianity is far from over. Certain issues are now agreed upon, others are still under debate, but the world-views of Darwinism and Christianity are, on a few fundamental issues, irreconcilable. The discussion continues, and, as we shall see, the problems raised for Christian theism by evolution have elicited creative new responses in the twentieth century.

We next turn to a movement of Protestant Liberalism (Ritschlianism) of the late nineteenth century that engaged the issues raised by both historical criticism and development and natural science. It did so in creative ways that proved extremely influential. The movement began in Germany but soon spread to the English-speaking world.

NOTES

1. *Allegemeine Bibliothek der biblischen Litteratur,* IV, Part 6 (1793), 997f.
2. J. W. Colenso, *The Pentateuch and Joshua,* I (London, 1862), 143f.
3. W. E. H. Lecky, *Democracy and Liberty,* Vol. 7 (1896), 424–425. Cited in E. Abbott and L. Campbell, *The Life and Letters of Benjamin Jowett,* Vol. I (London, 1897), 196.
4. Abbott and Campbell, *Life and Letters of Benjamin Jowett,* p. 345.
5. Ibid., pp. 275–276.
6. H. B. Wilson, "The National Church," in *Essays and Reviews* (London, 1860), p. 175. Unless otherwise indicated, future citations will be taken from this edition.
7. Ibid., p. 51.
8. Ibid., p. 56.
9. Ibid., p. 69.
10. Ibid., p. 77.
11. Ibid., p. 78.
12. Ibid.
13. C. W. Goodwin, "On the Mosaic Cosmogony," in *Essays and Reviews,* p. 211.
14. Ibid., pp. 224–225.
15. Ibid., p. 226.
16. Ibid., p. 227.
17. Ibid., pp. 227–228.
18. Ibid., pp. 239–240.
19. Ibid., p. 240.
20. Ibid., pp. 250–251.
21. B. Jowett, "On the Interpretation of Scripture," in *Essays and Reviews,* pp. 373–374.
22. Ibid., p. 374.
23. Ibid., p. 354.
24. Ibid., p. 358.
25. Ibid., pp. 337–338.
26. Ibid., pp. 379, 380.
27. Ibid., pp. 382–383.
28. Ibid., pp. 345–346.
29. Ibid., pp. 347, 348.
30. Ibid., p. 387.
31. Ibid., pp. 387–388.
32. Ibid.
33. Abbott and Campbell, op. cit., Vol. II, 273.
34. Ibid.
35. For full accounts of the responses to *Essays and Reviews,* see Josef Altholz, *Anatomy of a Controversy: The Debate over Essays and Reviews, 1860–64* (Andershot, 1994); and Ieuan Ellis, *Seven against Christ: A Study of 'Essays and Reviews'* (Leiden, 1980).
36. Geoffrey Faber, *Jowett* (London, 1957), p. 278.
37. *Aids to Faith,* ed. W. Thomson (London, 1861), p. 318.
38. Ibid., p. 314.
39. Cited in Faber, op cit., p. 288.
40. *Life and Letters of F. J. A. Hort,* I, ed. A. F. Hort (London, 1896), pp. 399–400.
41. Ibid., pp. 428, 440, 442.
42. Leonard Hodgson, *Biblical Theology and the Sovereignty of God* (Cambridge, 1947), pp. 16–17.

I am indebted to Basil Willey's *Nineteenth Century Studies* for this reference.

43. For an account of this period, see John Hedley Brooke, *Science and Religion: Some Historical Perspectives* (Cambridge, 1991).

44. *The Works of William Paley*, Vol. I, ed. G. W. Meadley (Boston, 1810), 16.

45. Francis Darwin, *Life and Letters of Charles Darwin* (London, 1887), II, 219.

46. Paley, op. cit., p. 311.

47. Charles Lyell, *Principles of Geology* (London, 1830–1833), I, 164.

48. Ibid., p. 144.

49. G. S. Carter, *A Hundred Years of Evolution* (London, 1957), p. 22.

50. Robert Chambers, *Vestiges of the Natural History of Creation,* 4th ed. (London, 1844).

51. Ibid., p. 232.

52. Ibid.

53. Ibid.

54. Charles Darwin, *On the Origin of the Species,* 4th ed. (London, 1866), XVIII.

55. *Vestiges,* p. 158.

56. Francis Darwin and A. E. Seward, *More Letters,* I (London, 1903), 194.

57. *The Autobiography of Charles Darwin,* ed. Nora Barlow (London, 1958), p. 87.

58. F. Darwin, *Life and Letters,* I, 83.

59. C. Darwin, op. cit., p. 577.

60. John C. Greene, *The Death of Adam* (Ames, 1959), p. 302.

61. C. Darwin, *The Descent of Man* (New York, 1962), p. 528.

62. John Dillenberger, *Protestant Thought and Natural Science* (London, 1961), pp. 217–218.

63. David Lack, *Evolutionary Theory and Christian Belief* (London, 1957).

64. The most reliable account of this event can be found in Adrian Desmond and James Moore, *Darwin* (New York, 1992), Chap. 33.

65. J. W. Clark and T. M. Hughes, eds., *Life of Adam Sedgwick,* II (Cambridge, 1890), 357–358.

66. Asa Gray, *Darwiniana* (New York, 1876), p. 69. Gray tried unsuccessfully to convert Darwin to a modified theistic teleology. Darwin vacillated in his own attitude toward teleology. At times he acknowledged a teleology but rejected most of the teleological speculation of his scientific contemporaries. His own view is probably best expressed in a letter to Gray, in which he wrote: "I cannot think that the world as we see it is the result of chance; and yet I cannot look at each separate thing as the result of design. . . . I am, and

shall ever remain, in a hopeless muddle." (F. Darwin, *Life and Letters,* II, p. 146).

67. D. A. Wilson and D. W. MacArthur, *Carlyle in Old Age* (London, 1834).

68. *Life and Letters of F. J. A. Hort,* I, 474.

69. *Life and Memories of Charles Kingsley,* II, ed. Mrs. Kingsley (London, 1877), 288.

70. Cited in Lack, op. cit., p. 19.

71. James R. Moore, in *The Post-Darwinian Controversies,* offers a helpful typology of theological responses to Darwinism which he calls Christian Darwinism, Christian Anti-Darwinism, and Christian Darwinisticism. We will cite examples of each type.

72. F. Temple, *The Relations between Religion and Science* (London, 1884), p. 115.

73. Aubrey Moore, *Science and the Faith* (London, 1889).

74. Ibid., pp. 184–185.

75. Ibid., p. 199.

76. Ibid., pp. 202–203.

77. Ibid., p. 204.

78. Ibid., p. 208.

79. Ibid., p. 210.

80. Ibid., p. 212.

81. Ibid., pp. 230–231.

82. C. Hodge, *What Is Darwinism?* (New York, 1874), pp. 142–143.

83. Ibid., pp. 144–145.

84. Ibid., pp. 131–132.

85. C. Hodge, *Systematic Theology,* II (New York, 1872), 19.

86. Ibid., pp. 29–47.

87. Ibid., pp. 40–47.

88. Ibid., p. 26.

89. Hodge, *What Is Darwinism?* p. 158.

90. Ibid., pp. 173–174.

91. Ibid., p. 60.

92. For this point regarding Hodge's appeal to the argument *to* design, I am dependent on Jonathan Wells, *Charles Hodge's Critique of Darwinism* (Lewiston, N.Y., 1988).

93. Hodge, *What Is Darwinism?* p. 44.

94. Henry Drummond, *The Ascent of Man* (London, 1894), p. 46.

95. Ira V. Brown, *Lyman Abbott* (Cambridge, 1953), p. 2.

96. Lyman Abbott, *The Theology of an Evolutionist* (London, 1897), p. 21.

97. Ibid., pp. 9–10.

98. L. Abbott, *The Evolution of Christianity* (London, 1892), p. 66.

99. Ibid., p. 249.

100. Ibid., p. 206.

101. Ibid., p. 227.
102. Ibid., pp. 250–251.
103. Abbott, *Theology,* pp. 188–189.
104. Ibid., p. 73.
105. Abbott, *Evolution,* p. 258.
106. T. H. Huxley, *Essays on Some Controverted Questions* (London, 1894), p. 89.

107. R. H. Hutton, *Aspects of Religious and Scientific Thought* (London, 1899), p. 48.
108. Thomas Huxley, *Evolution and Ethics and Other Essays* (New York, 1896), p. 83.

SUGGESTIONS FOR FURTHER READING

I. Biblical Criticism and Essays and Reviews

General Accounts of Biblical Criticism in the Nineteenth Century

Clements, R. E. "The Study of the Old Testament." In *Nineteenth Century Religious Thought in the West,* III, ed. Ninian Smart (Cambridge: Cambridge University Press, 1985).

Kümmel, Werner George. *The New Testament: A History of the Investigation of Its Problems* (London, 1973). A classic study of the history of New Testament criticism.

Neill, Stephen. *The Interpretation of the New Testament 1861–1961* (Oxford: Oxford University Press, 1966). The early chapters give a fine perspective on British biblical criticism in this period.

Niel, William. "The Criticism and Theological Uses of the Bible, 1700–1950." In *The Cambridge History of the Bible,* ed. S. L.Greenslade (Cambridge: Cambridge University Press, 1975).

O'Neill, J. C. "The Study of the New Testament." In *Nineteenth Century Religious Thought in the West,* III, ed. Ninian Smart (Cambridge: Cambridge University Press, 1985).

"Essays and Reviews" and Its Background

Altholz, Josef L. *Anatomy of a Controversy: The Debate over "Essays and Reviews" 1860–1864* (Andershot: Scholar, 1994).

Ellis, Ieuan. *Seven against Christ: A Study of "Essays and Reviews"* (Leiden: E. J. Brill, 1980). The studies of Altholz and Ellis are thorough explorations of the background, of the essays themselves, and the aftermath and significance of this controversy.

Willey, Basil. "Septem Contra Christum." In *More Nineteenth Century Studies* (New York: Harper and Row, 1966). A brief, highly readable account.

II. Darwinism and Christianity

General Works on Science and Theology in the Period

Bowler, Peter J. *Evolution: The History of an Idea* (Berkeley: University of California Press, 1984). This book does not focus specifically on science and religion, but it gives an excellent account of evolutionary theory since the eighteenth century and its religious and social significance.

Brooke, John Hedley. *Science and Religion: Some Historical Perspectives* (Cambridge: Cambridge University Press, 1991). Chapters 4–8 offer a superb account of the science and religion issues since Newton, including perceptive chapters on natural theology and on Darwinism. Includes an excellent bibliography of the most up-to-date literature.

Gillispie, Charles Coulston. *Genesis and Geology: The Impact of Scientific Discoveries upon Religious Beliefs in the Decades before Darwin* (New York: Harper and Row, 1959). This study remains an excellent source of information on the topic of its title, although its view of Catastrophic and Uniformitarian geology is now widely challenged.

On Darwin and Darwinism

Kohn, David, ed. *The Darwinian Heritage* (Princeton: Princeton University Press, 1985). This collection of essays by Darwin scholars covers Darwin's own development and that of his revolutionary theory; Darwin in his social context; the reception of Darwinism; and perspectives on Darwin and Darwinism.

Ruse, Michael. *The Darwinian Revolution* (Chicago: University of Chicago Press, 1979). This is one of the best general accounts of the social and scientific background of Darwinism, Darwin's theory, and the scientific, philosophical, and religious response.

On Darwin's Religious Views

Brooke, J. H. "The Relations between Darwin's Science and His Religion." In *Darwinism and Divinity: Essays on Evolution and Religious Belief,* ed. John Durant (Oxford: Basil Blackwell, 1985). This book includes other valuable essays on Darwinism and theology.

Brown, Frank Burch. *The Evolution of Darwin's Religious Views* (Macon, Ga.: Mercer University Press, 1986). This monograph gives a fine overview of the subject.

Desmond, Adrian, and James Moore. *Darwin* (New York: Warner Books, Inc., 1991). This masterful biography presents the most authoritative account and one that emphasizes the social and family context.

Gillespie, Neil C. *Charles Darwin and the Problem of Creation* (Chicago: University of Chicago Press, 1979). Emphasizes the residual theism in Darwin's writings.

The Reception of Darwinism

Ellegaard, Alvar. *Darwinism and the General Reader: The Reception of Darwin's Theory of Evolution in the British Periodical Press, 1859–1872* (Gothenburg, 1958). Important study of the initial response in Britain beyond the scientific community.

Gregory, Frederick. *Nature Lost: Natural Science and the German Theological Traditions of the Nineteenth Century* (Cambridge: Harvard University Press, 1992). A study of four different theological responses, primarily to Darwinism, by German theologians, including Strauss and Herrmann.

Hull, David. *Darwin and His Critics: The Reception of Darwin's Theory of Evolution by the Scientific Community* (Cambridge: Harvard University Press, 1973).

Livingstone, David N. *Darwin's Forgotten Defenders: The Encounter between Evangelical Theology and Evolutionary Thought* (Grand Rapids: Eerdmans Publishing Company, 1987). Valuable study that helps (with Moore below) to put to rest the view of an inevitable "warfare" between Darwinism and theology.

Moore, James R. *The Post-Darwinian Controversies: A Study of the Protestant Struggle to Come to Terms with Darwin in Great Britain and America 1870–1900* (Cambridge: Cambridge University Press, 1979). The finest study to date of the Protestant response to Darwin in the Anglo-American world.

Roberts, Jon H. *Darwinism and the Divine in America: Protestant Intellectuals and Organic Evolution, 1859–1900* (Madison: University of Wisconsin Press, 1988).

Wells, Jonathan. *Charles Hodge's Critique of Darwinism* (Lewiston: Edwin Mellon Press, 1988). Perceptive and sympathetic account of Hodge's critique of Darwinism.

Chapter 11
The Ritschlian Theology
and Protestant Liberalism

Albrecht Ritschl

In the last decades of the nineteenth century in Germany, Hegelian Idealism was in sharp decline. The time was ripe for a new effort to bring Christianity into a creative relationship with the intellectual *Zeitgeist*. The closing decades of the century witnessed a rather widespread repudiation of Speculative Idealism and a revival of the Critical Idealism of Kant. It was also a time of advance in the application of the methods of historical-critical research to the biblical texts and the history of dogma. The intellectual climate was, therefore, one of metaphysical agnosticism and historical positivism. Kant's critical epistemology had shown that knowledge is limited to the experience of phenomena. For Kant the only access to God, the only route out of our finitude is by way of the practical reason. With the demise of Hegelianism, the German Neo-Kantians returned to this position of Kant.

The rejection of philosophical speculation went hand in hand with a concentration on the empirical and historical. Even our moral value judgments do not emerge in a vacuum but are mediated to us through our participation in a historical tradition and social experience. Schleiermacher was quite correct in grounding religious faith in experience, but even he failed to see adequately that Christian experience is only appropriated through particular historical events mediated through a community. The new call, therefore, was not only "back to Kant" but also "back to the historical sources." The theological response to this call was the Ritschlian school of theology whose influence dominated Protestant thought in Germany from 1875 to World War I and in America from the turn of the century until as late as 1930.

The school is named after Albrecht Ritschl, whose writings influenced a generation of theologians who, though independent in many respects, reflected certain common tendencies that are traceable principally to Ritschl himself. By and large, the Ritschlian theologians turned aside from classical metaphysics or the investigation of the "universal foundations of all being," in large part because it failed to make the crucial differentiation between the realm of nature and that of the spiritual life [*geistige Leben*], the life of persons. Consequently, they rejected the speculative theology of the rationalists and their "proofs" of the existence of God. The Ritschlians also clearly distinguished between religion and dogma and often associated the latter with metaphysics. They did not reject dogma but, like Schleiermacher, saw it as derived from religious experience and as protecting religious truths. They were highly critical of what they considered to be the sterile dogmatism of the Protestant "confessionalists" and called for a reappropriation of the vital, living religion of biblical faith and of the Protestant Reformers, especially Luther. In addition, the Ritschlians were suspicious not only of speculative and dogmatic Christianity but of mystical and individualistic expressions of piety which they detected both in medieval Catholicism and in later German Pietism, and even in Schleiermacher and his followers. By contrast, the Ritschlians understood Christianity as essentially an historical and practical or moral religion, with emphasis on the historical revelation in Jesus Christ and on the theme of the kingdom of God—as the community of spiritually free persons—as the regulative principle of a Christian theology. Because they gave special attention to these themes, many consider Ritschlianism to be the perfect expression of Protestant Liberal theology. The identification is accurate, although the position of the Ritschlians has often been caricatured by their conservative and Neo-Orthodox critics. Many of the Ritschlians were theologians and historians of great erudition, whose ideas were more subtle and complex than is generally realized.

In the last decades of the nineteenth century, the major theological faculties in Germany—Berlin, Marburg, Tübingen, Jena, Leipzig—were dominated by Ritschl's pupils or under the influence of his writings. The major theological journals, such as *Die christliche Welt* and *Theologische Literaturzeitung*, became organs of the Ritschlian school. Among the numerous theologians inspired by Ritschl's ideas, the most important in Germany included Wilhelm Herrmann, Julius Kaftan, Theodor Häring, and Adolf von Harnack. In America most liberal theologians in the early decades of the twentieth century, men such as Henry Churchill King, Arthur Cushman McGiffert, William Adams Brown, and Walter Rauschenbusch, acknowledged their indebtedness to the Ritschlian school. Of necessity, we will confine our discussion of Ritschlian Liberalism to four significant figures: Ritschl himself, Herrmann, Harnack, and Rauschenbusch.

ALBRECHT RITSCHL

Albrecht Ritschl (1822–1889) was born in Berlin, the son of a prominent Lutheran preacher who became General Superintendent of the Lutheran Church of Pomerania when Albrecht was five years old. Young Ritschl grew up in Stettin amid a deep, vigorous Lutheran spirituality. When he entered the university in 1839, he was already committed to the study of theology. He attended lectures at Bonn, Halle, and Heidelberg but remained unsatisfied with the "mediating" theology he found there. At Tübingen he attached himself to the historian F. C. Baur and in his earliest work on the Gospels gave support to Baur's hypothesis concerning the origins of Christianity. A decade later in the second edition of his first important work, on the rise of the old Catholic Church, Ritschl rejected the Baurian and quasi-Hegelian theory that the early Church is a synthesis of primitive Jewish and Gentile Christianity. At this point, Ritschl began his own independent studies of the New Testament and the history of doctrine and of systematic theology.

Ritschl began his teaching career at Bonn in 1846. In 1864 he was invited to the chair at Göttingen, where he taught for a quarter century. He continued to lecture on the New Testament but devoted more of his time in these later years to systematic theology. Outside of his scientific work in theology, his life, like Kant's, was uneventful. Between 1870 and 1874 he published the three volumes of his magnum opus, *The Christian Doctrine of Justification and Reconciliation.* The

English translation of the important third volume appeared in 1900.

It was the publication of this great work that marks the beginning of Ritschl's wide influence which, by 1890, dominated Germany. Ritschl did not encourage the formation of a school, but attacks on his writings from the orthodox, the pietists, and those liberals opposed to his views soon drew men like Herrmann and Harnack together in defense of his position. Ritschl was not averse, however, to theological controversy and proved an energetic and sharp disputant. His works after 1874 reflect the controversy inspired by his new ideas. Principal among these writings is *Theology and Metaphysics* (1881) and the three-volume *History of Pietism* (1880–1886). The latter, while a work of great historical learning, sought also to discredit Pietism as a malignant revival of Catholic piety within evangelical Protestantism. Ritschl's reputation as the most influential Church theologian between Schleiermacher and Karl Barth does not rest, however, on these works but on *The Christian Doctrine of Justification and Reconciliation*. The attention that is given to this great work is, however, usually limited to Ritschl's "positive development" of the doctrines of justification and reconciliation in the third volume of this opus. This disregard of the exegetical and historical work in the first two volumes has rather distorted our understanding of Ritschl's own self-understanding of the theological task, as well as his influence on those who followed him.

Ritschl's distinctive constructive theology was dependent on decades of work as a painstaking historian and biblical exegete, reflected not only in a wide range of earlier studies of church history, but also in *The Christian Doctrine of Justification and Reconciliation* itself. Ritschl perceived his work as that of an historical theologian—and at least two-thirds of his published output is the work of an historian—and not that of a systematic theologian. He saw himself as carrying forward the "unfinished Reformation" of the sixteenth century, an event he understood to be of world-historical importance with great significance for modern culture. However, Ritschl also considered the Protestant Reformation as not only unfinished but also deformed by later

developments. The great Reformers such as Luther and Calvin reformed church practice and institutions, but they failed to carry out a thorough reformulation of theology; rather, they merely reintroduced older medieval and scholastic formulations in a new guise. And then Protestant theology in the seventeenth and eighteenth centuries only reinforced these tendencies in Lutheran and Reformed Orthodoxy.

Ritschl believed that this deformation of biblical-Reformation religion (as distinct from theology) had contributed to the impoverishment and marginalization of Protestantism in the modern world. Therefore, the task of the modern theologian is to reconstruct theology through a creative reinterpretation of the vital religious ideas of the Reformers, as those ideas illuminate the New Testament message. Ritschl was certain that such a reconstruction of this heritage would prove of great importance in meeting the problems of the modern world.[1]

As we turn now to Ritschl's constructive appropriation and development of the Christian theological tradition as he understood it, it is important that we remember that his "synthesis" is built upon his laborious work of scriptural exegesis and his study of church history and that he envisioned this historical work as serving the task of carrying forward the "unfinished Reformation."

Ritschl's Practical View of Religion

Ritschl agreed with Schleiermacher that religion is a matter of experience and that Christian theology is a matter of Christian experience. Where the two giants of Protestant Liberal theology differed was on the nature of religious experience. Ritschl considered Schleiermacher's definition of religion as "the feeling of absolute dependence" to be wrong on several counts. First, Schleiermacher's concentration on the "Christian consciousness" of the individual, while mediated through the Christian community, was, in Ritschl's view, dangerously close to subjectivism. For Ritschl the historian, the proper object of theology is not the individual's consciousness but the historical reality of the Gospel as given in the New Testament. Christian doctrine is to be formed solely by reference to the Gospel norm, i.e., the historical Jesus Christ. As one of Ritschl's disciples asserted, "A Ritschlian is spared the agony of self-analysis; nor is it for him by taking stock of himself to fix the factors by which he can best make clear, to himself or others, wherein the content of Christianity lies."[2] The theologian's task is simply to explicate the meaning of the content of God's *self-revelation* as historically given in the person of Jesus Christ.

Second, Schleiermacher's emphasis on feeling does not properly locate the essence of religious experience. For Ritschl religion is an entirely practical matter. It is neither mystical feeling nor, as with the Hegelians, metaphysical knowledge. Religion is fundamentally *the experience of spiritual freedom,* of being liberated from bondage to nature's blind necessity. Religious faith first emerges in relation to the human struggle with and overcoming of a mechanistic determinism. Humans are both creatures of nature and spiritual beings who recognize their natural limitations and capacity to posit and strive toward the achievement of spiritual ends. Religion is the answer to this contradiction in human existence in that only God or a Supreme Power can guarantee the victory of the world of ends and of the spiritual life:

> In every religion what is sought, with the help of the superhuman spiritual power reverenced by man, is a solution of the contradiction in which man finds himself, as both a part of the world of nature and a spiritual personality claiming to dominate nature. For in the former *role* he is a part of nature, dependent upon her, subject to and confined by other things; but as spirit he is moved by the impulse to maintain his independence against them. In this juncture, religion springs up as faith in superhuman spiritual powers, by whose help the power which man possesses of himself is in some way supplemented, and elevated into a unity of its own kind which is a match for the pressure of the natural world.[3]

Ritschl also disagrees with Schleiermacher's idea of God as the source or object of the mystical feeling of absolute dependence. For Ritschl such a conception is religiously too impersonal and misrepresents the Christian experience of God, since

Christians experience God through *faith in God's liberating grace as that is uniquely revealed in the person and work of Christ.* God is known neither passively and impersonally (mystically) nor theoretically (metaphysically) but actively and personally—what today we would call existentially—since God is personally experienced as the sole guarantor of our spiritual victory over the world.[4]

This does not mean that God is a "fiction" introduced to encourage us to think "as if" we had gained freedom over nature. God is experienced as that reality and power which *alone* can and does deliver us from helplessness. It is just that such a God cannot be *known* abstractly in terms of some metaphysical essence but only practically.

> Knowledge of God can be demonstrated as *religious knowledge* only when He is conceived as securing to the believer such a position in the world as more than counterbalances its restrictions. Apart from this value-judgment of faith, there exists no knowledge of God worthy of this content.[5] (Italics added.)

The Theory of Value Judgments and the Historical Jesus Christ

The theory of "value judgments" is one of the keys to Ritschl's theology and probably his most significant contribution to religious thought. Ritschl's theory of value judgments is dependent on the philosopher R. H. Lotze's (1817–1881) modification of Kant's theory concerning how the mind receives sensations or impressions from the phenomenal world. According to Lotze, the mind receives impressions of phenomena in a twofold way. On the one hand, the mind judges sensations in respect to the causal relations in an objective system of nature. This is the method of scientific or theoretical knowledge. On the other hand, the mind receives sensations according to their worth to an ego susceptible to feelings of pleasure and pain. This is the source of the mind's knowledge of value. These two functions of the mind—making causal judgments and value judgments—work simultaneously and both are indispensable to knowledge. In this view no form of scientific knowledge is completely disinterested. But just because "value-judgments are determinative in the case of all connected knowledge (scientific) of the world," Ritschl goes on to distinguish between what he calls "concomitant" and "independent" value judgments.

> The former are operative and necessary in all theoretical cognition, as in all technical observation and combination. But *independent* value judgments are all perceptions of moral ends or moral hindrances, in so far as they excite moral pleasure or pain, or, it may be, set in motion the will to appropriate what is good, or repel the opposite. . . . Religious knowledge moves in independent value-judgments, which relate to man's attitude to the world, and call forth feelings of pleasure or pain, in which man either enjoys the dominion over the world vouchsafed him by God, or feels grievously the lack of God's help to that end.[6]

It would be quite wrong to speak of these two modes of cognition as objective and subjective, if we mean by subjective value judgment a denial of the objective reality of the value. Both modes of cognition give us real, objective, though quite different, knowledge. Ritschl agrees with Kant that we cannot know things in themselves (*Ding an sich*), but with Lotze he asserts positively that we can know things through their qualities and effects on us and our response to them.

It is important to point out that Ritschl's discussion of the cognitive truth of value judgments is found in that section of *Justification and Reconciliation* which concerns the doctrine of God and the failure of the Scholastic "proofs" of the existence of God. Ritschl was convinced that the critique of natural theology carried out by Hume and Kant was entirely convincing. In the case of the ontological argument, the natural theologians had failed "to prove the *objective existence* of God as contrasted with His existence in thought." In the case of the cosmological and teleological arguments, the theologians failed to prove the existence *of God.*" What they proved was the necessity in thought of a first cause and last end, but these are theoretical ideas which, as Hume has shown, require none of the moral and personal attributes of the Christian God.

Now it is true that the Christian idea of God, our Father in Christ, includes in itself the ideas of a First Cause and Final End, as subordinate characteristics. But, posited as independent things, the conceptions of first cause and final end fail to transcend the conception of the world, and therefore fall short of the Christian idea of God.[7]

The fact is, according to Ritschl, that God cannot be known in himself but "only in his effects upon us," only as God is revealed to us as the guarantor of our victory over the natural world.

> Apart from this value-judgment of faith, there exists no knowledge of God worthy of this content. So that we ought not to strive after a purely theoretical and "disinterested" knowledge of God, as an indispensable preliminary to the knowledge of faith. To be sure, people say that we must know the nature of God and Christ ere we can ascertain their worth for us. But Luther's insight perceived the incorrectness of such a view. The truth rather is that we know the nature of God and Christ *only in their worth for us. For God and faith are inseparable conceptions;* faith, however, confessedly does not consist in abstract knowledge or knowledge which deals with *merely* historical facts. . . . For the "goodness and power" of God, on which faith casts itself, is in Luther's view revealed *in the work of Christ alone."*[8] (Italics added.)

God can be known only in his worth for us as revealed in the work of Christ and as appropriated by faith. In Ritschl's view, "by faith" is an absolutely necessary condition for any knowledge of God, for God is not revealed *merely* in historical facts. Actually, there are no such things as neutral, disinterested, historical facts. Facts are always interpreted facts. Take, for example, the crucifixion of Jesus. Can we know that event-in-itself? Do we not appropriate the meaning of that event through the quite different responses of a dutiful but indifferent Roman soldier, a pious but doubting Pharisee, or a faithful and believing disciple who sees in it the gracious action of God? A scientific description of the crucifixion can tell us some important facts, but it cannot judge of its religious worth. And judgments of worth are fundamentally more important than mere judgments of fact, for our existential attitude toward the world and our fellows is dependent on just such judgments of value.

Ritschl would wish to add, however, that it would be quite misleading to say that while for the Christian consciousness Jesus has the value of God, for the scientific consciousness he has *only* the valuation of a man. The point is that judgments of fact and judgments of value are always "mutually related" and operate simultaneously. The scientific consciousness per se can neither affirm nor deny anything about the value of Jesus, let alone about his divinity. Science simply overreaches its bounds when it attempts to make such value determinations. Therefore it cannot possibly be said that science as such gives us a "truer" picture of Jesus since it can never give us an estimate of his worth without stepping outside its limits.

The indissoluble relation between fact and value had important implications for Ritschl's whole method. It meant that we cannot know the objects of religious experience in themselves either by Hegelian ratiocination or by some special mystical sense. At the same time it implied that the norms of Christian theology are not grounded in the individual consciousness but in the concrete events of history. Yet the historical norm, i.e., the Christ, is never simply derived as an inference from the historical facts but is always a value judgment of faith. Thus Ritschl's view of the historical Jesus Christ sought to avoid the twin dangers of historical positivism and idealism. Historical positivism, as evidenced in the "back to Jesus" movement, wished to strip away the faith of the early Church and get back to the "bare facts" of the original Jesus. Ritschl has often been erroneously identified with just those positivists who wished to separate the "Jesus of history" from the "Christ of faith." Nothing could have been further from Ritschl's view. For Ritschl the historical Jesus cannot even be known in himself independent of the experience of the early Church and the effects he produces on us as members of the Christian community.

> Authentic and complete knowledge of Jesus' religious significance—His significance, that is, as a Founder of religion—depends on one's reckoning oneself part of the community which he founded. . . . This religious faith does not take an unhistorical view

of Jesus, and it is quite possible to reach an historical estimate of Him without first divesting oneself of this faith, this religious valuation of His Person. The opposite view is one of the characteristics which mark that great untruth which exerts a deceptive and confusing influence under the name of an historical "absence of presuppositions." *It is no mere accident that the subversion of Jesus' religious importance has been undertaken under the guise of writing His life,* for this very undertaking implies the surrender of the conviction that Jesus, as the Founder of the perfect moral and spiritual religion, belongs to a higher order than all other men. But for that reason *it is likewise vain to attempt to re-establish the importance of Christ by the same biographical expedient.* We can discover the full compass of His historical actuality solely from the faith of the Christian community.[9] (Italics added.)

Ritschl clearly had no interest in getting back to the historical Jesus in order to circumvent the risk of faith; nor was he guilty of subsuming the content or norm of the Christian religion *solely* within the subjective act of faith. Ritschl saw the hermeneutical interdependence of history *and* faith. He, therefore, called for the application of the most rigorous historical criticism in reconstructing the historical Jesus Christ, for he believed that only such historical honesty could save theology from subjective fancy and speculative flights from historical revelation. At the same time he saw the impossibility of getting back to the original Jesus on supposedly "objective" or "neutral" presuppositions concerning his person. Any such judgment of Jesus's person and work is a judgment of value. Ritschl thus sought to maintain an integral connection between the *fides quae creditur* (the faith that is believed) and the *fides qua creditur* (the personal act of faith or trust).

Ritschl's insistence on beginning with the witness of the early Church concerning the historical person of Jesus Christ does not mean that he took an uncritical attitude toward the primitive traditions. Ritschl did not accept the Gospel "picture" of Jesus Christ *as such* but recognized the necessity of making historical judgments concerning the various layers of Christological tradition. He held that all the Gospel traditions must find their "criterion in the historical figure presented by his [Christ's] life." For Ritschl this meant that all speculations concerning

Christ's pre-existence and post-existence must be checked by what we know concerning the historical figure. This check even extends to those "supernatural" events of the Gospels such as the Virgin Birth, the miracles, and the Resurrection. For Ritschl these "historical" traditions are not integral to any estimate of the historical figure of Jesus Christ.

It is just at this point that the ambiguities of Ritschl's hermeneutic become apparent. Ritschl appears to want to say that the "back to Jesus" movement erred in seeking to derive the normative Jesus Christ solely from the historical facts, and yet he himself proceeds to make judgments as to what traditions concerning Jesus Christ are normative for faith on the basis of the criterion of the "historical figure presented by His life."[10] It is clear that Ritschl wants to infer Christological normativeness only from certain strata of the historical traditions.

The Person and Work of Christ

Despite certain difficulties that one encounters in Ritschl's statements on the relation of faith and history, it is clear that he wished to begin with the historical Jesus Christ. He rejected the possibility of getting back to a Jesus behind the sources, but, on the other hand, he denied the validity of the traditional Christological formulae, since they tended to be abstractions unrelated to the historical person of Jesus Christ and having no genuine bearing on experience.

For Ritschl to know Christ's person is to know his work or, as the Lutheran theologian Philip Melanchthon would say, his benefits. To begin with an abstract definition of Christ, such as in the Nicene and Chalcedonian formulae, is to confuse a disinterested, scientific judgment with a judgment of faith. According to Ritschl, to speak of Christ as God

> is not a judgment which belongs to the sphere of disinterested scientific knowledge, like the formula of Chalcedon. When therefore, my opponents demand in this connection a judgment of the latter sort, they reveal their own inability to distinguish scientific from religious knowledge, which means that they are not really at home in the sphere of religion.[11]

To begin with a priori notions concerning God and Christ before examining historical revelation itself is a false method of theological cognition. Luther's approach to the person of Christ is, for Ritschl, the only valid one, for

> while assuming the formula of the two natures, *Luther really connects the religious estimate of Christ as God with the significance which Christ's work has for the Christian community.* . . . According to Luther, the Godhead of Christ is not exhausted by maintaining the existence in Christ of the Divine nature; the chief point is that *in His exertions as man His Godhead is manifest and savingly effective.*[12] (Italics added.)

The attribute of *divinity* in Christ "is to be found in the service He renders, the benefit He bestows, the saving work He accomplishes."[13] For this reason Ritschl contends that it is even false to attempt to extract a doctrine of the Godhead of Christ from Christ's own words or deeds alone as in some forms of biblicism. The reason is that

> the thought of Christ's Godhead *is never other than the expression of that unique acknowledgment and appreciation which the Christian community yields to its Founder.* . . . apart from that relation it is inconceivable.[14] (Italics added.)

It is crucial to emphasize here the importance of the Christian community's estimate and witness to Christ. It is *in* the community that one experiences the benefits of Jesus, just as did the apostolic community. The historical Jesus is the Jesus that is knowable through the community. For Christianity begins not with the birth of Jesus but with Peter's confession, "You are the Christ." However, Ritschl wishes to maintain that while the estimate of Christ's divinity is always made from within the community of faith, such an estimate is always based on "the greatest possible exactness to the historically certified characteristics of His active life."[15] What we see in the New Testament picture of Jesus Christ is the perfect living-out of an ethical calling or vocation, directed to the divine purpose of realizing the Kingdom of God. For Ritschl the universal ethical Kingdom of God is the supreme end of God

Himself. In Christ this idea first received shape historically and

> therefore He is that Being in the world in Whose self-end God makes effective and manifest after an original manner His own eternal self-end. Whose whole activity, therefore, in discharge of His vocation, forms the material of that complete revelation of God which is present in Him, in Whom, in short, the Word of God is a human person.[16]

Such is the manner in which the Christian community joins together its *ethical* and *religious* estimate of Christ through his unique *vocation*. Ritschl prefers to use the term "personal vocation" rather than the traditional term "office" to describe Christ's work, since the former gives greater place to the personal and volitional qualities of Christ's activity and underlines Christ's continuity with the human race. Ritschl also reverses the traditional procedure by holding that the *religious* estimate of Christ (as God perfectly revealed) can only follow from, and is therefore dependent on, the *ethical* estimate of Christ's own self-realization (as humanity perfectly realized). According to Ritschl, Christ's work for others is necessarily related to the fulfillment of his own end.

> The fundamental condition of the *ethical apprehension of Jesus* is contained in the statement, that what Jesus actually was and accomplished, that He is in the first place for Himself. Every intelligent life moves within the lines of a personal self-end. This the old theologians could not bring themselves to see, for they referred the obedience of Christ exclusively to the end of representing mankind, that is, to an end other than the personal self-end of Jesus. . . . These claim Christ so exclusively for their own salvation, that they will not concede to Him the honour of existing for Himself; although without this, how is it possible to render any real service to others?[17]

According to Ritschl, Christ is not merely the herald of the message of God's Kingdom but inaugurates or actualizes the moral will of God in his own person.

> Accordingly, the permanent significance of Jesus Christ for His community is based, *first,* on the fact

that He was the only one *qualified* for His special calling, the introduction of the kingdom of God; and that He devoted Himself to the exercise of this highest conceivable calling in the preaching of the truth and in loving action without break or deviation.[18] (Italics added.)

The ethical estimate of Jesus's own self-realization, nevertheless, involves the *religious* estimate of his vocation as revealer of God, since Christ clearly saw his own ethical vocation as the fulfilling of the will of God.

> As the Founder of the Kingdom of God in the world, in other words, as the Bearer of God's ethical lordship over men, He occupies *a unique position* toward all who have received a like aim from Him, *therefore He is that Being in the world in whose self-end God makes effective and manifest after an original manner His own eternal self-end.*[19] (Italics added.)

Christ's continuity with humanity is indicated by the fact that He is successful in reproducing His moral attributes in the lives of the members of His community, the Church. But He is also *unique* since He,

> being the first to realize in His own personal life the final purpose of the kingdom of God, is therefore alone of His kind, for should any other fulfil the same task as perfectly as He, yet he would be unlike Him because dependent on Him. Therefore, as the original type of the humanity to be united into the kingdom of God, He is the original object of the love of God, so that the love of God for the members of His kingdom also is *only* mediated through Him.[20]

In what does Christ's work consist? For Ritschl it consists in Christ's being God's instrument of redemption through the forgiveness of sins, the re-establishment of human communion with God, and the founding of a human community of reconciliation. In elucidating the nature of Christ's work, Ritschl is especially concerned to deny a purely objective conception of substitutionary atonement. For Ritschl the ethical condition necessary for a satisfactory theory of Christ's redemptive work must be "that Christ is first of all a Priest in His own behalf before he is a priest for others." That is, "it is not the mere fate of dying that determines the value of Christ's death as a sacrifice; what renders this issue of His life significant for others is *His willing acceptance of the death inflicted upon Him by His adversaries as a dispensation of God and the highest proof of faithfulness to His vocation.*"[21] (Italics added.)

Christ's fulfillment of his own *ethical vocation* leads directly to the *religious* valuation of his work for others.

> In the course of His life He in the first place *demonstrated* to men His Father's love, grace, truth, by exercising His divine vocation, to found the Kingdom of God. . . . This achievement of His life is also intelligible as being not only for His own sake, but for the purpose of introducing His disciples into the same position towards God.[22]

Christ's work for others is twofold—consisting of both *justification* and *reconciliation* accomplished through his moral influence on and through His community, the Church. The first aspect of Christ's work concerns the justification (forgiveness) of those who, through sin, are alienated from God.

> Their [the sinners] effective union with God is to be thought of as the forgiveness of their sins, as the ending of their separation from God, as the removal of their sense of guilt which is associated with distrust. . . . Their guilt is not taken into account in God's judgment, since they are admitted in the train of God's beloved Son to the position towards God which was assumed and maintained by Him. The verdict of justification or forgiveness is therefore *not to be formulated in such a way that the community has its relationship to Christ imputed to it, but in such a way that the community which belongs to Christ has imputed to it His position towards the love of God, in which He maintained Himself by His obedience.*[23] (Italics added.)

In this way Ritschl relates justification integrally to *reconciliation* and again denies a purely objective idea of Christ's substitutionary atonement and formal imputation of righteousness. This is made clear in the following statement:

In so far as justification is viewed as effective, it must be conceived as reconciliation, of such a nature that while memory, indeed, preserves the pain felt at the sin which has been committed, yet at the same time the place of mistrust towards God is taken by the positive assent of the will to God and his saving purpose.[24]

In Ritschl's view reconciliation is the affective or subjective coordinate of justification by which our adoption as unalienated disciples manifests itself in the carrying out of God's will.

> Thus in reconciliation the forgiveness of sins appears no longer merely as the purpose of God, but also as the result purposed. According to the conception of reconciliation with God, the individual has in faith and trust appropriated to himself the final purpose of God (the kingdom of God), and given up his enmity against God. In adoption (acceptance as children of God) the gracious purpose of the judgment of justification is carried into effect, so that God places Himself in relation of Father to the believer, and gives him the right to the full confidence of a child. *These effects of divine redemption, however, find practical application only on the condition that the believer takes at once an active part in the recognized purpose of the kingdom of God. . . .*[25]

Although Ritschl sees justification and reconciliation as inseparable, he does not confuse them. Justification or forgiveness is the necessary presupposition of reconciliation but does not ensure its accomplishment. The two aspects of redemption must be held together in tension, similar to the indispensable union of faith and works in the Christian life. In Ritschl's view orthodoxy, and even Luther, placed a one-sided emphasis on justification through Christ, to the neglect of the ethical dimension of reconciliation. According to Ritschl, the doctrine of redemption, like Christianity itself, resembles an ellipse with two foci: justification and reconciliation. In the words of a more recent commentator, for Ritschl

> every moment in the circumference of Christian existence is a function both of the graceful indicative and

of the moral imperative. Christ restores sinners to fellowship with God, but he also enlists their discipleship for the Kingdom. The imperative defines the sin which alienates us as well as the goal which engages our no longer alienated freedom. The indicative overcomes our alienation and bestows upon us the power freely to embrace the imperative as our own.[26]

Although it is correct to speak of Ritschl's view of Christ's work as a form of moral influence, it is quite wrong to draw the inference that Ritschl's theory is purely subjective. Ritschl stresses the fact that Christ is the "first" and therefore the "unique" bearer of God's ethical lordship over humanity, and for that reason God's justification is *only* mediated through Him. In Christ alone God's grace is fully manifest in such a way as to change objectively our own status before God by opening the way for a changed relationship to God in us.

Ritschl's doctrine of Christ's work cannot then, without significant qualification, be labeled subjective. He was seriously concerned to avoid an individualistic conception of salvation—a doctrine he discerned as central to both Catholicism and Pietism. For Ritschl salvation is always a social fact mediated through the Church, conceived as the community of believers. It is not as if a person experienced salvation and then joined the Church; rather, it is in and through the communion of believers that the individual is made aware of sin, hears the promise of divine forgiveness, is able to grow in grace, and is both receiver and agent of reconciliation. Ritschl, therefore, sets it down that

> the Evangelical Christian's right relation to Christ is both historically and logically conditioned by the fellowship of believers; historically because a man always finds the community already existing when he arrives at faith, nor does he attain this end without the action of the community upon him; logically, because no action of Christ upon men can be conceived except in accordance with the standard of Christ's antecedent purpose to found a community.[27]

Because salvation occurs *within* the community, Christianity is at its very center a social or communal reality.

Religion is always social. Christ did not aim at any action upon men which would merely be a moral instruction of individuals. On the contrary, His purpose in the latter direction was subordinated to the creation of a new religion. The individual believer, therefore, can rightly understand his position relative to God only as meaning that he is reconciled by God through Christ *in* the community founded by Christ.[28]

One can say that Ritschl has his own conception of *Extra ecclesiam nulla salus* (no salvation outside the Church), except that for him the Church is marked by the communion of believers, not by a hierarchical institution, legitimized by law and dogma.

Just as Christ's redemptive work has two inseparable components, justification and reconciliation, so the redeemed life is marked by two foci. First, the redeemed person is freed from bondage to nature's necessity, so that he or she enjoys a sense of spiritual freedom. This is the religious side of reconciliation. Ritschl expounded this aspect of the redeemed life with great feeling, for he considered it to be at the heart of Luther's understanding of the "freedom of the Christian." It is basically a serene faith in the providence of God.

> In this faith, although we neither know the future nor comprehend perfectly the past, yet we judge our temporary relation to the world according to our knowledge of the love of God, and according to the assurance which this knowledge gives us of the value of every child of God in comparison with the world, which is directed by God in accordance with His final purpose, i.e., our salvation. *From this faith springs that confidence which in all its degrees is equally removed from the growing anxiety which might arise from our relation to the superior power of nature,* and from dull indifference or bold recklessness or Stoic imperturbability, because no one of these is an expression of constant spiritual freedom. In particular, faith in providence furnishes a standard by which the first impression of misfortunes as limitations of freedom or as divine punishments is transformed into a recognition of their significance as blessings, i.e., as means of education or probation. *In this judgment of evil, he who trusts in providence gives evidence of his dominion over the world. . . .*[29] (Italics added.)

Ritschl indicates that such a faith in providence represents the "personal realization of Christianity *as a religion*" and that it guarantees "that it is not merely a doctrine of morals." Nevertheless, Ritschl sees this religious aspect of the Christian life as inseparably joined to its moral component— "labour for the Kingdom of God" in the fulfillment of one's vocation.

It is generally agreed that Ritschl, especially in his *Instruction in the Christian Religion,* gave greater place to this second, moral aspect of redemption— that is, to the Kingdom of God as "the organization of humanity through action inspired by love." According to many interpreters, the Kingdom of God is *the* regulative principle of Ritschl's theology and reveals his concentration on the social and tele- ological character of Christianity. For Ritschl Christianity is not principally a good already gained for the individual but a social ideal yet to be realized. The Kingdom of God is the highest good of the Christian community, but only insofar as "it forms at the same time the ethical ideal, for whose attain- ment the members of the community bind them- selves together through their definite reciprocal action."[30]

The ethical realization of the Kingdom is rooted in the motive of love of God and one's neighbor. Nevertheless, it is itself *supernatural* since it is real- ized by persons only in their union into the com- munity of their Lord Jesus Christ who uniquely *ini- tiated* the perfect will of God. The Kingdom of God is also *supramundane* in that it continues to exist "even when the present mundane conditions of spir- itual life are changed." At the same time the Kingdom of God is radically *mundane* in the sense that it is realized concretely in the moral transfor- mation of society through the personal vocation of selfless love as exemplified in the dutiful, virtuous lives of individuals.

Ritschl's emphasis on the Kingdom of God struck a true biblical theme that had long been neglected. That Ritschl's view of the Kingdom con- tained a strong element of late nineteenth-century moral optimism may be true, although Ritschl is frequently misread as believing in a simple, utopian progressivism. Such a position can with greater jus- tice be attributed to some of Ritschl's disciples, especially to those American liberals identified with the movement known as the "Social Gospel" as we will see.

Ritschl's theology was influential in Germany and in the Anglo-American world in the late nine- teenth and early twentieth centuries, fundamen- tally shaping the character of modern liberal Protestantism. And it was the very character of that influence that occasioned the powerful critique by Karl Barth and other proponents of Dialectical the- ology after 1914, who charged the Ritschlians with accommodating Christianity to the bourgeois cul- ture of Bismarck's Germany. This was true in some cases, but it ignores the recurrent theme of social transformation in the writings of several members of the school. Ritschl's so-called return to Kant often is unfairly interpreted as a reversion to the rationalism and the moral optimism of the Enlightenment. Further, Ritschl is charged with religious "subjectivism" and pragmatism, traceable to his doctrine of value- judgments and the episte- mological priority of faith. Most of these accusa- tions require qualification and are not a fair esti- mate of Ritschl's own teaching. Nevertheless, from the 1920s to the 1960s the writings of Ritschl and his followers were often caricatured. Especially damning is the claim that the Ritschlians gave ide- ological support to a spiritually impotent and degenerate bourgeois culture at the turn of the cen- tury. On this issue scholars today continue to differ. However, with the present interest in the historical, ethical, and social issues that had occupied the Ritschlians, there is a renewed interest in Ritschl's work.

Whether or to what extent Ritschlian theology is applicable in the very different context of the late twentieth century is debatable. But there is no ques- tion of Ritschl's historical importance. He represents a crucial bridge to the theologies of the twentieth century, largely by way of the directions taken by his students and disciples. They carried forward his interests in the historical and the ethical, even as they themselves moved beyond Ritschl and adopted positions opposed to his own. In volume two of this work, we will see that one stream of influence is, ironically, found in the Dialectical theology of Karl Barth and Rudolf Bultmann, by way of Wilhelm Herrmann. This is related to the ongoing preoccu- pation with the questions of "faith and history," especially the issues surrounding the relation of the "Jesus of history" and the "Christ of faith."

Another of Ritschl's critical legacies lies in the attention that he gave to the eschatological theme of the Kingdom of God. It was his student and son-in-law, Johannes Weiss, who was to pursue this theme in his influential book entitled *Jesus' Preaching of the Kingdom of God* (1892). But Weiss did not see Jesus's preaching of the Kingdom in terms of Ritschl's this-worldly moral ideal. Rather, he portrayed Jesus as a first-century Jewish apocalyptical prophet whose futuristic and other-worldly message was radically foreign to our modern sensibilities. Nevertheless, Ritschl's concentration on the biblical motif of the Kingdom of God has remained a fundamental theme in twentieth-century theology.

Ritschl's concern to ground Christian theology in history and his interest in the relations of Church and culture were carried forward by his student, Ernst Troeltsch, and by Adolf von Harnack but, again, in directions not taken by Ritschl himself. The concern of both Harnack and Troeltsch to discover the distinctive "essence" of a changing historical Christianity, that is, to find its "timeless" spirit or message that escapes the relativities of history, has its source in Ritschl's effort to distinguish between the authentic Christian Gospel and later inauthentic developments. Many other legacies of Ritschl could be discussed, for example, the impetus that he gave to the renaissance of studies of Luther at the turn of the century and to the movements of social Christianity in the first half of the twentieth century, to mention only two.[31]

"Ritschlianism" as a *movement* means, of course, not only Ritschl but Ritschl as appropriated and interpreted by his great disciples. Chief among these was the more philosophical Wilhelm Herrmann, who gave his own peculiar stamp to Ritschlian Protestant Liberalism.

WILHELM HERRMANN

Wilhelm Herrmann (1846–1922) was born into a family of Lutheran pastors. He received his early education in the Gymnasium in Stendal and entered the theological faculty of the University of Halle in 1866. He impressed the Neo-Pietist theologian F. A.

Tholuck, who invited the young Herrmann to be his secretary. He lived in the Tholuck household for two and a half years. The extent of Tholuck's influence on Herrmann is disputed, but it is difficult not to believe that Herrmann's abiding concern for the deeply personal experience of Christian faith was nurtured by Tholuck and his years at Halle. It was also in Tholuck's house that Herrmann first met Ritschl, although at the time he already was attracted to his writings and said that in Ritschl's work he saw a means of freeing himself from the pervasive influence of Halle Pietism.

Herrmann was the first important theologian to publicly declare his adherence to Ritschl's program. He strongly defended Ritschl's *Justification and Reconciliation* against its critics when it first appeared. What drew Herrmann to Ritschl was the latter's repudiation of Christianity's dependence on classical metaphysics and his recognition of the inadequacy, even the danger to theology, of theoretical knowledge and the modern hegemony of scientific naturalism and positivism. All of these concerns were united in their joint appeal to the Kantian critiques of pure and practical reason.

Herrmann was appointed a *Privatdozent,* or instructor, in theology at Halle in 1875, but his dissent from his own theological colleagues was marked by the publication of his first book, *Metaphysics in Theology* (1876), in which he defended the independence of religious faith from all forms of scientific knowledge. Herrmann explored the same theme more deeply in *Religion and its Relation to Science and Morality* (1879), again revealing his dependence on the Kantian critique of knowledge. Ritschl commended the book as representing the method most appropriate to his own theological system. In that same year, 1879, Herrmann was called to Marburg as a professor of systematic theology, and he remained there for the next thirty-eight years. In Marburg Herrmann was a highly influential teacher of future theologians, including Karl Barth and Rudolf Bultmann, and of numerous Americans who brought home with them the main features of the Ritschlian theology, adapting it to their own native forms of Liberal and Modernist theology. Herrmann was the most important philosophical and systematic theologian among the followers of Ritschl, just as Adolf von

Harnack was to be the leading historian of dogma. Herrmann's most influential work, *The Communion of the Christian with God,* appeared in 1884.

Science, Metaphysics, and Theology

As a true son of the Lutheran legacy, Herrmann saw it as his task to free Christian faith from all worldly justifications. This would include an inerrant Bible, the confessional standards of orthodoxy, the rational claims of the *Religionsphilosophie* espoused by his Neo-Kantian colleagues Hermann Cohen and Paul Natorp in Marburg, and the pretentious claims of a zealous natural science. Herrmann applies Luther's great discovery of justification by faith through grace apart from works of the law to his own understanding of science and metaphysics, considering both to be forms of autonomous intellectual "work" that obey *our* laws of logic and technical mastery.

In Herrmann's judgment, Christian theologians have been enticed to find support for religion in science and metaphysics which falsely claim to establish the universal grounds of knowledge. Just as scientists are not satisfied to explore the limits of phenomenal reality and are seduced into a search for "the idea of a world whole and a unified ground of things," so theologians hope that they can with such help "reach the rock bottom of reality and uncover the secret of the unified gigantic construct of the universe."[32] Neither scientists nor philosophers nor theologians understand the true limits of human knowledge. Within its proper limit, science is entirely free to hold sway, and even a mechanistic view of *nature's processes* should not be opposed by theology. It is only when science exceeds its bounds and imposes itself on the realm of human meanings and purposes that it must be opposed.

Herrmann believed that the same limits must apply to the metaphysician who also seeks the universal ground of being and knowledge but ends up in logical contradictions and antinomies. For theology to seek a basis in metaphysics is, Herrmann asserts, to lean on "an arm of flesh." Theology must be quite free of any particular metaphysical worldview. "Whether in other respects philosophy is deistic, pantheistic, theistic, or anything else, is a matter of indifference to us as theologians."[33] Beyond our

human drive for knowledge and the mastery of nature, and beyond our search for the universal forms of all being, lies a deeper human concern, namely, "an answer to the question, how is the world to be judged if there really is to be a highest good?"[34] Metaphysics does not address the reality of the human will, the vital question of the meaning and purpose of existence, and the fact of our freedom and our responsibility in the world.

Christian theology need not, then, occupy itself with the problems of metaphysics, for "the task of theology is the proof that the problems of the moral spirit are solved when, by appropriation of what Christianity regards as good, it participates in the religious view of the world which belongs to Christianity."[35] That is, in contrast to science and metaphysics, with their antagonism of nature and the human spirit and will, Christianity recognizes both nature and spirit as under the teleological guidance of a personal, loving God. Belief in God as revealed in Christ allows the Christian to see the world of nature not as an indifferent enemy of our hopes and purposes but as filled with moral meaning and ourselves as free agents with a moral destiny.

In Herrmann's dualism of science (knowledge) and religion (moral freedom), we can see the harbinger of twentieth-century religious Existentialism. Herrmann's existential separation of the religious life from the domination of natural science and philosophy is summarized in the following representative passage:

> . . . [L]ife creates its own justification through its act. This act cannot, as such, be proved to others, since the act alone brings the acting subject into the forum of life. The attempt to procure such a justification through scientific proof must be seen as profanation from the perspective of life or religion; from the perspective of science it would involve abandonment of its moral dignity and power over things. In generally valid knowledge we comprehend the real which, to the religiously alive, always becomes God's revelation. . . . The autonomy of individual religious life and the independence of scientific research belong together. . . . That their unity is however inscrutable for us is shown by the inharmonious opposition between what we experience and what our thinking creates.[36]

Doctrine, Revelation, and Faith

The most dangerous enemy of Christian faith for Herrmann is not, however, either natural science or metaphysics. The real enemy is found within the Church itself, namely, in the identification of Christian revelation with doctrine (*Lehrsätze*). In both Catholicism and Protestant orthodoxy, belief in doctrine is falsely understood as faith, for faith is conceived as *assent* to some normative doctrines (confessions), or to statements culled from Scripture, or to the Church's teaching authority. To Herrmann all of these are external sources of belief and represent various forms of legalism. True revelation and faith can never be an assent to what others say and believe. Such acts are not faith but mere intellectual consent:

> If we had received only information concerning God, it would still be left to us to obtain the certainty of a real communion of God with ourselves. And no such endeavour of ours could ever conquer doubt, for it is amidst such endeavours that doubt does always arise. . . . For in such doctrines, however, true they may be in themselves, we are not brought face to face with that reality which gives faith its certainty.[37]

The same applies to the authority of Scripture when biblical texts are fitted into a system of dogmatic theology. This simply leads "to the legitimation of a faith which is nothing more than a ready acceptance of unaccustomed thoughts." Pathetically, and "for the sake of so-called loyalty to Scripture," we "call our own those thoughts which still remain strange to us."[38] But true faith can neither be forced, artificially produced, nor appropriated outwardly. Faith is always a personal revelatory experience (*Erleben*) in which the individual comes to know the freedom and joy of the *beneficia Christi*, of Christ's liberating joy and call. And yet such genuine experiential knowledge yields no universal knowledge of the world, nor does it offer objective, demonstrable proof. Faith, Herrmann insists, is an unconditional trust in a Power which the Christian distinguishes from his or her own inner life but which brings with it a blessedness and a claim, a moral imperative, to take up the task of moral and spiritual self-denial.

Faith begins, then, in our human awareness of a moral sense which constitutes our unique inner life as human beings. But this very sense makes us painfully aware that our life is perpetually in conflict with the good. "So the very thoughts which we know are able to set free our inner life only throw us back again into discouragement and despondency. From this inward strife (*Anfechtung*) . . . we are saved when once we have come to understand the fact that Jesus belongs to this world of ours."[39] However, this liberation cannot be willed, only experienced in an encounter with a reality that cannot be produced from within but must be revealed to us. And, for Herrmann, it is the encounter with the historical fact of Jesus that awakens both the revelatory experience and personal faith as the individual discovers the inner life of Jesus and its liberating power. It is essential that the inner life of Jesus take hold personally and not simply that it be appropriated through the testimony of others. "Anything that has not the strength to force its way into this inner world of consciousness as an undeniable reality is not in a position to constitute with this inner world the fulcrum of a new life."[40]

The act of faith is always a personal one, and when it is experienced, it is self-authenticating. Against the doubt and reproach of others, "faith cannot defend itself." Herrmann insists that religious people who attempt such a defense of their faith show in the very doing that they are secretly ashamed of it before others. Yet "faith firmly maintains that God performs such miracles for the faithful."[41] For Herrmann faith is indeed miraculous, but not as something beyond or contrary to nature. Rather, while faith "as miracle originates from a transcendent reality," it nevertheless is "to be defined only in contrast with nature, though it is within the sphere of nature that it is experienced. The attempt to make miracle intelligible inevitably annuls the idea of miracle."[42] The individual need no longer look for the testimony of others to hold fast to the reality of Jesus's life, nor should he or she seek demonstrable proof in the face of the doubts of others.[43] And here we are led to Herrmann's highly distinctive response to the "quest of the historical Jesus" and to the growing challenge presented by the "assured results" of historical investigation.

History and the Inner Life of Jesus

In Herrmann's later writings his attention to the relations of religion to the spheres of natural science and metaphysics recedes, and the central issue becomes the relation between nature and the realm of the historical. The former represents the domain of demonstrable knowledge and the latter that of the inner life and the experienceable, the sphere of morality and religion, which are not amenable to universal, conclusive proof. They require acts of a free will, trust, and devotion to a task. According to Herrmann, Christian historical existence reveals two challenging facts: the demand of the moral law on conscience and the historical (*geschichtliche*) revelation of the inner life of Jesus. But the question presents itself: Does not the *fact* of Jesus presuppose an objective ground (Jesus's inner life) as the foundation of faith and one that is dependent on the work of the historical scholar?

It is true, Herrmann concedes, that we have no certain knowledge of Jesus without the historical narratives of the New Testament. But these written narratives are not the only fact that we incorporate into our picture of historical reality. "The content of those narratives may also become a fact for us." And this happens "only when we ourselves establish its reality." However, if the contents of these narratives are viewed only from the position occupied by the Gospel writers, for example, from the perspective of the culture of their age, we then must decide how far we can incorporate these features into *our* picture of what really happened, and we remain in the sphere of the merely probable. Herrmann points out that in such a circumstance, "we are always prepared to modify our results upon more exact examination of the narrative or upon the discovery of new information. It is obvious, then, that such decisions do not give us facts on which our religious faith could be based," since the sphere of the merely probable cannot be the ground of faith. The historian may well succeed, for example, in convincing us that the man Jesus lived, or lived in a certain way, but if the historian "seeks to base his faith in God upon this, his argument collapses immediately," for "once again doubt lifts its head."

Here Herrmann appeals to Lessing's judgment that we encountered in Chapter 2:

There comes back the feeling that it is a fatal drawback that no historical judgment, however certain it may appear, ever attains any more than probability. But what sort of religion would that be which accepted a basis for convictions with the consciousness that it was only probably safe? For this reason it is impossible to attach religious conviction to a mere historical decision. Here Lessing is right.

But neither, Herrmann goes on to insist, does Christianity deny the historical reality of Jesus, nor is faith won "by the forcible suppression of historical doubt." What is it, then, that removes all doubt from the historical picture of Jesus?

Here again, Herrmann appeals to Lessing's insight: The certitude of religion is to be found in "the proof of the spirit and of power," that is, in personal experience in its encounter with historical fact, when that fact no longer remains merely "accidental" but becomes a fact "necessary to me," a part of my own vital experience. Lessing spoke of the "beneficent shock of the electric current," an image congenial to Herrmann's sense of the effect of the power of the inner life of Jesus on the Christian. It is exactly that truth and power wrought by the personal influence of Jesus's life that, according to Herrmann, "sets us free from the mere record, because it presses upon us as a power that is present through its work upon us." And so the person "who has found the inner life of Jesus through the mediation of others . . . has become free even of that mediation." The individual, in other words, must start with the testimony of the Church in the New Testament, but we do not grasp its truth "until the enrichment of our own life makes us aware that we have touched the Living One . . . a power which we recognize as the best thing our life contains."

Herrmann then proceeds to insist that, having had this experience, one "can with heartfelt confidence allow the historical criticism of the New Testament writings to have full play," for no criticism can disfigure the clear features of Jesus's own inner life. "Whenever we come to see the person of Jesus, then, under the impress of that inner life that breaks through all the veils of the story, we ask no more questions as to the trustworthiness of the Evangelists. The question whether the portrait of Jesus belongs to history [*Geschichte*] or fiction is silenced."

Herrmann's confidence even extends to seeing the historical criticism of the New Testament as a real blessing. First, criticism demonstrates what a small foundation historical results can afford when it comes to "what the Person of Jesus shall signify for the Christian." And "in shattering such [scientific] hopes it destroys certain false props of faith, and that is a great gain." Second, the changing results of criticism point to the irresolute relativity of historical judgments compared to the portrait of Jesus which the believer holds as absolute truth. "And this helps us not to forget that the most important fact in our inner life cannot be given to us once for all, but must be continually laid hold of afresh with all our soul."[44]

Herrmann's theological position on the question of the Jesus of history and the Christ of faith is the most radical among the Ritschlians. He joins a fearless commitment to the work of historical (*historisch*) criticism with the conviction that the reality of the New Testament historical (*geschichtliche*) inner life of Christ is the unshakable ground of faith. Herrmann is insistent that Christ's inner life as appropriated by the believer is the *fides quae creditur,* the ground of faith, and not simply the *fides qua creditur,* the subjective act of believing. Or, more accurately perhaps, there is a joining of the two.

In any case, the ground of faith cannot be objectively demonstrated or serve as an external authority for others. Herrmann's position on the historical Christ and faith, we will see, is similar in many ways to the more celebrated position of Søren Kierkegaard, although Herrmann's use of the category of history appears to be inconsistent, resulting in a good deal of ambiguity. Later critical work on the New Testament, especially by Rudolf Bultmann and the exponents of Form Criticism, raises serious questions about the biographical value of the Gospel portraits of Jesus and especially about the possibility of recovering the personality and inner, psychological life of Jesus. Bultmann, in fact, will reject the entire effort to establish historically the inner life of Jesus, claiming that theologically such an historically constructed "inner life" is itself—though contrary to Herrmann's intention—a "false historical prop" of faith. One can argue that Herrmann did not appeal to the *historisch* inner life of Jesus, but rather to the *geschichtliche* Christ. Nevertheless, in

his use of "historical fact" when speaking of revelation and of Jesus's inner life, Herrmann appears to presuppose some *historische* features of that life that can be recovered by research.

The historical issues raised by Herrmann provoked an exchange with the Halle theologian Martin Kähler. The exchange was in response to Kähler's book, *The So-Called Jesus of History and the Historic Biblical Christ* (1892). In the second edition (1896) Kähler included an essay directed specifically at Herrmann. The two men actually shared a good deal in their views on the relationship of history and faith. Kähler put the issue as firmly as had Herrmann: How can Jesus Christ be the object of faith if the question of who he is can only be established by the fluctuating investigations of modern historical scholarship? According to Kähler, what we have in the New Testament proclamation about Jesus are not sources for a biography but only "a vast field strewn with the fragments of various traditions."

Kähler, however, goes beyond Herrmann in affirming that the man Jesus recovered by historical scholarship and the Christ of faith are "two fundamentally different things." In Kähler's estimation the Ritschlians, and especially Herrmann, focus exclusively on the earthly Christ, the figure retrievable by scientific historical (*historisch*) investigation, and not on the exalted Christ, the suprahistorical (*geschichtliche*) Christ of the New Testament apostolic witness. Kähler, like Barth and Bultmann later, sees the Gospels as essentially confessional documents, "proclamations of the messiahship of the crucified Jesus." The Gospels are not historical reports; they are testimonies of the earliest community's faith in the exalted Christ. It is, therefore, the full New Testament Christ, the resurrected and exalted Lord, who *"is himself the originator of the biblical picture of Christ."*[45]

According to Kähler, Herrmann's positing of the "inner life of Jesus" as the ground of faith is, therefore, inadequate, for he severs the pre-Easter and post-Easter Gospel witness, and there can be no such separation of the two. In his reply Herrmann agrees that the *historisch* cannot be the ground of faith, but he charges Kähler with confusing the *ground* and the *content* of faith. For Herrmann the apostolic witness to the post-Easter exalted Christ is the content of faith and not its ground, and to take this apostolic witness as ground is to return to an objective and external authority, to a form of "biblicism." For Herrmann the only ground of faith is the historically (*geschichtliche*) encountered inner life of Jesus in one's own inner life. While history (*Historie*) cannot establish or prove this historical fact for faith, it can help to properly elucidate (legitimate?) it in light of false portrayals of Jesus's person. Herrmann would say that, paradoxically, in joining the Jesus of history and the Christ of faith, Kähler actually denies any place for *Historie*. But Kähler and Bultmann would retort that Herrmann has not yet freed himself from the authorizing role of profane *Historie*.

As one commentator has observed with regard to both Herrmann's and Kähler's use of the distinction between *Historie* and *Geschichte:*

> Herrmann seemed more firmly committed to the neutral or presuppositionless character of Historie— even though he wavered in the consistency with which he employed the distinction, for the "objective fact" of the inner life of Jesus seems often to depend on the *historisch* reliability of the main features of the gospel portrait of Jesus. Kähler, on the other hand, saw the supposed presuppositionless nature of Historie as simply a myth. The critical historian, for Kähler, is fully committed to his dogmas . . . about what can and cannot be accepted as historical fact.[46]

Ritschl and his followers raised profound questions about the Christian faith and its relation to history and to historical research. But nothing points up the differences within the Ritschlian program as much as the responses of its members to this issue. Herrmann's response went far beyond that of Ritschl himself; and, as we will see, the responses of the two great historians, Adolf von Harnack and Ernst Troeltsch, were to oppose both the dualism of Wilhelm Herrmann and the radical responses of his students, Barth and Bultmann.

ADOLF von HARNACK

Adolf von Harnack (1851–1930) was born in 1851 in Dorpat in Estonia. His father, Theodosius Harnack, was a professor of theology at the university and a Lutheran in the strict Pietist tradition. Harnack was educated in Dorpat and Erlangen and in 1872 entered the University of Leipzig, where he completed the doctorate in Church history in 1873. His distinguished academic career began at Leipzig, first as a Privatdozent and in 1876 as a professor-extraordinary. He held professorships at both Giessen and Marburg and in 1888 was called to a chair at the University of Berlin. His appointment to Berlin was a cause of serious controversy, however; it was delayed for several months, and the matter was finally resolved by the Emperor William II's decision overruling the Church officials. Opposition to Harnack's appointment was based on his *History of Dogma,* the first volume of which had appeared in 1885. The publication of the multivolume *Dogmengeschichte* introduced Harnack to a lifetime of theological controversy and led to a painful break with his father. The shadow of suspicion was never completely removed from his career as a Church historian, and, despite his eminent position, he never was given any position of authority or honor by the Church. In spite of this fact, no person in Germany had a greater influence on Protestant Christianity at the turn of the century than Harnack. His influence was largely the result of his prolific writing which included over sixteen hundred books, monographs, and articles. The *History of Dogma,* his book on *Marcion,* and *The Mission and Expansion of Christianity* are classics in their field. Harnack's popular book *What Is Christianity?* is considered the finest and most influential statement of liberal Protestant theology.

It is difficult to believe that a man of such scholarly erudition and productivity could also be a man of action, yet Harnack held many time-consuming administrative positions during his career. In 1876 he founded the *Theologische Literaturzeitung* and for many years was its only editor. He served as Rector of the University of Berlin, and his counsel was frequently sought in the Ministry of Education. In 1906 he was appointed Director General of the Royal Library and in 1911 to the position of President of the Kaiser Wilhelm Foundation, established for the creation of numerous scientific research institutes. He was raised to the rank of the hereditary nobility in 1914 by Kaiser Wilhelm II, to whom Harnack was a friend and confidant. In 1921

Harnack was offered the post of German Ambassador to the United States, but he declined the honor.

The Historical Interpretation of Christianity

Of the many influences that helped to shape Harnack the historian and theologian, none was greater than that of Albrecht Ritschl. It was during his period in Leipzig that Harnack first identified himself with the Ritschlian school. A few years later Harnack acknowledged that his own *Dogmengeschichte* would have been impossible without Ritschl. What Ritschl contributed most to Harnack was a distaste for metaphysical speculation and a devotion to an historical interpretation of Christianity. It was in such a Ritschlian direction that Harnack believed "lay the future direction of Protestantism."[47] Harnack was even more rigorously historical in orientation than Ritschl, holding that Christianity could only be understood as an historical movement and by the methods of historical interpretation. He called upon Christians to take upon themselves the historical responsibility of appropriating critically their religious heritage and making it their own. To be worthy of study, history, for Harnack, must have a living relationship to the present.

> We study history in order to intervene in the course of history and we have a right and a duty to do so: for without historical insight we either permit ourselves to be mere objects put in the historical process or we shall have the tendency to lead people down the wrong way. To intervene in history—this means that we must reject the past when it reaches into the present only in order to block us. . . . There is no doubt that, with respect to the past, the historian assumes the royal function of a judge, for in order to decide what of the past shall continue to be in effect and what must be done away with or transformed, the historian must judge like a king. Everything must be designed to furnish a preparation for the future, for only the discipline of learning has a right to exist which lays the foundation for what is to be.[48]

Harnack agreed with the historian Ernst Troeltsch who was fond of saying that "one must overcome history by history," that is, one must come to know one's heritage, accept it, and then shape it into a living possibility in the present and for the future.

That Harnack acted on his own historical convictions is evident in his two most famous works, *The History of Dogma* and *What Is Christianity?* Harnack wrote the *History of Dogma* to show the origins and development of Christian dogma to the time of the Reformation. But, more important, he produced this massive study to demonstrate historically that if the Christian gospel was to remain a living force in the modern world, it must be freed from dogma—the reason being that "as the adherents of the Christian religion had not these dogmas from the beginning . . . the business of the history of dogma is to ascertain the origin of Dogmas and then to describe their development."[49] For by delineating the process by which dogmas originate and develop, "the 'history of dogma' furnishes the most suitable means for the liberation of the Church from dogmatic Christianity"[50]—or of overcoming history by history. Here we see a very different view of the development of dogma from that of Möhler or Newman.

According to Harnack, dogmatic Christianity is a definite step in the development of Christianity out of the faith that one encounters in the primitive Gospel. It is the intellectualizing or Hellenizing of the primitive faith, or, as he put it, "the work of the Greek spirit on the soil of the Gospel." Harnack did not consider the development of dogma an obviously bad thing. Understood historically, it becomes clear that dogma, like the retention of the Old Testament canon, preserved the Christian faith from powerful heresies that would have seriously distorted the Christian message. However, understood historically, it also becomes clear that dogma became embodied in an authoritarian, ecclesiastical institution which made and continues to make claims and demands that are very foreign to the primitive Gospel. The importance of the Reformation is to be seen in Luther's rediscovery of this Gospel freed from ecclesiastical authoritarianism. One can, therefore, acknowledge that the dogmatic Hellenization of the Gospel was historically necessary and at the same time recognize that those conditions no longer exist which require the retention of such an historical "form" of Christianity. Harnack believed that historical responsibility demanded the present liberation of Christian faith from an infallible authoritarianism that was contrary to the very spirit of the Gospel.

It is frequently commented that Harnack was a "primitivist" in that he criticized the whole history of Christianity from the normative standard of its earliest expression. Such a judgment needs rather careful qualification. Harnack the historian was very mindful of the fact that no particular historical "form" of Christianity can definitively represent its reality and, at the same time, that the reality of Christianity comes to us *only* through concrete historical traditions. However, Harnack believed that one could extract the unique essence of Christian faith from all of its historical forms which have come and gone. He saw the alternatives as follows:

> Either the Gospel is . . . identical with its earliest form, in which case it came with its time and has departed with it; or else it contains something which, under differing historical forms, is of permanent validity. The latter is the true view. The history of the Church shows us in its very commencement that "primitive Christianity" had to disappear in order that "Christianity" might remain; and in the same way in later ages one metamorphosis followed upon another.[51]

The Essence of Christianity

The distinctive essence of Christianity, that which is of "permanent validity" within the temporal forms, is what Harnack called the *gospel of Jesus Christ*. This gospel requires no definitive historical form and has in fact outlived numerous historical traditions which must be judged by it. If such a criticism is not carried out, church dogmas and institutions will be judged by some particular historical tradition.

It is evident that the key to Harnack's reconstruction is his conception of the gospel of Jesus Christ, for he lays it down as his most fundamental rule that "that only is Christian which can be established authoritatively by the Gospel."[52] While, for Harnack, the Gospel of Jesus Christ is the normative

essence of Christianity, the attempt to specify the content of this Gospel is more difficult. In Harnack's view the Gospel is *not* an intellectual doctrine but a *dynamic reality.* The Gospel *is* Jesus Christ, the living person who awakens life in those who will open themselves to his reality. Harnack wished to stress the point that the Gospel is the Gospel *of* Jesus, rather than a Gospel *concerning* him. However, he made the distinction not to exclude Jesus from the Gospel (he clearly does not[53]) but because he did not want the Gospel to be confused with an intellectual dogma concerning the Person of Christ.

In *What Is Christianity?* Harnack takes upon himself the historical responsibility of attempting to uncover the historical Jesus, as well as a definition of the Gospel and the permanent essence of Christianity. According to his famous definition, set forth in that book, the Gospel as taught by Jesus embraces three themes, each being "of such a nature as to contain the whole."

> *Firstly, the kingdom of God and its coming. Secondly, God the Father and the infinite value of the human soul. Thirdly, the higher righteousness and the commandment of love.*[54]

The boldness of Harnack's interpretation is evident in his handling of the first theme: the difficult question of Jesus's eschatology. Harnack acknowledges that Jesus's preaching concerning the coming of the Kingdom of God was ambiguous and that Jesus shared the Jewish apocalyptical world-view of his time. Yet Harnack disagrees with those historians of religion who see nothing in Jesus's preaching of the Kingdom but ideas already current in his time. Harnack believes that the historian has the responsibility of distinguishing between the traditional "husk" and the peculiar "kernel" in Jesus's message of the Kingdom. And it is clear to Harnack that while Jesus used the vivid apocalyptical language of his day, he did so only to put in striking relief the dynamic, moral relationship between God and humanity. The "kernel" of Jesus's preaching of the Kingdom is, Harnack claims,

> the rule of the holy God in the hearts of individuals; *it is God himself in his power.* From this point of view everything that is dramatic in the external sense has

vanished; and gone, too, are all external hopes for the future. . . . It is not a question of angels and devils, thrones and principalities, but of God and the soul, the soul and its God.[55]

The second theme expresses Jesus's most persistent message and the very essence of religion itself: God the Father and the infinite value of each human being. Here it is clear that Jesus's Gospel "contains no statutory or particularistic elements." By applying the idea of Providence to the whole world, Jesus shows that all life is rooted and safe in the Eternal. Such a faith is beautifully affirmed in the Lord's Prayer and in such passages as Luke 12:6—"Are not two sparrows sold for a farthing? and one of them shall not fall to the ground without your Father. But the very hairs of your head are all numbered." Also in the verse "What shall it profit a man if he gain the whole world and lose his own soul?" it is clear that Jesus puts the very highest value on the individual person. As a true Ritschlian, Harnack writes, "The man who can say 'My Father' to the Being who rules heaven and earth, is thereby raised above heaven and earth, and himself has a value which is higher than all the fabric of this world."[56]

Yet the circle of Jesus's Gospel does not include only the individual soul alone and secure with its God. It offers individuals this incomparable gift of assurance, but it also sets them a task. The Gospel is an ethical message of "the higher righteousness and the commandment of love." What distinguishes Jesus's Gospel from other ethical thought is that Jesus severed the connection between ethics and external forms of observance. Jesus goes straight to the root of morality, to the disposition and the intention. This is what is meant by the "higher righteousness." Jesus reduced the moral life "to *one* root and to *one* motive—love."

It was in this sense that Jesus combined religion and morality, and in this sense religion may be called the soul of morality, and morality the body of religion. We can thus understand how it was that Jesus could place the love of God and the love of one's neighbor side by side; the love of one's neighbor is the only practical proof on earth of that love of God which is strong in humility.[57]

Harnack, like most Ritschlian liberals, saw the ethical task of building a community inspired by love of neighbor as an indispensable dimension of Jesus's Gospel. Despite the individualistic tenor of much of what Harnack says about "God and the soul, the soul and God," like Ritschl he saw the Christian life as essentially social or corporate in nature. Harnack, too, was committed to a "social gospel." This is made especially clear in the section of *What Is Christianity?* where he discusses "The Gospel and the poor, or the social question." There is no doubt in Harnack's mind that if Jesus were present today, he would be championing those who work to relieve the hard lot of the poor. "The fallacious principle of the free play of forces, of the 'live and let live' principle—a better name for it would be the 'live and let die'—is entirely opposed to the Gospel."[58] Harnack believed that Jesus contemplated a community of persons "in which wealth, as private property in the strict sense of the word, was non-existent."

In this sense, [the Gospel] is profoundly socialistic, just as it is also profoundly individualistic, because it establishes the infinite and independent value of every human soul. . . . Its object is to transform the socialism which rests on the basis of conflicting interests into the socialism which rests on the consciousness of a spiritual unity.[59]

Harnack's views of the social gospel were not, however, the most provocative of his ideas. The section of *What Is Christianity?* that raised the greatest storm of protest had to do with "The Gospel and the Christological question." What alarmed many was Harnack's statement that *the Gospel, as Jesus proclaimed it, has to do with the Father only and not with the Son.* What Harnack meant to convey in this statement was his concern that the object of the Gospel not be identified with some metaphysical doctrine of the God-man unity. He did not mean to imply that Jesus stood outside the Gospel. It is true, nevertheless, that for Harnack Jesus's Divine Sonship is conceived as residing in His *knowledge of God.*

The consciousness which he possessed of being the *Son of God* is, therefore, nothing but the practical consequence of knowing God as the Father and as his

Father. Rightly understood, the name of Son means nothing but the knowledge of God.[60]

Harnack believed that this in no way detracted from the very highest view of Christ if one thing was kept in mind, namely, that

no one had ever yet known the Father in the same way in which Jesus knew Him, and to this knowledge of Him he draws other men's attention, and thereby does "the many" an incomparable service. He leads them to God, not only by what he says, but still more by what he is and does, and ultimately by what he suffers.[61]

In Harnack's view the Gospel, then, is not something taught *about* Christ, nor is Christ a mere *component* of the Gospel. Rather, *"he was its personal realization and its strength, and this he is felt to be still."*[62] Such a living faith demands no dogmatic guarantees of Christ's uniqueness.

Fire is kindled only by fire; personal life only by personal forces. Let us rid ourselves of all dogmatic sophistry, and leave others to pass verdicts of exclusion. The Gospel nowhere says that God's mercy is limited to Jesus' mission. But history shows us that he is the one who brings the weary and heavy laden to God; and again, that he it was who raised mankind to the new level; and his teaching is still the touchstone, in that it brings men to bliss and brings them to judgment.[63]

No one who understands this can fail to affirm that here the divine appeared in as perfect a form as it can appear on this earth. And such an affirmation requires no theoretical formulation but, rather, a life lived in accordance with this message, which is "something so simple, something that speaks to us with so much power, that it cannot easily be mistaken."[64] Harnack suffered little doubt that the real Jesus and the Gospel message could be recovered— and that it was relevant to modern life. In this he was one with Ritschl, but he differed markedly from Strauss, Johannes Weiss, and Albert Schweitzer.

What Is Christianity? was originally presented as a series of public lectures at the University of Berlin during the winter semester of 1899–1900. When published that same year, the book created great excitement and in the years that followed exerted an extraordinary influence on theologians and laypersons alike. The popular demand for the book is illustrated by the fact that in the year of its publication the main railway station in the city of Leipzig was blocked by freight cars which were going to ship *What Is Christianity?* throughout the world. More than any other book it represented the spirit of Protestant Liberalism in the decades just prior to World War I.

WALTER RAUSCHENBUSCH

In the quarter century before World War I, a host of young American theologians went to Germany to complete their theological studies. There they sat at the feet of many of the leaders of the Ritschlian school, teachers such as Herrmann, Harnack, and Kaftan. American liberal theology never became dominantly Ritschlian, but the leaders of the movement—people like William Adams Brown and Arthur C. McGiffert—were profoundly influenced by their Ritschlian mentors. This was true also of the greatest of the American liberal theologians, Walter Rauschenbusch (1861–1918). Like most of his American contemporaries, Rauschenbusch was theologically eclectic—drawing upon Schleiermacher, Idealism, Ritschl, and evolutionary doctrine. Nevertheless, as in the case of Brown and McGiffert, the dominant themes in his theology have a strong Ritschlian cast.

Rauschenbusch was born in Rochester, New York, the son of a German Baptist professor at the Rochester Theological Seminary. Walter was raised in an environment of conservative German Baptist piety. He was educated in both Germany and the United States, graduating from the University of Rochester and the Rochester Seminary. After graduation he was to take a mission post in India, but his appointment was blocked by one of his own professors who considered his views on the Old Testament too liberal. Rauschenbusch thus turned to the pastorate and accepted a call from the Second German Baptist Church in New York City. The church was located on the edge of Hell's Kitchen, one of the city's infamous slums. Here Rauschenbusch came face to face with the horrors of poverty and economic insecurity. Here he also discovered how ineffectual was pious, individualistic philanthropy in solving major social problems.

It was from his eleven years' ministry in Hell's Kitchen that Rauschenbusch emerged, as Reinhold Niebuhr has said, "the real founder of social Christianity in this country" and "its most brilliant and generally satisfying exponent." In 1897 Rauschenbusch accepted a position in the German faculty of the Rochester Theological Seminary. Five years later he became Professor of Church History in the regular faculty, a position which he held until his death. He wrote little as a Church historian, and what he did write in the field was related to his first interest, the social question.

In 1907, while on leave in Germany, Rauschenbusch published *Christianity and the Social Crisis.* It was a hard-hitting, prophetic attack on the social evils of the day, advocating radical social solutions. Rauschenbusch even considered it "a dangerous book" and feared that it would cost him his teaching position. To his amazement, it awakened a wide, positive response. It was a book born at the proper moment; for large numbers of Americans were now prepared for social change, and liberal theology was gaining a wider following. Rauschenbusch returned from Europe famous and cast in the role of leader of the "Social Gospel" movement. He responded with enthusiasm and gave of himself tirelessly as lecturer, preacher, and writer. In the last decade of his life, he produced two other major books, which also proved popular successes: *Christianizing the Social Order* (1912) and *A Theology for the Social Gospel* (1917). The latter book is on a par with Harnack's *What Is Christianity?* as a lucid statement of liberal theology.

Rauschenbusch was not a Ritschlian in the sense that, like Herrmann and Harnack, he saw himself as consciously carrying forward the program of a "school"; but the themes of his theology are extraordinarily similar to Ritschlian liberalism. Like the Ritschlians, he was disinterested in metaphysics and dogma, stressing rather the historical Jesus as the ini-

tiator of the divine community—the Kingdom of God. He saw persons as caught in the struggle between their spiritual and natural impulses and conceived of salvation in ethical and social terms. However, Rauschenbusch combined with these Ritschlian themes an evolutionary theism and a social progressivism more akin to trends in American thought.

A Theology of the Social Gospel

The key to Rauschenbusch's conception of Christianity is found in the words "social" or "solidaristic." He considered the heart of Jesus's teaching to be the message of the Kingdom of God; and, as preached by Jesus, the Kingdom was never thought of as a purely internal, spiritual possession of the individual.

> The purpose of all that Jesus said and did and hoped to do was always the social redemption of the entire life of the human race on earth. . . . Christianity set out with a great social ideal. The live substance of the Christian religion was the hope of seeing a divine social order established on earth.[65]

Just as Harnack saw the Hellenization of Christianity as a distortion of the Gospel, so Rauschenbusch discerned in the history of the Church a long "eclipse" of the social ideal of primitive Christianity. Only now, he believed, was it possible to see this *social Gospel* "bursting forth again with the indomitable energy of divine life." Rauschenbusch believed that the rediscovery of Jesus's message of social redemption demanded that modern theology be rewritten in accordance with this normative principle. The key to such a theological reconstruction would be the Kingdom of God. All other doctrines would then be formulated in accordance with this guiding motif. "We have a social gospel." What is needed is "a systematic theology large enough to match it and vital enough to back it."[66] This Rauschenbusch sought to provide in *A Theology for the Social Gospel.*

That Rauschenbusch did not properly understand the New Testament message concerning the Kingdom of God is today generally conceded.

However, Rauschenbusch was correct in recognizing it to be one, if not *the* basic, motif of both the Old Testament and the message of Jesus. This being so, Rauschenbusch contended, the old, individualistic conceptions of sin and salvation must be rethought and a more truly biblical and solidaristic view of humanity proposed. Rauschenbusch acknowledged that a frequent cause of distrust of liberal theology was its failure to appreciate the power of sin in human life. But this, too, was due to the inability of liberal theology to consider humanity in other than individualistic and voluntaristic terms and, therefore, to take into consideration the complex social matrix of sin. However, a theology focused on the Kingdom of God is prepared to see these more profound social characteristics of human depravity.

The shallowness of liberal anthropology was evidenced, for example, in the eagerness of many liberal theologians to abandon the doctrine of original sin. Rauschenbusch, on the contrary, wished to defend it.

> It is one of the few attempts of individualistic theology to get a solidaristic view of its field of work. This doctrine views the race as a great unity, descended from a single head, and knit together through all ages by unity of origin and blood.[67]

Science, to some extent, corroborates this ancient doctrine. "Evil does flow down the generations through the channels of biological coherence. Idiocy and feeble-mindedness, neurotic disturbances . . . and anti-social impulses in children must have their adequate biological causes. . . ."[68] Where theology went wrong was in seeing sin exclusively in biological transmission rather than along the lines of social tradition.

> One generation corrupts the next. The permanent vices and crimes of adults are not transmitted by heredity, but by being socialized. . . . Just as syphilitic corruption is forced on the helpless foetus in its mother's womb, so these hereditary social evils are forced on the individual embedded in the womb of society and drawing his ideas, moral standards and spiritual ideals from the general life of the social body.[69]

Rauschenbusch believed that there was general unanimity in theology that sin was essentially selfishness or egoism and that the social implication of such a definition "is proof of the unquenchable social spirit of Christianity."

> Sin is essentially selfishness. That definition is more in harmony with the social gospel than any individualistic type of religion. The sinful mind, then, is the unsocial and anti-social mind. To find the climax of sin we must not linger over a man who swears, or sneers at religion, or denies the mystery of the trinity, but put our hands on social groups who have turned the patrimony of a nation into the private property of a small class, or have left the peasant labourers cowed, degraded, demoralized, and without rights in the land.[70]

When viewed in the perspective of the Kingdom of God, theology will make much less of individual sins. Rather, Christians will reserve their horror for those in high places who use powerful lobbies to defeat poverty legislation and factory laws and for nations who set the world at war because of their colonial ambitions.

Rauschenbusch saw the cause of sin as rooted in the conflict between the selfish ego and the common good of humanity, which he equated with God.[71] However, we will never be able to think of the root of sin in such social terms as long as we continue to conceive of God in feudal, monarchical categories.

> The theological definitions of sin have too much the flavour of the monarchical institutions under the spiritual influence of which they were first formed. In an absolute monarchy the first duty is to bow to the royal will. A man may spear peasants or outrage their wives, but crossing the king is another matter.[72]

Sin, as taught by Jesus, is rarely depicted as a private transaction between the sinner and God. In Jesus's teaching our rebellion against God usually takes the form of profiting at the expense of our fellows. Therefore, an adequate doctrine of humanity and sin requires that "we democratize our conception of God."

> He (God) works *through* humanity to realize his purposes, and our sins block and destroy the Reign of

God in which he might fully reveal and realize himself. Therefore, our sins against the least of our fellowmen in the last resort concern God. Therefore, when we retard the progress of mankind, we retard the revelation of the glory of God. Our universe is not a despotic monarchy, with God above the starry canopy and ourselves down here; it is a spiritual commonwealth with God in the midst of us.[73]

Rauschenbusch's doctrine of God reflects the influence of the immanentism of Schleiermacher, the Hegelians, and the evolutionists, but also the insights of the Left-Wing Hegelians and the turn-of-the-century *religionsgeschichtliche Schule,* namely, that theological formulations reflect the patterns of a culture and that social change can revolutionize religious doctrines. This is not to say that Rauschenbusch believed that Christian doctrines were merely the relative products of social forces. He believed the teachings of Jesus constituted the *normative* doctrine of God. "Here," he said, "we see one of the highest redemptive services of Jesus to the human race. When he took God by the hand and called him 'our Father,' he democratized the conception of God."[74] Nevertheless, as in the case of sin, the Christian doctrine of God has undergone periods of distortion and restoration, and Rauschenbusch believed the Social Gospel was "God's predestined agent" to restore Jesus's normative vision of God. That Rauschenbusch was himself a product of the late nineteenth-century liberal, democratic spirit is nowhere more striking than in his doctrine of God. God is measured by the norms of a liberal, democratic socialism.

> A theological God who has no interest in the conquest of justice and fraternity is not a Christian. It is not enough for theology to eliminate this or that autocratic trait. Its God must join the social movement. . . . The development of a Christian social order would be the highest proof of God's saving power. The failure of the social movement would impugn his existence.[75]

Like the Ritschlians, Rauschenbusch did not concern himself with metaphysical questions of the existence and nature of God. God was the assumed ground of democratic, moral values and the supporting agent of moral redemption and progress.

Rauschenbusch's view of salvation also has affinities with Ritschlian liberalism, except that with Rauschenbusch the ethical and social dimension of salvation is given even greater place. Rauschenbusch did not overlook the importance of individual salvation but saw it as only an *essential part* of a necessarily enlarged conception of salvation. It was the job of the Social Gospel to make known this wider, social nature of redemption. That is, that personal salvation itself must be affected by the biblical, "solidaristic" view of humanity, now rediscovered by the Social Gospel.

> If our exposition of the superpersonal agents of sin and of the Kingdom of Evil is true, then evidently a salvation confined to the soul and its personal interests is an imperfect and only partly effective salvation.[76]

According to Rauschenbusch, individual salvation is inadequate on two counts. First, it tends to emphasize those qualities of personal egoism that are the antithesis of Jesus's teaching of discipleship in the Kingdom as that of servanthood and cooperation.

> If sin is selfishness, salvation must be a change which turns a man from self to God and humanity. His sinfulness consisted in a selfish attitude, in which he was at the center of the universe, and God and his fellowmen were means to serve his pleasures, increase his wealth, and set off his egoisms. Complete salvation, therefore, would consist in an attitude of love in which he would freely co-ordinate his life with the life of his fellows in obedience to the loving impulses of the spirit of God. . . . Salvation is the voluntary socializing of the soul.[77]

Those persons converted by an individualistic evangelism are thus frequently "worth no more to the Kingdom of God than they were before." Their vision of salvation is selfishly focused on themselves. Therefore, we must ask ourselves the following question:

> If we are converted, what are we converted to? If we are regenerated, does the scope of so divine a transformation end in our "going to heaven"? The nexus between our religious experience and humanity seems

gone when the Kingdom of God is not present in the idea of regeneration.[78]

Christianizing the Social Order

Not only does an individualistic view of salvation distort Jesus's message of discipleship in the Kingdom; it also fails to consider that social institutions must be redeemed in order to create an environment in which the individual can be healed and renewed. In some environments the historical and social conditions are such as not only to weaken but also actually to thwart the possibility of reconciliation and sanctification. Rauschenbusch held it imperative, then, that not only individuals but the "superpersonal forces," the "composite personalities" such as the state and the economic institutions be converted and redeemed. These superpersonal institutions are saved when they are freed from the law of Mammon and brought under the law of Christ.

> The fundamental step of repentance and conversion for professions and organizations is to give up monopoly power and the incomes derived from legalized extortion, and to come under the law of service. . . . The corresponding step in the case of governments and political oligarchies . . . is to submit to real democracy. Therewith they step out of the Kingdom of Evil into the Kingdom of God.[79]

Despite his considerable grasp of the social dimensions of human sin and alienation, many of Rauschenbusch's statements, such as the above, appear today naively voluntaristic and utopian. Nevertheless, Rauschenbusch did not believe in an inevitable movement toward social perfection. He did believe in the possibility of "Christianizing the social order," which for him meant bringing the orders of society into harmony with the teachings and spirit of Christ. Yet even Christianizing the social order was not to be confused with perfection. "As long as men are flesh and blood, the world can be neither sinless nor painless. . . . If perfection were reached today, new adjustments would be demanded tomorrow by the growth of new powers."[80] There is, however, *progress toward* Christianizing individuals and institutions, and Rauschenbusch believed he dis-

cerned clear evidence that most of the institutions of American society had been infused with a new life reflecting the spirit of Christ.

> Four great sections of our social order—the family, the organized religious life, the institutions of education, and the political organization of our nation—have passed through constitutional changes which have made them to some degree part of the organism through which the spirit of Christ can do its work in humanity.[81]

The one area of society Rauschenbusch considered still largely governed by selfish motives was the economic order. "Our business life is the seat and source of our present troubles. . . . Business life is the unregenerate section of our social order."[82] Yet Rauschenbusch was assured that, because "the larger part of the work of christianizing our social order is already accomplished,"[83] Christians could be confident that economic institutions would soon also come under the law of Christ. In any case, "there has been a speeding up of redemption," and every victory made progress surer.

Looking at humanity and society from the perspective of the twentieth century, the sanguine views of American liberal Protestantism appear today to be utopian, unreal, and even dangerous. However, Rauschenbusch and his followers in the Social Gospel movement should not be faulted for being of their own time. In fact, their social analyses and prescriptions were often entirely relevant to the conditions of their day. Where Rauschenbusch does fall short, perhaps, is in his understanding of some basic doctrines of Christianity. His conception of sin, though far superior to that of most liberals, failed to plumb the depths of human sin as the corruption of our spiritual freedom. His "democratized" God and his progressive conception of the Kingdom were more dependent on the ideals of a liberal culture than on the Bible and the theology of the Church. It is generally acknowledged that Rauschenbusch's theology was more subtle and profound than that of most of his liberal Protestant contemporaries. Nevertheless, those elements of his theology which most reflect his own culture, and were most in accord with the prevailing liberalism, were what were largely appropriated and emphasized by those in the Social Gospel movement. This is well expressed in the following assessment of Rauschenbusch:

> His keen sense of the kingdom of God as judgment, and of the deepening of the burden of guilt through the recognition of social sin; the new validity which he found in the doctrine of original sin through the recognition of the social transmission of sin; the sense of crisis in individual and social life, and the demand for repentance and rebirth; and the desperateness of the struggle against the "kingdom of evil" (the super-individual forces of evil infecting the whole social organism)—these elements of Rauschenbusch's theology were less influential than those which reinforced the characteristic liberal tenets.[84]

Protestant liberal theology reflected to a considerable degree the cultural climate at the turn of the century. Traditional metaphysics was under fire at the same time that the Bible and church dogma were undergoing rigorous historical scrutiny. There was a concern to reduce Christianity to its simplest terms, which meant for most liberal theologians a recovery of the ethical message of Jesus. Religious authority was located in the personal experience of justification and reconciliation through Jesus, rather than in the canonical Scriptures or ecclesiastical dogma. Salvation was interpreted in moral, social, and progressive terms.

If Paul Tillich is correct that a genuine theology is a "theology of correlation" between the cultural situation and the Christian message, then Ritschlian Liberalism would appear to be a near-perfect theology for its time. Its formulation of the Christian message was well suited to meet the metaphysical agnosticism, historicism, and moral optimism of the pre–World War I period. But the question that must be asked is whether, in their concern to meet the cultural situation, the liberals were guilty of formulating their "answers" in such a way as to distort the Christian message? In their concern to return "to the sources," were Harnack and his fellow liberals getting back to the historical Jesus and the primitive Christian message or were they, according to the

Jesuit Father George Tyrrell, seeing only an image of their own bourgeois Protestant faces? Did Ritschlianism involve an extensive accommodation of Christianity to the assumptions of modern culture? This was to be the judgment of two important theological movements, one of which had its beginnings at the end of the century, the other two decades later. Those movements were Roman Catholic Modernism and Protestant Neo-Orthodoxy. Both of these movements trace their beginnings, in part, to a repudiation of Protestant Liberalism. Yet it is interesting that neither movement simply represents a reactionary tendency away from Liberalism, as was the case with American Fundamentalism. Both Catholic Modernism and Neo-Orthodoxy accepted Liberalism's openness to biblical criticism, even radicalizing it. They were both to focus on Jesus's message of the Kingdom of God, but they interpreted this biblical motif in strikingly different ways. They were also skeptical of metaphysical speculation and natural theology. Beyond this, however, the two movements have little in common other than their concern to offer a viable alternative to what they considered a reactionary Orthodoxy, for example in the Princeton Theology or in Neo-Thomism, and the accommodating Liberalism of the Ritschlians.

In the next two chapters we will examine two important movements that represent efforts to counter the influence on Christian thought of the heritage of the Enlightenment and Modernity. We refer to them both as movements of recovery and conservation because they both seek to return to an earlier tradition of theology—one in the late Middle Ages, the other in the sixteenth and seventeenth centuries—that they consider to be a more orthodox and adequate expression of classical Christianity. Both movements began relatively early in the nineteenth century but gained greater authority and influence in the latter decades of the century. Both movements were also long-lived, and so we will be dropping back chronologically in introducing them, but we will also show how they were important in the theological discussions at the end of the nineteenth century and beyond, underlining the persistence of the debates over the issues raised by Modernity.

NOTES

1. On the importance of historical work and its "unfinished Reformation" in Ritschl's theology, see David Lotz, *Ritschl and Luther* (Nashville, 1974); and David Lotz, "Albrecht Ritschl and the Unfinished Reformation," *Harvard Theological Review*, 73 (1980), 337–372.

2. H. R. Mackintosh, *Types of Modern Theology* (London, 1952), p. 148. A quotation from F. Kattenbusch, the source not cited.

3. Albrecht Ritschl, *The Christian Doctrine of Justification and Reconciliation*, III, trans . H. R. Mackintosh and A. B. Macaulay (Edinburgh, 1900), 199. See also p. 17.

4. On this point, with regard to Schleiermacher and Ritschl on God, I am grateful for the suggestion made by Darrell Jodock.

5. Ritschl, op. cit., p. 212.

6. Ibid., pp. 204–205.

7. Ibid., p. 215.

8. Ibid., p. 212.

9. Ibid., pp. 2–3.

10. Ibid., p. 406.

11. Ibid., p. 398.

12. Ibid., p. 393.

13. Ibid., pp. 396–397.

14. Ibid., pp. 400, 404.

15. Albrecht Ritschl, *Instruction in the Christian Religion*, trans. A. M. Swing, in *The Theology of Albrecht Ritschl* (New York, 1901), p. 200.

16. Ritschl, *Justification and Reconciliation*, p. 451.

17. Ibid., p. 442.

18. Ritschl, *Instruction*, p. 195.

19. Ritschl, *Justification and Reconciliation*, p. 451.

20. Ritschl, *Instruction*, p. 197.

21. Ritschl, *Justification and Reconciliation*, p. 477.

22. Ibid., p. 546.

23. Ibid., pp. 546–547.

24. Ibid., p. 85.

25. Ritschl, *Instruction*, p. 214.

26. A. Durwood Foster, *A Handbook of Christian Theologians*, ed. Dean G. Peerman and Martin E. Marty (Cleveland, 1965), p. 64.

27. Ritschl, *Justification and Reconciliation*, p. 549.

28. Ritschl, *Instruction*, pp. 233–235.

29. Ibid., pp. 174–175.

30. Ibid., p. 179.

31. For a full discussion of Ritschl's influence on and relevance to theology in the twentieth century, see the essays by Jodock, Lotz, and Welch in Darrell Jodock, ed., *Ritschl in Retrospect* (Minneapolis, 1995).

32. Wilhelm Herrmann, *Die Metaphysik in der Theologie* (Halle, 1876), p. 2.

33. Ibid., p. 21.

34. Ibid., p. 8.

35. Ibid., p. 22.

36. W. Herrmann, *Schriften zur Grundlegung der Theologie,* II, ed. Peter Fischer- Appelt (Kaiser Verlag, 1966–1967), 261. Cited in Simon Fisher, *Revelatory Positivism? Barth's Earliest Theology and the Marburg School* (Oxford, 1988), p. 138.

37. W. Herrmann, *The Communion of the Christian with God,* trans. J. Sandys Stanyon (New York, 1906), p. 58.

38. Ibid., p. 239.

39. Ibid., pp. 99–100.

40. Ibid., p. 141.

41. W. Herrmann, *Systematic Theology* (London, 1927), p. 84.

42. Ibid., pp. 83–84.

43. Herrmann, *Communion,* p. 74.

44. Ibid., pp. 67, 69, 71, 72, 74, 75–76, 76–77.

45. M. Kähler, *The So-Called Historical Jesus and the Historic Biblical Christ,* trans. and ed. Carl E. Braaten (Philadelphia, 1964), pp. 49, 83, 87.

46. Claude Welch, *Protestant Thought in the Nineteenth Century,* II (New Haven, 1985), 156. Welch's exposition of the themes of Herrmann's theology and the Herrmann- Kähler discussion is the most lucid brief account available, and I have been dependent on it on some crucial points.

47. Agnes von Zahn-Harnack, *Adolf von Harnack* (Berlin, 1936), p. 91.

48. A. Harnack, "Über die Sicherheit und Grenzen geschichtlicher Erkenntnis," in *Reden und Aufsätze,* IV, 7. Cited in Wilhelm Pauck, *The Heritage of the Reformation* (Glencoe, Ill., 1961). See also Wilhelm Pauck, "Adolf von Harnack," in D. G. Peerman and M. E. Marty, *A Handbook of Christian Theologians,* for a brief, masterful treatment of Harnack's work.

49. *History of Dogma,* I, trans. from 3d German edition by Neil Buchanan (New York, 1958), 1.

50. *Grundriss der Dogmengeschichte,* 9th ed. (Berlin, 1921), p. 5. Cited in Pauck, "Adolf von Harnack," p. 97.

51. A. Harnack, *What Is Christianity?* trans. T. B. Saunders (London, 1901), pp. 13–14.

52. *History of Dogma,* I, p. 13.

53. Ibid., p. 58ff.

54. Harnack, *What Is Christianity?*, p. 51.

55. Ibid., p. 56.

56. Ibid., p. 67.
57. Ibid., p. 73.
58. Ibid., p. 100.
59. Ibid., pp. 99–100.
60. Ibid., p. 128.
61. Ibid., p. 144.
62. Ibid., p. 145.
63. Ibid.
64. Ibid.
64. Ibid., p. 14.
65. Walter Rauschenbusch, *Christianizing the Social Order* (New York, 1912), pp. 67, 69.
66. Walter Rauschenbusch, *A Theology for the Social Gospel* (New York, 1917), p. 1.
67. Ibid., p. 57.
68. Ibid., p. 58.
69. Ibid., p. 60.
70. Ibid., p. 50.
71. Ibid., pp. 46–47.
72. Ibid., p. 48.
73. Ibid., p. 49.
74. Ibid., pp. 174–175.
75. Ibid., p. 178.
76. Ibid., p. 95.
77. Ibid., pp. 97–99.
78. Ibid., pp. 100–101.
79. Ibid., p. 117.
80. Rauschenbusch, *Christianizing the Social Order,* p. 126.
81. Ibid., pp. 154–155.
82. Ibid., p. 156.
83. Ibid., p. 155.
84. John Dillenberger and Claude Welch, *Protestant Christianity Interpreted through Its Development* (New York, 1988), p. 228.

SUGGESTIONS FOR FURTHER READING

I. Ritschl and the Ritschlian Theology

Hefner, Philip, trans. *Albrecht Ritschl: Three Essays* (Philadelphia: Fortress Press, 1972). Includes three important essays: the "Prolegomena" to *The History of Pietism,* "Theology and Metaphysics," and "Instruction in the Christian Religion," and a fine Introduction.

———. *Faith and the Vitalities of History: A Theological Study Based on the Work of Albrecht Ritschl* (New York: Harper and Row, 1966). Relates Ritschl to issues central to more recent theological discussion. Excellent bibliography.

Jodock, Darrell, ed. *Ritschl in Retrospect: History, Community, and Science* (Minneapolis: Fortress Press, 1995). Valuable assessments by eight Ritschl scholars.

Lotz, David. *Ritschl and Luther* (Nashville: Abingdon Press, 1974). Also see Lotz, "Albrecht Ritschl and the Unfinished Reformation," *Harvard Theological Review,* 73 (1980), 337–372; and "Ritschl in Retrospect" in Jodock above.

Mueller, David L. *An Introduction to the Theology of Albrecht Ritschl* (Philadelphia: Westminster Press, 1969). A good introduction to the central themes and a critical assessment.

Richmond, James. *Ritschl: A Reappraisal* (London: Collins, 1978).

Rupp, George. *Culture-Protestantism: German Liberal Theology at the Turn of the Twentieth Century* (Missoula, Mont.: Scholars Press, 1977). This monograph counters the Neo-Orthodox critique of the Ritschlian theology and demonstrates the differences as well as commonalities shared by Ritschl, Herrmann, Kaftan, Troeltsch, Harnack, and others.

Welch, Claude. *Protestant Thought in the Nineteenth Century,* II (New Haven: Yale University Press, 1985). Includes a fine summary of Ritschl's theology, entitled "Faith, History, and Ethics in Balance." Also brief accounts of Herrmann and Harnack.

II. Wilhelm Herrmann

There are no thorough studies of Herrmann in English. The following include helpful surveys and special studies:

Barth, Karl. "The Principle of Dogmatics According to Wilhelm Herrmann." In *Theology and Church* (New York: Harper and Row, 1962). Both sympathetic and critical.

Deegan, Daniel L. "Wilhelm Herrmann: A Reassessment," *Scottish Journal of Theology,* 19 (1966), 188–203. Good, brief account of central themes in Herrmann's theology.

Fisher, Simon. *Revelatory Positivism? Barth's Earliest Theology and the Marburg School* (Oxford: Oxford University Press, 1988). Chapter 3 contains an examination of Herrmann in the context of Marburg Neo-Kantianism.

Gregory, Frederick. *Nature Lost? Natural Science and German Theological Traditions of the Nineteenth*

Century (Cambridge: Harvard University Press, 1992). Chapters 6–7 are a fine study of Herrmann's views on science and theology.

Voelkel, Robert. *The Shape of the Theological Task* (Philadelphia: Westminster Press, 1968). Chapter 1 contains a study of Herrmann, and the book explores further his theology in relation to the contemporary theological task. Also see Voelkel's "Introduction" to Wilhelm Herrmann, *The Communion of the Christian with God* (Philadelphia: Fortress Press, 1971).

III. Adolf von Harnack

Glick, Wayne. *The Reality of Christianity: A Study of Adolf von Harnack as Historian and Theologian* (New York: Harper and Row, 1967). The only extensive study of Harnack in English.

Pauck, Wilhelm. *Harnack and Troeltsch: Two Historical Theologians* (New York: Oxford University Press, 1968). A masterful essay on Harnack. Also see W. Pauck, "Adolf von Harnack's Interpretation of Church History." In *The Heritage of the Reformation* (Glencoe, Ill.: Free Press, 1961).

Rumscheidt, Martin. *Revelation and Theology: An Analysis of the Barth-Harnack Correspondence* (Edinburgh: Scottish Academic Press, 1972). Also see M. Rumscheidt, ed. "Introduction" to *Adolf von Harnack: Liberal Theology at Its Height* (Minneapolis: Fortress Press, 1991). A fine collection of selections from Harnack's vast writings.

IV. Walter Rauschenbusch and the Social Gospel in America

Handy, Robert T., ed. *The Social Gospel in America 1870–1920* (New York: Oxford University Press, 1966). Good selections from Rauschenbusch's writing, as well as from Washington Gladden and Richard Ely, with helpful introductions and bibliography.

Hopkins, Charles H. *The Rise of the Social Gospel in American Protestantism 1865–1915* (New Haven: Yale University Press, 1940). A detailed study, though now dated in some of its views.

May, Henry F. *Protestant Churches and Industrial America* (New York: Harper and Row, 1949; reissued 1967). A classic study of the variety of types of social Christianity in America.

Sharpe, Dores. *Walter Rauschenbusch* (New York: Macmillan Co., 1942). Full of valuable biographical information but weak on analysis of Rauschenbusch's theology and significance.

Chapter 12
Movements of Recovery and Conservation: The Princeton Theology

Charles Hodge

It is often said that the dominant trend of Protestant theology in the nineteenth century is inherently subjective. That is, the religious object, God, is present and real only in and through the experiencing, willing, and apprehending subject or self.[1] We have observed how this is true for Coleridge, Schleiermacher, and Bushnell, among many others, and that it is related to their opposition to objective "evidences," whether derived from natural theology or the Bible. Attention to the believing subject persists, in different ways, in the work of Feuerbach, Ritschl and his disciples, and Kierkegaard.

A feature of the movement of ideas, as of societies, is that when they are driven too far in one direction, counterforces emerge that inevitably prompt a reaction. In nineteenth-century theology this often takes the form of a move to assert a more "objective" view of theology, something indepen-

dent of the self and objectively given in, for example, Scripture or the Church. Such movements of reaction often demand a return to, and the conservation of, what earlier had proven "tried and true." We already have seen how the radically disruptive ideas and actions of the Enlightenment and the French Revolution were accompanied by a Counter-Enlightenment and a period of political restoration in Europe. It is not surprising then that the first half of the nineteenth century saw movements of reaction and restoration in both Church and theology, since the attack on orthodox belief and on ecclesiastical institutions and prerogatives continued apace in the decades after 1800. The corrosive work of the Deists and skeptics such as Voltaire, Hume, and Reimarus was followed by the shocks of Schleiermacher and Hegel, and then those of radicals such as Strauss and Feuerbach. Not only the

Romantic turn to religious experience ("subjectivism") but science and biblical criticism were now seen as a dire threat to theology and to the traditional "confessional" churches.

The short-lived Restoration after 1815 had itself been threatened by the European revolutions of 1848, just as the Tory establishment in the Church of England was profoundly shaken by the Reform Bill of 1832. The outcome of the latter threat was, as we have seen, the Oxford or Tractarian Movement. But everywhere both political events and intellectual developments appeared to be undermining the very foundations of both the Catholic and Protestant traditions. And the result was a general reaction against "Liberalism." In the Catholic Church it took the form of Ultramontanism and the restoration of Thomistic theology, movements that will be described in Chapter 13.

In Germany the theological reaction was expressed in a restoration of an older Lutheran confessionalism. Among the most important of these Lutheran confessional theologians were August Vilmar (1800–1868), F. A. Philippi (1809–1892), and E. W. Hengstenberg (1802–1869). The program of these theologians "was openly and vigorously restorative. Its spirit was that of a self-conscious minority seeking to defend the church against the dominance of rationalist and idealist views, to hold to the objectivities of Christian truth against subjective vagaries, and so to reprise the distinctive doctrine and order of the early Lutheran church."[2]

Because these Lutherans opposed all forms of progressive liberalism and called for a return to the "pure" Lutheranism of the older confessions, their work is often referred to as a "theology of repristination," that is, a movement to restore Lutheran theology to its original state. However, this theology not only placed great emphasis on the teachings of the classical Lutheran confessions but also upheld a conservative view of biblical inerrancy and verbal inspiration. This meant, of course, strong opposition to modern historical criticism of the Bible. There was to be no abiding of any position that was not willing to assent fully to the old Lutheran confessions as a rule of faith but also to the Bible's inerrancy. As we will see in the case of the Princeton Theology, these were to be the two pillars of many

of the movements of theological restoration that came to prominence in the middle decades of the nineteenth century.

BACKGROUND

It is generally recognized that historically the most influential of the indigenous American restorationist and "confessional" movements is the Princeton Theology, associated with four theologians who taught at Princeton Theological Seminary between 1812 and 1921. No movement associated with a single theological school has had greater impact on American religious life than the Princeton Theology. For over a century it remained the guardian of Presbyterian orthodoxy in the United States and beyond. Thousands of the seminary's students were shaped by the teaching of the four theologians, and scores of those students assumed the presidencies of American colleges, became leading scholars and teachers in their own right, and held some of the most influential pulpits in the country. It would not wholly please the Princeton theologians to know, however, that their influence continues into the late twentieth century not significantly in their own Presbyterian Church and seminary but, rather, among many nondenominational Fundamentalists and "enthusiastic" Evangelicals.

Like the movements of restoration in Europe, the Princeton Theology originated in reaction to Enlightenment "infidelity," but also to the new emotional religion associated with American "revivalism" that was rampant in the 1820s and 1830s and to the accompanying "liberalizing" spirit that was now taking hold. To understand the position of the Princeton Theology, something must be said of the theological disputes within the American Presbyterian Church at the beginning of the nineteenth century.

During the eighteenth century Presbyterianism became a significant force in American life, especially in the more cosmopolitan Middle Colonies that stretched from New York to South Carolina. The Presbyterian churches were a mixture of English Puritans, who had settled originally in New England and on Long Island in the seventeenth century, and the later Scotch-Irish immigrants. The first presbytery, or governing body, was established in Philadelphia in 1706 and reflected the Church's diversity with Scottish, Irish, and English ministers in its small membership. At the time of the American Revolution, Presbyterianism was identified as a champion of independence from Britain. In 1788 the Presbyterian general synod, consisting of sixteen presbyteries, constituted itself as a General Assembly in the new Presbyterian Church in the U.S.A. This union, however, did not erase important theological differences. When the Calvinist orthodoxy of some of the Scotch-Irish appeared to them to be threatened, and the teachings of the Westminster Confession of Faith (1647) to be compromised, controversy erupted. At the beginning of the nineteenth century, it took the form of a contest between what was called the conservative "Old School" and the more liberal and tolerant "New School."

The New School Presbyterians favored a plan of union with their Calvinist colleagues in the Congregational Church and favored a more decentralized church government and authority. The Old School represented a more "high church" conception of church order and government and a stricter reading of the Westminster standards with less latitude of interpretation. The New School tended to embrace the "New Divinity" associated with Jonathan Edwards's pupil Samuel Hopkins (1721–1803), who altered his mentor's Calvinism in a more subjective, voluntaristic direction, and with Nathaniel William Taylor (1786–1856), spokesman of the "New Haven Theology." The conflict between the two schools centered on the issue of unregenerate humanity. The Old School charged that the New School perceived sin as voluntary acts of the human will which made regeneration "the act of the sinner himself." The work of regeneration as portrayed in New Haven resembled that of divine persuasion "analogous to the influence which one now exerts over the mind of another." This allegation on the part of the Old School representatives was not wholly fair, but it expressed their apprehensions regarding any laxity toward what they perceived to be the classical Calvinism of the Westminster standards. Many of the Old School also disapproved of the New School's ties with other

evangelical denominations, for example, in forming cooperative societies such as the American Bible Society (1816) and the American Sunday School Union (1824). The Old School saw such alliances as opening the doors to dangerous toleration and laxity. Most crucial, however, were the different views the two schools held toward the revivals that marked the Second Evangelical Awakening in America in the early decades of the nineteenth century—and especially toward the "new measures" adopted by the great revivalist Charles Finney in his work in western New York state. Members of the New School thought the emotional excesses of Finney's revivalism were to be indulged, since they proved effective in saving souls. The Old School saw these very souls as being imperiled and destroyed by the false teaching that inevitably accompanied such enthusiasm. Finally, the two schools embraced very different philosophical frameworks. While deep into Scottish philosophy, the New School came to favor ethical intuitionism and philosophical idealism, which allowed for greater speculative freedom. The Old School adhered to common-sense Scottish Realist epistemology, which frowned on speculation and insisted that theology follow an inductive, "scientific" method. As we will see, these two philosophic orientations entailed very different theological starting points and approaches to the text of Scripture.

Before 1812 the Presbyterian Church had no school for the theological training of its clergy. Young men studied under clerical tutors for their ordination examinations administered by the presbytery. Archibald Alexander (1772–1851), a young minister serving the Third Presbyterian Church of Philadelphia, and previously president of Hampden-Sydney College in Virginia, believed that the time had come for the creation of a theological seminary to produce well-qualified ministers, especially in view of the threats of the "New Divinity" that he had observed during a tour of New England. In 1808 he proposed such a move to the General Assembly, and, after a few years of planning, Alexander was himself elected Princeton Seminary's first professor. The direction and central themes of the Princeton Theology, which were to guide its life for the next century, were firmly set by Alexander. He was joined and later succeeded by Charles

Hodge (1797–1878), who was named Professor of Exegetical and Didactic Theology in 1840. The third member of the Princeton school was Hodge's son, Archibald Alexander Hodge (1823–1886), who was called to be his father's associate in 1877 and succeeded to his chair in 1879. The last and most learned member of the school was Benjamin Breckinridge Warfield (1851–1921).

In his General Assembly sermon Alexander portrayed the special dangers of the time—theological error and infidelity—that made it imperative that Princeton Seminary be established. The one he associated with the eighteenth-century *rationalism* and Deism that he found in the ranks of Unitarianism; the other, which he called *enthusiasm,* he identified with the "New Divinity." Alexander saw enthusiasm and superstitious infidelity as akin to one another and as succeeding "each other as cause and effect." While he was an active revival preacher, he also could write: "The wild ebullitions of enthusiasm, when they subside, leave their subjects under the fatal influence of some absurd opinions which become the creed of a new sect."[3] For Alexander, the danger posed for evangelical truth by these two "signs of the times" was their self-sufficiency with regard to Scripture:

> The rationalist will not receive many of the doctrines of revelation because they do not accord with his preconceived notions, which he calls the dictates of reason. The enthusiast will not submit to the authority of scripture because he imagines that he is under the direction of a superior guide. The one makes his own reason the judge of what he will receive as true from the volume of revelation; the other determines every thing, whether it relate to opinion or practice, by the suggestion of his fancied inspiration.[4]

We can see in Alexander's influential sermon the key to the Princeton Theology and its guiding principle: the authority of Scripture as exempt from error as the source of all Christian doctrine and truth. In "Search the Scriptures," his inaugural address of 1812 as Princeton's first professor of theology, Alexander sets the keynote of the school's apologetic, namely, the proofs for the perfect integrity and authority of Scripture. Later, in his *Evidence of the Authenticity, Inspiration, and Canonical Authority of*

the Holy Scriptures, Alexander was to assert that the full inspiration of the Bible was "such a divine influence upon the minds of the sacred writers as rendered them exempt from error, both in regard to the ideas and the words." The entire edifice of Christian belief was, therefore, dependent on the inerrancy of Scripture. "Could it be shown," Alexander lays it down, "that the evangelists had fallen into palpable mistakes in facts of minor importance, it would be impossible to demonstrate that they wrote anything by inspiration."[5]

A second key to the Princeton Theology, and a guide to their theological program, is their unwavering commitment to a conservative Calvinist confessionalism, especially as systematized by the late seventeenth-century Genevan theologian, Francis Turretin (1623–1687). Turretin was a stalwart defender of the Genevan orthodoxy of his day, based on John Calvin's Catechism, (1545), the Second Helvetic Confession (1566), and the Canons of the Synod of Dort, (1619). While perhaps not as rigid as often depicted, Turretin held strict views of such orthodox Reformed doctrines as biblical inspiration and inerrancy, election, and reprobation. The developments of Reformed theology after Calvin proved to be highly complex as Calvinism spread in Switzerland, France, Holland, Britain, and America. But the Princeton theologians perceived its normative and unified character as represented in the Westminster standards and in the writings of the Reformed dogmaticians of the seventeenth century, especially Turretin.

When Alexander began teaching at Princeton, he was hard pressed to find an appropriate theological text for his students. He did not find any in English that were adequate and settled on Turretin. As his biographer reports, although Alexander found Turretin's *Institutio Theologiae Elencticae* to be "ponderous, scholastic, and in a dead language," he nevertheless had felt the influence of Turretin's "athletic sinewy reason" on his own mind and judged that those of his students who mastered him "were apt to be strong and logical divines."[6] Charles Hodge also drew heavily on Turretin, as well as on Calvin and the confessional standards, in writing his own three-volume *Systematic Theology,* which replaced Turretin's *Institutio* as the theology text at Princeton in the 1870s. Hodge spoke of Turretin's text as "one of the most perspicuous books ever written." A. A. Hodge's enlarged edition of his *Outlines of Theology* (1879) also was crucially inspired by Turretin, especially regarding scriptural inspiration and inerrancy.[7] Benjamin Warfield was the only member of the school of Princeton Theology not to be deeply influenced by Turretin and the seventeenth-century Reformed dogmaticians, although the president of Princeton Seminary in Warfield's day, F. L. Patton, called Turretin "the Thomas Aquinas of Protestantism."

A third vital key to understanding the assumptions and methods that guided the Princeton theologians is the influence of the philosophy known as Scottish "common-sense" realism.[8] The Princeton theologians' biblicism and confessionalism were undergirded and informed by this Scottish philosophy that had had a deep influence on American thought in general for a half century just before the American Revolutionary period. The Scottish "common-sense" philosophy was brought to Princeton from Scotland when the Reverend John Witherspoon (1723–1794), a minister of the Church of Scotland, became president of the College of New Jersey (later Princeton College) in 1768. He opposed the "New Divinity" and its idealist philosophy, established Scottish realism as the official philosophy of the college, and became the defender of orthodox Calvinism. His students were the teachers of both Archibald Alexander and Charles Hodge.

The "school" of Scottish realism was led by Thomas Reid (1710–1796) and Dugald Steward (1753–1828), the latter being the chief disseminator of Reid's philosophy and the one who had the greater influence in America and in Princeton. Reid was a strict empiricist. He opposed not only the idealism of Bishop Berkeley (1685–1753) but also the skepticism of David Hume, who, as we have seen, had disclosed the weakness of empiricism. Reid adopted the inductive, scientific realism of Aristotle, which grounded all knowledge in sensory experience. And he identified this inductive realism with the scientific method espoused a century earlier by Francis Bacon in his *Novum Organum*. Both Reid and Steward treated a wide range of scientific subjects in their philosophical lectures. They regarded Isaac Newton's scientific work as the culmination of the Baconian inductive philosophy.

The great issue for Reid was overcoming the skeptical dead end of British empirical philosophy. Hume had exposed the fallacy of John Locke's solution to the dualism of mind and matter, self and world. Locke claimed that what we perceive in the mind are not objects themselves but "ideas" formed by our consciousness. But, as Hume demonstrated, if all we know are ideas then we cannot be certain that things exist objectively and independently of those ideas. Reid cut this perplexing Gordian knot by simply asserting that all that exists are minds and matter and that the mind perceives not ideas but the real objects themselves. "Perception," Reid insists, "hath always an object distinct from the act by which it is perceived."[9] How does Reid know this? Well, by intuition, or what he called "judgment," an a priori "irresistible conviction" of the reality of external objects, a belief comparable to a religious faith. It is this "judgment" that secures our confidence in our sense perceptions and in scientific induction. Reid wrote:

> If there are certain principles, as I think there are, which the constitution of our nature leads us to believe, and which we are under a necessity to take for granted in the common concerns of life, without being able to give a reason for them—these are what we call 'the principle of common sense'; and what is manifestly contrary to them, is what we call absurd.[10]

The philosopher who boldly rejects the principles that guide the conduct of all humankind is foolish indeed.

This "common-sense" view of knowledge largely derived from Stewart by way of Reid—confident in Baconian scientific progress, practical and pragmatic in spirit, and democratic in its belief in the veracity of the common judgments of humanity—was well-suited to the "Gilded Age" in American history. And it was anchored in a common-sense belief in God. As Reid reasoned:

> Indeed, if we believe that there is a wise and good Author of nature, we may see a good reason why he should continue the same laws of nature, and the same connections of things, for a long time; because, if he did otherwise, we could learn nothing from what is past, and all our experience would be of no use to us.[11]

An important feature of this Scottish realism was its taken-for-granted conviction that true science and theology were not only compatible but mutually supportive. Protestant theology and Newtonian science, it was assumed, formed a natural kinship. When Archibald Alexander instituted the Princeton curriculum, he sought to adapt the Scottish philosophy to the needs of theological education. Theology was to be thoroughly guided by the method of Baconian empiricism, and for Alexander this meant that "unless the Christian religion is attended with sufficient evidence, we cannot believe in it even if we would."[12] As we will see, the principles and method of Scottish realism are especially evident in the theology and apologetics of Charles Hodge.

Scottish realism gave to the Princeton Theology a confidence that its theological work was established on the solid grounds of Baconian scientific induction. In the American intellectual ethos of the first half of the nineteenth century, it proved successful, for it shared the common intellectual assumptions of the day, namely, assurance of the truthfulness of the Baconian method and the Newtonian world-view. Hodge, for example, could say confidently that "the theologian must be guided by the same rules in the collection of facts as govern the man of science."[13] We can see in retrospect that the world-view of the Princeton theologians was essentially static, uniform, and unhistorical. It was impervious to the Romantic world of development and historical particularity—the world of Herder and Hegel. But such a theology, grounded in the principles of Scottish "common-sense" realism, was often to find itself in some perplexity when its scientific and epistemological assumptions were profoundly challenged by the inroads of historical criticism and science after mid-century. Ironically and unintentionally, this "common-sense" realism placed many inheritors of the Princeton Theology, and conservative Protestant theology generally, in the position of frequently initiating a largely fruitless "warfare" between science and theology.[14]

CHARLES HODGE

Three of the four theologians who comprise the "school" of Princeton Theology had long tenures at Princeton, but none so long as Charles Hodge (1797–1878). He taught there for fifty-eight years. On the day of the celebration of his fiftieth year of teaching, even the shops in Princeton closed to honor the great man. Hodge is the person most associated with and representative of the Princeton Theology. Born in Philadelphia, he early came under the influence of his Presbyterian pastor, Dr. Ashbel Green, one of the founders of Princeton Seminary who became president of Princeton College in 1812. Hodge's widowed mother also moved to Princeton in 1812 so that her two sons, Charles and Hugh, could have a college education. It was an auspicious year for the Princeton Theology since it also saw the founding of Princeton Seminary. Young Hodge attended Archibald Alexander's inaugural lecture as professor. Soon a friendship with the older man was established; Hodge became his pupil and later his colleague.

Hodge entered the sophomore class at Princeton College in the fall of 1812. Ashbel Green taught him moral philosophy, steeped in the principles of Scottish realism. Hodge then attended Princeton Seminary from 1815 to 1819, under the tutelage of Archibald Alexander. After graduation he did further study of Hebrew, taught seminary students the biblical languages, and served as a preacher in several churches. In 1820 he returned to Princeton and in 1822 was named Professor of Oriental and Biblical Literature. He remained at the seminary for the rest of his long career, except for a leave between 1826 and 1828 to study and to tour German theological centers. Conservative theologians such as August Tholuck in Halle and E. W. Hengstenberg in Berlin reinforced his suspicions of mysticism, rationalism, and the new higher criticism of the Bible.

In 1840 Hodge became Professor of Exegetical and Didactic Theology. However, he had long since made his reputation as an able opponent of the "New Divinity." He carried out his theological combat in the *Biblical Repertory* (1825), which was later called the *Biblical Repertory and Theological Review* and then the *Biblical Repertory and Princeton Review.* In the pages of this review, which he edited for forty-six years, Hodge took on the leading theologians and clergy of his day—Nathaniel Taylor, Edwards Amasa Park, Horace Bushnell, John W. Nevin, and Charles Finney—as well as the German rationalists and biblical critics. Hodge's *Repertory* had great influence in Presbyterian circles in America and beyond. It is generally agreed today that the breadth and complexity of Hodge's mind are far better revealed in the pages of the *Repertory* than in the two-thousand pages of his three-volume *Systematic Theology*, published late in his career. The latter, however, does set forth Hodge's systematic thought on a wide range of methodological and doctrinal questions, and it remains today an important text and resource in conservative evangelical theological circles.

Speaking retrospectively in 1868 about his journal, Hodge emphasized its lack of originality. "No article," he wrote,

> opposed to [the Presbyterian standards as taught in the Word of God] has ever appeared in its pages. . . . Whether it be a ground of reproach or approbation, it is believed to be true that an original idea in theology is not to be found in the pages of the *Biblical Repertory and Princeton Review* from the beginning until now. The phrase "Princeton Theology," therefore, is without distinctive meaning.[15]

What Hodge meant, of course, was that the Princeton Theology did not diverge from the true Word of God in Scripture as formulated in the Westminster standards. Hodge's words have been cited by later critics to demonstrate the uncreative, scholastic, and outdated character of Hodge's massive theological enterprise. Hodge doubtless would be displeased with the recent judgment of a Church historian who writes that both Charles Hodge and his critics are historically wrong. This historian points to the very new and distinctive character of the Princeton Theology that, appropriating aspects of the ethos of its time and responding to contemporary challenges, unknowingly contributed to one of the major anti-intellectual movements in American religion in the twentieth century. "A systematic theology of biblical authority which defended the common evangelical faith in the infallibility of the Bible had to be created in the midst of the nineteenth-century controversy. The formation of this theology in association with the growth of the millenarian movement determined the character of Fundamentalism."[16] Hodge cannot be blamed, of course, for the unexpected ways in which his theology was later appropriated or for its historical consequences. Addressing what he saw as the threats to orthodox Christianity, he fashioned a response that proved to be a distinctive and, in its own terms, imposing theology of restoration.

Hodge's writings over half a century touch on many important theological subjects, but there are four that are particularly representative of his thought. One has to do with theological method. This is closely related to his doctrine of the Bible, its inspiration and authority. A third theme dominates his polemics against the "rationalists" and "mystics" of his time, namely, his focus on the theme of Christian anthropology. Finally, Hodge's theology offered a distinctive position with regard to the relationship between theology and science, especially his encounter with Darwinism. Here we will discuss the first three themes; Hodge's treatment of Darwinism and science was discussed in Chapter 10.

Theological Method

It was earlier remarked that Hodge regarded his own theology as unoriginal, as simply a restatement of the classic Calvinist theology of the Reformation. In fact, his theology was profoundly shaped by other influences, particularly those derived from the Enlightenment confidence in reason, though for Hodge a reason rightly exercised. Hodge begins his *Systematic Theology* with a long introductory discussion of theological method, specifically the right and wrong use of reason. Under the influence of Turretin's scholastic method in the *Institutes*, Hodge surveys the "state of the question." This involves clarifying what the question is and what it is not, surveying various answers and demonstrating their inadequacies, and marshaling arguments in support of the correct position.

Hodge opens this analysis by describing how theology is a science similar to astronomy or chemistry. Any science involves both facts and the mind's grasp of their causal and logical relations. The mere collection of facts does not constitute science. As a science, theology "must embrace an exhibition of the internal relation of those facts, one to another, and each to all. It must be able to show that if one be admitted, others cannot be denied."[17] The work of the systematic theologian, therefore, involves not only collecting the facts of Scripture ascertained by the biblical theologian but also exhibiting the internal relation of these facts to one other and vindicating them by showing their harmony and consistency. Note that Hodge begins his "scientific" theology with two fundamental assumptions: that the Bible is, first of all, a compendium of facts and that, second, the divine revelatory authority of this biblical treasury is capable of being demonstrated to any rational person.

Every science is distinct in its peculiar method, as determined by its peculiar nature. God does not teach chemistry; he gives the chemist facts out of which the chemist constructs the science of chemistry. Similarly, God does not teach systematic theology. He gives us the facts in the Bible which, when properly arranged and understood, constitute the science of theology. As with any other science, however, it is crucial that theology adopt the right *method* to ensure the scientific validity of its investigation. "If a man adopts a false method, he is like one who takes a wrong road which will never lead him to his destination."[18] Now, there are two great methods, the *a priori* and the *a posteriori*. "The one argues from cause to effect, the other from effect to cause." The former method, which seeks to determine what the facts must be from a consideration of the laws of the mind, is what Hodge calls the "speculative method."

The speculative method, with its a priori departure, is represented by a variety of types of medieval and modern *rationalism,* from St. Anselm to Christian Wolff and Schelling. These theological rationalists "lay down certain principles, called axioms, or first truths of reason, and from them deduce the doctrines of religion by a course of argument as rigid and remorseless as that of Euclid. . . . The result of this method has always been to transmute, as far as it succeeded, faith into knowledge, and to attain this end the teachings of the Bible have been indefinitely modified. Men are expected to believe, not on the authority of God, but on that of reason."[19]

Some rationalists admit an external, supernatural revelation so that truths not discoverable by reason can be made known. But once known they must be shown to be in accord with reason. Therefore, these rationalists undertake to give rational demonstrations of such doctrines as the Trinity and the Incarnation *independent of Scripture.* Such was the method of Christian Wolff. The more radical theological rationalists of the Enlightenment accept no authoritative biblical revelation at all, but only such revelation as is found in humanity itself and in the historical development of the race. If these rationalists concede that the Bible contains truth, it is so only insofar as it is wholly in accord with philosophy. Among these latter rationalists are Karl Daub, a disciple of Schelling, and Marheineke and Strauss, who "find Hegelianism in the Bible, and they therefore admit that so far the Bible teaches truth."[20]

Rationalism represents for Hodge only one of the false forms of theological method. Its error is to assume that by autonomous reason one can attain knowledge of theological truth. There is, however, a second modern form of theological method, equally dangerous and erroneous, but antithetical to rational speculation. Hodge calls it the "Mystical Method" which, distrusting reason, takes as its point of departure the religious feelings and affections. Like rationalism, it represents the modern turn to the "subject" but, in this case, to the individual's intuitive feelings. Mysticism has taken two historical forms. Natural mysticism simply holds that the natural religious consciousness of individuals, shaped by their unique circumstances, is the source of religious knowledge. It does not require the agency of God. However, the more prevalent expression of mysticism in the West is supernatural and theistic. According to theistic mysticism, God "holds direct communion with the soul; and by the excitement of its religious feelings gives it intuitions of truth." But again, such divine truth is independent of the outward teaching of the Bible; "it is this inward light, and not the Scriptures, which we are to follow."

In Hodge's estimation the consequences of this experiential mysticism are devastating for a true theology. First, there can be no such things as revelation or inspiration in the traditional theological sense of these terms, that is, as a "supernatural guidance of the Spirit, which renders its subjects infallible in communicating truth to others." For according to this intuitive mysticism, no person is infallible as a teacher, since revelation and inspiration are common to all humans, although in different degrees. In some persons today it may be as perfect as it was in the days of the Apostles. It follows that the Bible is not an infallible authority in matters of doctrine. The doctrines enshrined in the Bible "are only the forms under which men of Jewish culture gave expression to their feelings and intuitions." Other forms and expressions would and have been equally useful to persons in different times and circumstances. Furthermore, according to this mystical method, Christianity is not fundamentally a system of doctrines; "it is a life, an influence, a subjective state," a power within each individual Christian that determines his or her view of divine things.[21] The consequence of this method is that it is no longer the duty of a theologian to interpret Scripture but rather to interpret and make known the contents of his or her own Christian consciousness—for example, to determine what truths concerning God are implied in the feelings and consciousness of the Infinite and Eternal, or what truths about sin or redemption emerge from one's consciousness of Christ. The most distinguished and influential practitioner of this method is, of course, Friedrich Schleiermacher in his *The Christian Faith*. For Hodge a true theology must find a way between the rationalism of Christian Wolff and the experiential mysticism of Schleiermacher, one that is true to the revelation in Scripture alone.

Such a true method, he believed, will be free of the vagaries of both individual autonomous reason and mystical intuitive feelings. It will be an *inductive*, not a deductive method. And it will agree with those inductive assumptions and principles that guide the natural sciences. It will, for example, assume the trustworthiness of the testimony of our sense perceptions. The facts of nature that we know by our faculties of sense are reliable. It will also take for granted the entire adequacy of our mental faculties of perception, memory, inference, and so on. And finally, Hodge's inductive method presupposes those truths that "are not learned from experience, but which are given in the constitution of our nature,"[22] such as our conviction that the same cause under similar circumstances will produce like effects. Hodge's Scottish "common-sense" belief that we can be sure that we can take things as they are perceived by us, just as they are, reveals that he is imbued with

the same Baconian scientific optimism that inspired Voltaire. But what is even more striking to a twentieth-century reader is the ease with which Hodge draws the strict correlation between scientific induction and the inductive method in theology.

In an oft-quoted passage on the inductive method as it applies to theology, Hodge writes that "the Bible is to the theologian what nature is to the man of science. It is his store-house of facts; and his method of ascertaining what the Bible teaches, is the same as that which the natural philosopher adopts to ascertain what nature teaches."[23] That is, the theologian assumes all those laws of belief not learned *from* experience but presupposed by the scientist. However, Hodge continues, these laws of belief will include some that are not applicable to the natural sciences, such as "the essential distinction between right and wrong; that nothing contrary to virtue can be enjoined by God . . . that sin deserves punishment, and other similar first truths, which God has implanted in the constitution of all moral beings, and which no objective revelation can possibly contradict."[24] These "first truths of reason" are not individual opinions, for they have passed the test of universality and necessity and hence are self-evident since they force themselves on the mind of every rational creature.

The duty of the Christian theologian is, then, to assume the validity of the beliefs arrived at by the inductive, scientific method. His or her duty is also to apply this method to ascertain, collect, and show the consistency of the facts in the Bible, the facts which God has revealed to humanity concerning the divine nature and our relation to God. These constitute the theologian's duty because everything revealed in nature or that concerns the constitution of humanity "is contained and authenticated in Scripture." So "lest we should err in our inferences from the works of God, we have a clearer revelation of all that nature reveals in his word."[25]

Another duty of the theologian is to hold to the rule that "principles are derived from facts and not impressed upon them." It would be unscientific for a theologian "to assume a theory as to the nature of virtue, of liberty, of moral obligation, and then explain the facts of Scripture in accordance with his theories. His only proper course is to derive his theory of virtue, of sin, of liberty, of obligation from the facts of the Bible. . . . If he cannot believe what the facts of the Bible assume to be true, let him say so." If the Bible teaches that all humans bear the guilt of Adam's sin or that Christ bears our guilt and pays the penalty of the law in our stead, "these are facts with which we must make our principles agree."[26]

It follows from Hodge's argument that the Bible contains all the facts of theology. In other words, those truths taught us by intuitions that are constitutive of our very nature, or by religious experience, "are recognized and authenticated in the Scriptures." Therefore, the Bible serves as a safeguard and limit against what we may erroneously regard as self-evident either intuitively or experientially. So the Bible not only gives us facts about God, Christ, and so on, "but also records the legitimate effects of those truths on the mind of believers. So that we cannot appeal to our own feelings or inward experience, as a ground or guide, unless we can show that it agrees with the experience of the holy men as recorded in the Scriptures."[27] In short, (1) the only true method of theology is the inductive method, and (2) the Bible contains all the facts and truths that constitute the contents of a theology. Hodge's method calls for further analysis of his defense of the Bible's inspiration and authority.

The Inspiration and Authority of the Bible

With few exceptions, the German higher-criticism of the Bible did not have a decisive influence on American theology before the mid-nineteenth century. And yet the writings of Coleridge and Schleiermacher were having an effect on traditional notions of biblical inspiration and inerrancy in America, as we have seen in the case of Horace Bushnell. It was, in fact, Bushnell's "Preliminary Dissertation on the Nature of Language" that Charles Hodge saw as a profound threat to the received view of the Bible's authority and that provoked Hodge to write his own long essay on "Inspiration" in 1857.[28] Hodge conceded Bushnell's claim about the symbolical, suggestive, and approximative nature of much religious language. But he felt that Bushnell had "pressed them out to the most absurd conclusions." Simply because language is an imperfect vehicle of thought, one need not infer,

Hodge argues, that authors cannot be trusted by their words, or that there can be no objective revelation of God to the human reason, but only to the imagination and feelings, or that there can be no such thing as a scientific theology. Furthermore, Bushnell's doctrine of religious language does not allow for the communication of objective truth to the understanding and thereby weakens all confidence in the authority of the Bible. Hodge was shocked at Bushnell's extravagant claims regarding Scripture's contradictions and absurdities, for example, his statement that "there is no book in the world that contains so many repugnances, or antagonistic forms of assertion, as the Bible." The danger posed by Bushnell, and Hodge saw him as becoming legion, is that he does not recognize that doctrinal matters such as the Trinity or the Incarnation are fundamentally *questions of scriptural interpretation.* It is, therefore, all the more imperative to establish the Bible's true authority and inspiration.

To Hodge the logic of Christian belief is obvious. Faith in Christ entails faith in the Bible as the word of God,

> and faith in the Scriptures as the word of God, is faith in their plenary inspiration. That is, the persuasion that they are not the product of the fallible intellect of man, but of the infallible intellect of God. . . . In saying that the Bible is the word of God, we mean that he is its author; that he says whatever the Bible says; that every thing which the Bible affirms to be true is true. . . . What the Scriptures teach is to be believed, not on the authority of Moses or the prophets, or of the apostles and evangelists, but on the authority of God, who used the sacred writers as his organs of communication. The Bible is the product of one mind.[29]

Hodge was a systematic theologian similar to Francis Turretin. And he conceived of Scripture statically, as a body of facts and propositions, the plan, unity, and meaning of which makes it clear that it comes from the same divine author. This ahistorical hermeneutic explains in large part Hodge's assumption that

> All Christians in every age and every name have regarded the Bible in all its parts as in such a sense the word of God as to be infallible and of divine

authority. . . . Greeks, Romans, and Protestants all agree in saying, that everything in the Bible which purports to be the word of God . . . is to be received with the same faith and submission, as though spoken directly by the lips of God himself.[30]

Hodge obviously quite mistakenly assumes that the universal Church in every age has held the doctrine of verbal inspiration as Hodge himself understands it. That is, he assumes that the Church has always denied one or another doctrine of partial inspiration, or degrees of inspiration, or that inspiration is confined to the Bible's religious and moral teaching, or that it has not held a doctrine that often confuses inspiration with revelation.

But for Hodge clarity on such matters as inspiration is imperative if theology is not to take the wrong direction at its very inception. This requires careful distinctions between divine inspiration, revelation, and illumination. According to Hodge, the object of revelation is to impart *knowledge* to its recipients; whereas the object of inspiration is to render a person *infallible* in communicating truth to others. These two gifts and operations are distinct and are not always united. For instance, many have received divine revelations who were not themselves inspired to communicate them, while the object of inspiration is to preserve the biblical writer from error in teaching. Conversely, many inspired authors were not the subject of special revelations. Hodge cites the authors of the historical books of the Bible who "in many cases needed no supernatural communication of the facts which they recorded. All that was required was that they be rendered infallible as narrators."[31]

The distinction between inspiration and illumination is even more obvious in terms of their purposes. "Spiritual illumination is designed to make men holy by imparting to them the discernment of the truth and excellence . . . of divine truths already objectively revealed."[32] All genuine believers are gifted with spiritual illumination, while only a few persons, selected by God as his spokespersons, are inspired. One gift does not imply the other, since wicked men, such as Caiaphas, have been inspired. Hodge reminds us of the apostle Paul's teaching that a person may be an inspired prophet, knowing all mysteries, "and yet he be a sounding brass or a tinkling symbol."

Here we encounter a conception of divine inspiration that was anathema to the great Romantic writers as well as to modern liberal Protestant theology. For Hodge inspiration has a specific and limited scope, namely, to preserve the biblical writers from error in what they teach. It follows that for Hodge theologians such as Schleiermacher and Bushnell have a radically false notion of inspiration. They suppose that inspiration "consists in a divine afflatus, analogous to the inspirations of genius, by which the powers of the mind are aroused and strengthened."[33] This implies degrees of spiritual sublimity and insight and the possibility that one part of Scripture may be more entitled to our spiritual attraction and submission. But if inspiration entails infallibility, then there cannot be differences or degrees of truth or authority between one portion of the Bible and another, no degrees of inspiration and infallibility.

Hodge proceeds to insist that a true conception of biblical inspiration extends to the very words of the sacred writers. "The prophets not only constantly say 'Thus saith the Lord' . . . but from the very nature of inspiration . . . the guidance of the Spirit extended to the words employed." Since the end of inspiration is the communication of divine truth, and since it is communicated in human language, that language itself must be determined by the Spirit or there is no guarantee that it is not merely human. For example, "in the historical portions of Scripture, there is little for inspiration to accomplish beyond the proper selection of the materials, and accuracy of statement."[34] In other words, there is nothing in the narratives themselves to distinguish them from the accounts of ordinary persons. So the singular purpose of the doctrine of inspiration is to ensure that the guidance of the Holy Spirit is at work in the selection of the very words that these historians employ.

As Coleridge might well ask, does not Hodge here propose a purely mechanical view of biblical inspiration? Does he not conceive the utterances of the sacred writers merely as those of "a superhuman Ventriloquist"? Hodge's own words leave some ambiguity on the matter. In a letter to the Scottish theologian Marcus Dods, written only months before his death, Hodge insisted that "the accepted formula to express the doctrine of the Church in all ages on this subject [of inspiration] is, that the Scriptures were written *dictante Spiritu Dei*,"[35] that is, *dictated* by the Spirit of God. But on other occasions Hodge denied that his view involved anything mechanical. "It does not," he wrote in the early essay on "Inspiration," "make the writer a machine. It is not a process of dictation. . . . The writer retains his consciousness and self-control," although he or she may be unconscious of the divine influence that is at work. "He speaks and writes as freely and as characteristically as though he were entirely uninfluenced by the Spirit of God."[36]

Hodge's distinctive position on verbal inspiration harks back to the traditional view that, while a mystery, God's providential guidance and human freedom are compatible and are not contradictory. "It is a fundamental principle of scriptural theology that a man may be infallibly guided in his free acts." "Verbal inspiration," he continues, "which controlled the sacred writers in the selection of their words, allowed them perfect freedom within the limits of truth. They were kept from error, and guided to the use of words which expressed the mind of the Spirit, but within these limits they were free to use such language . . . as suited their own taste or purpose." Hodge offers the example of four persons who witness the same series of events, all of whom describe them differently, using different words and highlighting different things that especially suit the purpose of their narrative. But "if they were all inspired, their narratives would retain all these differences, with this single limitation, that they would all be free from error."[37]

Hodge makes it clear that the infallibility of the biblical writers is not a personal infallibility. They were entirely fallible in their knowledge of ordinary affairs, and no doubt many did not understand what they wrote. An individual could not, indeed, teach by *inspiration* that the earth is the center of the universe, "but such may be his own conviction." Inspiration did not elevate the biblical authors to a *knowledge* beyond their own age, yet, puzzlingly, Hodge insists that inspiration did preserve them "from *teaching* error." Now this would appear to bind Hodge to two possible alternatives. One alternative would be that the biblical writers did express cosmological or historical knowledge that was true but that would be humanly impossible for them to

know within the limits of their knowledge and time. The consequences would appear to require some notion of divine dictation which would override genuine free human agency. The other alternative would be that the biblical writers spoke, again let us say, of matters cosmological or historical in the language and according to the knowledge of their time but that these assertions do not, when properly interpreted, contradict scientific truth. They may only contradict scientific theories or hypotheses. The narrative of the Creation in Genesis would be a case in point. However, this places Hodge in the sometimes awkward position of having to revise his claims about what is and is not scientific teaching that is in accord with Scripture.

It is obvious that Hodge is not entirely clear or consistent on these hermeneutical matters. It is specifically on the unity of Scripture and science that, over a long career, his doctrine of verbal inspiration appears, in retrospect, to be most vulnerable. And yet even in the early essay on "Inspiration," his response to the growing evidence of irreconcilable contradictions and errors of fact in the Bible is to downplay their significance. He occasionally acknowledges more telling errors but then argues—rightly from the perspective of his critics—that they do not affect the Bible's saving message. However, he usually retreats hastily to a more uncompromising doctrine of plenary verbal inspiration. Hodge's sometimes cavalier response to biblical criticism and the real difficulties that it posed was, to be fair, due to his own deep faith in the internal testimony of the Holy Spirit. Therefore, he could write that "the cases of contradictions or inconsistencies are, considering the age and character of the different books constituting the Bible, wonderfully few and trivial," or that "the difficulties are so minute as to escape the notice of ordinary intelligence" and "must be sought as with a microscope." Even acknowledging that there are objections "of a more serious kind," he shrugs them off with the assurance that "these difficulties are miraculously small." Moreover, they "do not concern matters of doctrine or duty." But, of course, as his critics were quick to point out, Hodge's doctrine of plenary inspiration was not meant to be limited to those religious matters. Finally, Hodge advises that in those cases where seeming errors cannot be explained "it is rational to confess our ignorance, but irrational to assume that what cannot be explained is inexplicable." "We are perfectly willing," he writes, "to let these difficulties remain, and to allow the objectors to make the most of them."[38] This may be wise spiritual advice, but it was begging the question with regard to the confident claims about plenary verbal inspiration and those ostensible biblical "facts."

With the increasing developments in science, especially in geology, historical criticism, and evolutionary biology, one can observe Hodge's recourse to several new strategies, although his view of Scripture and science remains remarkably consistent. In the 1857 essay on "Inspiration," his optimism is pronounced. While the Bible was written before the birth of science, it nevertheless "touches on all departments of human knowledge"; it speaks of the planets, of the earth, "of the origin, constitution, and destiny of man; yet what has science or philosophy to say against the Bible? . . . The universe is revealed to its profoundest depths, and the Bible is found to harmonize with all its newly discovered wonders." Nothing in the Bible, he writes, "is inconsistent with the highest results of astronomy" and "geology will soon be found side by side with astronomy in obsequiously bearing up the queenly train of God's majestic word."[39]

Hodge had committed the *Princeton Review* to an openness to the findings of natural science. In an article on "The Unity of Mankind," written the year Darwin published *The Origin of Species,* he confidently asserted: "The church, as we have said, bows to the facts of nature, because they are the voice of God. Theories are the stammering utterances of men before which she holds her head erect."[40] And yet we have seen that the findings of the geologists and biologists by mid-century were more difficult, to the minds of many clearsighted theists, to accommodate to the biblical accounts that touched on matters of science and history. We have noted that Hodge's response was to call these new discoveries "hasty generalizations" and to label them mere hypotheses. When a conflict between the "facts" of science and the "facts" of the Bible appeared unresolvable, Hodge increasingly appealed to the Bible against the "hypotheses" of the scientists, that is, he reclaimed the Bible's infallibility in *all* areas of human knowledge.

While Hodge grants no a priori status to any interpretation of the "facts," the Bible's "facts" are given a privileged a apriori status that flies in the face of Hodge's reputed inductive theological method. He now proceeds to lay down his "first principle" and *from it deduces the doctrines of science.* This is evident in his quarrel with the American naturalist Louis Agassiz, who had come to favor the polygenist theory of human origins that conflicted with Hodge's reading of Scripture. Hodge declares that Agassiz would never have fallen into error on the question of the origin of the race had he "appreciated the immense *a priori* probability against that theory [polygenism] arising from the teachings of the Bible."[41] Hodge's later appeal to a theological *a priorism* is pronounced in his encounter with Darwinism in the 1870s and particularly in his discussion of the crucial issue of nature's design, as we have seen in Chapter 10.

A final move taken by Hodge to shore up a conception of plenary inspiration under growing attack was to appeal to the inerrancy of the original autograph copies of the biblical texts. In the "Inspiration" article, Hodge had briefly commented that many difficulties encountered in Scripture could be explained "by errors of transcription," but he made little of this in his other writings. In the *Systematic Theology,* however, he once again affirms, in the teeth of his dispute with Darwinism, that the inspiration and inerrancy of the entire Bible extends "to the statements of facts, whether they be scientific, historical or geographical . . . to everything any sacred writer asserts to be true."[42] But this is now ensured by the perfect inerrancy of the autograph copies. In his final statement on the subject of inspiration, in his letter to Marcus Dods, Hodge rests much of his appeal on this premise: "It is the Bible as it came from the hands of the sacred writers, and of the Bible as properly interpreted, that this infallibility is asserted. There may be discrepancies between one part of the Scripture and another, arising from errors of transcribers. Far more numerous and important difficulties have their origin in erroneous interpretations."[43] Hodge had made only slight appeal to the argument from the original autographs in his public writings on inspiration, but it would become a staple argument in the work of his successors, A. A. Hodge and B. B. Warfield.

It is appropriate to emphasize, as we have done, Hodge's attention to the evidences of the Bible's plenary verbal inspiration. While it occupied a relatively small place in his enormous body of writing, it was fundamental to his theological method and to his apologetics. Moreover, it has had a lasting influence, both on the work of his successors at Princeton and among conservative Protestant theologians in the Anglo-American world in the twentieth century. Nevertheless, to give such importance to this theme is also to misrepresent the full range of Hodge's theological work and to ignore other issues that were critically important to him. One such issue was the crucial debate between Hodge and various representatives of the "New Divinity" on questions relating to Christian anthropology, especially to what Hodge perceived as a dangerous autonomy, Neo-Pelagianism, and "perfectionism" in this new Liberalism.

Christian Anthropology

Between 1847 and 1851 Hodge engaged in an extensive and often acrimonious debate with "New School" theologians and others, such as Horace Bushnell. The central issue was the "New School" attack on the Princeton theologians' view of a depraved human nature that the former believed held Christianity up to ridicule. The "New Schoolers," such as Nathaniel Taylor, particularly had singled out the Princeton teaching regarding the imputation of Adam's sin to his posterity. We have noted that the religious life in America in the early decades of the nineteenth century was deeply aroused by the effects of the Second Great Awakening and revivalism which, in turn, provoked new debates about human sin, conversion, and regeneration. Hodge perceived in the theology of Taylor and the "New Schoolers" and in the theology of the revivals of the Second Awakening a resurgence of Pelagianism, a heresy that Hodge viewed as the root of all modern rationalism and mysticism.

Hodge wrote at this time that from the very beginnings of Christianity the Church was confronted with two great systems of doctrine locked in perpetual conflict.

> The one begins with God, the other with man. The one has for its object the vindication of the divine su-

premacy and sovereignty in the salvation of men; the other has for its characteristic aim the assertion of the rights of human nature. It is specifically solicitous that nothing should be held to be true, which cannot be philosophically reconciled with the liberty and ability of man. It starts with a theory of free agency and of the nature of sin, to which all the anthropological doctrines of the Bible must be made to conform.[44]

This second "system of doctrine," Pelagianism, was for Hodge the great enemy that had to be eradicated before it, in turn, displaced the Christian gospel.

Hodge detected in the preaching of the popular revivalist and Oberlin theologian Charles Finney a "voluntarism" that exemplified the Pelagian threat. Many of the "New School" theologians had distinguished between regeneration as an act of God and conversion as the human response of the believer, thereby preserving the primacy and prevenience of divine grace while affirming human free agency. Finney, however, considered the distinction trivial and collapsed regeneration and conversion into one act, and in such a manner as to give priority to human initiative. "It is ridiculous," he wrote, "to say that a sinner is passive in regeneration, or passive in being converted, for conversion is his own act. The thing to be done is that which cannot be done for him. It is something *he must do,* or it will never be done."[45] Finney was not denying the sinner's dependence on God's grace; he merely assumed it as a gift. But it was the sinner who was required to exercise his or her free will. Finney perceived God as an "efficient Cause" of conversion. "True, there is a sense in which God changes the heart, but it is only this; God influences the sinner to change, and then the sinner does it. The change is the sinner's own voluntary act."[46]

For Finney God's work is essentially that of persuasion, but even here he works indirectly through others, for example through the preacher. "And ordinarily, He employs the agency of others also, in printing, writing, conversation, and preaching. God has put the Gospel treasure in earthen vessels."[47] Finney also spoke of conversion or regeneration as "a change in the choice." He writes: "It is a change in the supreme controlling choice of the mind. The regenerated or converted person prefers God's glory to everything else. He chooses it as the supreme object of affection. . . . Now, he chooses God's service in preference to his own best interest. When a person is truly born again, his choice is habitually right, and of course his conduct is in the main right."[48] Hodge considered such voluntaristic and perfectionistic language intolerable. Finney believed that, once converted, the believer's new disposition of disinterested benevolence would make further moral choices easier, that is, he taught a growth in sanctification or moral perfection. For him human fallenness or depravity was essentially a matter of free sinful choices, not a condition of the whole person. Therefore, infants are not in a state of sin until the age of moral discretion.

The disagreement between Hodge and Finney on regeneration focused on their different views of human free agency and sin. Finney rejected the traditional Calvinist belief that God's grace is irresistible, since he maintained that no person could be elected against his or her own will. Hodge held that grace *is* irresistible and that God already has chosen who will be saved. For Hodge regeneration is the entire work of God; the sinner is unable by the exercise of will to perform the duties required by God, yet this inability is *not* excusable because of the imputed guilt of Adam's sin which we legally, though not morally, bear. Our inherent depravity is, for Hodge, consequent upon Adam's Fall, since Adam is the federal head or representative of the entire race. We, therefore, sin in Adam, and our whole nature is corrupted. Every human is born in sin and is a child of wrath. Only Christ, in virtue of his federal union with us and on our behalf, can justify and redeem believers. Redemption is not, then, based on a believer's will or righteousness but solely on the judicial action of Christ, his obedience and suffering *on our behalf* and *in our name,* by which action grace is imputed to us. This was Hodge's understanding of the orthodox Calvinist scheme of salvation.

Underlying the "New Divinity's" heresy was, then, a fallacy regarding the primacy of the freedom of the will and what it entailed concerning sin. Hodge regarded Finney's exclusive focus on the human will and intention to be a result of his excessive reliance on reason rather than the Bible and to be the source of his superficial understanding of sin. "It is expressly asserted by our Lord," Hodge coun-

ters, "that moral character attaches to what lies deeper than any specific acts of the will . . . but also to that which lies lower than consciousness." For Hodge sin is spoken of in the Bible in such phrases as "conceived in sin," and "indwelling in sin." Therefore, sin is not reducible to sinful acts; it is a condition of the soul, "a principle which brings forth fruit unto death." According to Hodge, the universal faith of the Church has held that since our nature is corrupted since birth,

> all who die unbaptized, according to the Romanists, perish; and by baptism not only guilt, but also the pollution of sin is removed, and new habits of grace are infused into the soul. It is needless to remark that the Lutheran and Reformed churches agree in holding this important doctrine, that moral character does not belong exclusively to voluntary acts, but extends to dispositions, principles, or habits of mind. This is involved in all their authoritative decisions concerning original righteousness, original sin, regeneration, and sanctification.[49]

Hodge engaged in several polemical attacks on the "New Divinity" as he saw it represented in Horace Bushnell's writings between 1847 and 1866. Hodge was one with Bushnell in the attack on the "new measures" associated with Finney and his theology of revivals. He also sympathized with Bushnell's profound understanding of the organic character of the human race. He saw this theme in Bushnell as consistent with an Augustinian doctrine of sin and its effects and as being far deeper than Finney's individualistic doctrine of conscious intention. Commending Bushnell on this point, Hodge notes that *Christian Nurture* rightly perceives that "there is a common life of the race, of the nation, of the church, of the family, of which each individual partakes, and which reveals itself in each, under a peculiar form, determined partly by himself and partly by the circumstances in which he is placed."[50]

But despite this accord, Hodge found Bushnell's account of human nature and regeneration "defective and erroneous." Bushnell, we earlier observed, saw conversion and regeneration as occurring gradually by the agency of God's grace, but as mediated indirectly through natural means, primarily through the family. If sin can be communicated corporately from parent to child and through the generations, then so can grace be conveyed, insisted Bushnell. God uses natural social and psychological means to bring about individual regeneration. And so, while holding that regeneration is of God, Bushnell continued to urge

> that we not only want a supernatural salvation (for nothing less than that can possibly regenerate the fall of nature) . . . we must have it wrought into nature and made to be as it were, one of its own stock powers. It does not meet our intellectual conditions, till it satisfies, in a degree, the scientific instinct in us, and becomes rational and solid, by appearing to work inherently, or from within, as by a certain force of law.[51]

Hodge was not assured by Bushnell's talk of the supernatural prevenience of God. For he read Bushnell's insistence on it "appearing to work inherently" by natural means as, at best, appealing to God as a great "efficient cause" or, at worst, regressing to a pure rationalism and naturalism. According to Hodge, Bushnell fails to recognize that the Bible makes a crucial distinction between the agency of God in the ordinary operations of nature and the work of God's Spirit in the regeneration and sanctification of human beings. "Dr. Bushnell may choose to overlook this distinction, and claim to be a supernaturalist because he believes God is in nature, but he remains on the precise ground occupied by those who are wont to call them Rationalists."

Hodge not only claims that there is nothing in Bushnell's doctrine of conversion that "transcends the ordinary efficiency of natural causes as the vehicles of divine power," despite Bushnell's urgent denials. He also charges Bushnell with providing an inadequate account of the full effects of the imputation of Adam's sin and subsequent human depravity. He does not believe that humans are "by nature the children of wrath" and "involved in a spiritual death." On the contrary, Bushnell teaches that "the forming influence of parental character and life is fully adequate to his regeneration; education can correct what there is of natural corruption."[52] Hodge's concerns appeared to him to be justified when, twenty years later, Bushnell published his *Vicarious Sacrifice* (1866) on the subject of the

Atonement. In this book Bushnell sought to explain the spiritual meaning behind the orthodox legal view of Christ's suffering and death as a substitutionary punishment and at the same time to emphasize the "subjective" or experiential truth of God's suffering and sacrifice as teaching the human family the vicarious quality of all true love. To Hodge such a "moral influence" theory of Christ's atoning work failed to do justice to what Christ accomplished singularly and *objectively* on the Cross, while giving greater place to its moral effects on the individual consciousness and to the analogy between human and divine love.

Hodge's final polemical foray against the "New Divinity" was directed at the theology of Edwards Amansa Park (1808–1900), the Congregationalist theologian who taught at Andover Theological Seminary. Park was the last of the influential New Englanders who avowed a kinship with Jonathan Edwards while approving of the reconceptions of old Calvinism proposed by people like Nathaniel Taylor. With other new Calvinists, Park denied the imputation of Adam's guilt to his progeny, accepted the "rationalist" view of the necessity of human free agency. He equated sin with volitional acts of sin.

Park published a sermon on "The Theology of the Intellect and That of the Feelings," which he had addressed to a group of Congregational ministers in 1850. It launched an eighteen-month exchange between the two theologians in Park's journal, *Bibliotheca Sacra,* and in Hodge's *Princeton Review*—each man claiming to bear witness to the traditions of true Calvinism. We cannot begin to explore here the variety of complex issues argued with great skill and force by the two men; however, the three long articles written by Hodge nicely summarize his major concerns already directed against the likes of Finney and Bushnell. They demonstrate the dangerous inroads that he believed "rationalism" and "mysticism" had made on authentic Reformation theology. We, therefore, can close our account of Hodge with a brief summary of his lifelong concerns with liberalism and with a statement of his own enduring credo, articulated in his exchange with Park.

Hodge finds Park, the avowed Calvinist, tending toward Bushnell's subjective theory of the

Atonement and holding that "the work of Christ was not a satisfaction to law and justice in the proper sense." In Hodge's estimation Park perceives God's justice as simply "benevolence guided by wisdom" and "dispensing with the demands of the law." Furthermore, for Park "the righteousness of Christ is not imputed to believers." From these theological views others necessarily follow. Park considers sin to be present only when it is perceived as in violation of a known law; the ability to repent and to change one's heart must be accommodated, and so on. Against this entire system of liberal divinity, Hodge summarizes what he believes to be the authentic teaching of the Bible and the great Reformed confessions. It is a classic statement of the old Calvinism. It is a system, Hodge writes, that has for its object

the vindication of the supremacy of God in the whole work of man's salvation . . . because man being in fact utterly ruined and helpless, no method of recovery which does not so regard him is suited to his relation to God. . . . This system does not exalt a system of morals or liberty over Scripture. It accommodates its philosophy to the facts revealed in the divine word . . . . It acknowledges Adam as the head and representative of his posterity . . . in whom we sinned and fell, so that we come into the world under condemnation, born the children of wrath . . . not merely diseased, weakened, or predisposed to evil. . . . It admits that by this innate, hereditary, moral depravity men are altogether disabled, and made opposite to all good; so that their ability to do good works is not at all of themselves, but wholly of the Spirit of Christ. It recognizes justice as distinguished from benevolence, to be an essential attribute of God . . . which renders the punishment of sin as necessary. . . . It therefore regards the work of Christ as designed to satisfy justice . . . by his perfect obedience. . . . His righteousness is so imputed to believers that their justification . . . is an act of a judge declaring the law to be satisfied. . . . This life is sustained by the indwelling of the Holy Spirit, to whose influence all right exertions are to be referred. Salvation is thus . . . entirely of grace.[53]

As Hodge wrote these words at mid-century, the old Calvinism of the seventeenth century confes-

sional standards no longer spoke to the majority of American Protestants. He continued, nevertheless, to exert a powerful influence over American Presbyterianism at the time of his death. When the founder of Princeton Seminary, Archibald Alexander, lay dying in 1851, he called Charles Hodge to his bedside. He handed Hodge a white bone walking stick and said, "You must hand this to your successor in office, that it may be handed down as a kind of symbol of orthodoxy."[54] Hodge obediently lived up to this call; he passed on to his Princeton successors, A. A. Hodge and B. B. Warfield, the patrimony of orthodox Calvinism.

BENJAMIN BRECKINRIDGE WARFIELD

Archibald Alexander Hodge played an important but brief role in the remarkable stability and persistence of the Princeton Theology. He served in his father's chair for only seven years, until his death in 1886. His *Outlines of Theology* (1860; 2d ed., 1879) proved to be a valuable, lucid statement of the Princeton position. His collaboration with Benjamin Warfield, (1851–1921) in the publication of the essay on "Inspiration" in 1881 had a more lasting influence. As we will see, the article refined and developed Charles Hodge's position on the verbal inspiration of the Bible, engaging the most recent advances in biblical criticism. The essay proved, however, to be an important factor in the fateful breach between Progressives and Fundamentalists in American Protestantism in the twentieth century. Our focus here will be on the work of B. B. Warfield who, for over thirty years, was the foremost defender of orthodox Presbyterianism and of the Princeton Theology against the inroads of Modernism.

Benjamin Breckinridge Warfield was born near Lexington, Kentucky, and attended the College of New Jersey (Princeton), graduating with highest honors. He was raised in an orthodox Calvinist home, and his early interests were in science and mathematics. To his family's surprise he wrote home during a trip to Europe in 1871 announcing that he planned to enter the ministry. At Princeton

Theological Seminary he studied under Charles Hodge. After further study in Leipzig, he served as assistant minister of the First Presbyterian Church in Baltimore and then for nine years as Professor of New Testament Exegesis and Literature at Western Seminary in Pennsylvania before returning to Princeton as Professor of Didactic and Polemical Theology. During his thirty-three years at the seminary, he adhered to the foundational principles of his predecessors: the orthodox Calvinist standards, the Scottish "common-sense" view of objective truth, and the verbal inerrancy of Scripture. However, Warfield was required to defend these principles in a time of mounting criticism, both without and within his own Presbyterian communion. While estimates of the consequences of his stalwart, unbending defense of Calvinist orthodoxy and Scriptural inerrancy are mixed, his immediate influence was powerful. It is generally conceded that his views of biblical inspiration were adopted by large numbers of Presbyterians, as well as by a variety of other conservative Protestant groups. It is said that his theological ideas dominated the Presbyterian General Assembly between 1892 and 1910. During this period the General Assembly went on record five times officially stating that belief in the inerrant original manuscripts of the Bible was essential for membership in the Presbyterian Church. With Hodge, Warfield identified true doctrinal Christianity with the standards of the Westminster Confession, and he countenanced no deviation from either liberal enemy or conservative ally. Warfield was a very learned man and was devoted to specialist scholarship whether it be the study of the Bible, the Church Fathers, or Calvin and Calvinism. He was a fine historian and a prolific writer. Among his most important books—most of them collections of articles and studies still in print—are *The Inspiration and Authority of the Bible, Christology and Criticism, Studies in Tertullian and Augustine, Calvin and Calvinism, Perfection, Studies in Theology,* and *Critical Reviews.*

The Inspiration and Authority of the Bible

It was only after about 1870 that the impact of European biblical criticism began to exert a broader influence on American theological scholarship. Yet in Princeton Charles Hodge continued to direct his critical attention at other foes. It was his son, A. A. Hodge, and Benjamin Warfield who later sensed the need to address this new and fast-spreading threat. They did so in their joint essay "Inspiration," published in 1881. This restatement of the Princeton position on the inspiration and authority of Scripture was to dominate much conservative Protestant thinking for decades, and it remains influential even today. What strikes the reader of this essay are two themes that were not as central to the apologetic of either Archibald Alexander or the elder Hodge. One is the emphasis now placed on the marshaling of demonstrable proofs of the Bible's inerrancy; the second is their crucial resort to the argument that the verbal inerrancy of Scripture applies only to the original autograph copies of the texts, that is, to the documents as they came directly from the biblical writers themselves.

A. A. Hodge introduces the essay by insisting that the plenary verbal inspiration of Scripture in no way denies the full cooperation of both God and human beings in its composition—the union of both supernatural and natural agencies. And yet this genuine cooperation results in a record without error. Everything is so perfectly adjusted and controlled, writes Hodge, that "each works perfectly, according to the laws of its own nature, and yet all together infallibly bring about the result God designs."[55] Hodge suggests an analogy from nature to demonstrate that it is perfectly reasonable to believe that "God may inform or direct a free intelligence without violating its laws," namely, the relation of instinct to free intelligence. Instinct is impersonal and unconscious, yet operates in humans (and animals) as the intelligence of the Creator working through the finite creature spontaneously and, in the case of a human, "informing and directing, yet never violating any of the laws of his free intelligence." An example would be the aesthetic instinct of a great artist. The analogy shows that "as a matter of fact God does prompt from within the spontaneous activities of his intelligent creatures, leading them by unerring means to ends imperfectly discerned by themselves; and that this activity of God . . . does not in any wise reveal itself as interfering with the personal attributes or the free rational activities of the creature."[56]

The idiosyncrasies of human agency that impress themselves on Scripture affect not only verbal expression or literary style but also the very substance of what is written, reflective of the writer's "original endowments, education, special information . . . his own special limitations of knowledge and mental power, and his personal defects as well as his powers."[57] God's unfolding plan in Scripture, while always divine, is "largely natural in its method."[58] Here Hodge and Warfield oppose the view that the biblical writers were some kind of "spiritual geniuses." And yet the process of Scripture formation is throughout "divinely-regulated." The natural contributions of the authors come from traditions, documents, testimonies, memory, experience, intuition, feeling, and so on, and yet they are continuously under the direction of God's providence.

> Each sacred writer was by God specially formed, endowed, educated, providentially conditioned, and then supplied with knowledge naturally, supernaturally, or spiritually conveyed, so that he, and he alone could, and freely would, produce his allotted part. Thus God predetermined all the matter and form of the several books largely by the formation and training of the several authors, as an organist determines the character of his music as much when he builds his organ and when he tunes his pipes as when he plays his keys.[59]

The writers "builded better than they knew."

Hodge was aware that the conception of biblical inspiration that he and Warfield defended as that of the historic Church was both widely misunderstood and opposed. He, therefore, sought to clarify further what they meant by the *plenary verbal* inspiration of Scripture. First, "plenary" simply meant "full" or "complete" inerrant inspiration. This merely affirms that verbal inspiration applies to all the books of the Bible, not only selected books or passages. Second, verbal inerrancy does not entail the idea that inspiration implies a mechanical divine verbal dictation. All that is meant is "that the divine superintendence, which we call inspiration, extends to the verbal expression of the thoughts of the sacred writers as

well as to the thoughts themselves."[60] While the thoughts and words are both alike human, and subject to human limitations, a divine superintendence guarantees the words as much as the thoughts. To speak of the writers, as some do, as divinely assisted in their knowledge, but *left* in both their thinking and their composition to their natural limitations, implies the possibility of several versions of God's revelation, each more or less adequate. This, of course, gives up entirely an *immediate* divine authorship of the Bible and the belief in a plenary verbal inspiration. What the opponents of plenary verbal inspiration fail to appreciate is that "the Scriptures are a *record* of divine revelations, and as such consist of words; and as far as the record is inspired at all, and as far as it is in any element infallible, its inspiration must reach to its words. Infallible thought must be definite thought, and definite thought implies words." Hodge insists that, whether inspired or not inspired, fallible or infallible, "*the line can never rationally be drawn between the thoughts and words of Scripture.*"[61]

How, the critics asked, does one continue to defend plenary inspiration in light of the results claimed by modern criticism regarding dates, authors, sources, and so on? As we have seen, liberal theologians and biblical scholars now argued that the Bible remained an authoritative rule in matters of faith and practice but that in matters involving natural science or history the Scriptures might be shown to contain errors and discrepancies. Hodge and Warfield responded that, while they were convinced that the Bible in all of its elements is "absolutely errorless," the issue is one of fact, to be decided by an impartial examination of Scripture itself. While allowing this concession to a factual study of the sources, Hodge appeals, nevertheless, to two arguments: recourse to the original autograph copies and the claim of apostolicity.

Hodge acknowledges that "upon the surface" many propositions of Scripture may appear erroneous or inconsistent with the present findings of science or history.

> Such apparent inconsistencies and collisions with other sources of information are to be expected *in imperfect* copies of ancient writings, from the fact that the original reading may have been lost, or that we may fail

to realize the point of view of the author, or that we are destitute of the circumstantial knowledge which would fill up and harmonize the record. Besides, the human forms of knowledge by which the critics test the accuracy of Scripture are themselves subject to error.[62]

So it is, Hodge argues, that all the affirmations of Scripture, whether of exalted spiritual doctrine, or of practice, or of physical or historical fact, or of psychological principle, "are without error when the *ipsissima verba* of the original autographs are ascertained and interpreted in their natural and intended sense."[63] Hodge provides a distinction between exactness and accuracy that for him is crucial. Exactness implies an absolute literalness of details which, he insists, the Scriptures never profess. Accuracy, on the other hand, secures a correct and truthful statement of facts or principles as they were intended to be affirmed. It is this latter, Hodge argues, that the Church has always affirmed.

Hodge resorts, finally, to the internal evidence of apostolicity in his response to modern criticism. He would cheerfully acknowledge critical claims as to authors, dates, and sources so long as they "are not plainly inconsistent with the testimony of Christ or his apostles as to the Old Testament, or with the apostolic origin of the books of the New Testament, or with the absolute truthfulness of any of the affirmations of these books so authenticated."[64] Hodge simply lays it down that the "facts" inerrantly testify that the New Testament books were produced by the immediate apostles of Jesus or their companions, that is, "the men whom Christ commissioned, and to whom he promised infallibility in teaching." Any conclusion of biblical criticism that denies the apostolic origin of the New Testament is a priori both "inconsistent with the true doctrine of inspiration" and factually erroneous. Warfield argues similarly:

> The New Testament writers continually assert of the Scripture of the Old Testament . . . that they ARE THE WORDS OF GOD. What the writers said, God said. Christ sent out the apostles with the promise of the Holy Ghost, and declared that in hearing them, men would hear him. The apostles themselves claimed to speak as the prophets of God and with plenary authority in his name binding all consciences. . . . These

claims are a universal and inseparable characteristic of every part of Scripture.[65]

The circularity of both arguments is conspicuous. The New Testament is of apostolic origin and plenary inspired because written by individuals commissioned by Jesus and promised infallibility. If errors were to be admitted in the New Testament, it would be equivalent to saying that it was not plenary, that is, inerrantly, inspired.

Warfield proceeds to offer proofs of plenary verbal inspiration beyond the self-authenticating testimony that he and Hodge find within the New Testament itself. These additional arguments are bold. Today they will appear to many also as rash and their persuasion overestimated. First, he argues that despite the multiple authorship of the biblical texts, in radically different contexts and over sixteen centuries, the various books constituting the Scriptures' "evidently constitutes one system, all their parts minutely correlated."[66] Second, while the Scriptures were not designed to teach natural science, philosophy, or history as such, and while, because of our defective knowledge or interpretations these texts present us with apparent errors, "yet the outstanding fact is that the general conformableness of the sacred books to modern knowledge in all these departments is purely miraculous." When compared, for example, with other cosmogonies or philosophies, "their comparative freedom even from apparent error is amazing." This "demonstrates that a supernatural intelligence must have directed the writing," and this "proves that the scientific element of Scripture, as well as the doctrinal, was within the scope of inspiration."[67]

Third, Warfield appeals to the exercise of the sublime moral and spiritual teachings of the Bible, to its "plan of redemption," and to its "law of absolute righteousness . . . over the noblest men and over nations" as proof that it "has sufficed to maintain the unabated catholicity of the strict doctrine of inspiration through all change of time and in spite of all opposition."[68] Finally, Warfield claims that the doctrine of plenary inspiration that he and his colleague here propose "has always been the doctrine of the Church."[69] Warfield made this assertion on numerous occasions, often equating an earlier theologian's appeal to the inspiration of Scripture with his distinctive doctrine of plenary verbal inerrant inspiration. His references, for example, to Luther and to the Council of Trent are striking instances. Undoubtedly some of the "proofs" appealed to by Warfield would convince believers who already were persuaded by other factors—for example, by the personal testimony of the Holy Spirit—to accept the claims of the Bible's truth and spiritual power. But taken separately Warfield's proofs appear to lack force, even credibility, since from a modern historical perspective his claims regarding the Bible's "unity of system," its scientific truth, and the antiquity and continuity of belief in plenary verbal inspiration itself were by now problematic and suspect.

The major defense in Warfield's armory of proofs remained the appeal to the original autograph copies of the biblical texts. He wrote dozens of articles in the decades after 1880 clarifying and defending his doctrine of biblical inspiration and authority against his critics. Increasingly at issue was Warfield's appeal to "the inerrancy of the original autographs." In 1893 he sought to defend this doctrine in an essay by that title. The critics had long argued that recourse to the testimony of the original autographs was not only unfalsifiable, since none of these documents presently existed, but also a strain on the belief of the faithful, since it implied that the sources now available to us are corrupted. Many of his Presbyterian colleagues, appealing to God's providential transmission of the sacred texts, called upon the Church to accept "the Bible as it is," that is, as it has come down to us in what is called the "received text," the version that textual scholars regard as most authentic on the basis of the manuscript evidence.

"Would these controversialists," Warfield replies, "have the Church affirm the absolute truth of scribes' slips and printers' errors? If we were to take some of them 'at the root of the letter,' they would seem to represent it as easier to believe in the infallibility of compositors and proofreaders than the infallibility of God." Errors inevitably intrude into any printed, let alone any hand-copied, document or book, but we do not blame the author for that. So neither should we blame God for corrupted manuscripts or printers' errors. "It is *the Bible* that we declare to be 'of infallible truth'—the Bible that God gave us, not the corruptions and slips which scribes

and printers have given us, some of which are in every copy." To place one's confidence in a "received text" would, in Warfield's estimation, "amount to the strong asseveration of the utter untrustworthiness of the Bible."[70] Both parties charged the other with undercutting the confidence of believers in the reliability of Scripture.

Warfield was scornful of talk about "original autographs that have vanished" or about a Bible that no living person has ever seen, implying that it was now difficult, if not impossible, to say what was in the original Bible and what was not. He was certain that the text we now have is essentially the autographic text, since God would not have allowed the Bible to become hopelessly corrupt. Nor is it impossible that the original text can be fully restored. In the context of the textual evidence available to scholars at the time, Warfield was taking a minimalist view of the existing textual variations. On his own terms, however, it is clear that Warfield had an airtight argument. If textual critics had demonstrated that they could resolve apparent textual variations, Warfield could claim that, indeed, it was possible that additional apparent discrepancies would be solved. But if serious discrepancies persisted, Warfield could take refuge in the infallible autograph copy.

Warfield's appeal to the autograph text may have appeared initially as a brilliant apologetic move, but it was to prove an ambiguous tactic, and some believe that it played a major role in the growing impasse between progressive and conservative forces in American Protestantism, as we shall see. Warfield's recourse to the original texts in his effort to deny the possibility of any real errors or discrepancies in Scripture did, however, allow him to take the offensive on the grounds of having the presumption in his favor of prima facie internal evidence of Scripture's infallibility. The burden of proof was laid on those who disagreed with the doctrine of plenary inerrancy based on the testimony of Scripture itself. The critics, Warfield insisted, "may fairly be required to furnish *positive and conclusive evidence in each alleged instance of error* until the presumption has been turned over to the other side."

Warfield challenged his critics to let it

(1) be proved that each alleged discrepant statement certainly occurred in the original autograph of the

sacred book in which it is said to be found. (2) Let it be proved that the interpretation which occasions the apparent discrepancy is the one which the passage was evidently intended to bear. . . . (3) Let it be proved that the true sense of some part of the original autograph is directly and necessarily inconsistent with some certainly-known fact of history or truth of science, or some other statement of Scripture certainly ascertained and interpreted.[71]

Warfield is, of course, proposing the impossible since all three demands presuppose access to the original autographs of St. Paul or Isaiah. And Warfield is himself free of any proof at all, since his assumptions regarding the internal evidence of Scripture and plenary inspiration are circular; they are compelling only to those who already accept his presumptions.

There are additional questions that Warfield's contemporary critics, and even conservative scholars today, have put to him. His fundamental ground for holding the doctrine of plenary inspiration was that it is a teaching of the Bible itself. In his defense of this claim, he often focused attention on two decisive New Testament texts: 2 Tim. 3:16 and 2 Pet. 1:19–21, although he used others as well. In 2 Timothy the key phrase that Warfield cites is, "All Scripture is inspired by God"; and in 2 Peter the crucial words are, "No prophecy of Scripture is a matter of one's own interpretation, because no prophecy ever came by the impulse of man, but men moved by the Holy Spirit spoke from God." Now in the first passage Warfield simply assumes without proof or a glimmer of doubt that the writer's use of the words "inspired by God" explicitly means plenary verbal inspiration. In the passage from 2 Peter, the subject of divine inspiration ("moved by God") is explicitly prophecy. However, Warfield justifies his use of the passage by simply claiming that "these three terms, law, prophecy, scripture, were indeed, materially, strictly synonyms."[72] Furthermore, he presupposes that the writer of 2 Peter, in speaking of the prophets' writing by the inspiration of the Holy Spirit, expressly meant to assert that the genealogies or numerical figures cited in the Pentateuch were historically inerrant, as was the question of authorship, a subject of modern scholarly debate unknown to the ancients.[73]

Critical to Warfield's doctrine of biblical inspiration is his claim that the use of the word "inspiration" implied in the minds of the biblical writers Warfield's conception of *plenary verbal inspiration.* Warfield's contemporary critics and many later scholars find that his conception of the origin and transmission of the biblical writings, especially his understanding of a biblical text's point of origin, that is, his notion of the original autographs, is strikingly unhistorical. It assumes that one can simply separate a text's "moment of origin" from its prehistory in oral tradition, and so on. An eminent contemporary Hebraist and authority on biblical interpretation points to this blind spot in Warfield's understanding of the origin and character of the biblical literature.

> On modern and historical modes of understanding the Bible, even as the most conservative scholars use them, it is no longer possible to fix upon a moment when scripture, or any one book of scripture, was "originally given," a moment therefore to which inspiration could be uniquely attached. And this means, on the one hand, that there is no single unique form of words which could be counted as the one inspired text. If inspiration is to be thought of at all, it has to extend to sources used, to previous drafts, in some degree to variant texts, in some degree to books and sections of books which in the end have not been counted as within the canon of holy scripture, in some degree to translations of the original texts, and in some degree to post-biblical tradition, since not only the preservation but also the very formation of the text is in considerable measure a work of post-biblical traditionalists.[74]

Warfield's Critique of Liberal Theology

Warfield never wrote a substantial constructive theology, perhaps because Hodge's huge *Systematic Theology* served as a definitive summation of the Princeton Theology. Rather, Warfield devoted his energies to defending Reformed orthodoxy and his position on biblical inspiration. He devoted much of his energy to writing essays and reviews for various journals in which he responded to the flood of publications by Liberal and Modernist theologians of every stripe. While generous in commending the learning of these opponents, almost every review focused on the inadequacy of their conception of Scripture and the ways in which their biblical interpretation was shaped by their modern scientific assumptions, rather than by the Bible's own internal testimony. At the turn of the century, Warfield published numerous reviews of the works of the great contemporary German biblical scholars and theologians, including Wilhelm Bousset, Johannes Weiss, Ernst Troeltsch, Reinhold Seeberg, and the Ritschlian theologians Adolf von Harnack, Wilhelm Herrmann, and Theodor Haering.

Warfield's criticisms of these influential liberal scholars often is telling as he unmasks their accommodations to current scientific and scholarly fashions. But surely he was oversimplifying matters to insist so artlessly that "instead of stating Christian belief in terms of modern thought, an effort [should be] made, rather, to state modern thought in terms of Christian belief."[75] Warfield was confident that he had refuted his Liberal and Modernist opponents by showing that Harnack and Troeltsch, for example, could not at the same time logically commit themselves to both supernatural and naturalistic assumptions. For him it was an either-or choice. At issue, of course, was the fundamental question regarding the implications of the use of historical-critical methods in the interpretation of the Bible, Christian origins, and the development of dogma. This was the heart of the matter, and many have suggested that the weakness in Warfield's apologetic is apparent in his naive conception of historical fact (what he called "pure fact") that was rooted in his uncritical acceptance of Scottish "common-sense" realism. Warfield appears impervious to the genuine issues raised by post-Kantian thought regarding the relations of metaphysics, or the supernatural, and the realm of the phenomenal and historical. This is apparent, for example, in his critiques of both Seeberg and Haering.

Reinhold Seeberg (1859–1935) was professor at Dorpat, Erlangen, and Berlin, and author of an important textbook in the history of dogma (*Lehrbuch der Dogmengeschichte,* 1913–1923)

which, in its third edition, consisted of five large volumes. Seeberg was also a systematic theologian and a leader of a school which called itself "Modern-Positive theology." "Modern" implied an openness to contemporary currents of thought and science. "Positive" meant the attempt to be faithful to the historical tradition of the Church. Seeberg believed that it was possible to hold to the religious truth of the Bible while applying the strictest methods of historical criticism to its contents. To Warfield this required the separation of some religious "essence" or kernel from an alleged culturally outmoded biblical husk—a criticism he also directed at Ritschl, Harnack, and Haering. At the heart of Seeberg's belief—and the belief of all Liberals or Modernists—Warfield detected a false conception of biblical inspiration. Liberals such as Seeberg were guilty of mistaken ideas about revelation and inspiration. Seeberg understood revelation as a series of divine acts in history by which God reveals his redemptive work. Revelation is the "history of salvation" (*Heilsgeschichte*). Inspiration, on the other hand, "consists in the fact that the Spirit of revelation creates in His first witnesses the right, sufficient, and efficacious understanding of revelation." That is, the prophets and the apostles were inspired and thereby were enabled not only to understand God's redemptive acts in history but also to make their meaning intelligible to others.

Such a conception of inspiration was firmly rejected by Warfield, since it only provided for the original acquisition of divine truth but not for its inerrant transmission to others. "The Scriptures," Warfield insists, "lie between us and the prophets" to ensure that the revealed truth is trustworthily communicated to us. Seeberg, on the contrary, endeavors to show "that the Scriptures are not always trustworthy either in their record of facts or in their inculcation of principles." Seeberg is willing to concede that the Bible contains statements that are "notoriously false," that it presupposes outmoded cosmologies and world-views, and that it "even presents absurd interpretations of facts and prophecies." "It can scarcely escape us," Warfield concludes, "that precisely what we have here is an attempt to discover a basis for confidence in the great facts and the great ideas set forth in [the Bible] without implication of the historical trustworthiness or of the authority of the Bible itself."

The failure to secure the *plenary* trustworthiness of the Bible is connected with another theme prominent in the work of Seeberg and the Ritschlian theologians such as Herrmann and Haering. Not only do they accept the radical findings of "naturalistic historical criticism," but "the basis of confidence is shifted from the Bible to Christian experience." Only those contents of the Bible are accepted that are validated by Christian experience. This is "to shift the Christianity we are to teach from an objective to a subjective foundation," to those vital truths that Coleridge said will "find us." Warfield insists that such a doctrine leads to "the ultimate elimination of all objective bases for these 'vital' truths themselves and the relegation of them . . . to the subjective experience itself."[76]

The charge of theological "subjectivism" is the persistent theme of Warfield's attack on the Ritschlian theologians in the essays he wrote between 1890 and 1910. This charge is not entirely fair and would require significant qualification. However, Warfield was disturbed by the Liberal and Ritschlian theologians' repudiation of a propositional, "objective revelation" and their conception of revelation as purely "personal," as received only in faith. To Warfield, theologians such as Herrmann and Haering speak of divine revelation as if it were dependent on the personal appropriation or interpretation of faith. While Haering, for example, claims that the judgment of faith presupposes the reality of the object of faith whose value and truth is affirmed, he nevertheless appears to so qualify that claim as to ground divine revelation in the act of subjective appropriation itself. In the last analysis Haering concludes that "the validity of judgments of faith depend on the living conviction that the supreme reality in question [i.e., God] manifests itself, but only to one *who consents to recognize its reality as a value for him personally,* not in the irresistible way in which the laws of logic demand recognition." (Italics added.) This, for Warfield, is to fall into a pure voluntarism, subjectivism, and pragmatism. "All convictions," he responds, "are the product of evidence, and are not producible at will; and each conviction naturally

rests on evidence fitted to produce that particular conviction."

To illustrate Haering's subjectivism, Warfield focuses on Haering's, and the Ritschlians', treatment of the historical Jesus. Haering insists that it is all over for Christianity if Jesus is only a creation of faith. Nevertheless, Haering also insists that no historical evidence can make the reality of Jesus Christ so certain that any intelligent person, conversant with the historical evidence of the New Testament, would consider it as compelling and as requiring assent to it as indisputable. All that history can do is offer a sufficiently high probability so as to enable an already "religiously susceptible" person to surrender himself or herself to Jesus Christ in good conscience. Warfield considers such position with regard to the biblical evidence wholly inadequate. He writes: "If the religiously susceptible man makes this venture of faith, he may indeed attain through this to a certainty of the existence of this Jesus. But assuredly, then, the certainty he thus attains is the product of his faith, not of the historical evidence."[77] Haering, in Warfield's estimation, is perilously near to making Jesus the creation of faith itself—that is, the phantom of a dissolving subjectivism. It is clear to most scholars that Warfield does not do justice to Haering's perhaps overconfident trust in what "history" can tell us about the "personal life" of Christ, but that is not our concern here. What is striking is Warfield's unmovable confidence in the demonstrative force of the New Testament historical evidence ("the facts") as such, especially in light of his rather broad acquaintance with the work of New Testament higher criticism. Here again, the nineteenth-century question of religious faith and the claims of historical religion emerge as the critical issue.

The Princeton theologians, largely due to their "common-sense" realist and their Baconian assumptions about knowledge and truth, were confident that all rational minds were capable of directly apprehending the same "facts" in the external world, regardless of cultural perspective or other limits on human knowledge that anguished most post-Kantian theologians. Warfield proceeds in his apologetical efforts essentially untouched by these concerns. He appears untroubled, as George Marsden has remarked, by the question: "How is it that there are so many rational and upright people of good will who refuse to see the truth which consists of objective facts that are as plain as day?"[78] Despite the fact that America was increasingly characterized by a rich pluralism of diverse ethnic and religious groups and sects, Warfield could unabashedly write in 1903: "It is the distinction of Christianity that it has come into the world clothed with the mission to *reason* its way to domination. . . . It is solely by reasoning that it has come this far on its way to kingship. And it is solely by reasoning that it will put all its enemies under its feet."[79]

Benjamin Warfield's doctrine of biblical inspiration and inerrancy became perhaps the central theme of the Princeton Theology in its later years, and it had a profound, though ambiguous, aftereffect. It was cold comfort to some biblical conservatives to be assured by Warfield that there were inerrant original autographs but that the version of the Bible that they were presently reading was corrupt and untrustworthy in some parts. Nevertheless, it was Warfield's doctrine of an inerrant Scripture that was adopted by many influential conservative Protestant theologians and clergy after 1880, and it remains to this day a mainstay of biblical Fundamentalism. And so the Princeton Theology's doctrine of Scripture played a major role in the theological wars that preoccupied American Protestantism between 1880 and 1920.

The Presbyterian Church was especially rent by the controversy over the inerrancy of Scripture as those issues were defined by the Princeton theologians. In the 1890s biblical conservatives in the denomination brought formal charges of heresy against three of the denomination's most distinguished theological scholars and seminary professors—the biblical scholar Charles A. Briggs and the historians Henry Preserved Smith and Arthur Cushman McGiffert. All three left the Presbyterian Church as a result of this opposition from within the denomination. Union Theological Seminary in New York City separated itself from the official jurisdiction of the Presbyterian Church in 1892 and became an independent interdenominational seminary as a result of the Presbyterian General Assembly's actions against Professor Briggs. The

prominent conservative Presbyterians, most of whom were allied with Princeton Seminary, empowered conservatives and fundamentalists in other denominations to pursue their own attacks on liberal theology and to carry out their own heresy hunts. As George Marsden has shown, the recourse to ecclesiastical action taken by these Presbyterian ministers and scholars set a precedent for conservatives in other Protestant groups to pursue similar proceedings against their own progressives who dared to defend the methods and results of historical criticism. Furthermore, the Presbyterians' defensive actions resulted in efforts to establish a few doctrinal fundamentals that would characterize orthodox Christian belief, the rejection or reconception of which would be proof of doctrinal infidelity.[80] The upshot was the adoption by the Presbyterian General Assembly in 1910 of a five-point declaration of essential doctrinal beliefs. Briefly, these five essentials were: (1) the inerrancy of Scripture, (2) the Virgin Birth of Christ, (3) Christ's substitutionary atonement, (4) his bodily resurrection, and (5) the historical authenticity of the biblical miracles. In the 1920s these standards of orthodoxy became the famous "five points" of Fundamentalism. Premillennialism, or the belief that the Second Coming of Christ will occur *before* the advent of the millennium, after which Christ will reign over the earth, was substituted for the statement on miracles, which was presupposed by inerrancy.

What was occurring in the early decades of the twentieth century was the strange alliance of the Princeton Theology with groups, such as Bible Baptists, dispensationalists, and millenarianists, that earlier Princeton theologians would have repudiated. The Modernist-Liberal theologians and clergy were the common enemy of this new coalition. There is, however, a deep irony in the fact that the Princeton Theology, committed for a century to the resolute defense of the classical confessional standards of Reformation Christianity, especially the Calvinist Westminster Confession, should in its last years align itself with groups that looked upon the Church's ancient confessions of faith as irrelevant to, if not a deviation from, the plain teachings of an inerrant Bible.

NOTES

1. See Claude Welch, *Protestant Thought in the Nineteenth Century,* I (New Haven, 1972), p. 60. On the various Protestant movements of "restoration and conservation" after 1830, including German Confessionalism and the American Mercersburg School, see Chap. 9.
2. Ibid., p. 195.
3. Archibald Alexander, *A Sermon Delivered at the Opening of the General Assembly of the Presbyterian Church in the United States, May 1808.* Cited in Mark A. Noll, *The Princeton Theology 1812–1921* (Grand Rapids, Mich., 1983), p. 53.
4. Ibid.
5. Archibald Alexander, *Evidences of the Authenticity, Inspirations and Canonical Authority of the Holy Scriptures* (Philadelphia, 1836), pp. 229, 230.
6. James W. Alexander, *The Life of Archibald Alexander* (Philadelphia, 1855), p. 331.
7. For an introduction to and sampling of Reformed Scholastic theology of the seventeenth century, see John W. Beardslee III, ed. and trans., *Reformed Dogmatics* (New York, 1965).
8. On Scottish Common-Sense Realism and its influence on American thought and theology from the Revolution to the mid-nineteenth century, see the following: Sydney E. Ahlstrom, "The Scottish Philosophy and American Theology," *Church History,* 24 (1955), pp. 257–272; Henry F. May, *The Enlightenment in America* (New York, 1976), Part IV, Chap. 2; Theodore Dwight Bozeman, *Protestants in an Age of Science: The Baconian Ideal and Antebellum American Religious Thought* (Chapel Hill, 1977); Jack B. Rogers and Donald K. McKim, *The Authority and Interpretation of the Bible* (New York, 1979), Chap. 4 and 5.
9. Thomas Reid, *An Inquiry into the Human Mind,* ed. Timothy Duggan (Chicago, 1970), p. 206.
10. Thomas Reid. Cited in Henry Laurie, *Scottish Philosophy in Its Natural Development* (Glasgow, 1902), pp. 133–134.
11. Thomas Reid, *An Inquiry into the Human Mind, on the Principles of Common Sense* (Edinburgh, 1765), pp. 342–343.
12. A. Alexander, *Evidences,* p. 89.
13. Charles Hodge, *Systematic Theology,* I (New York, 1872), 11.
14. Men like Hodge and Warfield held more sophisticated views of science than they are credited with, including their views of evolution. This was also true of other nineteenth-century evangelical scholars, as the studies of J. Moore and D. Livingstone demonstrate.

See the "Suggestions for Further Reading" for Chapter 10.
15. A. A. Hodge, *The Life of Charles Hodge* (New York, 1880), pp. 256–257.
16. Ernest R. Sandeen, *The Roots of Fundamentalism: British and American Millenarianism 1800–1930* (Chicago, 1970), p. 106.
17. C. Hodge, *Systematic Theology,* I, 1.
18. Ibid., p. 3.
19. Ibid., p. 5.
20. Ibid., p. 6.
21. Ibid., pp. 7, 8.
22. Ibid., p. 9.
23. Ibid., p. 10.
24. Ibid.
25. Ibid., p. 11.
26. Ibid., pp. 13–14.
27. Ibid., p. 16.
28. Hodge's critique of Bushnell's "Dissertation" is found in the *Biblical Repertory and Princeton Review,* XXI (1849), 259–298.
29. Charles Hodge, "Inspiration," *Biblical Repository and Princeton Review,* XXIX (October 1857), 661–663. This is Hodge's first extensive treatment of biblical inspiration. The themes of this essay are also found in C. Hodge, *Systematic Theology,* I, 151–188.
30. C. Hodge, "Inspiration," p. 664.
31. Ibid., p. 665.
32. Ibid., pp. 665–666.
33. Ibid., p. 668.
34. Ibid., pp. 674–675.
35. Letter of November 2, 1877. Printed in *The Presbyterian,* 48 (January 1878), 9. Information on this source regarding Hodge's view of inspiration is found in James L. McAllister, Jr., "The Nature of Religious Knowledge in the Theology of Charles Hodge" (Ph.D. Diss., Duke University, 1957), p. 201f.
36. C. Hodge, "Inspiration," p. 677.
37. Ibid., pp. 677–678.
38. Ibid., pp. 686–687.
39. Ibid., p. 683.
40. Charles Hodge, "The Unity of Mankind," *Princeton Review,* 31 (January 1859), 148.
41. Ibid., pp. 104–105.
42. C. Hodge, *Systematic Theology,* I, 163.
43. Letter of November 2, 1877. McAllister, op. cit., p. 210. For the two citations from McAllister's original research, I am dependent on Rogers and McKim, op. cit.

44. Charles Hodge, "The Theology of the Intellect and That of the Feelings," *Princeton Review* (April 1851). Reprinted in *Essays and Reviews* (New York, 1879), pp. 573–574.

45. Charles G. Finney, *Lectures on Revivals of Religion,* ed. William G. McLaughlin (Cambridge, 1960), pp. 341–342.

46. Charles G. Finney, *Sermons on Gospel Themes* (Oberlin, 1876; reprinted, New York, n.d.), p. 93.

47. Finney, *Lectures on Revivals,* p. 19.

48. Charles G. Finney, *Lectures to Professing Christians* (New York, 1878), p. 322. These lectures were originally delivered in 1836 and 1837.

49. C. Hodge, *Systematic Theology,* II, 110. Hodge's full treatment of Christian anthropology is developed in the second volume of the *Systematic Theology,* Part II, including the origin and nature of humans, the unity of humans, the fall, sin, and free agency. His treatment of soteriology, Part III, also is found in volume two and includes his discussion of the covenant of grace, the person and the work of Christ, and theories of atonement.

50. Charles Hodge, "Bushnell on Christian Nurture," *Princeton Review* (October 1847). Reprinted in *Essays and Reviews,* p. 336.

51. Horace Bushnell, *Sermons on Christ and His Salvation* (New York, 1877), p. 274.

52. C. Hodge, "Bushnell on Christian Nurture." Reprinted in *Essays and Reviews,* p. 337.

53. C. Hodge, "The Theology of the Intellect and That of the Feelings," II. Reprinted in *Essays and Reviews,* pp. 577–582.

54. A. Hodge, op. cit., p. 382.

55. A. A. Hodge and B. B. Warfield, "Inspiration," *Presbyterian Review,* 2 (April 1881). Reprinted in M. Noll, *The Princeton Theology 1812–1921* (Grand Rapids, 1983), p. 222.

56. Ibid., p. 223.

57. Ibid., pp. 223–224.

58. Ibid., p. 224.

59. Ibid.

60. Ibid., p. 226.

61. Ibid., pp. 227–228.

62. Ibid., p. 229.

63. Ibid.

64. Ibid., p. 228.

65. Ibid., p. 230.

66. Ibid.

67. Ibid.

68. Ibid., p. 231.

69. Ibid.

70. B. B. Warfield, "The Inerrancy of the Original Autographs," *The Independent* (March 23, 1893). Reprinted in Noll, op. cit., pp. 268–274. Citations here are from Noll: pp. 270–271.

71. Hodge and Warfield, "Inspiration." Cited in Noll, op. cit., p. 232.

72. B. B. Warfield, *The Inspiration and Authority of the Bible* (Philadelphia, 1948), p. 139.

73. On these matters relating to Warfield's interpretive preconceptions, see David Kelsey, *The Uses of Scripture in Recent Theology* (Philadelphia, 1975), Chap. 2; and James Barr, *Fundamentalism* (Philadelphia, 1977), Chap. 9.

74. Barr, *Fundamentalism,* p. 294.

75. B. B. Warfield, *Critical Reviews* (Oxford, 1932), p. 322.

76. Ibid., pp. 236–237, 238, 239, 240.

77. Ibid., pp. 409, 410, 415.

78. George M. Marsden, *Fundamentalism and American Culture* (New York, 1980), p. 114. Marsden's Chapter XIII ("Presbyterians and the Truth") is a fine brief account of the outcome of the Princeton Theology's distinctive doctrine of biblical inerrancy. For a longer account of the controversy within the Presbyterian Church, see Lefferts A. Loetscher, *The Broadening Church* (Philadelphia, 1954).

79. B. B. Warfield, *Selected Shorter Writings of Benjamin B. Warfield,* II, ed. John E. Meeter (Nutley, N.J., 1973), 99–100.

80. Marsden, *Fundamentalism and American Culture,* Chap. 13.

SUGGESTIONS FOR FURTHER READING

I.

On the Intellectual and Theological Background of the Princeton Theology

Bozeman, Theodore Dwight. *Protestants in an Age of Science: The Baconian Ideal and Antebellum American Religious Thought* (Chapel Hill: University of North Carolina Press, 1977).

Loetscher, Lefferts. *The Broadening Church: A Study of Theological Issues in the Presbyterian Church since 1869* (Philadelphia: University of Pennsylvania Press, 1957).

Marsden, George. *The Evangelical Mind and the New School Presbyterian Experience* (New Haven: Yale University Press, 1970).

———. *Fundamentalism and American Culture: The Shaping of Twentieth Century American Evangelicalism* (New York: Oxford University Press, 1980).

May, Henry F. *The Enlightenment in America* (New York: Oxford University Press, 1976).

Sandeen, Ernest R. *The Roots of Fundamentalism: British and American Millenarianism 1880–1930* (Chicago: University of Chicago Press, 1970).

All of the above books are excellent studies and include valuable notes and bibliographies, as well as assessments, that bear on the background and the significance of the Princeton Theology.

II.

On the Princeton Theology and Theologians

Noll, Mark A. *The Princeton Theology 1812–1921* (Grand Rapids: Baker Book House, 1983). This is an excellent resource. It includes a long, well-informed introduction, judicious selections from Alexander, Charles Hodge, A. A. Hodge, and Warfield, and an excellent bibliography of primary and secondary works.

Rogers, Jack B., and Donald K. McKim. *The Authority and Interpretation of the Bible: An Historical Approach* (San Francisco: Harper and Row, 1979). Includes a good account and critical assessment of the views of Alexander, Charles Hodge, A. A. Hodge, and Warfield on the inspiration and authority of the Bible. For a more positive assessment of the Princeton theologians on the interpretation of the Bible, see the introduction and bibliography in Noll above.

Wells, David F., ed., *The Princeton Theology* (Grand Rapids: Baker Book House, 1989). A collection of essays, including ones on Charles Hodge, Warfield, and J. Gresham Machen, the scholar who finally broke with Princeton Seminary in the late 1920s to carry on what he considered to be the Princeton tradition at Westminster Theological Seminary in Philadelphia.

On Charles Hodge

In addition to the works cited above, see:

Hewitt, Glenn A. *Regeneration and Morality: A Study of Charles Finney, Charles Hodge, John W. Nevin, and Horace Bushnell* (Brooklyn: Carlson Publishing Inc., 1991).

Hodge, A. A. *The Life of Charles Hodge* (New York: Charles Scribner's Sons, 1880).

Nelson, John Oliver. "Charles Hodge (1797–1878): Nestor of Orthodoxy." In *The Lives of Eighteen from Princeton,* ed. Willard Thorp (Princeton: Princeton University Press, 1946).

On Benjamin Warfield

In addition to the works cited above, see:

Barr, James. *Fundamentalism* (Philadelphia: Fortress Press, 1977). Chapter 9 includes an incisive analysis and critique of Warfield's biblical interpretation by an eminent authority on the Hebrew Bible and biblical interpretation.

Kelsey, David H. *The Uses of Scripture in Recent Theology* (Philadelphia: Fortress Press, 1975).

Meeter, John E., ed. *Selected Shorter Writings of Benjamin B. Warfield,* 2 vols. (Nutley, N.J.: Presbyterian and Reformed Publishing Company, 1970).

Chapter 13
Movements of Recovery and Conservation: Ultramontanism and the Neo-Thomistic Revival

Désiré Joseph Cardinal Mercier

In Chapter 6 we explored some of the contours of Catholic Romantic thought in France in the early decades of the nineteenth century. Among the distinctive features of this period were the political restoration of the Bourbon monarchy and the Catholic reaction to the Enlightenment that took the form of Traditionalism. We noted the varieties of Romantic Traditionalism in writers as different as Joseph de Maistre and Félicité de Lamennais. However, the Traditionalists emphatically promoted Ultramontanism, the movement in support of the special prerogatives and the unique authority of the Pope. In this way they sought to free the Catholic Church from the jurisdiction and domination of the civil powers. We observed how Lamennais's Liberal Catholicism was crushed during the reign of Pope

Gregory XVI (1831–1846), despite Lamennais's defense of the Ultramontanist cause. The next century would prove that Liberalism and Ultramontanism were not to coexist easily.

During Pope Gregory's fifteen-year rule, support for Ultramontanism grew apace, and, as we will see, its victory was achieved in 1870 by his successor, Pope Pius IX. Ironically, as papal ecclesial power grew between 1830 and 1870, the Pope's influence on civil society and on the European nation-states steadily weakened. However, support for more centralized ecclesial power in Rome was by no means unchallenged in the Church; and to understand the theological and ecclesial significance of the First Vatican Council (1870), a sketch of the historical background will be helpful. The history leading up to the actions of the First Vatican Council will direct us to another related movement of restoration that also is critically important to an understanding of modern Catholicism, namely, the revival of Neo-Thomistic philosophy and theology. Both Ultramontanism and Neo-Thomism were well-considered efforts on the part of the Church to stem the tide of modernity and "liberalism" in the spheres of politics, ecclesiology, *and* thought.

THE VICTORY OF ULTRAMONTANISM

The Historical Background

On a number of occasions, we have noted that the question of religious authority is a distinctive feature of the modern era. As Kant remarked, an important legacy of the Enlightenment was humanity's "release from its self-incurred tutelage"—that is, its release from authoritarianism in all of its manifestations and the defense of individual liberty and political democracy. The Enlightenment gave pride of place to the authority of autonomous reason. Many Romantics, as well, appealed to the authority of personal religious experience; others, such as Lamennais, invoked the authority of the community itself, the *sensus communis.* Still other thinkers, such as Maistre, appealed to the absolute authority of the Church as embodied in the Pope. He was looked to as the sole means of "releasing" Catholicism from its own self-incurred "tutelage" to the growing secular governments and to the power of national bishops eager to retain their power and privileges.

The Catholic Church long had respected the guidance of natural reason when it was coupled with an implicit faith in the authoritative, revealed teachings of the Church. But the nature and the limits of papal authority in particular had long been a matter of dispute. While some form of a primacy of the Bishop of Rome had seldom been an issue, the relative ecclesial authority and jurisdiction of the Pope, the bishops, and the temporal power had been hotly contested since the fourteenth century.

The Movement of Gallicanism. The movement either to oppose or to minimize the authority of the papacy is generally referred to as Gallicanism, from the word referring to Gaul or France. It was especially pronounced in the seventeenth and eighteenth centuries, and it took two forms: political and theological Gallicanism. Political Gallicanism supported the dominant influence of the crown (the state) in the public affairs of the nation's church. Ecclesiastical Gallicanism insisted that primary responsibility for questions of worship and doctrine lay with the bishops of the national church, with the Pope having a role of rather remote supervision.

Two historical circumstances were important in the growth of Gallicanism after the fourteenth century and in the ongoing contest over authority between the papacy, the bishops, and the temporal sovereigns. The first was the so-called Babylonian Captivity of the Church and the Great Schism. These were precipitated by the contest over temporal authority between Pope Boniface VIII and Philip the Fair of France. Boniface had issued his bull *Unam Sanctam* (1302), which declared that no temporal power could claim independence of the Pope, the temporal authority being subordinate to the spiritual power, and that every human being was subject to the Pope. King Philip would have none of it and dispatched troops to Italy to bring Boniface to France for trial. Boniface was momentarily taken prisoner but shortly thereafter died in October 1303. The next Pope was a Frenchman who assumed the name Clement V and took up residency in the French city of Avignon, where future Popes resided for nearly seventy years. In 1378 Pope Gregory XI returned to Rome, but he soon died and thus began the Great Schism (1378–1417), during which time there was a dual papacy with Gregory XII in Rome and Benedict XIII in Avignon. This impossible situation resulted in the two colleges of cardinals calling the Council of Pisa (1409), an action which implied the authority of the bishops in council over that of the Pope. However, the two reigning Popes refused to resign, and the election of Alexander V left the Church with three Popes. The Council of Constance (1414–1417) deposed the three Popes and decreed that all persons, including the Pope, were to be subordinate to the ecumenical council of the bishops. When a General Council was in session, the supreme authority in the Church was vested in it and not in the Pope. This resulted in the movement known as Conciliarism with its theological center among the doctors at the University of Paris, a group which included the renowned theorist John Gerson. This Conciliarist form of theological Gallicanism henceforth did battle with the defenders of Roman papalism and its claim to unique prerogatives.

Political Gallicanism continued to exert itself through the trend toward strong, centralized monarchies throughout Europe after 1300. Later, in combating the spread of Protestantism, the papacy itself recognized the necessity of granting extraordinary powers over the Church to its own Roman Catholic princes in an effort to counter this religious menace. Thus, on all sides the papacy found itself confronting the rising power of the territorial monarchs and the threat of autonomous national Catholic churches. In seventeenth-century France, for example, King Louis XIV became the embodiment of absolute sovereignty, abiding no correction from either the bishops or the Pope. It was Louis XIV's differences with the Pope that resulted in the classic formulation of the Gallican principles in the Gallican Declaration of 1682, drawn up by none other than the great French bishop Jacques Bossuet (1627–1704), a frequent preacher at the royal court and the tutor of the king's eldest son. The Gallican Bossuet symbolized the spirit of France in the age of Louis XIV.

Though rejected by Pope Innocent IX, the Gallican Declaration was accepted by the French bishops and thereafter was imposed upon all of the French clergy. The king required that the articles be taught in all seminaries and universities. The declaration's famous "Four Articles" set forth the basic principles of Gallicanism:

1. That kings are not subject to any ecclesiastical power in temporal matters, and they cannot be deposed, directly or indirectly, by the authority of the Pope; nor can the sovereign's subjects be dispensed from their obedience to their temporal sovereign.

2. That the power over spiritual matters conferred upon St. Peter and his successors remains, though checked by General Councils as laid down by the decrees of the Council of Constance.

3. That the exercise of apostolic power must be regulated by the canons of the Church and, in France, by the laws, rules, and customs of the French Church.

4. That while the Pope has the chief voice in questions of faith, yet his decisions are not irreformable unless the consent of the Church is given.

The seventeenth and eighteenth centuries—the "Age of Absolutism"—witnessed national movements similar to those in France that sought to limit papal power in both Church and state—indeed, to give to the national sovereigns rule over their Church. In 1763 Johann von Hontheim, Suffragan Bishop of Trier, wrote a work under the pseudonym of "Febronius" in which he reasserted the principles of Conciliarism. While affirming the Pope's primacy of honor, he called for limiting the prerogatives of the Pope and rejected papal infallibility, while defending the supreme authority of bishops in council. In Austria the Holy Roman Emperor, Joseph II, instituted policies similar to Gallicanism and known as "Josephism." He asserted the right of the state to regulate ecclesiastical affairs and placed limits on the powers of the papacy in spiritual matters, including the requirement of temporal consent for the publication of any papal bull or document in Austria.

Policies such as the above directed at limiting papal authority did predominate in many parts of Europe up to the period of the French Revolution and Napoleon. However, Conciliarists and Gallicans were not the only voices to be heard on the issue of papal authority. Many European bishops and clergy, but especially the Italians and the Jesuits, continued to uphold not only papal primacy but also the Pontiff's preeminence over councils, as well as his infallibility in matters of faith. It was only with the Restoration in the early decades of the nineteenth century that the forces in support of the Pope's unique authority and infallibility were to gain the upper hand beyond Rome. The movement was called Ultramontanism, signifying that the European churches once again looked beyond the mountains, the Alps, to Rome itself and to the Pope as the seat of authority for the universal Church.

The Growth of Ultramontanism

In Chapter 6 we saw how closely the new Catholic apologetic in the early decades of the nineteenth century was related, in the writings of Maistre and Lamennais, to the defense of a centralization of authority in the papacy in response to the great damage done to the Church by the claims of the absolutist monarchies over church affairs and, finally, by the French Revolution. But theological and political arguments for the special privileges of the Pope had also been proposed earlier in response to the Conciliarists and to the threat of Protestantism. Chief among these was the work of the Jesuit Robert Bellarmine (1542–1621), *Controversies against the Heresies of Our Times* (1586). Bellarmine argued that the Petrine texts in the New Testament clearly teach that Christ appointed St. Peter to be the ruler of the Church by divine ordinance. While Christ remains the supreme spiritual head of the Church, the Pope, as St. Peter's successor, is the ministerial and *monarchical* head of the Church on earth. The Keys of St. Peter signify the Pope's absolute rule over the Church, which is neither a democracy nor an aristocracy, but a monarchy. We will hear clear echoes of Bellarmine's arguments on the relation of the Pope and the bishops and on the Pope's infallibility in the preamble to the First Vatican Council. On the relation between Pope and council, Bellarmine writes:

It belongs to the Pope to convoke a General Council; or to sanction its being convoked by another, as the Emperor; or, it suffices if he afterwards gives his confirmation to what has been done. But if it neither be convoked, nor approved, nor its acts confirmed by him, it is no true General Council.

The Pope simply and absolutely is above the Universal Church, in that he is the Head of the whole Church on earth; and so he is above a General Council, and can recognize no judge upon earth above himself.

On the Pope's infallibility, Bellarmine asserts:

The Pope is supreme judge in deciding controversies on faith and morals. When he teaches the whole Church in things pertaining to faith, he cannot err.

Nor can he err in moral precepts prescribed for the whole Church, and relating to things necessary for salvation, or in themselves good or evil.

The question arises, of course, as to why councils are necessary, if the Pope himself is infallible. Bellarmine replies that "even though infallibility be in the Pope . . . he ought not to neglect the human and ordinary means of arriving at a true knowledge of the matters in question: but by the ordinary means of a Council."[1] These doctrines are, in essentials, reasserted by Maistre in *Du pape* (1819).

The fortunes of the Catholic revival and the growth of Ultramontanism in Europe from the Bourbon restoration in 1815 to 1870 is a complex story. There were divisions within the Ultramontanist Movement, as we have seen in the case of the royalism of de Maistre and the liberalism of individuals like Charles Montalembert, the early follower of Lamennais. Suffice it to say that, slowly but surely, the conservative Ultramontanist Movement gained strength, largely through the support of the Vatican itself. Rome defended Ultramontanist publications, such as *Civiltà cattolica, L'Univers,* and *La Correspondance de Rome,* against the attacks of Gallican bishops. Rome also supported the publication of works directed at the refutation of Febronian and Gallican doctrines, and many of the Gallican texts were suppressed. The new national seminaries in Rome were imbued with anti-Modernist and Ultramontanist ideas which were taken back to the home countries. In 1853 Pope Pius IX published the encyclical *Inter Multiples,* which expressed strong disapproval of Gallican activities in France. In fact, the personal popularity of Pius IX and his resistance to the secular Italian nationalists were extremely important factors in explaining the growing support of the Ultramontanist cause.

When Pope Pius IX followed Gregory XVI to the papal throne in 1846, he was reputed to have liberal sympathies. However, political events changed him. Early in his reign he granted a political constitution to the papal states and allowed papal troops to join in the alliance of Italian states in their war against Austria and its designs on Lombardy. But Pius only allowed his troops to defend the borders of the papal states, that is, away from the northern front. The

Italian armies were defeated in 1848 by the Austrians in Lombardy, and the Pope was blamed. The same year the Pope's prime minister, Count de Rossi, was murdered, and the Pope's palace was besieged by revolutionary Italian nationalists. Pius escaped with the help of the French ambassador and fled to Gaeta in the kingdom of Naples, where he found asylum for a year.

After the events of 1848, Pius IX's position changed dramatically, such that Italians referred to him as "Pio Nono Secondo," Pius the Ninth, the Second. Through French intervention the Pope was restored to Rome in 1850, and henceforth the papal states, their days numbered, were virtually ruled as a theocracy. Pius IX increasingly took actions to oppose what he now perceived as the malignant spread of Liberalism: political, ecclesial, and intellectual. A number of papal actions after 1850 illustrate the growth of centralized papal power and the effort to eradicate the threat of Liberalism.

On December 8, 1854, Pius IX declared the dogma of the Immaculate Conception of the Blessed Virgin Mary. Beyond its theological significance, the definition established a critical precedent: that for the formal definition of a Catholic dogma it was sufficient that the Pope should act on his own authority, with only such consultation with the Church—the bishops—as appeared to him to be proper. There was, to be sure, wide and growing support for the dogma among the faithful. Nevertheless, Pius IX did not consider it necessary to receive the formal sanction of the bishops in council in pronouncing on such a fundamental doctrine of faith. The precedent for such authority proved to be very important sixteen years later at the First Vatican Council.

In 1863 Roman Catholic conferences held in Malines, Belgium, and Munich brought together progressive Catholic scholars and clergy from around Europe. At Malines Montalembert delivered two addresses calling for the Church to sever the alliance of Throne and Altar and to accept "a free Church in a free State." While it was a clear appeal for political and religious liberty, it was not a radical speech; nevertheless, it was attacked by conservatives, and Montalembert was rebuked by Pius IX. The "Munich congress" was under the leadership of the great Catholic historian Ignaz Döllinger. The subject of the deliberations was academic freedom and the right of Catholic scholars to pursue freely the methods of historical and scientific scholarship in their own work. Döllinger insisted that the ecclesiastical authorities should not interfere with free scholarly inquiry except in some rare cases of dogma. Pius IX responded with a brief insisting, on the contrary, that Catholic scholarship was indeed to be guided by the Rome authorities and the magisterium, the Church's teaching authority; he also banned the holding of similar conferences in the future.

The Pope's action had serious consequences for several of the Church's intellectual leaders. For example, the English lay Catholic historian Sir John Acton ceased publishing the Catholic periodical *The Home and Foreign Review* as a result of the Munich brief. In an article titled "Conflicts with Rome," Acton explained the reasons for the suspension:

> Its [the *Review's*] object has been to elucidate the harmony that exists between religion and the established conclusions of secular knowledge, and to exhibit the real amity and sympathy between the methods of [historical] science and the methods employed by the Church. That amity and sympathy the enemies of the Church refuse to admit, and her friends have not learned to understand. Long disowned by a large part of our Episcopate, they are now reflected by the Holy See; and the issue is vital to a Review which, in ceasing to uphold them, would surrender the whole reason of its existence.[2]

The congresses at Malines and Munich, the growing efforts of the Italian nationalists to annex the papal states to the kingdom of Italy, and other actions by liberals and by the secular governments convinced Pius IX that a bolder and more definitive action should be taken. In a measure mulled over for years and then abruptly taken, the Pope published in December 1864 the encyclical *Quanta cura,* to which was appended the notorious *Syllabus of Errors.* The *Syllabus* listed eighty errors, arranged in ten categories. They were propositions extracted from previous papal speeches and encyclicals and taken out of their specific context. For example, one was from an encyclical directed against the imposition of new anticlerical laws in the kingdom of

Piedmont. However, as stated, the condemnations appeared to be a sweeping rejection of political liberalism as such. Among the things condemned as erroneous were freedom of conscience and religion; freedom of the press; the sovereignty of the people; that the Catholic religion should not be the only religion recognized by the state; that Catholics have a right to question the compatibility of the Pope's temporal power with his spiritual power; and, in proposition eighty, "that the Roman Pontiff can and should reconcile himself to and agree with progress, liberalism, and civilization as lately introduced."

Catholics and non-Catholics alike were stupefied; they could not believe what they were reading. The bishops were perplexed as to how to interpret it to their people. The British prime minister William Gladstone and the American president Abraham Lincoln were profoundly concerned as to what the *Syllabus* meant with regard to the civil loyalty of their Catholic citizens in a democracy. Liberal newspapers throughout Europe and America ridiculed the document and fueled anti-Catholic feelings. The popular and influential French bishop F. A. D. Dupanloup angrily remarked that "if we do not succeed in checking this senseless Romanism, the Church will be outlawed in Europe for half a century." Pius IX later had to admit that his list of wholesale condemnations was "raw meat needing to be cooked."

It was Bishop Dupanloup who came to the rescue. He published a pamphlet in which he explained the Pope's denunciations in terms of what he called the "thesis" and the "hypothesis." What the Pope denounced was the "thesis," for example, that the Catholic Church would hold as its ideal rule that a society should have rival religious beliefs. However, the "thesis" does not negate the "hypothesis," for example, that in an imperfect world and in certain contexts it would not be wrong, but entirely prudent, for the Church to allow a wide margin of freedom of religion and of the press, such as in the United States. Dupanloup's interpretation was accepted unenthusiastically in Rome, but he received more than six hundred letters from bishops throughout the world expressing their gratitude for getting them out of an embarrassing situation with his tour de force. The Paris wits said that the "thesis" is when the Church condemns the Jews; the "hypothesis" is when the papal nuncio dines with the Baron de Rothschild, the wealthy Jewish banker.

The important point here is that it is a serious question whether the Pope himself intended the *Syllabus* to be of universal application and whether he considered it to be an infallible teaching. At any rate, it was received by many Vatican officials, theologians, and journalists as a dogmatic teaching of the Church. Many Catholic publications and learned treatises insisted on its binding force and asserted that all Catholics must assent to its teaching.

The Syllabus of Errors severely divided not only Catholic theologians and scholars but also the bishops and clergy. Many bishops, such as Dupanloup, and intellectual leaders, such as Montalembert, had supported a moderate Ultramontanism. A number of these individuals now became opponents of increased papal power and especially of any attempt to define the Pope's infallibility, whether their objection was on theological or on largely prudential grounds. But Pius's encyclical also had the opposite effect: It emboldened the more extreme Ultramontanists to accelerate their efforts to strengthen papal authority. During the 1860s the question of the Pope's spiritual and temporal authority, and by extension the general question of ecclesiology, was the critical subject of discussion in the Church.

By now there was wide acceptance of papal infallibility, but the actions of Pius IX obviously had caused many to hesitate and some, like Döllinger, to steel themselves against the doctrine. This uncertainty led to a growing sentiment among Ultramontanists that a council should be held to deal with a variety of matters touching on ecclesiology, including the persistent questions about relations between the Church and the state, but also with a view to confirming the juridical authority of the Pope in all matters.

Before we turn to the historic decisions of the First Vatican Council, it is important to look at some of the positions regarding the authority and the infallibility of the Pope that were taking shape in the years prior to 1870. The majority in favor of a definition of papal infallibility offered arguments similar to those of Robert Bellarmine almost two hundred years earlier. Yet there were extreme Ultramontanists who wished to go much further, creating what their critics called "a cult of the papacy." What the extremists did was to divide the Ultramontanist cause into two increasingly opposed factions. The modernizing party, represented by the likes of Montalembert and Dupanloup, wanted to protect the freedom of the Church, but it also recognized the need for Catholics to take an active role in the political life of the nation, which involved some compromise with secular political realities. The extremists, best exemplified in the figure of Louis Veuillot, accepted no such compromise. They came to be known as the "irreconcilables," and they preferred to resist what they saw as the corrupting influences of liberal politics and the dissolving effects of critical scholarship, that is, any concessions to modernity. What the extremists called for was an uncompromising pronouncement of what they perceived to be traditional Catholic claims. Pius IX sympathized with the aims of Veuillot and the "irreconcilables."

The principal voice of extreme Ultramontanism in France was the widely circulated newspaper *L'Univers,* edited by the layman Veuillot. In it Veuillot argued that the *Syllabus of Errors* must be understood as a formal condemnation of the modern republican state and that the parliamentary form of government was based on a heretical principle. He carried on a constant warfare with the bishops in his support of papal absolutism. He confused papal infallibility with spiritual inspiration and spoke of the Pope as alone carrying with him the thoughts of God, so that "we must unswervingly follow his inspired directions." "The infallibility of the Pope is," he wrote, "the infallibility of Jesus Christ Himself," and "when the Pope thinks, it is God who is thinking in him." In 1870 a follower of Veuillot was reported to have said that he did not like the definitions of the Vatican Council being spoken of as having been shaped by the council. "It is much simpler to think of them as whispered directly by the Holy Ghost into the Pope's ear."[3]

Extreme Ultramontanism was not confined to France and the reaction against Gallicanism. In England it was championed by the recent convert William George Ward in the pages of the *Dublin Review,* which he edited after 1863. Having rejected the Anglican *via media,* and fearful of the anarchy wrought by modern critical scholarship, Ward was convinced that the only assurance of the future unity and strength of the Christian Church was to be found on the rock of papal authority and infallibility. Cuthbert Butler's fair description of Ward's views shows how far Ward moved beyond the position of Bellarmine and most of the Ultramontane theologians:

> For him, all direct doctrinal instructions of all encyclicals, of all letters to individual bishops and allocutions, published by the Popes, are *ex cathedra* pronouncements and *ipso facto* infallible. . . . He did not shrink from saying that bulls, as the "Quanta Cura" of 1864, were to be accepted "as the Word of God." Thus he utterly rejected the idea that infallible pronouncements are few and far between . . . or require any theological tribunal to declare them *ex cathedra* or interpret their meaning.[4]

Like Veuillot, Ward equated infallibility with the Pope's personal spiritual inspiration. Among his most outrageous sallies was his remark that he wanted a papal encyclical every morning for breakfast along with his London *Times.*

The excesses of Ward's kind of Ultramontanism could be chronicled at length. While these were the extravagances of the few, individuals like Ward and Veuillot nevertheless had wide influence through their journalism. Ironically, their enduring significance as Ultramontanists lies in the fact that they energized a minority party of bishops who were to vigorously oppose a definition of papal infallibility in 1870 and even more so that they largely defined the issue for the public. Even after a relatively "moderate" definition was promulgated, their version of papal infallibility was what the broad Catholic world accepted as genuine Church teaching for generations after 1870.

The Debate over Papal Authority and Infallibility: Manning, Döllinger, and Kenrick

In the years immediately prior to 1870, it became clear to bishops on all sides that the council promoted by the *Civiltà cattolica* and *L'Univers* had to be convoked to settle issues that were causing consternation in their flocks and difficulties with their civil governments. Pamphlets and books defending one or another position began to appear.

On the question of papal infallibility, most of these writings came from the opposition, since the traditional Ultramontane position was well known. The opposition writings also were, on the whole, more scholarly, and several were produced by historians such as Döllinger, Acton, and Monsignor Maret, Dean of the theological faculty at the Sorbonne. There were also compelling, though not extreme, defenses of increased papal prerogatives and infallibility. One was a pastoral letter written by Monsignor Deschamps, Archbishop of Malines and a leader of the infallibilists at the council. He defended the definability of infallibility as being inherent in the New Testament Petrine texts, offered a defense of the doctrine, and countered the extremists by setting forth some of the theological limits of papal infallibility. For example, he insisted that *ex cathedra* pronouncements must teach doctrines that relate *directly* to matters of faith and morals. He also held that such pronouncements do not require or imply some new "inspiration."

Archbishop Henry Manning.

The most indefatigable of the traditional defenders of an Ultramontane Catholicism was Henry Manning (1808–1892), the Anglican convert who later was appointed Archbishop of Westminster in 1865 and raised to the cardinalate in 1875. He considered his efforts at securing a definition of papal infallibility in 1870 to be his major work. From the time of his conversion in 1845, he looked to Rome as his guide and, like Ward, as the only seat of infallible authority in an increasingly unstable world. For Manning Anglicanism and Gallicanism represented great threats to the Christian Church's unity. "Anglicanism," he wrote, "is essentially Erastian, and mistakes nations for churches."[5] Modern governments since before the Reformation had sought to establish national churches and thereby to draw the loyalty of their citizens away from the universal Church. Manning's Anglican experience of accommodation to the state gave him hope that a strengthened papacy would win the allegiance of Catholics back to Rome and would counter the splintering and weakening of the universal Church. "Gallicanism, Josephism, Anglicanism are," he wrote, "devices of government, and diseases of the ruling classes. . . . The choice lies between a State religion and the faith of Christendom, between a royal supremacy and the authority of the Vicar of Christ."[6]

Manning believed that the only thing that could save the Church and civilization was a reassertion of authority in an empowered and infallible papacy. While Manning was a man of action and not a theologian, he nevertheless wrote a profusion of letters, pamphlets, and drafts in defense of infallibility, before the meeting of the Vatican Council, during its sessions, and after its close. At the council he worked tirelessly as the "chief whip" of the majority party. His ideas, however, were largely drawn from other conservative scholars and theologians.

Manning agreed with de Maistre and Ward that the Catholic Church is a monarchy and that its rule extends to the temporal as well as the spiritual realm. He argued that without the necessary temporal privileges the spiritual work of the Church would be imperiled. As for spiritual sovereignty, Manning understood the infallibility of the Pope to be clearly established in the Petrine texts in the New Testament (Matt. 16:18; Luke 22:32; John 21:17), and he simply cites these passages as proof-texts. Concerning the gift of spiritual sovereignty given to Peter and to his successors, Manning writes:

> Our divine Lord communicated to His Church upon earth, and preeminently to His Vicar, the Head of the Church on earth, the Chief of His Twelve Apostles, a portion of His sovereignty. . . . The spiritual and supernatural sovereignty of His kingdom He vested in His Church on earth, in His Apostles, and above all, in him who was the Chief of the Apostles.[7]

The Petrine texts not only give sovereignty to Peter; their commission of the Chief Apostle to "strengthen the brethren" implies, for Manning, the gift of infallibility to Peter *and* to his successors. The indefectibility or infallibility of the Catholic Church is, therefore, indissolubly linked to St. Peter and to his papal successors. The Church's infallibility is, therefore, grounded in a *singular* privilege conferred on St. Peter and his successors. According to Manning, it is a unique "charisma," attached to the *office* of the Pope but freely given by God to the *person* holding the office, and therefore not dependent on the Church: "This divine assistance [of infallibility] is his [the Pope's] special prerogative depending on God alone; independent of the Church, which in dependence on him is endowed with the same infallibility."[8] The Pope need not consult with the Church in the exercise of infallibility.

Manning's view of the relation of the Pope and the bishops naturally follows from his reading of the meaning of the Petrine texts. Against the Gallicans, especially Bishop Maret of Paris, Manning insists that *ex cathedra* pronouncements of the Pope may be *apart from* the bishops. This did not imply that there was opposition between Pope and bishops, only that the Pope was not required to consult the bishops in order to exercise infallibility. It is the Pope's singular privilege, though enjoyed by the Church through him and working in union with him. In this way the infallibility of the Pope and the Church are never opposed, as was the case in the fourteenth century. Manning summarizes the relations as follows:

> I am unable to see that the primacy and infallibility of Peter in any way lessened or detracted from the authority and endowments of the Apostles; nor does it appear how the authority and endowment of his Successor shall lessen or detract from those of the Episcopate. Bishops are not less authoritative because their Head is more so. Bishops are not less the judges of doctrine in an Oecumenical Council because their Head, in the intervals between Council and Council is, by Divine assistance, guided and sustained so that he shall not err in interpreting the faith and expounding the Law of God.[9]

Manning worked hard for the removal of any council decree stating that the decisions of the Pope *required* the consent of the Church, for he saw in such a limitation a divisive Gallicanism threatening the unity of the universal Church.

When it appeared that a council was likely, many Church leaders who had not opposed some notion of papal infallibility in principle came, nevertheless, to consider its definition inopportune or counterproductive in light of the obvious disagreements that the issue was inciting, as well as for fears of the unforeseen political reactions to such a declaration in the present climate. The anxieties of the "inopportunists" are conveyed in a letter from John Henry Newman to the English bishop Ullathorne of Birmingham, written on January 28, 1870:

> When we are all at rest, and have no doubts, and at least practically, not to say doctrinally, hold the Holy Father to be infallible, suddenly there is thunder in the clear sky, and we are told to prepare for something we know not what to try our faith we know not how. No impending danger is to be averted, but a great difficulty is to be created. Is this the proper work for an Ecumenical Council?. . . I look with anxiety at the prospect of having to defend decisions, which may not be difficult to my private judgment, but may be most difficult to maintain logically in the face of historical facts. What have we done to be treated as the faithful never were treated before? When has a definition of a doctrine de fide been a luxury of devotion, and not a stern painful necessity?[10]

Manning and the traditional Ultramontanists would have nothing of the "inopportunist" fears and reservations. He addressed the question of "inopportunism" in his pastoral letter to his clergy in 1869. Against Newman's contention that a definition of infallibility is unnecessary, Manning argues that the fact that the great majority of the Church approves of papal infallibility is indication enough that a decision to authorize an existing doctrine would not be difficult. Against the claim that the difficulties raised by papal infallibility would make a definition either impossible or too obscure, Manning replies that, on the contrary, a definition would clarify the question once and for all. The "inopportunists" further argued that a definition would hinder any possible reunion with the Eastern Churches, would increase Protestant prejudice and hostility, would render relations with the secular states more difficult, and would risk placing the Church in a more disadvantageous position. To these concerns Manning responds that it is better to let the other Christian bodies know the full truth as to what is involved in any possible reunion with Rome and what is the Church's true belief with regard to the temporal power than to leave these matters ambiguous and open to misunderstanding. Manning and the conservatives were prepared to throw down the gauntlet, come what may.

Johann Joseph Ignaz von Döllinger. By and large, the German bishops and theologians were not fervent Ultramontanists. At the same time they did not look favorably on the nationalism of the extreme French Gallicans. But they maintained a high regard for the hierarchy and especially the prerogatives of the bishops in their dioceses. This was true, for example, of the Tübingen theologians. In contrast, the great Munich theologian and Church historian Johann Joseph Ignaz von Döllinger (1799–1890) was, until 1860, much more sympathetic to early nineteenth-century Ultramontanism. In his multivolume *History of the Church,* written in the 1830s, he held Ultramontane views of the Petrine texts and of the Pope's supremacy. He considered the decrees of the Council of Constance to be invalid. However, the actions of Pius IX, especially the *Syllabus of Errors,* and the spread of more extreme views among the Ultramontanists turned him into a single-minded critic of papal infallibility. An article in the Jesuit *Civiltá cattolica* of February 1869, predicting that the Pope's infallibility would be proclaimed by acclamation at the upcoming council, energized Döllinger to take action, and he responded with a series of articles in the German

Ignaz von Döllinger

newspaper *Allgemeine Zeitung.* The articles were immediately expanded, published as a book, and translated into several languages including English, under the title *The Pope and the Council* by "Janus."

By means of an accumulation of historical evidence, Döllinger protested against the ecclesiastical and political dangers of confusing the Church with the papacy by treating them as convertible terms. He portrays the Ultramontanist party as either ignorant of early Church history or of falsifying it since the ninth century by distorting the Pope's spiritual primacy into an absolute monarchy. True piety, Döllinger argues, demands an exposé of this historical error and its causes. Every faithful Catholic is convinced, of course, that papal primacy "rests on Divine appointment":

> But on this has followed, since the ninth century, a further development, artificial and sickly rather than sound and natural—of the Primacy into the Papacy, a transformation rather than a development. . . . The ancient Church found the need of a centre of unity, of a bishop possessed of primatial authority. . . . But when the presidency of the Church became an empire, when in the place of the first bishop deliberating and deciding in union with his "brethren" on the affairs of the Church, and setting them an example of submission to her laws, there was substituted the despotic rule of an absolute monarch. . . . Of the privileges afterwards obtained or laid claim to by the Popes not one can be traced up to the earliest times, and pointed to as a right uninterruptedly and everywhere exercized.[11]

Döllinger proceeds to elaborate on the actions of the papacy and the events of Church history that have led to the contemporary claims of the extreme Ultramontanists and to the demand for a dogmatic decree of papal infallibility. The immense catalogue of events, which Döllinger often portrays in conspiratorial terms, is impressive despite its obvious partisan character. Bishop Ullathorne judged it to be "the gravest and severest attack on the Holy See and the Jesuits and especially on the policy of Rome for a thousand years, and will be a great storehouse for the adversaries of the Church."[12]

Initially, Döllinger reviews the errors and contradictions of earlier Popes that were bound to raise serious doubts in contemporary minds about the trustworthiness of infallible pronouncements. For example, both Popes Innocent I and Gelasius I declared it indispensable that infants receive communion and that those who died without receiving it went straight to Hell. A thousand years later their teaching was anathematized at the Council of Trent. Döllinger enumerates many other papal pronouncements and actions that were contradicted by later Popes. Furthermore, he insists that some explanation is required for how only recently the idea of papal infallibility, which makes "the pope of the day the one vehicle of the Church's inspirations," arose. How should it have first been ascertained in the year of grace 1869?

> For thirteen centuries an incomprehensible silence on this fundamental article reigned throughout the whole Church and her literature. None of the ancient confessions of faith, no catechism, none of the patristic writings composed for the instruction of the people contain a syllable about the Pope, still less any hint that all certainty of faith and doctrine depends on him. For the first thousand years of Church history not a question of doctrine was finally decided by the Pope.

Döllinger points out the enormous differences in the role of the primacy of the bishop of Rome in the early centuries and its change in the later Middle Ages. In the earlier period "the Popes took no part in convoking Councils" which were convoked by emperors. "Nor were the Popes ever consulted about it beforehand." "They were not always allowed to preside, personally or by deputy, at the Great Councils." And "neither the dogmatic nor disciplinary decisions of these Councils required Papal confirmation." Döllinger then proceeds to trace the process by which the Popes increased their power over several centuries. One important factor was the forgery of documents, such as the pseudo-Isadorian Decretals of the ninth century, which put forth claims in support of papal authority. Another example was Gratian's *Decretum* of the twelfth century, a document that included the Isadorian forgeries and which became the official manual for canon law. It profoundly influenced the writings on papal prerogatives by such Scholastic theologians as Thomas Aquinas.

Döllinger turns next to a compendium of papal actions taken since the twelfth century that greatly helped to solidify the central authority of the papacy. These included the institution of papal legates or ambassadors who interfered in the administration of local dioceses; the use of papal dispensations and patronage; the influence of the Inquisition in strengthening the papal system; the use of the Index to suppress any criticism of Rome and to enhance the influence of Ultramontane teachings; the suppression of certain works that related to the condemnation of Pope Honorius for heresy by the Sixth Ecumenical Council; the *Liber Diurnus,* which included historical information that was impossible to reconcile with papal infallibility; and the efforts of the Jesuits, whose zealous loyalty to the Pope Döllinger perceives as a renunciation of personal intelligence and judgment.

The Pope and the Council concludes with a warning against papal power that anticipates Lord Acton's admonition that "power tends to corrupt, and absolute power corrupts absolutely":

> All absolute power demoralizes its possessor. To that all history bears witness. And if it be a spiritual power . . . the danger of self-exaltation is only so much the greater . . . while it is peculiarly conducive to self-deceit. . . . And if the man into whose hands this absolute power has fallen cherishes the further opinion that he is infallible, and an organ of the Holy Ghost . . . it seems almost impossible that his sobriety of mind should always be proof against so intoxicating a sense of power.[13]

Döllinger believed that the dogma of infallibility would place the Pope in a cloud of perpetual incense and adulation that was calculated to strengthen a belief in the Pope's own mind of his difference from other mortals, with all the dangers inherent in such a belief and power.

The Pope and the Council created a sensation and elicited numerous critical responses from the Ultramontanists. It also gained the support of fourteen influential German bishops against a declaration of the dogma, ostensibly on "inopportunist" grounds. It further helped to enlist European governments in efforts to persuade the Church against taking this action. While Döllinger was, in many respects, the early leader of the minority party opposing papal infallibility, he refused the entreaties of his supporters, including high ecclesiastics, to reside in Rome during the council. He thought that he could serve more effectively through his writings for the press. The actual leaders of the minority in Rome were the layman John Acton, the English historian and friend of Döllinger—who was responsible, because of his international connections, for organizing the somewhat disparate forces of the minority—and the French bishop Dupanloup, who raised many questions as to whether any official action was necessary in view of the complexity of defining infallibility and its unforeseen consequences. Dupanloup served as "chief whip" of the minority party at the council sessions.

Archbishop Peter Richard Kenrick.   Included among the minority party opposing papal infallibility was the Archbishop of St. Louis, Peter Richard Kenrick (1806–1896). He was, perhaps, the firmest critic of infallibility at the council itself. He was joined, at least initially, by the American archbishops McCloskey of New York and Purcell of Cincinnati. Half a dozen other American bishops opposed the final draft of the constitution on infallibility at the time of the trial ballot taken on July 13, which preceded the final vote on July 18, 1870. Kenrick wrote a speech which he had planned to read to the council, but he left Rome on July 17 with many other minority bishops when it became obvious what the final outcome of the vote would be. His speech, however, was printed in Latin in 1870 and later was published in English.

Kenrick begins his speech by acknowledging the primacy of the Pope in both honor and jurisdiction as being held universally by the Church. He denies, however, that the testimony of the ancient Church fathers' interpretation of the Petrine text—"On this rock will I build my church"—will support the modern Ultramontane interpretation:

> Either no argument at all, or one of the slenderest probability, is to be derived from the words, "On this rock I will build my church," in support of the primacy. Unless it is certain that on *the rock* is to be understood as the apostle Peter in his own person, and not in his capacity as the chief apostle speaking for

them all, the word supplies no argument whatever, I do not say in proof of papal infallibility, but even in support of the *primacy* of the bishop of Rome. If we are bound to follow the majority of the fathers in this thing, then we are bound to hold for certain that by *the rock* should be understood the faith professed by Peter, not Peter professing the faith.

According to Kenrick, what the Petrine text promises to Peter is inseparable from the rest of the apostles and not given solely to Peter himself. Kenrick insists that it is not by Scripture but by the testimony of Christian antiquity that Peter is given a special privilege above the other apostles. And again by this testimony it does appear that he is infallible but that "on this condition, he should use the counsel of his brethren, and should be aided by the judgment of those who are his partners . . . and should speak in their name."

Kenrick expresses particular concern regarding the Ultramontane belief that the Pope's gift of infallibility is a personal *charisma,* since the word is used only in association with a person. Archbishop Manning, for example, had made much of this personal spiritual gift and was, apparently, equating infallibility with spiritual inspiration. Furthermore, Manning would not consider "fixing the conditions for the exercise of the Pope's infallibility. He asserts that He who gave the charisma will give the means for its due exercise." But once the Pope is imbued with such an idea of spiritual inspiration "the holier in life . . . the more fervent is piety, the more dangerous he would prove both to himself and to the church, which (according to this system) derives its infallibility from him."

What need, one must ask, does a Pope who accepts this notion of infallibility have of the council of his brethren or the opinions of theologians? The very danger implied by such a question insists that the Church declare its belief that God alone is infallible. Kenrick proposes that the most that can be said of the Church is that it is *inerrant* or *indefectible,* that is, promised that because it is aided by the Holy Spirit "it may discover and distinguish truths divinely revealed . . . so that it shall not tolerate errors contradicting revealed truths."[14]

When Kenrick returned to St. Louis, he submitted to the decrees of the First Vatican Council in a public speech. He later explained to Lord Acton that the motive of his submission was "'simply and singly' the authority of the Church" and that it was "pure obedience" of faith; he would leave it to others to reconcile the council's action with the facts of history. Kenrick was able to justify his action intellectually by applying John Henry Newman's theory of development to the doctrine of papal infallibility. Kenrick wrote that the present dogma was so different from what was the case in the early Church "that it can only be supposed identical in substance by allowing a process of doctrinal development. This principle removed Newman's great difficulty and convinced him that, notwithstanding the difference, he might and should become a Catholic. I thought that it might justify me in remaining one."[15]

The First Vatican Council and Its Meaning

The Council of the Vatican opened on the anniversary of the Feast of the Immaculate Conception of Mary on December 8, 1869. It met in the south transept of St. Peter's in Rome. Not surprisingly, it was a more varied representation of bishops than was the case at the Council of Trent in the sixteenth century. There were about two hundred bishops present from outside Europe, including forty-nine from the United States and sixty from the Eastern Rite churches in union with Rome. There were two constitutions that were ultimately voted on: *De Filius,* on faith and reason (to which we will return later), and *Pastor Aeternus,* on the primacy and infallibility of the Pope. The former was approved unanimously (667 to 0) in April 1870. The really controversial schema on the Church was put forward on January 21. Originally it was proposed to deal with a variety of ecclesial issues. The juridical authority of the Pope in the Church was one important issue, but also scheduled for consideration were the nature of the temporal dominion of the Church, the rights and duties of the civil powers, and the relations between Church and state.

As the weeks moved on, it became clear to the majority party that the debates on the early chapters on the Church might take months. The minority party, opposing a declaration on infallibility, was eager to see these debates extended, thereby delaying

any action on infallibility until an adjournment might be reached. Their view was that "to do nothing was to do a lot." These tactics caused Archbishop Manning and others to urge Pius IX to place the schema on infallibility before other subjects on the agenda. Provoked by accounts of the actions of anti-infallibilists such as Père Gratry in Paris, Döllinger, and Acton, in seeking the intervention of European governments, Pius acceded to the request of the majority leadership on April 19.

From the beginning the minority found itself at a strategic disadvantage. No minority theologians had been appointed to the preparatory commissions to draw up the various schema, and the special Congregation, with responsibility to deal with proposed amendments to the schema, included no minority party members. Despite these disabilities, the debate on the schema on infallibility lasted from mid-May to mid-July. Speeches by Bishops Hefele, Maret, Strossmayer, and Darboy presented the full armory of the anti-infallibilist argument, questioning the timeliness, the definability, and the historical legitimacy of a declaration on papal infallibility. On July 13 a vote was taken on a conditional draft: 451 were in favor, 88 were opposed, and 62 were in favor conditionally.

There were two issues of special concern to the minority, and to those bishops giving only conditional assent, that faced the drafters of the final schema. First, there was the concern that it be made absolutely clear—against the extreme infallibilists— that infallibility not be personal or absolute, that is, that it not attach to any and every formal utterance of the Pope. Second, there was the disputed question whether the definition would ensure that, before making an *ex cathedra* pronouncement, the Pope must consult the Church, namely, the bishops. Wording to that effect was absent from the July 13 draft. When the members reassembled on July 16, a report was made on amendments. To the earlier draft, which stated that the decrees of the Pope were irreformable of themselves, the drafting deputation now added the words "and not from the consent of the church." The phrase was specifically directed against what was perceived as the Gallican tendencies of the minority. That evening a delegation of the minority, including archbishops and cardinals, sought an audience with Pius IX to request the insertion of either "relying on the testimony of the churches" or "the bishops not excluded." The Pope rejected the request.

Studies have shown that most of the majority party were moderate and were prepared to find a compromise formula that would bring about a reconciliation of the parties. But Pius IX stood with the more intransigent papal infallibilists. Earlier, when the Dominican theologian Cardinal Guido, a member of the majority, suggested the inclusion of a phrase that would require the Pope to examine tradition—normally involving consultation with the bishops—before speaking *ex cathedra,* Pius IX rebuked him: "Tradition! I am the Tradition!"

On July 18 the final vote was taken. Five hundred thirty-three council fathers voted yes, and only two voted no. The Pope then confirmed the constitution. A great many of the minority had, of course, already left Rome, knowing the outcome and either not wanting to be disrespectful of the Pope or fearing that a vote against the constitution might cause them to be anathematized for rejecting what would be a dogmatic teaching of the Church. On the next day war was declared between France and Prussia, and the French troops withdrew from Rome. On September 20 the Italian troops laid siege to the city and soon occupied it. On October 20 Pius IX suspended the council indefinitely. In the following days and months, the bishops who had not assented did so one after another. Lord Acton reproached minority bishops, such as Kenrick, for their lack of courage in ceasing their opposition and in accepting the decrees. Döllinger and some of his Catholic colleagues continued to attack the dogma and the constitutionality of the council. On April 17, 1871, Döllinger was excommunicated by the Archbishop of Munich, and other excommunications followed. The Catholic bishops throughout the world had the unenviable task of attempting to interpret the exact meaning of the Pope's infallibility to their flocks. Some, like Archbishop Manning, gave it a wide interpretation; others gave it narrow scope and a moderate reading.

What did the constitution *Pastor Aeternus* actually say regarding the Pope's authority and infallibility? Two canons, here cited, give an indication of the supreme, universal, ordinary, and immediate jurisdiction of the Pope as spelled out by the Council:

If, then, any one shall say that the Roman Pontiff has the office merely of inspection or direction, but not full and supreme power and jurisdiction over the Universal Church, not only in things pertaining to faith and morals, but also in things that relate to the discipline and government of the Church spread throughout the world; or that he possesses merely the principal part, and not all the fullness of this supreme power; or that this power which he enjoys is not ordinary and immediate, both over each and all the Churches and all the pastors and the faithful—*let him be anathema.*

We teach and define that it is a dogma divinely revealed: that the Roman Pontiff, when he speaks *ex cathedra,* that is, when in discharge of the office of Pastor and Doctor of all Christians, by virtue of his supreme apostolic authority he defines a doctrine regarding faith or morals to be held by the Universal Church, by the divine assistance promised him in Blessed Peter, is possessed of that infallibility with which the Divine Redeemer willed that his Church should be endowed for defining doctrine regarding faith or morals: and that therefore such definitions of the Roman Pontiff are irreformable of themselves and not from the consent of the Church. But if anyone, which God forbid, presume to contradict this Our definition—*let him be anathema.*[16]

The *supreme* power is indicated by the phrase that says the Pope's *ex cathedra* definitions are "irreformable of themselves and not from the consent of the Church." The Pope's jurisdiction is *universal* in that *all* bishops, clergy, and laity, and *all* Churches in communion with Rome, including the Eastern Rite churches, are subject to his authority. The Pope's jurisdiction is *ordinary* in the sense that powers are vested in his office and are not delegated. The council affirmed that this not-delegated power does not interfere and contradict the ordinary and immediate powers of the bishops in their dioceses, but the relationship of these powers is left unsatisfactorily imprecise. The Pope's *immediate* power means that he can exercise it directly without going through an intermediary, such as a secular sovereign or another ecclesiastic. The Pope does not require the permission of the president of a state or that of a local bishop if he wishes to carry out certain ecclesial functions.[17]

What of the Pope's infallibility? The prospect of great confusion regarding the meaning and the limits of the Pope's infallibility was largely resolved by a tract written in 1871 by the General Secretary of the council, Bishop Joseph Fessler of Austria. Entitled *The True and the False Infallibility of the Popes,* it offered a moderate interpretation of the canon on infallibility, and it received a warm commendation from Pius IX himself, who wrote to Fessler that he had "brought out the true meaning of the dogma of papal infallibility." Fessler's semiofficial interpretation not only relieved the fears of the minority bishops but also assisted them in their own efforts to interpret the decree. Fessler laid down the following conditions necessary for an infallible papal teaching:

1. The Pope must speak as Pope, not as a private person or as a theologian. He must be exercising his supreme authority over the entire Church.

2. The Pope's teaching must be a doctrine of faith or morals.

3. The Pope's pronouncement must not be merely advice or warning; it must be a dogmatic definition. It must intend to terminate a controversy and pronounce a final determination on the question.

4. The doctrine taught must be a truth necessary to salvation and one revealed by God.

5. And, while it need not be addressed to all believers—it may be directed to a single individual—it must virtually be intended for all believers, since it is defining something essential to the faith.

It is clear that Fessler excludes the regular utterances of the Pope in carrying out his daily tasks; pamphlets or books written by the Pope; ordinary briefs or utterances, even those to the entire Church; and utterances having to do with regular juridical and disciplinary matters. Fessler's conditions led him to say that the precise occasions on which the Pope declared an infallible doctrine were very few, but he does not specify what these were. The careful studies of the historians Chaupin and Dublanchy in the 1920s list only twelve such occasions up to 1870 and rule out the many encyclicals of Pope Leo XIII (1878–1903) and Pope Pius X (1903–1914). Such minimalist claims, that now have gained authority, would appear to have shown that the fears of Döllinger and Acton were unfounded, just as the extravagances of Veuillot and Ward were repudiated. The infallibility of the *Syllabus of Errors,* commonly defended in the 1860s and 1870s, is entirely rejected today. Some would even say that these minimalist interpretations give point to the witticism that the Pope is infallible so long as he defines nothing.[18]

The victory of moderation is today perceived as salutary. In conclusion, two points need to be stressed. The continuing uncertainty among Catholic scholars as to exactly what papal teachings are *ex cathedra* pronouncements raised the question as to what authority any lists of infallible teachings possess. Apparently none, since there is no infallible list of infallible teachings. Hence the further question that was asked: Was it in the Church's interest to declare a dogma whose actual exercise is so rare and that has resulted in division and uncertainty in the Church because it is not always clear what authoritative papal teaching is or is not infallible? The question continues to be debated by Catholic scholars and theologians, but the prevailing view is that, despite the inadequate language employed, it was a wise, necessary, and honest action, in accord with the doctrinal development of the Church's deposit of faith. What the majority of bishops wanted to affirm through their action was that God will be faithful to his Church. The judgment of one Catholic commentator would be broadly accepted as a proper assessment of the situation at the time:

> The defining of the position of the Pope as successor and heir of St. Peter, according to the mind of the Catholic Church, and the setting forth in unmistakable terms the implications of his primacy and infallible teaching authority, was surely a right act: in that it shuts out the possibility of anyone seeking union with the Catholic Apostolic Roman Church . . . doing so under the misapprehension of what is involved. . . . For centuries before the Vatican Council the dogmas it defined on the Papacy had been growing more and more predominant in Catholic schools of Western Christendom, so that anyone coming into the Church would have found himself practically bound to accept them as almost certain theological opinions, liable and likely to be defined.[19]

Times, of course, do change, and as we will see in volume two, the actions of the Second Vatican Council (1962–1965) were to add a new chapter to the Church's reflections on the question of ecclesial and papal authority.

THE NEO-THOMISTIC REVIVAL

Beginnings

The growth in the Ultramontanist movement that we have just surveyed was closely allied with the revival of medieval Scholastic philosophy and theology in Europe after roughly 1840. Both movements were centered in Rome; both had the strong support of the Jesuits; and both were directed at restoring unity, order, and authority in a Church and a culture that were divided and perceived to be increasingly influenced by modernist ideas, that is by the democratic, pluralistic, and even secular intellectual currents of the nineteenth century. The Neo-Scholastic or Neo-Thomistic revival began in Italy in the 1840s in an effort to counter the pluralism of the various schools and what was judged to be the errors of German Idealism, of the Tübingen School, of the antirationalism of French Traditionalism, of the doctrines of the Italian ontologists, of the Fideism of writers such as Bautain, and, later, of the historical work of Döllinger and the Munich School. The movement soon spread beyond Italy to centers such as Mainz and Münster in Germany, to Austria, Paris, and Spain, and to Louvain in Belgium.

While often used interchangeably, the terms "Neo-Scholasticism" and "Neo-Thomism" are not historically identical, at least, that is, until the encyclical *Aeterni Patris*. Neo-Scholasticism refers to the revival of interest in medieval Scholastic philosophy and theology in the nineteenth century as a bulwark against what the Church saw as a growing pluralism and subjectivism in Catholic theology in Italy, Germany, and France, in particular. It refers to the broad revival of interest in medieval philosophers such as Dun Scotus, St. Bonaventure, and Albert the Great, as well as St. Thomas Aquinas, as representing a definitive *philosophia perennis* in the service of Catholic theology. Neo-Thomism refers more narrowly to the recovery of the thought of

Thomas Aquinas. However, with the encyclical *Aeterni Patris* Thomas Aquinas's philosophy is given a privileged place among the Scholastic teachers, and thereafter the terms often are used interchangeably, although referring dominantly to the attempt to restore the thought of Thomas Aquinas. This change is nicely reflected in the words of the eminent historian of Scholasticism, Martin Grabmann: "The direction that has emerged since the mid-nineteenth century and usually found in Catholic theology and philosophy [takes] up again the connection with the ecclesiastical scholasticism interrupted by the Enlightenment, searching to make fruitful for contemporary problems the thought-world of medieval scholasticism, particularly of Thomas Aquinas."[20]

The restoration of the thought of Thomas Aquinas was given authoritative sanction with the issuance of Pope Leo XIII's encyclical *Aeterni Patris* on August 4, 1879. It is clear that Leo XIII saw a profound connection between the actions of the First Vatican Council, with its centralizing of ecclesial authority in Rome, and *Aeterni Patris*. He looked out at Europe and beyond and observed the breakdown of the Church's temporal authority, the growth of Modernist philosophy and secularism, and the need of the Church to address a host of complex questions regarding the Church and political sovereignty, industrialism and the economy, and other matters of personal and social ethics. To address these issues effectively, the Pope saw a decisive advantage in being able to ground the Church's teaching in a stable, authentic, and united philosophy. In other words, any reformation of the modern political, economic, and moral order required as its prerequisite the restoration of theology's intellectual integrity and unity. This, the Pope believed, could be accomplished by a return to "the golden wisdom of St. Thomas," the fountainhead of philosophical truth. Leo wrote at the time:

> There is none of us but can see the danger in which the family and civil society itself are involved owing to the plague of perverse opinions; they would certainly be much more tranquil and secure if a sounder doctrine, one more in conformity with the teaching of the Church, were taught in schools, such a doctrine as is contained in the works of Thomas Aquinas. For the

theses which St. Thomas maintains with regard to the true nature of liberty, now degenerated into licence, the divine origin of all authority . . . the just and paternal sovereignty of kings, the obedience due to the higher powers, and the necessity of mutual charity among all men and such like, are of supreme and irresistible efficacy.[21]

Leo XIII's call for the restoration of the teaching of St. Thomas, and for it to be "spread far and wide for the defense and beauty of the Catholic faith and for the good of society," was followed by a series of practical actions to implement the program. The Pope founded the Roman Academy of St. Thomas, established a commission to edit a critical text of all of St. Thomas's writings (the *Editio Leonina*), founded the Institut Supérieur de Philosophie in Louvain as a center for the study and dissemination of the doctrines of St. Thomas, and declared St. Thomas the patron of all Catholic universities, colleges, and schools throughout the world. A number of journals devoted to Neo-Thomism were founded, including *Divus Thomas* (1880), *St. Thomasblätter* (1888), *Revue thomiste* (1893), *La Revue néoscholastique de philosophie* (1894), and many others. In America the best known were begun after World War I: *The Modern Schoolman* (1923), *The New Scholasticism* (1927), and *The Thomist* (1939).

Not all Catholic institutions followed Leo XIII's directives. Some pursued older, eclectic forms of Scholasticism or tried to proceed in other philosophical frameworks. The Modernist crisis (see Chapter 14) of the 1890s and beyond caused Leo's successor, Pope Pius X, to make absolutely clear his understanding of Leo XIII's intention, against those Modernist theologians who simply "deride and heedlessly despise scholastic philosophy and theology." In his *motu proprio, Doctoris Angelici* of June 29, 1914, the Pope made it clear that by Scholasticism he meant "the principal teachings of St. Thomas Aquinas." He then decreed

that the capital theses in the philosophy of St. Thomas are not to be placed in the category of opinions capable of being debated one way or another, but are to be considered as the foundations upon which the whole science of natural and divine things is based. . . . We

therefore desired that all teachers of philosophy and sacred theology should be warned that if they deviated so much as a step, in metaphysics especially, from Aquinas, they exposed themselves to grave risk.[22]

The Pope concluded his directive by stating that it was "our will and We hereby order and command that teachers of sacred theology in Universities, Academies, Colleges, Seminaries and Institutions enjoying by apostolic indult the privilege of granting academic degrees . . . use the *Summa Theologica* of St. Thomas as the text . . . and comment upon it in the Latin tongue."[23] Pronouncements and actions of Pontiffs following Pius X gave increased support to the Thomistic Movement. The Code of Canon Law issued under Benedict XV in 1917 required all professors of philosophy and theology to hold and teach the doctrines of St. Thomas. Pius XI, in *Studiorum Ducem* (1923), declared that "St. Thomas should be called . . . the Common or Universal Doctor of the Church: for the Church has adopted his philosophy for her very own."

As a result of the threat of new forms of "Modernism" after World War II in the work of writers such as Henri de Lubac and Teilhard de Chardin, Pius XII lamented in *Humani Generis* (1950) that the teachings of Thomas Aquinas are now "scorned by some who shamelessly call it outmoded in form and rationalistic, as they say, in its method of thought." Only with the reign of John XXIII, beginning in 1958, was the rigid adherence to Thomas Aquinas relaxed and a new openness to other philosophical approaches possible in Roman Catholic theology.

Among the best and most open-minded leaders of the second generation of the Thomist revival was Désiré Cardinal Mercier, founder of the Institut Supérieur de Philosophie at Louvain University. Mercier's colleague at Louvain, Maurice de Wulf (1867–1947), was the greatest historian of the new Scholasticism in the earlier period of the movement. His *History of Medieval Philosophy* and his *Introduction to Scholastic Philosophy* are standard works in the field. Among the outstanding Neo-Thomist apologists in the early decades of the twentieth century were Ambroise Gardeil (1859–1931), Antonin Sertillanges (1863–1948), and Réginald Garrigou-Lagrange.

Neo-Thomism represents, in brief, the attempt to bring the traditional teachings of St. Thomas Aquinas into the very different philosophical climate of the nineteenth century in an effort to show that this body of doctrine is as relevant to the problems of Modernity as it was to those of the thirteenth century. The theme of the Louvain school in particular can be stated thus: As a body of doctrine the truth of Thomism is the child of eternity, independent of time; as the elaboration of that doctrine in the course of human history, Thomism is the child of time and required to adapt to changing conditions. The theme is *continuity* and *adaptation.* This is well expressed by Maurice de Wulf:

> When the new scholastic philosophy proclaims by its very name its continuity with a glorious past, it is merely recognizing this incontestable law of organic relationship between the doctrines of the centuries. It does more, however. Its endeavor to re-establish and to plant down deeply amid the controversies of the twentieth century the principles that animated the scholasticism of the thirteenth is in itself an admission that philosophy cannot *completely* change from epoch to epoch; that the truth of seven hundred years ago is still the truth of today; that down through all the oscillations of historical systems there is ever to be met with a *philosophia perennis*—a sort of atmosphere of truth, pure and undiluted, whose bright, clear rays have lighted up the centuries even through the shadows of the darkest and gloomiest clouds.
>
> At the same time, let us hasten to add, that the new scholasticism inscribes on its programme, side by side with this respect for the fundamental doctrines of tradition, *another essential principle* of equal importance with the first—which it supplements—and expressed with equal clearness by the name it has chosen for itself: the principle of *adaptation to modern intellectual needs and conditions.*[24]

The Thomists sought to show that the *philosophia perennis,* as classically formulated by Thomas Aquinas, alone can meet the crisis of modern thought which is the result of subjectivism and relativism. At the same time, these Neo-Scholastics contend that Thomas Aquinas is supple and resilient enough to incorporate those genuine truths which modern philosophers have brought to light but have either exaggerated or have failed to integrate into a larger and more adequate conceptual scheme. Thus it is that many of the Thomists have sought to show both the general inadequacies of modern philosophical positions and ways in which the authentic truths present in these philosophies are not only consistent with but more compatible with Thomistic realism.

Thomism, like Aristotelianism, is a system which incorporates the widest of philosophical and scientific concerns, including logic, physics, psychology, ethics, metaphysics, and aesthetics. It is not our purpose here to survey the contributions of Thomism to all of these diverse fields but to focus, rather, on the distinctive contribution of Neo-Thomism to a few of the vital issues confronting modern Christian theology. However, before pursuing this it is necessary for us to know something about the fundamental doctrines of Thomistic philosophy itself.

Thomistic Metaphysics

Thomism is fundamentally Aristotelian in its epistemology and metaphysics. The Thomists insist on the empirical or sensory basis of all knowledge, while rejecting both a positivist phenomenalism and a Kantian idealism which would deny that science can reach through phenomena to a genuine knowledge of metaphysical reality. Nevertheless, Thomism begins with existent being, the natural world, and inquires what it is and how it exists and *from* this inquiry moves to the question of that Being which is its own existence, whose essence is to exist. Knowledge of God can be attained by reflection on created being. The starting point of any metaphysics must then be sense experience of material objects. However, reflection on such experience leads the mind to make certain distinctions. Objects in nature change while remaining substantially the same. Animals grow and change their shape and color. Hence a distinction must be drawn between a being's substance and its accidents. Moreover, we can even discern substantial changes in being as well as accidental ones. Material being can undergo changes which alter the substantial character of the material. When the pig eats corn, the corn does not remain what it was but becomes pork. At the same time, the corn does not cease to be. It undergoes a substantial change. This observation leads to further distinctions. There appears to be an underlying material substrate of change which in itself is not any definite thing, what Thomas Aquinas called "prime matter." On the other hand, matter is always determinate matter, some substantial form, corn or pork or some intermediate substance. Form is what places matter in some specific class. All material substance is thus made up of matter and form.

This analysis leads Thomas Aquinas to the doctrines of potency and act as well as essence and existence. Prime matter is pure potentiality, whereas substantial form is act, that is, that which places the material being in its specific class and determines its essence. The distinction between matter and form is that between potency and act. The potential is not yet in act but can become so. The child has the power to become a pianist and so is potentially a pianist. Potency is to essence what act is to existence.

No finite being exists necessarily. We can conceive of a finite essence without knowing if it exists. I can conceive of a Martian, for example. Existence (*esse*) is the act by which an essence is or has being (*ens*). "Esse," says Thomas Aquinas, "denotes a certain act; for a thing is not said to be (esse) by the fact that it is in potentiality, but by the fact that it is in act" (*Contra Gentiles,* I, 22). Through existence essence has being. Nevertheless, act is also determined by essence, in the sense that to be is always the existence of this or that essence. Neither essence nor existence should be conceived of as independent of the other. There is no essence without existence and no existence without essence. And yet, existence is the more fundamental, since created existence is the actualization of a potentiality. Existence is the highest perfection of any essence.

As we have observed, for Thomas Aquinas no finite being exists necessarily. All finite existence is contingent. This, in Thomas Aquinas's view, points to that Being which is the source of finite creatures. Such a Being cannot itself be the conjoining of essence and existence but must have existence as its essence, a Being who exists necessarily. According to him, God is *Qui est,* He who is. Existence itself (*ipsum esse*) is the essence of God.

Thomism holds that no finite, created being is necessary nor is it the sufficient ground of the union of its essence and existence. Such a union must,

finally, have recourse to a Being in whom essence and existence are identical. But humans have no intuitive or innate a priori knowledge of God's nature or existence. That such a Being exists can be known only through demonstrations from its effects, that is, a posteriori. While Thomists acknowledge that no perfect knowledge of God can be obtained through a purely natural knowledge of effects, proof can be given that such a cause (i.e., God as *ipsum esse*) does exist, assuming the finitude and contingency of the effects. This is possible because the human mind, while dependent upon the senses for its knowledge, can transcend sensory objects in that objects of sense bear a relation or analogy to things that transcend them. This analogy of being (*analogia entis*) is the key to Thomistic metaphysics and theology.

While Thomas Aquinas gave great attention to the nature of human knowledge, he did not have to respond to the kinds of epistemological questions posed, first, by Descartes's universal doubt or by the criticisms of Hume and Kant that we have examined in Chapter 3. The Neo-Thomists of the late nineteenth century were called upon, however, to defend a genuine rational knowledge of God in a post-Kantian context that was skeptical of the claims to metaphysical *knowledge.* Among the many influential Neo-Thomists at the turn of the century who took up the challenge of modern philosophy and science were Désiré Mercier and Réginald Garrigou-Lagrange. Both devoted their energies to restoring Thomistic philosophy and to countering their modern adversaries: Cartesian Dualism, post-Kantian Subjectivism and Fideism, and the vitalism and anti-intellectualism of Henri Bergson.

Désiré Joseph Mercier

Désiré Joseph Mercier (1851–1926) was not only a noted philosopher and an important leader of the revival of Thomism at the turn of the century; he was also a distinguished archbishop who was made a cardinal in 1907. Born in the Brabant province of Belgium, Mercier entered the Malines Seminary after secondary school in order to prepare for the priesthood. After five years at Malines, he studied at the University of Louvain. He was ordained in 1874 and was named Professor of

Philosophy at the Malines Seminary in 1877, the year he received his licentiate in theology. In 1882 a chair of Thomistic philosophy was established at Louvain, and Mercier was appointed its first incumbent. As part of Pope Leo XIII's efforts to restore Thomistic philosophy, the Institute of Philosophy for the study of Scholasticism was established at Louvain, with Mercier as its president. Under his direction the institute flourished and gained an international reputation for the study of philosophy. Mercier repudiated the superficial dismissal of modern philosophy that characterized the work of many contemporary Thomists, and his critical work on Kant was taken seriously by Kantian scholars. In 1906 Mercier's academic career was interrupted when he was appointed Archbishop of Malines; he was made a cardinal the following year. He became deeply engaged in practical pastoral matters , as well as in political and scientific activities. During World War I he gained international attention and respect for his resistance to German aggression.

Mercier's greatest contribution to a Thomism adapted to the modern situation was in the general field of epistemology, with the objective of establishing certitude regarding our natural knowledge of God. To do so it was necessary for Mercier to demonstrate the fallacies of Descartes, Kant, and all subsequent modern forms of skepticism, subjectivism, and fideism, or *doctrines* of immanence. He begins with Descartes and charges him with a failure to carry out consistently his own methodic doubt. Since, for Descartes, all *acts* of consciousness have been brought into doubt "for the same reasons it should be possible to reject its testimony when it assures me of my existence." That is, "to be logical Descartes ought to have said: I am aware that I doubt; it is possible that I exist, but I may be deceived." But, Mercier argues, whether "fictitious or real, *universal* doubt leads nowhere and without a violation of reasoning it can never be a means of leading us to certitude."

Modern philosophers had, in large measure, conceded that Kant was correct in his critique of natural theology when he argued that knowledge, i.e., science, stops at the threshold of supersensible reality. These philosophers accepted Kant's contention that only those human cognitions are scientific that are synthetic a priori judgments conditioned by our pure intuitions of space and time. Mercier regarded Kant's denial of any objective or scientific knowledge of immaterial being as the source of all modern immanentism, subjectivism, and fideism—hence the need to challenge Kant on this fundamental doctrine and to lay claim to a genuine *knowledge* beyond the realm of phenomena. Mercier took up this epistemological challenge in a series of influential publications. As we have learned, according to Kant the mind "synthesizes" unconnected sensory impressions, placing them in space and time, and through the "categories" of understanding—such as causality and substance—connects these sensory impressions which become phenomena. However, when our judgments deal with things-in-themselves, that is, with *noumena,* they lose all objective value and are devoid of the status of knowledge. Mercier argues, on the contrary, that the forms or predicates that we attribute to the subject of our judgments are not merely known by the mind, are not merely subjective, but are things-in-themselves existing in nature. He defends a modified epistemological and metaphysical realism against all forms of Kantian and Neo-Kantian Idealism.

According to Mercier's doctrine of judgment, our ideas faithfully represent concrete things in the world. "It is clear to me," he writes,

> from my own consciousness that when I experience a sensation I am the subject of an impression, that there take place within me some passive impressions. Now my sensations, as indeed all contingent beings, require a sufficient cause and, since these phenomena are passive, the cause of their existence is not to be found in any adequate manner within myself. It follows, therefore, that there must be, outside me the subject who feels, one or more real beings capable of producing sensible impressions within me.

One may object that we can have experience of the external world without the necessity of having recourse to the principle of causality. To this Mercier replies that "although we can acquire the notion of a real being without having recourse to the principle of causality . . . nevertheless it is impossible to affirm *with certainty* the existence of the external world without having recourse to the principle of causality." That is, not only do we all have spontaneously forced upon us the irresistible conviction that a world external to ourselves really exists; we also are aware that "a fact so remarkable requires a sufficient reason for its explanation. But no other sufficient reason can be assigned for that conviction but the real existence of the external world." Idealistic proposals, such as Kant's theory of the a priori forms of cognition, are not adequate as explanations, for they fail to bridge over the world as mere subjective experience, in terms of our representations of it, to its objective reality. But once we acknowledge the reality and the nature of the external world, we are carried inevitably to a reasoned analysis of the nature not only of contingent being but of its cause. At issue here between Mercier and Kant is the question of certain judgment, that is, what justifies us in asserting that a particular predicate in a proposition, say redness or rationality, agrees with the subject. According to Kant, when we make the judgment "this is a cause," our knowledge of the predicate "cause" is not derived from the object but from the mind's own application of the category of causality to the object. It is the mind that forms the judgment "this is a cause." Universal predicates, such as cause, are constituted by the mind and are not included in a sensible object, since sense experience is about particular things. On the contrary, according to Mercier, in the act of judgment we apprehend something, an object, but also a quality in that object which *is* its subject, that is, that does *exist* in the subject. Judgment is the act of perceiving the agreement of predicate with subject in our apprehension of an object. Such an act is more than the act of simple conception, since such acts of judgment give us objective evidence and certain knowledge of the world.

Modern philosophy and theology have, however, generally followed Kant and agnosticism in asserting that God cannot be an object of knowledge derived from our sensory experience of the world. Traditionalism, too, has agreed that the mind is incapable of proving the existence of God and that God can only be known by faith that is grounded upon a primal revelation. Alternatively, the new "spiritualist philosophy" of Bergson, Laberthonnière, and Le Roy asserts that God is known only through the activity of the whole person, through an experiential intuition. The post-Kantian agnostics all claim as an a priori truth that we cannot rise to a true knowledge or science of that which transcends the phenomenal or material order. But, Mercier replies,

> a very elementary introspection proves that being, and not necessarily material being, is the object of intelligence. . . . If indeed after mature reflection we find that the material world requires for its *adequate* interpretation that immaterial things also exist, we shall not be wrong in listening to what our reason informs us about those immaterial things.

A thorough reflection on the material world will disclose one indisputable fact, namely, that it is contingent and that it is not the sufficient reason or explanation of its being, cause, or intelligible order.

Against the Traditionalists Mercier argues that if they are right that the mind is incapable of divine *knowledge,* revelation alone will not be sufficient to explain how we arrive at a certain knowledge of God's existence and nature. For

> if we receive a revealed truth, that is not by an act of blind credence but only after we have satisfied ourselves about the claims that this proposition has to be received by faith; and it is only by the exercise of our reason that we can satisfy ourselves about its credibility. Yet traditionalism is based on the assertion that the reason is totally incapable.[25]

Réginald Garrigou-Lagrange

Marie-Aubin-Gontran Garrigou-Lagrange (1877–1964) was born at Auch, France, in 1877. His intellectual gifts were early recognized at the *lycée*. He first studied medicine at the University of Bordeaux but underwent a conversion in 1897 and joined the Dominican order and received the name Réginald Marie. In 1904 he was sent to study philosophy at the Sorbonne where he, like the great Thomistic philosopher Jacques Maritain (see volume two), attended the lectures of Henri Bergson. In 1907 he was appointed Professor of the History of Philosophy at Le Saulchoir. From 1909 to 1918 he taught at the Angelicum in Rome, and during the period 1918 to 1959 he occupied the chair of spiritual theology at the Angelicum. During his long career he lectured weekly on the metaphysics of Thomas Aquinas.

Unlike more venturesome Neo-Thomists such as Mercier and Maritain, Garrigou-Lagrange is conservative and is referred to rather amusingly by some as a leader of "Strict-Observance Thomism." He reached rather definite philosophical and theological views early which appear to have developed hardly at all. Nevertheless, he enjoyed controversy, and his first book, *Le Sens commun* (1909), is a thorough-going criticism of the Modernism of Édouard Le Roy, a student of Bergson (see Chapter 14). After World War II Garrigou-Lagrange became a vocal critic of "la nouvelle theologie" in France. But despite the fact that he was not a path-breaking thinker, Garrigou-Lagrange played a highly significant role as an apologist and polemicist in the cause of Neo-Thomism. He also is a good representative of conservative Neo-Thomism at the turn of the century.

Garrigou-Lagrange's extensive treatment of the proofs of the existence and nature of God are especially characteristic of Neo-Scholastic apologetics at the time of the Modernist crisis. He begins his major work on the subject by citing in detail the definitions of the First Vatican Council on the question of the ability of human reason to know God with certainty. He also cites the council statements and those set forth in the anti-Modernist oath, prescribed in the papal *motu proprio Sacrarum antistitum* (1910), that describe the errors of fideism, traditionalism, and all forms of immanentism and subjectivism. On the knowledge of God accessible to the natural light of reason, the council had decreed: "The same Holy Mother Church holds and teaches that God . . . may be known for certain by the natural light of human reason, by means of created things; and if anyone shall say that the one true God . . . cannot be certainly known by the natural light of human reason through created things; let him be anathema" (*Dei Filius,* Chap. 2). Garrigou-Lagrange then proceeds to show that *Dei Filius* was directed specifically against fideism, traditionalism, and all forms of Kantianism.

The Proofs of the Existence of God. In the *Summa Theologica* and the *Summa Contra Gentiles*

St. Thomas Aquinas had offered five proofs of the existence of God. Garrigou-Lagrange perhaps goes beyond Aquinas in the belief that the proofs are not only fully in accord with the first principles of human reason but presuppositionless, and that all other proofs can be reduced to them. In typical Thomistic fashion, he begins a posteriori with an analysis of created being. Whether it be a stone or an angel, created being can be taken as the starting point for the theistic proofs, since the demonstration of God's existence is deduced from a knowledge of effects, that is, of created being. Every *created thing,* we discover, is subject to change, is caused, is contingent, is composite or imperfect, and is directed to some end. From this the Thomistic proofs conclude that there must be a being that is not moved, not caused, that is necessary, simple, or perfect and directs all things to their proper end.

Garrigou-Lagrange begins his exposition of the proofs by offering a general proof which, in fact, he believes includes all the others, namely, that "the greater cannot proceed from the less." A prime instance is that becoming depends on being. However, this general proof is only *scientifically* established by the cumulative demonstration of the five other proofs. The first proof is that from movement or motion. We observe that things in the world, both physical and spiritual (for example, the human will), are in motion, that is, move from potency to act. But a thing cannot be moved, so the argument goes, from potency to act except by something that is already in act. Therefore, "(1) Whatever is in motion, is set in motion by another; and (2) in a series of actually and essentially subordinate movers, there is no regress to infinity. Hence we must finally arrive at a first mover which is itself not moved by a kind of motion."[26]

In his exposition of each proof, Garrigou-Lagrange seeks to address those objections offered by modern science and philosophy. We cannot here attempt to survey all of the numerous objections, nor is it necessary to give examples of Garrigou-Lagrange's rebuttal to the objections in the case of each proof; it will suffice to illustrate his mode of argument in a few instances. In the discussion of the first proof, the very adequacy of the concept of motion as movement by another is questioned by modern physics. Garrigou-Lagrange responds that these new and proper insights do not, however, touch the fundamental metaphysical distinction between potency and act. The principle objection, however, comes from the new process philosophy or philosophy of becoming, associated with Bergson and his disciples. They argue that the Thomistic idea of distinct, independent movers is based on an outmoded, mechanistic conception, on a spatial imagery that is obsolete and guilty of the fallacy of "misplaced concreteness." Édouard Le Roy had pressed this objection based on the postulate of morcellation or the mental process of dividing an organism:

> This distinction between mover and moved, between motion and its subject, and the primacy of act over potency, all proceed from the same postulate of common thought. . . . Criticism shows that this morcellation of matter is but the result of a mental process, prompted by the dictates of practical utility and discourse. . . . If the world consists of an immense continuity of unceasing transformations, it is no longer a question of a graduated and innumerable series of beings which necessarily calls for an absolute beginning. . . . *Why not simply identify being with becoming?* . . . *As things* are motion, there is no longer any need of asking whence they derive their motion.[27]

Motion does not demand an explanation; it explains everything else.

To this challenge of the new philosophy of process, Garrigou-Lagrange argues that being and becoming cannot be identified because

> *becoming* is not, like *being,* intelligible by itself. *Becoming* is a successive union of diverse elements. This union cannot be unconditional, for diversity, of itself and as such, cannot be one. Becoming is the transition from indetermination to determination, and hence presupposes a determinate cause; to deny this is to say that nothingness can be a cause of *being,* which is a denial of the principle of identity and a setting up in its place of the principle of Pantheism. . . . [But] even if the world were but one substance, *as long as there is in it such a thing as becoming,* it demands a mover *which is not subject of any becoming,* and which consequently is distinct from it.[28]

Garrigou-Lagrange perceives, correctly or not, that the new philosophy of becoming initiated by Bergson tends toward an immanental Pantheism that fails adequately to protect the transcendence, independence, and impassibility of God. As we will see in volume two, the issue of God's independence of or interdependence with the world and God's unchangeableness become major issues of debate in twentieth-century theology.

The second proof focuses on the nature of efficient causation. Nothing exists of itself or it would have to exist before itself, which is impossible. In nature we observe a certain order of efficient causes, but these causes cannot cause themselves, for before anything can be a cause of something else, it must be first in existence. If, therefore, the order of efficient causes

> are not self-existent, their existence depends upon higher causes. . . . But we cannot proceed *ad infinitum,* but must finally arrive at a primary cause, itself uncaused which has *being* from itself, which can give to, and preserve in, others, and without which nothing that actually exists could continue to exist.[29]

We are, then, led by this proof to a supreme efficient cause *whose essence is to exist* and who is the source of all *becoming.*

The third proof concentrates not on the dependence of becoming or being or an analysis of the causes of being but on the contingency of all things, the fact that things need not exist.

> We observe that some beings are contingent, that is to say, do not exist forever, but, on the contrary, are born and die. Of such a nature are the minerals which decompose or form a constituent part of fresh matter, such as plants, animals, and human beings. This we know to be a fact. From it we proceed to deduce the existence of a necessary being, or one which always existed *per se* and cannot cease to exist.[30]

That any contingent thing exists implies a necessary being.

Modern critics of this third proof argue that the demonstration does not solve the theistic problem because it fails to establish conclusively that the necessary being is distinct from the world and is infinitely perfect. It only proves that there is some thing that is necessary. Perhaps the necessary being is an aggregate of contingent beings, or a law governing such beings, or a substrate beneath all phenomena. Garrigou-Lagrange responds that the necessary being cannot be an *aggregation* of contingent beings, for an aggregation of parts, even if it were infinite in time and space, could not constitute a necessary being. "For a thing to have a semblance of reality it would be necessary to add to these parts a dominating principle, be it either the law which governs them, or the process of *becoming* through which they must pass, or the substance common to all the parts." However, the necessary being cannot be the law which unites the contingent elements, for such a law

in order to be the necessary being, would have to have its sufficient reason within itself and also contain the sufficient reason for all the phenomena that it has controlled, now controls, and will control in the future. Now a law is nothing but a constant relation between various phenomena or beings, and as every relation presupposes the extremes upon which it is based, the existence of a law presupposes the existence of the phenomena which it unites, instead of being presupposed by them. It exists only if they exist.[31]

The scientific Positivists often appealed to the law of the conservation of energy, since it is primordial and universal; and if "nothing is lost and nothing is created" as the law affirms, "then the necessary being is the material world itself, governed by this law."[32] This argument fails to recognize, however, that far from being a primordial necessity, the law of conservation of energy is itself contingent and requires an extrinsic sufficient reason or cause. Finally, the necessary being can neither be the *becoming* which forms the substratum of phenomena nor their common substance. Garrigou-Lagrange, following the great sixteenth-century Dominican philosopher Cardinal Cajetan, argues that the third proof, taken in conjunction with the two preceding proofs, establishes conclusively that the prime mover and the first cause *are essentially distinct from the world* since the world is subject to becoming which they are not. Similarly, the neces-

sary being "cannot be a *substance common* to all *beings,* for such a substance would be the subject of *becoming.*"[33] But we have observed that the process of becoming demands a cause that is not itself subject to the same becoming.

A point of clarification is perhaps needed here regarding the first three proofs. They do not, as sometimes is claimed, have to do with the possibility or impossibility of an infinite mathematical series. The order of dependence for which Garrigou-Lagrange and the Thomists are arguing is not temporal but logical and ontological. The fact of a series of contingent beings without a temporal beginning still does not make them necessary. The entire series is eternally insufficient. It requires some ontological explanation—a prime, efficient, necessary cause or being.

The fourth or "henological argument" (because it argues from the many to the one, from the composite to the simple) begins with our experience of the fact that there are beings who possess varying degrees of goodness, truth, nobility, and the like and that these degrees of perfection require that there be a being who is absolutely Good or True, and so on. Garrigou-Lagrange states the argument as follows:

When a perfection, the concept of which does not imply any imperfection, is found in various degrees in different beings, none of those which possess it imperfectly contains a sufficient explanation for it, and hence its cause must be sought in a being of a higher order, which is this very perfection. As St. Thomas remarks: More or less are predicated of different things, according as they resemble in different ways something which is the maximum.[34]

This proof is of Platonic origin, and many Thomists believe that it lacks the rigor of the other arguments. They would argue that it assumes too much, for example, that because we observe degrees of human striving and perfection, say of goodness, such a naturalistic aspiration proves a good God, as if the object necessarily corresponds to our natural desire for it which cannot be denied or frustrated. Garrigou-Lagrange gives considerable attention to this proof and considers it absolutely valid. In his view the argument is based on the same principles used in the earlier arguments, namely, that beings which possess certain qualities or perfections cannot account for such attributes by themselves but are dependent on some other being. Ultimately, such perfections must be derived from a being who possesses the perfection in its highest degree, which *is* the perfection. Therefore, for goodness and truth to exist there must be Goodness and Truth, just as there must be a Being who is *ipsum esse* if there are lesser beings.

The fifth proof is the teleological proof based on the order observed as prevailing in the world. Garrigou-Lagrange sees this proof as closely allied with the preceding "henological" proof "which concludes from the *multiplicity* of things to the existence of a *higher unity.* The fifth proof argues from the *orderly arrangement in multiplicity* to the existence of a *unity of concept* and an intelligent designer."[35] Garrigou-Lagrange states the essentials of Thomas Aquinas's argument briefly in the form of a syllogism: "A means cannot be directed to an end except by an intelligent cause. Now, we find in nature, in the things that lack intelligence, means directed to ends. Therefore, nature is the result of an intelligent cause."[36]

The modern objections to the teleological proof have been directed against both the minor premise (that "things which lack intelligence act for an end") and the major premise (that "things which lack intelligence cannot tend toward an end, unless they are directed by an intelligent being which knows the end"). Critics of the minor premise attack the claim that, for example, the bird's wings are made *for* flying. Evolutionary theorists such as Darwin would argue not that the bird has wings for the purpose of flying but that it flies because it has wings—and that apparent finality in living beings can be explained by natural causes such as natural selection. Garrigou-Lagrange responds that the denial of *intrinsic* finality in things that lack intelligence is contrary to both science and philosophical reason. He appeals to the work of the German philosopher Eduard von Hartmann (1842–1906), who defended the teleological character of nature mathematically by a calculation of probabilities. He demonstrated that "in an organic structure such as the eye the act of seeing presupposes the simultaneous presence of thirteen conditions, and each of the conditions presupposes many others. . . . According to the law of probabili-

ties, without any designing cause, there are 9,999,985 chances against 15 for the possibility of these thirteen conditions meeting so as to make seeing possible."[37]

The philosophical objection to the modern evolutionary and mechanistic denials of *intrinsic* finality is based on their appeal to both *chance* and *necessity,* neither of which, Garrigou-Lagrange argues, offers a sufficient explanation. Marvelous things do happen by chance, such as finding a treasure while digging a grave. However,

> Aristotle has proven convincingly that reason can see in chance only something which is accidental. It is the accidental cause of an effect produced without any intention, either natural or conscious, such that it could be said to have been directly intended. The chance effect is an *accidental* effect which happens so as to make it seem that the action which brought it about was meant for that purpose. One digs a grave, which is the end intended, and accidentally finds a treasure. But precisely because it is *accidental*, chance cannot be considered a cause, in the *natural* order, of each agent which produces its own effect. We cannot claim that all the effects produced in nature are accidental; *for the accidental necessarily presupposes what is essential.* One finds a treasure in digging a grave, but it is intentionally that one digs the grave, and previous to this, the treasure was intentionally buried in the ground. Chance is but the coming together of two actions which in themselves are not fortuitous, but intentional.[38]

Chance, Garrigou-Lagrange insists, leaves everything to be explained.

What of the mechanistic materialist's appeal to *necessity,* that is, the appeal only to the *efficient cause* and whatever determining elements it may itself possess? For example, that fire *must* burn or that a bird *must* fly but does not have wings *for* flying, for the *purpose* of flying. However, if the nonteleologist "seeks to explain the flight of a bird by the necessary conformation of its wings, the necessity of this conformation has still to be explained."[39] If the mechanistic nonteleologist then appeals

> to the presence of a prior efficient cause, and, in the final analysis, to a general law, such as the law of the

conservation of energy, they merely evade the question. We still ask . . . why the force operates in a certain determined manner, and why there is conservation of the same. . . . The law of the conservation of energy is not a necessary truth, a supreme law from which nature cannot escape. . . . Therefore, *necessity* is not sufficient to explain, anteriorly to the "survival of the fittest", the origin of adaptations. The necessity of physical laws is merely *hypothetical; i.e.,* it presupposes something. And precisely what does it presuppose? Finality.[40]

Garrigou-Lagrange argues that even if necessity existed throughout nature, it would still presuppose finality. The principle of finality is simply reducible to the principle of sufficient reason. The true formula of the principle of finality is given by both Aristotle and Thomas Aquinas: "Every agent necessarily acts for an end." The necessity of a final cause is an immediate necessity for every agent, *for the final cause is the raison d'être of the efficient cause.*

As noted earlier, the major premise of the fifth proof argues that the orderly arrangement of things demands *an intelligent cause.* Hume, Kant, and others have argued that order does not entail an intelligent or infinite designer. Kant insisted that, granting order, we cannot prove that it is the result of an intelligent designer, we can only resort to analogies and *say* that it is so because we know of no other cause. Garrigou-Lagrange responds that order is indeed the result of intelligent design, not only because change and necessity explain nothing, "but also because *order* presupposes that the means find their *raison d'être* in the end, and because it is the very essence of intelligence to perceive the *raison d'être,* which is its formal object."

Kant also insisted that this proof could, at best, lead to the existence of a great architect of the world, but not its creator. Garrigou-Lagrange's answer is that the fifth proof remains sufficient if it leads only to intelligence, "since the four preceding proofs have demonstrated the existence of a prime mover, of a first cause, of a necessary being, and of a first being."[41] The proofs are interdependent, and their force is embodied in the coherent combination of all of the five ways.

Conclusion

The modern Neo-Thomistic revival remained a vital intellectual force almost to the time of the Second Vatican Council in the 1960s. Despite present disfavor, several of the Neo-Thomistic thinkers made significant contributions to nineteenth- and twentieth-century thought. But it is also true that in the first half of the twentieth century the development of Thomism produced a split between the more traditional Neo-Thomists, represented by figures like Garrigou-Lagrange and, more especially, Jacques Maritain and his followers, and the movement known as Transcendental Thomism, represented by Pierre Rousselot (1878–1915) and Joseph Maréchal (1878–1944). Both movements claimed to follow the principles set forth in the epistemology and metaphysics of St. Thomas Aquinas. But the issues between them proved to be great, and the differences converged most pointedly on the issues of history and philosophical pluralism. The emerging school of Transcendental Thomism argued for the legitimacy of a plurality of philosophies congruent with diverse historical contexts. Since the Second Vatican Council theologians in the transcendental tradition, such as Karl Rahner (1904–1984) and Bernard Lonergan (1904–1984), though continuing to be informed by the thought of Thomas Aquinas, no longer can be considered as belonging to the Neo-Thomistic revival as it was conceived by Leo XIII and heralded in *Aeterni Patris* over a century ago. (On this development of Thomism, see volume two.)

Despite *Humani Generis,* issued by Pope Pius XII in 1950, there has been a growing chorus of anti-Thomist criticism within the Church. The complaint continues to be heard that Thomism is out of touch and is unable to understand and address itself relevantly to the contemporary situation because of its highly intellectualist and essentialist approach to problems. Some Catholic critics go so far as to claim that modern Thomism has given considerable impetus to contemporary atheism by upholding an outmoded Greek metaphysics and that the obsolescence of Thomism is inevitable with the shedding of Christianity's Greek-Hellenistic cultural form.

For many Catholic intellectuals Thomism no longer remains an adequate guide because it is so lacking in historical-critical methods that are essential to modern theological work. Such a complaint is made by the Jesuit biblical scholar J. L. McKenzie:

> What I find lacking in the Thomistic synthesis . . . and in speculative theology as a whole—are historical and critical methods and approach. In modern education and in the modern intellectual world these have a place in the training of the educated man which they did not have in the thirteenth century. . . . The historical and critical attitude exhibited by St. Thomas . . . does not meet the standards of modern historians and critics. . . . For this a theology . . . different from the scholastic synthesis as it is currently taught in seminaries, seems necessary.[42]

There also are those both in and outside the Church who regard Thomistic natural theology, as found in the writings of either a Garrigou-Lagrange or the more creative Jacques Maritain, to be fundamentally unacceptable, either because they believe that the Kantian critique of natural theology, especially in its more recent formulations, is compelling or that a natural knowledge of God is incompatible with a genuine Christian theism. In view of these kinds of criticism, can Thomism serve as a foundation for theology in the future? It is likely that the answer will depend on whether it can creatively integrate into its system the advances in knowledge and the experience of human beings in the twenty-first century. The genius and wisdom of St. Thomas Aquinas is a legacy of Christian thought certainly as rich as that of St. Augustine and Luther and not one to dismiss heedlessly without great loss.

NOTES

1. Robert Bellarmine, *Controversies* (1586). Cited in Dom Cuthbert Butler, *The Vatican Council 1869–1870* [1930] (London, 1962), pp. 40–41.

2. Lord Acton, *The Home and Foreign Review,* IV (April 1864). Included in *History of Freedom and Other Essays* (London, 1907), p. 489.

3. These and other statements of Veuillot, *L'Univers,* as well as those of other extreme Ultramontanists, are discussed in Butler, *Vatican Council;* Derek Holmes, *The Triumph of the Holy See* (London, 1978); and Wilfrid Ward, *William George Ward and the Catholic Revival* (London, 1893).

4. Butler, *Vatican Council,* pp. 57–58.

5. E. S. Purcell, *Life of Cardinal Manning* (London, 1896) p. 42.

6. Henry Edward Manning, *The Centenary of St. Peter and the General Council: A Pastoral Letter to the Clergy* (London, 1867), pp. 56–57.

7. H. E. Manning, *The Temporal Power of the Vicar of Christ,* 2d ed. (London, 1862), pp. 6–7.

8. H. E. Manning, *The Vatican Council and Its Definitions: A Pastoral Letter to the Clergy* (London, 1870), p. 91.

9. H. E. Manning, *The Oecumenical Council and the Infallibility of the Roman Pontiff: A Pastoral Letter to the Clergy,* pp. 147–148.

10. Charles S. Dessain and Thomas Gornall, eds., *The Letters and Diaries of John Henry Newman,* XXV (Oxford, 1973), 18–19.

11. "Janus" [Ignaz von Döllinger], *The Pope and the Council* (London, 1869), p. xxii.

12. Butler, *Vatican Council,* p. 89.

13. "Janus," *Pope and the Council,* pp. 64, 77–78.

14. Peter Richard Kenrick, *Concio in Concilio Vaticano habenda at non habita* (Naples, 1870); an English translation is in Leonard W. Bacon, ed., *An Inside View of the Vatican Council in the Speech of the Most Reverend Archbishop Kenrick of St. Louis* (New York, n.d.). My citations are from the Bacon translation of Kenrick's speech more recently included in Joseph Fitzer, *Romance and the Rock* (Minneapolis, 1989), pp. 245, 249, 262, 261.

15. Letter of March 29, 1871, to Lord Acton. Quoted extensively in James Hennesey, S. J., *The First Council of the Vatican: The American Experience* (New York, 1963), p. 321ff.

16. Joseph Neuner and Heinrich Roos, *The Teaching of the Catholic Church* (Staten Island, N.Y., 1967) no. 382, 388.

17. For a good discussion of the prerogatives and limits of the papacy's authority after Vatican I, see Patrick Granfield, *The Limits of the Papacy* (New York, 1987).

18. This is the observation of Butler, *Vatican Council*, p. 473.

19. Ibid., pp. 487–488.

20. Cited in Thomas O'Meara, *Church and Culture: German Catholic Theology, 1860–1914* (Notre Dame, 1991), pp. 33–34.

21. Pope Leo XIII, *Aeterni Patris,* Appendix I, in Jacques Maritain, *St. Thomas Aquinas* (London, 1946), p. 151.

22. Pope Pius X, *Doctoris Angelici,* Appendix II, in Maritain, op. cit., pp. 156–157.

23. Ibid., p. 159.

24. Maurice de Wulf, *An Introduction to Scholastic Philosophy* (New York, 1956), pp. 161, 163.

25. Cardinal Mercier, *A Manual of Scholastic Philosophy,* I, [1916] trans. T. L. Parker and S. A. Parker (London, 1932), I:356, 380–381, 381, 394; II: 17, 22.

26. R. Garrigou-Lagrange, O P., *God, His Existence and His Nature,* I, [1909] trans. Dom Bede Rose (St. Louis, 1934), 262.

27. Ibid., p. 280.

28. Ibid., pp. 281–282.

29. Ibid., pp. 290–291.

30. Ibid., p. 293.

31. Ibid., p. 295.

32. Ibid., p. 296.

33. Ibid., p. 299.

34. Ibid., p. 346.

35. Ibid., p. 345.

36. Ibid., p. 346.

37. Ibid., p. 351.

38. Ibid., pp. 352–353.

39. Ibid., p. 357.

40. Ibid., pp. 358–359.

41. Ibid., p. 369.

42. J. L. McKenzie, S. J., "Theology in Jesuit Education," *Thought* (Autumn 1959), pp. 353–354.

SUGGESTIONS FOR FURTHER READING

I.

Background on Modern Ultramontanism

Aubert, Roger. *The Church in a Secularized Society* (New York: Paulist Press, 1978). Part one, Chapters 1–4 offer a fine survey.

Holmes, J. Derek. *The Triumph of the Holy See: A Short History of the Papacy in the Nineteenth Century* (London: Burns and Oates, 1978). Chapters 1–4 are relevant to the developments from the French Revolution to 1870.

Jedin, Hubert, and John Dolan. *History of the Church,* VIII. This volume, entitled *The Church in the Age of Liberalism,* is edited by Roger Aubert et al. (New York: Crossroad Publishing Company, 1981). Chapters 17–22 are an excellent account of this period, written by Aubert who is one of the finest authorities, but the English translation is inferior to the Aubert volume cited above.

Steinfels, Peter. "The Failed Encounter: The Catholic Church and Liberalism in the Nineteenth Century." In *Catholicism and Liberalism,* ed. R. Bruce Douglass and David Hollenbach (New York: Cambridge University Press, 1994), pp. 19–44. Why and when Ultramontanism went antiliberal. Excellent background.

II.

The Vatican Council and Its Outcome

Butler, Cuthbert. *The Vatican Council 1869–1870* [1930] (London: Collins and Harvill Press, 1962). A slightly abridged edition of the 1930 book. A classic, sympathetic, yet quite evenhanded treatment.

"Janus" [Ignaz von Döllinger]. *The Pope and the Council* (London: Rivingtons, 1869). One of the most influential criticisms of the Ultramontanist claims and of papal infallibility by a Catholic historian.

"Quirinus" [Ignaz von Döllinger]. *Letters from Rome on the Council by Quirinus,* 2 vols. [1870] (New York: Da Capo Press, 1973). Sixty-nine letters from Döllinger commenting on the council from May 1869 to July 1870 and representing the intransigent anti-infallibilist position.

Hennesey, James, S. J. *The First Council of the Vatican: The American Experience* (New York: Herder and Herder, 1963). A fine account of the participation at the council by American bishops, many of whom opposed a definition on infallibility. Good on Archbishop Kenrick.

Manning, Henry Edward, Cardinal. *The Vatican Council and Its Definitions* (London: Longmans, Green and Co., 1870).

————. *The True Story of the Vatican Council,* 2d ed. (London: Burns and Oates, 1877).

These books represent an interpretation of the council and its decrees from the perspective of a confirmed infallibilist and leader of the majority party.

O'Gara, Margaret. *Triumph in Defeat: Infallibility, Vatican I, and the French Minority Bishops* (Washington, D.C.: Catholic University of America Press, 1988). An interesting study of the position of the French minority bishops at Vatican I and their reasons for opposing papal infallibility.

Sparrow Simpson, W. J. *Roman Catholic Opposition to Papal Infallibility* (London: John Murray, 1909). While questionable in some of its interpretations and judgments, this book gives a sense of the extent of Catholic opposition to a definition on infallibility.

III.

Later Reflections on the First Vatican Council and Its Meaning

Granfield, Patrick. *The Limits of the Papacy: Authority and Autonomy in the Church* (New York: Crossroad Publishing Co., 1987). A valuable reflection on papal authority and its limits in the perspective of Vatican I and Vatican II.

Journal of Ecumenical Studies, 8 (Fall 1971). A valuable collection of essays on papal infallibility by leading scholars.

Küng, Hans. *Infallible?: An Inquiry* (London: William Collins Sons, 1971). A controversial book by the Catholic Tübingen theologian in which he raises serious questions regarding the Church's teaching on papal infallibility.

Papal Primacy and the Universal Church, ed. Paul C. Epie and T. Austin Murphy (Minneapolis: Augsburg, 1974). A pioneering joint Lutheran and Catholic statement with accompanying articles. Also see companion volume in the series, *Teaching Authority and Infallibility in the Church* (1980).

IV.

The Neo-Thomistic Revival

Chesterton, G. K. *Saint Thomas Aquinas* (London: Hodder and Stoughton, 1956). A lively discussion of Aquinas, his philosophy, and the concerns of the Thomistic revival.

DeWulf, Maurice. *An Introduction to Scholastic Philosophy* (New York: Dover Publications, 1956). A broad introduction by a noted historian to the concerns and doctrines of both medieval and modern Scholasticism and the revival under Pope Leo XIII.

Gilson, Etienne. *The Christian Philosophy of St. Thomas Aquinas* (New York: Random House, 1956). An authoritative study by a leading twentieth-century historian.

McCool, Gerald A. *Nineteenth Century Scholasticism: The Quest for a Unitary Method* (New York: Fordham University Press, 1989). A valuable study that shows how Neo-Scholasticism emerges out of a reaction to other schools of Catholic theology in the nineteenth century.

————. *From Unity to Pluralism: The Internal Evolution of Thomism* (New York: Fordham University Press, 1992). A sequel to the book cited above that explores the development from the unitary doctrine of late nineteenth-century Thomism to the emergence of pluralism through a study of Rousselot, Maréchal, Maritain, and Gilson.

————. *The Neo-Thomists* (Milwaukee: Marquette University Press, 1994). A broader, briefer, more popular treatment.

Chapter 14
Roman Catholic Thought
at the End of the Century:
____ The New Apologetics and Modernism ____

Maurice Blondel

INTRODUCTION

In Chapter 6 we traced the typical forms of Catholic apologetic among the Traditionalists, especially in de Maistre and Lamennais, and concluded with an account of the Fideism and moderate Traditionalism of Louis Bautain. For all their differences, these writers were influenced by Romanticism and were united in their attack on the rationalism and individualism of the Enlightenment. Chateaubriand initiated a new apologetic that looked to the beauty and to the cultural institutions of the past that were, he argued, the achievement of the Catholic genius. The Traditionalists turned away from abstract argument and appealed, rather, to the "givenness" of a

primal divine revelation, passed on over the centuries in the Catholic Church, and to its fittingness to meet the needs of a society threatened by autonomous reason and a divisive polity.

In Germany and in England, we observed rather different apologetic strategies, for example, in the work of the Tübingen theologians and in J. H. Newman. Again, however, they were united in their repudiation of rationalism and the traditional demonstrations of the existence of God and the proofs of revelation. They also shared a common commitment to a new philosophy of faith and to a new conception of the relationship of reason and the will, as it is most fully developed by Bautain and Newman. In the latter decades of the century, a question was incessantly raised regarding this new apologetic: Can such a philosophy of faith avoid falling into voluntaristic and pragmatic interpretations of Christian faith? That is, did these new philosophies of faith not only reject the excessive claims of an autonomous rationalism but also deny that human reason is capable of knowing any divine truth with intellectual certitude? Bautain, of course, was judged by his ecclesiastical superiors to have stepped over the line into fideism and voluntarism, and Newman's *Grammar of Assent* was similarly suspect in the eyes of many Roman theologians.

In this chapter we will explore two important movements of Catholic thought roughly between 1880 and 1910, both having their origins in France, but also moving beyond its borders into other parts of Europe. The first movement is philosophical and is concerned primarily with the role of the will and action in the attainment of religious knowledge and certitude. It has been called the "philosophy of action" in reference to the major work of its most prominent representative, Maurice Blondel. The second movement had more to do initially with the effort to bring Catholic scholarship up to date with regard to developments in biblical studies and the historical study of Catholic tradition, investigations that were flourishing in Protestant centers of learning. Since both movements ran afoul of the Thomistic revival, they both are comprised under the name "Modernism." The name and the defining characteristics of Catholic Modernism actually were the contrivance of its ecclesiastical opponents. The so-called movement included an interesting array of Catholic scholars and writers whose interests varied considerably but who were joined together by their common commitment to bring the Catholic Church into serious dialogue with the intellectual and social currents at the turn of the century. While only some of the leaders of Modernism were professional philosophers, the major figures—Alfred Loisy, Blondel, Lucien Laberthonnière, Friedrich von Hügel, Édouard Le Roy, and George Tyrrell—all engaged in religious apologetic endeavors, and most of these proved to be highly provocative and, finally, anathema to the authorities.

Before we discuss these two movements, a brief sketch of the intellectual context will give us a better sense of the philosophical movements in France

that preceded 1880 and that were found to be highly congenial, both intellectually and spiritually, to thinkers such as Tyrrell and Le Roy. Since the days of the French Enlightenment, the period of Helvetius and Condorcet, there were French thinkers who sought to counter the behaviorist and materialist doctrines of some of these influential *philosophes*. They did so by proposing one or another form of "spiritualist" philosophy, that is, philosophies that were devoted to a defense of the freedom of the will and the unique creative activity of the human spirit. These philosophies were to insist that the human will and action are as basic as, if not more basic than, reason and thought in our understanding of human consciousness and knowledge.

Among the earliest of these philosophers is François-Pierre Maine de Biran (1766–1824), who attacked the prevailing materialist psychologies in France. While physical science advances from facts to general causes, Maine de Biran argued that the study of psychology must begin with the distinctive internal experience of human effort. Apart from this fundamental fact of consciousness, such activities as perception, memory, habit, and judgment are inexplicable. Descartes, therefore, was wrong in asserting, "I think, therefore I am" (*Cogito ergo sum*). He should have said, "I will, therefore I am" (*Volo, ergo sum*). It is not thought alone but the "whole person" who is active in thought—volition, effort, will—the total free and striving personality. And the implication of such a fact of human consciousness is a *personalist philosophy* that insists on the reality of "spirit," that is, on free will and deliberative action that involves a propensity, indeed, an exigency or need, for religion. According to Maine de Biran, not only materialism but Spinozistic Pantheism and the rationalists' proofs of the existence of God all are incompatible with such a spiritual religion. For they all either deny the reality of the free personality or, in the latter case, make God into an external object demonstrated by discursive reason. In such philosophies freedom and faith, the very heart of religion, are simply dead.

Initially, Maine de Biran rejected the idea that belief in God was required to live the moral life, where values and ends could be achieved by human effort and action. But later he became more certain that human reason itself was powerless to fire the will and action, and he looked to a third level of reality, to divine grace and the need for a self-abandonment and "absorption in God." Maine de Biran is recognized as the founder of nineteenth-century French "spiritualist" philosophy, a tradition that would continue in the work of Ravaisson, Boutroux, and Bergson and would profoundly influence the Christian "philosophy of action" that came to prominence at the end of the century.

Jean Ravaisson (1813–1900) carried forward the tradition of Maine de Biran. He briefly taught philosophy but was a man of wide interests in education, the arts, and classical antiquity. In 1870 he was appointed Curator of Antiquities at the Louvre in Paris. In his most influential work, *De l'habitude*, he argued that our habitual activity reflects the reversion of our free and spontaneous activity back to the sphere of the mechanical and the routine. Nevertheless, this habitual and instinctive behavior in turn provides the basis for new creative and purposeful human action. According to Ravaisson, the stability of habit and instinct correspond to the world of space and mechanism. On the other hand, freedom and creativity correspond to the sphere of time, freedom, and change. "Thus," he writes, "habit gives us the living demonstration of this truth, that mechanism is not self-sufficient: it would be only, so to speak, the fossilized residue of a spiritual activity." Here we note a theme that will be developed with great sophistication by Henri Bergson, especially in *The Two Sources of Morality and Religion* (1932). Like Bergson, Ravaisson was a powerful critic of all forms of scientific reductionism, for example, the efforts to explain the mind in physico-chemical terms. Rather, he argued that the lower must be explained by the higher. The spiritual life, the life of the human mind or soul, is this higher life and is characterized by the will, freedom, and purpose.

The final representative of the "spiritualist" philosophy that we will mention is Emile Boutroux (1845–1921), a teacher of Maurice Blondel when Boutroux was a lecturer at the École Normale in Paris from 1877 to 1886. He then moved to the Sorbonne, where he occupied a chair of philosophy. Boutroux's work centered on the philosophy of science and its relation to religion, beginning with his thesis on *The Contingency of the Laws of Nature*

(1874). There he argued that all natural laws are approximations and, as we move sequentially from the laws of physics to the sciences of biology, psychology, and sociology, it is clear that mechanistic-deterministic reductive explanations are neither exhaustive nor wholly adequate.

Boutroux argues that the whole of nature reveals what he calls a "a degree of contingency," a fact that mechanistic laws leave out of account. And as we move to those higher levels of life and consciousness, this irreducibly contingent factor becomes more apparent and significant. Human consciousness, which involves reason, is inherently holistic in its active engagement with the world and in its account of life, including judgments of meaning and value. While science does not presuppose such metaphysical needs, it does assume the creative and systematic activities of the mind that are a portent of these spiritual exigencies, for the life of the mind also involves such creative and symbolic reflections in the realms of art, morality, and religion.

THE NEW APOLOGETICS: CHRISTIAN PHILOSOPHIES OF ACTION

The French "spiritualist" philosophies that we have reviewed were not alone in criticizing the materialism and scientific positivism of the mid-century. After 1880 a widespread reaction set in against these perceived threats to human freedom and to spiritual values. Nietzsche, as we will see, mocks pretentious "pure thought" and argues for the primacy of the will. In England the psychologist and philosopher James Ward (1843–1925) spent his career demonstrating the limits of scientific positivism and the fact that psychology reveals the fundamental role of the will and practical action in all human experience and knowledge. The American psychologist-philosopher William James, a founder of Pragmatism, was similarly engaged in showing the limits of abstract thought and the crucial role of the will, action, and faith in human life. We will return to James in our account of early twentieth-century thought in volume two. In France the most influential criticism of all forms of scientific reductionism was the "vitalist" philosophy of Henri Bergson and the significance it placed on the unceasing, creative, and vital impetus (*élan vital*) in all life. Bergson was contemporary with the thinkers with whom we are especially concerned here, three figures who not only best represent the "philosophy of action" but devoted their energies to applying this philosophy in the cause of Christian apologetics.

Léon Ollé-Laprune

From the time of Louis Bautain in the 1830s, there continued a line of Catholic scholars in France who remained committed to his teaching. While they balanced the roles of reason and faith in a more traditional manner than Bautain, they too were sharp critics of rationalism. They not only denied discursive reason's capacity to prove the existence of God but insisted that such a religious rationalism led logically to one or another form of Pantheism. Among these writers were the Parisian professor, then bishop, H. L. Maret and Alphonse Gratry, Bautain's pupil. We briefly met both of these priests in their roles as active opponents of papal infallibility in the period just before 1870. Both men rejected theological rationalism, especially the idea that demonstrations of God's existence were possible independent of the moral preparation of the individual and the activity of faith. Gratry insisted that faith and reason so penetrate one another that, while they can be distinguished, they cannot be divided. Among Gratry's closest followers was the devout Catholic layman Léon Ollé-Laprune (1839–1898).

Ollé-Laprune studied at the École Normale Supérieure in Paris, taught philosophy in several *lycées,* and then was given a permanent post at the École Normale in 1870. He was influenced by Pascal and by Newman's *Grammar of Assent,* as well as by Ravaisson and Gratry. Thus his conviction that the will and action are integrally bound up with our thinking and knowing had a long pedigree. Knowledge and the discovery of truth imply attention, and attention is a voluntary action. But Ollé-Laprune, like Blondel, wished to avoid charges of both voluntarism and pragmatism. Against both tendencies he insists that truth is independent of our will. The will, nevertheless, helps us to recognize and receive it, but the will does not create truth.

Ollé-Laprune distinguishes assent, which is involuntary, and consent, which is voluntary. One may, for example, give an intellectual assent to a proof of God's existence, but true belief involves the act of consent which is an unconditional, *personal* certitude that requires the total engagement of the self. Such certitude includes intellectual judgment, which is not a free act, *and* the free act of the will. The will also may be called upon to intervene to overcome some hesitation, but such an intervention of the will is not simply due to a desire to believe. Rather, it is due to the fact that the hesitation to consent is deemed unreasonable. This philosophy of the will and action is worked out fully in Ollé-Laprune's most important work, *De la certitude morale* (1880).

According to Ollé-Laprune, in the sphere of the moral and spiritual life, will and knowledge are inseparable, since the truth cannot simply be assented to; it must be personally embraced, loved, and acted on:

> Moral truth is not given merely to look at; it is not an object purely of contemplation. Essentially practical, it requires of us a practical assent, and if we fall into the habit of refusing this the liveliness of our first impressions diminishes. As the measure of the responses to the interior call becomes weaker and less satisfactory, so the appeal itself becomes less satisfactory, so the appeal itself becomes less forceful. . . . There is a light which shines in the mind, but one has to make use of it. Otherwise, it becomes feeble and seems to go out.[1]

In passages that remind one of the later writings of William James, Ollé-Laprune argues that our reason often leaves us helpless to consent. Furthermore, alternative choices often are truly live but also ambiguous, which makes the personal engagement of the will and faith necessary in such instances. Neither knowledge nor certitude will be forthcoming without action. And so not only the will but faith as trust (*fiducia*) must play its role in the life of moral reason:

> Trust is of the nature of love. It presupposes two terms between which an accord freely comes about. The object works through its appeal, and the power of

its attraction seems irresistible. But if, on the other side, the will is inactive, nothing is achieved. Such is the character of all things *moral*.[2]

Ollé-Laprune's *De la certitude morale* was a passionate and compelling religious apologetic, but it was not rigorous philosophy. He had, however, considerable influence on Maurice Blondel, who was his student at the École Normale Supérieure. Blondel wrote that it was Ollé-Laprune who taught him that "the viewpoint of the mind is always interdependent with the life of the person." At a time when scientific positivism was dominant in the schools, Ollé-Laprune "brought to light the unnoticed essential."[3] It was left to Blondel, however, to develop this essential insight with more philosophical rigor in his work, *L'Action*.

Maurice Blondel

Maurice Blondel (1861–1949), the chief representative of the "philosophy of action," was born in Dijon and attended the *lycée* there before entering the École Normale Supérieure in 1881. He remained there for five years and was assisted by Ollé-Laprune and Emile Boutroux. After passing his qualifying examinations, he taught at several *lycées*. He then retreated to his family country house near Dijon where, in solitude for two years, he worked on seven drafts of his thesis, *L'Action,* which was submitted to the Sorbonne and published in 1893. The subject was thought unsuitable by many philosophical colleagues in Paris, and only through the efforts of Boutroux were they won over. Even after the thesis was published, Blondel was refused teaching posts because it was thought that his religious conclusions compromised a necessary philosophical impartiality. However, again through Boutroux's efforts, Blondel was appointed to a post at the University of Lille in 1895, and, in 1896, he became Professor of Philosophy at the University of Aix-en-Provence, where he taught until 1927.

Blondel's philosophical work is often divided into three periods. The first, ending as early as 1896, is for our purposes his most creative. It includes the crucial work, *L'Action,* and the important *Letter on Apologetics* (1896) which is related to it. With the essay "History and Dogma" (1904), these works

constitute Blondel's contribution to a new Christian apologetics at the turn of the century. They also are the writings that engulfed Blondel in disputes with several of the leading Catholic Modernist historical-critical scholars and in attacks by both Scholastic theologians and the ecclesial authorities. Here we will focus on these critical early writings.

Blondel described himself as a Christian apologist and was convinced of the need for an authentic Christian philosophy. What he meant by "authentic" was quite opposed to the then-conventional notions of a Christian philosophy—namely, Aristotelian scholastic philosophy as the handmaiden of theology, used to prove certain theological doctrines such as the existence and nature of God. For Blondel a Christian *philosophy* will exhibit both the limitations of philosophy itself and the lack of human self-sufficiency. Furthermore, it will reveal that human beings naturally aspire to that which transcends nature, that they possess an exigency for the supernatural. Moreover, such a philosophy will be entirely autonomous and will be modern, not backward-looking. And this will require that it be a philosophy that pursues the *method of immanence*.

L'Action. What the method of immanence entails is a phenomenology of human consciousness and experience and the drawing out of its spiritual implications. In the *Letter on Apologetics* Blondel describes why such a method is now needed:

> The conflict of modern thought, with a jealous susceptibility, considers the notion of *immanence* as the very condition of philosophizing; that is to say, if among current ideas there is one which it regards as marking a definitive advance, it is the idea, which is at bottom perfectly true, that nothing can enter into a man's mind which does not come out of him and correspond in some way to a need for development.[4]

For Blondel such a method of immanence demands what he calls a "philosophy of action." The term has been misunderstood. By "action," Blondel does not mean simply the exercise of the "will" that either precedes or accompanies thought. For him thought itself is a form of activity. Action is vital, conscious life itself. "There is," he writes, "nothing in the properly subjective life that is not as an individual initiative and as a unique case . . .; nothing that is not an act."[5] The error of philosophy has been to confine itself to ideas and abstract theories, not only to distinguish but actually to separate and isolate thought, instinct, the will, and faith. Blondel wants to find the point where all of these converge. And "action" is the term that Blondel adopts to speak of this primal source of spiritual activity which he intends to explore.

What we discover as distinct about our spiritual activity is an exigency, an aspiration to self-fulfillment, the reaching out to achieve goals. But what is also evident is that this primal action always ends in failure. Blondel writes:

> For me to will myself fully, I have to will more than I have yet been able to find. As I come up against the supreme necessity of the will, therefore, I have to determine what I will so that I may be able, in all fullness, *to will to will*. Yes, I have to will myself; but it is impossible for me to reach myself directly; from myself to myself, there is an abyss that nothing yet has been able to fill.[6]

Our basic, latent, actuating human will (*la volonté voulante*) constitutes our life in its continuous striving to fulfill itself through the manifest or actuated will (*la volonté voulue*). But these latter distinct acts of will are never satisfied. Some persons will seek to meet this existential fact by a pessimistic negation, that is, to will nothing, as with the philosopher Schopenhauer. But to will nothing is itself an act of will, an intentional refusal of life. The same is true of the skeptic or the dilettante who seeks satisfaction in the moment. The latter exhibits a willful commitment, if only to the self at the moment. Other persons seek to satisfy the exigency of their basic will to life, which of course is never satisfied by their manifest will, by seeking the infinite itself in some finite object or cause, in what Blondel calls "superstition":

> Strange condition this! What man cannot grasp, express, or produce, is precisely what he projects outside of himself to make it the object of a cult, as if in his inability to touch it within himself, he hoped to reach it better by placing it in the infinite. . . . What he sets infinitely above himself is precisely what he pre-

tends to dominate, monopolize, absorb. . . . Thus we want to realize outside what escapes us inside, with the secret aim of somehow imprisoning this infinite in the finite of a real object . . . and of finally having, in a perfect action, the coveted conclusion, security and repose.[7]

It is the yearning that lies in the gap between our potentials and our strivings and our illimitable reach and achievement that opens the way to genuine transcendence or the supernatural as the goal of the will. The transcendent, we discover, is in but not of us. It is more than we can capture or conceptualize or objectify. This presents us with an option, a choice: whether some merely finite end is to become for us "the one thing needful," or whether we, by a deliberate act of "mortification" and self-surrender, give our will over to the transcendent, to God. Blondel believes that our exigence for the transcendent makes it "impossible not to recognize the insufficiency of the whole natural order and not to feel an ulterior need; it is impossible to find within oneself something to satisfy this religious need. *It is necessary;* and *it is impracticable.* Those are, in brutal form, the conclusions of the determinism of human action."[8] So it is that philosophy can point to the need for the transcendent, or God, as a live hypothesis, but it cannot compel belief. That demands an existential choice, a personal act of self-surrender. Only in practice, only in living action, in "mortification," will knowledge of God be forthcoming.

Blondel does not claim that philosophy can bring *positive knowledge* of the transcendent or supernatural. The philosophy of action reveals only our human need of the transcendent, of a Will that we cannot create and that is not our own. The method of immanence can only point to this "undetermined supernatural." As a Christian, Blondel believes that the positive reality of the supernatural is given only in an historical revelation, but that such a revelation lies beyond the province of philosophy itself and cannot be proven to be true. Having said that, it must also be recognized that even the revealed knowledge of God would not be a possibility for human beings if there were not the immanent exigency and striving for the transcendent and eternal in the human soul itself.

Blondel believed that he had shown that an exploration of human action leads us beyond the natural order of things and that philosphy no longer can ignore the supernatural; to do so is contrary to the openness of the philosophical quest. Blondel, therefore, sought to provide a religious apologetic that adhered to the modern demand to follow the method of immanence and, at the same time, to the truth of Catholic supernaturalism. His hopes were soon dashed. He was attacked in the *Revue thomiste* in 1896, charged with supporting a Neo-Kantian subjectivism. Other theological criticism would follow. He was censured for supporting a *doctrine* of immanence (which his critics erroneously equated with Blondel's explicit *method* of immanence), fideism, voluntarism, and anti-intellectualism. Blondel's *Letter on Apologetics* was sent to the Holy Office in Rome, but no disciplinary action was taken against him. Unlike some of his Modernist colleagues and friends, Blondel never was officially condemned. Later Popes, in fact, were to commend his work.

Blondel's unwelcome immersion in controversy was not, however, only due to the attacks of the conservative theologians. His criticism of Alfred Loisy and others in *Histoire et Dogma* (1904) brought him into a dispute on matters of historical criticism and its relation to dogma, a field in which he was not fully comfortable. He thus found himself opposed by the Neo-Thomists on one side and by some of the Modernists on the other. As a result, he determined not to publish further on the subject of religion, and his resolve lasted for almost three decades. Yet Blondel was to come into his own again in the 1930s in a burst of creative activity. In these pre–World War II years, his early apologetic works became, once again, the subject of great interest among some French Jesuits. It has been shown, for example, that Blondel did, in fact, have an influence on the rethinking of Thomistic philosophy in the early decades of the twentieth century by men such as Pierre Rousselot and Joseph Maréchal. And the French theologian Yves Congar, an advisor at the Second Vatican Council, judged that the theological style represented at the council was that set out by Blondel early in the century. Finally, his philosophy also had an influence on the post-war French Existentialist philosophers, particularly Gabriel Marcel and Maurice Merleau-Ponty.

Lucien Laberthonnière

Our third representative of the "new apologetic" was a priest who in 1886 became a member of the Oratorians, the order of Alphonse Gratry and John Henry Newman. Lucien Laberthonnière (1860–1932) taught philosophy at the Oratorian College of Juilly, near Paris. In 1887 he was appointed the director of a school in Paris, only to return to Juilly as rector of the college. However, the French government's anticlerical legislation of 1902, which prohibited religious congregations from engaging in their traditional educational roles without state authorization, caused Laberthonnière to leave Juilly and return to Paris, where he directed his energies to study and writing. His two most important books soon appeared: *Essays in Religious Philosophy* (1903) and *Christian Realism and Greek Idealism* (1904). In 1905 he assumed the editorship of the influential *Annales de Philosophie Chrétienne,* at the height of its involvement in the Modernist crisis. The next year, Laberthonnière's two principal works were put on the Index of prohibited books. And in 1913 the *Annales* and two other books of his were also consigned to the Index, and he was forbidden by the ecclesiastical authorities to publish anything further. Unlike Blondel, Laberthonnière was a courageous combatant, but he submitted to the authority's ban. He said that he stood for resistance and not revolt since the latter, expressing a desire to dominate, was but another form of the authoritarianism that he opposed. He wrote to Loisy that "silent, persevering, mortified work will do more than anything else."[9] Laberthonnière continued to write in the hope that the ban would be lifted; and, if not, for posthumous publication. He also composed works that were published by others, including, ironically, a pastoral letter for the bishop of Nice in 1915 which, after its publication, received the assent of sixty French bishops. After his death, many of Laberthonnière's manuscripts were published by a friend, and several also found their way onto the Index.

Laberthonnière stood in the philosophical line that proceeds from St. Augustine through Pascal, Maine de Biran, Bautain, and Blondel. And among the more immediate influences on him were Boutroux, Newman, and Blondel. Though he was a close disciple and friend of Blondel in the early years, their relations later cooled when Laberthonnière felt that Blondel was conceding too much to the Neo-Thomists in light of their criticisms of Blondel's work. While philosophically united with Blondel, Laberthonnière was an independent thinker and many of his ideas were developed before the appearance of *L'Action*. He was also far more persistent and uncompromising in his critique of Neo-Thomism, some would say to the point of fanaticism.

Laberthonnière's "personalist" philosophy echoes many of the themes that we have encountered in Ollé-Laprune and Blondel. More insistently than either, he sees Christian philosophy as itself an authentic option as it is expressed in its Augustinian form, freed of the abstractions of Aristotle or Descartes. He refers to his philosophy as *Le dogmatisme moral*. By dogmatism he means belief as a living, moral reality, as an existential affirmation of being, in contrast to belief as assent to abstract propositions. Every person begins with some prepossession, that is, with some moral motivation or animating principle which is then tested in experience and action. "We do not," he writes, "set out from knowledge so that faith may follow. We believe as we know and we know as we believe. The outcome is a complete transformation of the soul."[10] Philosophy, for Laberthonnière, is essentially *moral,* in that it begins with the problem of the self. Philosophy is not an abstract inquiry; it has to do with the meaning of life. And every metaphysics implies a way of life and every life assumes a metaphysics. Being, for Laberthonnière, as with the twentieth-century Existentialists, concerns existence, what it means to be, not as a person already made, but as a person having to fashion a life through choice and action. Abstract ideas are dead until they are taken up into lived experience. Here Newman's distinction between a merely notional and a real, personal assent comes into play.

This does not mean that we create ourselves by some Promethean effort. To know being as it is *outside* the self, one must begin by *knowing it in oneself.* For example, "to suppose that we can will *not* to be is no whit less to submit to being. However, what we are depends on us, because it is for us to choose the end that gives meaning to our existence . . . [and]

what we are comes from what we cleave to, from what we love." This, Laberthonnière reminds us, is what St. Augustine teaches in his *Confessions,* for in that book "one sees how knowledge transforms itself and discovers being, according as the will is purified by disengagements from the love of vain appearances."[11]

Laberthonnière's writings are a sustained attack on abstraction and on the separation of reason and faith, of nature and the supernatural. In an often-cited phrase, he insists that faith is "to be seen as a union of two loves, rather than as a combination of two ideas. It is not an abstract conclusion but a vital action."[12] If we acknowledge that there are two orders, the natural and the supernatural, they nevertheless interpenetrate one another and do not represent separate realities in actual life. God comes to a person from within that person's being for, as St. Augustine insists, God is closer to us than we are to ourselves. Religious belief is, then, entirely different from the act of understanding the relationship between abstract ideas and joining them into some logical connection. It is always a personal act. To affirm this is not to deny that God is the prevenient motive for faith but, rather, only to say that faith manifests itself in the interior life of the person.

In an important essay on Pascal, Laberthonnière criticizes the theological juxtaposition of natural reason and supernatural revelation, as if the latter were some kind of appendage. Unless there is something of the supernatural already within us, the revealed truth will be merely a heteronomous, foreign object without meaning, not capable of being seen as a response to our real existential need, and therefore not a vital truth for us. Something in us must correspond with any extrinsic revelation. Otherwise, "religion would thus be nothing more than a *superstition* . . . foreign to moral life; and the God of religion would have for us no other character than that of a *power* commanding us from on high, arbitrarily as slaves are commanded. It would therefore become truly something *heteronomous,* that is to say, a slavery."[13] The dualism understood by Pascal is that of the method of immanence, a dualism of the divided self that must, by grace, be freed from egocentrism and undergo a moral conversion, a change of heart. True self-affirmation is to rest one's will in the will of God; it is at once our affirmation without ceasing to be God's.

Laberthonnière's apologetic of immanence is, it should be clear, a resolute attack on all forms of radical dualism—of reason and faith, of nature and supernature, of God and the human soul. To separate them is to commit the sin of *extrinsicism,* that is, of seeing God, revelation, faith, and grace as something external and imposed from outside. And he associates this error with the theology of the Neo-Thomists and their dependence on Aristotle. Laberthonnière's attack on what he regards as this fatal turn of Christian theology is brought out most thoroughly in his second important collection of essays, *Christian Realism and Greek Idealism.* We need comment only briefly on the theme of the book; it reveals, however, why Laberthonnière's dogged attack on Thomism, which was held in almost exclusive favor in Rome, understandably was a leading factor in his condemnation as a Modernist, since other Modernists, too, were dismissive of Scholastic "medievalism."

Under the tag of "idealism" Laberthonnière lumps the entire tradition of Greek intellectualism, especially Aristotelianism, which he finds abstract, speculative, and dualistic. His attack on "idealism" has some interesting parallels with Ritschl. Idealism represents the separation of intellect and will, and it conceives of faith as an intellectual assent to propositions, rather than as a lived experience. For Aristotle God is the unmoved-Mover, self-sufficient, and the object of scientific proof, that is, a truth imposed on the intellect from without. Laberthonnière believed that the Thomistic proofs of the existence of God were illusory, since such a philosophy cannot account for the obvious fact that such "proofs" generally fail to gain assent to faith in the living God of Christianity. Thomism simply superimposes Christianity onto a foreign Greek metaphysics that is autonomous and wholly independent of Christianity. For Laberthonnière being a Christian is not the adding of some supernatural facts onto the substructure of natural facts. Christianity means seeing all of reality concretely and as reflecting the penetration of the supernatural in the natural. Christianity teaches that God is the supreme personal reality, living and acting presently in the human consciousness, and that faith is a living possession of truth experienced from within the self. The great evil of Thomistic theology is the introduction of a pagan conception of God and the world into Christianity itself.

In reply to Laberthonnière, the Thomistic theologians sought to show that his characterization of St. Thomas Aquinas and Thomistic philosophy was a caricature. Technically, they appear to be correct, but it can also be argued that Laberthonnière was more farsighted in recognizing that it could no longer be assumed that classical metaphysics and Christianity were compatible or that it was the appropriate vehicle for a Christian apologetic in an era responsive to historicism, evolutionary thought, and personalist philosophies. Laberthonnière clearly was a philosophical Modernist, although far from holding the crude "immanentism," "pragmatism," and "naturalism" denounced in the Vatican condemnations. Laberthonnière was not, however, a biblical critic or historian. While he accepted modern biblical criticism and thought that it could humanize biblical revelation, he also was convinced that such criticism would not touch the doctrinal truths of the New Testament since, for him, they were confirmed in experience. He was, in other words, as innocent as Blondel of the deeper issues involved in matters of historical fact and interpretation, issues that had exercised the German theologians since early in the century. These questions soon engaged the Catholic Modernists and their opponents, and they were launched with the appearance of the "biblical question" and the work of Alfred Loisy.

ROMAN CATHOLIC MODERNISM

Like the word "liberalism," the terms "Modernism" and "Modernist" have been used in a great variety of ways in the past century. Frequently "Modernist" is used simply to designate any religious idea or movement that is progressive or unorthodox. The word often is used as a synonym for Protestant Liberalism, particularly Ritschlian Liberalism, while conservatives and fundamentalists often use the word as a term of abuse for all of those who disagree with them. However, in its stricter and more historical sense, the term "Modernism" refers to a movement so designated by the Roman Catholic Church and which began around 1890 and lasted for a few years after its condemnation in the papal encyclical *Pascendi Gregis* in 1907.

To refer to Catholic Modernism as a *movement* also requires some clarification. *Pascendi Gregis* gives the impression that there was a highly organized school of thinkers with a clear intellectual platform who cleverly sought to undermine the traditional teachings of the Church from within. Actually, Catholic Modernism was not a single movement but a general tendency among quite independent individuals who sought, in the words of Alfred Loisy, "to adapt the Catholic religion to the intellectual, moral and social needs of the present time." What drew the Modernists together, as happened in some cases, was a common concern to adapt the teaching of the Church to the modern age.

It is also difficult to trace the intellectual precursors of Modernism. The assumption that the Modernists stood in a discernible line of intellectual descent is not supported by the evidence. It has been said that they were dependent on J. A. Möhler and the Tübingen School, but this has been denied by the Modernists themselves. Newman has sometimes been called "the father of Modernism," but this claim contains only a modicum of truth. In most respects Newman was a conservative, especially in his defense of ecclesiastical authority. The views of Loisy and George Tyrrell would have shocked him. Nevertheless, Newman's struggle with the problem of history and dogma and his subsequent theory, as worked out in *An Essay on the Development of Christian Doctrine* (1846), was congenial to the Modernists. And it is easy to see how Loisy and Tyrrell, both of whom studied Newman's work, could interpret and develop his thought along lines that Newman never intended. In any case, Newman's *Essay* and *Grammar of Assent* were helpful to some of the Modernists and, because of Newman's high position in the Church, were also useful. Certainly, however, the most significant influence on Loisy and Tyrrell was exposure to the new historical criticism of the Bible and tradition.

The Modernist Movement began in France where it also had its greatest impact and largest following. Its beginnings can properly be associated with the Abbé Louis Duchêsne (1843–1922), for

Duchêsne was the first important Catholic scholar in France at the end of the nineteenth century to be censured for his historical-critical studies. It was he who, perhaps more than anyone else, influenced Alfred Loisy. Duchêsne had been Professor of Church History at the Catholic University of Paris since 1877. He was noted for his bold application of scientific principles to the study of ecclesiastical history and gained a wide following among the younger scholars. As a result of his criticisms, Duchêsne was suspended from the Institut Catholique for a time and was named Director of the École Française in Rome in 1897. However, from as early as 1890 Duchêsne apparently resolved that the full acceptance by the Church of the new historiography was not possible and so removed himself from any position of leadership among the Modernists. His position was soon filled by Loisy.

Alfred Loisy

Alfred Loisy (1857–1940), referred to by a noted Catholic scholar as "one of the most dangerous adversaries whom the Church has ever encountered,"[14] was a Catholic priest until his excommunication in 1908. He is known as the intellectual leader of the Modernist Movement and as one of

Alfred Loisy

the finest biblical scholars of his generation. His religious vocation began when he entered the seminary at Chalons in 1874. There he distinguished himself by not only his intellectual brilliance but his exemplary piety and was sent by his bishop to complete his training in Paris where he came under the influence of Duchêsne. Due to ill health, Loisy was forced to leave Paris but was ordained priest in 1879 and briefly served as a parish priest.

Largely because of Duchêsne's presence there, Loisy returned to the Institut Catholique in 1881 and soon after was appointed to the faculty of theology as a lecturer in Hebrew. About this same time Loisy began to attend the lectures of Ernst Renan at the Collège de France. Renan, best known for his rationalistic *Vie de Jésus,* was now in his old age but at the height of his renown. Loisy's devotion to critical scholarship flowered under Renan's tutelage, although Loisy claimed to reject the great man's rationalistic conclusions. In his *Mémoires* Loisy writes: "I instructed myself at his school in the hope of proving to him that all that was true in his science was compatible with Catholicism sanely understood."[15] There is no doubt that in those early years Loisy's resolve was to serve the Church by establishing a sounder apologetic on a solid, scientific—that is, historical-critical—base.

In 1890 Loisy defended a thesis at the Institut Catholique on the Canon of the Old Testament. Although the thesis passed, it clearly opposed traditional teaching on the inspiration of Scripture. This victory sparked a decade of fearless critical work on the Bible marked by a series of controversies. The history of the Canon of the Old Testament was followed by one on the New Testament (1891), and the following year Loisy tackled the early chapters of Genesis, raising questions concerning their historicity. As a result, students from the Seminary of Saint-Sulpice were forbidden to attend Loisy's lectures, which caused a sensation in the Catholic intellectual world.

In 1893 Mgr. d'Hulst, Rector of the Institut Catholique, published an article on *La question biblique,* whose veiled purpose was a defense of the progressive study of the Bible and of his professor, the suspect Loisy. The result could not have been further from the intention. The article provoked a heated controversy which ended in Loisy's dismissal from his professorship and the issuance of

the encyclical *Providentissimus Deus* by Leo XIII. The encyclical, addressed the question of biblical study, counseled against the danger of rationalism in biblical interpretation and condemned those who set aside the traditional conception of divine inspiration.

Removed from his academic post, Loisy was appointed chaplain to a girl's school at Neuilly. He submitted to the encyclical but, with less rigorous demands upon him, was able to continue his biblical studies in earnest. His catechetical duties also broadened his theological interests and made him more conscious of the apologetic task. It was during his five years at Neuilly that the groundwork was laid for his most publicized book, *L'Évangile et l'Église* (*The Gospel and the Church*). His position by this time was outside Catholic orthodoxy, although his own sense of devotion to the service of the Church remained genuine. He was sincerely committed to bringing about a union of Catholicism and modern knowledge and was still confident it could be done.

After a series of articles on the religion of Israel were condemned by Cardinal Richard in late 1900, Loisy became a lecturer at the École des Hautes Études at the Sorbonne. This gave him a position of distinction in the scholarly world and greater independence from the institutional Church. In the spring of 1902, Loisy actually began writing *The Gospel and the Church.* He had long desired to write a modern apology for Catholicism, and the popularity, in 1902, of the French translation of Adolf von Harnack's *Das Wesen des Christentums* (*What Is Christianity?*) gave him a perfect foil. Neither he nor his friends and advisers realized the sensation the book would cause—that it would be regarded as the summation of all the heresies of Modernism and would ultimately lead to Loisy's excommunication.

Because of the significance of *The Gospel and the Church* in the Modernist controversy, an analysis of its contents is the best way to gain an understanding of the Modernist doctrine and program. The book purports to be a refutation of Liberal Protestantism, but this was not its principal object. The critique of Harnack's Liberal Protestantism was the perfect occasion for the development of the outlines of a truly modern Catholic position. It was a shrewd stroke, but it is quite unfair to assert, as some have, that Loisy sought thereby to disguise his own unorthodox doctrines. There is no pretense in the book. The radicalness of his Catholicism is never veiled.

Each chapter begins with a statement of the Liberal Protestant position as developed by Harnack in *What Is Christianity?* and then argues for the historical and experiential validity of the Catholic view. Since we have examined Harnack's doctrine in a previous chapter, there is no need to rehearse it here. Loisy begins his critique of Harnack's rendition of essential Christianity on the grounds laid out by Harnack himself—by appeal to the facts of history. If we take the historical view, can we derive, as Harnack has done, the complex reality of early Christianity from a single idea, such as faith in God the Father? Do the sources warrant such a judgment or, Loisy asks, is it the a priori assumption "of a theologian who takes from history as much as suits his theology"?[16] Appeal to history is not necessarily the same as what appeals to us. "The gospel has an existence independent of us." Therefore, Loisy urges, let us "try to understand it in itself, before we interpret it in the light of our preferences and our needs."[17] Honest criticism forbids that we resolve as historically nonessential all that we today find unacceptable. Picking and choosing a small number of texts in support of our theories is uncritical.

> Herr Harnack has not avoided this danger, for his definition of the essence of Christianity is not based on the totality of authentic texts, but rests, when analysed, on a very small number of texts, practically indeed on two passages: "No man knoweth the Son, but the Father: neither knoweth any man the Father save the Son" and "The Kingdom of God is within you," both of them passages that might well have been influenced, if not produced, by the theology of the early times.[18]

This leads Loisy to a second critical point. Literary analysis does not allow us to make the clear distinction between Jesus and the primitive tradition that Harnack appears to make. What we have in the Gospel is "but an echo, necessarily weakened and a little confused, of the words of Jesus."

Whatever we think, theologically, of tradition, whether we trust it or regard it with suspicion, we know Christ only by tradition, across the tradition, and in the tradition of the primitive Christians. This is as much as to say that Christ is inseparable from His work, and that the attempt to define the essence of Christianity according to the pure gospel of Jesus, apart from the tradition, cannot succeed, for the mere idea of the gospel without tradition is in flagrant contradiction with the facts submitted to criticism.[19]

The tradition includes the appropriation of Jesus's life and message by the Christian community, and, in Loisy's opinion, no other Christ is historically available.* Nor should this be regretted. Why should the essence of a tree be identified with "but a particle of the seed from which it sprung" rather than with the complete tree? According to Loisy, Harnack has peeled away the fruit of primitive Christianity with such abandon that it is doubtful if anything will remain.

> This method of dismembering a subject does not belong to history, which is a science of observation of the living not a dissection of the dead. Historical analysis . . . does not destroy what it touches nor think all movement digression, and all growth deformity.[20]

Loisy believed that if we examine the message of Jesus, freed from a priori notions and personal prejudices, we will see that it was radically eschatological, couched in the contemporary Jewish apocalypticism of the first century.** As we have seen, Harnack was not entirely daunted by this fact. He

---

*Here Loisy was in accord with the views of the *Formgeschichte* school, soon to gain prominence through the work of the Protestant scholars Martin Dibelius, K. L. Schmidt and R. Bultmann—viz., that the New Testament is largely the work of the early Christian communities and that it is almost impossible to extract the history and message of Jesus from the primitive Christian traditions about him. See volume two.

**Here again Loisy was in advance of most New Testament scholars of his time. His recognition of the centrality of apocalyptic eschatology in the message of Jesus was contemporary with that of Johannes Weiss and predated Albert Schweitzer's famous *Quest of the Historical Jesus* (1906) in which the theory of thoroughgoing eschatology is given its classic expression. Recognition of the eschatological message of Jesus did more than anything else to destroy the liberal, Ritschlian picture of the historical Jesus.

believed that, although it was difficult, it was not impossible to distinguish what was traditional from what was new and personal, the kernel from the husk, in the preaching of Jesus concerning the kingdom of God. For Harnack the husk was, of course, traditional Jewish apocalypticism. The kernel of Jesus's own view had to do simply with faith in a merciful Father. But this, according to Loisy, was to play fast and loose with the New Testament sources.

> Christ nowhere confounds the kingdom with the remission of sins. . . . Nowhere does He identify the kingdom with . . . God's power acting in the heart of the individual.[21]

The authenticity of the single text (Luke 17:20) on which Harnack most depends is, in Loisy's view, uncertain and its meaning not clearly the one Harnack gives it. In any case "to sacrifice the rest of the gospel to the doubtful interpretation of a solitary passage would be to go contrary to the most elementary principles of criticism."[22] Examined in its totality, Jesus's message is seen as an urgent and radical announcement of the approaching kingdom of God, envisioned in bold apocalyptical terms. Concern for all else, for life in this world, for law and culture "is as though non-existent."[23] Jesus made no attempt to reconcile his radical demands to the prudential realities of life. Loisy argues that it is for this very reason that it was later absolutely necessary to detach the message from its earliest connections. The very preservation of the gospel demanded that it develop and change to meet new historical conditions.

Harnack's interpretation of Christology is open to similar criticism. His identification of Sonship with Jesus's knowledge of God is based on a single text (Matt. 11:27) which is probably not from Jesus himself but the product of the early tradition. Moreover, "the gospel conception of the Son of God is no more a psychological idea signifying a relation of the soul to God than is the gospel conception of the kingdom."[24] Jesus thought of himself as the Son of God "to the extent he avowed himself the Messiah." That is, the divine Sonship was linked to Jesus's vocation of announcing the approaching kingdom. Viewed in this perspective the gospel is not about "God and the soul, the soul and its God";

rather, at the very heart of the gospel is "the reality of the kingdom that is to come, the certainty of the gospel message concerning it, and the mission of Him who announces it."[25] Loisy readily admits that this "entire gospel" is bound up with a view of the world that is no longer ours; but at least it is the whole gospel and not some imagined essence. The very fact that the gospel detached itself, little by little, from its original form shows that that *form* was only temporary. Humans change with the ages, and it is only appropriate that the gospel "not fail to accommodate itself" to those changes.

> The truly evangelical part of Christianity today is not that which has never changed . . . and has never ceased to change, but that which in spite of all external changes proceeds from the impulse given by Christ, and is inspired by His Spirit.[26]

The primitive gospel, which centered on the coming kingdom and the mission of the Messiah, was a "simple idea" for Loisy, one which the historian is now able to see as "the concrete, rudimentary, indistinct symbol of subsequent events"—e.g., the anticipation of the kingdom of God in the Church. "It was the certain presentiment of what we see today." Development, then, is not an "abasement," as Harnack claimed, for the form of the gospel necessarily had to change.

Since the Church is the historical embodiment of the gospel, it is also natural that it should grow and change and take on new forms. Struggle, movement, and modification are the very laws of life.

> These struggles do not prove a diminution of life but that life is threatened: when the crisis is over, and the power of the organism is augmented, it is to be praised for its vitality, not blamed because it suffered or because it did not succumb. The Church can fairly say that, in order to be at all times what Jesus desired the society of his friends to be, it had to become what it has become: for it has become what it had to be to save the gospel by saving itself.[27]

For Loisy it is a fact that the institutional Church is as necessary to the gospel as is the gospel to the Church. The indispensability of the Church and its authority for the very preservation of the gospel does not mean, however, that Jesus consciously established the institutional Church.

> It is certain that Jesus did not systematize beforehand the constitution of the Church as that of a government established on earth and destined to endure for a long series of centuries . . . . *Jesus foretold the kingdom, and it was the Church that came;* she came, enlarging the form of the gospel, which it was impossible to preserve as it was. . . . The preservation of its primitive state was impossible, its restoration now is equally out of the question, because the conditions under which the gospel was produced have disappeared forever. History shows the evolution of the elements that composed it. . . . *It is easy today to see in the Catholic Church what stands today for the idea of the heavenly kingdom, for the idea of the Messiah . . . and for the idea of the apostolate.* . . . The tradition of the Church keeps them, interpreting them and adapting them to the varying conditions of humanity.[28] (Italics added.)

The marks of the Church today are the same as those of the primitive community, only "grown and fortified." Loisy comments that the continuity of the gospel has no more need to reproduce exactly the Galilean form than a person has need to preserve, at fifty, the features and manners of life of the day he or she was born in order to be the same individual. Since the Church has undergone continuous change in the past, there is no reason to doubt that this process will continue in the future. Loisy even conjectures, prophetic of Vatican II, that the extreme centralization of authority in the Pope which was required by historical circumstance may have reached its limit and that a new consideration of ecclesiastical authority may bring about a reaction to the present policy. At least, "theological reflection has not yet spoken its final word on the subject."[29] And, he adds, it should not be forgotten that "the Church is an educator, rather than a dominating mistress: she instructs rather than directs, and he who obeys her only does so according to his conscience, and in order to obey God."[30] As the institutional Church evolved and changed to meet the challenge of changing circumstances and to preserve itself, so Christian dogma constantly develops new forms to conform to the thought patterns of contemporary knowledge and the facts of religious experience. The Hellenization of early Jewish Christianity is the most obvious illustration of this process, which continues to the present day. The doctrines of the Incarnation and Trinity are Greek dogmas, "unknown to Judaic Christianity." But they, too, can expect to undergo transformations.

> Anyone who has followed the progress of Christian thought from the beginning must perceive that neither the Christological dogma nor the dogma of grace nor that of the Church is to be taken for a summit of doctrine. . . . The conceptions that the Church presents as revealed dogmas are not truths fallen from heaven and preserved by religious tradition in the precise form in which they first appeared. . . . Though the dogmas may be Divine in origin and substance, they are human in structure and composition. It is inconceivable that their future should not correspond to their past. Reason never ceases to put questions to faith, and traditional formulas are submitted to a constant work of interpretation.[31]

According to Loisy, dogmatic *definitions* are always relative and variable. They are always related to the general form of human knowledge at the time of their constitution. It thus follows that a considerable revolution in knowledge renders necessary a reinterpretation of the old formula which no longer adequately expresses the original religious experience or idea. Thus a distinction should always be made between the material image of the formula and its proper religious meaning or idea. The former is relative; the latter is enduring and can be reconciled with changing knowledge. Take, for example, the statement from the Creed, "He descended into Hell, He ascended into Heaven."

> These propositions have for many centuries been taken literally. Generations of Christians have followed one another believing Hell the abode of the damned to be beneath their feet, and Heaven, the abode of the elect, above their heads. Neither learned theology nor even popular preaching maintains this localization today. . . . May we not say, looking at the transformation that the apparent sense of the formulas has undergone, that the theology of the future will again construct a more spiritual idea of their content?[32]

The very need for ceaseless interpretation and development of dogmatic formulae makes plain the essentially spiritual character of such doctrines. They are meant to be flexible and imprecise, an aid to faith. They allow for individuality of interpretation and, contrary to Protestant opinion, do not demand a narrow subserviency.

> The Church does not exact belief in its formulas as the adequate expression of absolute truth, but presents them as the least imperfect expression that is morally possible. . . . The ecclesiastical formula is the auxiliary of faith, the guiding line of religious thought: it cannot be the integral object of that thought, seeing that object is God Himself, Christ and His work; each man lays hold of the object as he can, with the aid of the formula. As all souls and all intelligences differ one from the other, the gradations of belief are also of infinite variety, under the sole direction of the Church and in the unity of her creed. The incessant evolution of doctrine is made by the work of individuals, as their activity reacts on the general activity, and these individuals are they who think for the Church while thinking with her.[33]

It is difficult to believe that Loisy thought that his book represented a position acceptable to the ecclesiastical authorities. In fact, of course, he was quite aware that it did not. Loisy was presenting the Church with a program of modernization which, he was soon to learn, it had no intention of adopting. Loisy's orthodox critics have argued that his book left no place for certain fundamental Christian beliefs, for supernaturalism, or for the historical Incarnation. A careful reading of *The Gospel and the Church* does not support such a claim. What the book does do is to call for a radical reform of the Church's attitude toward biblical research, the nature of its authority, and its conception of dogma. That Loisy's own theological views were later to become heterodox and skeptical is true, and perhaps it can be argued that his Modernist program was the first step in that inevitable direction. But this, too, is highly questionable since there were Catholics of liberal but orthodox faith, such as Baron Friedrich von Hügel and Wilfred Ward, who considered *The Gospel and the Church* an important apology for Catholicism and who never took the path Loisy later was to follow.

The book was enthusiastically received by many Catholic intellectuals, but within a few months of its appearance it was vigorously attacked and condemned by the Archbishop of Paris. Why was it considered dangerous, even heretical? The charges against it were numerous. Loisy had denied the Church's teaching concerning the inspiration of Scripture; he had depicted Jesus as a herald of the kingdom, as initiator of a religious spirit and movement, but not as the revealer of infallible truths. He had considered Jesus limited and fallible in his judgments, and dogma relative because conditioned by changing historical circumstances. He also viewed the bodily resurrection as mythical and took a highly personal view of the nature and authority of the papacy and the Church's teaching office. But, above all, what was anathema to the Church was Loisy's equivocal use of the terms "development" and "change." The Church taught that dogma was the necessary and logical *development* of the original deposit of faith—the making explicit what was implicit in the New Testament revelation. This development was carried out on the basis of certain logical and historical principles. The doubt raised earlier by Newman's *Essay on Development* now became unmistakably clear in *The Gospel and the Church*: development involves real doctrinal change. That is, Loisy

> does not treat of the New Testament as a *depositum fidei* to be explained and developed, but never *changed* by the Church, he treats it rather as something in itself subject to change, and it was in treating *development* as though it were *change* that the essence of his heresy consisted.[34]

Loisy offered a somewhat qualified "submission" to Cardinal Richard of Paris in February 1903 but continued to pursue his historical work. Late that same year he published *Autour d'un petit livre*, a frank defense and elaboration of the principles expressed in *The Gospel and the Church*. This was a clear challenge to the authorities. They had but two alternatives: to accept Loisy's program or to condemn his views as heretical and excommunicate him from the Church. Both of the latter steps were delayed for a few years; the first occurred with the appearance of *Lamentabili* and *Pascendi Gregis* in 1907, the second a year later.

Before examining these measures taken by Pius X, the thought of two other major figures in the Modernist Movement must be considered.

George Tyrrell

If Loisy exemplified the scientific commitment of Modernism, George Tyrrell (1861–1909) embodied the Catholic spirit of the movement. Tyrrell was born an Irishman and raised in the Anglican Church of Ireland. As a young man he came under the influence of High Church Anglican friends, but High Anglicanism did not long satisfy him. At eighteen Tyrrell moved to London and was received into the Roman Catholic Church that same year. He had for some time held a rather idealized picture of the religious life of the Society of Jesus and, in 1880, entered the novitiate of that order. However, from the beginning there was a deep tension in Tyrrell's vocation between unselfish devotion and submission and a scrupulous independence of judgment.

During his seven years of training, Tyrrell became an ardent student and disciple of St. Thomas Aquinas, opposing the more narrow Scholasticism of the Jesuit Suarez (1548–1617) which was then dominant in the society. Tyrrell was ordained priest in 1891, spent a few years in parish mission work, and then taught philosophy at the Jesuit college at Stonyhurst from 1894 to 1896. It was during these latter years that new intellectual influences began to unsettle Tyrrell's theological tranquility and he began to question the compatibility of his thought and office. The newly developed friendship with the Catholic layman Baron Friedrich von Hügel was of greatest consequence, for it was largely through von Hügel that Tyrrell was introduced to the philosophical work of Maurice Blondel and Lucien Laberthonnière as well as to German biblical criticism.

The first of Tyrrell's writings that clearly revealed a serious break with tradition was an article on eternal punishment entitled "A Perverted Devotion," published in 1899. Tyrrell called for an agnosticism concerning the punishment of the damned and criticized the rationalistic attitude of Scholasticism toward the mysteries of the faith. In this essay the beginnings of Tyrrell's Modernist program are evident. Thereafter he was under suspicion, and his priestly work was reduced. He moved to Richmond in Yorkshire where he lived from 1900 to 1905 in virtual retirement at a little Jesuit mission. During this period he continued to write articles and books, often anonymously or pseudonymously, which led inevitably to a break not only with the society but with the Roman Church itself. Refusing to repudiate what he had written in "A Letter to a Friend," published in 1903, Tyrrell was dismissed from the Society of Jesus in February 1906. Efforts were made to heal this breach with the Church, but these ended when Tyrrell wrote two letters to *The Times* of London publicly criticizing the encyclical *Pascendi gregis*. As a result he was deprived of the sacraments.

By this time Tyrrell saw himself as a prophet who, though never to see the Promised Land himself, was heralding a revolution in the Roman Church which would ultimately waken it from its "medieval dreams." He asked at this time:

> May not Catholicism like Judaism have to die in order that it may live again in a greater and grander form? Has not every organism got its limits of development after which it must decay, and be content to survive in its progeny? Wineskins stretch, but only within measure, for there comes at last a bursting-point when new ones must be provided.[35]

From 1906 until his death in 1909, Tyrrell called for a complete revolution of Catholicism and denounced the conservatives, often in bitter, scathing language—none more so than his attack upon Cardinal Mercier in *Medievalism* (1908). Tyrrell did not claim to have all the answers to meet the Church's need, but in his last books the general theological principles of a Modernist revolution are sketched. The most important of these books are *Lex Orandi* (1903), *A Much Abused Letter* (1906), *Lex Credendi* (1906), *Through Scylla and Charybdis* (1907), *Medievalism* (1908), and *Christianity at the Cross Roads* (1910). The last book was published posthumously and, as Loisy remarked, went far beyond the "modest program of reforms" contained in *The Gospel and the Church*.

George Tyrrell died of Bright's disease in July 1909. Although he received the sacraments on his deathbed, he made no retraction of his "errors" and was, therefore, denied a Roman Catholic burial. "When Tyrrell died," Loisy wrote, "it may be said that Modernism, considered as a movement of overt resistance to the absolutism of Rome, died with him."[36] It is significant that Tyrrell refused through the end to acknowledge he was outside the Catholic Church; rather "he died professing to defend Catholic principles against the Vatican heresies."[37] This is important in revealing Tyrrell's devotion to what he saw as Catholicism. Like Loisy, he was committed to modern critical scholarship but entirely opposed to Liberal Protestantism. Unlike Loisy, Tyrrell kept his criticism and Catholic spirituality in finer balance.

In the public mind Modernism had come to mean detachment from tradition, the equivalent of Protestant Liberalism. Nothing could have been further from Tyrrell's mind. In his last book he makes this absolutely clear.

Of the avowed adherents or admirers of Modernism a large proportion understand it in this loose sense (as detachment from tradition). They believe in modernity . . . but he (the Modernist) also believes in tradition. . . . By a Modernist I mean a churchman, of any sort, who believes in the possibility of a synthesis between the essential truth of his religion and the essential truth of modernity.[38]

Whether or not such a program could have been carried out within the Roman Church at the time is doubtful, and Tyrrell's own view of Catholicism was highly personal. But it is clear that his Modernism was worlds apart from Liberal Protestantism. *Christianity at the Cross Roads* was a passionate repudiation of Protestantism.

To suppose that Modernism is a movement away from the Church and is converging towards Liberal Protestantism is to betray a complete ignorance of its meaning—as complete as that of the Encyclical *Pascendi*. With all its accretions and perversions Catholicism is for the Modernist the only authentic Christianity. Whatever Jesus was, He was in no sense a Liberal Protestant.[39]

Tyrrell accepted the apocalyptical interpretation of Jesus and his message as set forth by Loisy, Weiss, and Schweitzer and agreed that such a picture of Jesus made the Jesus of Liberalism historically untenable. In Tyrrell's classic statement, "The Christ that Harnack sees, looking back through nineteen centuries of Catholic darkness, is only the reflection of a Liberal Protestant face, seen at the bottom of a deep well."[40] But what of the Christ of Catholicism? Is he compatible with the apocalyptic visionary of the New Testament? Tyrrell believed he was—*if* we see Jesus's apocalypticism as the expression of an essential "religious idea in a certain stage of development." That religious *idea* is transcendentalism or otherworldliness. It is this idea which is so lacking in Liberal Protestantism but is the very essence of both Jesus's eschatology and Catholic spirituality.

This contempt of the world preached by Jesus was not Buddhistic in its motive. It was a contempt for a lower and transitory form of existence in favour of a higher—a proximate pessimism but an ultimate optimism. That the world was thought to be in its death-agony made it doubly contemptible. But when this thought was dropped by the Church, the world still remained contemptible. It was but a preparation and purgatory; the theatre of the great conflict between the forces of good and evil—a conflict that could be decided in favour of Good only by the Coming of the Son of Man. . . . The emphatic Persian dualism of Good and Evil, of the Kingdom of God and of Satan, is common to the idea of Jesus and the idea of Catholicism. . . . It is not between Jesus and Catholicism but between Jesus and Liberal Protestantism that no bridge, but only a great gulf, is fixed.[41]

What Jesus and Catholicism have in common, then, is the spiritual truth of his apocalyptic message. That Jesus was mistaken in his literal belief in a coming new age is not significant. Jesus was possessed by the truth of a great idea and necessarily had to embody it in the limited thought forms of his day. We, too, must interpret the transcendent and supernatural in the thought forms of our culture, recognizing that such forms are mere human efforts to give expression to deeply felt religious truths.

The Modernism of Tyrrell, and that of Loisy, is markedly distinguished from Ritschlian Protestantism in its contention that it is the *idea* and not the historical *fact* that is the basis of Christianity. According to Tyrrell, religion is the embodiment of the spiritual ideal in changing historical forms; hence religious statements are always *symbolic*.

> Religion, as such, deals entirely with the transcendent. Its "idea" unfolds itself and comes into clearer consciousness in an infinity of directions and degrees, dependent on its mental, moral and social environment—on the materials out of which it has to weave an embodiment for itself. But, from the nature of the case, its presentiment of the transcendent order, and of the present order in its relation to the transcendent, can never be more than symbolic . . . the transcendental can never be expressed properly. Translated into the terms of our present philosophy, the "ideal" of Jesus remains symbolic. To whatever degree we dematerialize our symbols of the spiritual, material they must remain. Our own symbolism would be as unacceptable for a later age as the apocalyptic symbolism is for us. The only remedy lies in a frank admission of the principles of symbolism. With this admission we have no need to abolish the Apocalypse, which as the form in which Jesus embodied His religious "idea" is classical and normative for all subsequent interpretations of the same. . . . What each age has to do is to interpret the apocalyptic symbolism into terms of its own symbolism.[42]

Implicit in Tyrrell's doctrine of religious symbolism and spiritual truth is a distinctive conception of revelation, doctrine, and development. For Tyrrell revelation is not the receiving of propositional knowledge, nor is it essentially an instruction of the mind. Therefore, it is not to be confused with doctrine or theology. Rather, revelation is experience. It is, Tyrrell came to insist, "a showing on the part of God, a seeing on the part of the receiver. Prophecy is but the communication of this vision to others. Theology must take prophecy not as statement, but as experience." The prophet's aim is to kindle in others the direct, personal experience of revelation. Thus, every revelation is a "showing of God" and is equidistant to the Eternal.

All preconceptual revelatory experience seeks, of course, to communicate its spiritual reality to others, but all such efforts "require a certain translation of inward vision into outward language and symbolism—a translation that can never be exhaustive or adequate, but at most suggestive." In fact, it may be translated conceptually as history or as theology—and thereby only "puzzle, perplex, and annoy." Theology is necessary and especially so as an effort to protect the truth of revelatory experience, but it is at best only the after-reflection, the statement of the experience. Therefore, theology is an intellectual exercise, a science, and a necessary one. But theology must never be granted an infallible status. This is the error of the Scholastic theologians and the Ultramontanists—an error that Tyrrell refers to as "theologism." "We know," he liked to remind his colleagues, "more theology than St. Peter or St. Mary Magdalene or St. Paul, but do we believe more or hope more or love more?"

Since revelation is the divine "presence," it is latent in the depths of being, else we would not be able to recognize it. Nevertheless, the revelation experienced by Christ remains for Tyrrell the summit and norm of all divine disclosure.

> As the spirit did not cease with the apostles, so neither did revelation and prophecy. But a peculiar character rightly attached to that which was the effect of immediate contact with Christ, and of the spirit as it was breathed forth from his very lips. This has rightly been regarded as alone classical and normative, as the test by which all spirits and revelations in the Church are to be tried.

Because others may manifest the same spirit of Christ does not imply that they can complete or supersede it, as Lessing assumed, or that it can be organically developed. Tyrrell insists that there can be no development of revelation any more than there can be a development of what is good or right. There can, however, be a development "in ethics, i.e., in the *understanding* of what is right. There is no progress in religion . . . but only in theology, i.e., in the understanding of things divine"; for, like ethics, theology is a science. Christ's revelation is the Church's *depositum fidei*, its deposit of faith, what

Tyrrell came to call the "Spirit of Christ." And in the Church's subsequent history the *depositum* does not develop like an acorn develops into a mighty oak tree. Here Tyrrell rejects several conceptions of development: the High Anglican idea of a return to a fixed apostolic norm; the older Catholic idea of the development, logically or organically, of the implicit into the explicit; and even Newman's conception of the development of the deposit of faith, for, despite its merit, it does not sufficiently take into account the limits of the organic analogy or properly distinguish the deposit *as revelation* and its conceptual formulation in doctrine.

According to Tyrrell, the Church's responsibility is to serve as *custos depositi* (guardian of the deposit), and it must never claim to have developed the *depositum.* Therefore, there will never be a perfect equation between the language of prophetic and scientific truth, between revelation and theology. And this is the root error of "theologism." Nevertheless, there not only can but *must* be a development of theology, just as there is development in the science of biblical criticism. The work of the theologian, Tyrrell insists, "is as variable as his intelligence and information; today different from yesterday; tomorrow from today."[43] For this reason Tyrrell rejects Newman's physiological model of development. It represents, Tyrrell came to believe, a too-passive and organic idea of the development of theological doctrine; the organism is potentially in the beginning what it will later become. The "idea" is present from the first and shapes itself into deeper and fuller expressions. On the contrary, for Tyrrell the development of theology, and the spiritual life itself, is more unpredictable and creative. So long as theology serves as guardian of the revelatory *depositum,* it may take future forms wholly unpredictable. For example, contrary to Newman's tests, a development may not reveal retrospectively a logical coherence or be foreshadowed in earlier teachings. Older forms such as Platonic and Aristotelian certainly may prove inauthentic, incapable of adequately communicating or protecting the living truth, the "Spirit of Christ." This is not to say that the past should be wiped out as wholly worthless, as is claimed by the fanaticism of some Protestant "pseudo-revolutionaries." Nevertheless, there is a crucial difference between physiological and spiritual development, of

which Newman does not take proper account. Like the arranging and rearranging of a bouquet of flowers, in the development of the spiritual life

the final arrangement is not implied in or exacted by the first. It is not a process of passive unfolding, but of active reconstruction. . . . And this holds of the collective as of the individual spirit life. . . . The "law" of spiritual development is a freely chosen path to good—one of many; that of organic development is a fixed path to a fixed form or determination of good; my bodily future is predictable, not my spiritual future. Who knows how a child will "turn out"?[44]

In Tyrrell's account of doctrine and development, we encounter an aspect of Modernism that was unacceptable to liberal Protestant and traditional Catholic alike. The Modernists often were careless about or disinterested in the question of the factual bases of Christian claims and were negligent in distinguishing fact from religious value. This is clear in Tyrrell's letter to von Hügel, where he summarizes his views of dogmatic formulae:

What value, then, do I attach to ecclesiastical definitions? . . . *What* she says is often absolutely wrong, but the truth in whose defence she says it is revealed, and to that truth alone we own adhesion. . . . In all controversies the Church must instinctively take the side that best protects the spiritual life. Her criticism is purely opportunist. In all her utterances she only repeats the truth revealed—their *meaning* is just the revealed truth which they protect. That a lie should be sometimes protective of truth is a consequence of the view of truth as *relative* to the mentality of a person or people. Hence, no definition of the *historicity* of the Virgin Birth could *mean* more than that the Virgin Birth was part of revelation. *Because and so long as the denial of its historicity seems to destroy its religious value, she will and must affirm its historicity in order to affirm those values.* In the implicit affirmation she is right of necessity; in the explicit protective affirmation she may be quite wrong. . . . about history, she makes quite fallible affirmations protective of those implicitly affirmed revealed truths.[45] (Last italics added.)

If the truth of the "idea," the revelation, is independent of, or at least indifferent as to, its historical or even rational verification, how does the Modernist make any distinction between religious ideas, between the revelations of one prophet and those of another? Tyrrell's answer is given most fully in *Lex Orandi*. It is essentially experiential and pragmatic. Revelation is the communication of a spiritual experience, and its aim is to kindle that experience in others. Revelation is not conceptual statement; that is theology, or the after-reflection of the experience.

> The *religiously* important criticism to be applied to points of Christian belief, whether historical, philosophic or scientific, is not that which interests the historian, philosopher or scientist; but that which is supplied by the spirit of Christ, the *spiritus qui vivificat:* Is the belief in accord with, is it a development of, the spirit of the Gospel? What is its religious value? Does it make for the love of God and man? Does it show us the Father and reveal to us our sonship?[46]

Such a test of religious truth, however, cannot be merely private and idiosyncratic. Religious truth must possess what Tyrrell called "representative value"; otherwise it is not rooted in what is universally real and fruitful. Religious truth must be in accord, then, with the very nature and laws of spiritual reality, and only beliefs "that have been found by continuous and invariable experience to foster and promote the spiritual life of the soul" can be so regarded. Tyrrell believed that Christians could be confident that their Creed bore the closest analogy to the realities of the spiritual world.

> And the reason of this assurance is found in the universally proved value of the Creed as a practical guide to the eternal life of the soul—a proof which is based on the experience not of this man or that, however wise or holy, but of the whole Christian people and of the Church of the Saints in all ages and nations, on the consensus of the ethical and religious *orbis terrarum*.[47]

Tyrrell's criterion of the truth of Christian dogmas and beliefs "is simply the practical one of proved universal religious value." But what, one may ask, if the scholar demonstrates that the "faith of millions" can indeed be wrong, since what they presently believe is based on a fiction? Tyrrell answers that "in case of conflict, he (the believer) is justified in preferring to hold on to an otherwise rationally indefensible belief until its religious value is accounted for and saved in some higher truth. . . . Faith will never allow him to deny a belief of proved religious value."[48] Take, for example, the question of historical criticism.

> Certain concrete historical facts enter into our creed as matters of faith. Precisely as historical facts they concern the historian and must be criticised by his methods. But as matters of faith they must be determined by the criterion of faith, i.e. by their proved religious values as universally effectual of spiritual progress. . . . The believer will desire and endeavour to play the part of historian and to harmonise every seeming discord. . . . But he will always be justified in holding to the faith-taught facts until he is convinced that their religious value is in no way imperilled by the results of historical criticism.[49]

Tyrrell was, of course, partially right. The historian is concerned with the historical and experiential consequences of "events" and ideas irrespective of the nature of their origin. Origin does not necessarily determine value or truth. Nevertheless, Tyrrell and the other Modernists, like the Idealist theologians, paid little attention to a fundamental tenet of Christian theology—i.e., that its claims are grounded in an historical revelation, in certain facts open to the scrutiny of historical investigation. Beliefs could be substantively affected one way or another by the historical evidence. Not so for Tyrrell; for him the historical and the religious judgment each have their place, but, somehow, they never can conflict.

> We must see in her [the Virgin Mary] the revelation of a new aspect of the Divine Goodness. . . . Who can deny that the Christian spirit has been fed and fostered by this belief? . . . Yet plainly, it is not the flesh but the spirit that quickeneth; it is not the physical facts that matter, but the religious values which they symbolize. . . . As in other matters (e.g., in His Transfiguration and Ascension) so, too, in this, the spiritual truth is given to us not in the language of parable but in that of historical fact, *which as such is*

subject to the criteria of history, though as the vehicle of religious value, as the earthen vessel of a heavenly treasure, it is subject only to the criterion of faith.[50] (Italics added.)

Édouard Le Roy

This practical and experiential conception of dogma which characterized Modernism was most systematically formulated by the Frenchman Édouard Le Roy (1870–1954). Le Roy was a distinguished mathematician turned philosopher, who sought a synthesis of Catholicism, evolution, and the vitalistic philosophy of Henri Bergson. He was Bergson's successor at the Collège de France. His book *Dogme et Critique* (1907) is one of the clearest philosophical expressions of French Catholic Modernism, and a chapter of that book entitled "What Is a Dogma?" is the most succinct formulation of the Modernist view on the subject.

Le Roy rejected the Scholastic conception of dogma, for he believed the attempt to formulate conceptually the truth of revelation always results in either a crude anthropomorphism or, if we mean by the dogmatic term something incommensurate with human experience, agnosticism. But neither of these alternatives is required if we recognize the true nature and function of dogma. So considered, it will become clear that, intellectually, dogmas function in two important ways. Negatively, they serve as protections against false beliefs. Positively, the function of dogma "is, above all, the formulation of a rule of practical conduct."[51] Take, for example, the doctrines "God is personal" and the "resurrection of Christ." Consider first the negative value of these dogmas.

On the dogma: "God is personal"—I don't see any definition of the divine personality. It tells me nothing of this personality; it doesn't reveal its nature to me; it does not furnish me with a single explicit idea. But I see very well that it says to me: "God is not a simple law, a formal category, an abstract entity. . . ." The resurrection of Christ gives rise to the same comments. At no point does the dogma inform me . . . of what comprises Jesus' second life. In a word, it doesn't communicate a concept to me. But, on the contrary, it ex-

cludes certain conceptions that I would be tempted to make for myself. Death didn't put an end to Christ's activity in the things of this world; he still intervenes and lives among us. . . .[52]

These dogmas serve to exclude certain false notions but, above all, serve to guide us in our religious life. Dogmas are essentially prescriptive, calling us to act in a certain way. For example,

"God is personal" means "Conduct yourselves in your relation to God as you do in your relations with a human being." Similarly "God is resurrected" means "Be in regard to Him as you would have been before his death, like you are now toward a contemporary.[53]

Le Roy denied that his experiential interpretation of dogmas involved theological or historical skepticism. He insisted that dogma interpreted as a rule of conduct involved *implicitly* the affirmation that ultimate reality is such as to justify such conduct. However, his critics, including both Blondel and Laberthonnière, argued that Le Roy's quite appropriate emphasis on religious experience as necessary for the recognition of revelation and dogma did not, however, give proper attention to the affirmation of the object of experience *in its form as dogma* which comes to be known in one's own experience. Laberthonnière saw Le Roy as caught in the following difficulty.

If dogma gives us no information about the object toward which we act, then the command becomes something to be blindly and irresponsibly obeyed. If the command does not so impugn the responsible exercise of our freedom, then it is because it first gives us a reasonable motive for the action and practice enjoined on us, and this means it tells us about supernatural and divine reality.

As Laberthonnière asked: "How can it be wrong to say 'God is personal' if it is correct to say 'act toward God as toward a person.'"[54]

It would appear that Le Roy's agnosticism concerning the actual perfections of the Divine Being and his rejection of the bodily resurrection of Christ belied his denials of skepticism. In any case, his conception of dogma was seen as a radical innovation, incompatible with the traditional view and perilously close to subjectivism. *Dogme et Critique* was placed on the Index in the same year in which it was published.

A further characteristic of Catholic Modernism, which clearly distinguished it from Liberal Protestantism, was the great stress the Modernists placed on the Church and the social or corporate dimension of Catholic belief and practice. A true religion proved itself by its durability in time and its universality in scope. Like Newman, Tyrrell felt strongly that *quod semper, quod ubique, quod ab omnibus* was the true test of a religion and that no religion had greater durability and scope than Catholicism. This aspect of Modernism is especially prominent in Tyrrell's "A Letter to a Friend," which was addressed to an anonymous Catholic scholar who was drifting from the faith because of intellectual doubts. It is true, Tyrrell concedes, that if adherence to Catholicism means mental assent to a system of conceptions, then his friend should separate himself from the communion of the Church. But, Tyrrell argues, Catholicism is not primarily a theological system but "a spiritual organism in whose life we participate." The essence of the Church is not doctrine or hierarchy but "the collective subconsciousness of the 'Populus Dei'." Tyrrell asks:

> Is it not because you forget this that the prospect seems to you so hopeless? Is it not because you are . . . taking no account of the inscrutable voiceless life which it (Catholicism) strives feebly to formulate of the eternal truths, the Divine instincts that work themselves out irresistibly in the heart of the whole people of God?[55]

It is this subconscious spiritual *consensus gentium* that Tyrrell identifies with Catholicism—a universal spiritual society, expressing the deepest-felt religious beliefs and hopes of the race.

> To belong to this world-wide authentic and original Christian society, to appropriate its universal life as far as possible, to be fired with its best enthusiasms, to devote oneself to its services and aims is to go out of

one's selfish littleness and to enter into the vast collective life—the hopes and fears and joys and sorrows, failures and successes—of all those millions who have ever borne, or bear, or shall yet bear the name Catholic, and who have in any degree lived worthy of that name.

> Reasons like these may hold a man fast to the Church by a thousand ties of affection and loyalty, of moral, religious, and Christian sentiment, which can in no way be weakened by any collapse of his intellectual formulation of Catholicism.[56]

Clearly the "friend" to whom Tyrrell was addressing these sentiments was himself. And here he summarizes his understanding of what constitutes genuine Catholicism and gives his own reasons for remaining in the Church despite the "Vatican heresies."

THE OUTCOME OF CATHOLIC MODERNISM

Modernism was not a single movement, as *Pascendi Gregis* would lead one to believe. However, Catholics such as Loisy, Tyrrell, Le Roy, and Laberthonnière held certain things in common which gave them a sense of participation in a common cause. They all felt strongly that the Roman Church had closed its mind, and even its heart, to intellectual difficulties that were besetting the Church and which were disturbing countless loyal Catholics. Most of the Modernists were critical of Scholasticism. They felt it had served Christian apologetic well in a previous age but that its categories and doctrine were foreign to a culture whose thought forms were imbued with an historical sensibility and with evolution and a vitalistic life philosophy. Tyrrell also felt that the overly intellectualistic character of Scholastic theology was responsible for a drying up of the spiritual life. In addition, the Modernists all were committed to historical-critical scholarship and believed the Church could and must survive such critical analysis. In this they differed from those who lost confidence in the Church's capacity to absorb the new learning. The Modernists called for a new conception of dogma and dogmatic development. But it is significant that they wished to preserve the dogmatic tradition, while radically reconceiving its nature experientially. In this they again represented a position between Catholic orthodoxy and Protestant Liberalism. The Modernist program had certain affinities with the movement, a generation later, of Christian Existentialism—especially with Rudolf Bultmann's program of "demythologizing" the New Testament. Bultmann also attempted to steer a course between orthodoxy and Liberalism. The common elements in these two movements are summarized as follows by B. M. G. Reardon:

> Both Bultmann and the Modernists would have agreed that the proof of the Gospel rests not in historical claims likely to satisfy the requirements of the technical historian but in its capacity to act as a medium of an actual experience. . . . Both alike are at odds with liberalism no less than with conventional orthodoxy. For they deny that the Gospel can be equated with the Jesus of History, of whom historically we know very little. . . . Moreover for the representation of Christian truth which they envisage Bultmann and his predecessors alike turn to a specific philosophy. This, in the former case, is the current existentialism of Martin Heidegger. . . . (The Modernists) turned to "Activism" or personalism . . . and to the fashionable . . . pragmatism of C. S. Peirce.[57]

Modernism represented a threat to the Roman Church, as Bultmann's program has done to orthodox Protestantism, because it not only aimed at a single dogma but sought to reorient the entire theological tradition. Though the Modernists were small numerically, they were to be found in all levels of the Church—laypersons, priests, and prelates* such as Mgr. Mignot, Archbishop of Albi—and especially in places of intellectual influence. Their importance, therefore, was disproportionate to their numbers. Modernist ideas were penetrating every stratum of the Church and society. New reviews and magazines were devoted to disseminating

*Estimates range from forty thousand priests to a few hundred priests and laypersons. Loisy's estimate of "fifteen hundred at the most" is probably a fair guess. Daniel-Rops remarks that in France, where Modernism had its widest following, the movement was led by "no more than half a dozen men."

Modernist ideas. Among these were *Demain, Revue du clergé français,* and the highly esteemed *Annales de philosophie chrétienne.* The issues were soon given a public airing in the popular press. Rome faced the real possibility that Modernism might spread widely and penetrate deeply into the life of the Church. While the aged Leo XIII was still Pontiff, no urgent measures were taken. This changed with the accession of Pius X to the throne in 1903. Already in the same year five works of Loisy were placed on the Index, followed shortly after by condemnations of works by Laberthonnière and Le Roy. The most decisive measures were to wait until 1907 when Pius X had two documents prepared—a catalog of errors, modeled after Pius IX's *Syllabus of Errors,* and an encyclical.

The catalog, entitled *Lamentabili Sane Exitu,* condemns sixty-five Modernist "errors" concerning Sacred Scripture and the doctrinal teachings of the Church. Most of the condemned propositions were extracts from the writings of Loisy, a few from Tyrrell, and at least one from Le Roy. The decree called a halt to a genuinely historical study of the Scriptures and tradition. This is evident in the fact that it condemned such propositions as the following:

> 11. Divine inspiration does not so extend to the whole Sacred Scripture so that it renders its parts, all and single, immune from all error.
> 18. John claims for himself the quality of a witness concerning Christ; but in reality he is only a distinguished witness of . . . the life of Christ in the Church, at the close of the first century.
> 34. The critic cannot ascribe to Christ a knowledge circumscribed by no limits except on a hypothesis which cannot be historically conceived and which is repugnant to the moral sense, viz., that Christ as man had the knowledge of God and yet was unwilling to communicate the knowledge of a great many things to His disciples and to posterity.
> 35. Christ had not always the consciousness of His Messianic dignity.
> 52. It was foreign to the mind of Christ to found a Church as a Society which was to last on the earth for a long course of centuries; nay in the mind of Christ the Kingdom of Heaven together with the end of the world was about to come immediately.[58]

The wording of many of the propositions was, as in some of the cases above, a curious mixture of acceptable and unacceptable notions. But acceptance of the condemnation, as such, would clearly compromise the historian's critical freedom. For example, it is legitimate to condemn an unqualified assertion that Christ did not have a Messianic consciousness or that He thought the world was about to end "immediately." But does this mean that the critic must agree that Christ "always" had a consciousness of his Messianic dignity or was minded "to found a Church which was to last for a long course of centuries"?

Two months later appeared the encyclical letter *Pascendi Dominici Gregis.* This encyclical expounds at great length the theoretical principles underlying the Modernist position, weaving them together as if constituting a coherent system. The central heresies were labeled "agnosticism" and "vital immanence." The letter replies with a reaffirmation of the Church's traditional teaching and concludes by enumerating certain specific steps to be taken to remedy the growing contagion. Among these practical remedies was the order that Thomistic philosophy be made the basis of the sacred sciences. Anyone not subscribing to Thomistic doctrine was instantly suspect. Furthermore, anyone tainted with Modernism was excluded without compunction from teaching and administrative positions in seminaries and Catholic universities. Bishops were to prohibit the publication of Modernist writings and not permit such literature to be read by seminarians and university students. Finally, vigilance committees were instituted to collect evidence of Modernist writing or teaching.[59]

Three years later, in 1910, these measures were strengthened by the imposition of the anti-Modernist oath (*motu proprio Sacrarum antistitum*). This was a detailed statement which was required to be signed by all priests and until recently was required of all candidates for the priesthood before ordination. It includes submission to *Lamentabili* and *Pascendi* and acceptance of certain other theological doctrines.

Accompanying these actions was an anti-Modernist campaign supported by Pius X, due to his anxiety that the Modernist errors were more dangerous than those of Luther. The so-called poisonous doctrines of the Modernists allowed the Pope to justify the use of "extraordinary means," including acts of denunciation, intimidation, and injustice that amounted to a veritable reign of terror. The campaign was called "Integralism" because its followers saw themselves as defending the "integrity" of traditional Catholicism. The zealots in the movement had few scruples about their tactics, even engaging in espionage. The most notorious instance was the *Sodalitium Pianum,* a small society serving as a kind of secret service, organized by Mgr. Umberto Benigni, working within the Vatican Secretariat of State. Members of the society spied on Modernist suspects, secretly placed the names of priests and scholars on blacklists, which often led to the loss of their positions, and defamed their enemies in Catholic publications. Even Cardinal Mercier, a leader of the Thomistic revival and target of George Tyrrell's wrath in *Medievalism* (1908), was placed on the blacklist because of his reservations about the society's intolerant zeal. Support for the "Integralist" cause far exceeded the relatively small circle of the *Sodalitium Pianum.*

With the anti-Modernist oath, Modernism came to an end within the Roman Church. By this time Loisy was excommunicated, Tyrrell was dead, and their works, as well as those of Le Roy and Laberthonnière, were on the Index. Several of the Modernist journals, by now under condemnation, ceased publishing. Many of the Modernists followed the lead of Le Roy and Laberthonnière by submitting and continuing to attempt to reform the Church from within. Only a few dozen priests left the Church. Modernism was defeated, since the result of the effort was a Church more deeply committed to entrenched positions, with strong safeguards against any differences of viewpoint. Catholic biblical scholarship was not to recover any real vitality until after World War II. Critical scholarship was severely limited.

However, it is the view of some Catholic scholars today that Pius X's action saved the Church from serious error and that, if the crushing of Modernism stifled creative, progressive thought in the Roman Catholic Church for several decades, it certainly did not kill it. This is evident, for example, in the appearance of Karl Adam's popular *The Spirit of Catholicism* as early as 1924. In that book Adam reinterprets the decrees of Pius X in such a way as to give new scope for critical scholarship. "The Church," writes Adam,

> cannot possibly be an enemy to sober criticism, least of all to the so-called historico-critical method. Even the much-attacked anti-modernist encyclical of Pope Pius X and the anti-modernist oath, do not forbid this method, but rather presuppose it. What they forbid is simply this, that men should make the affirmation of supernatural faith dependent exclusively on the results of this method.[60]

Today a great many distinguished Catholic theologians and scholars readily admit that the Modernists were right on one score at least: that there *were* serious intellectual difficulties facing the Church *and* that with the condemnation of Modernism these problems merely went underground, only to re-emerge in the 1940s. It is also widely conceded that the Modernists were right in certain of their aims and that after Vatican II many of these are now legitimately pursued. Daniel-Rops contends that the Modernist error was originally tactical, only subsequently degenerating into a doctrinal one, but that this is

> no reason for rejecting what was useful and necessary in the desire to enable Christianity to resist her enemies by adopting their own weapons and methods. The condemnation fixed the limits beyond which a Catholic cannot go without falling into error; it did not forbid Catholics to tread the road along which the

Modernists had gone too far. So true is this that it would be easy to show how certain currents of thought, which can be reasonably said to be more or less descended from Modernism, are today accepted by the Church.[61]

It is not quite correct, then, to say that the Modernist Movement was killed in the Roman Church. Its aims and influence are still present, as is evident in post–Vatican II Catholic theology. This theology, as we will see later, is far more pluralistic. Thomism is recognized as only one of several legitimate theological sources. The focus in recent Catholic theology is similar to that of many of the Modernists, for example, on what can be called Christian "personalism"; on human consciousness and its natural, intuitive knowledge of God—on what Karl Rahner calls the "supernatural existential." Recent theology also stresses the nonpropositional character of revelation and its experiential appropriation and the symbolic and contextual character of doctrinal formulations and rejects a purely "logical" or "cumulative" idea of doctrinal development. Finally, recent theology gives significant attention to the universal human spiritual quest and to the authentic glimpses of religious truth beyond the orbit of the Catholic Church and, therefore, the need for ecumenical discussion. If not all of these themes are the direct result of the Modernist movement, Catholic theology in the late twentieth century clearly does reflect many of the Modernists' most urgent concerns.

NOTES

1. L. Ollé-Laprune, *La certitude morale,* 2d ed., p. 67f. Cited in Bernard Reardon, *Liberalism and Tradition: Aspects of Catholic Thought in Nineteenth Century France* (Cambridge, 1975), p. 214.
2. Ibid., p. 215.
3. Jean Lacroix, *Maurice Blondel: An Introduction to the Man and His Philosophy* (New York, 1968), pp. 13–14.
4. M. Blondel, "The Letter on Apologetics," in *The Letter on Apologetics and History and Dogma,* trans. and intro. Alexander Dru and Illtyd Trethowan (New York, 1964), pp. 151–152.
5. M. Blondel, *Action: Essay on a Critique of Life and a Science of Practice* [1893], trans. Oliva Blanchette (Notre Dame, 1984), p. 105.
6. Ibid., p. 313.
7. Ibid., p. 286.
8. Ibid., p. 297.
9. Laberthonnière to Loisy, October 11, 1907, Bibliothèque Nationale. Cited in Alec Vidler, *A Variety of Catholic Modernists* (Cambridge, 1970), p. 87. On the details of Laberthonnière's ban and subsequent publications, see Vidler's characteristically wry account.

10. L. Laberthonnière, *Essais de philosophie religieuse* (Paris, 1903), p. 84. Cited in Gabriel Daly, *Transcendence and Immanence: A Study in Catholic Modernism and Integralism* (Oxford, 1980), p. 106.
11. L. Laberthonnière, *Essais,* pp. 40–41. Cited in Bernard Reardon, ed., *Roman Catholic Modernism* (London, 1970), pp. 196–197.
12. Laberthonnière, *Essais,* XVI. Cited in Reardon, *Liberalism and Tradition,* p. 245.
13. Laberthonnière, *Essais,* p. 173. Cited in Daly, op. cit., p. 107.
14. Henri Daniel-Rops, *A Fight for God* (London, 1966), p. 215.
15. A. Loisy, *Mémoires,* I (Paris, 1930), 118.
16. A. Loisy, *The Gospel and the Church,* trans. Christopher Home, 2d English ed. (London, 1908), p. 4.
17. Ibid., p. 8.
18. Ibid., pp. 11–12.
19. Ibid., p. 13.
20. Ibid., p. 19.
21. Ibid., p. 66.
22. Ibid., p. 72.
23. Ibid., p. 86.
24. Ibid., p. 96.
25. Ibid., p. 113.
26. Ibid., pp. 115–116.
27. Ibid., p. 150.
28. Ibid., pp. 166–167.
29. Ibid., p. 210.
30. Ibid., p. 175.
31. Ibid., pp. 210–211.
32. Ibid., pp. 216–217.
33. Ibid., pp. 224–225.
34. E. E. Y. Hales, *The Catholic Church in the Modern World* (London, 1958), p. 192.
35. *A Letter to a Friend, A Professor of Anthropology in a Continental University* (1903), p. 44.
36. Loisy, *Mémoires,* III, 127.
37. See A. Vidler, *The Modernist Movement in the Roman Church* (Cambridge, 1934), pp. 179–181, for a brief comparison of the Modernism of Loisy and Tyrrell.
38. G. Tyrrell, *Christianity at the Crossroads* (London, 1909), p. 4.
39. Ibid., pp. xx–xxi
40. Ibid., p. 44.
41. Ibid., pp. 69–73.
42. Ibid., pp. 100, 103.
43. G. Tyrrell, *Through Scylla and Charybdis* (London, 1907), pp. 289, 303, 304, 325, 292, 295–296, 345.
44. G. Tyrrell, *Essays on Faith and Immortality,* ed. M. Petre (London, 1914), pp. 126–127.
45. Ibid., pp. 59–60. See *Lex Orandi,* Chap. XXIII.
46. *Lex Orandi* (London, 1903), p. 55. See Tyrrell, *Christianity at the Crossroads,* pp. 80–87.
47. Ibid., p. 58.
48. Ibid., pp. 167–168.
49. Ibid., pp. 169–170.
50. Ibid., pp. 175–176.
51. E. Le Roy, *Dogme et Critique* (Paris, 1907), p. 25.
52. Ibid., pp. 19–20.
53. Ibid., p. 25.
54. L. Laberthonnière, *Dogme et theologie* (Paris, 1977), p. 61. See Guy Mansini, *What Is Dogma?* (Rome, 1985), for an account of Laberthonnière's critique of Le Roy.
55. *A Letter to a Friend,* p. 21.
56. Ibid., p. 25.
57. "Demythologizing and Catholic Modernism," *Theology,* Vol. LIX (Nov. 1956).
58. *Lamentabili Sane Exitu,* in Paul Sabatier, *Modernism* (London, 1908), App. III, p. 217ff.
59. Ibid., p. 324ff. Also, see Daly, op. cit., Chap. 8 and 9.
60. K. Adam, *The Spirit of Catholicism* (New York, 1958), pp. 231–232.
61. Daniel-Rops, *A Fight for God,* p. 237.

SUGGESTIONS FOR FURTHER READING

I. FRENCH RELIGIOUS THOUGHT IN THE LATE NINETEENTH CENTURY

There are surprisingly few studies in English that explore in depth French religious thought and theology in the nineteenth century. The following are recommended:

Copleston, Frederick. *A History of Philosophy,* IX (New York, Newman Press, 1975). Includes lucid brief accounts of the thought of Maine de Biran, Ravaisson, Boutroux, Bergson, Ollé-Laprune, Blondel, and Laberthonnière.

Dansette, Andrien. *Religious History of Modern France,* II (New York: Herder and Herder, 1961). A good introduction to the ecclesiastical and political background. Chapters 7–8 deal with thought.

Reardon, Bernard. *Liberalism and Tradition: Aspects of Catholic Thought in the Nineteenth Century* (Cambridge:

Cambridge University Press, 1975). The latter chapters include fine studies of Maine de Biran, Maret, Gratry, Ollé-Laprune, Blondel, Laberthonnière, and Loisy.

II. MAURICE BLONDEL

In addition to the above, see:

Bouillard, Henri. *Blondel and Christianity*, trans. James M. Somerville (Washington, D.C.: Corpus Books, 1969). Chapter 1 is a general account of *L'Action* and Blondel's later works. The remainder of the book is a full exploration of Blondel's views on the supernatural and Christian philosophy.

Daly, Gabriel. *Transcendence and Immanence: A Study in Catholic Modernism and Integralism* (Oxford: Clarendon Press, 1980). Chapters 2 and 4 are on Blondel.

Dru, Alexander, and Illtyd Trethowan, trans. *Maurice Blondel: The Letter on Apologetics and History and Dogma* (New York: Holt, Rinehart and Winston, 1964; reprint, Grand Rapids, 1994). The translations of these important essays are accompanied by a long and helpful introduction.

Lacroix, Jean. *Maurice Blondel: An Introduction to the Man and His Philosophy*, trans. John C. Guinness (New York: Sheed and Ward, 1968). A brief account of Blondel's life and writings, with short extracts and a bibliography.

Somerville, James M. *Total Commitment: Blondel's L'Action* (Washington, D.C.: Corpus Books, 1968). The fullest account in English of *L'Action,* but hard to come by.

Lucien Laberthonnière

There is no thorough study of Laberthonnière in English. There are interesting brief accounts in Daly, Copleston, and Reardon above, and in Alec Vidler, *A Variety of Catholic Modernists* (Cambridge: Cambridge University Press, 1970), pp. 82–90.

III. ROMAN CATHOLIC MODERNISM

Among the many books on Roman Catholic Modernism, the following are recommended:

Appleby, Scott R. *"Church and Age Unite!" The Modernist Impulse in American Catholicism* (Notre Dame: University of Notre Dame Press, 1992). A comprehensive examination of the role of Modernism in American Catholic thought.

Daly, Gabriel. *Transcendence and Immanence* (see above). A valuable study of such figures as Blondel,

Laberthonnière, Loisy, von Hügel, Tyrrell, and Le Roy, especially in relation to the reigning Thomistic theology of the time.

Loome, Thomas Michael. *Liberal Catholicism, Reform Catholicism, Modernism: A Contribution to a New Orientation in Modernist Research* (Mainz: Matthias-Grünewald-Verlag, 1979). A valuable but tendentious study that relates Modernism to other forms of liberal Catholic thought, thereby seeing the "Modernism" of Loisy, for example, as only a singular manifestation of a much wider and complex crisis in the Church and "a tragic deviation from the modernist tradition." An extremely valuable bibliographical resource.

O'Connell, Marvin R. *Critics on Trial: An Introduction to the Catholic Modernist Crisis* (Washington, D.C.: Catholic University of America Press, 1994). A well-written account of the Modernists, their initiatives, and the outcome of the crisis.

Ranchetti, Michele. *The Catholic Modernists: A Study of the Religious Reform Movement 1864–1907* (London: Oxford University Press, 1969). One of the few studies in English that examines the Italian Modernists, such as Buonauiti, Murri, and Fogazzaro.

Reardon, Bernard M. G. *Roman Catholic Modernism* (London: Adam and Charles Black, 1970). A fine selection from the writings of the principal Modernists, preceded by a long, informative introduction.

Vidler, Alec. *The Modernist Movement in the Roman Church* (Cambridge: Cambridge University Press, 1934). An early and, therefore, somewhat dated study, still full of knowing interpretations and judgments.

———. *A Variety of Catholic Modernists* (Cambridge: Cambridge University Press, 1970). A delightful series of studies, full of interesting detail based on unpublished sources. Especially valuable on the "Lesser Lights and Fellow Travellers" of the Modernist cause.

Alfred Loisy

There is no full-scale study of Loisy in English. The books by Daly, Ranchetti, Reardon, and Vidler above all include studies of aspects of Loisy's scholarly work and thought. In addition, see the following:

Petre, M. D. *Alfred Loisy: His Religious Significance* (Cambridge: Cambridge University Press, 1944). A brief, interesting account of Loisy's relations with other Modernists and assessments of his thought.

Scott, Bernard, ed., Alfred Loisy, *The Gospel and the Church* (Philadelphia: Fortress Press, 1976). This edition includes a long and helpful introduction that includes discussions of Loisy, Newman, and Harnack.

Turvasi, Francesco. *The Condemnation of Alfred Loisy and the Historical Method* (Rome: Edizioni di Storia e Letteratura, 1979). An interesting account of Loisy, biblical criticism, and relations with the Roman authorities, largely explored through Loisy's correspondence with the suspect Roman professor of scripture, Giovanni Genocchi.

George Tyrrell

In addition to the books by Daly, Loome, Reardon, and Vidler cited above, the following are recommended:

Barmann, Lawrence F. *Baron Friedrich von Hügel and the Modernist Crisis in England* (Cambridge: Cambridge University Press, 1972). A fine study of von Hügel and Modernism and includes much on Tyrrell.

Leonard, Ellen. *George Tyrrell and the Catholic Tradition* (Ramsey, N. J.: Paulist Press, 1982). Good on Tyrrell's contribution to ecclesiology and the idea of Catholicism.

Livingston, James C., ed. *Tradition and the Critical Spirit: Catholic Modernist Writings, George Tyrrell* (Minneapolis: Fortress Press, 1991). Collection of representative writings of Tyrrell, some difficult to come by. Introduction and bibliography.

Petre, Maude D., ed. *George Tyrrell's Letter's* (London: T. Fisher Unwin, 1920). Important source for understanding Tyrrell and his spirituality.

———. *Von Hügel and Tyrrell: The Story of a Friendship* (London: J. M. Dent and Sons, 1937).

———. *Autobiography and Life of George Tyrrell,* 2 vols. (London: Edward Arnold, 1912). Vol. 1: *Autobiography of George Tyrrell, 1861–1884,* arranged with supplements by M. Petre. Vol. 2: *Life of George Tyrrell from 1884 to 1909.*

Sagovsky, Nicholas. *"On God's Side": A Life of George Tyrrell* (Oxford: Oxford University Press, 1990). An up-to-date brief biography.

Schultenover, David G., S. J. *George Tyrrell: In Search of Catholicism* (Shepherdstown, W. Va.: Patmos Press, 1981). The best study available of Tyrrell's developing philosophy of religion and apologetic to 1903.

Édouard Le Roy

There are brief treatments of Le Roy in Daly, Reardon, and Vidler above. For the best study in English, see

Mansini, Guy, OSB. *"What Is a Dogma?": The Meaning and Truth of Dogma in Édouard Le Roy and His Scholastic Opponents* (Rome: Editrice Pontificia Universita Gregoriana, 1985).

Chapter 15
Kierkegaard and Nietzsche: Toward
the Twentieth Century

Søren Kierkegaard

If we were to specify the two dominant theological movements at the end of the nineteenth century, they would be the Neo-Thomistic revival in Roman Catholicism and Ritschlianism in Protestantism. The first represents, in large part, a conservative return to and restoration of an older theological tradition. The second was an effort, among several though not all of its members, to engage in a "theology of correlation" between the cultural situation and the Christian message—an effort that sometimes involved an accommodation of Christianity to the assumptions of the current culture. Both movements, for reasons that will become clear, would have been repudiated by both Kierkegaard and Nietzsche. These two prophetic figures represent a *new* situation, or, as some would argue, they embody the true spiritual meaning of the entire rev-

olution called Modernity. Through their seductive irony, their masks of indirect communication, and their startling and dangerous attacks, they bring to the fore significant features of the Modern age. After World War I the German philosopher Karl Jaspers wrote the following:

> The present philosophic situation is determined by the fact that the two philosophers, Kierkegaard and Nietzsche, who did not count during their own lifetime . . . are constantly growing in importance. Whereas the philosophers after Hegel recede into the background next to Kierkegaard and Nietzsche, they stand before us today basically unquestioned as the really great thinkers of their time. . . . This affinity between them in the whole course of their lives, down to the particulars of their thinking, is so compelling, that their essential

character seems to have been born out of the needs arising from the spiritual situation of their century.[1]

The "situation" of their century is revealed, first and foremost, in a series of impressive critiques of reason and of classic epistemological foundationalism. This critique, it must be said, is not the unique province of twentieth-century post-Modernism. Kierkegaard and Nietzsche carry this radical critique to its end but without repudiating reason as such. As Karl Jaspers and others have shown, they use all the devices of reason to unmask doctrinaire rationalism. Neither writer appeals merely to feeling or sentiment; neither is a dogmatic systematizer or a skeptic. Both attempt to unmask a false rationality in the defense of what they see as authentic truth.

Both writers are opponents of "systems." Both are unconditionally honest, and both rage against the thoughtless conventionality, what they see as the inauthentic, bourgeois nihilism of their day. As a result, both men were driven into solitude and suffering. They both attack Christendom, that is, an effete and acculturated Church that they judge to be a blasphemy—what Kierkegaard calls "making a fool of God." Kierkegaard is drawn to the demanding truth of New Testament discipleship and to its indifference to worldly expectations and values. Nietzsche looks, rather, to the ideal of early pre-Socratic Hellenism, to the superior individual and the liberation of the "eternal return." And they both call others to take on their own hazardous thought-experiments and their own risks of freely shaping a life without the safeguards of popular approbation—to embrace what Nietzsche calls "the dangerous Perhaps."

What Kierkegaard and Nietzsche themselves offer are not primarily solutions; they offer, rather, a series of questions and challenges: about knowledge, truth, ethics, the nature of Christianity and, foremost, what it means to exist as an individual. We need not follow them; we must judge their teaching for ourselves. For they were essentially "awakeners" and, therefore, they frequently had to shout. But if one reads them with any care, one is bound to be attracted by a sense of power, of exhilaration, of being in the presence of authentic truth-seekers.

SØREN KIERKEGAARD

Introduction

Søren Kierkegaard (1813–1855) remains one of the great, seminal Christian writers of the Modern period. But few, if any, of the influential thinkers since the Enlightenment present more difficulties for the historian and expositor. His collected works and papers in Danish constitute thirty volumes. Much of his most important work was written pseudonymously and presents complex problems for the interpreter faced with Kierkegaard's use of indirect communication, irony, the introduction of various alternative points of view and existential stages or forms of life. A further difficulty lies in the fact that Kierkegaard wrote in Danish. While his more polemical and overtly religious writings had an influence on the religious life of Copenhagen at mid-century, his influence was not seriously felt in Europe and beyond until the early years of the twentieth century. Yet it is important to understand Kierkegaard in his own political and social context in Denmark between the 1830s and the 1850s if we are to understand the specific sources and motivations of his writing.

It is also crucial to recognize that Kierkegaard must be appreciated as a Christian thinker in the context of the wider movement of European thought at mid-century. This would include, for example, the special influence of German Romanticism and his response to Kant, Hegel, Hamann, and Schleiermacher, among others. Kierkegaard can be understood only when he is seen in terms of both the more circumscribed context of Copenhagen *and* the wider European thought in the first half of the century. Our discussion of Kierkegaard's thought will take into account these contexts. Like the work of all great thinkers, however, Kierkegaard's work transcends these cultural contexts and addresses perennial issues that have engaged Christianity since its beginning. His impact on early twentieth-century religious thought was momentous and continues to be crucial today. It is, therefore, quite appropriate to place Kierkegaard here, with Nietzsche, as one whose discovery and whose influence at the turn of the century proved to be critical for an understanding of philosophical as well as religious thought throughout the twentieth century. As was indicated earlier, both Kierkegaard and Nietzsche radicalize many of the questions that had been directed at Christianity by others in the nineteenth century, but they do so in a manner that is more attuned to the post-Modern sensibilities of the late twentieth century.

The complexities of Kierkegaard's authorship have resulted in several readings of his work, with critical implications for an interpretation of his own thought and position. There are, for example, scholars who ignore the pseudonyms and read Kierkegaard's writings as a whole and as representing his personal views. Other scholars, often influenced by contemporary literary criticism, especially deconstructionism, see Kierkegaard as a poet and ironist who does not represent a single or dominant point of view but, on the contrary, offers various open possibilities for existential appropriation by the reader. In this view much of Kierkegaard's important pseudonymous body of work is essentially an effort to question, to subvert, and even to destroy conventional and orthodox positions without offering any resolution or higher existential option.

The prevailing view represents something of a middle position and appears to be in accord with a reading of Kierkegaard's entire body of work and his own statements about his aim as an author. Scholars in this tradition take seriously the pseudonyms and the fact that these texts are often meant to be humorous, ironical, and subversive, but they also hold that this literary method of indirect communication is put to the service of a serious encounter with a Christian point of view that represents Kierkegaard's own position.[2] In other words, even the explorations of the pseudonymous works ultimately serve, though not in any predetermined way, a definite religious authorship, namely, the subversive and then undisguised attack on "Christendom," as it is joined with the challenge of an authentic Christian discipleship—the Christianity of the New Testament.

In his *The Point of View for My Work as an Author,* written in 1848 but published posthumously, Kierkegaard speaks of the ambiguity and duplicity of his entire authorship and notes that it was a "conscious one" and that it had "a deeper reason." He rejects the contention that he was first an aesthetic author "and then in course of years *changed* and became a religious author," although he acknowledges that it was not his intention to become a religious writer at all, but to become a country pastor after completing the pseudonymous *Concluding Unscientific Postscript* (1846). But later in *The Point of View* he stresses the dialectical and reciprocal relationship between the aesthetic and the religious writings that he, at least now, sees as having been present from the beginning (for example, the relationship between *Either/Or* and *Two Upbuilding Discourses*) to 1848. These are followed by the signed series of Christian writings, but then Kierkegaard stopped publishing in 1851. He resumed publication in 1854 with a flurry of hard-hitting polemical writings in the last year of his life. In a private journal entry in 1848, Kierkegaard had concluded: "Right now the totality is so dialectically right. *Either/Or* and the two upbuilding discourses. . . . The illusion that I happened to get older and for that reason became a decisively religious author has been made impossible."[3] It is appropriate, therefore, to say that Kierkegaard came to see a unity in his authorship between his indirect, his signed, and his late polemical writings, that unity consisting of a criticism of a mediating, bourgeois Christianity as contrasted with his vision of what it truly means to be a Christian.

Søren Kierkegaard was born in Copenhagen, the seventh and last child of Michael Kierkegaard and Ane Lund, a woman who before becoming Michael's second wife had been a servant in his house. Ane bore her husband a daughter only four months after his first wife's death. This knowledge played a decisive role in Kierkegaard's own religious pilgrimage. Though Michael Kierkegaard was a wealthy merchant, he was a melancholy man who brooded over his moral lapses. The melancholy of his elderly father had an indelible effect on the young and precocious son. As a young boy Kierkegaard compensated for a crooked back and a lack of physical robustness with vast learning and a sharp wit, developing a sense of his own superiority at an early age. He acquired the nickname "the fork."

Kierkegaard entered the University of Copenhagen in 1830 to study theology. However, his early interests were in philosophy and literature, and he finally took his theological examinations and degree in 1840, out of deference to his dead father. He then completed his master's degree with a dissertation on *The Concept of Irony* in 1841. It took him ten years to complete his university education, with much of that time being spent in dilettante intellectual endeavors and as a brilliant, charming man-about-town. A series of events then brought about a spiritual crisis in Kierkegaard's life which dedicated him to the problems of religious existence, specifically to what it means *to be* a Christian.

The first event was his father's confession of the sin he had committed with his servant girl Ane. The second event was Kierkegaard's broken engagement. In 1837 he had met and fallen in love with Regine Olsen. They were engaged, but Kierkegaard immediately felt he had done the wrong thing and broke off the engagement. His reasons were never revealed, although in his last days he described his life as a great and incomprehensible suffering, saying "I had my thorn in the flesh, and therefore did not marry and could not take on an official position."[4] Most biographers identify the "thorn in the flesh" with his melancholy.

The break with Regine began what Kierkegaard was to call his "aesthetic authorship," and the works produced during this early period included *Either/Or, Repetition, Fear and Trembling, The Concept of Anxiety, Stages on Life's Way,* and *The Sickness unto Death.* All these books were written under pseudonyms. It was during this period, shortly after completing the *Concluding Unscientific Postscript* (1846), that another crucial event determined Kierkegaard's vocation. He had written against P. L. Møller, an aesthete and editor of a scandalous paper called the *Corsair.* Kierkegaard expected that his attack on this libelous publication would elicit considerable support. However, this did not occur. Instead the *Corsair* turned on him in a series of savage articles and cartoons, holding him up to public ridicule. Kierkegaard suffered a martyrdom of laughter which isolated him further from the masses, whom he came to liken to a flock of dumb geese. The experience was crucial in his growing recognition that "outer" as well as "inner" suffering would be required of a Christian. Kierkegaard interpreted the event as providential and increased his resolve to pursue his religious authorship. From 1843 until a year before his death, Kierkegaard's life was outwardly uneventful, being spent almost entirely in writing. During this period he completed his two pseudonymous philosophical masterpieces, *Philosophical Fragments* (1844) and the *Concluding Unscientific Postscript* (1846), as well as innumerable religious works, including *Works of Love* (1847), *Purity of Heart* (1847), *Christian Discourses* (1850), *Training in Christianity* (1850), *For Self-Examination* (1851), and *Judge for Yourself* (1851–1852).

During the last years of his life, Kierkegaard came to a profound awareness of Christian faith and the realization that he was called to witness to this truth as he saw it. He knew that this would entail suffering for him at the hands of the majority. Such, he came to believe, was the vocation of Christian discipleship. The writings of these years all point to the difficulty of becoming a Christian and the hypocrisy of conventional Christianity and the institutional Church. When even these works failed to gain a response, Kierkegaard was moved to make a direct and unsparing attack on the state Church of Denmark. The articles and pamphlets that appeared in 1854 and 1855 were published in English as *Attack upon Christendom.* What provoked Kierkegaard's initial assault was Bishop Martensen's funeral oration for Bishop J. P. Mynster, in which he referred to Mynster as "a true witness to the truth," a man of humility, suffering, and poverty. For Kierkegaard such a peroration was outrageous. Bishop Mynster was a clever man, very much at home in the world—a man who, in Kierkegaard's view, had nothing in common with the early Christian martyrs. The state Church of Denmark was itself apostate, the clergy self-satisfied functionaries of the government who spent their time baptizing, marrying, and burying people who otherwise considered the ministrations of the Church irrelevant. According to Kierkegaard, where everyone is considered Christian by the conventional act of baptism, Christianity *eo ipso* does not exist.

In the New Testament the Saviour, our Lord Jesus Christ, represents the situation thus: The way that leadeth unto life is straitened, the gate narrow—few be they that find it!—Now, on the contrary, to speak only of Denmark, we are all Christians, the way is broad as it possibly can be, the broadest in Denmark, since it is the way in which we are all walking, besides being in all respects as convenient, as comfortable as possible; and the gate is as wide as it possibly can be, wider surely a gate cannot be than through which we are all going *en masse. Ergo* the New Testament is no longer truth.[5]

In Kierkegaard's view New Testament Christianity was so foreign to the comfortable congregations of Denmark that they weren't even capable of seeing the ludicrous disparity between the primitive Christian message and the elegant preachments of their bishops.

> In the magnificent cathedral the Honorable and Right Reverend *Geheime-General-Ober-Hof-Prädikant,* the elect favorite of the fashionable world, appears before the elect company and preaches *with emotion* upon the text he himself elected: "God hath elected the base things of the world, and the things that are despised." And nobody laughs.[6]

So Kierkegaard's scathing polemic continued until, at the height of his passionate attack, he was stricken with an infection of the lungs. He spent several weeks in the hospital during which time he refused to retract what he had said about the Church and refused to receive communion from a priest. Yet he died strong in his religious convictions and in a state of great spiritual peace.

The Dialectic of Existence

Kierkegaard's writings defy easy systematization, yet they are characterized by certain prominent themes.

Hegelianism was the reigning philosophy in the Denmark of Kierkegaard's day, and his work must be seen in large part as an effort to overthrow the rational pretensions of Hegel's theology. In fact, Kierkegaard's work can be viewed as a sustained attack on all forms of rational theology, whether it be the moral idealism of the Kantians or the absolute idealism of the Hegelians. This becomes especially clear in Kierkegaard's own existential dialectic, which he develops in his earliest writings.

Like Hegel, Kierkegaard approaches the religious problem by means of a dialectical method. But, unlike Hegel, Kierkegaard's dialectic is existential; that is, it does not move within a closed, necessary logical system but begins with the single individual confronted with the possibilities of existence. Each pseudonym represents a different view or form of life. Kierkegaard's existential dialectic moves within three chief spheres of existence: the aesthetic, the ethical, and the religious. For Kierkegaard these three existential possibilities are not to be conceived of so that the third is the logical synthesis of the first two. The triadic dialectic does not imply a necessary progression, nor does it remove the necessity of facing an ultimate "either-or" leap from one stage to another. Neither does the "leap" from the ethical to the religious stage mean that the existential choice between the aesthetic and religious is forever put behind. The three spheres of existence are continually present possibilities, although for Kierkegaard the religious stage represents authentic selfhood. Aesthetic life is examined in the first parts of *Either/Or* (1843) and *Stages on Life's Way* (1845), while ethical existence is explored in the second part of each of these works. The religious stage is examined from the "distanced" perspective of the outsider, or of nonbelief, in such pseudonymous works as *Philosophical Fragments, Concluding Unscientific Postscript,* and *Fear and Trembling.* The religious and affirmatively Christian point of view is expressed in the pseudonymous *Sickness unto Death* and *Training in Christianity,* as well as in the late Christian discourses.

Kierkegaard identifies the aesthetic sphere of existence with Romantic sensibility and sees this sensibility expressed in numerous moods, especially in sensual immediacy (Don Juan), doubt (Faust), and despair (Ahasuerus, the Wandering Jew). The chief characteristic of the aesthetic sphere is the lack of involvement, the sense of detachment. It is marked by experiment and the inability to make a determined, permanent decision. The aesthete lacks moral will and, therefore, loses power over him or herself.

The aesthetic stage is portrayed in both "quantitative" and "qualitative" terms, the former represented by the sensualist wooer and seducer Don Juan. He becomes the melancholy victim of his own search for the pleasurable moment which is never satisfied. He is in a state of dread but is unconscious of it. Kierkegaard sees Goethe's Faust as a "reflective" seducer, illustrated as well by "A" and by Johannes of the "Seducer's Diary" in *Either/Or*. The difference between Faust and Don Juan is that between a "qualitative" or intensive and a "quantitative" or extensive aesthetic existence. Kierkegaard contrasts them by reference to two methods in the "rotation" of crops. Don Juan's seductions are inartistic and unreflective. They are like the weary "extensive" movement from one city to another. Faust and Johannes, however, represent another method of rotation; not one involving the change of soil, but "in changing the methods of cultivation and the kinds of crops." Here a principle of limitation is adopted which is more artistic and resourceful. It seeks relief from boredom "not through extensity but through intensity." Faust seeks to assuage his doubting soul through his erotic love of Margarete, "not because he believes in it but because it has an element of presentness in which there is momentary rest and a striving that diverts and that draws attention away from the nothingness of doubt. His pleasure, therefore, does not have the cheerfulness that characterizes a Don Juan."[7]

The melancholy and despair that result from the attempt to live aesthetically are powerfully described in "The Unhappy One" who lives without hope forever. But Faustian doubt is only a qualified form of despair, for frequently it can long remain satisfied, like Lessing, with the search for truth, though skeptical of ever finding it. Nevertheless, such doubt is frequently the covering for a deeper despair.

Recognition of complete despair is invoked in the figure of the Wandering Jew, in whom lurks the profounder despair which results in complete absence of hope. In *Sickness unto Death* Kierkegaard analyzes the dialectic of despair with brilliant psychological insight. He agrees with Hegel that despair is something a person must taste before he or she comes to true consciousness of life. Thus despair is dialectical and not wholly negative, for it opens up divergent possibilities of response. Despair can lead to a spiritual hardening and death; it can also serve to awaken a person to his or her eternal validity. But there is no salvation except in passing through despair.

> So when I say "Despair," it is no overexcited youth who wants to whirl you into the maelstrom of passions. . . . But I shout to you not as a consolation, not as a state in which you are to remain, but as an act that takes all the power and earnestness and concentration of the soul. . . . [A]ny human being who has not tasted the bitterness of despair has fallen short of the meaning of life.[8]

To despair absolutely is to break one's bondage to the finite perspective, for "in despairing a person chooses again, and what then does he choose? He chooses himself, not in his immediacy, not in this accidental individual, but he chooses himself in his eternal validity."[9] Such a change does not involve a smooth dialectical mediation. There is no rational escape from the sickness unto death. Anxiety and despair simply bring one before a decision, and this decision, filled with pathos, requires a "leap" to a new stage.

The leap to the ethical stage is summed up in the imperative: "Choose thyself." That is, affirm an absolute choice. For Kierkegaard the ethical life is defined not so much by the content of one's choices as by the manner of choice. To choose ethically is to choose with passion, in an unconditional way. The ethical demand is that one become infinitely interested in existing. The aim of the ethical life, therefore, is not simply to know the truth but to become it, not to produce objective truth but to transform one's subject self. According to Kierkegaard, it is ethical decision that gives a person a sense of inner coherence, as well as a task and vocation.

While Kierkegaard does not regard ethical existence as the highest stage of selfhood, he has a deep respect for the ethical vocation, as illustrated in the figure of Judge William in *Either/Or* and *Stages of Life's Way*. Like Kant, the judge is devoted to the realization of those values that are universal and eternal. Unlike aesthetic existence, the ethical vocation may appear bland, like Judge William's devotion to the civic virtues; nevertheless, such a vocation requires *passion,* or the wholehearted commitment of the self to its vocational choice. This sphere of ethical humanism is integrally related to what Johannes

Climacus describes as Religiousness A, or immanent religiousness, both in the *Fragments* and the *Postscript.*

The *Postscript,* however, also describes the ethical as inherent in "faith" or Christian existence, but there it is expressed in the pathos of guilt and suffering that are characteristic of Religiousness B. Regarding *Either/Or,* Kierkegaard remarks that "there were only two components and the Judge [the ethical] was unconditionally the winner."[10] However, in *Stages on Life's Way* Judge Williams's preoccupation with temporal concerns reveals how close he is to aesthetic existence, and his belief in a secular vocation begins to fall apart. He is divided and struggling and recognizes that the next movement is in the direction of the religious.

Kierkegaard was not an extravagant ethical intuitionist, but he believed that most ethical theories were "formalistic" and thus did not give adequate consideration to the single individual and the unique situation. Ethical judgment requires reflection, but such reflection cannot overlook the uniqueness of each person and each situation. This is exactly what is wrong with most ethical systems, such as Kant's. They are overly formal and, therefore, cannot take into account certain indispensable existential realities. According to Kierkegaard, a moral theology like Kant's founders on three basic issues. First, it tends to make evil and sin superficial rather than radical. Kant recognized radical evil, but Kierkegaard sees this as inconsistent with Kant's strong commitment to autonomy. Second, Kant's ethics fails to deal adequately with the motivation or will to carry out the moral imperative. Kant erroneously assumed that the "ought implies the can." In Kantian ethics the ethical is situated in the *ideal* (the categorical imperative), but the *real* involves sin. As Kierkegaard observes:

> An ethic that ignores sin is an altogether useless science, but if it recognizes sin it is *eo ipso* beyond its sphere. . . . Ethics fails over repentance, for repentance is the supreme expression of ethics, but as such contains the most profound ethical contradiction.[11]

Kant's theology erroneously conceived of sin in quantitative terms. Kierkegaard, on the other hand, sees sin as "total guilt"—and total guilt is not a condition that can be determined by adding up particular guilty acts.

> The priority of the total guilt is no empirical qualification, is no sum total, because a totality-qualification is never produced numerically. The totality of guilt comes into existence for the individual by joining his guilt, be it just one, be it utterly trivial, together with the relation to an eternal happiness.[12]

That is, the person who justifies him or herself does so by judging the self by an all-too-human standard.

> The person who turns toward himself with the absolute criterion will of course not be able to go on living in the bliss that if he keeps the commandments and has received no sentence for anything and is regarded by the clique of revivalists as a really sincere person he then is a good fellow, who, if he does not die soon, will in a short time become all too perfect for this world. He will, on the contrary, again and again discover guilt and in turn discover it within the totality-category: guilt.[13]

To maintain a quantitative view of guilt is, in Kierkegaard's opinion, to remain religiously immature. "With regard to guilt-consciousness, childishness assumes that today, for example, he is guilty in this or that, then for eight days he is guiltless, but then on the ninth day everything goes wrong again."[14]

Kantian moral theology not only makes trivial the serious human condition of sin and guilt but, finally, fails to deal adequately with the question of the moral will, the power to carry out the moral imperative. The categorical imperative convinces the individual of his or her duty but leaves the person powerless to effect it. The ethical idealist illicitly assumes "the ought implies the can." But that which we would do we do not; sin is a surd which proves the universal imperative an ineffectual ideal. According to Kierkegaard, only the theonomous influence of grace can resolve the ethical problem. But to speak of grace is to enter the religious stage— the stage of dogma which Kant disallowed. Kierkegaard writes:

With dogmatics begins the science that in contrast to that science called ideal, namely, ethics, proceeds from actuality. It begins with the actual in order to raise it up to ideality. It does not deny the presence of sin; on the contrary, it presupposes and explains it by presupposing hereditary sin. However, since dogmatics is very seldom treated purely, hereditary sin is often brought within its confines in such a way that the impression of the heterogeneous originality of dogmatics does not always come clearly into view but becomes confused. . . . Therefore dogmatics must not explain hereditary sin but rather explain it by presupposing it . . . something that no science can grasp.[15]

Kierkegaard's third criticism of the ethical stage is that its formalism leaves no place for the individual exception to the universal imperative. Kierkegaard's argument for the irreducible singularity of the individual's status before God is portrayed most effectively in *Fear and Trembling.* There Kierkegaard offers a sustained analysis of the story of Abraham's sacrifice of his son Isaac. For Kierkegaard Abraham is the prototype of the *exception,* the person called by God to perform a task which is a scandal to ethical rationalism. By means of this story, Kierkegaard asks whether there can be a "teleological suspension of the ethical." Can there be situations in which one's absolute obedience to God contravenes the categorical imperative? The answer is yes because, as Kierkegaard remarks, one who knows the living God "determines his relation to the universal by his relation to the absolute, not his relation to the absolute by his relation to the universal."[16]

According to Kierkegaard, Abraham is even defensible in keeping his purpose a secret before Sarah and Isaac, for the "Knight of Faith" obeys God without seeking to be justified before others. There is something unique and ineffable about one's relation to God. Both Kant and Hegel conceived of morality as the subordination of the self to the universal—at the expense, as Kierkegaard saw it, of elements indispensable to the life of the individual.

For all the reasons we have enumerated, all "first ethics" or idealistic ethics fail and require an existential leap of faith to the religious stage of existence. *Fear and Trembling* reveals the third sphere of existence, the religious.

Faith and the Absolute Paradox

The religious stage itself offers two possibilities—what Kierkegaard calls "Religiousness A" and "Religiousness B"—in other terms, the religion of immanence and the religion of transcendence, or the religion of Socrates and the religion of Jesus Christ. Kierkegaard develops the differences between these two religious options and his view of Christianity in the *Philosophical Fragments* and the *Postscript.* The distinction between the two options and the problem of Christianity is posed by Kierkegaard in the title page motto of the *Fragments:* "Can a historical point of departure be given for an eternal consciousness; how can such a point of departure be of more than historical interest; can an eternal happiness be built on historical knowledge?"[17] Here, through Johannes Climacus, Kierkegaard raises in the form of a question the thesis that Lessing had put to Christianity as a fact: "Incidental truths of history can never furnish the proof of necessary truths of reason."

Climacus begins this "project of thought" with the Socratic problem: "How far does the truth admit of being learned?" In answering the question, he contrasts the view of Socrates, who is Kierkegaard's symbol of all philosophical Idealism, with the Christian doctrine of revelation. Religiousness A, or the religion of Socrates, presupposes that religious truth is present *within* every human being, for, as Plato taught in the *Meno,* all true knowledge is merely recollection. All humans possess truth from eternity; what is required is a teacher or midwife who, by skillful means, can induce the student to give birth to the truth. This implies that the person of the teacher and the occasion have no special significance.

Viewed Socratically, any point of departure in time is *eo ipso* something accidental, a vanishing point, an occasion. Nor is the teacher anything more. . . . In the Socratic view, every human being is himself the midpoint, and the whole world focuses only on him because his self-knowledge is God-knowledge.[18]

In such a view whether one has been instructed "by Socrates or by Prodicus or by a servant-girl" is incidental.

What if the Socratic approach to truth is wrong, however? What if a specific *moment* in time is of vital significance for the acquisition of the truth? The consequence would be that the teacher ceases to be an incidental occasion in the student's own coming to the truth but the indispensable and unique bearer of the truth. It follows that the student is destitute of the truth and in a state of error:

> Now if the moment is to acquire decisive significance, then the seeker up until that moment must not have possessed the truth, not even in the form of ignorance, for in that case the moment becomes only a moment of occasion; indeed, he must not even be a seeker. . . . Consequently, he has to be defined as being outside the truth (not coming toward it like a proselyte, but going away from it) or as untruth. He is, then, untruth.[19]

Now, if the learner is to acquire the truth, the teacher must *bring it to him or her and give the condition necessary for understanding it.*

> But the one who not only gives the learner the truth but provides the condition is not a teacher. Ultimately, all instruction depends upon the presence of the condition; if it is lacking, then a teacher is capable of nothing, because in the second case, the teacher, before beginning to teach, must transform, not reform, the learner. But no human being is capable of doing this; if it is to take place, it must be done by the god himself. . . . The teacher, then, is the god, who gives the condition and gives the truth. Now, what shall we call such a teacher, for we surely do agree that we have gone far beyond the definition of a teacher.[20]

A teacher who gives the learner both the requisite condition and the truth is no ordinary teacher but should be called *Saviour* and *Redeemer.* The moment is also unique and decisive; let us call it the *Fullness of Time.* The disciple who, in a state of error, receives the condition and the truth "becomes a different person . . . becomes a person of a different quality, or as we can also call it, a *new* person."[21]

It is clear that Climacus's "project of thought" is not his own invention but takes its departure from the Christian Gospel. Accordingly, God is not *in* humanity, for humanity is separated from God by

sin. Therefore, God must come to the individual from outside by his own grace. We start then with God, not humanity. But God does not need humanity for fulfillment, nor is the moment of God's self-revelation demanded of God. God chooses out of love to become humanity's teacher. Here is met what appears to be an impasse—the incommensurability between God and humanity.

> Out of love, therefore, the god must be eternally resolved in this way, but just as his love is the basis, so also must love be the goal, for it would indeed be a contradiction for the god to have a basis of movement and a goal that do not correspond to this. The love, then, must be for the learner, and the goal must be to win him, for only in love is the different made equal, and only in equality or in unity is there understanding. . . . Yet this love is basically unhappy, for they are very unequal, and what seems so easy—namely, that the god must be able make himself understood—is not so easy if he is not to destroy that which is different.[22]

To accomplish the divine aim, God can neither draw the person up nor appear before the person in awesome glory and majesty. The union can only be accomplished by God's descent and appearance, not in glory, but in the form of a servant. "But," Kierkegaard reminds the reader, "the form of the servant was not something put on. Therefore God must suffer all things, endure all things . . . thirst all things, be forsaken in death, absolutely the equal of the lowliest of human beings—look, behold the man!"[23] The truth of Christianity comes then at a particular moment in history in which the eternal God appears in the form of a humble human servant.

Socrates had considered human nature a great *paradox,* for when he reflected on the human being he could not decide whether it was a stranger monster than Typhon or a creature partaking of the divine. But, compared with the Socratic paradox, the Incarnation of the Eternal in time exceeds all the limits of human comprehension. It is, in Kierkegaard's words, the *Absolute Paradox,* the *Miracle,* the *Absurd* to which we can respond either in Faith or in Offense. The paradox of the Incarnation is doubly absurd, for it claims that God has become human, that the Eternal has become temporal, and that our eternal happiness can have its point of departure in an historical event the very historicity of which can only be accorded probability.

Kierkegaard recapitulates as follows:

> If we do not assume the moment, then we go back to Socrates, and it was precisely from him that we wanted to take leave in order to discover something. If the moment is posited, the paradox is there, for in its most abbreviated form the paradox can be called the moment. Through the moment, the learner becomes untruth; the person who knew himself becomes confused about himself and instead of self-knowledge he acquires the consciousness of sin, etc. . . . And the moment of decision is *foolishness,* for if the decision is posited, then the learner becomes untruth. . . . The expression of offense is that the moment is foolishness, the paradox is foolishness. . . . (But) the offense remains outside the paradox—no wonder, since the paradox is the wonder.[24]

The coming of the Eternal into time is the wonder or miracle and, as such, lies outside the realm of objective proof. The relationship between the disciple and the paradox is always that of faith. This is made clear by Kierkegaard in his discussion of the contemporary disciple and the disciple at second-hand. It is frequently assumed that the original disciples were in a more favorable position than the believer of today. But such is not the case. It is true that a contemporary of Jesus may have been an historical eyewitness, but historical knowledge does not make the eyewitness a disciple. On the contrary, it may well make discipleship more difficult. The belief that God is incarnate in the rabbi of Nazareth walking around in the city of Jerusalem is an absurdity and an offense to reason. The eyewitness has no advantage.

> The contemporary can go and observe the teacher—does he then dare to believe his eyes? Yes, why not? As a consequence, however, does he dare to believe that he is a follower? Not at all, *for if he believes his eyes, he is in fact deceived, for the god cannot be known directly.* Then may he close his eyes? Quite so. But if he does, then what is the advantage of being contemporary?[25] (Italics added.)

How, then, does the original learner become a disciple? Kierkegaard answers:

> When the understanding is discharged and he receives the condition. When does he receive this? In the moment. This condition, what does it condition? His understanding of the eternal. . . . In the moment, therefore, he receives the eternal condition, and he knows this from having received it in the moment, for otherwise he merely calls to mind that he had it from eternity. He receives the condition in the moment and receives it from that teacher himself. All extravagant talking and trumpeting from the housetops about being crafty enough, even though he did not receive the condition from the teacher, to discover the god's incognito . . . that he could detect it in himself, for he felt so strange every time he looked at the teacher, that there was something in that teacher's voice and countenance, etc., etc.,—this is blather, by which no one becomes a follower but only mocks the god.[26]

According to Kierkegaard, the disciple believes *only* because he has received the condition from God. The disciple knows that he would have nothing without God's grace, for without grace he is blinded by error and cannot possibly pierce the *Absolute Paradox,* God's incognito. In that case Faith is as paradoxical as the Paradox, for "Faith is itself a wonder, and everything that holds true of the paradox is also true of faith."[27]

It follows that there is no advantage or disadvantage to being a contemporary of Jesus or a disciple at second hand. "For one who has what one has from the god himself obviously has it at first hand, and one who does not have it from the god himself is not a follower."[28]

Two questions do remain, however. What, if anything, can the original disciple do for his successors? He can, Kierkegaard concedes, "tell someone who comes later that he himself has believed that fact." But that is not, in the strict sense, a communication but merely affords an occasion.

> Thus if I say that this and this occurred, I speak historically, but if I say, "I believe and have believed that this happened, *although it is folly to the understanding and an offense to the human heart,*" I have in the very same moment done everything to prevent anyone else

from making up his mind in immediate continuity with me and to decline all partnership, because every single person must conduct himself exactly the same way.[29]

The original disciple can relate the content of his or her faith, but the content exists only to be appropriated by faith. There is no shortcut, no immediacy whereby the leap of faith can be removed or its indubitability assured. Likewise, the *credibility* of the contemporary witness cannot be the basis of the secondary disciple's belief. This would be the case if the *fact* referred to were a simple historical fact, but the fact in question is the *Moment,* the *absolute* or *eternal fact.* Purely historical facts are relative, and so whatever can be clearly differentiated by time is *eo ipso* not the Absolute. However, if the fact referred to is an eternal fact, then every age is equally near it, for there is only one tense in relation to the eternal and that is the present. The sum of the matter is simply that if the credibility of a contemporary witness is to have any interest for a successor, it must be with respect to historical fact. But if we are talking about the *Moment,* we must ask, What historical fact? What historical "fact" that can become an object only for faith and which one human being cannot ever communicate immediately to another? If we are talking about this "fact," we are talking about *revelation,* which cannot be contained within the relativities and probabilities of historical research.

> If the fact of which we speak were a simple historical fact, the historiographer's scrupulous accuracy would be of great importance. This is not the case here, for faith cannot be distilled from even the finest detail. The heart of the matter is the historical fact that the god has been in human form, and the other details are not even as important as they would be if the subject were a human being instead of a god.[30]

Climacus thus concludes his "project of thought" with one of the most-discussed passages in modern theology:

> Even if the contemporary generation had not been left anything behind except these words, "We have believed that in such and such a year the god appeared in the humble form of a servant, lived and taught among

us, and then died"—this is more than enough. The contemporary generation would have done what is needful, for this little announcement, this world-historical *nota bene,* is enough to become an occasion for someone who comes later, and the most prolix report can never in all eternity become more for the person who comes later.[31]

The question on the title page of the *Fragments* has now been answered. There can be an historical point of departure for an eternal consciousness which can have more than a mere historical interest—that is, if it is a *unique* historical fact, the Paradox, the Moment of the Eternal entering into time. However, one's eternal happiness cannot be based upon historical knowledge alone, for history is the sphere of the relative and probable. Eternal truth can be appropriated only by a faith in the paradox held in infinite passion. Kierkegaard's understanding of the relationship between faith, subjectivity, and truth requires further analysis.

Truth Is Subjectivity

As we have seen, the theme of the paradox is central to Kierkegaard's thought. The necessary counterpart to that theme is Kierkegaard's doctrine that *Truth is subjectivity.* Kierkegaard did not deny that there were truths independent of the knower. What he did insist on was that it is wrong to think of religious truth, that is, faith, as acquired in the same way that one obtains information. To do so is to consider the person as somehow abstracted from the truth. It does not consider the existential role of the self in the appropriation of religious truth. But this is just the problem that confronts the existing individual.

In the *Postscript* Kierkegaard develops the thesis that it is not the objective truth of Christianity but the relationship of the existing individual to Christianity that is the fundamental problem. In religion the truth is subjective because it is a truth that requires personal appropriation. The objective point of view overlooks this very factor.

> Objectively viewed, Christianity is a *res in facto posita* [given fact], the truth of which is asked about in a purely objective way. . . . With regard to the subject's

relation to known truth, it is assumed that if only the objective truth has been obtained, appropriation is an easy matter; it is automatically included as a part of the bargain, and in the end the individual is a matter of indifference. Precisely this is the basis of the scholar's elevated calm and the parroter's comical thoughtlessness.[32]

The scholar misses the real point, for he or she confuses historical results with the appropriation of eternal truth. But history cannot produce such faith. On the contrary, scientific "results" impede faith.

> Faith does not result from a straightforward scholarly deliberation, nor does it come directly; on the contrary, *in this objectivity one loses that infinite, personal, impassioned interestedness, which is the condition of faith.*[33] (Italics added.)

Where there is undisputed evidence there is no passion, hence no faith, and therefore "Whereas up to now faith has had a beneficial taskmaster in uncertainty, it would have its worst enemy in this certainty."[34]

It is important to be clear, in the light of his provocative language about subjectivity, uncertainty, faith, and the "leap," that Kierkegaard was not opposed to objective knowledge in the sphere of science, nor was he a subjective idealist. He was, like the average person, a naive realist. Unlike Descartes and Kant he took for granted the factual reality and objectivity of the external world and other persons. In the sciences "objectivity" is necessary but, like mathematics, can often entail an "indifferent truth." The danger of scholarly objectivity is that it leads to an "approximation-process" that never can be completed and may never lead to a decision or action. And even in science, complete objectivity is not attainable since it, too, is probable, approximate, and open to correction. Kierkegaard, it is crucial to understand, applies his "subjectivity is truth" thesis to what he calls "ethico-religious" knowledge.[35] This kind of knowledge has to do with human existence, and, as Climacus notes, it is impossible to think about existence *in existence* without passion: "All existence-issues are passionate, because existence, if one becomes conscious of it, involves passion. To think about them so as to leave out passion is not to

think about them at all, is to forget the point that one indeed is oneself an existing person."[36]

In Kierkegaard's opinion passion—or inwardness—is the very criterion of religious faith, for faith is by definition the appropriation of the Absolute Paradox, that which for discursive reason is absurd and historically only probable. Only a faith which exhibits a passionate appropriation of its object is a true faith. Hence, for Kierkegaard, as for all twentieth-century Existentialists, the *how,* or mode of decision, takes precedence over the *what,* or object of one's devotion.

> If someone who lives in the midst of Christianity enters, with knowledge of the true idea of God, and prays, but prays in untruth, and if someone lives in an idolatrous land but prays with all the passion of infinity, although his eyes are resting upon the image of an idol—where, then, is there more truth? The one prays in truth to God although he is worshipping an idol; the other prays in untruth to the true God and is therefore in truth worshipping an idol.[37]

The inward "how" of appropriation is the passion of the infinite, and the passion of the infinite is the truth. "But," adds Kierkegaard,

> the passion of the infinite is precisely subjectivity, and thus subjectivity is truth. . . . Only in subjectivity is there decision, whereas wanting to become objective is untruth. The passion of the infinite, not its content, is the deciding factor, for its content is precisely itself. In this way the subjective "how" and subjectivity are the truth.[38]

If subjectivity is the truth, then any expression of such truth must include its antithesis to objectivity and an indication of the tension and risk involved in subjective inwardness. Kierkegaard offers the following definition of existential truth: "An objective uncertainty, held fast through appropriation with the most passionate inwardness, is the truth, the highest truth there is for an existing person."[39] The truth is the existential venture which chooses an objective uncertainty with the passion of the infinite.

Here it is necessary, once again, to stress a point. When Kierkegaard speaks of truth as subjectivity, as an objective uncertainty held in infinite passion, it is necessary to remember that he is referring to truth that cannot be known through a "parrot-like echo" but only through one's own activity. Such is the nature of ethical and religious truth—for the simple reason that such truths are incapable of being reduced to irrefutable demonstrations. In other words, when Kierkegaard speaks of the "leap," he is not speaking of a method of choosing a brand of refrigerator! The "leap of faith" is a moral and religious category and has to do with what William James called "live options"—those existential decisions of life involving "limit situations" in which certainty remains impossible.

A further question requires clarification. If truth is subjectivity, is not Kierkegaard's doctrine open to a radical subjectivism and individualism in theology? Is not Kierkegaard encouraging irrationalism? The question has been widely debated, and the issue is a complex one. There is little doubt that Kierkegaard's position lends itself to subjectivism and irrationalism. That he himself is guilty of either of these charges is doubtful. Book One of the *Postscript* makes it clear that the question of religious truth can be dealt with objectively but that such a stance is by itself *inadequate*. In the sphere of religion, all statements about the religious object involve the interdependence of object and subject—i.e., fact and appropriation, event and interpretation. Kierkegaard's own theology was in one sense extremely objectivist in that he largely accepted the biblical traditions and the Church's dogmatic formulae uncritically and was untouched by the radical historical work of scholars such as D. F. Strauss. His almost exclusive emphasis on subjective appropriation in faith was possible, perhaps, because of his unconscious *assumption* of the tradition's reliability. Kierkegaard's apparent disinterest in the historical bases of faith is, therefore, more understandable and much less radical than that of Karl Barth and his followers who, while following Kierkegaard in this regard, do so in full knowledge of modern historical-critical research on the Gospels and Church dogma.

It must also be kept in mind that most of the attention given to "truth as subjectivity" in the *Postscript* has to do with the ethico-religious sphere, and it is clear that it is not the whole truth regarding Christian faith. If one concentrates on the

Fragments, it is easy to interpret even Christian faith as an *intellectual* act, that is, as assent to the Absolute Paradox as an absurd proposition or dogma. But in the *Postscript* it is clear that such an intellectualistic conception is rejected. Christian faith has to do, rather, with the relationship to a Person (Christ, the God-man). Kierkegaard writes:

> The object of faith, then, is the actuality of the god in existence, that is, as a particular individual, that is, that the god has existed as an individual human being. Christianity is not a doctrine about the unity of the divine and the human. . . . In other words, if Christianity were a doctrine, then the relation to it would not be one of faith, since there is only an intellectual relation to a doctrine. . . . What holds as the maximum in the sphere of intellectuality, to remain completely indifferent to the actuality of the teacher, holds in just the opposite way in the sphere of faith—its maximum is the infinite interestedness in the actuality of the teacher.[40]

What does faith as "infinite interestedness" in the teacher involve? For Kierkegaard it entails *a consciousness of one's own inability and of one's total guilt.* In other words, Christian faith draws one into a qualitatively different subjectivity—what Kierkegaard calls *"subjectivity as untruth."* Such a subjectivity plunges one into a deeper consciousness than is possible in the ethico-religious sphere and the Socratic paradox, that is, of an objective uncertainty grasped with infinite passion by a finite, existing individual. For to be in *untruth,* the self or believer is wholly dependent on the other, on God. It is to embrace the *double paradox* or the Absolute Paradox in which the learner is given not only the truth by the teacher but also the capacity to apprehend the truth. The consciousness of sin requires that through grace the person be given the gift of truth by God. "Subjectivity as untruth" is, therefore, something that neither paganism nor the natural reason can know, since it is a blow against human pride and involves knowing sin, total guilt, and grace.

A final question involves the "leap of faith" in the religious sphere and the claim that Kierkegaard in fact renounces any *intelligible* choice or action on the part of the individual, despite the attention that he gives to existential passion and inwardness. Scholars differ considerably in their interpretation of Kierkegaard on this point. Some, perhaps most, appear to deny that Kierkegaard offers an "argument from need" or that he appeals to what Pascal calls "reasons of the heart." They argue that the Absolute Paradox leaves no place for such a volitionalist role for the human will or emotions, since faith is a pure gift of God. As one scholar asserts: "This faith is not produced by an act of the will on the part of the believer, but rather is an act of God. All that the believer can do is to be open to God's gift of grace."[41] Other scholars point to the passages in the *Discourses* and the *Journals* that do appear to stress the role of the emotions and will and which also appear to imply a real existential "need," implying a "point of contact" between human need and the divine response. In the *Journals,* for example, one reads: "There is only one proof of Christianity and that, quite rightly, is from the emotions, when the dread of sin and a heavy conscience tortures man into crossing the narrow line. . . . There lies Christianity."[42] In the *Discourses* Kierkegaard gives much attention to human "need," "concern" and "seeking" as bringing *with them* the "nutriment" that comes from God.

Finally, there are scholars who, while rejecting "volitionalist" interpretations of the "leap of faith," also decline to accept what they see as a false dichotomy between God's grace and human activity in Kierkegaard's conception of the "leap of faith." These scholars argue that Kierkegaard's theology is not an appeal to irrationalism. Kierkegaard is, of course, aware of the limits of human reason and of the laughable pretensions of those rationalists who assume a position *sub specie aeternitatis.* Therefore, his valuable polemic against the presumptuous "immediacy" of certain philosophers and historians, and his insistence on the objective uncertainty and the passionate quality of the act of faith, may lead a reader to view Kierkegaard as an irrationalist whose position is immune to criticism. But this is a mistaken reading. For Kierkegaard the religious life entails reasons, but they are not the same kind of reasons that we employ in science, nor will they ever amount to indisputable proofs, since the religious life is one of choice and passionate commitment. However, Kierkegaard is not an irrationalist, these

scholars argue, because he does not demand a thorough discontinuity between divine grace and human decision in the act of faith. The *leap* of faith is neither a blind act of the will nor a movement based solely on the heteronomous and extrinsic act of God, despite the fact that the "leap" does convey graphically both the *decisiveness* and the *transformative* character of religious faith.

This interpretation insists that Kierkegaard's understanding of the "leap of faith" is opposed to all dualistic notions of the will and knowledge, or of divine prevenience and human choice. The divine gift of grace and the human decision are not mutually exclusive. Coming to faith is like undergoing a radical reenvisionment of the world or like a moral transformation that is irresistible and yet is not coerced. For Kierkegaard, as for J. H. Newman, the argument goes, faith is an imaginative reconception or envisionment of life based on a *gestalt* shift, or a convergence of factors that, taken as a whole, reach a "critical threshold" which results in a *qualitative change,* a *decisive transition.* This is not the immediate result of a choice or act of will in the normal sense, yet in retrospect this new vision is experienced as at once compelled and the freest of human acts. Moreover, this new envisionment makes complete sense—indeed, it appears to be the only real option or possibility and is entirely compelling. Such a view, it is argued, paradoxically preserves both discontinuity and continuity in the act of religious faith or the revisioning of life.[43] Critics of this interpretation claim that, while countering the charge of irrationalism, it presents a too-rational account of Kierkegaard's Absolute Paradox and the leap to the religious sphere of existence and that it does not take seriously enough what Kierkegaard calls "the breach of continuity." No attempt will be made to resolve these differences in interpretation here; one must read Kierkegaard and judge for oneself.

FRIEDRICH NIETZSCHE

Introduction

Because this book is fundamentally concerned with the encounter between Christianity and modern thought, it is appropriate to conclude our

Friedrich Nietzsche

account of the nineteenth century with Friedrich Nietzsche (1844–1900). Like that of Feuerbach and Strauss, Nietzsche's work was profoundly shaped by his encounter with Christianity, and his critique of Christianity remains a powerful challenge even today. Strauss raised crucial historical questions about Christianity that continue to engage biblical scholars and theologians. Feuerbach's psycho-genetic criticism has, through Freud and others in the twentieth century, continued to influence thinking about the root and function of religion and of Christianity in particular. Marx's socioeconomic and ideological critique of religion has, of course, had a profound influence in large parts of the world for the better part of the twentieth century, and it continues to inform the work of scholars who are not orthodox Marxists. Nietzsche's "suspicion" is different; it is fundamentally a *moral* criticism and is based on a naturalistic anthropology and psychology that reflects the influence of nineteenth-century evolutionary theory. Ironically, Nietzsche's scorn for what he saw as Christianity's psychological "slave" or "herd" morality has been found congenial to notorious versions of "social Darwinism," as well as to varieties of libertar-

ians and moral hedonists. Both groups represent views of life that were abhorrent to Nietzsche and his ideal of "self-overcoming" and mastery.

Nietzsche's relationship to Christianity is rather more complex than is generally understood. He has been both praised and dismissed as the archenemy of Christianity, and it is foolish to minimize his virulent hatred of what he saw as Christianity's resentful slave morality and nihilism. As we will see, however, his view of Jesus is more complicated. During the Nazi period Nietzsche was interpreted as offering a new form of Christian life and thought.[44] The philosopher Karl Jaspers has placed great importance on the Christian roots of Nietzsche's thought and refers to Nietzsche as a man who knew and admitted the Christian basis of his real motivating forces.[45] Nietzsche respected "genuine Christianity" and said that he was honored "to come from a breed which was in earnest about its Christianity." At the same time, he could call "Christianity the one great curse . . . the one great instinct of revenge . . . the one immortal blemish of mankind."[46]

Many critics have pointed to Nietzsche's rather myopic and, therefore, simplistic view of Christianity based, as they see it, on the narrow moralistic piety that was fostered in his home during his childhood. Be that as it may, our task is to attempt to describe the nature of Nietzsche's critique of Christianity which, though not as broadly influential as others, is, like Kierkegaard's attack on Christendom, ruthless and, with regard to certain expressions of Christianity, also impressive.

Friedrich Nietzsche was the child of a Lutheran parsonage. His father as well as his mother's father and grandfather were Lutheran pastors. Nietzsche's father died when he was only five years old, and he was brought up in Naumberg in an excessively feminine environment with his mother, sister, grandmother, and two aunts. We are told that young Nietzsche was serious and introspective and was known by his companions as "the little pastor."

During his early school years Nietzsche's lifelong admiration of Greek culture was aroused, and his alienation from Christianity began. At eighteen his religious doubts were already matured. This is evident in an early essay entitled "Fate and History," in which he admits that, regarded with an impartial eye, many conclusions would have to be drawn concerning Christianity that would conflict with commonly held opinions. He then adds that an attempt at such a free, impartial inquiry

> is the work not of a few weeks, but of a lifetime. To dare to launch out on the sea of doubt without compass or steersman is death and destruction for undeveloped heads; most are struck down by storms, very few discover new countries. From the midst of this immeasurable ocean of ideas one will often long to be back on firm land.[47]

In 1864 Nietzsche entered the University of Bonn but the following year moved to Leipzig to continue his philological studies. While in Leipzig, Nietzsche first read Schopenhauer's *World as Will and Idea.* While he was to reject Schopenhauer's pessimism, the book's theme of blind Will and its atheism were appealing to the young classicist whose break with Christianity was by now complete.

In 1869, on the recommendation of F. Ritschl, Nietzsche was appointed to the chair of philology at the University of Basel without yet having completed his doctorate. It was during these early years in Basel that Nietzsche became a close friend of the composer Richard Wagner, whose villa on Lake Lucerne Nietzsche frequently visited. Nietzsche's attachment to Wagner at this time is reflected in his first important work, *The Birth of Tragedy,* published in 1871. During these years of teaching, Nietzsche also published *Thoughts Out of Season,* which consisted of attacks on historical learning and on D. F. Strauss as the "philistine of culture" and essays extolling Schopenhauer and Wagner. Nietzsche resigned his professorship at Basel in 1879 because of persistent ill health and a growing dissatisfaction with what he considered academic pedantry. For the next ten years he led the life of a wanderer, seeking a cure for his physical ailments at various places in Italy, Switzerland, and Germany. During the early years of this period, he produced *Human—All Too Human, The Dawn of Day,* and *Joyful Wisdom,* all of which reflect a new phase of his career. Then began his attack on metaphysics, traditional morality, self-renunciation, and Christianity, which, for Nietzsche, represented the amalgam of all of these evils.

Nietzsche's most famous work, *Thus Spake Zarathustra,* appeared in four parts between 1883 and 1885. In this visionary and poetical work he presents two of his most significant ideas: the transvaluation of values and the *Übermensch.** *Zarathustra* was followed by *Beyond Good and Evil* (1886) and *A Genealogy of Morals* (1887). *Beyond Good and Evil* was meant to be a prologue to Nietzsche's greatest work, one on which he was already at work but which he never completed. The notes for this were published posthumously as *The Will to Power.*

During this period Nietzsche found himself more and more alienated from old friends and isolated by his failure to communicate his innermost thoughts. He wrote to his sister: "A profound man needs friends, unless indeed he has a God. And I have neither God nor friend!" He came to see himself as an exception, one given the unique vocation of heralding the coming of the superior individual. But the conflict between his deep emotional desire for companions and disciples and his growing isolation, coupled with his feverish mental activity, brought him to the brink of exhaustion. The writings of 1888, *Nietzsche contra Wagner, The Twilight of the Idols, The Antichrist,* and *Ecce Homo,* are the work of a hostile, frenzied, but brilliant and powerful mind—a mind pushed to the extreme of mental tension. The extravagant self-exaltation of *Ecce Homo* borders on madness.

In January of 1889 Professors Jacob Burckhardt and Franz Overbeck of Basel received bizarre letters from Nietzsche, who was then living in Italy. Overbeck rushed to Turin, where he found his friend in a state of insanity. Nietzsche never recovered. He lived the remaining years under the care of his mother and then his sister and died in Weimar on August 25, 1900.

The "Death of God" and the Revaluation

Nietzsche judged the modern world to be in a state of cultural decline—in what he called a condition of nihilism. Like Matthew Arnold, Nietzsche saw himself "between two worlds, one dead, the

---

*Since the term "Superman" may connote something supernatural and has come to be identified with Nazi racial theories and with a comic book character, it is preferable to translate Nietzsche's term *Übermensch* as "Overman" or superior individual.

other powerless to be born." Speculative philosophy was spent, but its place was taken by an effete liberalism and a crude, acquisitive materialism. A complacent, philistine optimism was rife. Nietzsche expressed this condition of cultural nihilism in a powerful parable entitled "The Madman," cited here in its entirety.

The Madman

Have you not heard of that madman who lit a lantern in the bright morning hours, ran to the market place, and cried incessantly, "I seek God! I seek God!" As many of those who do not believe in God were standing around just then, he provoked much laughter. Why, did he get lost? said one. Did he lose his way like a child? said another. Or is he hiding? Is he afraid of us? Has he gone on a voyage? or emigrated? Thus they yelled and laughed. The madman jumped into their midst and pierced them with his glances.

"Whither is God?" he cried. "I shall tell you. *We have killed him*—you and I. All of us are his murderers. But how have we done this? How were we able to drink up the sea? Who gave us the sponge to wipe away the entire horizon? What did we do when we unchained this earth from its sun? Whither is it moving now? Whither are we moving now? Away from all suns? Are we not plunging continually? Backward, sideward, forward, in all directions? Is there any up or down left? Are we now straying as through an infinite nothing? Do we not feel the breath of empty space? Has it not become colder? Is not night and more night coming on all the while? Must not lanterns be lit in the morning? Do we not hear anything yet of the noise of the gravediggers who are burying God? Do we not smell anything yet of God's decomposition? Gods too decompose. God is dead. God remains dead. And we have killed him. How shall we, the murderers of all murderers, comfort ourselves? What was holiest and most powerful of all that the world has yet owned has bled to death under our knives. Who will wipe this blood off us? What water is there for us to clean ourselves? What festivals of atonement, what sacred games shall we have to invent? Is not the greatness of this deed too great for us? Must not we ourselves become gods simply to seem worthy of it? There has never been a greater deed; and whoever will be born after us—for the sake of this deed he will be part of a higher history than all history hitherto."

Here the madman fell silent and looked again at his listeners; and they too were silent and stared at him in astonishment. At last he threw his lantern on the ground, and it broke and went out. "I come too early," he said then; "my time has not come yet. This tremendous event is still on its way, still wandering—it has not yet reached the ears of man. Lightning and thunder require time, the light of the stars requires time, deeds require time even after they are done, before they can be seen and heard. This deed is still more distant from them than the most distant stars—*and yet they have done it themselves*."

It has been related further that on that same day the madman entered divers churches and there sang his *requiem aeternam deo.* Led out and called to account he is said to have replied each time, "What are these churches now if they are not the tombs and sepulchers of God?"[48]

For Nietzsche the "death of God" is not the result of philosophical analysis but a cultural fact, the consequences of which have not yet been fully revealed to Western consciousness. Yet we are living in the shadow of the dead God, and, when we awaken to the fact that God is truly dead, madness will erupt. For the death of God means the death of the ultimate ground and support of all traditional values.[49] For over two thousand years Western civilization has derived its "thou shalt" and "thou shalt not" from God, but that is now coming to an end. Humanity will be thrown back upon itself where "there is no one to command, no one to obey, no one to transgress." Humanity will be caught in a terrifying dilemma: To proclaim the death of God will be to deny everything its ultimate meaning and value, but to believe in the existence of God will be to live in a world of fictions, to embrace nihilism. For, according to Nietzsche, it is primarily Christianity, which he calls the "Platonism of the people," that destroyed truth, the truth of life proclaimed by the early Greeks, and has substituted the fictional supports of God, moral universals, grace, and immortality. This problem of nihilism is "far too great, too distant, too far from the comprehension of the many," but it is on its way and must be faced. It is crucial to Nietzsche's conception of Western nihilism that people are unaware of it, as witnessed by the response to the announcement of the death of God. Nevertheless, the alternatives are a return to decadence, to the nihilism of Christianity, or a courageous "transvaluation of values" in which individuals decide for themselves what is good and evil, true and beautiful.

Nietzsche believed that many had come to see through the dogmas created by Christianity but that they hadn't the courage to face the consequences of being thrown back on their own resources. At this point Nietzsche develops the interesting idea that it was the truth-seeking which was encouraged by Christianity that led to its own death. Nietzsche admits that "even we devotees of knowledge today, we godless ones and anti-metaphysicians, still take *our* fire too from the flame which a faith thousands of years old has kindled: that Christian faith, which was also Plato's faith, that God is truth, that truth is divine."[50] Atheism is, then, the last evolutionary phase of that Christian ideal of divine truth.

> *What,* strictly speaking, has actually *conquered* the Christian God . . . Christian morality itself, the concept of truthfulness which was taken more and more seriously, the confessional punctiliousness of Christian conscience, translated and sublimated into scientific conscience, into intellectual purity at any price. Regarding nature as though it were a proof of God's goodness and providence; interpreting history in honour of divine reason, as a constant testimonial to an ethical world order . . . now all that is *over,* it has conscience *against* it, every sensitive conscience sees it as indecent, as a pack of lies. . . . All great things bring about their own demise through an act of selfsublimation: that is the law of life. . . . In this way, Christianity *as a dogma* was destroyed by its own morality, in the same way Christianity *as a morality* must also be destroyed— we stand at the threshold of *this* occurrence. After Christian truthfulness has drawn one conclusion after another, it will finally draw the *strongest conclusion,* that *against* itself; this will, however, happen when it asks itself, "What does all will to truth mean?"[51]

Naturalism, the Will to Power, and Perspectivism

"What does all will to truth mean?" The question directs us to several doctrines that are central to Nietzsche's developing thought. First, it is impor-

tant to understand Nietzsche's naturalism, deeply informed as it is by nineteenth-century evolutionary theory. It is critical to his understanding of the "will to power." Contrary to some commentators, Nietzsche was not a materialist; but neither did he believe that the distinctive feature of the human species was reason; indeed, he found rationalism and idealism abhorrent. He saw humanity as a species of animal, and he mocked the high-flown "verbal pomp" of human vanity that interprets humans as having an extra-natural or super-natural origin and essence. One must be "deaf to the siren songs of old metaphysical bird catchers who have been piping at him all too long, 'you are more, you are higher, you are of a different origin.' " Nietzsche calls for a transference of humanity "back into nature."[52]

This does not mean that humanity is not a *distinctive* species of animal; for Nietzsche it is "the most interesting." But even the emergence of human "spirituality" and "soul"—which have profoundly altered life on earth—must be understood naturalistically. The entire evolution of humanity's spiritual life is a question of the body, but "it is the history of the development of a higher body that emerges into our sensibility. The organic is rising to yet higher levels."[53]

Again, Nietzsche is not speaking here in the optimistic terms of a social-Darwinian human progress, for humanity's developed spirituality can also be a cunning "sickliness" and "resentment." Spiritual life can manifest itself in "life-enhancement" and ascent, or in "weakness" and decay, in a turning away from the higher instincts of life. But in either case Nietzsche undertakes the task of a "moralistic naturalism," by which he means the tracing back of "moralities" to their natural, *extra-moral* origins, as well as the natural explanation of their development in their specific contexts. In this he is very much a product of the nineteenth-century *Zeitgeist;* for from the 1860s to the turn of the century, the historical and social sciences were especially preoccupied by the Darwinian questions of the origin and the development of social institutions, beliefs, and customs.

Nietzsche's thinking was deeply permeated with evolutionary ideas, and, as Walter Kaufmann rightly observes, it was Darwin who aroused Nietzsche from his dogmatic slumbers, just as Kant had been aroused earlier by Hume.[54] Darwin posed the questions that Nietzsche felt it necessary to confront. But Nietzsche's own response was not Darwinian; it was in fact anti-Darwin. What shocked Nietzsche was that someone like D. F. Strauss could cheerfully renounce his Christianity, embrace Darwin "as one of the greatest benefactors of mankind," and yet think that his own bourgeois, optimistic ethics was untouched. Nietzsche, too, renounced Christianity but agonized over the consequences of a godless world of blind, meaningless becoming. The future consequences horrified him:

> If the doctrines of sovereign Becoming, of the fluidity of all . . . species, of the lack of any cardinal distinction between man and animal . . . are hurled into the people for another generation . . . then nobody should be surprised when brotherhoods with the aim of robbery and exploitation of the nonbrothers . . . will appear on the arena of the future.[55]

Nietzsche's own project is to offer a vision of a "truly *human* being," of the superior being who can rise above the beasts. But this condition is not the destiny of a species, only that of the rare artist, philosopher, or saint. The "will to power" is not, then, to be confused with Darwin's adaptive "fitness" in the struggle for existence. Self-enhancement, not the preservation of the type, is Nietzsche's doctrine: "Basic error of biologists hitherto: it is not a question of the species, but of more powerful individuals. The many are only a means." The superior individual is one who must risk *existence itself* to achieve his or her "overcoming" and mastery. "Life," Nietzsche insists, "is not the adaptation of inner circumstances to outer ones, but will to power, which, working from within, incorporates and subdues more and more of that which is 'outside.' "[56] And it is this "higher type" of humanity that is, therefore, more vulnerable to extinction. In a note entitled "Anti-Darwin," Nietzsche writes:

> There are no *transitional forms*. . . . Every type has its limits: beyond this there is no evolution. . . . *My general view. First proposition:* man as a species is not progressing. Higher types are indeed attained, but they do not last. The level of the species is *not* raised. *Second*

> *proposition:* man as a species does not represent any progress compared to any other animal. The whole animal and vegetable kingdom does not evolve from the lower to the higher. . . . The richer and the more complex forms—for the expression "higher type" means no more than this—perish more easily: only the lowest preserve an apparent indestructibility. . . . Among men, too, the higher types . . . perish most easily. . . . The brief spell of beauty, of genius, of Caesar is *sui generis.*[57]

If Nietzsche's evolutionary naturalism is not Darwinian, it does smack at times of a now-discredited Lamarckian doctrine that once again gained credibility in the last decades of the nineteenth century. Nietzsche speaks often of biological breeding, and he appears to assume the heritability of acquired characteristics, including moral virtues. He writes: "All the virtues and efficiency of body and soul are acquired laboriously and little by little, through much obstinate, faithful repetition of the same labors, the same renunciations; but there are men who are the heirs and masters of this slowly-acquired manifold treasure of virtue and efficiency."[58]

Whatever Nietzsche's relation to the evolutionary doctrines of his time, the fact of *becoming* is fundamental to his doctrine. Everything, he asserts, is becoming, but he adds: "Becoming must be explained without recourse to final intentions."[59] Nietzsche rejects the doctrine of creation; the world is infinite, and it does not have a purpose or goal. According to Nietzsche, all becoming is characterized by relative fields of force that he calls the "will to power"—the most elemental fact of nature. The world is simply "a monster of energy, without beginning, without end" and the "*solution* for all its riddles? . . . The *will to power—and nothing besides!*"[60] In a passage in the posthumous *Will to Power*, Nietzsche indicates the vast scope of this extraordinary conception:

> The will to accumulate force is special to the phenomena of life, to nourishment, procreation, inheritance—to society, state, custom, authority. Should we not be permitted to assume this will as a motive cause in chemistry, too?—and in the cosmic order? Not merely conservation of energy, but maximal economy

in use, so the only reality is the will to grow stronger of every center of force—not self-preservation, but the will to appropriate, dominate, increase, grow stronger.[61]

It is clear that Nietzsche understands the "will to power" as a protean process or activity and that it is not to be construed solely in *psychological* terms of willing or desiring. As one commentator has rightly suggested, Nietzsche "wants to show that willing is . . . not a desire but a complicated activity, not a causally privileged part of human behavior but the behavior itself . . . without regard to its outcome. Willing so construed is independent of intention. . . . It is therefore independent of its traditional association with living, and perhaps only conscious, organisms."[62]

The entire sequence of phenomena in the world does not demonstrate any "law" but rather a complex of power relationships between various forces: "Life would be defined as an enduring form of processes of the establishment of force, in which the different contenders grow unequally. To what extent resistance is present even in obedience; individual power is by no means surrendered. . . . 'obedience' and 'commanding' are forms of struggle."[63] We cannot explore Nietzsche's odd and problematic personification of nature and his attributing to inorganic phenomenon psychic powers. Suffice it to point out that for Nietzsche this personification is applied to knowledge at the inorganic level: "The will to power *interprets*." Nietzsche explains: "Mere variations of power could not feel themselves to be such: there must be present something that wants to grow and interprets the value of whatever else wants to grow. . . . In fact, interpretation is itself a means of becoming master of something."[64] Knowledge is a form of "will to power." Despite the problems inherent in his scientific and cosmological claims for this doctrine, "the will to power" remains one of Nietzsche's most interesting ideas. It has proven of special interest to philosophers and post-Modernist literary figures who are attracted to its connection to forms of epistemological and axiological perspectivism or relativism.

The connection of knowledge with power has been useful as well to writers who see the will to knowledge as a form of imposition and control of others, be it domination by class, race, gender, religion, or whatever. Fundamental to Nietzsche's view of knowledge is Kant's insight into the active role of the mind in the shaping of reality; Nietzsche, however, substitutes for Kant's "categories of understanding" the vital need to impose and master by the interpretive will to power. Nietzsche characterizes scientific endeavor itself as the transformation of nature into our human conceptual schemes for the purpose of governing nature. Our interests, therefore, influence *all* of our perceptions. And so for Nietzsche there is no one perception of the "object" out there, or one interpretation of the text that lies before us and that can claim to be *the* "factual" or "true" one.

Let us be on guard against the hallowed philosopher's myth of a "pure, will-less, painless, time-less knower"; let us beware of the tentacles of such contradictory notions as "pure reason," "absolute knowledge," "absolute intelligence." All these concepts presuppose an eye such as no living being can imagine, an eye required to have no direction, to abrogate its active and interpretive powers—precisely those powers that alone make of seeing, seeing *something*. All seeing is essentially perspective, and so is all knowing.[65]

The perspective by which alone we can *see any thing* is shaped by our hopes, fears, and needs. Our intellect and knowledge are determined by these *affective* conditions of existence. We would not have knowledge "if we did not *need* to have it, and we would not have it *as it is,* if we could live otherwise."[66] Even such a strongly believed "truth" as the law of causality is, for Nietzsche, a "provisional assumption," so essential to us that not to believe it would make life impossible. But are such beliefs for that reason truths? "What a conclusion! As if the preservation of man were a proof of truth!" "Truth," Nietzsche contends, "is the kind of error without which a certain species could not live. The value for *life* is ultimately decisive." Such beliefs as freedom and the self or soul are necessary fictions, without which we could no longer think or act. The entire notion of truth must now legitimize itself before this new tribunal—"as a means of the preservation of man, as *will to power.*"[67]

If all of our sense perceptions and knowledge are permeated with judgments that derive fundamentally from our affective senses of what is harmful, useful, and needful, so are our *moral* judgments determined by these affects. According to Nietzsche, all moral distinctions are conditioned by the individual's perspective. His genealogical project is then

> to demonstrate how everything praised as moral is identical in essence with everything immoral and was made possible, as in every development of morality, with immoral means and for immoral ends—; how on the other hand, everything decried as immoral is, economically considered, higher and more essential, and how a development toward a greater fullness of life necessarily also demands the advance of immorality.[68]

A genealogy of morals, furthermore, reveals the emergence of two basic types of morality—"the morality with which the healthy instinct defends itself against incipient decadence—and another morality with which this very decadence defines and justifies itself and leads downwards"[69]—the morality that Nietzsche identifies with Christianity.

Here in the realm of moral valuation, however, it is plain that, for the perspectivist Nietzsche, not all perspectives are of equal value or truth. The superiority of his *own* conception of moral value and truth is unequivocally dogmatic. Furthermore, it is an aristocratic morality, a morality of domination that represents a thorough "transvaluation" of all decadent Judeo-Christian "higher values." The healthy aristocratic instincts embody the will to power which "strives to grow, spread, seize, become predominant—not from any morality or immorality but because it is *living* and because life simply *is* will to power."[70] In these terms Nietzsche proceeds to defend his noble "inequality of rights" and his hierarchical view of society as grounded, he believes, in nature itself, the result of certain physiological conditions that struggle against nihilistic decadence. We will return to Nietzsche's personal answer to the pervasive nihilism of the "herd" after considering rather more fully his interpretation of Christianity as the embodiment of this decadence that he so abhors.

The Critique of Christianity

From what has been said, it is clear that for Nietzsche atheism is based not on rational skepticism concerning God's existence but on the belief that the God of the Christian tradition is no longer worthy of support.

> That we find no God—either in history or in nature or behind nature—is not what differentiates *us,* but that we experience what has been revered as God, not as "godlike" but as miserable, as absurd, as harmful, not merely as an error but as a *crime against life.* We deny God as God. If one were to *prove* this God of the Christians to us, we should be even less able to believe in him.[71]

For Nietzsche the Christian God is a degenerate conception, representing the very contradiction of life, "the declaration of war against life, against nature, against the will to live ! . . . the deification of nothingness, the will to nothingness pronounced holy!"[72] Like Marx, Nietzsche hit upon a theory of rationalization that he believed explained the persistence of the alienated and other-worldly consciousness of Christian civilization. Christian belief and practice are the unconscious product of *ressentiment*—the *resentment* of the weak masses against their aristocratic superiors. Nietzsche believed that Christianity, being the quintessential expression of resentment, was the root of Western decadence.

Strange as it may seem, resentment is in fact a form of power. As Nietzsche observed, the will to power expresses itself in a great variety of ways, e.g., in monastic asceticism as well as in Titanic physical prowess. The will to power often is channeled in ways that disguise its true character. The principal manifestation of this disguised will to power is *resentment,* the exact opposite of genuine sublimation of Dionysian power.

Related to the concept of resentment is Nietzsche's theory of the two types of morality—master-morality and slave-morality. Slave-morality has its origins in Judaism and its fruition in Christianity. In both cases this form of morality is the result of the frustration and resentment of a weak, priestly class in revolt against its aristocratic masters, the Romans. The Jews started the slave revolt in morals, for it was the Jews who first suc-ceeded in avenging themselves on their enemies by radically inverting the cultural values of their mas-ters. Their weapon was their own impotence. "It is their impotence," says Nietzsche, "which makes their hate so violent and sinister, so cerebral and poi-sonous." The Jews avenged themselves by an act of the most spiritual vengeance, "a strategy entirely appropriate to a priestly people in whom vindictive-ness had gone most deeply underground."

> It was the Jew who, with frightening consistency, dared to invert the aristocratic value equations, good—noble—powerful—beautiful . . . and to hang on to this inversion with their teeth, the teeth of the most abysmal hatred (the hatred of impotence), saying "the wretched alone are the good; the poor, impotent, lowly alone are the good; the suffering, deprived, sick, ugly alone are pious, alone are blessed by God . . . and you, the powerful and noble, are on the contrary the evil, the cruel, the lustful, the insatiable, the godless to all eternity; and you shall be in all eternity the un-blessed, the accursed, and damned."[73]

The slave revolt in morals had its beginnings in a resentment turned malevolently creative. Resenting the power of the strong, the Jews and Christians, perhaps unconsciously, condemned the morally strong, their own morals of pity, mercy, self-denial being but shrewd compensation for their own weak-ness. Resentment is, therefore, at the heart of all herd morality, for the herd is made up of those who "love one another" because of fear of their superiors. All the values of the master are thus condemned as "evil" because these are the very traits that are lack-ing in and, therefore, feared by the weak.

For Nietzsche Christian love is not the manifes-tation of a strong self-discipline but the product of resentment.

> From the trunk of that tree of vengefulness and hatred, Jewish hatred—the profoundest and sub-limest kind of hatred capable of creating ideals and re-versing values, the like of which has never existed on earth before—there grew something equally incom-parable, a *new love*, the profoundest and sublimest kind of love—and from what other trunk could it have grown?

> One should not imagine it grew up as the denial of that thirst for revenge, as the opposite of Jewish hatred! No, the reverse is true! That love grew out of it like its crown . . . spreading itself farther and farther into the purest brightness and sunlight, driven as it were into the domain of light and the heights in pursuit of the goals of that hatred—victory, spoil, and seduction—by the same impulse that drove the roots of that hatred deeper and deeper and more and more covetously into all that was profound and evil. This Jesus of Nazareth, the incarnate gospel of love, this "Redeemer" who brought blessedness and victory to the poor, the sick, and the sinners—was not this seduction in its most uncanny and irresistible form, a seduction and bypath to precisely those *Jewish* values and new ideals?[74]

Jesus and the Christian Church have merely uni-versalized the Jewish transvaluation of values. "Everything," says Nietzsche, "is becoming Judaized or Christianized, or mobized. . . . The progress of this poison through the entire body of mankind seems irresistible."[75]

Nietzsche's attitude toward Jesus and his repudi-ation of Christ is rather complex and deserves special attention. He attacks both the historical Jesus and the Christ of Church dogma; but, while he despises the latter, he respects the former for his integrity. There was, in truth, "only *one* Christian," Nietzsche asserts, "and he died on the cross. The 'evangel' *died* on the cross. What has been called 'evangel' from that moment was actually the opposite of that which *he* had lived: 'ill-tidings,' a *dysangel*."[76]

Nietzsche interprets Jesus as being the prototype of a particular human psychological type—one who realized in his own inner life a serene sense of redemption from the cares of the world, a sense of blessedness which allowed him to pass through the world without anxiety or care. What Jesus exempli-fies is the Eastern achievement of an otherworldly serenity which the trampling power of external events can never disturb. This is perfectly manifest in Jesus's life of love and nonresistance, a love that is nonprudential and unconditional. It is perfectly summed up in Jesus's attitude toward death:

> This "bringer of glad tidings" died as he had lived, as he had taught—*not* to "redeem men" but to show how one must live. This practice is his legacy to

mankind: his behavior before the judges, before the catchpoles, before the accusers and all kinds of slander and scorn—his behavior on the *cross*. He does not resist, he does not defend his right, he takes no step which might ward off the worst; on the contrary he *provokes* it. And he begs, he suffers, he loves *with* those, *in* those, who do him evil. *Not* to resist, *not* to be angry, *not* to hold responsible—but to resist not even the evil one—to *love* him.[77]

Nietzsche scorns the attempts of liberal historians, such as Ernst Renan, to picture Jesus as a "genius" and "hero."

M. Renan, that buffoon *in psychologicis,* has introduced the two most inappropriate concepts possible into his explanation of the Jesus type: the concept of *genius* and the concept of the *hero*. But if anything is unevangelical it is the concept of the hero. Just the opposite of all wrestling, of all feeling-oneself-in-a-struggle, has here become instinct: the incapacity for resistance becomes morality here ("resist not evil"—the most profound word of the Gospels, their key in a certain sense), blessedness in peace, in gentleness, in not *being able* to be an enemy. . . . To make a *hero* of Jesus! And even more, what a misunderstanding is the word "genius"!. . . Spoken with the precision of a physiologist, even an entirely different word would still be more nearly fitting here—the word *idiot*.[78]

Jesus is seen by Nietzsche after the image of the "idiot," for he represents all the childlike qualities.

The "glad tidings" are precisely that there are no longer any opposites; the kingdom of heaven belongs to the *children*. . . . it is, as it were, an infantilism that has receded into the spiritual. The case of puberty being retarded and not developing in the organism as a consequence of degeneration.[79]

Earlier Nietzsche had proclaimed through Zarathustra that Jesus "died too early; he himself would have recanted his teaching had he reached my age. Noble enough was he to recant."[80]

Nietzsche admired Jesus's noble integrity, the fact that he lived his doctrine to the end. Yet he rejects Jesus, for Jesus exemplifies the psychological type set on rejecting the world—one possessed of an instinctive will to nothingness!* If such a way of life were to be universally followed, it would lead to nihilism, to the extirpation of all the higher values of culture and the destruction of humanity.

Nietzsche's critique of Christianity is not principally directed against Jesus, however. His most violent attack is aimed at the Church's transformation of the "good tidings" of Jesus into the doctrine of faith in Christ. Nietzsche believed that Christianity constituted the complete distortion of Jesus's life and teaching. Walter Kaufmann has shown that Nietzsche's critique of the Church's faith in Christ was twofold: a criticism of *faith versus action* and of *faith versus reason*.[81]

The whole transformation of Jesus's "glad tidings" began with his death on the Cross. This unexpected, disgraceful event confronted the disciples with several questions:

Who was this? What was this? Their profoundly upset and insulted feelings, and their suspicion that such a death might represent the *refutation* of their cause . . . this state is only too easy to understand. Here everything *had* to be necessary, had to have meaning, reason. . . . Only now the cleft opened up: "*Who* killed him? *Who* was his natural enemy?" This question leaped forth like lightning. Answer: *ruling* Jewry, its highest class. From this moment one felt oneself in rebellion against the existing order, and in retrospect one understood Jesus to have been *in rebellion against the existing order*. Until then this warlike, this No-saying, No-doing trait had been *lacking* in his image; even more, he had been its opposite.[82]

What now gripped the disciples was a most unevangelical feeling, the desire for *revenge*. "Once more the popular expectation of a Messiah came to

---

*Again, Nietzsche's interpretation here of the Jesus of the Gospels is widely repudiated, even by those critics most sympathetic to Nietzsche. See Kaufmann's *Nietzsche,* Chap. 12. To Nietzsche the strong, apocalyptical Jesus is the product of the Gospel editors and totally foreign to Jesus's own consciousness. Was Nietzsche the victim of the nineteenth-century liberal lives of Jesus after all?

the foreground; a historic moment was envisaged: the 'kingdom of God' comes as a judgement over his enemies."[83] A second question emerged:

> "How *could* God permit this?" To this the deranged reason of a small community found an altogether horribly absurd answer: God gave his son for the remission of sins, as a *sacrifice*. In one stroke, it was all over with the evangel!. . . Jesus had abolished the very concept of "guilt"—he had denied the cleavage between God and man; he *lived* this unity of God and man as his "glad tidings". . . . From now on there enters into the type of the Redeemer, step by step, the doctrine of judgement and return, the doctrine of death as a sacrificial death, the doctrine of the *resurrection* with which the whole concept of "blessedness" . . . is conjured away—in favor of a state *after* death.[84]

For Nietzsche it was the apostle Paul who was most responsible for transforming the gospel into a doctrine of revenge and decadence. "In Paul was embodied the opposite type to that of the 'bringer of glad tidings' ": the genius in hatred. . . . *How much this dysangelist* sacrificed to hatred!"[85] According to Nietzsche, Paul "invented his own history of Christianity," and at the center of his nihilistic doctrine was erected the belief in "justification by faith." It was this, more than anything else, that denied Jesus's emphasis on practice. Faith now became the substitute for action. The doctrine of justification by faith was but a shrewd *rationalization* for Paul's, and later for Luther's, own weakness and failure to live out the radical demands of Jesus:

> "Faith," was at all times, for example, in Luther, only a cloak, a pretext, a *screen* behind which the instincts played their game. . . . "Faith" . . . the characteristic Christian *shrewdness*—one always *spoke* of faith, but one always *acted* from instinct alone.[86]

Not only did the doctrine of faith serve the Christian community as a rationalization for its failure in practice, but it justified a *sacrificium intellectus* and the maintenance of a double standard of truth. "Faith," says Nietzsche, "is the *veto* against

*"Bringer of ill tidings"

science."[87] Faith divides the world into two spheres, one known by reason, the other based on belief or conviction. This allows the Christian a double standard by which to judge matters which others must judge by reason alone. Nietzsche was especially incensed by the double standard used by Christian scholars in his own field of philology.

The Philology of Christianity

How little Christianity educates the sense of honesty and justice can be seen pretty well from the writings of its scholars: they advance their conjectures as blandly as dogmas and are hardly ever honestly perplexed by the exegesis of a Biblical verse. Again and again they say, "I am right, for it is written," and the interpretation that follows is of such impudent arbitrariness that a philologist is stopped in his tracks, torn between anger and laughter, and keeps asking himself: Is it possible? Is it honest? Is it even decent?[88]

At the conclusion of a note in *The Will to Power,* Nietzsche adds the remark: "A very popular error: having the courage of one's convictions; rather it is a matter of having the courage for an *attack* on one's convictions!!"[89] No individual has the "right" to believe something, even if reason cannot decide the issue. Neither happiness nor utility is a proper criterion for judging matters of truth. Nietzsche found a theological pragmatism abhorrent:

> How many people still make the inference: "one could not stand life if there were no God . . . . consequently there *must* be a God (or an ethical significance of existence)!" . . . what presumption to decree that all that is necessary for my preservation must also really *be there*! As if my preservation were anything necessary![90]

Nietzsche was so opposed to utilitarian and pragmatic proofs that he believed appeals to pleasure and utility were, in fact, "counter-proofs" against any truth claims that might be advanced. There is no necessary correlation between truth and pleasure.

> The experience of all severe, of all profoundly inclined spirits teaches the *opposite*. At every step one has to wrestle for truth; one has had to surrender for

it almost everything to which the heart, to which our love, our trust in life, cling otherwise. That requires greatness of soul; the service of truth is the hardest service. What does it mean after all to have *integrity* in matters of the spirit? That one is severe against one's heart, that one despises "beautiful sentiments," that one makes of every Yes and No a matter of conscience. Faith makes blessed: consequently it lies![91]

Faith, for Nietzsche, is a sure sign that not even a beginning has been made in the discipline of truth-seeking. Moreover, it is the sign of a

> need born of *weakness.* The man of faith, the "believer" of every kind, is necessarily a dependent man—one who cannot posit *himself* as an end. . . . The "believer" does not belong to *himself.* . . . Every kind of faith is itself an expression of self-abnegation, of self-alienation.[92]

Strength and freedom are born only of a fearless openness to truth. All "great spirits," Nietzsche says, "are skeptics." And yet the great mass prefer the martyrs and fanatics, the sick spirits, for "the fanatics are picturesque; mankind prefers to see gestures rather than to hear *reasons.*"[93]

We are back, once again, to Nietzsche's original critique: Christian faith is the manifestation of a weakness which supports an escape from, and contempt for, all strong and honest instincts and values. Nietzsche, thus, concludes *The Antichrist: A Curse on Christianity* with this thunderous denunciation:

> I *condemn* Christianity. I raise against the Christian church the most terrible of all accusations that any accuser ever uttered. It is to me the highest of all conceivable corruptions. . . . Parasitism is the *only* practice of the church; with its ideal of anemia, of "holiness," draining all blood, all love, all hope for life; the beyond as the will to negate every reality; the cross as the mark of recognition for the most subterranean conspiracy that ever existed—against health, beauty, whatever has turned out well, courage, spirit, *graciousness* of the soul, *against life itself.* . . . I call Christianity the one great curse . . . the one great instinct of revenge. . . . I call it the one immortal blemish of mankind.[94]

The *Übermensch* and the Eternal Recurrence

The Antichrist closes with Nietzsche's call for a new reckoning of time. We have until now calculated time from the first day the "calamity" of Christianity began. "*Why not,*" he asks, "*rather after its last day? After today?* Revaluation of all values!"[95] Nietzsche looked to the coming of a new type of human existence in which there would be a transvaluation of all values. The new values would be embodied in the new individual, the *Übermensch* or superior person, who would emerge after the death of nihilism. However, Nietzsche did not believe that the superior person was inevitable. "Progress," he said, "is a merely modern idea. . . . further development is altogether *not* according to any necessity in the direction of elevation, enhancement, or strength."[96] The higher type of humanity, Nietzsche believed, could be discovered in widely different times and cultures and "such fortunate accidents of great success . . . *will* perhaps always be possible."[97] And yet, despite Christianity's fight to the death against this higher type, Nietzsche prophesied that such individuals would emerge after the madness brought on by the consciousness of the "death of God" had been fully vented.

The *Übermensch* will be "God's successor."

> Once one said God when one looked upon distant seas; but now I have taught you to say: overman. God is a conjecture; but I desire that your conjectures should not reach beyond your creative will. Could you *create* a god? Then do not speak to me of any gods. But you *could* create the overman. . . . Away from God and gods this will has lured me; what could one create if gods existed?. . . But my fervent will to create impels me even again toward man. . . . The beauty of the overman came to me as a shadow. O my brothers, what are the gods to me now?[98]

The *Übermensch* succeeds God but will also supersede humanity. "Man is something that should be overcome," and the person who has overcome him or herself has achieved self-possession. What Nietzsche means by "self-overcoming" is highly significant and should make clear that Nietzsche's superior individual is the antithesis of the cruel, tyrannical Nazi, with whom the *Übermensch* has frequently been identified. Self-possession has, once again, to do with the will power. As we have learned, all creatures, without exception, are possessed of the will to power, but what sets humanity apart from the animals is the fact that humans can channel their will to power toward *self-mastery.* In fact, that which requires the greatest exercise of power is the overcoming or mastery of oneself. The superior individual demands just such self-discipline and hardness toward him or herself. The *Übermensch,* in the words of Walter Kaufmann,

> has overcome his animal nature, organized the chaos of his passions, sublimated his impulses, and given style to his character—or, as Nietzsche said of Goethe: ". . . he disciplined himself into wholeness, he *created* himself" and became "the man of tolerance, not from weakness, but from strength," "a spirit who has *become free.*"[99]

The key to the superior individual is, first of all, self-discipline.

> The most spiritual men, as the *strongest,* find their happiness where others would find their destruction: in the labyrinth, in hardness against themselves and others, in experiments; their joy is self-conquest; asceticism becomes in them nature, need, instinct. Difficult tasks are a privilege to them; to play with burdens that crush others, a recreation. . . . They are the most venerable kind of man; that does not preclude their being the most cheerful and kindliest.[100]

Hardness toward oneself and achievement of self-conquest does not result in the superior individual self-importantly lording it over others. It is only the weaklings who think "themselves good because they have no claws"; the superior individual has claws but does not use them. "When the exceptional human being treats the mediocre more tenderly than himself and his peers, this is not mere politeness of heart—it is simply his *duty.*"[101] In the superior individual graciousness is a sign of strength rather than weakness. Most of the powerful heroes of history—e.g., Cesar Borgia and Napoleon—lack the virtues of the exceptional individual, especially the realization of self-mastery through sublimation

of power. Julius Caesar came close to it, but the ideal would be the Roman Caesar with Christ's soul.

The *Übermensch's* life is just that: overabundant, overjoyed. It is the Dionysian life, possessed of the yea-saying instinct. It is just this affirmation of the moment that gives joy to the superior individual's life, despite the loss of all belief in an ultimate meaning in history, in human progress, or in any supramundane redemption or existence.

It is here that Nietzsche joins his portrayal of the *Übermensch* with his controversial teaching of the Eternal Recurrence. The connection is important. Nietzsche's numerous references to the eternal recurrence have elicited a variety of interpretations. And because Nietzsche speaks of the eternal recurrence as "the most *scientific* of all possible hypotheses," a great deal of attention has been given to its cosmological meaning and its empirical plausibility. Recent commentators, however, have focused instead on its existential meaning, independent of its cosmological validity; on how it relates to Nietzsche's attitude to life as envisioned in the *Übermensch* and the overcoming of nihilism.

Nietzsche's solution to the question of how life and the world are to be "justified" came to him suddenly in August 1881 in the Swiss mountains near Sils Maria, "6000 feet beyond people and time." It came to him as the doctrine of the eternal recurrence, the revelation that the individual who masters him or herself achieves a perfect joy, an *amor fati,* a love of fate, that liberates one from all concerns about "justifying" the world and its ways. The first statement of the eternal recurrence appears as an aphorism in *The Gay Science:*

> *The greatest stress.* How, if some day or night a demon were to sneak after you into your loneliest loneliness and say to you, "This life as you now live it and have lived it, you will have to live once more and innumerable times more; and there will be nothing new in it, but every pain and every joy and every thought and sigh and everything immeasurably small or great in your life must return to you. . . ." Would you not throw yourself down and gnash your teeth and curse the demon who spoke thus? Or did you once experience a tremendous moment when you would have answered him, "You are a god, and never have I heard anything more godly." If this thought were to gain

possession of you, it would change you, as you are, or perhaps crush you. The question in each and everything, "Do you want this once more and innumerable times more" would weigh upon your actions as the greatest stress. Or how well disposed would you have to become to yourself and to life to *crave nothing more fervently* than this ultimate eternal confirmation and seal?[102]

The eternal recurrence of pain and joy, of the immeasurably small or great, what Zarathustra calls the "abysmal thought," becomes for Nietzsche's *Übermensch* a liberation, a joy in life without any ultimate meaning, goal, or justification but, paradoxically, in the realization that all recurs—the evil with the good, the small and the petty with the noble and the superior. One cannot have one without the other. Zarathustra says:

> Have you ever said Yes to a single joy? O my friends, then you have said Yes too to all woe. All things are entangled, ensnared, enamored; if ever you wanted one thing twice, if ever you said, "You please me, happiness! Abide, moment!" then you would want *all* back. All anew, all eternally, all entangled, ensnared, enamored.[103]

If we were to have another life, Nietzsche is saying, it would have to be the same life—our life with all its joys and horrors and not some other idealized life. Nietzsche passionately rejects the belief that the meaning of life resides in some future *telos* or goal in history, or in development and progress, or in some other worldly beyond; meaning and joy are to be found in the love of life *as it is,* in all its fatedness and capricious becoming. The world's aimless becoming is redeemed only by giving each moment its eternal validity. "To impose upon becoming the character of being—that is the supreme will to power."[104] As Walter Kaufmann describes it, the eternal recurrence is a thorough rejection of both the Judeo-Christian redemptive history *and* its modern secular surrogates in the West:

> The doctrine of eternal recurrence is the most extreme repudiation of any depreciation of the moment, the finite, and the individual—the antithesis of any faith which pins its hopes on infinite progress, whether

it be evolution, Faust's unbounded striving, or the endless improvement of the human soul in Kant's conception of immortality. It is the antithesis too, of any faith which looks to another world; it is the creed of one whose message began: "I beseech you, my brothers, *remain faithful to the earth* and do not believe those who speak to you of other worldly hopes."[105]

Nietzsche's teaching of the eternal recurrence can be viewed as his "countermyth" to Platonism and Christianity, the two dominant Western narratives that despise and/or repudiate becoming.[106] To Nietzsche they both represent an appeal to the beyond, a belittling of our natural, finite experience, in short, decadence. The *Übermensch* alone can overcome this nihilism and will that every moment of life recur eternally. The *Übermensch* has, therefore, passed beyond the need to justify the ways of the world. The overman's song is "Once More"; the overman's motto is *Amor fati.** The *Übermensch* not only bears necessity; he or she loves it and has become what Nietzsche longed to become—only an affirmer, a yeasayer.

Like Marx, Nietzsche offered to what he considered a resentful and repressed humanity a new naturalistic religious vision. It is his substitute for a Christianity which he felt to be inherently self-alienating. In place of God, Nietzsche envisions the *Übermensch.* Healing will come not by supernatural grace but by a superhuman will to power—power sublimated into a form of perfect self-mastery. In place of eternal life, Nietzsche offers the ecstatic joy of eternal return.

Nietzsche was among those visionary prophets of the nineteenth century who, like Dostoevsky and Kierkegaard, sensed the decadence and death ingenerate in modern bourgeois culture. Nietzsche believed this nihilism was rooted in the soil of Christian values. His equation of Christianity and what he saw as the sickness of nineteenth-century European culture may be partially true but was one-sided and myopic. As George Santayana has remarked, Nietzsche was "living in the light of the ideal," and in that light popular Christianity could appear only weak, resigned, and hypocritical. He could not appreciate the simple virtues of the

*"Love of fate"

unsung life of countless Christians, virtues expressive of a noble sublimation of power; nor, apparently, could he understand the freedom and life-affirming joy that was at the center of genuine Christian faith.

Nietzsche can be viewed, nevertheless, as right in his rejection of those elements in European culture which, through the influence of Christianity, had become the source of weakness, self-deprecation, and suffering. There is an element of "world-weariness" in certain expressions of Christianity, traceable to the very beginnings of the Christian movement, which has been the cause of needless pessimism, apathy, and failure to will a more complete and better life. There is also a tradition of radical asceticism in Christianity which, psychologically, can manifest itself in self-hatred and a morbid, perverted attitude toward the body and sexuality. And Nietzsche was correct in his observation that Christian love too often degenerates into a sentimentalized emotion of pity and that pity is degrading, condescending, and the hidden source of self-gratification. In attacking this weak, exploitative form of love, Nietzsche served the Christian faith well. In fact, one of his contributions to Christianity and to the modern world is his insight into the concealed and perverse motivations of many of our "virtuous" deeds and the role of the egoistic "will to power" in even our most altruistic actions.

Nietzsche's significance for Christian thought lies also in his parable of the "death of God." For Nietzsche the death of God was a cultural fact that had not yet fully reached Western consciousness. However, it symbolized the fact that for many God, or the Ultimate, and the moral sanctions imposed by the Ultimate were no longer real. Hence, God could not continue for long to be the bearer of a system of values. Humanity would be thrown back upon itself. Nietzsche believed that humanity was not yet aware of this fact and was still living off those standards and values rooted in the soil of Christian belief. But, once uprooted, the flowers of Christian civilization, such as democracy, would wither and die, leaving humanity to find itself, as J. S. Mill said of Victorian England, "destitute of faith, but terrified at skepticism." The tension brought on by the breakdown of belief, Nietzsche prophesied, would usher in a period of active nihilism which would lead to violence and "wars such as there have never been on earth before."

It may very well be the case, however, that Nietzsche's principal significance for Christianity lies in the fact that, as Karl Barth has shrewdly observed, Nietzsche *understood* Christianity and its doctrine of sacrificial love all too well—*and he rejected it.* Nietzsche was essentially an ethicist, and he saw in Christian practice *the* mortal threat to his ideal of humanity: the lonely, proud, strong Zarathustra. As Barth remarks, what is new about Nietzsche, and what sets him apart from critics like Strauss, Feuerbach, Marx, or the "cool and good-tempered" Goethe, is his championing of a new morality of "the man of 'azure isolation,' six thousand feet above time and man . . . utterly inaccessible to others, having no friends and despising women."*

> And the true danger in Christianity, which [Nietzsche] alone saw . . . was that Christianity—what he called Christian morality . . . confronts him with the figure of the suffering man. . . . Christianity places before the superman the Crucified, Jesus, as the Neighbour, and in the person of Jesus a whole host of others who are wholly and utterly ignoble and despised in the eyes of the world . . . the hungry and thirsty and naked and sick and captive. . . . It aims to bring [Nietzsche] down from his height, to put him in the ranks which begin with the Crucified . . . Dionysius—Zarathustra is thus called to live for others and not himself.

Nietzsche, unlike the other critics, penetrates to the truly offensive and demanding heart of the Christian Gospel itself. And as Barth concludes, "by having to attack it in this form, he has done us the good office of bringing before us the fact that we have to keep to this form as unconditionally as he rejected it, in self-evident antithesis not only to him, but to the whole tradition on behalf of which he made this final hopeless sally."[107] Kierkegaard was, of course, one of a handful of great nineteenth-century writers who saw, as did Nietzsche, what was, in

---

*The post-Modern critics who are tempted to tame Nietzsche should attend more closely to his view of women. Barth considers Nietzsche's misogyny to be a key to his hatred of Christianity. I am grateful to Garrett Green for this observation.

fact, the heart of the Christian Gospel and what a terrible offense its call to live and suffer unconditionally with and for the neighbor represented.

Kierkegaard's influence, we have noted, was negligible outside of Denmark for half a century after his death. But he is rightfully seen as the "father" of the school of Dialectical theology that emerged early in the twentieth century under the leadership of Karl Barth. The themes of Kierkegaard's major works run like a thread through the early writings of that circle of German theologians whose program also came to be known as the "Theology of Crisis." Crucial to this theology was the rediscovery, with Kierkegaard, of the true nature of the moral stumbling block and the deep resentment that the "Crucified and his hosts" embodied for a modern autonomous and complacent humanity.

In volume two we will see that, like Kierkegaard, these theologians sought to divorce Christianity from a bourgeois culture and to direct attention to the infinite qualitative difference between the transcendent, crucified God and proud, self-satisfied humanity. They, too, will turn away from the liberal emphasis on the immanence of God and the immediacy of revelation and stress the crisis of faith and the paradoxicality and moral costliness of belief. With Kierkegaard they, too, will insist that faith is an "objective uncertainty" and that there are no historical or natural "proofs" of Christianity. And with Kierkegaard they will show little interest in the quest of the historical Jesus and consider that quest a vain and faithless search for an "objective revelation" which is, by their definition, a contradiction in terms.

In closing we observe that in their different ways the Enlightenment and Romanticism both had called for a return to the individual, a turn to the subject and its authenticity, as reflected, for example, in that Janus-faced writer J. J. Rousseau. Kierkegaard's powerful attack on bourgeois European culture is intensely directed at realizing that authentic "individual self." A few years later Nietzsche was to write: "I believe that everything which we in Europe want to honor as the values of 'humanity' . . . in the long run means only the depreciation of the entire species called 'man'—its reduction to mediocrity." For Nietzsche the chief cause of this cultural "nihilism" is Christianity itself and its conception of true humanity. Kierkegaard found the authentic self portrayed in the Gospels in the figure of the Crucified.

NOTES

1. Karl Jaspers, *Basic Philosophical Writings,* ed. and trans. Edith Ehrlich et al. (Athens, Ohio, 1986), p. 38.
2. For a brief discussion of the various readings of Kierkegaard's works and his aim, see C. Stephen Evans, *Passionate Reason: Making Sense of Kierkegaard's 'Philosophical Fragments'* (Bloomington, Ind., 1992), Chap. 1.
3. S. Kierkegaard, *Papirer,* IX, A241, 136. Cited in Howard V. Hong and Edna H. Hong, *Kierkegaard's Writings,* XII, 2 (Princeton, 1992), p. 138.
4. Josiah Thompson, *Kierkegaard* (New York, 1973), p. 232ff.
5. Søren Kierkegaard, *Attack on Christendom,* trans. Walter Lowrie (Boston, 1956), pp. 166–167.
6. Ibid., p. 181.
7. Søren Kierkegaard, *Either/Or,* Part I. Cited in *Kierkegaard's Writings,* III, ed. and trans. Howard V. Hong and Edna H. Hong (Princeton, 1987), 292, 206.
8. Søren Kierkegaard, *Either/Or,* Part II. Cited in *Kierkegaard's Writings,* IV (Princeton, 1987), 208.
9. Ibid., p. 211.
10. Kierkegaard, *Papirer,* VI, A41. Cited in *Journals and Papers,* V, ed. and trans. Howard V. Hong and Edna H. Hong (Bloomington, Ind., 1978), 278.
11. S. Kierkegaard, *Fear and Trembling,* trans. Walter Lowrie (New York, 1939), p. 147.
12. S. Kierkegaard, *Concluding Unscientific Postscript.* Cited in *Kierkegaard's Writings,* XII, 1 (Princeton, 1992), 529.
13. Ibid., p. 549.
14. Ibid., p. 531.
15. S. Kierkegaard, *The Concept of Anxiety.* Cited in *Kierkegaard's Writings,* VIII (Princeton, 1980), 19–20.
16. S. Kierkegaard, *Fear and Trembling* (Princeton, 1941), p. 105.
17. S. Kierkegaard, *Philosophical Fragments.* Cited in *Kierkegaard's Writings,* VII (Princeton, 1985), 1.

18. Ibid., p. 11.
19. Ibid., p. 13.
20. Ibid., pp. 14–15.
21. Ibid., p. 18.
22. Ibid., p. 25.
23. Ibid., pp. 32–33.
24. Ibid., pp. 51–52.
25. Ibid., p. 63.
26. Ibid., p. 64.
27. Ibid., p. 65.
28. Ibid., p. 100.
29. Ibid., p. 102.
30. Ibid., pp. 103–104.
31. Ibid., p. 104.
32. Kierkegaard, *Concluding Unscientific Postscript,* pp. 21–22.
33. Ibid., p. 29.
34. Ibid.
35. I am grateful to Earl McLane for pointing out the importance of stressing this point about science, objectivity, and "existence-issues" for Kierkegaard.
36. Kierkegaard, *Concluding Unscientific Postscript,* pp. 350–351.
37. Ibid., p. 201.
38. Ibid., p. 203.
39. Ibid., p. 203.
40. Ibid., pp. 326–327.
41. C. Stephen Evans, "Does Kierkegaard Think Beliefs Can Be Directly Willed?" *International Journal for Philosophy of Religion,* 26 (Dec. 1989), 198.
42. S. Kierkegaard, *Journals,* ed. and trans. Alexander Dru (New York, 1938), 926.
43. On this interpretation of Kierkegaard, see M. Jamie Ferreira's valuable study, *Transforming Vision: Imagination and Will in Kierkegaardian Faith* (Oxford, 1991). On the importance of these current interpretations of Kierkegaard, I am especially indebted to Earl McLane.
44. Ernst Benz, "Nietzsche's Ideen zur Geschichte des Christentums," *Zeitschrift für Kirchengeschichte,* 56 (1937).
45. Karl Jaspers, *Nietzsche and Christianity* (Chicago, 1961).
46. F. Nietzsche, *The Antichrist.* Cited in *The Portable Nietzsche,* selected and trans. Walter Kaufmann (New York, 1954), p. 656.
47. R. J. Hollingdale, *Nietzsche: The Man and His Philosophy* (Baton Rouge, 1965), p. 30.
48. F. Nietzsche, *The Gay Science.* Cited in Kaufmann, *Portable Nietzsche,* pp. 95–96.
49. Martin Heidegger interprets Nietzsche's words "God is dead" as the pronouncement that metaphysics can no longer concern itself with the "beyond" or with a supersensory, transcendent ground of Being but returns us to the pre-Socratic concern with things-that-are-within-this-world. See "Nietzsches Wort, 'Gott ist tot,' " in *Holzwege* (Frankfurt, 1950).
50. Nietzsche, *Gay Science.* Cited in Kaufmann, *Portable Nietzsche,* p. 450. This and other passages support Jasper's contention that Christian faith constitutes a basis of Nietzsche's own radical truthfulness and his uncompromising approach to life and its problems.
51. F. Nietzsche, *On the Genealogy of Morality,* ed. Keith Ansell-Pearson (Cambridge, 1994), pp. 126–127.
52. F. Nietzsche, *Beyond Good and Evil,* trans. Walter Kaufmann (New York, 1966), p. 161.
53. Friedrich Nietzsche, *The Will to Power* [1883–1888] trans. W. Kaufmann and R. J. Hollingdale (New York, 1967), p. 358.
54. Walter Kaufmann, *Nietzsche: Philosopher, Psychologist, Antichrist* (New York, 1956), p. 142.
55. F. Nietzsche, *Of the Use and Disadvantages of History for Life* (1874). Cited in W. Kaufmann, *Nietzsche* (1956), p. 82.
56. Nietzsche, *Will to Power,* pp. 360–361.
57. Ibid., pp. 362–363.
58. Ibid., p. 518.
59. Ibid., p. 377.
60. Ibid., p. 550.
61. Ibid., p. 367.
62. Alexander Nehamas, *Nietzsche: Life as Literature* (Cambridge, 1985), p. 78.
63. Nietzsche, *Will to Power,* p. 342.
64. Ibid.
65. F. Nietzsche, *Kritische Gesamtausgabe,* VI, 2 (Berlin, 1967), 383. Cited in Bernd Magnus, *Nietzsche's Existential Imperative* (Bloomington, Ind., 1978), pp. 27–28. I am indebted to Magnus's discussion of Nietzsche's concept of knowledge and the "will to power."
66. Nietzsche, *Will to Power,* p. 273.
67. Ibid., pp. 273, 272.
68. Ibid., p. 155.
69. Ibid., p. 153.
70. Nietzsche, *Beyond Good and Evil,* p. 203. I am indebted to Mark Fowler for insight into the conflict between Nietzsche's perspectivism and the will to power—and the problem for those, such as Alexander Nehamas, who interpret the perspectivism benignly. See Mark Fowler, "Nietzschean Perspectivism: 'How Could Such a Philosophy— Dominate'?" *Social Theory and Practice: An International and Interdisciplinary Journal of Social Philosophy,* 16 (Summer 1990), 119–162.

71. Nietzsche, *Antichrist,* 47. Cited in Kaufmann, *Portable Nietzsche,* p. 627.

72. Ibid., pp. 585–586.

73. F. Nietzsche, *On the Genealogy of Morals,* trans. Walter Kaufmann and R. J. Hollingdale (New York, 1967), p. 34.

74. Ibid., pp. 34–35. It is generally agreed that Nietzsche was not attacking genuine Christian love but a sentimentalized conception of love as pity. Erich Fromm has referred to this latter as "symbiotic love," which is based on weakness and unconscious exploitation.

75. Ibid., p. 36.

76. Nietzsche, *Antichrist,* 39. Cited in Kaufmann, *Portable Nietzsche,* p. 612.

77. Ibid., pp. 608–609.

78. Ibid., pp. 601–602.

79. Ibid., p. 604.

80. F. Nietzsche, *Thus Spoke Zarathustra.* Cited in Kaufmann, *Portable Nietzsche,* p. 185.

81. We will follow Kaufmann's analysis at this point. Our account of Nietzsche's portrayal of Jesus is also dependent, in part, on Kaufmann's interpretation. See Walter Kaufmann, *Nietzsche: Philosopher, Psychologist, Antichrist* (New York, 1956), Chap. 12.

82. Nietzsche, *Antichrist.* Cited in Kaufmann, *Portable Nietzsche,* pp. 614–615.

83. Ibid., p. 615.

84. Ibid., p. 616.

85. Ibid., p. 617.

86. Ibid., p. 613.

87. Ibid., p. 627.

88. F. Nietzsche, *The Dawn,* 84. Cited in Kaufmann, *Portable Nietzsche,* p. 80.

89. F. Nietzsche, *Will to Power,* 318. Cited in Kaufmann, *Nietzsche* (1956), p. 303.

90. Nietzsche, *Dawn,* 90. Cited in Kaufmann, *Nietzsche* (1956), p. 305.

91. Nietzsche, *Antichrist,* 50. Cited in Kaufmann, *Portable Nietzsche,* p. 632.

92. Ibid., pp. 638–639.

93. Ibid., pp. 638–639.

94. Ibid., pp. 655–656.

95. Ibid., p. 656.

96. Ibid., p. 571.

97. Ibid.

98. Nietzsche, *Thus Spoke Zarathustra.* Cited in Kaufmann, *Portable Nietzsche,* pp. 197, 199–200.

99. Kaufmann, *Nietzsche* (1956), p. 274.

100. Nietzsche, *Antichrist,* 57. Cited in Kaufmann, *Portable Nietzsche,* pp. 645–646.

101. Ibid., p. 647.

102. Nietzsche, *Gay Science,* 341. Cited in Kaufmann, *Portable Nietzsche,* pp. 101–102.

103. Nietzsche, *Thus Spoke Zarathustra,* Fourth Part, 19. Cited in Alexander Nehamas, *Nietzsche: Life as Literature,* p. 155.

104. Nietzsche, *Will to Power* (1968), p. 330.

105. Kaufmann, *Nietzsche* (1956), p. 277.

106. On the theme of Nietzsche's eternal recurrence as his "countermyth" to Christianity, see Bernd Magnus's fine study, *Nietzsche's Existential Imperative* (1978).

107. Karl Barth, *Church Dogmatics,* III, 2 (Edinburgh, 1960), 240–242.

SUGGESTIONS FOR FURTHER READING

I. SØREN KIERKEGAARD

There is an immense body of literature on Kierkegaard in English, including a large number of valuable studies on specific aspects of his thought and authorship. Here we cite only some of the best and more general studies.

Biography

Kirmmse, Bruce H. *Kierkegaard in Golden Age Denmark* (Bloomington: Indiana University Press, 1990). An important study that situates Kierkegaard and his later development and authorship in the social context of nineteenth-century Denmark.

Lowrie, Walter. *Kierkegaard* (Oxford: Oxford University Press, 1938). This is the most widely read and influential biography of Kierkegaard in English. Some regard its attention to the influence of certain biographical details on Kierkegaard's authorship to be exaggerated and unfortunate. See also Lowrie, *A Short Life of Kierkegaard* (Princeton: Princeton University Press, 1942; paperback ed., 1965).

Thompson, Josiah. *Kierkegaard* (New York: Alfred A. Knopf, 1973). A highly readable and interesting life of Kierkegaard that depicts him in less heroic terms.

Studies

Collins, James. *The Mind of Kierkegaard* (Chicago: Henry Regnery, 1953; reprint, Princeton University Press, 1983). A fine survey and analysis of central themes in Kierkegaard's thought.

Diem, Hermann. *Kierkegaard's Dialectic of Existence* (Edinburgh: Oliver and Boyd, 1959; reprint, Greenwood Press, 1978).

Evans, C. Stephen. *Kierkegaard's "Fragments" and "Postscript": The Religious Philosophy of Johannes Climacus* (Atlantic Highlands, N.J: Humanities Press, 1983). A helpful guide and analysis of central themes in these important works.

————.*Passionate Reason: Making Sense of Kierkegaard's "Philosophical Fragments"* (Bloomington: Indiana University Press, 1992).

Ferreira, M. Jamie. *Transforming Vision: Imagination and Will in Kierkegaardian Faith* (Oxford: Clarendon Press, 1991). A reconsideration of Kierkegaard's conception of faith, proposing a position between volitionalism and rationalism, and reflecting certain commonalities with the position of J. H. Newman. For advanced students.

Mackey, Louis. *Kierkegaard: A Kind of Poet* (Philadelphia: University of Pennsylvania, 1971). Mackey rejects the association of Kierkegaard with a particular point of view and interprets him as offering, even in the nonpseudonymous books, a series of literary *persona.*

Malantschuk, Gregor. *Kierkegaard's Thought,* ed. and trans. Howard V. Hong and Edna Hong (Princeton: Princeton University Press, 1971). An important work, considered by some to be the best study of Kierkegaard's thought. For advanced students.

Swenson, David F. *Something about Kierkegaard,* ed. Lillian Marvin Swenson (Minneapolis: Augsburg, 1945; reprint, Mercer University Press, 1983). An early study, by a pioneer in Kierkegaard studies, that remains valuable.

II. Friedrich Nietzsche

As with Kierkegaard, there is a large body of literature in English on Nietzsche. Some of the finest studies are in German and French and have not been translated. Some of the best studies in English are cited below, and several of these include good bibliographies. The most accurate and readable English translations of Nietzsche's works are those of Hollingdale and Kaufmann.

Biography

Hayman, Ronald. *Nietzsche: A Critical Life* (New York: Oxford University Press, 1980).

Hollingdale, R. J. *Nietzsche: The Man and His Philosophy* (Baton Rouge: Louisiana State University Press, 1965).

Studies

Barth, Karl. *Church Dogmatics,* III, 2 (Edinburgh: T. & T. Clark, 1960). This brief excursus on Nietzsche includes many brilliant insights.

Danto, Arthur C. *Nietzsche as Philosopher* (New York: Macmillan Company, 1965). An interesting critical analysis that points up the problems and the radical consequences of several of Nietzsche's doctrines.

Jaspers, Karl. *Nietzsche: An Introduction for the Understanding of His Philosophical Activity* [1936], trans. Charles F. Wallraff and Frederick J. Schmitz (Tucson: University of Arizona Press, 1980). Writing during the Nazi period, Jaspers counters the pro-Nazi interpretation of Nietzsche and portrays him as a nonideological thinker who attacks all normative positions.

————*Nietzsche and Christianity,* trans. E. B. Ashton (Chicago: Regnery, 1961). Nietzsche's dependence on and interpretation of Christianity.

Kaufmann, Walter. *Nietzsche: Philosopher, Psychologist, Antichrist* (Princeton: Princeton University Press, 1950; Vintage, 1975). An important study that rehabilitated Nietzsche as a thinker after World War II. Valuable on Nietzsche and Christianity. Some critics see Kaufmann as domesticating the more wild and dangerous aspects of Nietzsche's thought.

Magnus, Bernd. *Nietzsche's Existential Imperative* (Bloomington: Indiana University Press, 1978). A fine study that focuses on Nietzsche's Eternal Recurrence as his "countermyth" to Christianity.

Nehamas, Alexander. *Nietzsche: Life as Literature* (Cambridge: Harvard University Press, 1985). An important work that gives central attention to Nietzsche's perspectivism and represents the newer literary interest in Nietzsche. Critics argue that he, too, tames Nietzsche's dogmatism and elitism.

Schacht, Richard. *Nietzsche* (London: Routledge and Kegan Paul, 1983). This vast work offers critical analyses of the major themes in Nietzsche's works.

Solomon, Robert C., and Kathleen M. Higgins. *Reading Nietzsche* (New York: Oxford University Press, 1988). A valuable collection of essays on Nietzsche's major works by leading Nietzsche scholars.

Acknowledgments

The following publishers and organizations have generously granted permission to use extended quotations from their publications or to reprint photographs.

EXCERPTED TEXT:

Samuel Taylor Coleridge, *Confessions of an Inquiring Spirit*, edited by H. St. J. Hart, 1956. Reprinted by permission of A&C Black (Publishers) Limited.

J. M. Creed and J. S. Boys Smith, *Religious Thought in the Eighteenth Century*, 1934. Reprinted by permission of Cambridge University Press.

Excerpts from *The Essence of Christianity* by Ludwig Feuerbach and translated by George Eliot. Copyright 1957 by Harper & Row, Publishers, Inc. Reprinted by permission of HarperCollins Publishers, Inc.

David Hume, *Dialogues Concerning Natural Religion*, second edition, edited by Norman Kemp Smith, 1949 by Bobbs-Merrill Co. Used by permission of Prentice-Hall, Inc.

Immanuel Kant, *Critique of Pure Reason*, translated by Norman K. Smith, 1958. Reprinted by permission of Macmillan Press Ltd.

Immanuel Kant, *Religion within the Limits of Reason Alone*. Torchbook edition, 1960. Reprinted by permission of the Open Court Publishing Company, La Salle, Illinois.

Kierkegaard, Søren; *Philosophical Fragments: Kierkegaard's Writings* VII. Howard and Edna Hong, editors and translators. Copyright © 1985 and 1995 Poetscript, Inc. Reprinted by permission of Princeton University Press.

John Locke, *An Essay Concerning Human Understanding*, edited by A. S. Pringle-Pattison, 1956. Reprinted by permission of Oxford University Press.

Walter Rauschenbusch, *A Theology for the Social Gospel* (New York: Macmillan, 1917). Used by permission of the publisher.

Jean-Jacques Rousseau, *Emile: Or Education*, translated by Barbara Foxley, 1961. Everyman's Library Edition. Reprinted by permission of Everyman's Library, David Campbell Publishers Ltd.

Excerpts from *On Religion: Speeches to Its Cultured Despisers* by Friedrich Schleiermacher and translated by John Oman. Copyright © 1958 by Harper & Row, Publishers, Inc. Copyright © renewed 1986 by Harper & Row, Publishers, Inc. Reprinted by permission of HarperCollins Publishers, Inc.

David Friedrich Strauss, *The Life of Jesus Critically Examined*, copyright © 1972 Fortress Press. Used by permission of Augsburg Fortress.

God and Incarnation in Mid-Nineteenth Century German Theology, edited by Claude Welch, 1965. Reprinted by permission of Oxford University Press.

Reprinted from *Lessing's Theological Writings*, translated and edited by Henry Chadwick, with the permission of the publishers, Stanford University Press. Copyright 1956 by A. and C. Black Ltd.

The Oxford Movement, edited by Eugene R. Fairweather, 1964. Reprinted by permission of Oxford University Press.

From *The Portable Nietzsche* by Walter Kaufmann, editor, translated by Walter Kaufmann, Translation copyright

PHOTOGRAPHS:

5: Routledge Publishers.

14: New York Public Library Picture Collection.

22: Courtesy of Yale University Library.

40: From John Hill Burton, *Life and Correspondence of David Hume* I, 1846.

71:Bettmann.

83: Bettmann.

116: Archive Photos.

141: Bettmann.

142: Stock Montage, Inc.

162: From Wilfred Ward, *The Life of John Henry Cardinal Newman* I (London: Longmans, Green, and Co., 1912).

185: Courtesy Kösel-Verlag Publishers.

187: Courtesy Kösel-Verlag Publishers.

214: The Granger Collection.

221: Bettmann.

237: Bettmann.

270: From Karl Barth, *Die prot. Theologie im 19, Jahrhundert* (Zurich: Evangelisher Verlag, 1947).

299: Archive Photos.

336: Archive Photos.

327: From *A Manual of Scholastic Theology* I (London: Kegan, Paul, Trench, Trubner and Co., 1917).

365: Cambridge University Press.

356: From Maurice Blondel, *The Letter on Apologetics and History and Dogma* (New York: Holt, Rinehart and Winston, 1964).

384: National Historical Museum, Frederiksborg/ Danish Embassy.

398: From Paul Elmer More, *Nietzsche* (1912).

Index

Only those works quoted or given significant attention in the text are cited.